Revenue Statistics in Africa 2022

Statistiques des recettes publiques en Afrique 2022

1990-2020

Please cite this publication as:
OECD/AUC/ATAF (2022), *Revenue Statistics in Africa 2022*, OECD Publishing, Paris, https://doi.org/10.1787/ea66fbde-en-fr.

Merci de citer cet ouvrage comme suit :
OCDE/CUA/ATAF (2022), Statistiques des recettes publiques en Afrique 2022, Éditions OCDE, Paris, https://doi.org/10.1787/ea66fbde-en-fr.

ISBN 978-92-64-44808-7 (print/imprimé)
ISBN 978-92-64-72871-4 (pdf)

Revenue Statistics in Africa/*Statistiques des recettes publiques en Afrique*
ISSN 2617-6521 (print/imprimé)
ISSN 2617-653X (online/en ligne)

Photo credits/Crédits photo: Cover © some of the graphic elements in the main cover illustration were adapted from Freepik.com.
Couverture © certains des éléments graphiques de l'illustration de la couverture principale ont été adaptés de Freepik.com.

Corrigenda to publications may be found on line at: www.oecd.org/about/publishing/corrigenda.htm.
Les corrigenda des publications sont disponibles sur : www.oecd.org/fr/apropos/editionsocde/corrigendadepublicationsdelocde.htm.

Foreword

Revenue Statistics in Africa is a joint publication by the OECD Centre for Tax Policy and Administration, the OECD Development Centre, the African Tax Administration Forum and the African Union Commission, with technical support from the African Development Bank and the Cercle de réflexion et d'échange des dirigeants des administrations fiscales and with the financial support of the European Union within the framework of the Pan-African Statistics Program (PAS 2) implementation.

The report presents detailed, internationally comparable data on tax and non-tax revenues for 31 African countries. Its approach is based on the well-established methodology of the *OECD Revenue Statistics* database, which has become an essential reference source for OECD member countries and many more. Comparisons are also made with the average for OECD economies and for the economies featured in *Revenue Statistics in Latin America and the Caribbean* and *Revenue Statistics in Asia and the Pacific*.

The term "taxes" in this publication is confined to "compulsory, unrequited payments to general government". Taxes are "unrequited" in the sense that benefits provided by government to taxpayers are not normally in proportion to their payments. The OECD methodology classifies a tax according to its base: income, profits and capital gains (classified under heading 1000), payroll (heading 3000), property (heading 4000), goods and services (heading 5000) and other taxes (heading 6000). Compulsory social security contributions paid to general government are treated as taxes and classified under heading 2000. The concept and classification of taxes are set out in greater detail in the *OECD Interpretative Guide* in Annex A.

The term "non-tax revenues" includes all general government revenues that do not meet the OECD definition of taxation. Revenues that do not constitute taxation include grants (e.g. foreign aid), returns on government market investments, rents on the extraction of resources from public lands, sales of government-produced goods and services, and the collection of fines and forfeits. More details on these types of revenues are provided in Annex B.

Chapter 1 and Chapter 2 of this report provide an overview of the main trends in tax and non-tax revenues respectively in the 31 participating countries from 2010 to 2020. They include a specific focus on the impact of the COVID-19 crisis on revenues. Chapter 3 is a special feature on efficient taxation of the informal sector in Africa. Chapter 4 explores the level of tax revenues by main tax category and how the respective tax structures of the 31 countries have evolved since 1990. Chapters 5 and 6 provide detailed information on tax and non-tax revenues on a country-by-country basis as well as a comparison of the non-tax revenue mix over time in the 31 countries.

Avant-propos

Les *Statistiques des recettes publiques en Afrique* est une publication conjointe du Centre de politique et d'administration fiscales de l'OCDE, du Centre de développement de l'OCDE, du Forum sur l'administration fiscale africaine et de la Commission de l'Union africaine, avec l'assistance technique de la Banque africaine de développement et du Cercle de réflexion et d'échange des dirigeants des administrations fiscales et le soutien financier de l'Union européenne dans le cadre de la mise en œuvre du Programme statistique panafricain (PAS 2).

Le rapport fournit des données détaillées et comparables à l'échelle internationale, sur les recettes fiscales et non fiscales de 31 pays africains. Son approche repose sur la méthodologie bien établie des *Statistiques des recettes publiques de l'OCDE*, devenue une source de référence essentielle pour les pays membres de l'Organisation et au-delà. Des comparaisons sont également effectuées avec la moyenne des économies de l'OCDE et avec celle des économies couvertes par les *Statistiques des recettes publiques en Amérique latine et dans les Caraïbes* et les *Statistiques des recettes publiques en Asie et Pacifique*.

Dans cette publication, le terme « impôts » fait référence uniquement aux « versements obligatoires sans contrepartie aux administrations publiques ». Les impôts sont « sans contrepartie » en ce sens que les prestations fournies par les administrations aux contribuables ne sont pas normalement proportionnelles à leurs paiements. La méthodologie de l'OCDE consiste à classer les impôts en fonction de l'assiette : le revenu, les bénéfices et les gains en capital (rubrique 1000), les salaires et la main-d'œuvre (rubrique 3000), le patrimoine (rubrique 4000), les biens et les services (rubrique 5000) et autres impôts (rubrique 6000). Les cotisations obligatoires de sécurité sociale versées aux administrations publiques sont aussi traitées comme des impôts et classées dans la rubrique 2000. Des informations plus détaillées sur la notion et la classification des impôts sont présentées dans le *Guide d'interprétation de l'OCDE* figurant à l'annexe A.

Le terme « recettes non fiscales » recouvre toutes les recettes des administrations publiques qui ne sont pas considérées comme des « impôts » selon la définition de l'OCDE. Les recettes non fiscales incluent les dons (comme l'aide extérieure), les rendements d'investissements publics, les rentes tirées de l'extraction de ressources du domaine public, la vente de biens et de services produits par le secteur public, et les amendes et confiscations. On trouvera, à l'annexe B, des informations plus détaillées sur ces catégories de recettes.

Le chapitre 1 et le chapitre 2 du rapport offrent une vue d'ensemble des grandes tendances de 2010 à 2020, dans les 31 pays participants, des recettes fiscales et non fiscales respectivement avec un accent particulier sur l'impact de la crise du COVID-19 sur les recettes publiques. Le chapitre 3 est une étude spéciale expliquant comment taxer efficacement le secteur informel en Afrique. Le chapitre 4 examine le niveau des recettes fiscales par principaux types d'impôts et l'évolution des structures fiscales des 31 pays depuis 1990. Les chapitres 5 et 6 fournissent respectivement des données détaillées sur les recettes fiscales et non fiscales par pays ainsi qu'une comparaison des structures des recettes non fiscales dans le temps dans les 31 pays.

Acknowledgements

Revenue Statistics in Africa has been jointly produced by the Organisation for Economic Co-operation and Development (OECD) Centre for Tax Policy and Administration (CTPA), the OECD Development Centre (DEV), the African Tax Administration Forum (ATAF) and the African Union Commission (AUC), with the technical support of the African Development Bank (AfDB) and the Cercle de réflexion et d'échange des dirigeants des administrations fiscales (CREDAF) and with the financial support of the European Union.

The staff from these organisations with responsibility for producing the publication were: Emmanuelle Modica, Leonie Cedano, Talita Yamashiro Fordelone, Michael Sharratt, Melary Muñoz Rodriguez, Alexander Pick and Michelle Harding of CTPA under the supervision of the former Director Pascal Saint-Amans, the Director Grace Perez-Navarro, the Acting Deputy Director David Bradbury, and the Acting Head of the Tax Policy and Statistics Division Kurt Van Dender; Sébastien Markley and Arthur Minsat of DEV under the supervision of the Director of the Development Centre Ragnheiður Elín Árnadóttir, the Deputy Director Federico Bonaglia and the Senior Communications Manager Henri-Bernard Solignac-Lecomte; Frankie Mbuyamba, Manager: Regional Coordination and Senior Specialist: Applied Research and Statistics at ATAF, Ezera Madzivanyika, Research Manager at ATAF; Ndinaye Sekwi Charumbira, Policy Officer, Rumbidzai Treddah Manhando, Economist, Adoum Gagoloum, Head of Economics Statistics Division, African Union Institute for Statistics (STATAFRIC), and Jose Awong Alene, Senior Statistician under the supervision of Djamel Ghrib, Director of Economic Development, Integration, and Trade, Leila Ben Ali, Head of STATAFRIC, at the AUC; Chaouch Anouar, Statistician at AfDB under the Director of the Statistics Department Charles Leyeka Lufumpa, and Koua Louis Kouakou at AfDB; Manager of Economic and Social Statistics Division; Secretary General Catherine Lemesle of CREDAF; Policy Officer Gaëlle Doléans, Team Leader Economic Integration, Transport, Digital and Science, Technology and Innovation Fabio Di Stefano, and Team Leader Fiscal Policies Benedikt Madl at the European Commission (DG International Partnerships). The special feature (Chapter 3) was written by Michael Masiya and Ezera Madzivanyika (ATAF), with contributions from Asuo Afram (focal point for Ghana), Alex Muhanji (focal point for Kenya) and Cephas Tiye (focal point for Nigeria). Elizabeth Nash and Delphine Grandrieux (DEV) and Marie-Aurélie Elkurd (CTPA) assisted with the production and publication of this report and Stephanie Coic produced the cover.

The authors would like to thank the officials at the finance ministries, national tax agencies and national statistical institutes of the countries participating in this project who gathered and compiled the national data and provided their invaluable knowledge and expertise on their country's revenue collection systems and data. In particular, the authors would like to thank the focal points appointed for each country and their colleagues who facilitated the technical work: Seitebaleng Fologang for Botswana; Mariame Dabo and Michel Yaméogo for Burkina Faso; Carlos José Oliveira Bentub and Hamilton Cabral Fortes for Cabo Verde; Rogangoum Kodindouma Hervé and Hassan Adoum Mbodou Mbami for

Chad; Edouard Kalawa and Eritch Nghogue for Cameroon; Yacouba Fofana and Alex Koula Pouhe for Côte d'Ivoire; Christophe Bitasimwa Bahii, Liliane Bilonda, Elisabeth Dikisha Dietu, Dieudonné Bukasa Kabongo, Floribert Masuku Mambambu, Yvette Barhashishwa Shabani Mwangu, Richard Kabila Mutshi and Popol Mukoko Akabuele for the Democratic Republic of the Congo; Alaa Abdel-Rahman and Yasmine Kamel for Egypt; Teodoro Mbá, Benita Ebang Nzang, Bindang Ndong Okiri and Santiago Obama Benga for Equatorial Guinea; Eric Thembinkosi Dlamini, Mvuselelo B. Mdluli, Khulekani Innocent Mncina and Yvonne Ntfombiyenkhosi Mthombo for Eswatini; Asuo Afram and Francis Bright Mensah for Ghana; Alex Muhanji and Alex Mwangi for Kenya; Donah for Madagascar; T'sele Mokhathali, Haleokoe Jopo and Makananelo Puseletso for Lesotho; Laurent Kalonga, Chimvano Thawani, Alick Wella and Natasha Kandoje for Malawi; Siaka Samaké and Boubacar Diakité for Mali; Mohamed Falilou Gueye for Mauritania; Meeshrani Balgobin, Dharmarajen Changeya and Roshan Oree for Mauritius; El Moustapha Bennani and Abderrahim Mezroui for Morocco; Idi Itope and Nelago Ekandjo for Namibia; Mahamadou Djibrilla for Niger; Cephas Tiye for Nigeria; Frédéric Ngolele for the Republic of the Congo; Roy Valence Gasangwa and Denis Mukama for Rwanda; Pape Malick Diallo for Senegal; Sophie Belle, Francesco Estico, Rudy Sinon, Roseline Lepathy, Ayda Noel and Yannick Vel for Seychelles; Philippe Kargbo for Sierra Leone; Mampho Baholo, Paul Dreyer, Lawrence Gqesha, Mamiky Leolo, Tshepo Makgoro, Denis Marais, Nontokozo Mnqayi, Vivienne Smithdorf and Darlington Zhou for South Africa; Ouro-Adoï Abdelganiou and Imrane Moussa for Togo; Saoussen Boumaiza, Raja Hadj Khalifa and Rihab Ben Challadia for Tunisia; Jova Mayega, Ronald Nyenje Makumbi, Milly Isongoma Nalukwago and Allen Nassanga for Uganda.

The authors would like to add a special remembrance for Agnes Kanyangeyo, from Rwanda, who passed away in February 2022 and was a key contributor to the *Revenue Statistics in Africa* project since its inception in 2014.

Revenue Statistics in Africa is part of the *Global Revenue Statistics* Initiative. The authors would also like to thank the governments of Ireland, Japan, Luxembourg, the Netherlands, Norway, Sweden, Switzerland, the United Kingdom and the European Union for their support to the broader *Global Revenue Statistics* Initiative.

This document was produced with the financial assistance of the European Union. The views expressed herein can in no way be taken to reflect the official opinion of the European Union.

Remerciements

La publication des *Statistiques des recettes publiques en Afrique* a été produite conjointement par le Centre de politique et d'administration fiscales (CPAF) de l'Organisation de coopération et de développement économiques (OCDE), le Centre de développement de l'OCDE (DEV), le Forum sur l'administration fiscale africaine (ATAF) et la Commission de l'Union africaine (CUA), avec l'assistance technique de la Banque africaine de développement (BAfD), du Cercle de réflexion et d'échange des dirigeants des administrations fiscales (CREDAF), et avec le soutien financier de l'Union européenne.

Les agents de ces organisations auxquels la responsabilité de la publication a été confiée sont : Emmanuelle Modica, Leonie Cedano, Talita Yamashiro Fordelone, Michael Sharratt, Melary Muñoz Rodriguez, Alexander Pick et Michelle Harding du CPAF sous la supervision du Directeur précédent du CPAF Pascal Saint-Amans, de Grace Perez-Navarro, Directrice du CPAF, de David Bradbury, Directeur adjoint par intérim du CPAF et de Kurt Van Dender, Chef par intérim de la Division des politiques fiscales et statistiques ; Sébastien Markley et Arthur Minsat de DEV sous la supervision du Directeur du Centre de développement Ragnheiður Elín Árnadóttir, du Directeur adjoint Federico Bonaglia et de Henri-Bernard Solignac-Lecomte, Chef de la communication ; Frankie Mbuyamba, Responsable: Coordination régionale et spécialiste principal : Recherche appliquée et statistiques à l'ATAF et Ezera Madzivanyika, Responsable de recherche appliquée et statistiques à l'ATAF; Ndinaye Sekwi Charumbira, Chargée de mission, Rumbidzai Treddah Manhando, Économiste, Adoum Gagoloum, Chef de la division des statistiques économiques (STATAFRIC) et Jose Awong Alene, statisticien principal sous la supervision de Djamel Ghrib, directeur du développement économique, de l'intégration et du commerce et Leila Ben Ali, chef de l'Institut de statistiques de l'Union africaine (STATAFRIC), de la CUA ; Chaouch Anouar, statisticien à la BAfD, sous la supervision de Charles Leyeka Lufumpa, Directeur du département des statistiques et Koua Louis Kouakou, de la BAfD, Chef de la Division des statistiques économiques et sociales ; Catherine Lemesle, Secrétaire général du CREDAF; Chargée de mission Gaëlle Doléans, Chef d'équipe Intégration économique, Transport, Numérique et Science, Technologie et Innovation Fabio Di Stefano et Chef d'équipe Politiques fiscales Benedikt Madl à la Commission européenne (DG Partenariats internationaux). L'étude spéciale (chapitre 3) a été rédigée par Michael Masiya et Ezera Madzivanyika (ATAF), avec les contributions des points focaux Asuo Afram (point focal pour le Ghana), Alex Muhanji (point focal pour le Kenya) et Cephas Tiye (point focal pour le Nigéria). Elizabeth Nash et Delphine Grandrieux de DEV et Marie-Aurélie Elkurd du CPAF ont aidé à la production de la publication et Stephanie Coic a produit la couverture.

Les auteurs souhaitent remercier les responsables des ministères des finances, des administrations fiscales nationales et des instituts nationaux de statistiques des pays participant au projet, qui ont collecté et rassemblé les données nationales et ont partagé leur connaissance et expertise inestimable sur les systèmes de collecte de recettes et les données de leur pays. Les auteurs souhaitent en particulier remercier les points focaux désignés pour chaque pays et leurs collègues qui ont facilité le travail technique : Seitebaleng

Fologang pour le Botswana ; Mariame Dabo et Michel Yaméogo pour le Burkina Faso ; Carlos José Oliveira Bentub et Hamilton Cabral Fortes pour le Cabo Verde ; Edouard Kalawa et Eritch Nghogue pour le Cameroun ; Yacouba Fofana et Alex Koula Pouhe pour la Côte d'Ivoire ; Christophe Bitasimwa Bahii, Liliane Bilonda, Elisabeth Dikisha Dietu, Dieudonné Bukasa Kabongo, Floribert Masuku Mambambu, Yvette Barhashishwa Shabani Mwangu, Richard Kabila Mutshi et Popol Mukoko Akabuele pour la République démocratique du Congo ; Alaa Abdel-Rahman et Yasmine Kamel pour l'Égypte ; Teodoro Mbá, Benita Ebang Nzang, Bindang Ndong Okiri et Santiago Obama Benga pour la Guinée équatoriale ; Eric Thembinkosi Dlamini, Mvuselelo B. Mdluli, Khulekani Innocent Mncina et Yvonne Ntfombiyenkhosi Mthombo pour l'Eswatini ; Asuo Afram et Francis Bright Mensah pour le Ghana ; Alex Muhanji et Alex Mwangi pour le Kenya ; T'sele Mokhathali, Haleokoe Jopo et Makananelo Puseletso pour le Lesotho ; Donah pour Madagascar ; Laurent Kalonga, Chimvano Thawani, Alick Wella et Natasha Kandoje pour le Malawi ; Siaka Samaké et Boubacar Diakité pour le Mali ; Mohamed Falilou Gueye, pour la Mauritanie ; Meeshrani Balgobin, Dharmarajen Changeya et Roshan Oree pour Maurice ; El Moustapha Bennani et Abderrahim Mezroui pour le Maroc ; Idi Itope et Nelago Ekandjo pour la Namibie ; Mahamadou Djibrilla pour le Niger ; Cephas Tiye pour le Nigéria ; Frédéric Ngolele pour la République du Congo ; Roy Valence Gasangwa et Denis Mukama pour le Rwanda ; Pape Malick Diallo, pour le Sénégal ; Sophie Belle, Francesco Estico, Rudy Sinon, Roseline Lepathy, Ayda Noel et Yannick Vel pour les Seychelles ; Philippe Kargbo pour la Sierra Leone; Mampho Baholo, Paul Dreyer, Lawrence Gqesha, Mamiky Leolo, Tshepo Makgoro, Denis Marais, Nontokozo Mnqayi, Vivienne Smithdorf et Darlington Zhou pour l'Afrique du Sud ; Rogangoum Kodindouma Hervé et Hassan Adoum Mbodou Mbami pour le Tchad ; Ouro-Adoï Abdelganiou et Imrane Moussa pour le Togo ; Saoussen Boumaiza, Raja Hadj Khalifa et Rihab Ben Challadia pour la Tunisie ; et Jova Mayega, Ronald Nyenje Makumbi, Milly Isongoma Nalukwago et Allen Nassanga pour l'Ouganda.

Les auteurs souhaitent rendre un hommage particulier à Agnes Kanyangeyo du Rwanda, qui est décédée en février 2022 et qui a été une contributrice clé à l'initiative des *Statistiques des recettes publiques en Afrique* depuis sa création en 2014.

Les statistiques des recettes publiques en Afrique font partie de la *Base de données mondiale des statistiques des recettes publiques*. Les auteurs tiennent également à remercier les gouvernements de l'Irlande, du Japon, du Luxembourg, de la Norvège, des Pays-Bas, du Royaume-Uni, de la Suède et de la Suisse ainsi que l'Union européenne pour leur soutien à l'initiative des statistiques mondiales des recettes publiques.

Ce document a été produit avec le soutien financier de l'Union européenne. Les opinions exprimées ici ne peuvent en aucun cas être considérées comme reflétant les opinions officielles de l'Union européenne.

Table of contents

Table des matières

LIST OF TABLES/LISTE DE TABLEAUX

Chapter 1/Chapitre 1

Tax revenue trends, 2010-20/ Tendances des recettes fiscales, 2010-20

Chapter 3/Chapitre 3

Efficient taxation of the informal sector in Africa/ Imposer efficacement le secteur informel en Afrique

Chapter 4/Chapitre 4

Tax levels and tax structures, 1990-2020/ Niveaux et structures des impôts, 1990-2020

Chapter 5/Chapitre 5

Country tables, 1995-2020 – Tax revenues/ Tableaux pays, 1995-2020 – Recettes fiscales

Chapter 6/Chapitre 6

Non-tax revenue tables, 1995-2020/ Tableaux des recettes non fiscales, 1995-2020

LIST OF FIGURES/LISTE DE GRAPHIQUES

Chapter 1/Chapitre 1
Tax revenue trends, 2010-20/ Tendances des recettes fiscales, 2010-20

Chapter 2/Chapitre 2

Non-tax revenue trends, 2010-20/ Tendances des recettes non fiscales, 2010-20

Chapter 3/Chapitre 3

Efficient taxation of the informal sector in Africa/ Imposer efficacement le secteur informel en Afrique

Executive summary

Achieving the United Nations' Sustainable Development Goals (SDGs) and implementing the Addis Ababa Action Agenda and the African Union's Agenda 2063 require mobilising additional finance, in particular domestic resources, to fund public goods and services. The COVID-19 crisis has significantly affected government revenues, increasing the financing gap to achieving the SDGs and Africa's development agenda. As a consequence, the need for additional revenues has become even more critical.

Revenue Statistics in Africa 2022 presents internationally comparable indicators on tax and non-tax revenues that can help track progress on domestic resource mobilisation, and inform tax policy analysis and reforms. It also contributes to the implementation of the second phase of the Pan-African Statistics Programme – a joint initiative between the European Union and the African Union that aims to improve measurement of progress in the process of African Integration by promoting the use of statistical data of quality in the decision making process and policy monitoring. This report provides data on 31 countries and includes a special feature examining the taxation of the informal sector in Africa.

Tax revenues

In 2020, against the backdrop of the COVID-19 crisis, the unweighted average tax-to-GDP ratio for the 31 countries in this publication (the "Africa (31) average") was 16.0%, a decrease of 0.3 percentage points (p.p.) relative to 2019. The tax-to-GDP ratio refers to total tax revenues, including compulsory social security contributions, as a percentage of gross domestic product (GDP). The Africa (31) average in 2020 was below the averages of Asian and Pacific economies (19.1%), Latin America and the Caribbean (LAC) (21.9%), and the OECD (33.5%).

Tax-to-GDP ratios varied widely across the African region in 2020, ranging from 5.5% in Nigeria to 32.5% in Tunisia. More than three-quarters (24) of the African countries recorded a decline in their tax-to-GDP ratio between 2019 and 2020, largely due to the impact of COVID-19. Most of the decreases recorded over the period were smaller than one percentage point of GDP, but they exceeded this amount in seven countries. Namibia registered the largest decrease, of 1.7 p.p. In contrast, Chad's tax-to-GDP ratio rose by 6.6 p.p., the largest increase in the region, followed by the Republic of the Congo (1.7 p.p.).

Seventeen of the 31 countries recorded declines in nominal tax revenues in 2020, which fell by 0.5% on average. Nominal GDP increased by 0.2% on average, with 18 countries recording increases in nominal GDP. In a third of African countries, a decline in nominal tax revenues was accompanied by a decline in nominal GDP, mostly resulting in lower tax-to-GDP ratios in 2020 relative to 2019. However, the declines in GDP in the Republic of the Congo and Tunisia were larger than the drop in tax revenues, resulting in increases in their tax revenues as a share of GDP.

As was the case in Africa, about three-quarters of countries in the LAC and Asia-Pacific regions recorded decreases in tax revenues as a share of GDP between 2019 and 2020. However, tax-to-GDP ratios in the LAC and Asia-Pacific regions were more strongly affected by the COVID-19 crisis on average, decreasing by 0.8 p.p. and 1.2 p.p., respectively, over the period. In contrast, the OECD average increased by 0.1 p.p., and more than half of OECD countries recorded higher tax-to-GDP ratios in 2020 than in 2019.

Taxes on goods and services were the tax type most strongly impacted by the COVID-19 crisis across the 31 African countries, decreasing by 0.4% of GDP on average between 2019 and 2020. This decline was driven by a fall in revenues from value-added taxes (VAT) as a share of GDP of 0.3 p.p. In contrast, revenues from personal income taxes (PIT) remained unchanged over this period while those from corporate income taxes rose by 0.1 p.p., an increase driven entirely by Chad.

In 2020, the Africa (31) average tax-to-GDP ratio recorded its first year-on-year decline since 2010, although it was 1.6 p.p. higher than in 2010. In comparison, the average tax-to-GDP ratios for the LAC region and the OECD increased by 1.0 p.p. and 1.9 p.p. over this period. Tax-to-GDP ratios rose in 25 African countries between 2010 and 2020 and declined in six. The COVID-19 crisis has reversed a decade of gains in tax revenues as a share of GDP for several countries, notably Kenya and Namibia.

The increases in the Africa (31) average tax-to-GDP ratio between 2010 and 2020 were mainly generated by VAT and PIT. In 2020, taxes on goods and services remained the main source of tax revenues in Africa, accounting for an average of 50.4% of total tax revenues, with VAT accounting for 27.8%. Taxes on income and profits accounted for 39.3% of tax revenues. Taxes on goods and services were the principal source of tax revenues for 22 of the countries included in this report in 2020. For the other nine countries, taxes on income and profits accounted for the principal share.

Non-tax revenues

In 2020, average non-tax revenues reached 6.8% of GDP in Africa, ranging from 0.5% of GDP in South Africa to 35.1% of GDP in Lesotho. Non-tax revenues exceeded 10% of GDP in five countries, four of which (Botswana, Eswatini, Lesotho and Namibia) received most of their non-tax revenues in the form of funds from the Southern African Customs Union (SACU) Common Revenue Pool. Non-tax revenues were lower than tax revenues in all countries except Botswana, the Republic of the Congo and Lesotho. Between 2010 and 2019, average non-tax revenues decreased by 1.7 p.p. of GDP while tax revenues increased by 1.8 p.p. In 2020, the first year of the COVID-19 crisis, these trajectories reversed: while tax revenues declined by 0.3 p.p., non-tax revenues increased by 0.6 p.p., yielding an average increase in government revenues of 0.3 p.p. in 2020.

The COVID-19 crisis led to a decrease in oil royalties in a number of countries due to lower fuel prices and demand, while foreign aid increased over the same period. Grant revenues increased by 0.4 p.p. of GDP between 2019 and 2020 while property income decreased by 0.2 p.p., due to lower revenues from natural resources.

Sources of non-tax revenues vary by country. For 11 countries, a majority of non-tax revenues came from grants in 2020. Five countries (Cameroon, the Republic of the Congo, Equatorial Guinea, Mauritania and Nigeria) received most of their non-tax revenues from rents and royalties, in particular oil royalties. The 11 remaining countries, excluding the four net recipient SACU countries, relied more on other sources of non-tax revenues, such as interest and dividends and fees for goods and services.

Efficient taxation of the informal sector in Africa

Revenue Statistics in Africa 2022 includes a special feature examining challenges and potential solutions to taxing the informal sector in Africa. The chapter, which is based on the Guidebook produced by the African Tax Administration Forum (ATAF), summarises experiences and good practices of African countries in this area. While eight out of ten workers in Africa are in informal employment, the informal sector contributes little to domestic revenue mobilisation. Recommendations for the effective taxation of the informal sector include institutionalising exchanges between tax authorities and tax payers in the informal sector, simplifying and incentivising registration, rationalising the number of taxes and creating a database of actors in the informal sector.

Résumé

Pour atteindre les Objectifs de développement durable (ODD) des Nations Unies et mettre en œuvre le Programme d'action d'Addis-Abeba et l'Agenda 2063 de l'Union africaine, il est nécessaire de mobiliser des moyens financiers supplémentaires, et notamment des ressources intérieures, afin de financer l'offre de biens et de services publics. La crise du COVID-19 a un impact négatif significatif sur les recettes publiques, creusant le déficit de financement pour atteindre les ODD et réaliser le programme de développement de l'Afrique. Aussi, la nécessité de mobiliser des recettes supplémentaires est devenue encore plus impérieuse.

L'édition 2022 des *Statistiques des recettes publiques en Afrique* contient un ensemble d'indicateurs internationalement comparables sur les recettes fiscales et non fiscales qui peuvent aider à mesurer les progrès en matière de mobilisation des ressources intérieures et à éclairer les politiques et les réformes fiscales. Ce rapport contribue aussi à la mise en œuvre de la seconde phase du Programme statistique panafricain, une initiative conjointe de l'Union européenne et de l'Union africaine qui vise à améliorer la mesure des progrès dans l'intégration africaine, en encourageant l'utilisation de données statistiques de qualité dans le processus d'élaboration des politiques et leur suivi. Ce rapport livre des données sur 31 pays d'Afrique et contient une étude spéciale qui décrit l'imposition du secteur informel en Afrique.

Recettes fiscales

En 2020, dans le contexte de la crise du COVID-19, le ratio moyen non pondéré impôts/PIB dans les 31 pays d'Afrique couverts par cette publication [désigné ci-après « moyenne des pays d'Afrique (31) »] s'est établi à 16.0 %, soit une baisse de 0.3 point de pourcentage par rapport à 2019. Le ratio impôts/PIB correspond aux recettes fiscales totales, y compris les cotisations obligatoires de sécurité sociale, exprimées en pourcentage du produit intérieur brut (PIB). En 2020, la moyenne des pays d'Afrique (31) était inférieure à celle de la région Asie-Pacifique, de 19.1 %, à celle de la région Amérique latine et Caraïbes (ALC), de 21.9 % et de la zone OCDE (33.5 %).

En 2020, les ratios impôts/PIB ont affiché de grandes variations entre les pays de la région africaine, allant de 5.5 % au Nigéria à 32.5 % en Tunisie. Plus des trois quarts (24) des pays africains ont vu leur ratio impôts/PIB reculer entre 2019 et 2020, en grande partie à cause des répercussions du COVID-19. La plupart des baisses qui se sont produites pendant la période étaient inférieures à un point de PIB, mais elles ont dépassé ce montant dans sept pays. C'est la Namibie qui a accusé la plus forte baisse, soit 1.7 point de pourcentage. À l'inverse, le ratio impôts/PIB du Tchad a augmenté de 6.6 points, soit la plus forte hausse de la région, suivi de la République du Congo (1.7 point).

Dix-sept des 31 pays étudiés ont enregistré une baisse de leurs recettes fiscales nominales, qui se sont contractées de 0.5 % en moyenne. Le PIB nominal a progressé de 0.2 % en moyenne, et 18 pays ont vu leur PIB nominal s'accroître. Dans un tiers des pays africains, le recul des recettes fiscales nominales s'est accompagné d'un repli du PIB nominal, aboutissant le plus souvent à des ratios impôts/PIB plus faibles en 2020 qu'en 2019. Toutefois, la diminution du PIB en République du Congo et en Tunisie était plus marquée que l'érosion des recettes fiscales, conduisant à une augmentation de leurs recettes fiscales en pourcentage du PIB.

Comme en Afrique, environ les trois quarts des pays des régions ALC et Asie-Pacifique ont connu une baisse de leurs recettes fiscales en pourcentage du PIB entre 2019 et 2020. Toutefois, les ratios impôts/PIB dans les régions ALC et Asie-Pacifique ont été plus négativement touchés par la crise liée au COVID-19, puisqu'ils ont reculé de respectivement 0.8 point et 1.2 point au cours de la période. En revanche, la moyenne des pays de l'OCDE s'est accrue de 0.1 point et plus de la moitié des pays de l'OCDE ont vu leur ratio impôts/PIB augmenter entre 2019 et 2020.

Les impôts sur les biens et services représentaient la catégorie d'impôts la plus sévèrement touchée par la crise du COVID-19 dans les 31 pays d'Afrique, puisque les recettes correspondantes ont reculé de 0.4 % du PIB en moyenne entre 2019 et 2020. Cette baisse était due à la diminution des recettes tirées des taxes sur la valeur ajoutée (TVA) en pourcentage du PIB, soit 0.3 point. À l'inverse, les recettes générées par les impôts sur le revenu des personnes physiques (IRPP) sont restées inchangées au cours de cette période, tandis que celles provenant des impôts sur les bénéfices des sociétés ont augmenté de 0.1 point, une hausse exclusivement portée par le Tchad.

En 2020, le ratio impôts/PIB moyen de l'Afrique (31) a baissé par rapport à l'année précédente pour la première fois depuis 2010, même s'il était encore supérieur de 1.6 point à son niveau de 2010. Par comparaison, les ratios impôts/PIB moyens pour la région ALC et la zone OCDE se sont accrus de respectivement 1.0 point et 1.9 point au cours de cette période. Les ratios ont augmenté dans 25 pays d'Afrique entre 2010 et 2020, et ils ont diminué dans six. La crise du COVID-19 a porté un coup d'arrêt à une décennie de progression des recettes fiscales en pourcentage du PIB dans plusieurs pays, notamment au Kenya et en Namibie.

Les augmentations du ratio impôts/PIB moyen de l'Afrique (31) entre 2010 et 2020 étaient principalement dues à l'évolution favorable des recettes de la TVA et de l'IRPP. En 2020, les impôts sur les biens et services sont restés la principale source de recettes fiscales en Afrique, puisqu'ils ont généré 50.4 % du total des recettes fiscales en moyenne, la TVA à elle seule contribuant à 27.8 % du total. Les impôts sur le revenu et sur les bénéfices ont procuré 39.3 % des recettes fiscales. En 2020, les impôts sur les biens et services représentaient la principale source de recettes fiscales pour les 22 pays africains couverts par ce rapport. Dans les neuf autres pays, la plus grande partie des recettes fiscales provenait des impôts sur le revenu et les bénéfices.

Recettes non fiscales

En 2020, les recettes non fiscales moyennes équivalaient à 6.8 % du PIB en Afrique. Elles s'échelonnaient entre 0.5 % du PIB en Afrique du Sud et 35.1 % du PIB au Lesotho. Elles dépassaient 10 % du PIB dans cinq pays, dont quatre (Botswana, Eswatini, Lesotho et Namibie) percevaient la majeure partie de leurs recettes non fiscales sous la forme de fonds versés par le fonds commun des recettes de l'Union douanière d'Afrique australe (SACU). Le total des recettes non fiscales était inférieur à celui des recettes fiscales dans l'ensemble des pays à l'exception du Botswana, du Lesotho et de la République du Congo. Entre 2010 et 2019, les recettes non fiscales moyennes ont reculé de 1.7 point de PIB, tandis que les recettes fiscales augmentaient de 1.8 point. En 2020, la première année de la crise du COVID-19, ces trajectoires se sont inversées : alors que les recettes fiscales se sont contractées de 0.3 point, les recettes non fiscales ont progressé de 0.6 point, générant une hausse moyenne des recettes publiques de 0.3 point en 2020.

La crise du COVID-19 a provoqué une chute des redevances pétrolières dans un certain nombre de pays sous l'effet de la baisse des prix des combustibles et de la demande, tandis que l'aide étrangère s'est accrue au cours de la même période. Les recettes provenant des dons ont augmenté de 0.4 point de PIB entre 2019 et 2020, tandis que les revenus de la propriété ont fléchi de 0.2 point en raison de la baisse des recettes provenant des ressources naturelles.

L'origine des recettes non fiscales diffère selon les pays. Pour 11 pays, les dons constituaient la majorité des recettes non fiscales en 2020. Cinq autres pays (Cameroun, Guinée équatoriale, Mauritanie, Nigéria et République du Congo) tiraient quant à eux la majeure partie de ces recettes de loyers et de redevances, et notamment de redevances pétrolières. Les 11 pays restants, à l'exception des quatre pays bénéficiaires nets de la SACU, ont tiré l'essentiel de leurs recettes non fiscales d'autres sources telles que les intérêts et dividendes et les frais au titre de la vente de biens et services.

Imposer efficacement le secteur informel en Afrique

L'édition 2022 des *Statistiques des recettes publiques en Afrique* contient une étude spéciale qui examine les défis et solutions possibles pour taxer le secteur informel en Afrique. Ce chapitre, qui s'appuie sur le Manuel publié par le Forum sur l'administration fiscale africaine (ATAF), résume les expériences et bonnes pratiques des pays africains dans ce domaine. En Afrique, huit travailleurs sur dix appartiennent à l'économie informelle, mais ce secteur contribue peu à la mobilisation des ressources intérieures. Pour taxer efficacement le secteur informel, ce chapitre préconise d'institutionnaliser les relations entre autorités fiscales et contribuables du secteur informel, de simplifier et d'encourager l'enregistrement des entreprises, de réduire le nombre d'impôts et de créer une base de données des acteurs de l'économie informelle.

Chapter 1

Tax revenue trends, 2010-20

Chapitre 1

Tendances des recettes fiscales, 2010-20

Revenue Statistics in Africa 1990-2020/Statistiques des recettes publiques en Afrique 1990-2020

Chapter 1

Tax revenue trends, 2010-20

Achieving the United Nations' Sustainable Development Goals (SDGs) and implementing the Addis Ababa Action Agenda and the African Union's Agenda 2063 require mobilising additional finance, in particular domestic resources, to fund public goods and services. Taxation provides a predictable and sustainable source of government revenue, in contrast with the volatility of other important sources of public revenues, such as grants and mineral royalties.

Revenue Statistics in Africa presents an internationally comparable set of indicators on tax and non-tax revenues which can be used to track progress on domestic resource mobilisation (as envisaged in Agenda 2063, the SDGs, the Addis Ababa Action Agenda as well as related initiatives such as the Addis Tax Initiative) and to inform tax policy and reform. The report and its data also contribute to the Pan-African Statistics Programme, a joint effort between the European Union and the African Union to support statistical capacity in Africa by providing quality revenue statistics data that can inform decision-making processes and policy monitoring towards African integration.

This edition of the report includes data for 2020 and focuses on the impact of the COVID-19 crisis on tax systems across Africa. The pandemic significantly weakened public finances across the world, leading to sharp declines in revenues and higher debt levels. This report examines the pandemic's impact on tax revenues in absolute terms and as a percentage of GDP, in aggregate and for different tax types. It also compares the impact on African countries with those in other regions.

This chapter discusses trends in the tax-to-GDP ratio, tax structure and share of tax revenue by level of government in 31 African countries: Botswana, Burkina Faso, Cabo Verde, Cameroon, Chad, the Republic of the Congo, the Democratic Republic of the Congo, Côte d'Ivoire, Equatorial Guinea, Egypt, Eswatini, Ghana, Lesotho, Kenya, Madagascar, Malawi, Mali, Mauritania, Mauritius, Morocco, Namibia, Niger, Nigeria, Rwanda, Senegal, the Seychelles, Sierra Leone (included for the first time in this edition), South Africa, Togo, Tunisia and Uganda. It also compares the averages of the 31 African countries with the averages of 28 Asian and Pacific economies (OECD, 2022[1]), 26 Latin American and Caribbean (LAC) countries (OECD et al., 2022[2]), and 38 OECD countries (OECD, 2021[3]). The discussion supplements the detailed country information on tax revenue in Chapter 5.

Tax-to-GDP ratios in Africa

Tax-to-GDP ratios in 2020

The unweighted average tax-to-GDP ratio of the 31 African countries in this publication (referred to as the "Africa (31) average") was 16.0% in 2020 (Figure 1.1). The tax-to-GDP ratio is measured as tax revenues (including compulsory social security contributions paid to general government) as a proportion of gross domestic product (GDP).[1] In comparison, the average tax-to-GDP ratios in Asia and the Pacific, Latin America and the Caribbean, and the OECD were 19.1%, 21.9% and 33.5% respectively in 2020.

Tax-to-GDP ratios varied widely across the countries included in this publication in 2020, ranging from 5.5% in Nigeria to 32.5% in Tunisia. Morocco, Tunisia, the Seychelles and South Africa had tax-to-GDP ratios above 25%, 22 countries recorded tax-to-GDP ratios between 10.0% and 21.0% while the Republic of the Congo, the Democratic Republic of the Congo, Equatorial Guinea, Niger and Nigeria had tax-to-GDP ratios below 10%.

Figure 1.1. **Tax-to-GDP ratios and total tax revenue (excluding social security contributions) as a percentage of GDP, 2020**

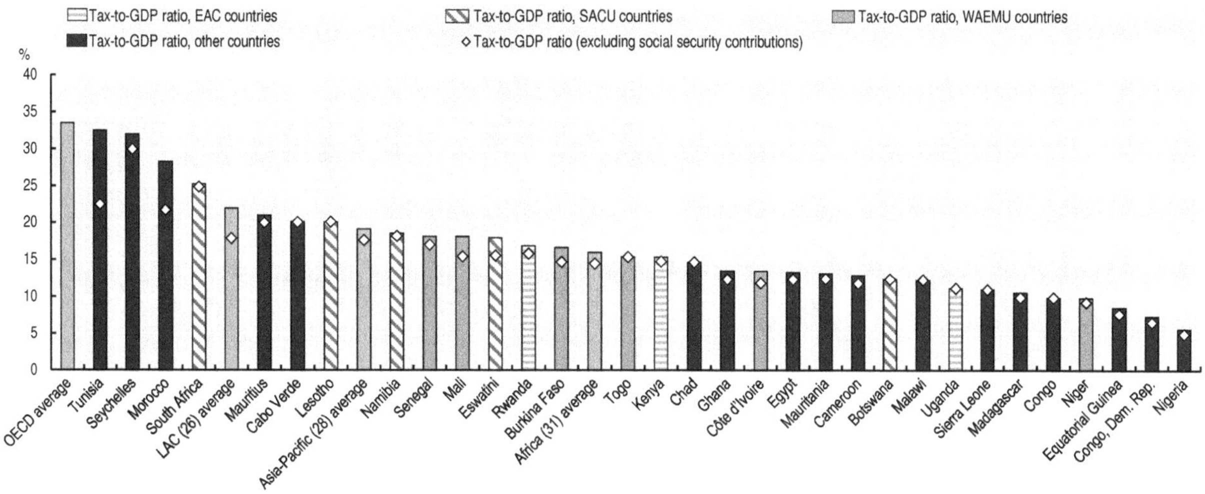

Note: Data include sub-national government tax revenues for Eswatini, Mauritius, Morocco, Nigeria (state revenues only) and South Africa for 2020. The Africa (31) average and the averages for Asia-Pacific (28 economies), LAC (26 countries) and the OECD (38 countries) are unweighted.

The Africa (31) average should be interpreted with caution as data on social security contributions are not available for Chad, the Republic of the Congo, Sierra Leone, Togo and Uganda and are only partially available for Cameroon and Senegal. Social security contributions for Botswana, Lesotho and Malawi are deemed to be null as they do not meet the criteria to be classified as social security contributions set out in the OECD classification of taxes in the Interpretative Guide. See the country tables in Chapter 5 for further information.

The tax-to-GDP ratio for South Africa includes payments made by South Africa to the Southern African Customs Union pool.

Source: Tables 4.1 and 4.2 in Chapter 4 and (OECD/ATAF/AUC, 2022[4]), "Revenue Statistics in Africa: Comparative tables", OECD Tax Statistics (database), *http://dx.doi.org/10.1787/be755711-en.*

StatLink *https://stat.link/e2rlxg*

Impact of COVID-19 on tax revenues: Changes in 2020 relative to 2019

The average tax-to-GDP ratio of the African countries covered in this report decreased by 0.3 percentage points (p.p.) between 2019 and 2020, largely as a result of the sharp decline in economic activity caused by the COVID-19 pandemic, which had a substantial effect on public revenues. The fall was primarily driven by the reduction in revenues from taxes on goods and services, which declined by 0.4 p.p. of GDP on average between the two years.

Tax-to-GDP ratios decreased in 24 countries and increased in 7 countries between 2019 and 2020 (Figure 1.2). Most decreases over the period were smaller than one percentage point of GDP; the fall exceeded this threshold in seven countries: Botswana, Cabo Verde, Egypt, Equatorial Guinea, Kenya, Lesotho and Namibia. Namibia registered the largest decrease, of 1.7 p.p. In contrast, Chad's tax-to-GDP ratio increased by 6.6 p.p., the largest increase across the region, followed by the Republic of the Congo (1.7 p.p.); in the other five countries where the tax-to-GDP ratio increased in 2020 relative to 2019, the increases were smaller than one percentage point.

Figure 1.2. **Year-on-year changes in tax-to-GDP ratios in 2019 and in 2020**

Percentage points of GDP

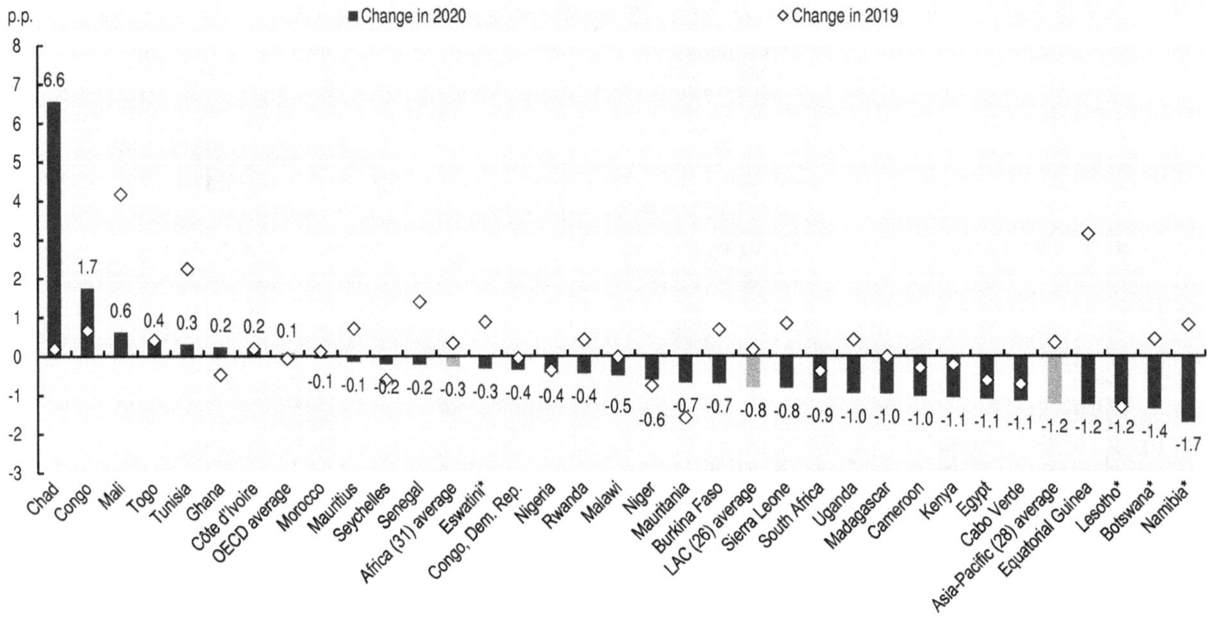

Note: The figures include sub-national government tax revenues for Eswatini, Mauritius, Morocco, Nigeria (state revenues only) and South Africa for 2020.

*Eswatini, Lesotho, Namibia and Botswana report their figures using an April-March fiscal year. This means 2020 figures for these countries include revenues up to 31 March 2021.

The Africa (31) average and the averages for Asia-Pacific (28 countries), LAC (26 countries) and the OECD (38 countries) are unweighted. The change in the Africa (31) average should be interpreted with caution as data for social security contributions are not available or are partial in a few countries. See the country tables in Chapter 5 for further information.

Source: Authors' calculations based on data in Table 4.1 in Chapter 4 and (OECD/ATAF/AUC, 2022[4]), *Revenue Statistics in Africa*: Comparative tables", OECD Tax Statistics (database), *http://dx.doi.org/10.1787/be755711-en*.

StatLink *https://stat.link/imqknv*

Overview of changes in tax revenues and in GDP in nominal terms

To provide further insights into the impact of the COVID-19 crisis on tax revenues, this section analyses changes in nominal tax revenues and nominal GDP between 2019 and 2020 in Africa. The value of the tax-to-GDP ratio depends on two components; its numerator (tax revenue) and its denominator (GDP) (see Box 1.1). This means that the changes in tax-to-GDP ratios between 2019 and 2020 reflect changes in nominal tax revenues as well as changes in nominal GDP over the same period.

The COVID-19 pandemic resulted in historic falls in nominal tax revenues and nominal GDP. Seventeen out of 31 countries covered by this report recorded declines in nominal tax revenues between 2019 and 2020, and nominal tax revenues fell by 0.5% on average over the period (unweighted figure). However, Chad experienced a significant increase in nominal tax revenues (73.6%) between 2019 and 2020; excluding Chad, the region's nominal tax revenue fell by 3.0% on average over the period. Although thirteen African countries recorded decreases in nominal GDP between 2019 and 2020, nominal GDP increased by 0.2% on average in the 31 countries of this publication (unweighted figure).

Figure 1.3 shows the changes in tax revenues and GDP in nominal terms between 2019 and 2020. In 11 African countries, a decline in nominal tax revenues accompanied a decline in nominal GDP and for nine of these countries nominal tax revenues fell by more than nominal GDP, leading to a decline in their tax-to-GDP ratio. For two countries (the Republic of the Congo and Tunisia), nominal tax revenues fell by less than nominal GDP between 2019 and 2020, leading to an increase in their tax-to-GDP ratios. A further six African countries reported decreases in nominal tax revenues while their nominal GDP increased, decreasing their tax-to-GDP ratios.

Figure 1.3. **Change in tax revenue and GDP in nominal currency, 2019-20**

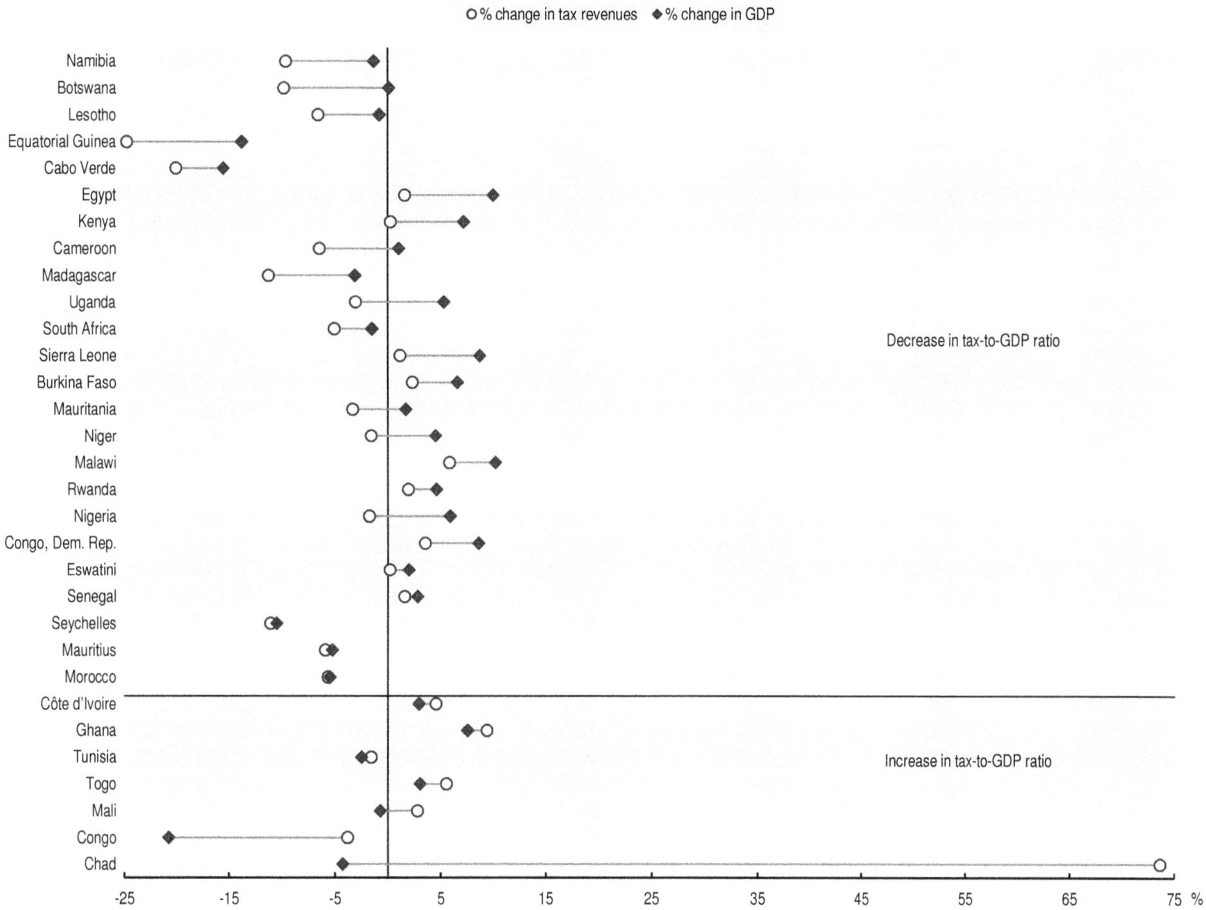

Note: The figures include sub-national government tax revenues for Eswatini, Mauritius, Morocco, Nigeria (state revenues only) and South Africa for 2020.

The change in the Africa (31) average should be interpreted with caution as data for social security contributions are not available or are partial in a few countries. See the country tables in Chapter 5 for further information.

*Eswatini, Lesotho, Namibia and Botswana report their figures using an April-March fiscal year. This means 2020 figures for these countries include revenues up to 31 March 2021. See the notes to the country tables in Chapter 5 for further information.

Source: Authors' calculations based on data in (OECD/ATAF/AUC, 2022[4]), "*Revenue Statistics in Africa*: Comparative tables", *OECD Tax Statistics* (database), *http://dx.doi.org/10.1787/be755711-en*.

StatLink https://stat.link/o34eb6

The Seychelles recorded large decreases in 2020 relative to 2019 (over 10%) in nominal GDP as well as in nominal tax revenues. Although these falls were significant, the decline in tax revenues as a percentage of GDP between 2019 and 2020 was relatively modest (0.2 p.p.) due to the similar magnitude of the falls in nominal tax revenues and nominal GDP.

Twelve African countries recorded increases in nominal tax revenues and in nominal GDP; for three of these countries, nominal tax revenues increased by more than nominal GDP, leading to an increase in the tax-to-GDP ratio. Two countries (Chad and Mali) experienced an increase in nominal tax revenues and a decrease in nominal GDP, resulting in a higher tax-to-GDP ratio in 2020 relative to 2019.

The COVID-19 crisis impacted the tax revenues and GDP of countries around the world. Across African countries, the impact was smaller than in LAC countries and in Asia-Pacific economies but greater than in OECD countries on average. The Africa (31) average tax-to-GDP ratio decreased by 0.3 p.p. between 2019 and 2020 while the LAC and Asia-Pacific (28) averages decreased by 0.8 p.p. and 1.2 p.p., respectively, and the OECD average increased by 0.1 p.p. over the period. Slightly more than half of the OECD countries had higher tax-to-GDP ratios in 2020 relative to 2019. In contrast, about three quarters of countries recorded decreases in tax revenues as a share of GDP in the other regions between 2019 and 2020.

In each region, most countries recorded falls in nominal tax revenues between 2019 and 2020, with the largest decrease observed in the Asia-Pacific region on average. Nominal tax revenues declined by 8.8% on average in Asia-Pacific economies, similar to the average decline observed in the LAC region (8.0%) but a much larger fall than the decline in nominal tax revenues of 0.5% for the Africa (31) average and 2.1% for the OECD average. Asia-Pacific (28) is the only region where some economies (three) experienced a fall in nominal tax revenues in excess of 30% between 2019 and 2020. Differences in the percentage change in nominal tax revenues across the regions may be partly explained by the level of inflation, which differed greatly in these regions in 2020: the average consumer price index in Africa in 2020 was 10.8%, while it was 3.2% in Asia-Pacific, and 1.1% in Europe (IMF, 2022[5]).

Figure 1.4. **Changes in nominal tax revenue and nominal GDP in Africa, Asia-Pacific, LAC and OECD countries, 2019-20**

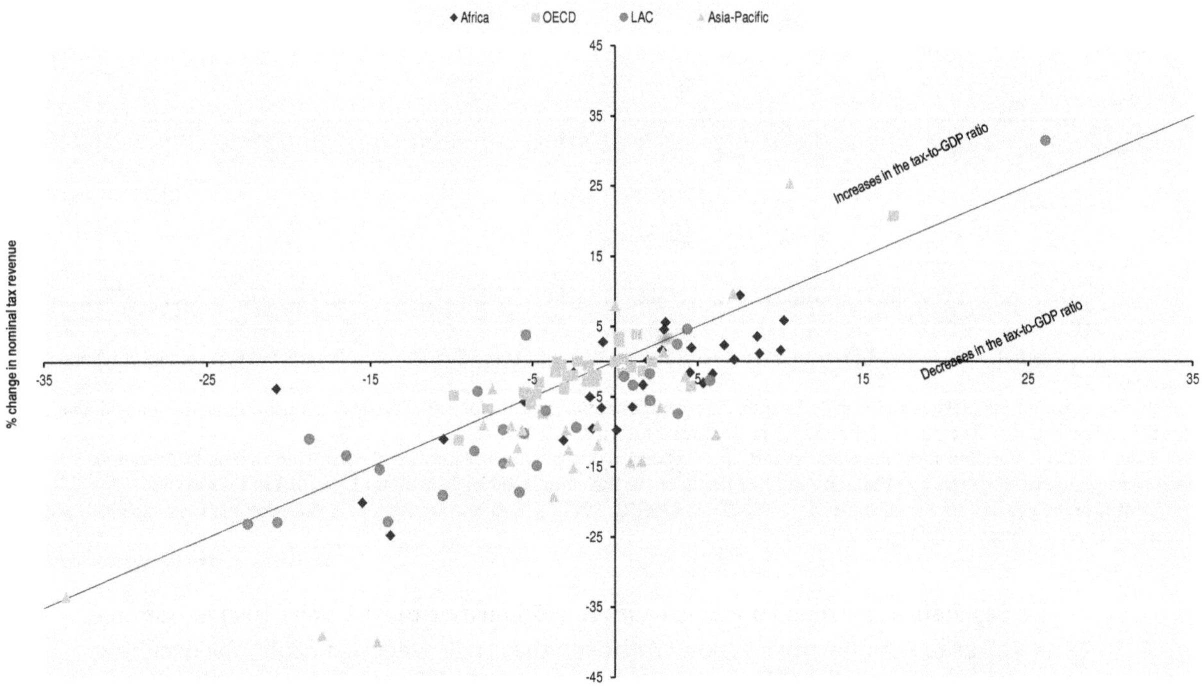

Note: Data include sub-national government tax revenues for Eswatini, Mauritius, Morocco, Nigeria (state revenues only) and South Africa for 2020. Total tax revenues for Chad, the Republic of the Congo, Sierra Leone, Togo and Uganda do not include social security contributions as they are not available.

Source: Authors' calculations based on data in (OECD/ATAF/AUC, 2022[4]), "*Revenue Statistics in Africa*: Comparative tables", *OECD Tax Statistics* (database), *http://dx.doi.org/10.1787/be755711-en*, (OECD, 2022[1]), (OECD et al., 2022[2]) and (OECD, 2021[3]).

StatLink *https://stat.link/5a6kog*

Between 2019 and 2020, eleven out of the 31 African countries in this publication recorded declines in both nominal GDP and nominal tax revenues, whereas this was the case for the majority of OECD and LAC countries. However, only a small number of African and LAC countries recorded nominal tax revenues falling by less than nominal GDP, resulting in higher tax-to-GDP ratios in 2020. This contrasts with the OECD, where nominal tax revenues fell by less than GDP in 14 of 25 countries that recorded declining nominal tax revenues and GDP.

Box 1.1. **Methodology: the tax-to-GDP ratio**

The tax ratios shown in this publication express aggregate tax revenues as a percentage of GDP. The value of this ratio depends on its denominator (GDP) as well as its numerator (tax revenue). Both the numerator and the denominator, may be subject to historical revision.

The numerator (tax revenues)

This publication uses revenue figures that are submitted annually by focal points from national Ministries of Finance, tax administrations or statistics offices. Historical tax revenue data are subject to revisions each year, with more important revisions in latest years. Past figures may also change from one edition to the next when new data are obtained by focal points to improve the publication.

In 23 African countries covered in this report, the reporting year coincides with the calendar year. The remaining eight countries report on a fiscal year basis. For these countries, the reporting year 2020 includes one quarter of 2021 (five countries with fiscal year from April to March) or two quarters of 2019 (four countries with fiscal year from July to June)[2]. This means that the revenue data for 2020 for countries on a fiscal year basis includes revenues from periods that were less significantly affected by the COVID-19 pandemic.

The denominator (GDP)

The GDP figures used in this publication are sourced from the *World Economic Outlook* (WEO) published by the IMF. Using these GDP figures ensures a consistency across countries, as well as international comparability. GDP figures are also revised and updated to reflect better data sources and improved estimation procedures, or to move towards new internationally-agreed guidelines for measuring the value of GDP.

The most recent available figures from WEO were published in April 2022 (IMF, 2022[6]) and include GDP revisions made by some countries to align with the most recent System of National Accounts (SNA 2008). The GDP figures in this edition were revised compared to last year's edition notably for Botswana, Kenya, Madagascar, Malawi, Seychelles, Tunisia and South Africa (the 2019 GDP for example for these countries were revised by 3% or more). The difference between the 2019 tax-to-GDP ratios in the 2021 and 2022 editions ranged from -2.1 p.p. in Tunisia and the Seychelles to 1.1 p.p. in Botswana; the 2019 average for the 30 countries included in last year's edition is 0.2 p.p. lower in this edition as a result of the revisions.

Impact of the pandemic on different tax types

Between 2019 and 2020, taxes on goods and services decreased more than taxes on income or other taxes, such as social security contributions and property taxes. In 2020, the largest decrease in tax revenues as a share of GDP was seen in value added taxes (VAT), which decreased by 0.3 p.p. on average. Other taxes on goods and services decreased by 0.1 p.p. over the period, driven by declining tax revenues from customs duties (0.1 p.p.).

No change was seen in personal income tax (PIT) revenues as a share of GDP, on average, while revenues from corporate income tax (CIT) and social security contributions (SSCs) increased by 0.1 p.p. on average between 2019 and 2020.

Figure 1.5 shows changes in tax revenues by tax category as a share of GDP in Africa between 2019 and 2020. VAT fell widely across the African countries in 2020, with three-quarters of the countries (24) in this report experiencing decreases. VAT revenues increased between 2019 and 2020 in the remaining 7 countries.

Namibia observed the largest drop in VAT as a share of GDP between 2019 and 2020, of 1.7 p.p. Namibia is among the quarter of the African countries in this publication that recorded the largest falls in nominal tax revenues between 2019 and 2020, of 9.6%. In April 2020, Namibia announced the launch of an Economic Stimulus and Relief Package to mitigate the impact of COVID-19 that included accelerated repayment of overdue and undisputed VAT refunds to businesses (EY, 2020[7]). This measure contributed to the lower collection of VAT revenues in Namibia in 2020 relative to 2019.

Revenues from customs duties across African countries were affected by the COVID-19 in 2020, but to a lesser extent than VAT. Nearly two thirds of African countries (19) recorded decreases in revenues from customs duties.

Figure 1.5. **Changes in tax revenues by tax category as a share of GDP, 2019-20**

Percentage points of GDP

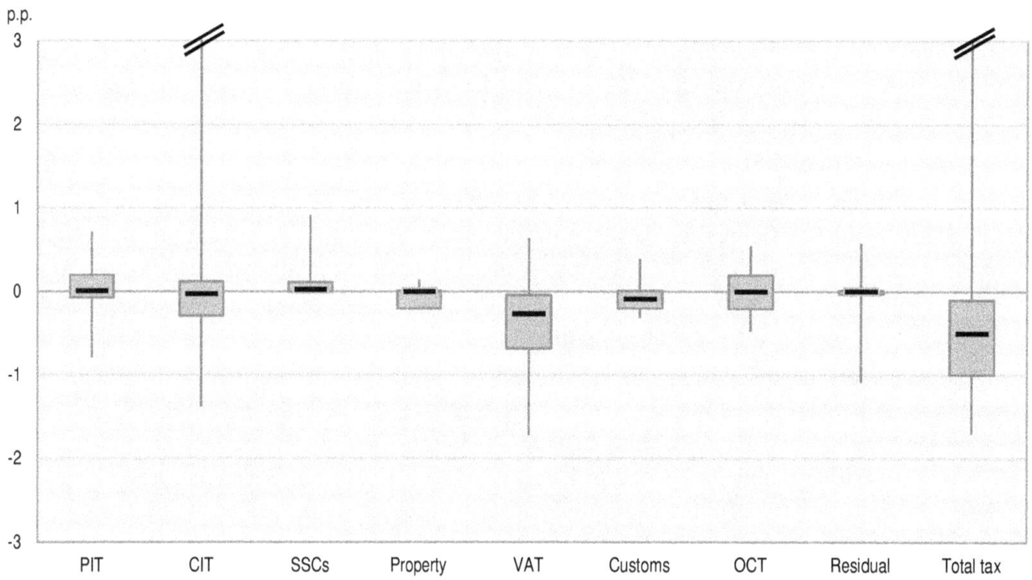

Note: The change in the Africa (31) average should be interpreted with caution as data for social security contributions are not available or are partial in a few countries. See the country tables in Chapter 5 for further information.
OCT stands for "Other consumption taxes" and includes all taxes on goods and services (heading 5000) excluding VAT (heading 5111) and customs duties (heading 5123). "Residual" includes taxes unallocable between PIT and CIT (heading 1300), payroll taxes (heading 3000) and other taxes (heading 6000).
In the figure, the lowest point represents the minimum country change for the tax type between 2019 and 2020; the box represents the changes for countries between the lower and upper quartiles (i.e. 50% of the African countries in this publication had changes within the range shown by each box); and the upper point for each tax type represents the maximum country change. The line in each box represents the median country change (i.e. half of African countries in this publication were above this line and half were below). CIT and total tax in this figure are cut off for visibility purposes excluding changes for Chad between 2019 and 2020 as a share of GDP (CIT and total tax increased by 5.2 p.p. and 6.6 p.p. respectively over the period).
Source: Authors' calculations based on data in (OECD/ATAF/AUC, 2022[4]), "Revenue Statistics in Africa: Comparative tables", *OECD Tax Statistics* (database), *http://dx.doi.org/10.1787/be755711-en*.

StatLink *https://stat.link/ea4twb*

Changes in CIT revenues as a share of GDP between 2019 and 2020 demonstrate a wide variation across African countries. They ranged from a decrease of 1.4 p.p. in Equatorial Guinea to an increase of 5.2 p.p. in Chad. The Africa (31) average for CIT revenues as a share of GDP increased by 0.1 p.p. between 2019 and 2020 (excluding Chad, the Africa (31) average for CIT revenues as a share of GDP fell by of 0.1 p.p. over the period). CIT declined as a share of GDP in about a third of African countries (12) in this publication of which 6 countries saw decreases greater than 0.3 p.p.

Major changes in tax-to-GDP ratios in African countries in 2020

Figure 1.6 presents changes in tax-to-GDP ratios between 2019 and 2020 by main tax heading across the 31 countries and on average. Namibia's tax-to-GDP ratio saw the biggest decrease, of 1.7 p.p., that was due to a decrease in VAT revenues as explained in the previous section. Botswana, Equatorial Guinea and Lesotho experienced the next largest decreases, of between 1.2 p.p. and 1.4 p.p. These decreases were driven by sharp declines in income taxes (1.1, 1.3 and 0.8 p.p., respectively). Lesotho's decline was mainly driven by a fall in PIT (1.4 p.p.) and Equatorial Guinea by CIT (1.4 p.p.). Lesotho also reported a significant decrease in VAT receipts (0.8 p.p.).

Figure 1.6. **Change in tax-to-GDP ratios by main tax heading between 2019 and 2020 and by country (percentage points)**

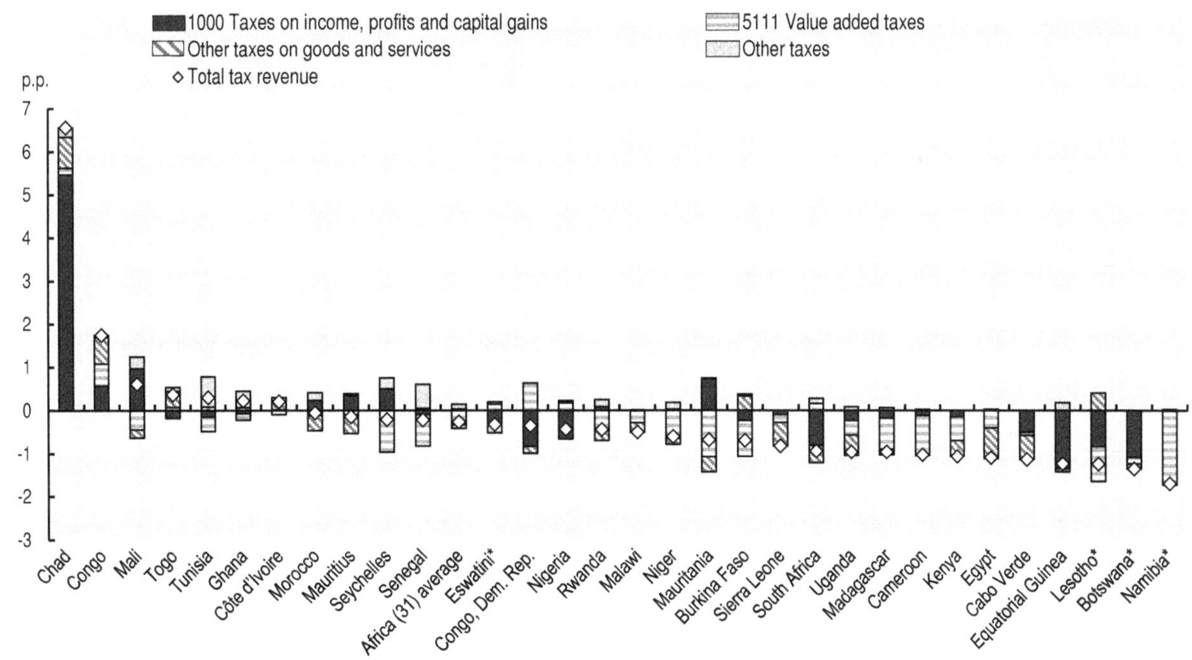

Note: The Africa (31) average should be interpreted with caution as data for social security contributions are not available or are partial in a few countries. See the country tables in Chapter 5 for further information.

*Eswatini, Lesotho, Namibia and Botswana report their figures using an April-March fiscal year. See the notes to the country tables in Chapter 5 for further information.

Source: Authors' calculations based on data in (OECD/ATAF/AUC, 2022[4]), "Revenue Statistics in Africa: Comparative tables", *OECD Tax Statistics* (database), *http://dx.doi.org/10.1787/be755711-en*.

StatLink https://stat.link/4sni1b

The increase of 6.6 p.p. in Chad's tax-to-GDP ratio between 2019 and 2020 was driven by an increase in CIT revenues from oil companies (5.2 p.p.). Despite the simultaneous drop in production volume in Chad and falls in the price of crude oil in 2020, the increase in

CIT from the oil sector in 2020 is mostly explained by CIT receipts on oil profits accrued in previous years (Minister of Finance and Budget of Chad, 2021[8]). The increase in CIT revenues contributed to the 74% increase in nominal tax revenues between 2019 and 2020 overall. Nominal GDP in Chad declined by 4% over the period, which magnified the increase in tax revenues as a share of GDP between 2019 and 2020 (see Box 1.1)

In the Republic of the Congo, the tax-to-GDP ratio increased by 1.7 p.p. between 2019 and 2020. Although nominal tax revenues fell by 4%, this decline was smaller than the fall in nominal GDP (21%), leading to an increase in the tax-to-GDP ratio. Revenues from all main tax categories fell between 2019 and 2020, with the decline in taxes on goods and services accounting for 63% of the total fall in nominal tax revenues.

Impact of the pandemic on different tax types across regions

The impact of COVID-19 on different tax types varied significantly across different regions. Falls in revenues from taxes on goods and services drove the decline of the average tax-to-GDP ratios in Africa, LAC and Asia-Pacific between 2019 and 2020. In contrast, the OECD average recorded an increase in tax revenues as a share of GDP over the period driven by increases in labour tax revenues (PIT and SSCs).

It is important to note that most tax revenues in OECD countries are reported on an accruals basis (when the tax liability is determined, rather than at the time of payment), whereas tax revenues in countries in the other regions are mainly reported on a cash basis. Tax revenues in some OECD countries may include liability amounts – notably for VAT – that will not be remitted by businesses to tax authorities in the short term or at all in the future due to tax measures adopted in some OECD countries in response to the COVID-19 crisis, such as deferrals of VAT payments or write-offs for the output-VAT for unpaid invoices. This means that tax revenues in some OECD countries may be overestimated in 2020, in particular for VAT. On the other hand, reporting on a cash basis in the other regions may mean that changes in the crisis are more pronounced due to the impact of deferrals in the payment of tax liabilities as part of countries' COVID-19 response.

Table 1.1. **Changes in tax revenues by main tax categories in Africa, LAC, Asia-Pacific and OECD, 2019-20**

	p.p.				% change			
	Africa (31)	LAC	Asia/Pacific (28)	OECD	Africa (31)	LAC	Asia/Pacific (28)	OECD
PIT	0.0	0.0	0.0	0.3	3.7	-3.0	-2.2	1.4
CIT	0.1	-0.2	-0.1	-0.4	5.0	-5.6	-5.3	-12.1
SSCs	0.1	0.1	0.0	0.3	8.9	-0.7	1.1	2.0
Property	0.0	-0.1	0.0	0.1	20.3	-14.2	3.4	0.0
VAT	-0.3	-0.2	-0.6	0.0	-4.1	-8.1	-11.9	-2.6
Customs	-0.1	-0.1	0.0	0.0	-1.5	-14.7	-5.8	-7.1
OCT	0.0	-0.4	-0.4	-0.2	1.7	-12.5	-12.4	1.9
Residual	-0.1	0.0	-0.1	0.0	0.9	-12.1	-27.0	14.4
Total tax	**-0.3**	**-0.8**	**-1.2**	**0.1**	**-0.5**	**-8.0**	**-8.8**	**-2.1**

Note: Data for 2020 for the OECD are preliminary and should be interpreted with caution.
OCT stands for "Other consumption taxes" and includes all taxes on goods and services (heading 5000) excluding VAT (heading 5111) and customs duties (heading 5123). Res. stands for "Residual" and includes taxes unallocable between PIT and CIT (heading 1300), payroll taxes (heading 3000) and other taxes (heading 6000).
Source: Authors' calculations based on data in (OECD/ATAF/AUC, 2022[4]), "*Revenue Statistics in Africa*: Comparative tables", *OECD Tax Statistics* (database), *http://dx.doi.org/10.1787/be755711-en*, (OECD, 2022[1]), (OECD et al., 2022[2]) and (OECD, 2021[3]).

In nominal terms, the negative impact of COVID-19 was clearly visible for all tax categories for the LAC and the Asia-Pacific regions (except for SSCs and property taxes in the Asia-Pacific region, which increased slightly in nominal terms between 2019 and 2020).

In contrast, five tax categories out of the eight did not decline in 2020 for the Africa (31) and OECD averages, notably labour tax revenues.

Revenues as a share of GDP from taxes on goods and services were less affected by the COVID-19 pandemic in Africa than in the LAC and Asia-Pacific regions: these revenues decreased by 0.4% of GDP on average between 2019 and 2020, compared to decreases of 0.7% and 1.0% of GDP over the same period in the LAC and Asia-Pacific regions, respectively. VAT revenues as a percentage of GDP decreased in the three regions, with Asia-Pacific registering the largest fall (of 0.6 p.p.), followed by Africa (0.3 p.p.) and LAC (0.2 p.p.). In comparison, VAT revenues as a share of GDP were unchanged over the period in the OECD on average. The Africa (31) average revenues as a percentage of GDP from other consumption taxes (OCT), including non-VAT general taxes, excises and export duties, were unchanged between 2019 and 2020, in contrast with decreases of 0.2 p.p. in the OECD and 0.4 p.p. in both the LAC and Asia-Pacific regions on average (Table 1.1).

Africa is the only region that recorded an increase in CIT revenues as a share of GDP between 2019 and 2020 (entirely due to the large CIT revenue increase in Chad over the period). The OECD average saw the largest fall in CIT revenues as a share of GDP, of 0.4 p.p., while the LAC and the Asia-Pacific (28) averages experienced smaller declines (0.2 p.p. and 0.1 p.p., respectively).

In all regions and as a share of GDP, average revenues from PIT and SSCs did not decline between 2019 and 2020. These revenues remained relatively stable as a share of GDP in all regions, except in the OECD. In 2020, the OECD averages for PIT revenues and SSCs both increased by 0.3 p.p. on average, the largest increases in revenues as a share of GDP observed for any tax category.

Impact of the pandemic on African's regional groups

Many of the countries in this publication belong to regional organisations whose members adopt common tax and external tariff rules and form a customs union. The average tax-to-GDP ratios of the three East Africa Community (EAC)[3] countries and the six West African Economic and Monetary Union (WAEMU)[4] countries included in this publication were 14.4% and 15.2%, respectively, in 2020, below the Africa (31) average. The average tax-to-GDP ratio for countries in the Southern African Customs Union (SACU) was 18.8% in 2020 (see Box 2.2 in Chapter 2).

The three sub-regions were all affected negatively by the COVID-19 pandemic but the magnitude of the decreases of tax-to-GDP ratios between 2019 and 2020 varied greatly between them. On average, SACU countries experienced the largest fall in tax revenues as a share of GDP, of 1.1 p.p., followed by the three EAC countries (0.8 p.p.). In contrast, the six WAEMU countries recorded a smaller decline in average tax revenues as a share of GDP, of 0.1 p.p., over the period (Figure 1.7).

The COVID-19 pandemic affected revenues from taxes on goods and services, especially from VAT, for all these groups. On average, the decreases in revenues from taxes on goods and services were 0.3 p.p. for the six WAEMU countries, 0.5 p.p. for SACU countries and 0.8 p.p. for the three EAC countries. The average falls in VAT revenues as a share of GDP between 2019 and 2020 ranged from 0.4 p.p. for the six WAEMU countries to 0.5 p.p. for the SACU countries. COVID-19 weighed more on income tax revenues in SACU countries[5], where these fell by 0.6 p.p. on average, while revenues from taxes on goods and services were the most affected in the other two sub-regions. Income tax revenues were relatively stable over the period in the WAEMU and EAC countries on average.

Figure 1.7. **Change in tax-to-GDP ratios by main tax heading and by sub-regional groups, 2019-20**

Percentage points

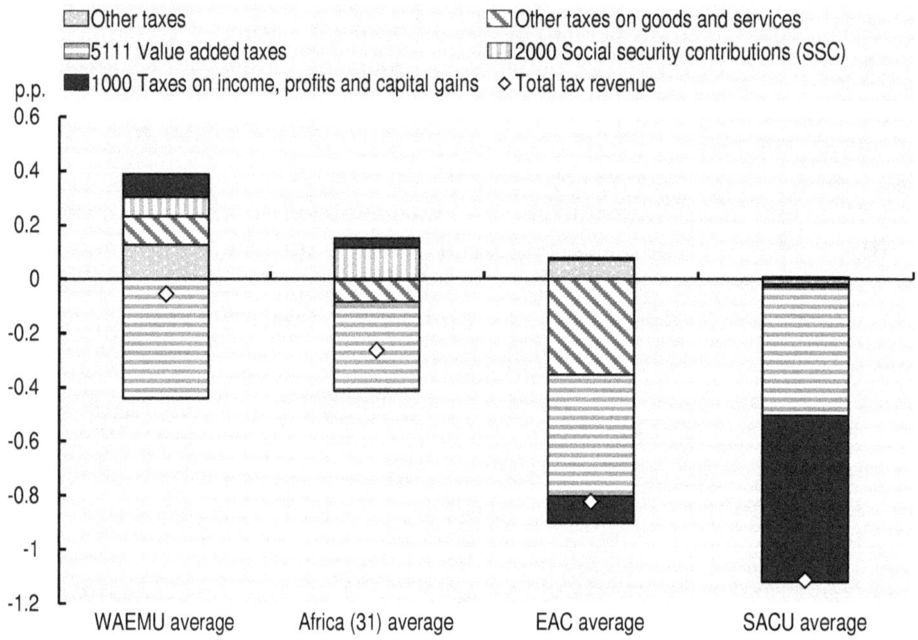

Source: Authors' calculations based on data in (OECD/ATAF/AUC, 2022[4]), "*Revenue Statistics in Africa*: Comparative tables", *OECD Tax Statistics* (database), *http://dx.doi.org/10.1787/be755711-en.*

StatLink *https://stat.link/nq9jpg*

Support measures implemented in Africa

African countries adopted a range of tax measures to mitigate the negative impact of COVID-19 pandemic on businesses and households. Lockdowns and other restrictions directly affected business profits, household spending and labour participation in Africa, resulting in a reduction of economic activity in 2020. Tax measures in response to COVID-19 further exacerbated falls in public revenues in Africa as well as across the world in 2020. This section provides examples of tax measures that were implemented in African countries included in this publication in response to the COVID-19 crisis. The analysis is not intended to be exhaustive but rather to illustrate various tax instruments African countries used to alleviate the impact of the crisis.[6]

Many tax measures adopted by African countries were related to CIT and VAT, and aimed to support businesses in addressing liquidity and cash flow issues. They included deferrals of tax payments, filing extensions and flexible tax payment plans; Egypt, Cabo Verde, Eswatini, Lesotho, Mauritius and Rwanda adopted such measures (see Box 1.2).

For example, CIT payments in Rwanda were deferred for all businesses, with longer deadlines for SMEs. Deadlines for the payment of CIT debt instalments were extended in Cabo Verde for all businesses. Large businesses in debt in South Africa were allowed to defer tax payments without incurring penalties by applying directly to the South African Revenue Service (SARS). In some countries, measures were applied to specific sectors such as tourism (Mauritius, the Seychelles). This was also the case for Egypt, which allowed businesses in affected industries to pay their CIT liability for 2019 over a three-month period ending in June 2020 instead of paying the full amount in April.

Other measures in support of businesses included tax waivers. Mali waived taxes on a case-by-case and sector-by-sector basis for private companies affected by the COVID-19 prevention measures. In addition, Mali temporarily suspended the "taxe synthétique" (a turnover tax) and property tax for companies. In Burkina Faso, businesses in the passenger transport, hotel and tourism sectors were granted a 25% reduction in their license fees.

Meanwhile, tax measures in relation to VAT included payment deferrals, filing extensions and acceleration of refunds as well as waivers and rates reductions. In Mali, a three-month VAT deferral was applied on electricity and water bills for all consumers. Several countries accelerated VAT refunds to enhance cash flow, for example Madagascar, Namibia and South Africa. In South Africa, small vendors were temporarily permitted to file VAT returns monthly instead of every two months, thereby accelerating the input tax refund.

VAT/GST waivers and reductions were adopted across Africa, targeting the medical, hospitality, cultural and sports sectors, or applied more generally. Burkina Faso, Rwanda and Mauritius applied VAT exemptions in the medical sector (on the sale of equipment used to fight Covid-19 in Burkina Faso, on masks produced domestically in Rwanda, and on goods and in medical research in Mauritius). Burkina Faso and Cabo Verde reduced VAT rates from 15% to 10% in the hotel and restaurant sectors.

African countries introduced a range of tax policies in relation to PIT and SSCs to support households during the pandemic. Those measures were similar to those applied to companies, such as partial deferral of payments (South Africa, the Seychelles), filing extensions (Eswatini, Lesotho) and tax waivers (South Africa, Rwanda). While these measures decreased or postponed the amount of tax revenues to be collected by governments, two countries (Egypt and Mauritius) increased PIT rates to finance the response to COVID-19. Egypt introduced a 1% "income tax salary" on all public and private sector salaries (except for those earning less than EGP 2 000) for a 12-month period. Individuals with a taxable income above a certain threshold in Mauritius had to pay a solidarity levy at a rate of 25%.

A number of African countries waived fines, penalties and interest payments for either households or companies (or both) during the COVID-19 pandemic in 2020. Such measures were adopted in Burkina Faso, Egypt, Lesotho, Mauritius and Rwanda.

Box 1.2. **Tax measures in Eswatini and in Lesotho in response to COVID-19**

This box shows examples of the major changes made in Eswatini and Lesotho to their tax policy in order to help businesses and individuals through the COVID-19 crisis in 2020.

Eswatini

The deadline for filing returns was extended by three months with no penalties for CIT and PIT. Other measures were mainly aimed at companies, especially those facing losses or cash-flow issues. Companies that projected losses benefited from the postponement of provisional tax payments by three months. These companies were required to fill in provisional returns in June and September 2020, with payments due in December 2020 and March 2021. Some companies in difficulty were considered for payment arrangements on provision of evidence of their cash-flow problems. Penalties and interest for older debts were waived only if the principal were paid between April and September 2020. As a result, companies prioritised debts where the interest payments and penalties were more significant and a greater amount of VAT debts was written-off compared to income tax debts.

Box 1.2. **Tax measures in Eswatini and in Lesotho in response to COVID-19** *(cont.)*

To help SMEs, Eswatini's government set up a SLZ 90 million relief fund for compliant SMEs. SMEs with a turnover of up to SLZ 8 million were provided a refund of the company tax paid in the 2019 tax year. The government exempted taxes (VAT and customs duties) for all COVID-19 related equipment (masks, sanitisers, personal protective equipment and any other medical items).

Lesotho

Lesotho introduced a number of tax-related relief measures and administrative relief measures for compliant businesses. The tax relief measures were largely underpinned by deferrals of payments of between six and eight months for specific taxes (PIT, CIT, Simplified Business Tax [SBT], PAYE and VAT).

As regards CIT, large businesses benefited from partial deferral for their first and second quarter instalments while SMEs were allowed full deferral of their first quarter instalment. All businesses were required to pay deferred amounts from the end of October 2020; these could be spread out into six equal monthly instalments to the end of March 2021. Businesses subject to the SBT in non-essential sectors saw their SBT waived during the lockdown whereas essential businesses (such as retail) that continued to operate during lockdown were due to pay the SBT as per the standard payment periods. Similarly, PAYE and VAT payments were deferred for non-essential businesses but not for essential businesses.

Goods imported to address the COVID-19 crisis were exempted from import VAT and import duties. Additional taxes, penalties and storage fees accrued as a consequence of unavoidable effects of the lockdown were waived.

The administrative relief measures included quick clearance of all imported essential goods and goods imported for relief of COVID-19. Revenue Services Lesotho expedited refund applications to enable businesses to obtain quick access to cash inflows while the verifications were made at a later date.

Source: Information provided by focal points in Eswatini Revenue Authority and in Revenue Services Lesotho.

Evolution of tax-to-GDP ratios since 2010

The COVID-19 pandemic put a stop to steady growth in tax revenues in Africa since 2010. In 2020, the Africa (31) average tax-to-GDP ratio was 1.6 p.p. higher than in 2010. In comparison, the LAC and OECD averages increased by 1.0 p.p. and 1.9 p.p., respectively, between 2010 and 2020.

The average tax-to-GDP ratio for the 31 African countries recorded an annual increase of 0.7 p.p. in 2011, marking the recovery from the global financial crisis. Between 2012 and 2019, the Africa (31) average increased steadily, from 15.0% of GDP in 2012 to 16.2% in 2019. The COVID-19 pandemic caused the first decline in the Africa (31) average tax-to-GDP ratio since 2010 (Figure 1.8).

PIT contributed most to the increase in the Africa (31) average tax-to-GDP ratio observed between 2010 and 2020, rising from 2.3% of GDP in 2010 to 3.1% in 2020 driven by higher incomes and improvements in taxation of high-net-worth individuals in Sub-Sahara Africa (Moore, Prichard and Fjeldstad, 2018[9]). CIT revenues did not contribute to the increase over this period, registering a steady decline as a share of GDP for the countries covered in this publication between 2012 and 2016. Falls in oil and mineral prices between 2013 and 2016 and decreases in CIT rates across the continent accounted for the fall in CIT revenues, as a result of which the proportion of income tax revenues attributable to PIT has grown in Africa over the last decade. In 2020, PIT revenues accounted for 51% of total income tax revenues, compared to 42% in 2010.

Figure 1.8. **Average tax-to-GDP ratios for Africa (31), LAC and OECD, 2000-20**

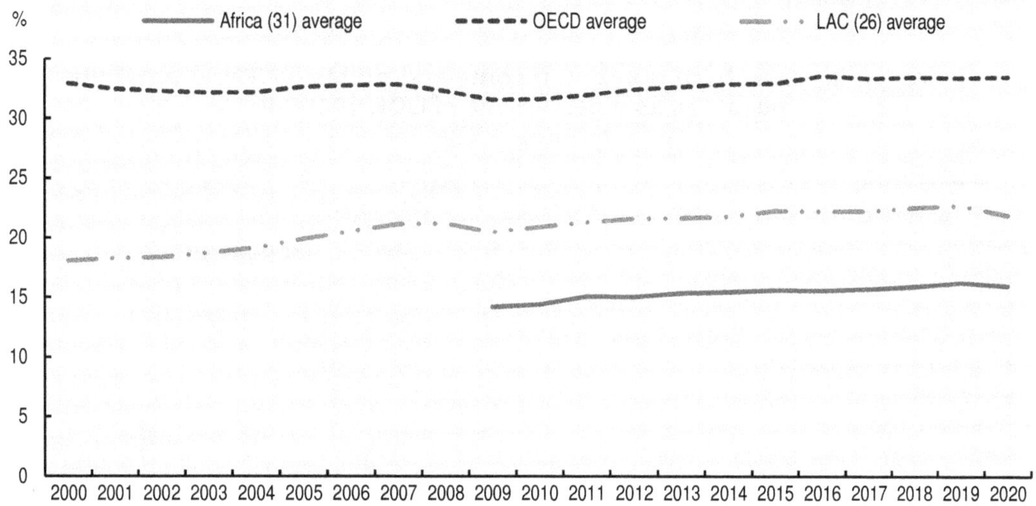

Note: The Africa (31) average should be interpreted with caution as data for social security contributions are not available or are partial in a few countries. See the country tables in Chapter 5 for further information.
The figures include sub-national government tax revenues for Eswatini, Mauritius, Mauritania (until 2018), Morocco, Nigeria (state revenues only) and South Africa for 2002-2020.
The Africa (31) average is estimated for 2009 as the data are not available for Chad and Nigeria. No estimation was made prior to 2009 because of the unavailability of data for a few countries.
The Africa (31) average and the averages for LAC (26 countries) and the OECD (38 countries) are unweighted. The Asia-Pacific (28) average is not available for years prior to 2018.
Source: Table 4.1 in Chapter 4 and (OECD/ATAF/AUC, 2022[4]), "Revenue Statistics in Africa: Comparative tables", *OECD Tax Statistics* (database), *http://dx.doi.org/10.1787/be755711-en*.

StatLink *https://stat.link/uyvm3i*

The second-largest driver of the increase in Africa's tax-to-GDP ratio between 2010 and 2020 was VAT receipts, which increased by 0.7 p.p. to reach 4.5% of GDP in 2020. The largest annual increase in average VAT revenues as a percentage of GDP was registered between 2012 and 2013 (0.3% of GDP) following the introduction of VAT in the Democratic Republic of the Congo and in Eswatini in 2012. A slight increase in the average standard VAT rate in the region during this decade (from 15.9% in 2010 to 16.2% in 2020) may also have contributed to the increase of VAT receipts as a percentage of GDP over the same period (Figure 1.9).

Average revenues from other taxes on goods and services, equivalent to 3.5% of GDP in 2020, have decreased slightly as a percentage of GDP since 2010, in part due to declines in revenues from trade taxes. This decline is associated with trade liberalisation across the continent that resulted in the reduction of import tariffs, the narrowing of the base of products and services subject to excises, and the elimination of taxes on exports. Tariffs will be further reduced under the implementation of the African Continental Free Trade Area (AfCFTA) (OECD/ATAF/AUC, 2021[10]).

The drivers of changes in tax revenues in the LAC region over the same period were similar to those in Africa. As with the Africa (31) average, revenues from PIT and VAT contributed significantly to the increase in the LAC region's average tax-to-GDP ratio; both increased by 0.5 p.p. between 2010 and 2020. Higher revenues from SSCs (up by 0.7 p.p.) also contributed to the overall increase in the average tax-to-GDP ratio in the LAC region. There is a large gap between the level of SSCs as a percentage of GDP between the respective regions: in 2020, SSCs amounted to 4.0% of GDP in the LAC region compared with the Africa (31) average of 1.5% (Figure 1.9).

Figure 1.9. **Revenue from taxes on income and profits, VAT and other tax headings as a percentage of GDP, 2010-20**

Percentage of GDP

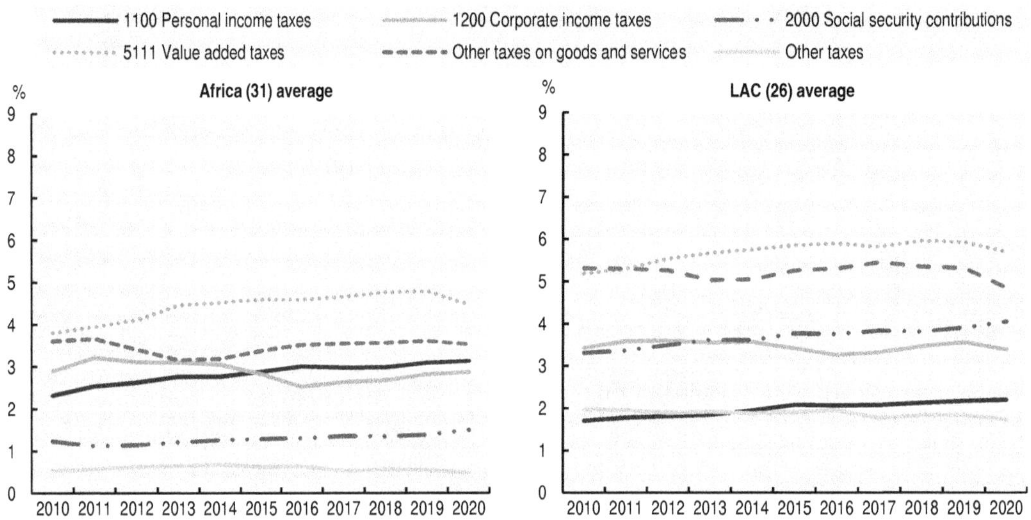

Note: The figures for the Africa (31) average include sub-national government tax revenues for Eswatini, Mauritania (up to 2018), Mauritius, Morocco, Nigeria (state revenues only) and South Africa for 2002-2019.
Source: Authors' calculations based on (OECD/ATAF/AUC, 2022[4]) "Revenue Statistics in Africa: Comparative tables", *OECD Tax Statistics* (database), *http://dx.doi.org/10.1787/be755711-en.*

StatLink *https://stat.link/8mtw0p*

Tax-to-GDP ratios rose in 25 African countries between 2010 and 2020 and declined in six. Rwanda and Tunisia recorded the largest increases over the period (of 4.5 p.p. and 6.6 p.p., respectively), while the largest decline occurred in Botswana (3.5 p.p.) (Figure 1.10).

The first year of the COVID-19 pandemic wiped out a decade of gains in tax revenue mobilisation for several countries, notably for Kenya and Namibia. Kenya recorded an increase in tax revenues as a share of GDP between 2010 and 2019 of 0.7 p.p. while Namibia recorded an increase of 1.6 p.p. After the COVID-19 crisis, their level of tax revenues as a share of GDP was lower in 2020 than in 2010.

Figure 1.11 presents the changes in tax revenues as a share of GDP across the 31 countries and for the Africa (31) and LAC averages between 2010 and 2020 by tax type. The increase in Tunisia's tax-to-GDP ratio between 2010 and 2020 was mainly attributable to higher revenues from PIT (3.5 p.p.) and SSC (3.0 p.p.). During this period, Tunisia undertook extensive reforms to its tax policy and administration to mobilise tax revenues. In addition, increases in PIT and SSC revenues came partly from the 147% increase in salaries on average (OECD/ATAF/AUC, 2021[10]).

Figure 1.10. **Change in tax-to-GDP ratios between 2010 and 2020**

Percentage points

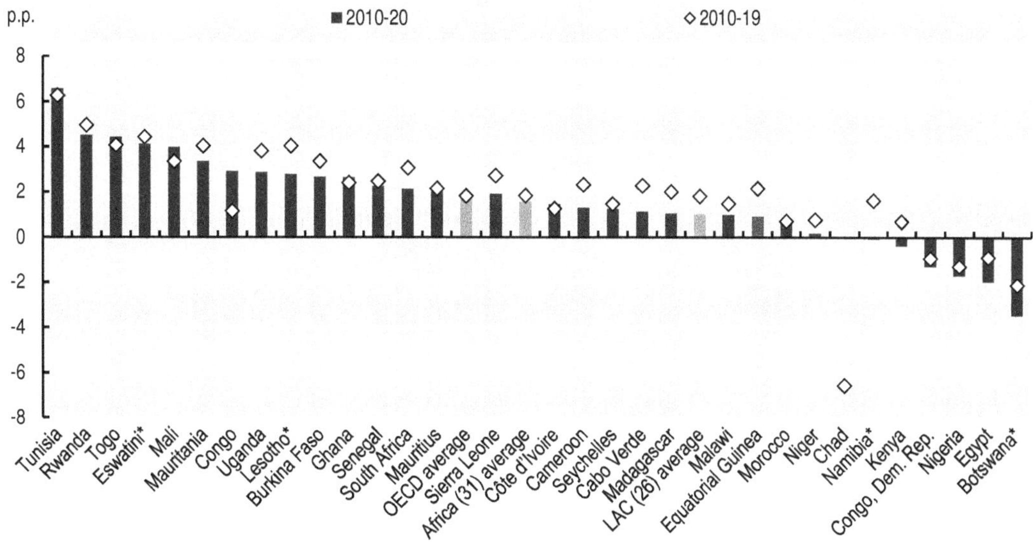

Note: The figures include sub-national government tax revenues for Eswatini, Mauritius, Morocco, Nigeria (state revenues only) and South Africa for 2020.

*Eswatini, Lesotho, Namibia and Botswana report their figures using an April-March fiscal year. This means 2020 figures for these countries include revenues up to 31 March 2021. See the notes to the country tables in Chapter 5 for further information.

The Africa (31) average and the averages for LAC (26 countries) and the OECD (38 countries) are unweighted. The Asia-Pacific (28) average is not available for years prior to 2018.

Source: Tables 4.1 and 4.2 in Chapter 4 and (OECD/ATAF/AUC, 2022[4]), "*Revenue Statistics in Africa*: Comparative tables", *OECD Tax Statistics* (database), *http://dx.doi.org/10.1787/be755711-en*.

StatLink *https://stat.link/vkb4az*

The increase in Rwanda's tax-to-GDP ratio between 2010 and 2020 was driven principally by revenues from income taxes (2.5 p.p.) and VAT revenues (1.3 p.p.). With the exception of 2020, tax collection in Rwanda has risen steadily from 2010 onwards by an average of 0.6 p.p. per year as a result of tax policy and administration reforms aiming to offset declines in foreign aid and trade tax revenues.[7] Administrative changes included the digitalisation of taxpayer tools, the modernisation of collection and audit processes, and increased collection of VAT arrears. With respect to tax policy, Rwanda expanded the PIT base, introduced withholding taxes (VAT and income taxes), removed tax exemptions and increased tax rates for several excises and import duties over the period. These reforms resulted in higher tax compliance, notably for VAT, and a significant increase in tax revenues across the main tax categories (Akitoby et al., 2019[11]) (PwC, 2019[12]) (IMF, 2020[13]). More recently, Rwanda enacted a new income tax law in 2018 that removed ambiguities and expanded the income tax base, contributing to the increase of income tax revenues of 0.7 p.p. between 2017 and 2019 (Economist Intelligence, 2018[14]). In 2020, tax revenues in Rwanda declined by 0.4% of GDP.

Botswana experienced a significant decrease in tax revenues as percentage of GDP between 2010 and 2020, from 15.8% to 12.4%.This is primarily explained by a decrease in income tax revenues (revenue from unallocable income tax between PIT and CIT, classified in "other taxes" in Figure 1.11) of 2.8 p.p. over the same period, representing an annual average decline of 0.3 p.p. VAT revenues also influenced the decline in tax-to-GDP, falling from 5.0% of GDP in 2010 to 4.3% in 2020.

Figure 1.11. **Change in tax-to-GDP ratios by main tax headings between 2010 and 2020 and by country**

Percentage points

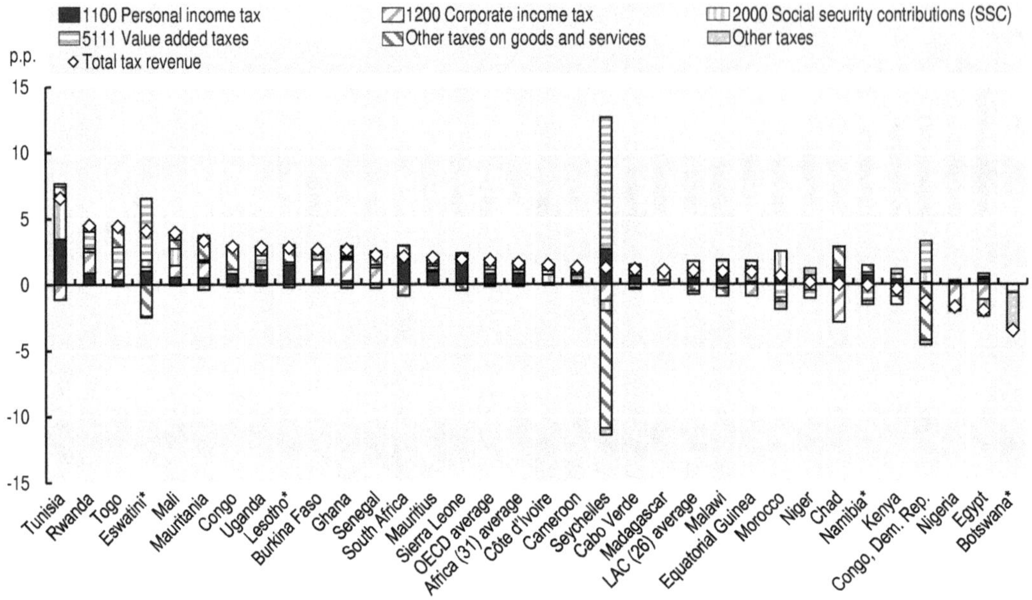

Note: The figures include sub-national government tax revenues for Eswatini, Mauritius, Mauritania (until 2018), Morocco, Nigeria (state revenues only) and South Africa.

*Eswatini, Lesotho, Namibia and Botswana report their figures using an April-March fiscal year. This means 2020 figures for these countries include revenues up to March 31, 2021.

The Africa (31) average and the averages for LAC (26 countries) and the OECD (38 countries) are unweighted. The Asia-Pacific (28) average is not available for years up to 2018. The data for the OECD are for 2019 as final data for 2020 are not available.

Source: Authors' calculations based on (OECD/ATAF/AUC, 2022[4]), "*Revenue Statistics in Africa*: Comparative tables", *OECD Tax Statistics* (database), *http://dx.doi.org/10.1787/be755711-en.*

StatLink *https://stat.link/5r7o2j*

Large changes also took place in the Seychelles between 2010 and 2020. VAT revenues as a share of GDP increased by 10 p.p. while other taxes on goods on services declined by 8.9 p.p. over the period. This was due to the introduction of VAT in 2013 to replace the Goods and Services Tax, which was levied on the importation of all goods and on the sales turnover of specific companies (OECD, 2020[15]).

Box 1.3. **Changes in tax-to-GDP ratios in SACU countries**

Five of the 31 countries included in this publication belong to the Southern African Customs Union (SACU): Botswana, Eswatini, Lesotho, Namibia and South Africa. SACU was founded in 1910, making it the oldest customs union in the world (SACU, 2020[16]). The five SACU members have a revenue-sharing agreement that provides for common external tariffs and for the payment of customs and excise duties into a common pool to be shared between the SACU countries. In this publication, revenue from excises, tariffs and customs duties are included as tax revenues in the SACU country that collected the revenue (South Africa) and revenues received from the SACU Common Revenue Pool are included as miscellaneous revenue in non-tax revenues (Botswana, Eswatini, Lesotho and Namibia) (see Box 2.2 in Chapter 2).

In 2020, the average tax-to-GDP ratio of the SACU countries (the SACU average) was 2.9 p.p. higher than the Africa (31) average and amounted to 18.8%. The evolution of the tax-to-GDP ratio between 2010 and 2020 in SACU countries was, on average, similar to the evolution of the Africa (31) average over the same period.

Box 1.3. **Changes in tax-to-GDP ratios in SACU countries** *(cont.)*

While the average tax-to-GDP ratio of the Africa (31) rose from 14.4% in 2010 to 16.0% in 2020, the SACU average rose from 17.7% of GDP in 2010 to 18.8% in 2020 (Figure 1.12).

VAT was the main driver of the increase in the SACU average during this period, increasing by 0.7 p.p., similar to the Africa (31) average. Tax-to-GDP ratios increased in Eswatini (4.1 p.p.), Lesotho (2.8 p.p.) and South Africa (2.1 p.p.), while the tax-to-GDP ratios of Namibia and Botswana declined by 0.1 p.p. and 3.5 p.p., respectively, over the period.

Figure 1.12. **Tax-to-GDP ratios (levels and changes) in SACU countries, 2010-20**

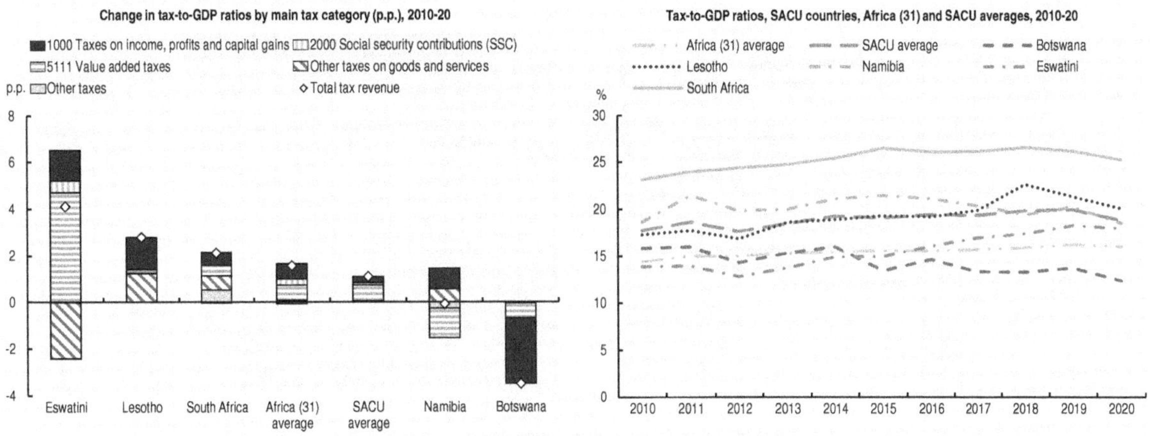

Source: Authors' calculations based on (OECD/ATAF/AUC, 2022[4]), "*Revenue Statistics in Africa*: Comparative tables", *OECD Tax Statistics* (database), *http://dx.doi.org/10.1787/be755711-en*.

StatLink *https://stat.link/k7rzwp*

Factors influencing tax-to-GDP ratios

Tax-to-GDP ratios are influenced by a variety of factors. These include macroeconomic characteristics such as the diversification of an economy, the importance of agriculture in the economy, resource endowments, openness to trade, debt and the size of the informal economy. Changes in the political situation in countries, such as social unrest and corruption, can also influence tax-to-GDP ratios. The capacity of tax administrations and tax morale (or willingness of companies and individuals to pay taxes) are also strongly linked to the level of tax revenues (OECD, 2014[17]) (OECD, 2019[18]). Location is relevant: landlocked countries are less able to impose taxes on goods and services entering the country than island countries.

Tax-to-GDP ratios tend to be higher in high income countries: in general, OECD countries collect a higher amount of tax revenues than non-OECD countries, measured as a percentage of GDP. Most of the countries included in this publication have lower income per capita and lower tax-to-GDP ratios than OECD and LAC countries. Levels of GDP per capita vary more among African countries than among LAC and OECD countries (Figure 1.13).

Countries' financing needs depend in part on their income level, which is an important consideration in understanding tax levels in different countries. The gap between public revenues and development financing needs tends to be larger in countries with lower per capita incomes, making mobilisation of additional public revenues particularly critical (Gaspar et al., 2019[21]). The COVID-19 crisis reduced tax revenues in most countries while resulting in significant increases in spending needs and public debt. Renewed efforts to reform tax policy and administrations with a view to increasing revenues have become even more of a priority in the aftermath of the COVID-19 crisis.

Figure 1.13. **Tax-to-GDP ratios and GDP per capita (in PPP) in African, LAC, OECD and selected Asian and Pacific economies, 2020**

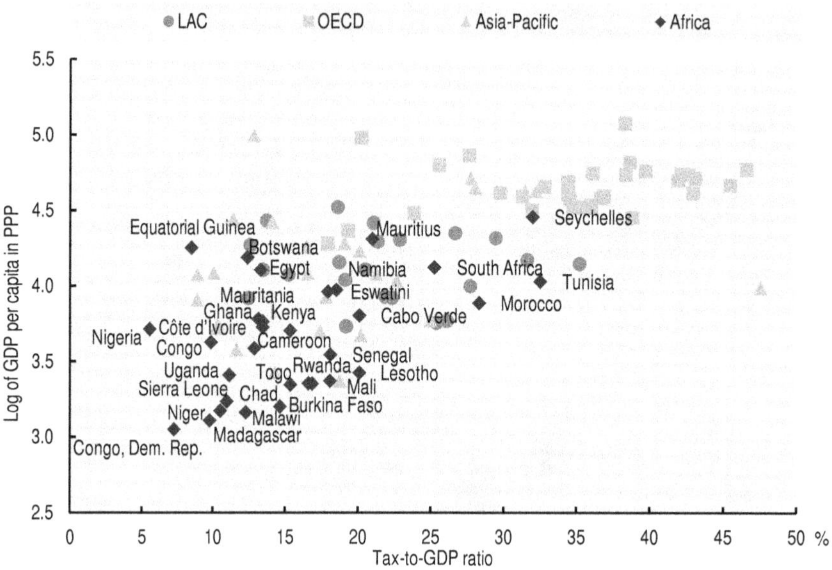

Note: The y-axis is on a logarithmic scale. The purchasing-power-parity (PPP) between two countries is the rate at which the currency of one country needs to be converted into that of a second country to ensure that a given amount of the first country's currency will purchase the same volume of goods and services in the second country as it does in the first. The implied PPP conversion rate is expressed as national currency per current international dollar. An international dollar has the same purchasing power as the US dollar has in the United States. An international dollar is a hypothetical currency that is used as a means of translating and comparing costs from one country to the other using a common reference point, the US dollar (definitions derived from (IMF, 2019[19])and ((WHO, 2015[20]).
Source: (IMF, 2022[6]) for figures of GDP per capita. Tax-to-GDP ratios are sourced (OECD/ATAF/AUC, 2022[4]), "*Revenue Statistics in Africa*: Comparative tables", *OECD Tax Statistics* (database), *http://dx.doi.org/10.1787/be755711-en*, (OECD, 2022[1]), (OECD et al., 2022[2]) and (OECD, 2021[3]);

StatLink *https://stat.link/smv9tw*

Figure 1.14 shows the distribution of tax-to-GDP ratios for the 31 African countries in this publication within three income groups in 2020 using the World Bank classification (World Bank, 2022[22]). It also presents changes in tax-to-GDP ratios by income group between 2019 and 2020 (low income countries, lower middle income countries, and upper middle income and high income countries grouped together[8]).

In 2020, 25 of the 31 African countries in this publication were classified as low income or lower middle income, with 11 in the low income group. This group of countries showed the smallest dispersion compared to countries at higher income levels; all low income countries registered a tax-to-GDP ratio below 19% in 2020, ranging from 7.3% of GDP in the Democratic Republic of the Congo to 18.1% in Mali, with an average level of 13.0%. In eight of the 11 countries, tax-to-GDP ratios were below 16%, a level that the IMF considers too low for them to finance the additional spending required to achieve the SDGs (Gaspar et al., 2019[21]).

For the 14 lower middle income countries, the average tax-to-GDP ratio was 16.7% in 2020. While this group demonstrates the widest range of tax-to-GDP ratios, including the highest (Tunisia) and the lowest (Nigeria), 10 countries had tax-to-GDP ratios near or below 20%. Within this income group, Tunisia and Morocco stand apart, with tax-to-GDP ratios above 28%. In high- and upper middle income countries, tax revenues as a percentage of GDP vary greatly, from 8.5% in Equatorial Guinea to 32.0% for the Seychelles, with an average of 19.6% of GDP.

Between 2019 and 2020, high- and upper middle income countries in *Revenue Statistics in Africa* on average experienced the largest decline in tax revenues as a percentage of GDP, of 0.9 p.p. The lower middle income group recorded a decrease in 0.3 p.p. while the low income group saw a rise in 0.2 p.p. over the period. However, when excluding Chad from the latter group, the average tax-to-GDP ratio in low income countries of this publication reported a decline of 0.4% of GDP on average in 2020 relative to 2019.

All three groups mobilised higher tax revenues in 2020 relative to 2010. Lower-middle income countries in *Revenue Statistics in Africa* registered the largest increase (2.1 p.p.) on average between 2010 and 2020, followed by low income countries (1.7 p.p. on average), while the upper middle income and high income group observed an increase of 0.5 p.p. on average over the same period. In all three income groups, increases in tax-to-GDP ratios over the last decade were on average below 5 p.p., a level that the IMF estimated – before the COVID 19 pandemic occurred – to be "ambitious and appropriate" target for many countries to meet the SDGs (Gaspar et al., 2019[21]). This represents a challenging goal for African countries in light of results in the previous decade and the impact of the COVID-19 pandemic.

Figure 1.14. **Tax-to-GDP ratios (levels and annual changes) by income group, 2020**

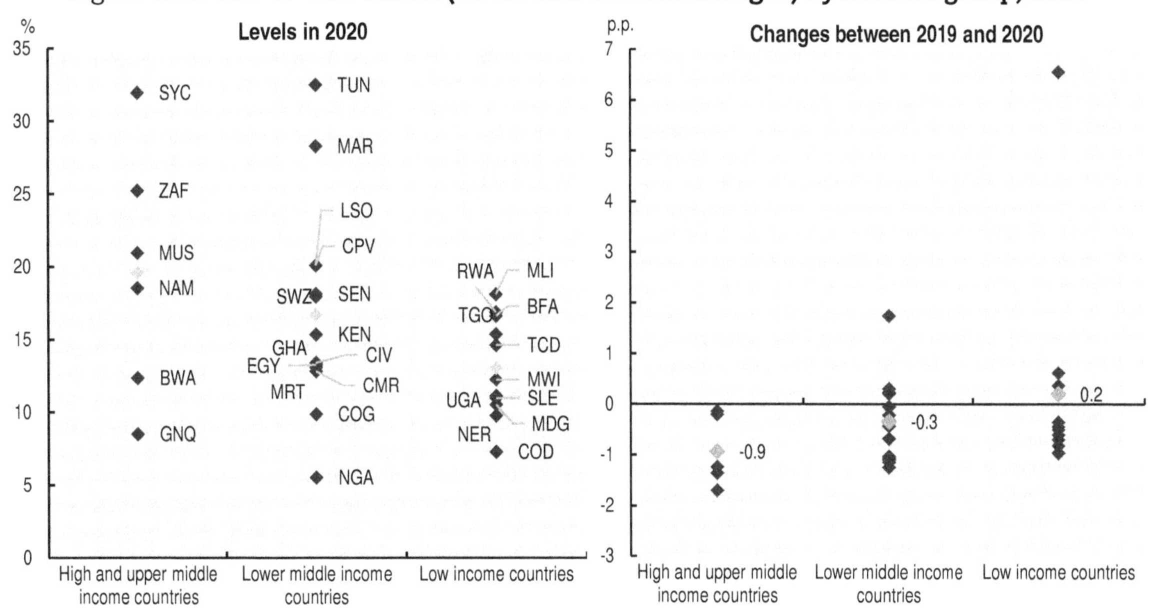

Note: The figures include sub-national government tax revenues for Eswatini, Mauritius, Morocco, Nigeria (state revenues only) and South Africa.

Eswatini, Lesotho, Namibia and Botswana report their figures using an April-March fiscal year. This means 2020 figures for these countries include revenues up to March 31, 2021.

The Seychelles is the only high income country in this report. For this reason, upper middle income (five countries) and high income countries (one country) are grouped together.

Source: Authors' calculations based on (OECD/ATAF/AUC, 2022[4]), "*Revenue Statistics in Africa*: Comparative tables", *OECD Tax Statistics* (database), *http://dx.doi.org/10.1787/be755711-en*. Country income classification according to the World Bank classification (World Bank, 2022[22]).

StatLink https://stat.link/e8lfyr

Countries that receive substantial revenues from natural resources often exhibit low tax-to-GDP ratios. Figure 1.15 shows the distribution of tax-to-GDP ratios of resource-rich countries compared to non-resource rich countries. Five countries in this publication are defined as resource-rich (countries for whom over 10% of GDP came from oil, gas, coal and mineral production for at least five years between 2010 and 2019 were classified as "resource-rich" (AUC/OECD, 2022[23])): Chad, the Republic of the Congo, Equatorial Guinea and Nigeria are oil-rich countries (countries for whom over 10% of GDP came from oil and natural gas production for at least 5 years between 2010 and 2019 were classified as "oil-rich" (AUC/OECD, 2022[23])) while Mauritania benefits from substantial mineral resources such as iron ore, copper, gold and silver and also depends on agriculture, livestock and fishing activities.

Figure 1.15. **Tax-to-GDP ratios (levels and annual changes) in resource-rich and non-resource rich countries, 2020**

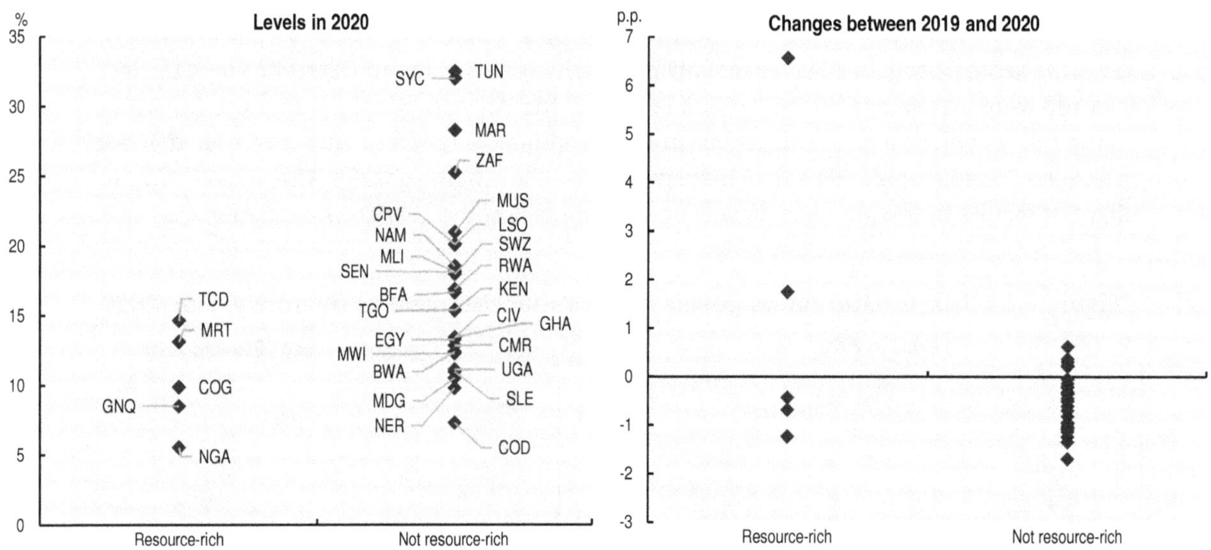

Note: The figures include sub-national government tax revenues for Eswatini, Mauritius, Morocco, Nigeria (state revenues only) and South Africa.

Source: Authors' calculations based on (OECD/ATAF/AUC, 2022[4]), "Revenue Statistics in Africa: Comparative tables", *OECD Tax Statistics* (database), *http://dx.doi.org/10.1787/be755711-en*. Country classification by resource level is based on (AUC/OECD, 2022[23]).

StatLink *https://stat.link/1d2o7t*

Figure 1.15 confirms that resource-rich countries included in this publication observe lower tax-to-GDP ratios than the non-resource-rich countries. In 2020, all resource-rich countries had tax-to-GDP levels of below 15%. The oil-rich economies of the Republic of the Congo, Equatorial Guinea, Nigeria and Chad had tax-to-GDP ratios below 10%. Oil revenues are mainly generated through oil rents and royalties, which are not classified as taxes (see Chapter 2). Developing countries encounter significant challenges in taxing extractive sectors because of longstanding tax exemptions or contracts between the country and the extractive industries benefiting local elites (Gwaindepi, 2021[24]), (Brautigam, Fjeldstad and Moore, 2008[25]).

The COVID-19 crisis had a large impact on resource-rich countries, in particular oil-rich countries. Sharp fluctuations in oil prices in 2020 affected the GDP of oil-rich countries; three of the four oil-rich countries recorded an annual decrease in nominal GDP that ranged from 4.3% in Chad to 20.3% in the Republic of the Congo. Falling oil prices in 2020 affected public revenues mainly through their impact on non-tax revenues (see Chapter 2). With respect to tax revenues, Figure 1.15 shows that annual changes of tax revenues as a percentage of GDP between 2019 and 2020 for resource-rich countries in this publication were not larger than changes for countries that are not resource-rich.

Tax structures in Africa

The composition of a country's tax revenues across different tax types is known as its tax structure or tax mix. This is an important indicator, since different taxes have different economic and social effects. The tax structures in the 31 countries in this publication reflect different policy choices, economic structures and conditions, tax administration capabilities and historical factors. Countries can be divided into three broad groups according to their principal source of revenue: VAT, other taxes on goods and services and income taxes.

Evolution of tax structures, 2010-20

Since 2010, the share of PIT and VAT revenues in the average tax structure for the countries in this publication has risen. Increases in both tax categories were significant in driving the overall increase in the tax-to-GDP ratio on average across the period. Revenues from PIT as a percentage of GDP increased by 0.8 p.p. while VAT increased by 0.7 p.p. between 2010 and 2020, reaching 3.1% and 4.5% of GDP, respectively, in 2020 (Figure 1.16).

The share of VAT and PIT in total tax revenues has also increased. The share of revenues from VAT increased by 0.8 p.p. to 27.8% of total taxation in 2020, continuing the longer-term shift toward VAT from other taxes on goods and services. The share of tax revenues from PIT increased by 3.0 p.p. over this period to 18.5% of total tax revenues in 2020, while the share of CIT revenues decreased by 2.0 p.p. Nonetheless, the average share of PIT revenues in total tax revenues remained lower than the share of CIT revenues in 2020, at 19.3% of total taxation.

Figure 1.16. **Tax structure, Africa (31) average as a percentage of total tax revenue and percentage of GDP, 2010 and 2020**

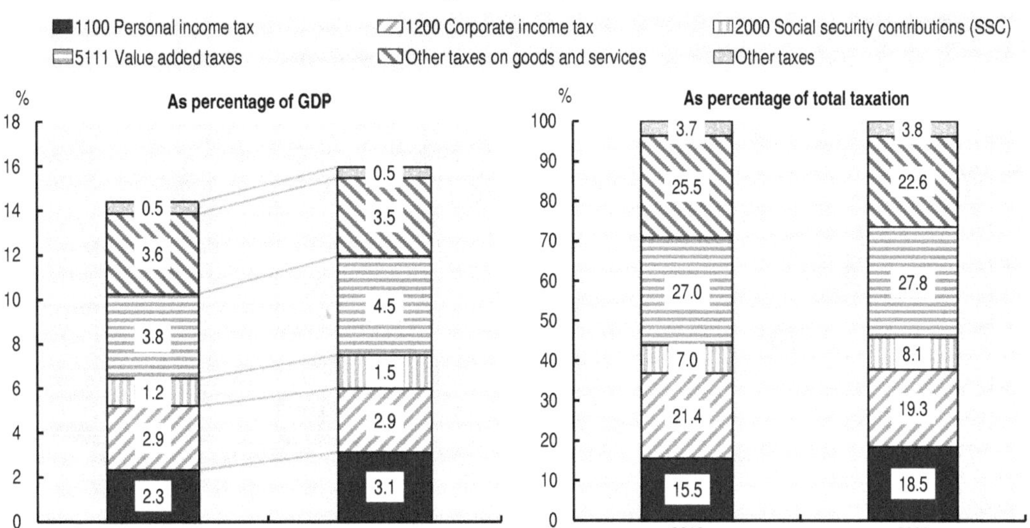

Note: The Africa (31) average is unweighted. The Africa (31) average should be interpreted with caution as data for social security contributions are not available or are partial in a few countries. See the country tables in Chapter 5 for further information.

Source: Authors' calculations based on data on (OECD/ATAF/AUC, 2022[4]), "Revenue Statistics in Africa: Comparative tables", *OECD Tax Statistics* (database), *http://dx.doi.org/10.1787/be755711-en.*

StatLink *https://stat.link/lqh94s*

During the COVID-19 pandemic, the Africa (31) average tax structure shifted further toward revenues from income tax and away from taxes on goods and services in 2020 due to the sharp decline in revenues from taxes on goods and services and stable income tax revenues as a percentage of GDP. The share of consumption tax revenues in total taxation declined by 1.5 p.p. on average between 2019 and 2020, whereas the share of PIT and CIT revenues in total tax revenues increased by 0.7 and 0.8 p.p., respectively, over the period.

Tax structures in 2020

In 2020, VAT generated the largest share of tax revenues on average for the countries included in this publication (Figure 1.17). Revenues from VAT accounted for 27.8% of total tax revenues on average, a share similar to the LAC average of 27.5% but 7.5 p.p. higher than the OECD average (2019 figure) and 4.7 p.p. higher than the Asia-Pacific (28) average. VAT revenues for the Africa (31) average were lower than the LAC and OECD averages when measured as a share of GDP (4.5% of GDP in Africa, compared to 5.7% in LAC and 6.7% in the OECD [2019 figure]) but were higher than the Asia-Pacific (28) average of 4.1% of GDP.

The average share of CIT revenues in total tax revenues in Africa was 19.3% in 2020, above the Asia-Pacific (28), LAC and OECD average shares (18.8%, 15.6% and 9.6% [2019 figure], respectively). Reported as a percentage of GDP, the average shares of CIT revenues for Africa, Asia-Pacific and the OECD were similar (2.9%, 3.1% and 3.0% of GDP [2019 figure], respectively); all were lower than the LAC average of 3.4% in 2020 (Figure 1.17).

In contrast, the Africa (31) average share of PIT revenues (18.5% of total tax revenues) was lower than the OECD average of 23.5% (2019 figure) and higher than the LAC and Asia-Pacific (28) averages (9.8% and 16.0%, respectively). As a percentage of GDP, the average level of PIT revenues across the OECD was more than double the Africa (31) average.

Figure 1.17. **Tax structure for the Africa (31), LAC, Asia-Pacific and OECD averages as a percentage of total tax revenues and as a percentage of GDP, 2020**

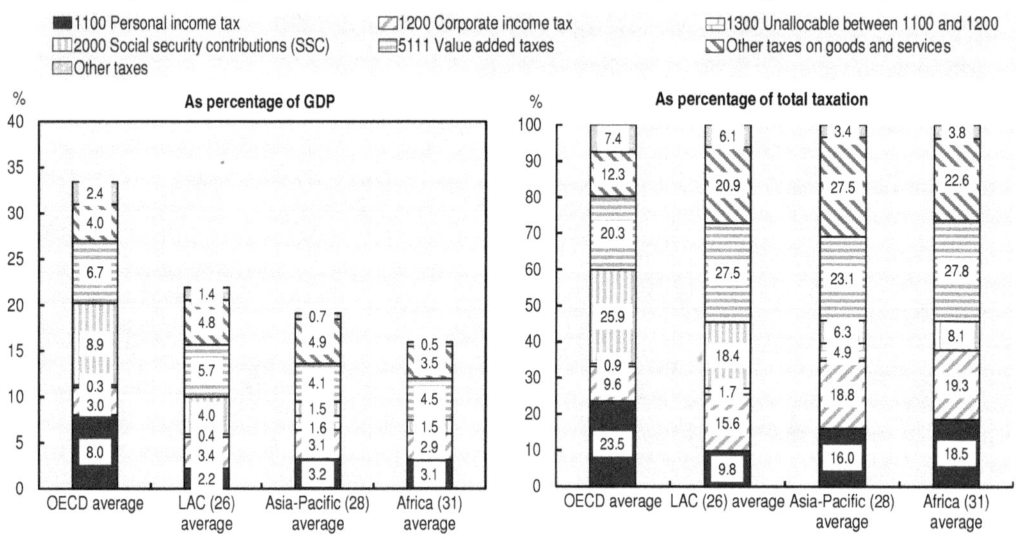

Note: The Africa (31) average, the averages for Asia-Pacific (28 economies), LAC (26 countries) and the OECD (38 countries) are unweighted.

The Africa (31) average should be interpreted with caution as data for social security contributions are not available or are partial in a few countries. See the country tables in Chapter 5 for further information.

The data for the OECD are for 2019 as final data for 2020 are not available.

Source: Authors' calculations based on data on (OECD/ATAF/AUC, 2022[4]), "*Revenue Statistics in Africa:* Comparative tables", *OECD Tax Statistics* (database), *http://dx.doi.org/10.1787/be755711-en.*

StatLink https://stat.link/0mnype

Figure 1.18 shows the decomposition of tax revenues across all countries included in this publication, differentiating between income taxes (both personal and corporate), SSCs, and taxes on goods and services (including VAT and other goods and services taxes).

Taxes on goods and services were the principal source of tax revenues for 22 of the 31 countries included in this publication (the first two groups of countries in Figure 1.18). Among these countries, taxes on goods and services generated between 34.5% of tax revenues in Tunisia and 77.0% of tax revenues in Togo. VAT accounted for the largest share of revenues from taxes on goods and services in this group of countries, except in the Republic of the Congo, Côte d'Ivoire, Ghana, Kenya, Mauritania and Uganda.

Figure 1.18. **Tax structure by country, 2020**

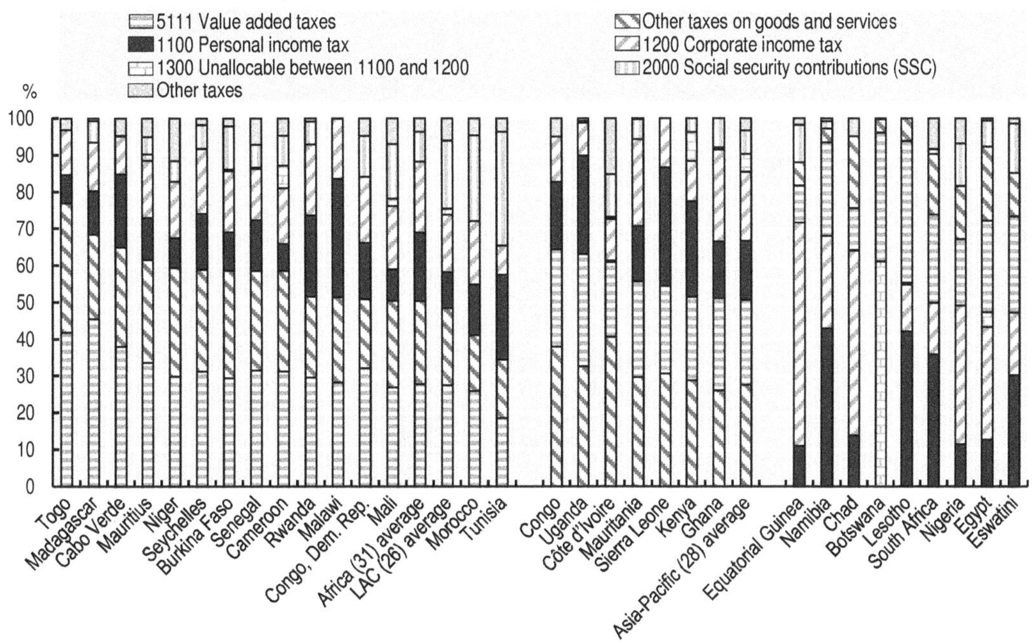

Note: Figures include sub-national government tax revenues for Eswatini, Mauritius, Morocco, Nigeria (state revenues only) and South Africa for 2020. The Africa (31) average and the averages for Asia-Pacific (28 countries), LAC (26 countries) and the OECD (38 countries) are unweighted.

The Africa (31) average should be interpreted with caution as data for social security contributions are not available or are partial in a few countries. See the country tables in Chapter 5 for further information.

The breakdown of revenue from income tax by personal income tax and corporate income tax is not available in Botswana.

The data for the OECD are for 2019 as final data for 2020 are not available.

Source: Authors' calculations based on data from (OECD/ATAF/AUC, 2022[4]), "Revenue Statistics in Africa: Comparative tables", *OECD Tax Statistics* (database), *http://dx.doi.org/10.1787/be755711-en.*

StatLink *https://stat.link/4ahp1j*

For nine countries (Botswana, Chad, Egypt, Equatorial Guinea, Eswatini, Lesotho, Namibia, Nigeria and South Africa), taxes on income and profits accounted for the principal share of total tax revenues. In all these countries, taxes on income and profits represented a greater share of total tax revenues than for the OECD and LAC averages, ranging from 47.2% of total tax revenues in Egypt and Eswatini to 71.6% in Equatorial Guinea.

Eighteen of the 31 countries covered in this publication received a higher share of tax revenues from CIT than from PIT. The share of CIT revenue was particularly large in Chad and Equatorial Guinea, where CIT revenues accounted for 50.2% and 60.6% of total taxes, respectively, while Lesotho and Namibia received more than 40% of total revenue from PIT in 2020. In 23 countries, revenues from VAT accounted for a larger share of total taxation than revenue from other taxes on goods and services. Eight countries received a higher share of revenues from other taxes on goods and services: Chad, Côte d'Ivoire, the Republic of the Congo, Ghana, Kenya, Mauritania, Sierra Leone and Uganda. By contrast, Botswana, Lesotho and Namibia, which are all members of SACU,[9] received less than 7.0% of total tax revenues from other taxes on goods and services. The revenue sharing agreement between SACU countries explains their relatively low share of other taxes on goods and services in comparison to other countries.

The importance of SSCs[10] in total tax revenues varies greatly across the 31 countries in this publication. The share was highest in Morocco and Tunisia, at 23.3% of total tax revenues in Morocco and 30.9% in Tunisia; in the remaining countries, SSCs ranged from less than 0.2% of total tax revenues in Cabo Verde to 14.8% in Mali. This variation reflects a diversity of social security programmes and contribution rates, with many countries making use of a variety of systems to fund social security benefits. For example, SSCs in South Africa finance the Unemployment Insurance Fund while other benefits, such as social assistance programmes covering old age, sickness and maternity, are financed by general revenues. In contrast, social security schemes in Morocco and Tunisia are modelled on the French system and provide a wide range of benefits on a contributory basis, including old age, disability, sickness and maternity, work injury (Tunisia), unemployment (Morocco) and family benefits (SSA, 2015$_{[26]}$).

Environmentally related tax revenues

Through the Paris Agreement of 2016, countries have committed to decarbonising their economies by the middle of this century, implying a shift away from fossil fuels as a source of energy. Environmentally related taxes, and price-based policy instruments more generally, play an increasingly significant role in many countries. By incorporating a price signal into consumer decisions, these taxes give effect to the polluter-pays principle and encourage businesses and households to consider the environmental costs of their behaviour.

An environmentally related tax is a tax whose base is a physical unit (or a proxy of a physical unit) of something that has a proven, specific harmful impact on the environment regardless of whether the tax is intended to change behaviours or is levied for another purpose (OECD, 2005$_{[27]}$). Revenues from taxes on energy can increase in the medium term if countries increase effective tax rates on the carbon content of fuels (Marten and Van Dender, 2019$_{[28]}$). A joint ITF and OECD study (OECD/ITF, 2019$_{[29]}$) shows how revenues from road transport can be stabilised in the long term through a mix of taxing distance driven, vehicles and fuel.

Although environmentally related tax revenues cannot be identified in the standard OECD classification of tax revenues, they can be identified through the detailed list of specific taxes included for most countries within this overarching classification. It is on this basis that they are included in the OECD Policy Instruments for the Environment (PINE) database (OECD, 2022$_{[30]}$).[11]

A detailed examination of country-specific taxes for the 31 African countries in this report demonstrates that, on average, revenue from environmentally related taxes amounted to 1.1% of GDP in 2020, a higher level than the average in Asia-Pacific[12] and LAC (0.8% and 1.0% of GDP, respectively) but lower than the OECD unweighted average of 2.2% of GDP. Across countries, environmentally related tax revenue ranged from less than 0.1% of GDP in the Republic of the Congo and Nigeria to 4.8% in the Seychelles (Figure 1.19). These figures need to be treated with caution as it is not possible to identify the precise level of environmentally related tax revenue for each country; the level of revenues shown in Figure 1.19 depends on the granularity of tax revenue data available.

Figure 1.19. **Environmentally related tax revenue by countries and main tax base, 2020**

Percentage of GDP

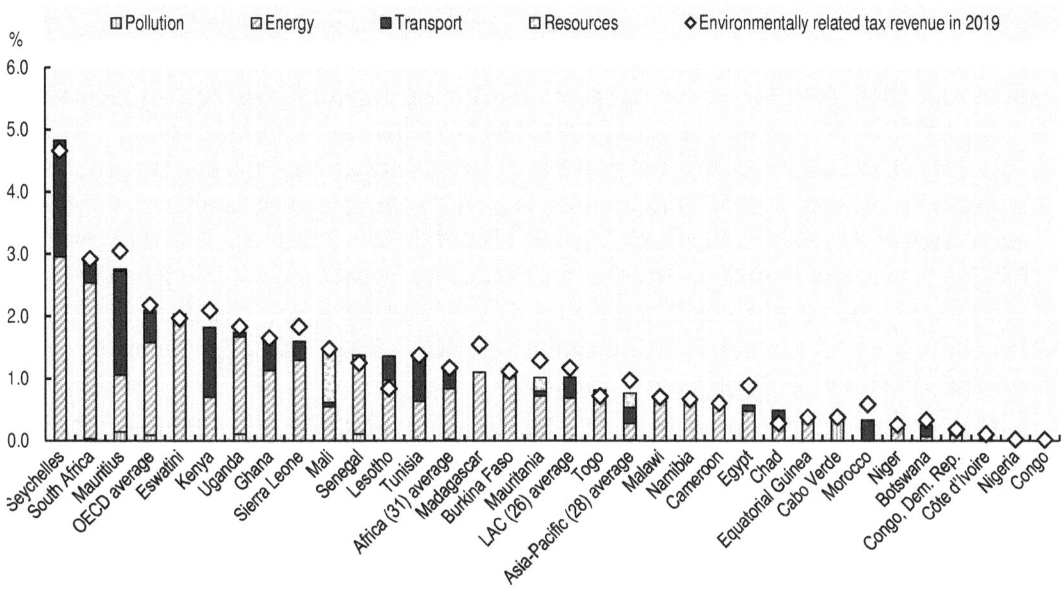

Note: These figures need to be treated with caution as it is not possible to identify the precise level of environmentally related tax revenue for each country. The figures of environmentally related tax revenues depend on the granularity of tax revenue data provided by participating countries. Rwanda is excluded as it has not been possible to identify environmentally related tax revenue.

Source: Authors' calculations based on data on (OECD/ATAF/AUC, 2022[4]), (OECD, 2022[30])PINE database for the OECD average, (OECD et al., 2022[2]) for the LAC average and (OECD, 2022[1]) for the Asia-Pacific average.

StatLink https://stat.link/7dgynw

In 2020, tax revenues from energy products generated the highest level of environmentally related tax revenue for the countries in this publication (0.8% of GDP on average). Revenues from taxes on energy products, most commonly from taxes on diesel and gasoline, amounted to approximately two-thirds of environmentally related tax revenue on average. Revenues from motor vehicle and transport taxes represented most of the remainder and revenues from other environmentally related bases were negligible, at 0.02% of environmentally related tax revenues on average. This is very similar to the breakdown of these revenues for OECD and LAC countries. In contrast, Asia-Pacific economies relied more on resource and transport taxes than energy taxes in 2020.

Taxes on energy products accounted for the largest share of environmentally related tax revenues in all but eight countries. Taxes on motor vehicles and transport were the main source of environmentally related revenues for Botswana, Côte d'Ivoire, Kenya, Mauritius, Morocco, Nigeria and Tunisia. Cabo Verde, Equatorial Guinea and Mali generated the main part of their environmentally related tax revenues either from resource taxes or pollution taxes.

Between 2019 and 2020, environmentally related tax revenues in the Africa (31) region remained unchanged. The OECD experienced a decrease of 0.1% of GDP, a smaller decrease than those for the LAC and Asia-Pacific averages over the same period (both amounting to 0.2 p.p.). In Africa, the decline in environmentally related tax revenues was principally driven by decreases in energy tax revenues followed by decreases in resource-related tax revenues. Most decreases in energy taxes were partly caused by falls in fuel excises due to pandemic-related mobility restrictions, lockdowns and teleworking.

South Africa has one of the highest levels of revenue from environmentally related taxes, amounting to 2.9% of GDP in 2020, with the fuel levy providing the largest share (1.4% of GDP). Over the past decade, South Africa has introduced the incandescent light bulb levy (2009/10); the electricity levy (2009/10); the CO_2 tax on vehicle emissions (2010/11) and the tyre levy (2016/17). More recently, South Africa introduced a carbon tax in 2019 with a tax rate of ZAR 120 (USD 8.34) per ton of carbon dioxide equivalent (SARS, 2020[31]) (Reuters, 2019[32]) (OECD, 2020[33]). From 1 January 2022, the carbon rate in South Africa has increased to ZAR 144 (about USD 9). South Africa plans to progressively increase the rate to reach USD 20 in 2026 to meet its COP26 commitments. From 2026, South Africa intends to increase carbon rates at a more rapid pace to reach at least USD 30 by 2030 and USD 120 beyond 2050 (The conversation, 2022[34]). In other four countries, a carbon tax is being finalised or under consideration (Botswana, Côte d'Ivoire, Morocco and Senegal) (News Ghana, 2022[35]) (The Institute for Research in Economic and Fiscal Issues (IREF), 2021[36]) (Carbon Pricing Leadership Coalition, 2018[37]) (UNFCCC, 2021[38]).

In the context of the introduction of a carbon border adjustment mechanism (CBAM) by the European Union (EU) from 2023 as part of a package that aims to cut greenhouse-gas emissions in the EU by 55% by 2030, African countries will face new taxes on certain of their exports to the EU. CBAM puts a carbon price on imports to the EU on the basis of the emissions required to produce them. The objective of the CBAM is to reduce the risk of carbon leakage by encouraging producers in non-EU countries to green their production processes, i.e. to tax carbon in their own industries. If the CBAM will initially apply to the highest-emitting products (iron and steel, cement, fertilisers, aluminium, and electricity generation), other products will be included in the future. Mozambique will be particularly affected as it is estimated that 54.1% of Mozambican aluminium CBAM sector exports are to the EU (European Commission, 2021[39]). Some policy makers in Africa have already started to implement new measures to mitigate the CBAM's effects on their economies. For example, Morocco is working on the certification of the carbon footprint of products as well on ensuring access for Moroccan exporting industries to renewable energies (Telquel, 2022[40]).

In general, the use of taxation to address environmental issues is low in the region and there is a significant scope to strengthen this type of taxation. The underutilisation of environmental taxes in the Africa region also needs to be understood in the context of the extensive use of fossil fuel subsidies. Fossil fuel subsidies in Africa were estimated to amount to 3.8% of GDP in 2020 (IEA, 2021[41]). Among the countries in this publication, Egypt, Ghana and Nigeria provided fossil fuel subsidies amounting about USD 7.9 billion, USD 200 million and USD 400 million, respectively, in 2020. The COVID-19 pandemic significantly affected these subsidies; in Egypt and Nigeria fossil fuel subsidies fell in 2020 by more than 50% relative to 2019. The International Energy Agency estimated that fossil fuel subsidies stood at USD27.7 billion for Africa and USD 180 billion globally in 2020, down 40% from 2019 levels to the lowest level in 14 years (IEA, 2021[42]) (Chuku and Ajayi, 2021[43]).

Reforming fossil fuel subsidies while at the same time implementing environmental taxation has the potential to mobilise significant government revenues and help to meet Agenda 2063 and the Sustainable Development Goals (SDGs).

Taxes by level of government

Analysis of taxation by level of government for the countries participating in this publication is limited by the fact that data on sub-national tax revenues are only available for five countries: Eswatini, Mauritius,[13] Morocco, Nigeria[14] and South Africa. In 2020, sub-national government revenues accounted for 0.3% of total tax revenues in Mauritius, 1.0% in Eswatini, 2.9% in Morocco and 6.9% in South Africa. In contrast, sub-national government tax revenues amounted to 15.3% of total tax revenues in Nigeria. Revenues collected at sub-national level are generally considered to be low in the region as a whole.

The COVID-19 pandemic has caused a significant decline in sub-national tax revenues around the world and Africa's sub-national tax revenues were no exception. These declined for Eswatini (0.2 p.p.), Morocco (0.1 p.p.) and Nigeria (0.1 p.p.) whereas they increased slightly for South Africa (0.1 p.p.) and remained unchanged In Mauritius.

In general, sub-national governments in Africa tend to have limited tax collection responsibilities. Many local governments receive a significant share of their total revenues from central government transfers. Local governments across Africa have limited resources and many local tax administrations are not adequately equipped to collect taxes or to account for them. This results in high collection costs and a large number of low-yield taxes. Moreover, processing of data on revenue collections and the exchange of information with other public institutions is poor and there is usually little co-operation with the central government. This can lead to a duplication of taxes or a levying of taxes that are contrary to national objectives (such as local taxes on export crops).

Revenues from property taxes are the most important source of tax revenue for sub-national governments in Eswatini, Mauritius, Morocco and South Africa. They accounted for all the reported tax revenue collected locally in Eswatini, Mauritius and South Africa and for more than 80% in Morocco. Most of the remainder derives from taxes on goods and services. In contrast, sub-national government tax revenues in Nigeria are mostly sourced from income taxes.

There are wide differences in local taxation among African countries and many countries do not levy any local taxes on buildings and landholdings or on economic activities (AfDB/OECD/UNDP, 2015[44]). Apart from South Africa, property registers are lacking or incomplete, which is a major challenge for the collection of property taxes (Fjeldstad; Chambas; Brun, 2014[45]). In Mauritius, for instance, property tax provides a low yield partly due to outdated cadastres and valuations of property (IMF, 2014[46]).

Some countries have been working on improving their property taxes, which has led to improved land registries and better administrative tools. Morocco has been reforming local government tax systems and administrations since 2007 to strengthen local tax revenue (Boisard; de Freitas; Hidouci, 2014[47]). Côte d'Ivoire has introduced GIS software in their land registries. South Africa has successfully decentralised urban property tax collection and has developed a modern system to collect property tax revenue including use of statistical techniques to conduct computer-assisted mass-appraisals (Monkam and Moore, 2015[48]).

Notes

1 The Africa (31) average should be interpreted with caution as data on social security contributions are not available for Chad, the Republic of the Congo, the Democratic Republic of the Congo (prior to 2012), Equatorial Guinea (prior to 2013), Madagascar (prior to 2011), Namibia (prior to 2009), Sierra Leone, Togo and Uganda and are only partially available for Cameroon and Senegal. Social security contributions for Botswana, Lesotho and Malawi are deemed to be null as they do not meet the criteria to be classified as social security contributions set out in the OECD classification of taxes in the *Interpretative Guide*. See the country tables in Chapter 5 for further information.

2 The fiscal year in Eswatini, Lesotho, Namibia, and Botswana runs from April to March. This means that reporting year 2020 is Q2/2020–Q1/2021. The fiscal year for Egypt, Kenya, Malawi, Mauritius (years prior to 2010 and for 2016 onwards) and Uganda ends on 30 June. The reporting year 2020 includes Q2/2019–Q2/2020. Some countries report certain components of tax revenues on a different basis depending on the nature of the revenues. For example, revenues in Rwanda are reported on a calendar year except for SSCs, which are reported on a fiscal year basis ending 30 June since 2008. Another example is South Africa, whose data is on a calendar year except for SSCs and taxes at provincial and local levels (reported on a fiscal year basis ending 30 March).

3 Burundi, South Sudan, Tanzania, Kenya, Rwanda and Uganda belong to the East Africa Community (EAC).

4 Burkina Faso, Benin, Côte d'Ivoire, Guinea Bissau, Mali, Niger, Senegal and Togo belong to the West African Economic and Monetary Union (WAEMU, also known by its French acronym, UEMOA).

5 In this publication, revenue from excises, tariffs and customs duties are included as tax revenues in the SACU country that collected the revenue (South Africa) and revenues received from the SACU Common Revenue Pool are included as miscellaneous revenue in non-tax revenues (Botswana, Eswatini, Lesotho and Namibia).

6 The information in this section was provided by focal points of participating countries (Burkina Faso, Cabo Verde, Egypt, Eswatini, Lesotho, Mali, Namibia and Rwanda) or from (OECD, 2021[49]) (Mauritius, Nigeria, the Seychelles and South Africa).

7 After the East African Community (EAC) Common Market was established in 2010, Rwanda adopted the EAC Common External Tariff Framework leading to a decline of revenues from trade taxes in 2010 by 0.3 p.p.

8 The Seychelles is the only country in this report to be a high income country. For this reason upper middle income (5 countries) and high income countries (1 country) are grouped together.

9 The five SACU members have a revenue-sharing agreement that provides for common external tariffs and for the payment of customs and excise duties into a common pool to be shared between the SACU countries. In this publication, revenue from excises, tariffs and customs duties are included as tax revenues in the SACU country that collected the revenue (South Africa) and revenues received from the SACU Common Revenue Pool are included as miscellaneous revenue in non-tax revenues (Botswana, Eswatini, Lesotho and Namibia).

10 Data on social security contributions are not available for Chad, the Republic of the Congo, the Democratic Republic of the Congo (prior to 2012), Madagascar (prior to 2011), Namibia, Sierra Leone, Togo and Uganda and are only partially available for Cameroon and Senegal. See the country tables in Chapter 5 for further information.

11 The PINE database classifies environmentally related taxes under four bases:

- Energy: This covers taxation of energy products such as fossil fuels and electricity also including fuels for transportation such as petrol and diesel. All CO_2-related taxes are in this category.
- Motor vehicles and transport services: This category includes imports or sales taxes on transport equipment, recurrent taxes on ownership, registration or road use of motor vehicles, and other transport-related taxes.
- Resources: This category includes taxes on mining and quarrying, forestry, wildlife and fisheries.
- Pollution: This category includes taxes on ozone-depleting substances, water and wastewater, waste management.

12 The Asia-Pacific average represents an average of 22 countries and not 28 as it has not been possible to identify environmentally related tax revenue for six countries due to data availability issues.

13 Data from Mauritius were derived from financial statements produced by Statistics Mauritius.

14 Sub-national tax revenues figures include state revenues but exclude local government revenues.

References

AfDB/OECD/UNDP (2015), *African Economic Outlook 2015: Regional Development and Spatial Inclusion*, OECD Publishing, Paris, *https://doi.org/10.1787/aeo-2015-en.* [44]

Akitoby, B. et al. (2019), *Case Studies in Tax Revenue Mobilization in Low-Income Countries*, *https://www.imf.org/en/Publications/WP/Issues/2019/05/14/Case-Studies-in-Tax-Revenue-Mobilization-in-Low-Income-Countries-46719* (accessed on 20 September 2021). [11]

AUC/OECD (2022), *Africa's Development Dynamics 2022: Regional Value Chains for a Sustainable Recovery*, AUC, Addis Ababa/ OECD Publishing, Paris, *https://doi.org/10.1787/2e3b97fd-en.* [23]

Boisard; de Freitas; Hidouci (2014), *Renforcer les recettes fiscales locales pour financer le développement urbain en Afrique*, Fonds Mondial pour le Développement des Villes (FMDV), Paris, *http://delog.org/web/wp-content/uploads/2016/03/Etude-FMDV-Fiscalite%CC%81-locale-Villes-Afrique-8-Cas.pdf.* [47]

Brautigam, D., O. Fjeldstad and M. Moore (2008), *Taxation and State-Building in Developing Countries: Capacity and Consent – ICTD, CMI*, *https://www.ictd.ac/publication/taxation-and-state-building-in-developing-countries-capacity-and-consent/* (accessed on 20 September 2021). [25]

Carbon Pricing Leadership Coalition (2018), *Launch of the PMR project on carbon taxation in côte d'ivoire*, *https://www.carbonpricingleadership.org/calendar/2018/7/12/launch-of-the-pmr-project-on-carbon-taxation-in-cte-divoire.* [37]

Chuku, C. and V. Ajayi (2021), *Accelerating Africa's green economy transition*, *https://www.brookings.edu/blog/africa-in-focus/2021/11/04/accelerating-africas-green-economy-transition/.* [43]

Economist Intelligence (2018), *New income tax law comes into force*, *http://country.eiu.com/article.aspx?articleid=1636776147&Country=Rwanda&topic=Economy&subtopic=Fo_2* (accessed on 20 September 2021). [14]

European Commission (2021), *Proposal for a regulation of the european parliament and of the council establishing a carbon border adjustment mechanism*, *https://ec.europa.eu/info/sites/default/files/carbon_border_adjustment_mechanism_0.pdf#page=194.* [39]

EY (2020), *Namibia announces Economic Stimulus and Relief Package to mitigate impact of COVID-19*, *https://taxnews.ey.com/news/2020-0884-namibia-announces-economic-stimulus-and-relief-package-to-mitigate-impact-of-covid-19?uAlertID=Sd%2FG8rua1oj6%2Fl58EZ2AiA%3D%3D* (accessed on 29 August 2022). [7]

Fjeldstad; Chambas; Brun (2014), *Local government taxation in Sub-Saharan Africa: a review and an agenda for research*, 2, Chr. Michelsen Institute, Bergen, *http://www.cmi.no/publications/file/5098-local-government-taxation-in-sub-saharan-africa.pdf.* [45]

Gaspar, V. et al. (2019), *Fiscal Policy and Development: Human, Social, and Physical Investments for the SDGs*, *https://www.imf.org/en/Publications/Staff-Discussion-Notes/Issues/2019/01/18/Fiscal-Policy-and-Development-Human-Social-and-Physical-Investments-for-the-SDGs-46444* (accessed on 20 September 2021). [21]

Gwaindepi, A. (2021), "Domestic revenue mobilisation in developing countries: An exploratory analysis of sub-Saharan Africa and Latin America", *Journal of International Development*, Vol. 33/2, pp. 396-421, *https://doi.org/10.1002/JID.3528.* [24]

IEA (2021), *Fossil fuels database*, *https://www.iea.org/data-and-statistics/data-product/fossil-fuel-subsidies-database* (accessed on 13 September 2022). [41]

IEA (2021), *Tracking the impact of fossil-fuel subsidies*, *https://www.iea.org/topics/energy-subsidies* (accessed on 13 September 2022). [42]

IMF (2022), "Inflation rate, average consumer prices", World Economic Outlook, *https://www.imf.org/external/datamapper/PCPIPCH@WEO/OEMDC/ADVEC/WEOWORLD* (accessed on 19 September 2022). [5]

IMF (2022), *World Economic Outlook Database, April 2022*, *https://www.imf.org/en/Publications/WEO/weo-database/2022/April* (accessed on 20 September 2021). [6]

IMF (2020), *The Development Path Less Travelled-The Experience of Rwanda*, *https://www.imf.org/en/Publications/Departmental-Papers-Policy-Papers/Issues/2020/08/17/The-Development-Path-Less-Travelled-The-Experience-of-Rwanda-49609.* [13]

IMF (2019), *World Economic Outlook - Frequently Asked Questions*, *https://www.imf.org/external/pubs/ft/weo/faq.htm#q4d* (accessed on 6 September 2019). [19]

IMF (2014), *Mauritius: 2014 article IV consultation-staff report (2014b)*, IMF, *http://www.imf.org/external/pubs/ft/scr/2014/cr14107.pdf.* [46]

Marten, M. and K. Van Dender (2019), *The use of revenues from carbon pricing. OECD Taxation Working Papers*, OECD, *https://doi.org/10.1787/3cb265e4-en.* [28]

Minister of Finance and Budget of Chad (2021), *Note de conjoncture sur le secteur pétrole au Quatrième trimestre 2020, https://observatoire.td/upload/publications/2021/NCSP%20Q4%202020%20%20VF.pdf* (accessed on 30 August 2022). [8]

Monkam, N. and M. Moore (2015), *How Property Tax Would Benefit Africa*, Africa Research Institute, *http://www.africaresearchinstitute.org/publications/property-tax-benefit-africa.* [48]

Moore, M., W. Prichard and O. Fjeldstad (2018), *Taxing Africa: Coercion, Reform and Development – ICTD*, Zed Books, *https://www.ictd.ac/publication/taxing-africa-coercion-reform-and-development/* (accessed on 20 September 2021). [9]

News Ghana (2022), *Botswana finalizing plans for introduction of carbon tax, https://newsghana.com.gh/botswana-finalizing-plans-for-introduction-of-carbon-tax/.* [35]

OECD (2022), *PINE database, http://www.oecd.org/environment/tools-evaluation/environmentaltaxation.htm.* [30]

OECD (2022), *Revenue Statistics in Asia and the Pacific 2022: Strengthening Tax Revenues in Developing Asia*, OECD Publishing, Paris, *https://doi.org/10.1787/db29f89a-en.* [1]

OECD (2021), *Country tax measures in response to COVID-19 pandemic, https://www.oecd.org/tax/covid-19-tax-policy-and-other-measures.xlsm.* [49]

OECD (2021), *Revenue Statistics 2021*, OECD Publishing, Paris, *https://doi.org/10.1787/6e87f932-en.* [3]

OECD (2020), "OECD analysis of budgetary support and tax expenditures. 2020 country notes", *Inventory of Support Measures for Fossil Fuels databas, http://www.oecd.org/fossil-fuels/data/.* [33]

OECD (2020), *OECD Tax Policy Reviews: Seychelles*, OECD Publishing, *https://doi.org/10.1787/cba38d19-en.* [15]

OECD (2019), *Tax Morale: What Drives People and Businesses to Pay Tax?*, OECD Publishing, *https://doi.org/10.1787/f3d8ea10-en.* [18]

OECD (2014), *Development Co-operation Report 2014: Mobilising Resources for Sustainable Development*, OECD Publishing, Paris, *https://doi.org/10.1787/dcr-2014-en.* [17]

OECD (2005), *Glossary of statistical terms, https://stats.oecd.org/glossary/detail.asp?ID=6437.* [27]

OECD/ATAF/AUC (2022), *Revenue Statistics in Africa: Comparative tables*, OECD Publishing, Paris. [4]

OECD/ATAF/AUC (2021), *Revenue Statistics in Africa 2021: 1990-2019*, OECD Publishing, Paris, *https://doi.org/10.1787/14e1edb1-en-fr.* [10]

OECD et al. (2022), *Revenue Statistics in Latin America and the Caribbean 2022*, OECD Publishing, Paris, *https://doi.org/10.1787/58a2dc35-en-es.* [2]

OECD/ITF (2019), *Tax revenue implications from the decarbonisation of road transport: scenarios for Slovenia*, OECD, *https://doi.org/10.1787/87b39a2f-en.* [29]

PwC (2019), *Sustaining the momemtum. Rwanda's 2019/20 National Budget Bulletin, https://www.pwc.com/rw/en/pdf/rwanda-budget-analysis-2019-20.pdf.* [12]

Reuters (2019), *South African carbon tax finally becomes law, https://www.reuters.com/article/us-safrica-carbontax/south-african-carbon-tax-finally-becomes-law-idUSKCN1SW0K6* (accessed on 6 September 2019). [32]

SACU (2020), *What is SACU?, http://www.sacu.int/about/what_is.html* (accessed on 10 September 2020). [16]

SARS (2020), *Tax statistics 2020, https://www.sars.gov.za/wp-content/uploads/Docs/TaxStats/2020/Tax-Statistics-2020.pdf.* [31]

SSA (2015), *Social Security Through the World: Africa*, SSA Publication Social Security Administration, Washington, DC, *http://www.ssa.gov/policy/docs/progdesc/ssptw/2014-2015/africa/ssptw15africa.pdf.* [26]

Telquel (2022), *Maroc-UE : Ryad Mezzour dévoile ses mesures d'adaptation à la nouvelle taxe carbone, https://telquel.ma/instant-t/2022/06/03/maroc-ue-ryad-mezzour-devoile-ses-mesures-dadaptation-a-la-nouvelle-taxe-carbone_1770177/.* [40]

The conversation (2022), *South Africa's carbon tax rate goes up but emitters get more time to clean up, https://theconversation.com/south-africas-carbon-tax-rate-goes-up-but-emitters-get-more-time-to-clean-up-177834#:~:text=Carbon%20tax%20rate%20increase%3A%20The,until%20it%20reaches%20US%2420.*[34]

The Institute for Research in Economic and Fiscal Issues (IREF) (2021), *Morocco's tax policy: the urgent need for tax system reform*, *https://en.irefeurope.org/publications/online-articles/article/morocco-s-tax-policy-the-urgent-need-for-tax-system-reform/*. [36]

UNFCCC (2021), *Stakeholders consultation in Senegal under the consultancy study on carbon tax*, *https://unfccc.int/about-us/regional-collaboration-centres/rcc-lome/stakeholders-consultation-in-senegal-under-the-consultancy-study-on-carbon-tax*. [38]

WHO (2015), *Purchasing Power Parity 2005*, World Health Organization, *http://www.who.int/choice/costs/ppp/en/*. [20]

World Bank (2022), *World Bank Country and Lending Groups*, *https://datahelpdesk.worldbank.org/knowledgebase/articles/906519* (accessed on 20 September 2021). [22]

Chapitre 1

Tendances des recettes fiscales, 2010-20

Pour atteindre les Objectifs de développement durable (ODD) des Nations Unies et mettre en œuvre le Programme d'action d'Addis-Abeba et l'Agenda 2063 de l'Union africaine, il est nécessaire de mobiliser des moyens financiers supplémentaires, et notamment des ressources intérieures, afin de financer l'offre de biens et de services publics. L'impôt représente une source de recettes publiques prévisible et stable, qui contraste avec la volatilité d'autres sources importantes de recettes publiques, comme les dons et les redevances minières.

Les *Statistiques des recettes publiques en Afrique* contiennent un ensemble d'indicateurs internationalement comparables sur les recettes fiscales et non fiscales qui peuvent servir à mesurer les progrès en matière de mobilisation des ressources intérieures (comme le prévoient l'Agenda 2063, les ODD, le Programme d'action d'Addis-Abeba, ainsi que des initiatives connexes telles que l'initiative fiscale d'Addis-Abeba), et à éclairer les politiques et les réformes fiscales. Ce rapport et les données qu'il contient contribuent aussi au Programme statistique panafricain, une initiative conjointe de l'Union européenne et de l'Union africaine visant à renforcer les capacités statistiques en Afrique, en fournissant des données statistiques de qualité sur les recettes publiques. Ces données faciliteront le processus d'élaboration des politiques et leur suivi, de manière à soutenir l'intégration africaine.

La présente édition du rapport contient des données portant sur l'année 2020 et examine l'impact de la crise du COVID-19 sur les systèmes fiscaux en Afrique. La pandémie a lourdement pesé sur les finances publiques dans le monde, entraînant une chute des recettes et une augmentation des niveaux de la dette. Ce rapport analyse les répercussions de la pandémie sur les recettes fiscales en valeur absolue et en pourcentage du PIB, pour le total des recettes fiscales et pour différents types d'impôt. Il compare également l'impact du COVID-19 sur les pays africains par rapport à d'autres régions.

Ce chapitre examine l'évolution du ratio impôts/PIB, de la structure fiscale et de la part des recettes fiscales par niveau d'administration dans 31 pays d'Afrique : Afrique du Sud, Botswana, Burkina Faso, Cabo Verde, Cameroun, Côte d'Ivoire, Guinée équatoriale, Égypte, Eswatini, Ghana, Kenya, Lesotho, Madagascar, Malawi, Mali, Maroc, Maurice, Mauritanie, Namibie, Niger, Nigéria, Ouganda, République démocratique du Congo, République du Congo, Rwanda, Sénégal, Seychelles, Sierra Leone (incluse pour la première fois dans cette édition), Tchad, Togo et Tunisie. Il compare également les moyennes de ces 31 pays d'Afrique avec celles de 28 pays d'Asie et du Pacifique (OCDE, 2022[1]), 26 pays d'Amérique latine et des Caraïbes (ALC) (OCDE et al., 2022[2]), et celle des 38 pays de l'OCDE (OCDE, 2021[3]). L'analyse proposée vient compléter les informations détaillées par pays consacrées aux recettes fiscales figurant au chapitre 5.

Ratios impôts/PIB en Afrique

Ratios impôts/PIB en 2020

Le ratio impôts/PIB moyen non pondéré dans les 31 pays d'Afrique couverts par la publication [désigné ci-après « moyenne des pays d'Afrique (31) »] s'est établi à 16.0 % en 2020 (Graphique 1.1). Le ratio impôts/PIB correspond aux recettes fiscales (y compris les cotisations de sécurité sociale obligatoires versées à l'administration générale) exprimées en pourcentage du produit intérieur brut (PIB)[1]. À titre de comparaison, les ratios impôts/PIB moyens pour la région Asie-Pacifique, Amérique latine et Caraïbes, et pour la zone OCDE étaient respectivement de 19.1 %, 21.9 % et 33.5 % en 2020.

En 2020, les ratios impôts/PIB ont affiché de grandes variations entre les pays couverts par la publication, allant de 5.5 % au Nigéria à 32.5 % en Tunisie. L'Afrique du Sud, le Maroc, les Seychelles et la Tunisie affichaient des ratios supérieurs à 25 %. Dans 22 pays, les ratios étaient compris entre 10.0 % et 25.0 %, tandis que la République du Congo, la République démocratique du Congo, le Niger et le Nigéria avaient un ratio inférieur à 10 %.

Graphique 1.1. **Ratios impôts/PIB et total des recettes fiscales (hors cotisations de sécurité sociale) en pourcentage du PIB, 2020**

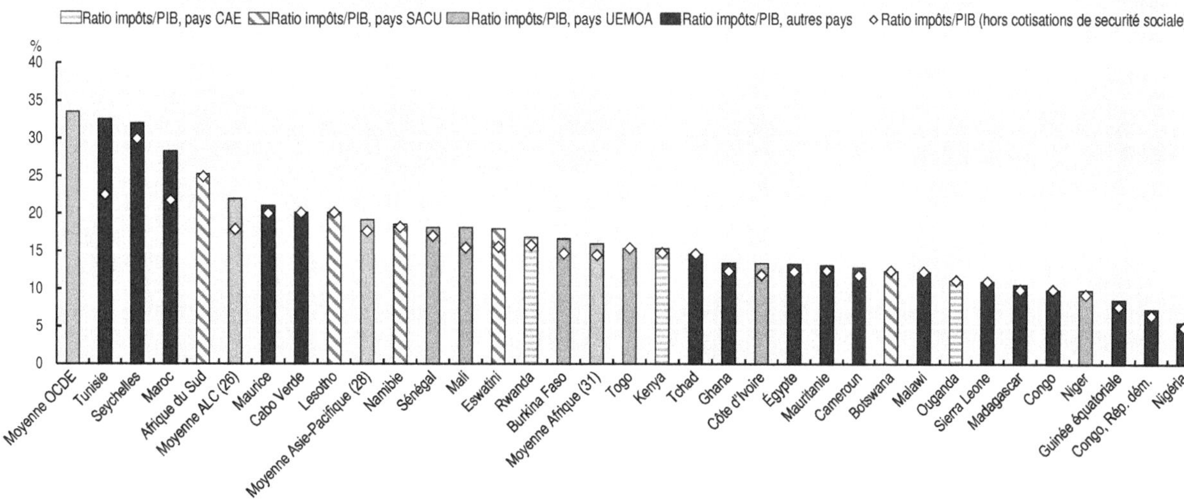

Notes : Les chiffres prennent en compte les recettes fiscales des administrations infranationales pour l'Afrique du Sud, l'Eswatini, le Maroc, Maurice et le Nigéria (recettes des États uniquement) pour l'année 2020. La moyenne Afrique (31) et les moyennes Asie-Pacifique (28 pays), ALC (26 pays) et OCDE (38 pays) sont des moyennes non pondérées.
Il convient d'interpréter la moyenne Afrique (31) avec précaution car des données relatives aux cotisations de sécurité sociale sont indisponibles pour l'Ouganda, la République du Congo, la Sierra Leone, le Tchad et le Togo, et elles sont incomplètes pour le Cameroun et le Sénégal. Les cotisations de sécurité sociale pour le Botswana, le Lesotho et le Malawi sont égales à zéro dans la mesure où elles ne remplissent pas les critères retenus pour être considérées comme des cotisations de sécurité sociale, selon la classification des impôts de l'OCDE figurant dans le Guide d'interprétation. Pour plus de précisions, se reporter aux tableaux par pays présentés dans le chapitre 5.
Le ratio impôts/PIB de l'Afrique du Sud prend en compte les sommes recouvrées par l'Afrique du Sud au profit de l'Union douanière de l'Afrique australe.
Source : Tableaux 4.1 et 4.2 figurant au chapitre 4 et (OCDE/ATAF/CUA, $2022_{[4]}$), « Statistiques des recettes publiques en Afrique : Tableaux comparatifs », *Statistiques fiscales de l'OCDE* (base de données), *https://doi.org/10.1787/7f54581d-fr*.

StatLink *https://stat.link/w4sv0o*

Impact du COVID-19 sur les recettes fiscales : variations en 2020 par rapport à 2019

Le ratio moyen impôts/PIB dans les pays d'Afrique couverts par ce rapport a baissé de 0.3 point de pourcentage entre 2019 et 2020, en grande partie à cause de la forte contraction de l'activité économique due à la pandémie de COVID-19, qui a eu un effet considérable sur les recettes publiques. Cette chute s'explique essentiellement par la diminution des recettes tirées des impôts sur les biens et services, qui ont reculé de 0.4 point de PIB en moyenne entre ces deux années.

Les ratios impôts/PIB ont diminué dans 24 pays et augmenté dans 7 pays entre 2019 et 2020 (Graphique 1.2). La plupart des baisses intervenues au cours de cette période étaient inférieures à un point de PIB ; le recul a été plus prononcé dans 7 pays : Botswana, Cabo

Verde, Égypte, Guinée équatoriale, Kenya, Lesotho et Namibie. C'est la Namibie qui a accusé la plus forte baisse, soit 1.7 point. À l'inverse, le ratio impôts/PIB a augmenté de 6.6 points au Tchad, qui enregistre la plus forte hausse de la région, suivi de la République du Congo (1.7 point) ; dans les cinq autres pays où le ratio impôts/PIB a augmenté en 2020 par rapport à 2019, les hausses étaient inférieures à un point.

Graphique 1.2. **Variation en glissement annuel des ratios impôts/PIB en 2019 et 2020**

Points de pourcentage de PIB

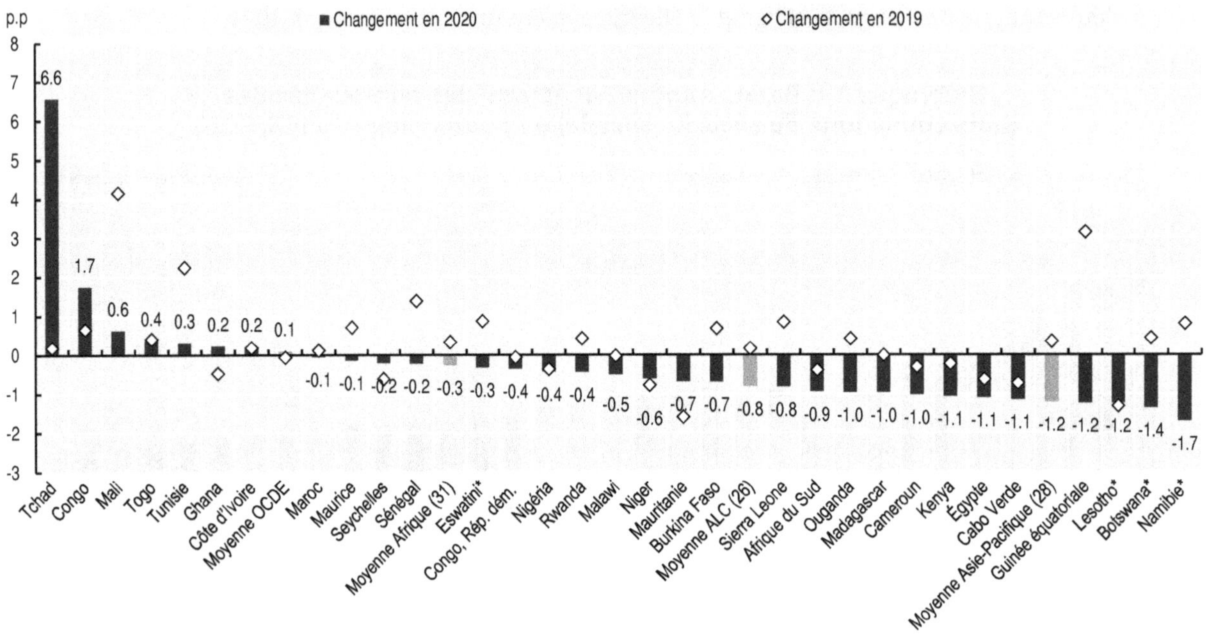

Notes : Les chiffres prennent en compte les recettes fiscales des administrations infranationales pour l'Afrique du Sud, l'Eswatini, le Maroc, Maurice et le Nigéria (recettes des États uniquement) pour l'année 2020.

*Au Botswana, en Eswatini, au Lesotho et en Namibie, l'année fiscale court du mois d'avril au mois de mars. Les chiffres de 2020 pour ces pays incluent donc les recettes perçues jusqu'au 31 mars 2021.

La moyenne Afrique (31) et les moyennes Asie-Pacifique (28 pays), ALC (26 pays) et OCDE (38 pays) sont des moyennes non pondérées.

Il convient d'interpréter l'évolution de la moyenne des pays d'Afrique (31) avec précaution, car des données relatives aux cotisations de sécurité sociale sont indisponibles ou incomplètes pour quelques pays. Pour plus de précisions, se reporter aux tableaux par pays présentés dans le chapitre 5.

Source : Calculs des auteurs basés sur des données figurant dans le tableau 4.1 du chapitre 4 et (OCDE/ATAF/CUA, 2022[4]), « Statistiques des recettes publiques en Afrique : Tableaux comparatifs », *Statistiques fiscales de l'OCDE* (base de données), *https://doi.org/10.1787/7f54581d-fr.*

StatLink *https://stat.link/hqtvi8*

Aperçu de l'évolution des recettes fiscales et du PIB en valeur nominale

Pour mieux comprendre l'impact de la crise du COVID-19 sur les recettes fiscales, cette section analyse les variations des recettes fiscales nominales et du PIB nominal entre 2019 et 2020 en Afrique. La valeur du ratio impôts/PIB dépend de deux composantes : son numérateur (recettes fiscales) et son dénominateur (PIB) (voir Encadré 1.1). Cela signifie que les variations des ratios impôts/PIB entre 2019 et 2020 reflètent des variations des recettes fiscales nominales et du PIB nominal au cours de la même période.

La pandémie de COVID-19 a provoqué une chute historique des recettes fiscales nominales et du PIB nominal. Dix-sept des 31 pays couverts par ce rapport ont vu leurs recettes fiscales nominales baisser entre 2019 et 2020, et la baisse s'est établie en moyenne à 0.5 % au cours de la période (chiffre non pondéré). Toutefois, le Tchad a connu une augmentation significative de ses recettes fiscales nominales (73.6 %) entre 2019 et 2020 ; hormis ce pays, les recettes fiscales nominales dans la région ont reculé de 3.0 % en moyenne pendant la période. Treize pays d'Afrique ont vu leur PIB nominal baisser entre 2019 et 2020 ; toutefois, il a augmenté de 0.2 % en moyenne dans les 31 pays couverts par cette publication (chiffre non pondéré).

Le Graphique 1.3 montre l'évolution des recettes fiscales et du PIB en valeur nominale entre 2019 et 2020. Dans 11 pays d'Afrique, le déclin des recettes fiscales nominales s'est accompagné du recul du PIB nominal et, pour 9 d'entre eux, les recettes fiscales nominales ont baissé davantage que le PIB nominal, entraînant une diminution de leur ratio impôts/PIB. Dans deux pays (République du Congo et Tunisie), les recettes fiscales nominales ont moins diminué que le PIB nominal entre 2019 et 2020, se soldant par une augmentation de leurs ratios impôts/PIB. Six autres pays d'Afrique ont connu un recul de leurs recettes fiscales nominales tandis que leur PIB nominal progressait, de sorte que leur ratio impôts/PIB a diminué.

Graphique 1.3. **Variations des recettes fiscales et du PIB en monnaie nominale, 2019-20**

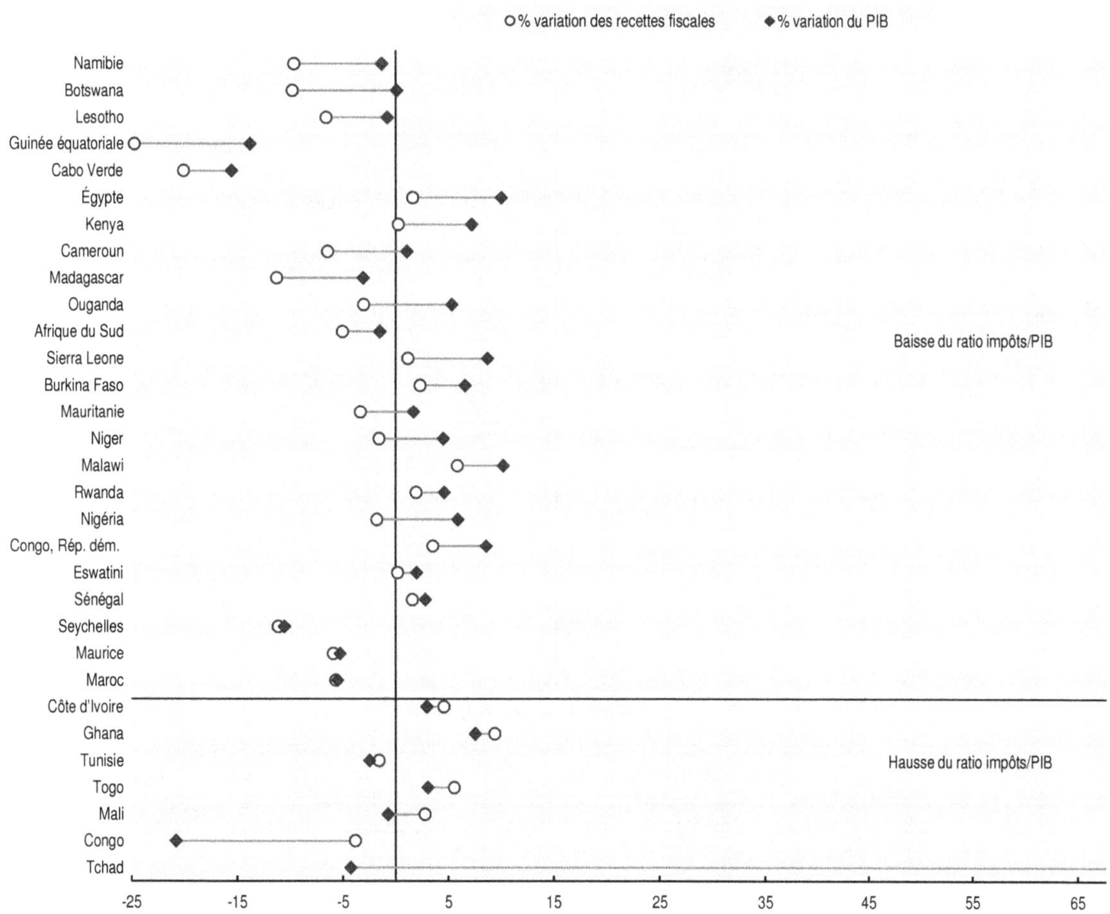

Notes : Les chiffres prennent en compte les recettes fiscales des administrations infranationales pour l'Afrique du Sud, l'Eswatini, le Maroc, Maurice et le Nigéria (recettes des États uniquement) pour l'année 2020.

Il convient d'interpréter l'évolution de la moyenne des pays d'Afrique (31) avec précaution, car des données relatives aux cotisations de sécurité sociale sont indisponibles ou incomplètes pour quelques pays. Pour plus de précisions, se reporter aux tableaux par pays présentés dans le chapitre 5.

*Au Botswana, en Eswatini, au Lesotho et en Namibie, l'année fiscale court du mois d'avril au mois de mars. Les chiffres de 2020 pour ces pays incluent donc les recettes perçues jusqu'au 31 mars 2021. Pour plus de précisions, se reporter aux notes des tableaux par pays présentés dans le chapitre 5.

Source : Calculs des auteurs basés sur des données figurant dans (OCDE/ATAF/CUA, 2022[4]), « Statistiques des recettes publiques en Afrique : Tableaux comparatifs », *Statistiques fiscales de l'OCDE* (base de données), *https://doi.org/10.1787/7f54581d-fr*.

StatLink *https://stat.link/zic9ny*

Entre 2019 et 2020, les Seychelles ont enregistré une forte contraction (plus de 10 %) de leur PIB nominal comme de leurs recettes fiscales nominales. Bien que ces baisses soient significatives, l'érosion des recettes fiscales en pourcentage du PIB entre 2019 et 2020 était relativement modeste (0.2 point), en raison de l'ampleur similaire des baisses des recettes fiscales nominales et du PIB nominal.

Dans 12 pays d'Afrique, l'augmentation des recettes fiscales nominales s'est accompagnée d'une hausse du PIB nominal et, pour 3 d'entre eux, les recettes fiscales nominales ont augmenté davantage que le PIB nominal, entraînant un accroissement de leur ratio impôts/PIB. Deux pays (Mali et Tchad) ont enregistré une progression de leurs recettes fiscales nominales et une diminution de leur PIB nominal, se traduisant par un ratio impôts/PIB plus élevé en 2020 qu'en 2019.

Graphique 1.4. **Variations des recettes fiscales nominales et du PIB nominal dans les pays d'Afrique, d'Asie-Pacifique, de la région ALC et de l'OCDE, 2019-20**

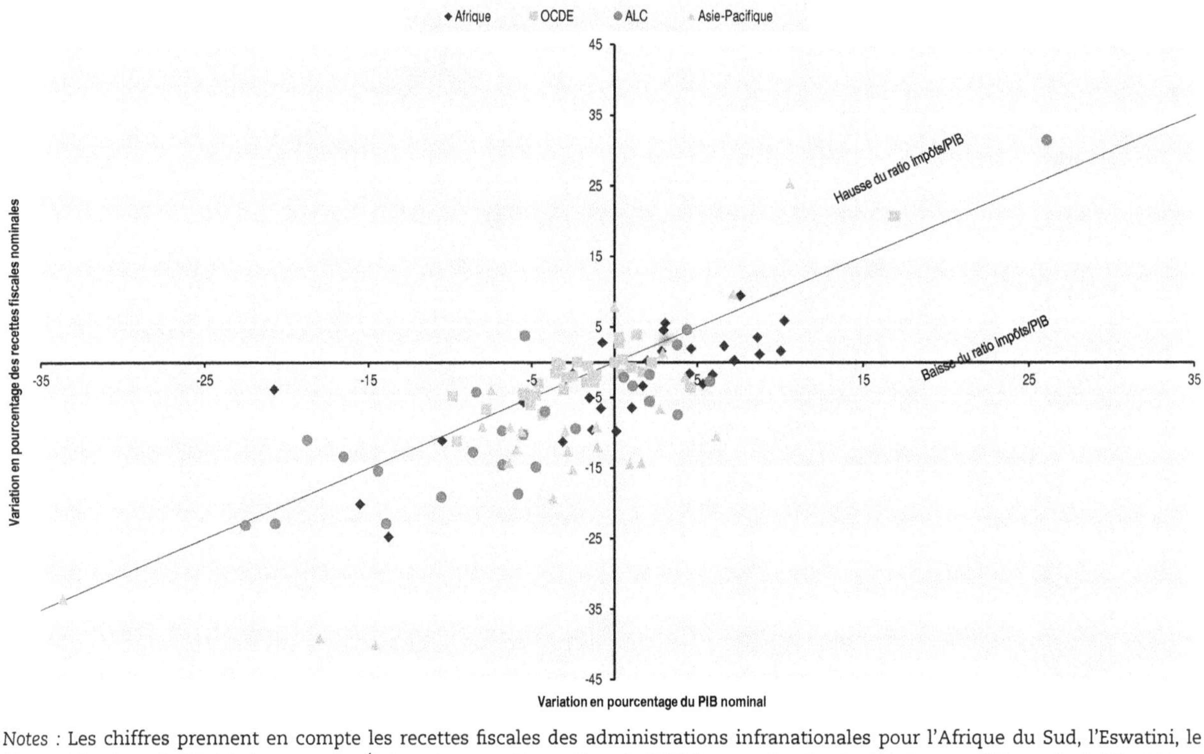

Notes : Les chiffres prennent en compte les recettes fiscales des administrations infranationales pour l'Afrique du Sud, l'Eswatini, le Maroc, Maurice et le Nigéria (recettes des États uniquement) pour l'année 2020. Les recettes fiscales totales pour l'Ouganda, la République du Congo, la Sierra Leone, le Tchad et le Togo n'incluent pas les cotisations de sécurité sociale car elles ne sont pas disponibles.
Source : Calculs des auteurs basés sur des données figurant dans (OCDE/ATAF/CUA, 2022[4]), « Statistiques des recettes publiques en Afrique : Tableaux comparatifs », *Statistiques fiscales de l'OCDE* (base de données), *https://doi.org/10.1787/7f54581d-fr*, (OCDE, 2022[1]), (OCDE et al., 2022[2]) et (OCDE, 2021[3]).

StatLink *https://stat.link/1zhrts*

La crise du COVID-19 a eu un impact sur les recettes fiscales et le PIB des pays du monde entier. Dans les pays d'Afrique, les répercussions de la pandémie ont été moins fortes que dans les pays de la région ALC et Asie-Pacifique, mais plus prononcées que dans les pays de l'OCDE en moyenne. Le ratio moyen impôts/PIB des pays d'Afrique (31) a baissé de 0.3 point entre 2019 et 2020, tandis que les moyennes des régions ALC et Asie-Pacifique (28) ont diminué de respectivement 0.8 point et 1.2 point, et la moyenne de l'OCDE a augmenté de 0.1 point au cours de la période. Un peu plus de la moitié des pays de l'OCDE avaient un ratio impôts/PIB plus élevé en 2020 qu'en 2019. En revanche, trois quarts des pays environ ont accusé une baisse de leurs recettes fiscales en pourcentage du PIB dans les autres régions entre 2019 et 2020.

Dans chaque région, la plupart des pays ont vu leurs recettes fiscales nominales reculer entre 2019 et 2020, la plus forte baisse concernant la région Asie-Pacifique. Les recettes fiscales nominales se sont contractées de 8.8 % en moyenne dans les pays de la région Asie-Pacifique, soit le même ordre de grandeur que celui observé dans la région ALC (8.0 %), mais beaucoup plus que la moyenne des pays d'Afrique (31) de 0.5 % et celle des pays de l'OCDE de 2.1 %. La région Asie-Pacifique (28) est la seule où certains pays (trois) ont subi une baisse de leurs recettes fiscales nominales supérieure à 30 % entre 2019 et 2020. Les différences de variation en pourcentage des recettes fiscales nominales entre ces régions peuvent s'expliquer en partie par le niveau d'inflation très hétérogène dans ces régions en 2020 : l'indice moyen des prix à la consommation en Afrique en 2020 était de 10.8 %, contre 3.2 % en Asie-Pacifique et 1.1 % en Europe (FMI, 2022[5]).

Entre 2019 et 2020, 11 pays d'Afrique sur les 31 couverts par cette publication ont enregistré à la fois une baisse de leur PIB nominal et de leurs recettes fiscales nominales, ce qui a été le cas pour la majorité des pays de l'OCDE et de la région ALC. Toutefois, seul un petit nombre de pays d'Afrique et de la région ALC ont vu leurs recettes fiscales nominales diminuer dans une proportion moindre que leur PIB nominal, aboutissant à une progression de leur ratio impôts/PIB en 2020. Dans la zone OCDE, en revanche, les recettes fiscales nominales ont moins baissé que le PIB dans 14 des 25 pays qui ont enregistré à la fois une diminution de leurs recettes fiscales nominales et de leur PIB nominal.

Encadré 1.1. **Méthodologie : le ratio impôts/PIB**

Les ratios impôts/PIB utilisés dans cette publication expriment les recettes fiscales totales en pourcentage du PIB. La valeur de ce ratio varie suivant son dénominateur (PIB) et son numérateur (recettes fiscales). Le numérateur et le dénominateur sont susceptibles de faire l'objet de révisions rétrospectives.

Le numérateur (recettes fiscales)

Cette publication utilise les chiffres des recettes qui sont transmis chaque année par les points de contact au sein des ministères des Finances, des administrations fiscales ou des offices statistiques nationaux. Les données rétrospectives sur les recettes fiscales font l'objet de révisions annuelles, des révisions plus importantes ayant lieu pour les années les plus récentes. Les chiffres antérieurs peuvent également changer d'une édition à l'autre lorsque de nouvelles données sont obtenues par des points de contact pour améliorer la publication.

Dans 23 pays africains couverts par ce rapport, l'année fiscale coïncide avec l'année civile. Les huit pays restants communiquent leurs données sur la base de l'année fiscale. Pour ces pays, les déclarations pour l'année 2020 couvrent un trimestre de 2021 (quatre pays ont une année fiscale allant d'avril à mars) ou deux trimestres de 2019 (cinq pays ont une année fiscale allant de juillet à juin)[2]. Cela signifie que les données relatives aux recettes pour 2020 concernant les pays qui communiquent leurs données sur la base de l'année fiscale comprennent des recettes se rapportant à des périodes qui ont été moins touchées par la pandémie de COVID-19.

Le dénominateur (PIB)

Les chiffres du PIB utilisés dans cette publication proviennent des *Perspectives de l'économie mondiale* publiées par le FMI. L'utilisation de ces chiffres du PIB garantit une

Encadré 1.1. **Méthodologie : le ratio impôts/PIB** *(suite)*

cohérence entre les pays, ainsi qu'une comparabilité internationale des ratios impôts/PIB. Les chiffres du PIB sont également révisés et actualisés pour tenir compte de l'amélioration des sources de données et des procédures d'estimation, ou pour appliquer de nouvelles lignes directrices convenues à l'échelle internationale pour mesurer la valeur du PIB.

Les chiffres les plus récents provenant des *Perspectives de l'économie mondiale* ont été publiés en avril 2022 (FMI, 2022[6]), et incluent les révisions du PIB effectuées par certains pays pour s'aligner sur l'édition la plus récente du Système de comptabilité nationale (SCN 2008). Dans cette édition, les chiffres relatifs au PIB ont été révisés par rapport à l'édition précédente, notamment pour l'Afrique du Sud, le Botswana, le Kenya, Madagascar, le Malawi, les Seychelles et la Tunisie (par exemple, le PIB de 2019 de ces pays a été révisé de 3 % ou plus). La différence entre les éditions 2021 et 2022 des ratios impôts/PIB de l'année 2019 s'échelonnait entre -2.1 points en Tunisie et aux Seychelles et 1.1 point au Botswana ; du fait de ces révisions, la moyenne pour 2019 des 30 pays d'Afrique couverts par l'édition de l'année dernière est inférieure de 0.2 point dans la présente édition.

Impact de la pandémie sur différentes catégories d'impôt

Entre 2019 et 2020, les impôts sur les biens et services ont baissé davantage que les impôts sur le revenu ou d'autres prélèvements, comme les cotisations de sécurité sociale et les impôts fonciers. En 2020, la plus forte baisse des recettes fiscales en pourcentage du PIB a concerné les taxes sur la valeur ajoutée (TVA), qui ont reculé de 0.3 point en moyenne. Les autres impôts sur les biens et services ont diminué de 0.1 point sur la période, pénalisés par le recul des recettes fiscales tirées des droits de douane (0.1 point). Les recettes de l'impôt sur le revenu des personnes physiques (IRPP), en pourcentage du PIB, sont restées identiques en moyenne, tandis que celles provenant de l'impôt sur les bénéfices des sociétés (IS) et des cotisations de sécurité sociale (CSS) ont augmenté de 0.1 point en moyenne entre 2019 et 2020.

Le Graphique 1.5 montre les variations des recettes fiscales par catégorie d'impôt en pourcentage du PIB en Afrique entre 2019 et 2020. En 2020, les recettes de la TVA ont reculé dans les trois quarts des pays d'Afrique (24) étudiés dans ce rapport. Elles ont progressé entre 2019 et 2020 dans les sept pays restants.

C'est en Namibie que la chute des recettes de TVA en pourcentage du PIB a été la plus marquée entre 2019 et 2020, soit 1.7 point. La Namibie est un des pays d'Afrique couverts par cette publication qui ont subi la plus forte baisse de leurs recettes fiscales nominales entre 2019 et 2020, soit 9.6 %. En avril 2020, la Namibie a annoncé le lancement d'un programme de relance et de soutien à l'économie visant à atténuer les conséquences du COVID-19, prévoyant le remboursement accéléré aux entreprises des trop-versés de TVA non litigieux (EY, 2020[7]). Cette mesure a contribué à réduire la collecte des recettes de TVA dans le pays en 2020 par rapport à 2019.

Les recettes des droits de douane dans les pays d'Afrique ont été pénalisées par le COVID-19 en 2020, mais moins que la TVA. Dans près des deux tiers des pays d'Afrique (19), les recettes tirées des droits de douane ont accusé un recul.

Les variations des recettes de l'IS en pourcentage du PIB entre 2019 et 2020 sont très hétérogènes entre pays d'Afrique. Elles s'échelonnaient entre une baisse de 1.4 point en Guinée équatoriale et une hausse de 5.2 points au Tchad. Entre 2019 et 2020, la moyenne pour les recettes de l'IS des 31 pays d'Afrique en pourcentage du PIB a progressé de 0.1 point (hors Tchad, cette moyenne a reculé de 0.1 point au cours de la période). La part des recettes de l'IS en pourcentage du PIB a décliné dans un tiers des pays d'Afrique (12) couverts par cette publication, et 6 pays ont subi une baisse supérieure à 0.3 point.

Graphique 1.5. **Variations des recettes fiscales par catégorie d'impôt en pourcentage du PIB, 2019-20**

Points de pourcentage de PIB

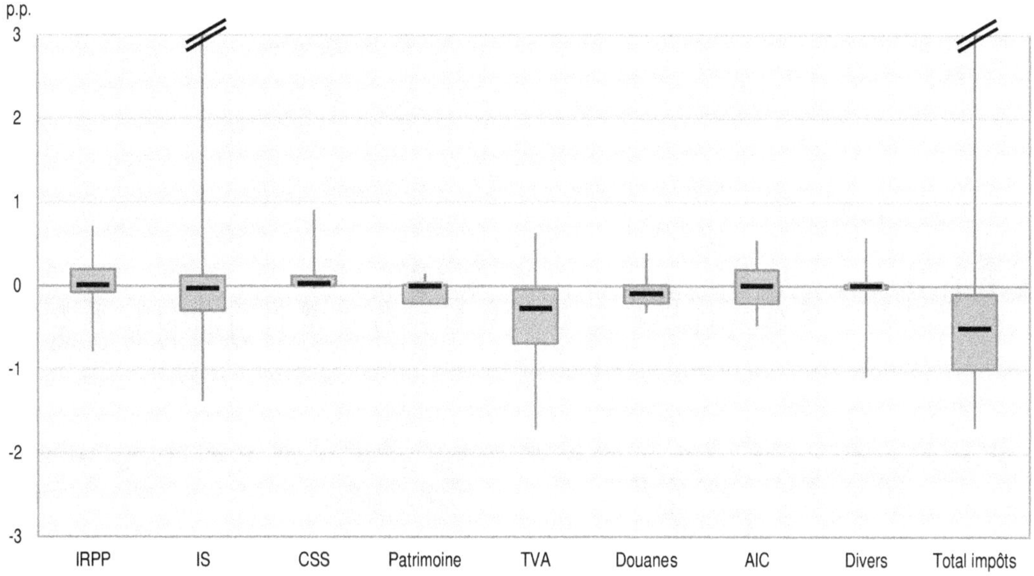

Notes : Il convient d'interpréter l'évolution de la moyenne des pays d'Afrique (31) avec précaution, car des données relatives aux cotisations de sécurité sociale sont indisponibles ou incomplètes pour quelques pays. Veuillez vous reporter aux notes des tableaux par pays au chapitre 5 pour plus d'informations.

AIC signifie « Autres impôts sur la consommation » et englobe tous les impôts sur les biens et services (rubrique 5000) hors TVA (rubrique 5111) et droits de douane (rubrique 5123). DIvers comprend les impôts non ventilables entre l'IRPP et l'IS (rubrique 1300), les impôts sur le main-d' œuvre (rubrique 3000) et d'autres impôts (rubrique 6000).

Dans ce graphique, le point le plus bas correspond à la variation minimale survenue dans le pays pour ce type d'impôt entre 2019 et 2020 ; la case représente les variations pour les pays qui se situent entre le quartile inférieur et le quartile supérieur (50 % des pays d'Afrique couverts par cette publication ont connu des variations comprises dans l'intervalle matérialisé par chaque case) ; et le point le plus haut pour chaque type d'impôt correspond à la variation maximale survenue dans le pays. La ligne dans chaque case représente la variation médiane (la moitié des pays d'Afrique couverts par cette publication se situaient au-dessus et l'autre moitié en dessous de cette ligne). Dans ce graphique, les recettes de l'IS et les recettes fiscales totales sont coupées à des fins de visibilité, et ne tiennent pas compte des variations survenues au Tchad entre 2019 et 2020 en pourcentage du PIB (les recettes de l'IS et les recettes fiscales totales au Tchad ont augmenté respectivement de 5.2 points et de 6.6 points sur la période).

Source : Calculs des auteurs basés sur des données figurant dans (OCDE/ATAF/CUA, 2022[4]), « Statistiques des recettes publiques en Afrique : Tableaux comparatifs », *Statistiques fiscales de l'OCDE* (base de données), *https://doi.org/10.1787/7f54581d-fr*.

StatLink *https://stat.link/dy4tmk*

Principales variations des ratios impôts/PIB dans les pays d'Afrique en 2020

Le Graphique 1.6 présente les variations des ratios impôts/PIB entre 2019 et 2020 par principale rubrique d'impôt dans les 31 pays et en moyenne. C'est le ratio impôts/PIB de la Namibie qui a le plus baissé, soit 1.7 point, à cause du recul des recettes de TVA, comme l'explique la section précédente. Le Botswana, la Guinée équatoriale et le Lesotho ont enregistré les plus fortes diminutions, comprises entre 1.2 point et 1.4 point. Ces diminutions étaient imputables à des baisses significatives des recettes des impôts sur le revenu (respectivement 1.1, 1.3 et 0.8 point). La baisse au Lesotho résulte principalement du repli des recettes de l'IRPP (1.4 point) et, en Guinée équatoriale, des recettes de l'IS (1.4 point). Le Lesotho a également connu une baisse sensible des recettes de la TVA (0.8 point).

Graphique 1.6. **Variations des ratios impôts/PIB (en points de pourcentage) observées entre 2019 et 2020 par principales rubriques d'impôt et par pays**

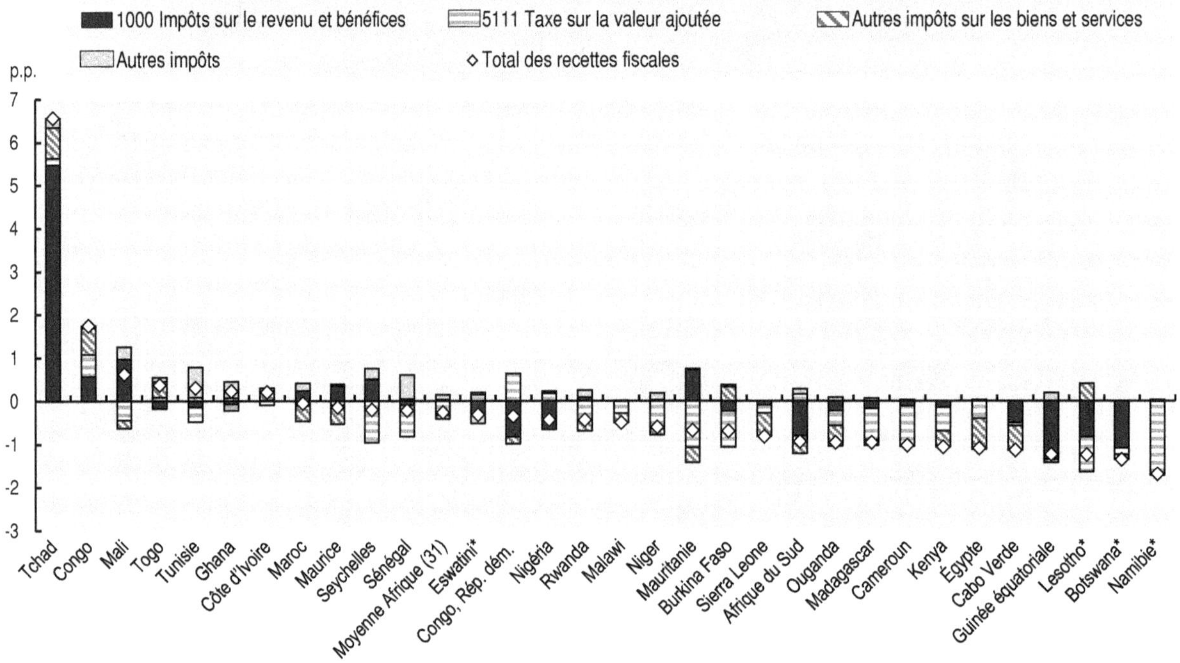

La moyenne Afrique (31) doit être interprétée avec précaution car des données relatives aux cotisations de sécurité sociale sont indisponibles ou incomplètes pour quelques pays. Veuillez vous reporter aux notes des tableaux par pays au chapitre 5 pour plus d'informations.

*Au Botswana, en Eswatini, au Lesotho et en Namibie, l'année fiscale court du mois d'avril au mois de mars. Pour plus de précisions, se reporter aux notes des tableaux par pays présentés dans le chapitre 5.

Source : Calculs des auteurs basés sur des données figurant dans (OCDE/ATAF/CUA, 2022[4]), « Statistiques des recettes publiques en Afrique : Tableaux comparatifs », *Statistiques fiscales de l'OCDE* (base de données), *https://doi.org/10.1787/7f54581d-fr*.

StatLink https://stat.link/by57xi

L'augmentation de 6.6 points du ratio impôts/PIB du Tchad entre 2019 et 2020 était portée par la progression des recettes de l'IS provenant des compagnies pétrolières (5.2 points). Malgré la baisse simultanée du volume de production au Tchad et la chute des cours du pétrole brut en 2020, l'augmentation des recettes de l'IS provenant du secteur pétrolier en 2020 s'explique principalement par les recettes de l'IS sur les bénéfices pétroliers accumulés au cours des années précédentes (Ministère des Finances et du Budget du Tchad, 2021[8]). Globalement, la progression des recettes de l'IS a contribué à la hausse de 74 % des recettes fiscales nominales entre 2019 et 2020. Le PIB nominal du Tchad a reculé de 4 % sur la période, ce qui a amplifié la hausse des recettes fiscales en pourcentage du PIB entre 2019 et 2020 (voir Encadré 1.1).

En République du Congo, le ratio impôt/PIB a augmenté de 1.7 point entre 2019 et 2020. Bien que les recettes fiscales nominales aient baissé de 4 %, ce recul a été moindre que la diminution du PIB nominal (21 %), entraînant une progression du ratio impôts/PIB. Les recettes provenant de toutes les principales catégories d'impôts ont reculé entre 2019 et 2020, et la baisse des impôts sur les biens et services représente 63 % de la baisse totale des recettes fiscales nominales.

Impact de la pandémie sur différents types d'impôt entre régions

Le COVID-19 a eu des effets très hétérogènes sur les différents types d'impôt d'une région à l'autre. Le recul des recettes tirées des impôts sur les biens et services est la principale cause de la baisse des ratios moyens impôts/PIB en Afrique, dans la région ALC et dans la région Asie-Pacifique entre 2019 et 2020. À l'inverse, dans les pays de l'OCDE en moyenne, les recettes fiscales ont augmenté en pourcentage du PIB sur la période, tirées par la hausse des recettes des impôts sur le travail (IRPP et CSS).

Il est important d'observer que la plupart des recettes fiscales dans les pays de l'OCDE sont comptabilisées selon la méthode des droits constatés (au moment où la charge fiscale est déterminée, et non au moment du paiement), tandis que les recettes fiscales dans les pays des autres régions sont principalement comptabilisées sur la base des encaissements. Dans certains pays de l'OCDE, les recettes fiscales peuvent inclure des dettes - notamment pour la TVA - qui ne seront pas acquittées par les entreprises aux autorités fiscales à court terme, voire qui ne le seront jamais, en raison des mesures fiscales parfois adoptées en réponse à la crise du COVID-19, comme les reports de paiements de TVA ou les effacements de TVA due sur les factures impayées. Cela signifie que, dans certains pays de l'OCDE, les recettes fiscales peuvent être surestimées en 2020, en particulier pour la TVA. D'un autre côté, la comptabilisation sur la base des encaissements dans les autres régions peut avoir pour effet que les variations survenues pendant la crise sont plus prononcées du fait des reports de paiement des impôts dus dans le cadre de la réponse des pays à la pandémie de COVID-19.

Tableau 1.1. **Variations des recettes fiscales par principales catégories d'impôt en Afrique, dans la région ALC, en Asie-Pacifique et dans l'OCDE, 2019-20**

	Point de pourcentage				% de variation			
	Afrique (31)	ALC	Asie-Pacifique (28)	OCDE	Afrique (31)	ALC	Asie-Pacifique (28)	OCDE
IRPP	0.0	0.0	0.0	0.3	3.7	-3.0	-2.2	1.4
IS	0.1	-0.2	-0.1	-0.4	5.0	-5.6	-5.3	-12.1
CSS	0.1	0.1	0.0	0.3	8.9	-0.7	1.1	2.0
Patrimoine	0.0	-0.1	0.0	0.1	20.3	-14.2	3.4	0.0
TVA	-0.3	-0.2	-0.6	0.0	-4.1	-8.1	-11.9	-2.6
Douane	-0.1	-0.1	0.0	0.0	-1.5	-14.7	-5.8	-7.1
AIC	0.0	-0.4	-0.4	-0.2	1.7	-12.5	-12.4	1.9
Divers	-0.1	0.0	-0.1	0.0	0.9	-12.1	-27.0	14.4
Total	**-0.3**	**-0.8**	**-1.2**	**0.1**	**-0.5**	**-8.0**	**-8.8**	**-2.1**

Notes : Les données pour 2020 pour l'OCDE sont préliminaires et doivent être interprétées avec précaution.
AIC signifie « Autres impôts sur la consommation » et englobe tous les impôts sur les biens et services (rubrique 5000) hors TVA (rubrique 5111) et droits de douane (rubrique 5123). Divers comprend les impôts non ventilables entre l'IRPP et l'IS (rubrique 1300), les impôts sur la masse salariale (rubrique 3000) et d'autres impôts (rubrique 6000).
Source : Calculs des auteurs basés sur des données figurant dans (OCDE/ATAF/CUA, 2022[4]), « Statistiques des recettes publiques en Afrique : Tableaux comparatifs », *Statistiques fiscales de l'OCDE* (base de données), *https://doi.org/10.1787/7f54581d-fr*, (OCDE, 2022[1]), (OCDE et al., 2022[2]) et (OCDE, 2021[3]).

En valeur nominale, l'impact négatif du COVID-19 était manifeste pour toutes les catégories d'impôt dans les régions ALC et Asie-Pacifique (sauf pour les CSS et les impôts fonciers dans la région Asie-Pacifique, qui ont légèrement progressé en valeur nominale entre 2019 et 2020). À l'inverse, les moyennes des 31 pays d'Afrique et de l'OCDE n'ont pas baissé en 2020 pour cinq des huit catégories d'impôt présentées dans le tableau 1.1, et notamment les recettes des impôts sur le travail.

En pourcentage du PIB, les recettes issues des impôts sur les biens et services ont été moins touchées par la pandémie de COVID-19 en Afrique que dans les régions ALC et Asie-Pacifique : elles ont baissé de 0.4 % du PIB en moyenne entre 2019 et 2020, contre respectivement 0.7 % et 1.0 % du PIB au cours de la même période dans les régions ALC et Asie-Pacifique. Les recettes de TVA, exprimées en pourcentage du PIB, ont reculé dans les trois régions, la plus forte baisse ayant été enregistrée en Asie-Pacifique (0.6 point), suivie de l'Afrique (0.3 point) et de la région ALC (0.2 point). Par comparaison, les recettes de TVA en pourcentage du PIB sont restées inchangées sur la période dans l'OCDE en moyenne. Exprimées en pourcentage du PIB, la moyenne des recettes des 31 pays d'Afrique provenant d'autres impôts sur la consommation, y compris les impôts généraux hors TVA, les droits de douane et les droits à l'exportation, est restée inchangée entre 2019 et 2020, contrairement à une baisse de 0.2 point dans la zone OCDE et de 0.4 point à la fois dans les régions ALC et Asie-Pacifique, en moyenne (Tableau 1.1).

L'Afrique est la seule région qui a vu ses recettes de l'IS progresser en pourcentage du PIB entre 2019 et 2020 (entièrement sous l'effet de la forte augmentation des recettes de l'IS au Tchad au cours de cette période). C'est dans les pays de l'OCDE que les recettes de l'IS en pourcentage du PIB ont le plus baissé en moyenne, soit 0.4 point, tandis que le recul a été plus limité dans les régions ALC et Asie-Pacifique (respectivement 0.2 et 0.1 point).

Dans toutes les régions et en pourcentage du PIB, les recettes moyennes de l'IRPP et des CSS n'ont pas diminué entre 2019 et 2020. Elles sont restées relativement stables en pourcentage du PIB dans toutes les régions, sauf dans la zone OCDE. En 2020, les moyennes OCDE des recettes de l'IRPP et des CSS se sont accrues de 0.3 point, soit la plus forte hausse de recettes en pourcentage du PIB observée, toutes catégories d'impôt confondues.

Impact de la pandémie sur les groupes régionaux en Afrique

La plupart des pays couverts par cette publication appartiennent à des organisations régionales dont les membres adoptent des règles communes en matière fiscale et douanière et forment une union douanière. Le ratio moyen impôts/PIB des trois pays de la Communauté d'Afrique de l'Est (CAE)[3] et des six pays de l'Union économique et monétaire ouest-africaine (UEMOA)[4] inclus dans cette publication s'établissait à respectivement 14.4 % et 15.2 % en 2020, soit moins que la moyenne des 31 pays d'Afrique. Le ratio moyen impôts/PIB des pays membres de l'Union douanière de l'Afrique australe (SACU) atteignait 18.8 % en 2020 (voir encadré 2.2 au chapitre 2).

Ces trois sous-régions ont toutes été pénalisées par la pandémie de COVID-19, mais l'ampleur des baisses des ratios impôts/PIB entre 2019 et 2020 varie beaucoup d'une région à l'autre. En moyenne, les pays de la SACU ont connu la plus forte baisse des recettes fiscales en pourcentage du PIB, soit 1.1 point, suivis des trois pays de la CAE (0.8 point). À l'inverse, les six pays de l'UEMOA ont subi une baisse plus modérée de leurs recettes fiscales moyennes en pourcentage du PIB, soit 0.1 point, pendant la période (Graphique 1.7).

La pandémie de COVID-19 a affecté les recettes tirées des impôts sur les biens et services, et notamment de la TVA, pour l'ensemble de ces groupes. En moyenne, les baisses de recettes issues des impôts sur les biens et services s'établissaient à 0.3 point pour les six pays de l'UEMOA, 0.5 point pour les pays de la SACU et 0.8 point pour les trois pays de la CAE. Entre 2019 et 2020, les baisses moyennes des recettes de TVA en pourcentage du PIB s'échelonnaient entre 0.4 point pour les six pays de l'UEMOA et 0.5 point pour les pays de la SACU. Le COVID-19 a davantage pesé sur les recettes de l'impôt sur le revenu dans les pays de la SACU[5], avec un recul de 0.6 point en moyenne, tandis que les recettes tirées des impôts sur les biens et services ont été les plus touchées dans les deux autres sous-régions. Les recettes de l'impôt sur le revenu sont restées relativement stables au cours de la période dans les pays de l'UEMOA et de la CAE, en moyenne.

Graphique 1.7. **Variation des ratios impôts/PIB par principale rubrique d'impôt et par groupe infrarégional, 2019-20**

Points de pourcentage

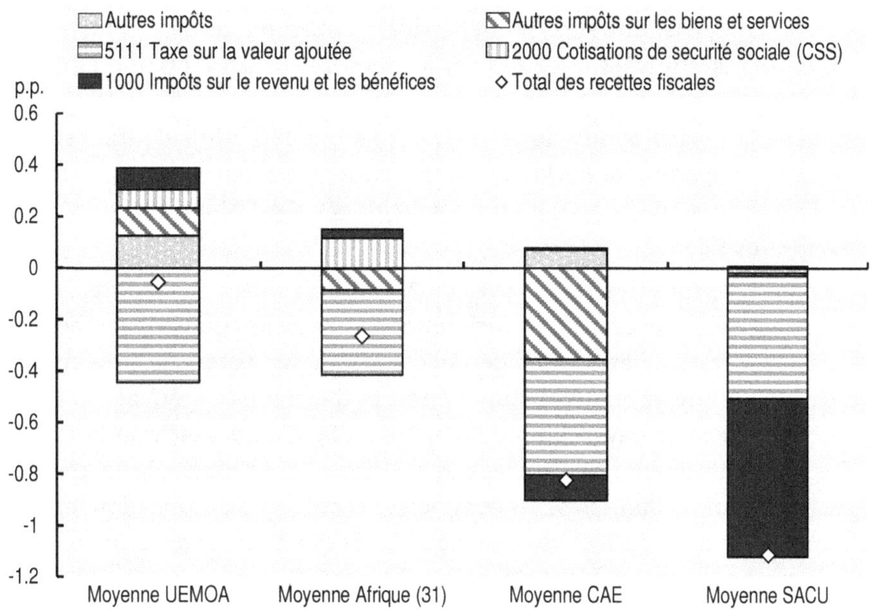

Source : Calculs des auteurs basés sur des données figurant dans (OCDE/ATAF/CUA, 2022[4]), « Statistiques des recettes publiques en Afrique : Tableaux comparatifs », *Statistiques fiscales de l'OCDE* (base de données), *https://doi.org/10.1787/7f54581d-fr*.

StatLink *https://stat.link/gz7mjr*

Mesures d'aide déployées en Afrique

Les pays d'Afrique ont adopté une série de mesures fiscales visant à atténuer les conséquences négatives de la pandémie de COVID-19 sur les entreprises et les ménages. Les confinements et autres restrictions ont eu un impact direct sur les bénéfices des entreprises, les dépenses des ménages et la participation au marché du travail en Afrique, entraînant une contraction de l'activité économique en 2020. Les mesures fiscales prises en réaction au COVID-19 ont aggravé la chute des recettes publiques en Afrique comme dans les autres régions du monde en 2020. Cette section donne des exemples de mesures fiscales qui ont été appliquées dans les pays d'Afrique couverts par la présente publication en réponse à la crise du COVID-19. Sans vouloir être exhaustive, cette analyse illustre les divers instruments fiscaux employés par les pays d'Afrique pour atténuer l'impact de la crise[6].

De nombreuses mesures fiscales adoptées par les pays d'Afrique concernaient l'IS et la TVA et visaient à aider les entreprises à faire face à leurs problèmes de liquidité et de trésorerie. Elles comprenaient des reports du paiement de l'impôt, l'allongement des délais de dépôt des déclarations et l'établissement d'échéanciers de paiement souples ; l'Égypte, le Cabo Verde, l'Eswatini, le Lesotho, Maurice et le Rwanda ont adopté de telles mesures (voir Encadré 1.2).

Par exemple, les paiements de l'IS au Rwanda ont été reportés pour toutes les entreprises, avec un allongement des délais pour les PME. Les délais de paiement des échéances de l'IS ont été allongés au Cabo Verde pour toutes les entreprises. En Afrique du Sud, les grandes entreprises endettées ont été autorisées à reporter le paiement des impôts sans pénalité, en s'adressant directement au South African Revenue Service (SARS). Dans certains pays, les mesures ont concerné des secteurs spécifiques, tels que le tourisme (Maurice, Seychelles).

Cela a également été le cas en Égypte, qui a autorisé les entreprises de secteurs affectés à payer leur IS pour 2019 sur une période de trois mois se terminant en juin 2020, plutôt que d'acquitter le montant total en avril.

Dans certains pays, les entreprises ont bénéficié d'exemptions du paiement de l'impôt. Au Mali, les entreprises privées affectées par les mesures de prévention du COVID-19 ont bénéficié d'exemptions au cas par cas et secteur par secteur. En outre, le Mali a suspendu temporairement la « taxe synthétique » (une taxe sur le chiffre d'affaires) et la taxe foncière sur les entreprises. Au Burkina Faso, les entreprises des secteurs du transport de voyageurs, des services hôteliers et du tourisme ont bénéficié d'une réduction de 25 % de leurs redevances de licence.

Pour leur part, les mesures en lien avec la TVA comprenaient des reports de paiement, l'allongement des délais de dépôt des déclarations et l'accélération des remboursements, ainsi que des exonérations et baisses de taux. Au Mali, un report de trois mois pour le paiement de la TVA afférente aux factures d'eau et d'électricité a été accordé à tous les consommateurs. Plusieurs pays, comme l'Afrique du Sud, Madagascar et la Namibie, ont accéléré les remboursements de TVA afin d'améliorer la situation de la trésorerie des entreprises. En Afrique du Sud, les petits commerçants ont reçu l'autorisation temporaire de déposer leurs déclarations de TVA chaque mois plutôt que tous les deux mois, permettant d'accélérer le remboursement de la TVA sur les intrants.

Des exonérations et réductions de la TVA/TPS ont été pratiquées, axées sur les secteurs de la médecine, de l'hôtellerie, de la culture et des sports, ou d'application plus générale. Le Burkina Faso, Maurice et le Rwanda ont appliqué des exemptions de TVA au secteur médical (sur la vente d'équipements utilisés pour lutter contre le COVID-19 au Burkina Faso, sur les masques fabriqués dans le pays au Rwanda et sur les biens et la recherche médicale à Maurice). Le Burkina Faso et le Cabo Verde ont ramené les taux de TVA de 15 % à 10 % dans les secteurs de l'hôtellerie et de la restauration.

Les pays d'Afrique ont mis en place un ensemble de politiques fiscales liées à l'IRPP et aux CSS afin d'aider les ménages pendant la pandémie. Ces mesures s'apparentaient à celles appliquées aux entreprises, comme le report partiel des paiements (Afrique du Sud, Seychelles), l'allongement des délais de dépôt des déclarations (Eswatini, Lesotho) et les exonérations d'impôts (Afrique du Sud, Rwanda). Ces mesures ont eu pour effet de réduire le montant des recettes fiscales perçues par les États ou d'en retarder le recouvrement, mais deux pays (Égypte et Maurice) ont relevé leurs taux de l'IRPP pour financer les mesures d'aide face au COVID-19. L'Égypte a mis en place un prélèvement de 1 % au titre de l'impôt sur le revenu sur tous les salaires des secteurs public et privé (à l'exception des titulaires d'un salaire inférieur à 2 000 EGP) pour une période de 12 mois. À Maurice, les personnes physiques percevant un revenu imposable supérieur à un certain seuil ont dû acquitter une taxe de solidarité au taux de 25 %.

Un certain nombre de pays africains ont renoncé aux amendes, pénalités et paiements d'intérêts pour les ménages ou les entreprises (ou les deux) pendant la pandémie de COVID-19 de 2020. C'est le cas au Burkina Faso, en Égypte, au Lesotho, à Maurice et au Rwanda.

Encadré 1.2. **Mesures fiscales adoptées en Eswatini et au Lesotho pour faire face à la crise du COVID-19**

Cet encadré illustre par un exemple les principales modifications que l'Eswatini et le Lesotho ont apportées à leurs politiques fiscales afin d'aider les entreprises et les particuliers à surmonter la crise du COVID-19 en 2020.

Eswatini

Le délai de dépôt des déclarations a été prolongé de trois mois sans pénalité pour l'IRPP et l'IS. D'autres mesures visaient principalement les entreprises, surtout celles déficitaires ou connaissant des difficultés de trésorerie. Les entreprises qui anticipaient des pertes ont bénéficié du report de trois mois du paiement des acomptes provisionnels de l'impôt. Ces entreprises étaient tenues de déposer des déclarations provisoires en juin et septembre 2020, l'impôt étant dû en décembre 2020 et mars 2021. Certaines entreprises en difficulté ont pu bénéficier de facilités de paiement à condition de fournir la preuve de leurs problème de trésorerie. Les pénalités et intérêts afférents à des dettes plus anciennes ont été annulés uniquement en cas de paiement du principal entre avril et septembre 2020. Aussi, les entreprises ont donné la priorité aux créances donnant lieu aux paiements d'intérêts et aux pénalités les plus élevés, et les radiations de créances de TVA ont été plus nombreuses que celles de créances d'impôt sur le revenu.

Pour aider les PME, le gouvernement d'Eswatini a mis en place un fonds de soutien de 90 millions SLZ pour les entreprises éligibles. Les PME réalisant un chiffre d'affaires n'excédant pas 8 millions SLZ ont reçu un remboursement de l'impôt sur les bénéfices des sociétés payé pendant l'exercice 2019. Le gouvernement a exonéré d'impôts (TVA et droits de douane) tous les équipements liés au COVID-19 (masques, désinfectants, équipements de protection individuelle et tout autre article médical).

Lesotho

Le Lesotho a adopté un certain nombre de mesures d'allégement à caractère fiscal et administratif à l'intention des entreprises éligibles. Les mesures fiscales reposaient largement sur des reports de paiement de six à huit mois pour certains impôts (IRPP, IS, système simplifié d'imposition des sociétés, retenues à la source et TVA).

S'agissant de l'IS, les grandes entreprises ont bénéficié du report partiel de leurs premier et deuxième acomptes trimestriels, tandis que les PME ont pu reporter intégralement le paiement de leur premier acompte trimestriel. Toutes les entreprises devaient payer les montants d'impôt différés depuis fin octobre 2020, par échelonnement en six mensualités égales jusqu'à fin mars 2021. Les entreprises assujetties au système simplifié d'imposition des sociétés (SBT) dans les secteurs non essentiels ont été exonérées pendant le confinement, tandis que les entreprises essentielles (vente au détail, par exemple) qui sont restées en activité pendant le confinement étaient redevables du SBT selon les échéances normales. De même, les paiements au titre des retenues à la source et de la TVA ont été reportés pour les entreprises non essentielles mais pas pour les entreprises essentielles.

Les biens importés pour faire face à la crise du COVID-19 étaient exonérés de la TVA et des droits à l'importation. Les impôts supplémentaires, pénalités et frais de stockage dus induits par les effets inévitables du confinement ont été annulés.

Les mesures de nature administrative comprenaient le dédouanement rapide de tous les biens essentiels importés et des biens importés destinés à lutter contre le COVID-19. Le Revenue Services Lesotho a accéléré le traitement des demandes de remboursements pour permettre aux entreprises de percevoir rapidement des liquidités, en reportant les vérifications à une date ultérieure.

Source : Informations communiquées par les points de contact au sein de l'Eswatini Revenue Authority et du Revenue Services Lesotho.

Évolution des ratios impôts/PIB depuis 2010

La pandémie de COVID-19 a stoppé la croissance régulière des recettes fiscales en Afrique depuis 2010. En 2020, le ratio impôts/PIB moyen dans pays d'Afrique (31) était supérieur de 1.6 point à son niveau de 2010. Par comparaison, les moyennes de la région ALC et de l'OCDE ont augmenté de respectivement 1.0 et 1.9 point entre 2010 et 2020.

Le ratio moyen impôts/PIB des 31 pays africains avait enregistré une hausse de 0.7 point en 2011, dans un contexte de reprise après la crise financière mondiale. Entre 2012 et 2019, la moyenne Afrique (31) a régulièrement augmenté, passant de 15.0 % du PIB en 2012 à 16.2 % en 2019. La pandémie de COVID-19 a provoqué la première baisse du ratio moyen impôts/PIB des pays d'Afrique (31) depuis 2010 (Graphique 1.8).

Graphique 1.8. **Ratios moyens impôts/PIB pour l'Afrique (31), l'ALC et l'OCDE, 2000-20**

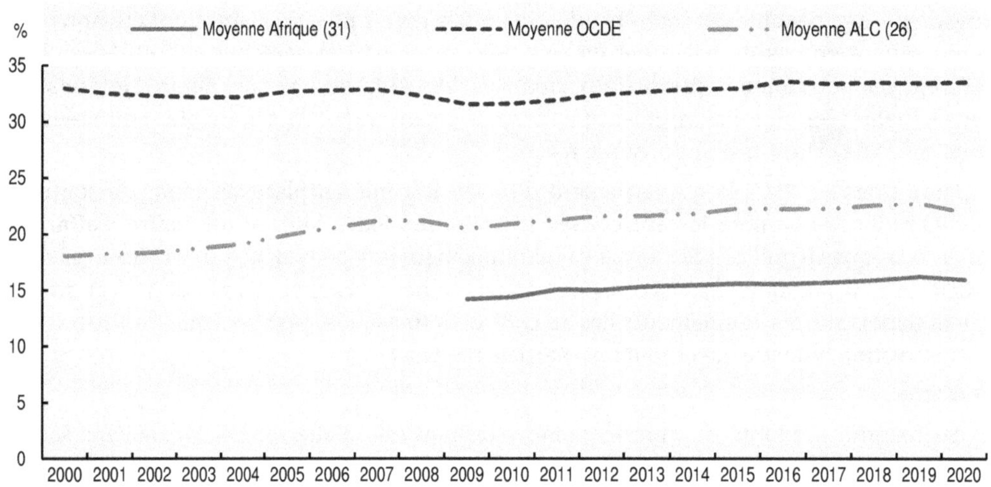

Note : Il convient d'interpréter la moyenne Afrique (31) avec prudence, car les données relatives aux cotisations de sécurité sociale ne sont pas disponibles ou ne sont que partielles pour quelques pays. Pour plus de précisions, se reporter aux tableaux par pays présentés dans le chapitre 5.
Les chiffres prennent en compte les recettes fiscales des administrations infranationales pour l'Afrique du Sud, l'Eswatini, le Maroc, Maurice, la Mauritanie (jusqu'en 2018) et le Nigéria (recettes des États uniquement) pour la période 2002-2020.
La moyenne Afrique (31) est une estimation pour 2009, car les données ne sont pas disponibles pour le Nigéria et le Tchad. On ne dispose pas d'estimation antérieure à 2009 faute de données relatives à quelques pays.
La moyenne Afrique (31) et les moyennes ALC (26 pays) et OCDE (38 pays) sont des moyennes non pondérées. La moyenne pour les pays d'Asie-Pacifique (28) n'est pas disponible pour les années antérieures à 2018.
Source : Tableau 4.1 figurant au chapitre 4 et (OCDE/ATAF/CUA, 2022[4]), « Statistiques des recettes publiques en Afrique : Tableaux comparatifs », *Statistiques fiscales de l'OCDE* (base de données), *https://doi.org/10.1787/7f54581d-fr*.
StatLink *https://stat.link/ts5lga*

C'est l'IRPP qui explique pour l'essentiel l'augmentation du ratio moyen impôts/PIB observé en Afrique (31) entre 2010 et 2020, passant de 2.3 % du PIB en 2010 à 3.1 % en 2020, sous l'effet de la progression des revenus et d'une imposition plus efficace des particuliers fortunés dans les pays d'Afrique subsaharienne (Moore, Prichard et Fjeldstad, 2018[9]). Les recettes tirées de l'IS n'ont pas contribué à cette hausse au cours de cette période, puisqu'elles ont régulièrement diminué en pourcentage du PIB dans les pays étudiés principalement entre 2012 et 2016. La baisse des cours du pétrole et des minéraux entre 2013 et 2016, et la diminution des taux de l'IS sur l'ensemble du continent expliquent la baisse des recettes de l'IS, de sorte que la part des recettes de l'impôt sur le revenu imputable à l'IRPP a augmenté en Afrique au cours de la dernière décennie. En 2020, les recettes tirées de l'IRPP représentaient 51 % du total des recettes de l'impôt sur le revenu, contre 42 % en 2010.

Les recettes de TVA ont représenté le deuxième principal moteur de l'augmentation du ratio impôts/PIB des pays d'Afrique, en hausse de 0.7 point à 4.5 % du PIB en 2020. La plus forte hausse annuelle des recettes moyennes de TVA en pourcentage du PIB s'est produite entre 2012 et 2013 (0.3 % du PIB) à la suite de l'introduction de la TVA en 2012 en République démocratique du Congo et en Eswatini. La légère augmentation du taux normal moyen de TVA enregistrée dans la région au cours de cette décennie (de 15.9 % en 2010 à 16.2 % en 2020) pourrait aussi expliquer la hausse des recettes de TVA en pourcentage du PIB sur la même période.

Les recettes moyennes provenant d'autres taxes sur les biens et services, soit l'équivalent de 3.5 % du PIB en 2020, ont légèrement diminué en pourcentage du PIB depuis 2010, en partie en raison de la baisse des recettes provenant des taxes sur les échanges. Ce déclin est associé à la libéralisation des échanges à l'échelle du continent, qui s'est traduite par l'abaissement des droits à l'importation, le rétrécissement de l'assiette des produits et services soumis à des droits d'accise, et l'élimination des taxes sur les exportations. Les droits de douane seront de nouveau réduits dans le cadre de la mise en place de la Zone de libre-échange continentale africaine (ZLECAf) (OCDE/CUA/ATAF, 2020[10]).

Les facteurs influant sur l'évolution des recettes fiscales dans la région ALC au cours de la même période sont similaires à ceux observés en Afrique. De même que pour la moyenne Afrique (31), les recettes tirées de l'IRPP et de la TVA ont fortement contribué à l'augmentation du ratio moyen impôts/PIB de la région ALC (en hausse de 0.5 point entre 2010 et 2020). La hausse des recettes provenant des cotisations de sécurité sociale (en hausse de 0.7 point) a également favorisé l'augmentation globale du ratio moyen impôts/PIB de la région ALC. Les niveaux de CSS en pourcentage du PIB diffèrent nettement entre les deux régions : en 2020, les recettes provenant des CSS s'établissaient à 4.0 % du PIB dans la région ALC, contre 1.5 % en moyenne pour les pays d'Afrique (31) (Graphique 1.9).

Graphique 1.9. **Recettes tirées des impôts sur le revenu et les bénéfices, de la TVA et d'autres catégories d'impôts, en pourcentage du PIB, 2010-20**

Percentage of GDP

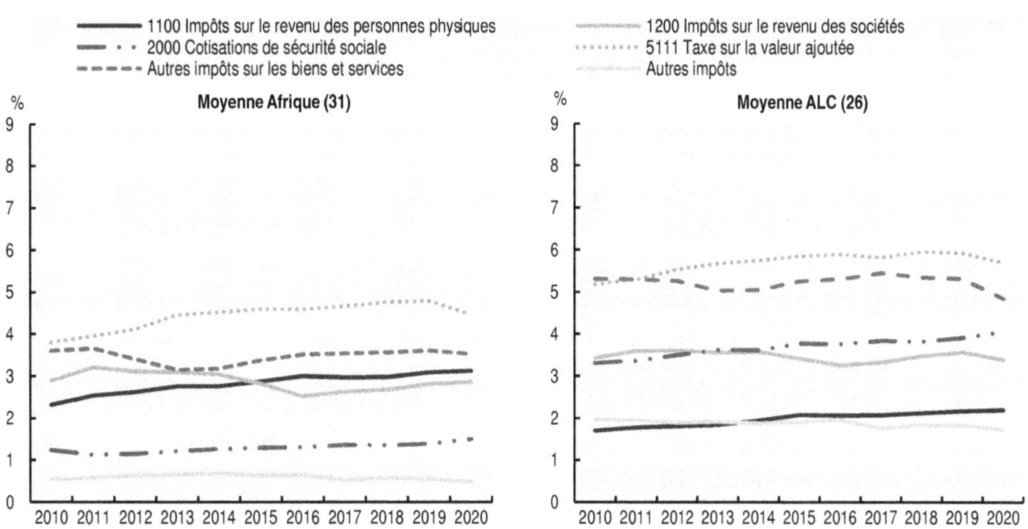

Note : Les chiffres relatifs aux pays d'Afrique (31) prennent en compte les recettes fiscales des administrations infranationales pour l'Afrique du Sud, l'Eswatini, le Maroc, Maurice, la Mauritanie (jusqu'en 2018) et le Nigéria (recettes des États uniquement) pour la période 2002-2019.

Source : Calculs des auteurs basés sur (OCDE/ATAF/CUA, 2022[4]), « Statistiques des recettes publiques en Afrique : Tableaux comparatifs », *Statistiques fiscales de l'OCDE* (base de données), *https://doi.org/10.1787/7f54581d-fr*.

StatLink *https://stat.link/q8rua9*

Les ratios impôts/PIB ont augmenté dans 25 pays entre 2010 et 2020, et ils ont diminué dans six. Le Rwanda et la Tunisie ont enregistré les plus fortes hausses au cours de la période (respectivement 4.5 points et 6.6 points), alors que c'est au Botswana que la baisse a été la plus prononcée (3.5 points) (Graphique 1.10).

La première année de la pandémie de COVID-19 a stoppé une décennie de gains en matière de mobilisation des recettes fiscales pour plusieurs pays, notamment le Kenya et la Namibie. Entre 2010 et 2019, le Kenya et la Namibie ont enregistré une hausse de leurs recettes fiscales équivalente respectivement à 0.7 point et 1.6 point de PIB. Après la crise du COVID-19, leur niveau de recettes fiscales en pourcentage du PIB était plus faible en 2020 qu'en 2010.

Graphique 1.10. **Variation des ratios impôts/PIB entre 2010 et 2020**

Points de pourcentage

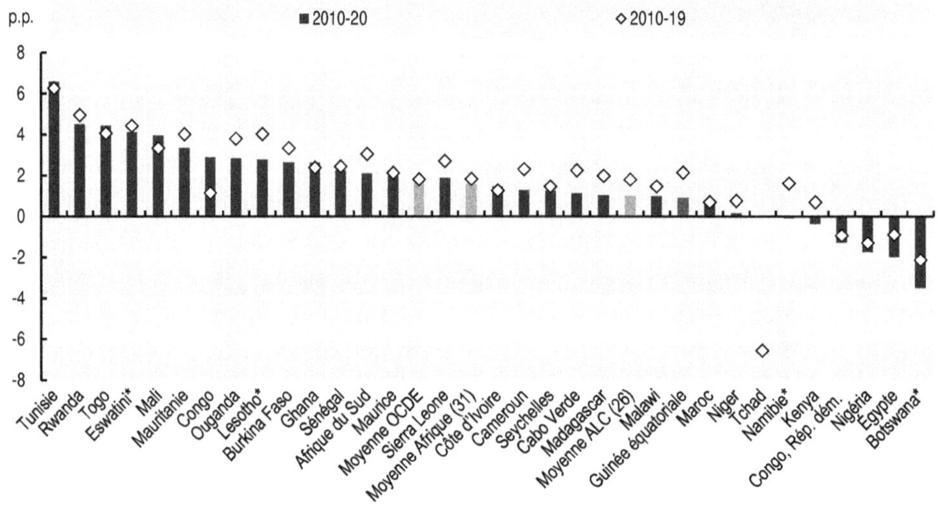

Notes : Les chiffres prennent en compte les recettes fiscales des administrations infranationales pour l'Afrique du Sud, l'Eswatini, le Maroc et le Nigéria (recettes des États uniquement) pour l'année 2020.

*Au Botswana, en Eswatini, au Lesotho et en Namibie, l'année fiscale court du mois d'avril au mois de mars. Les chiffres de 2020 pour ces pays incluent donc les recettes perçues jusqu'au 31 mars 2021. Veuillez vous reporter aux notes des tableaux par pays au chapitre 5 pour plus d'informations.

La moyenne Afrique (31) et les moyennes ALC (26 pays) et OCDE (38 pays) sont des moyennes non pondérées. La moyenne pour les pays d'Asie-Pacifique (28) n'est pas disponible pour les années antérieures à 2018.

Source : Tableaux 4.1 et 4.2 figurant au chapitre 4 et (OCDE/ATAF/CUA, 2022[4]), « Statistiques des recettes publiques en Afrique : Tableaux comparatifs », *Statistiques fiscales de l'OCDE* (base de données), *https://doi.org/10.1787/7f54581d-fr*.

StatLink *https://stat.link/4uby1n*

Le Graphique 1.11 présente l'évolution des recettes fiscales en pourcentage du PIB dans les 31 pays d'Afrique ainsi que les moyennes Afrique (31) et ALC entre 2010 et 2020, par type d'impôt. L'augmentation du ratio impôts/PIB de la Tunisie entre 2010 et 2020 s'explique essentiellement par la hausse des recettes provenant de l'IRPP (3.5 points) et des CSS (3.0 points). Au cours de cette période, la Tunisie a réformé en profondeur ses politiques et son administration fiscales afin de mobiliser des recettes fiscales. En outre, la hausse des recettes tirées de l'IRPP et des CSS s'explique en partie par l'augmentation de 147 % en moyenne des salaires (OCDE/CUA/ATAF, 2020[10]).

L'augmentation du ratio impôts/PIB du Rwanda entre 2010 et 2020 s'explique essentiellement par la hausse des recettes provenant des impôts sur le revenu (2.5 points) et de la TVA (1.3 point). Si l'on fait abstraction de l'année 2020, depuis 2010, les recettes fiscales augmentent régulièrement au Rwanda, de 0.6 point par an en moyenne, sous l'effet des réformes de la politique et de l'administration fiscales engagées en vue de compenser la baisse recettes provenant de l'aide extérieure et des taxes sur les échanges[7]. Les changements administratifs portent notamment sur la dématérialisation des outils destinés aux contribuables, la modernisation des procédures de recouvrement et de contrôle, et un meilleur recouvrement des arriérés de TVA. S'agissant de la politique fiscale, le Rwanda a élargi l'assiette de l'IRPP, instauré des retenues à la source (TVA et impôts sur le revenu), supprimé les exonérations fiscales, et relevé les taux de plusieurs droits d'accise et droits à l'importation au cours de la période considérée. Ces réformes se sont traduites par une amélioration de la discipline fiscale, notamment en ce qui concerne la TVA, et par une augmentation significative des recettes fiscales dans les principales catégories d'impôts (Akitoby et al., 2019[11]) (PwC, 2019[12]) (FMI, 2020[13]). Plus récemment, le Rwanda a adopté en 2018 une nouvelle loi relative à l'impôt sur le revenu qui a levé les ambiguïtés et élargi l'assiette de l'impôt, et contribué à accroître les recettes de l'impôt sur le revenu de 0.7 point entre 2017 et 2019 (Economist Intelligence Unit, 2018[14]). En 2020, le Rwanda a vu ses recettes fiscales diminuer de 0.4 % du PIB.

Le Botswana a enregistré une baisse significative de ses recettes fiscales en pourcentage du PIB entre 2010 et 2020, de 15.8 % à 12.4 %, qui s'explique principalement par une baisse de 2.8 points des recettes de l'impôt sur le revenu (recettes provenant de l'impôt sur le revenu non ventilables entre l'IRPP et l'IS, classées dans la catégorie « autres impôts » dans le Graphique 1.11) sur la même période, ce qui représente un recul annuel moyen de 0.3 point. Les recettes de TVA ont également joué un rôle dans la baisse du ratio impôts/PIB, qui est passé de 5.0 % du PIB en 2010 à 4.3 % en 2020.

Graphique 1.11. **Variation des ratios impôts/PIB par principales rubriques d'impôt entre 2010 et 2020 et par pays**

Points de pourcentage

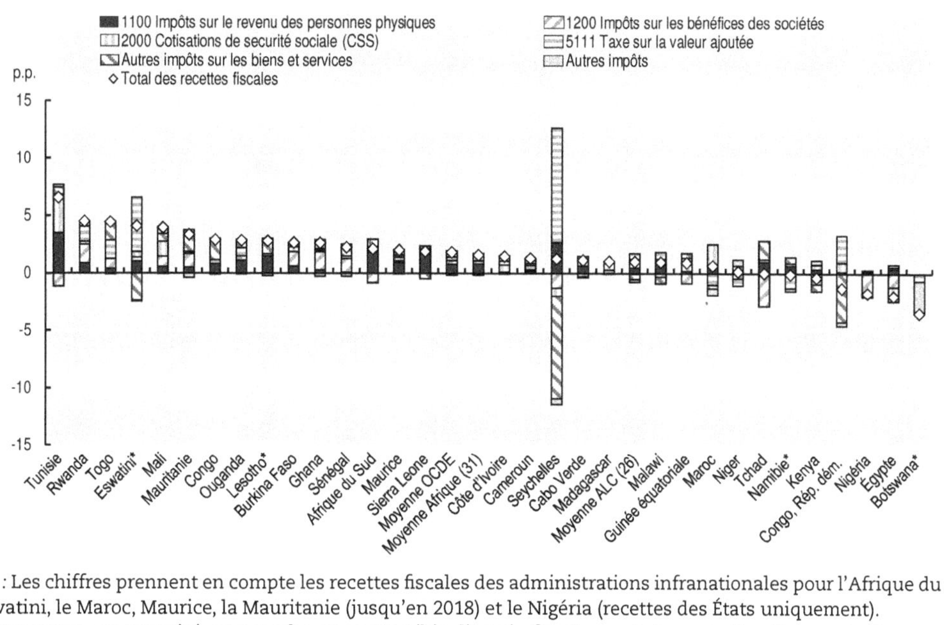

Note : Les chiffres prennent en compte les recettes fiscales des administrations infranationales pour l'Afrique du Sud, l'Eswatini, le Maroc, Maurice, la Mauritanie (jusqu'en 2018) et le Nigéria (recettes des États uniquement).

*Au Botswana, en Eswatini, au Lesotho et en Namibie, l'année fiscale court du mois d'avril au mois de mars. Les chiffres de 2020 pour ces pays incluent donc les recettes perçues jusqu'au 31 mars 2021.

La moyenne Afrique (31) et les moyennes ALC (26 pays) et OCDE (38 pays) sont des moyennes non pondérées. La moyenne pour les pays d'Asie-Pacifique (28) n'est pas disponible pour les années antérieures à 2018. Les données concernant l'OCDE portent sur l'année 2019, car les données définitives relatives à l'année 2020 ne sont pas disponibles.

Source : Calculs des auteurs basés sur (OCDE/ATAF/CUA, 2022[4]), « Statistiques des recettes publiques en Afrique : Tableaux comparatifs », *Statistiques fiscales de l'OCDE* (base de données), *https://doi.org/10.1787/7f54581d-fr*.

StatLink *https://stat.link/p0ahnm*

On observe d'importants changements aux Seychelles entre 2010 et 2020. Les recettes de TVA en pourcentage du PIB ont progressé de 10 points, tandis que les autres impôts sur les biens et services ont diminué de 8.9 points sur la période. Cela s'explique par la mise en place d'une TVA en 2013 destinée à remplacer la taxe sur les biens et services, qui était prélevée sur l'importation de tous les biens et sur le chiffre d'affaires de certaines entreprises (OCDE, 2020[15]).

Encadré 1.3. **Variations des ratios impôts/PIB dans les pays membres de la SACU**

Cinq des 31 pays inclus dans cette publication font partie de l'Union douanière d'Afrique australe (SACU) : Afrique du Sud, Botswana, Eswatini, Lesotho et Namibie. La SACU a été fondée en 1910, ce qui en fait l'union douanière la plus ancienne au monde (SACU, 2020[16]). Les cinq pays membres de la SACU sont liés par un accord de partage des recettes qui prévoit l'application de tarifs extérieurs communs et une répartition des droits de douane et d'accise perçus par les pays membres. Dans la présente publication, les recettes issues des droits de douane et d'accise sont incluses dans les recettes fiscales du pays de la SACU qui les a collectées (Afrique du Sud), et les montants redistribués par le fonds commun des recettes de la SACU sont classés dans les tableaux des recettes non fiscales, sous la rubrique des recettes diverses pour le Botswana, l'Eswatini, le Lesotho, et la Namibie (voir encadré 2.2 au chapitre 2).

En 2020, le ratio moyen impôts/PIB des pays de la SACU (la moyenne SACU) était supérieur de 2.9 points au ratio moyen de l'Afrique (31), et s'élevait à 18.8 %. L'évolution du ratio impôts/PIB entre 2010 et 2020 dans les pays de la SACU a été, en moyenne, similaire à celle de la moyenne de l'Afrique (31) au cours de la même période. Alors que le ratio moyen impôts/PIB de l'Afrique (31) a progressé de 14.4 % du PIB en 2010 à 16.0 % en 2020, la moyenne SACU est passée de 17.7 % du PIB en 2010 à 18.8 % en 2020 (Graphique 1.12).

La TVA a été le principal moteur de l'augmentation de la moyenne SACU au cours de cette période, avec une hausse de 0.7 point, comparable à la moyenne Afrique (31). Les ratios impôts/PIB ont augmenté en Eswatini (4.1 points), au Lesotho (2.8 points) et en Afrique du Sud (2.1 points), et ont diminué en Namibie, de 0.1 point, et au Botswana, de 3.5 points au cours de la période.

Graphique 1.12. **Ratios impôts/PIB (niveaux et variations annuelles) dans les pays de la SACU, 2010-20**

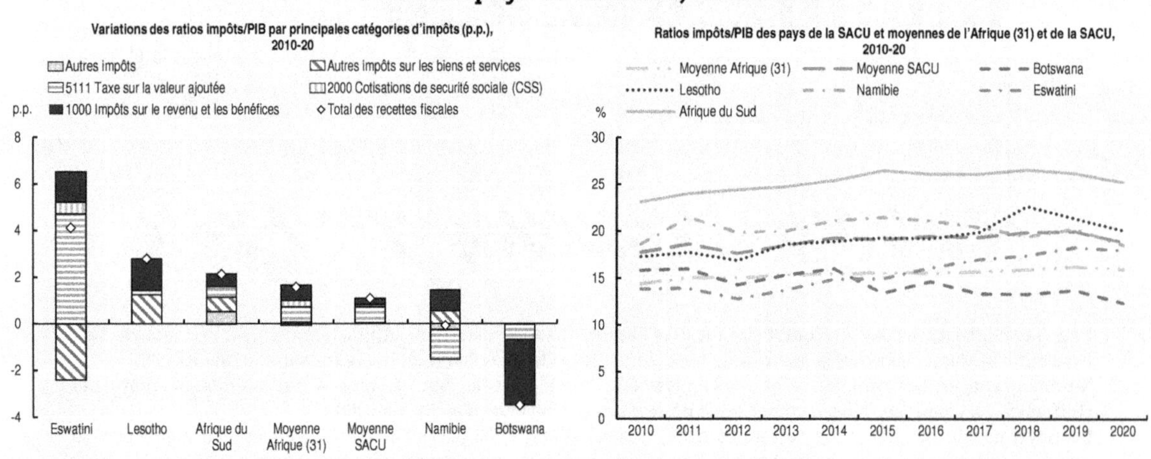

Source : Calculs des auteurs basés sur (OCDE/ATAF/CUA, 2022[4]), « Statistiques des recettes publiques en Afrique : Tableaux comparatifs », *Statistiques fiscales de l'OCDE* (base de données), *https://doi.org/10.1787/7f54581d-fr*.

StatLink *https://stat.link/kfb2yd*

Facteurs ayant un effet sur les ratios impôts/PIB

Les ratios impôts/PIB sont influencés par plusieurs facteurs. Il s'agit entre autres des caractéristiques macroéconomiques, telles que la diversification d'une économie, l'importance de l'agriculture, les dotations en ressources, l'ouverture aux échanges et la taille de l'économie informelle. L'évolution de la situation politique des pays, qu'il s'agisse de troubles sociaux, de corruption, etc., peut également influer sur les ratios impôts/PIB. La capacité des administrations fiscales, et le civisme fiscal (le consentement à l'impôt de la part des entreprises et des particuliers) sont aussi étroitement liés au niveau des recettes fiscales (OCDE, 2014[17]) (OCDE, 2019[18]). L'emplacement géographique peut exercer une influence sur les niveaux d'imposition : par exemple, les pays enclavés peuvent plus difficilement taxer les biens et services au port d'entrée que les pays disposant d'un accès à la mer.

Les ratios impôts/PIB sont habituellement supérieurs dans les pays à haut revenu : en général, les pays de l'OCDE collectent des recettes fiscales plus importantes que les pays hors OCDE, en pourcentage du PIB. La plupart des pays couverts dans cette publication affichent des niveaux de revenu par habitant et des ratios impôts/PIB plus bas que les pays de l'OCDE et de la région ALC. Les niveaux de PIB par habitant varient davantage entre les pays africains qu'entre les pays ALC et les pays de l'OCDE (Graphique 1.13).

Graphique 1.13. **Ratios impôts/PIB et PIB par habitant (en PPA) dans les pays d'Afrique, d'Amérique latine et des Caraïbes, de l'OCDE et dans certaines économies d'Asie et du Pacifique, 2020**

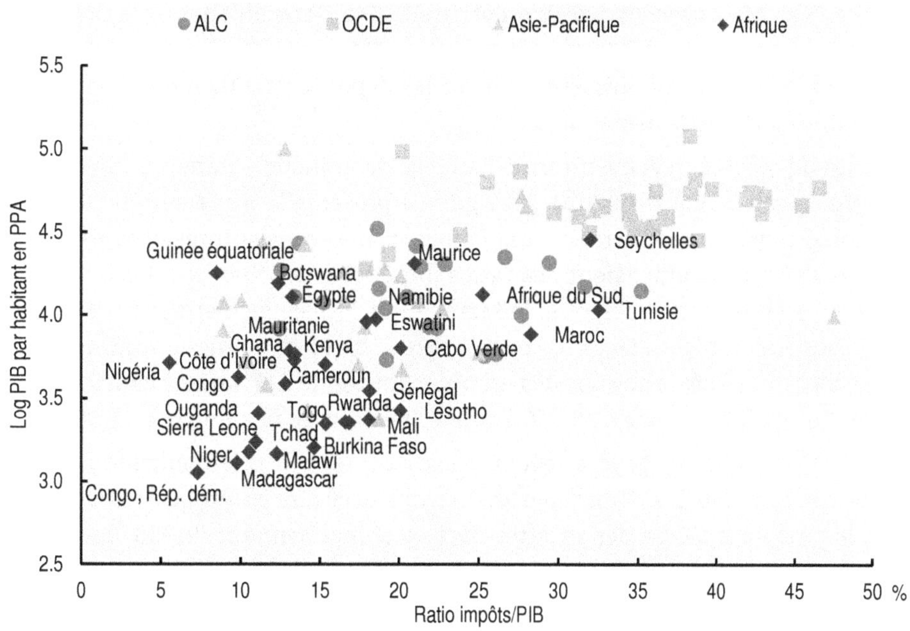

Note : L'axe y est sur une échelle logarithmique. La parité de pouvoir d'achat (PPA) entre deux pays est le taux auquel la monnaie d'un pays doit être convertie dans celle d'un second pays pour qu'un volume donné de monnaie du premier pays permette d'acheter la même quantité de biens et de services dans chaque pays. Le taux de conversion PPA est le taux utilisé pour convertir une monnaie nationale en dollar international courant. Un dollar international a le même pouvoir d'achat que le dollar US aux États-Unis. Un dollar international est une monnaie hypothétique utilisée comme moyen pour convertir et comparer les coûts d'un pays à l'autre grâce à un point de référence commun, le dollar US (définitions issues de (FMI, 2019[19])) et (OMS, 2015[20]).

Source : (FMI, 2022[6]) pour les chiffres du PIB par habitant. *Source :* Calculs des auteurs basés sur des données figurant dans (OCDE/ATAF/CUA, 2022[4]), « Statistiques des recettes publiques en Afrique : Tableaux comparatifs », *Statistiques fiscales de l'OCDE* (base de données), *https://doi.org/10.1787/7f54581d-fr*, (OCDE, 2022[1]), (OCDE et al., 2022[2]) et (OCDE, 2021[3]).

StatLink *https://stat.link/ycin14*

Les besoins de financement des pays sont fonction en partie de leur niveau de revenu, qui constitue un élément important à prendre en compte pour comprendre les niveaux d'imposition dans les différents pays. L'écart entre les recettes publiques et les besoins de financement pour le développement est généralement plus important dans les pays où le revenu par habitant est faible, ce qui fait que la mobilisation de recettes publiques supplémentaires y est particulièrement cruciale (Gaspar et al., 2019[21]). La crise liée au COVID-19 s'est traduite par une baisse des recettes fiscales dans la plupart des pays, et par une hausse sensible des besoins de financement et de la dette. Les efforts renouvelés pour réformer la politique et les administrations fiscales en vue d'augmenter les recettes fiscales ont pris une importance encore plus grande au lendemain de la crise sanitaire.

Le Graphique 1.14 montre la répartition des ratios impôts/PIB des 31 pays africains couverts par la présente publication pour trois catégories de revenu en 2020 selon la classification de la Banque mondiale (Banque mondiale, 2022[22]). Il présente aussi l'évolution des ratios impôts/PIB par catégorie de revenu entre 2019 et 2020 (les pays à faible revenu, les pays à revenu intermédiaire de la tranche inférieure, ainsi que les pays à revenu intermédiaire de la tranche supérieure et les pays à revenu élevé qui forment une seule catégorie[8]).

En 2020, 25 des 31 pays africains figurant dans cette publication étaient classés parmi les pays à faible revenu ou à revenu intermédiaire de la tranche inférieure, dont 11 dans la catégorie des pays à faible revenu. Ce groupe de pays présentait la dispersion la plus faible par rapport aux pays à revenu élevé ; tous les pays à faible revenu ont enregistré un ratio impôts/PIB inférieur à 19 % en 2020, de 7.3 % du PIB en République démocratique du Congo à 18.1 % au Mali, avec un niveau moyen de 13.0 %. Dans huit des onze pays, les ratios impôts/PIB étaient inférieurs à 16 %, niveau que le FMI considère comme trop faible pour que les pays à faible revenu puissent financer les dépenses supplémentaires nécessaires pour atteindre les ODD (Gaspar et al., 2019[21]).

Pour les 14 pays à revenu intermédiaire de la tranche inférieure, le ratio moyen impôts/PIB s'élevait à 16.7 % en 2020. Si ce groupe présente la dispersion la plus forte des ratios impôts/PIB, y compris les ratios impôts/PIB les plus élevés (Tunisie) et les plus faibles (Nigéria), 10 d'entre eux affichaient des ratios impôts/PIB proches de 20 % ou inférieurs à ce niveau. Au sein de cette catégorie, le Maroc et la Tunisie se distinguent avec un ratio impôts/PIB supérieur à 28 %. Dans les pays à revenu élevé et à revenu intermédiaire de la tranche supérieure, les recettes fiscales en pourcentage du PIB varient considérablement, de 8.5 % en Guinée équatoriale à 32.0 % aux Seychelles, avec une moyenne à 19.6 % du PIB.

Entre 2019 et 2020, les pays à revenu élevé et à revenu intermédiaire de la tranche supérieure couverts par les *Statistiques des recettes publiques en Afrique* ont enregistré en moyenne la plus forte baisse des recettes fiscales en pourcentage du PIB, de 0.9 point. Le groupe des pays à revenu intermédiaire de la tranche inférieure a accusé une baisse de 0.3 point, tandis que celui des pays à faible revenu a enregistré une hausse de 0.2 point sur la période. Toutefois, si l'on exclut le Tchad de ce dernier groupe, le ratio moyen impôts/PIB dans les pays à faible revenu couverts par cette publication a connu une baisse de 0.4 % du PIB en moyenne en 2020 par rapport à 2019.

Les trois groupes ont accru leurs recettes fiscales entre 2010 et 2020. Les pays à revenu intermédiaire de la tranche inférieure étudiés dans les *Statistiques des recettes publiques en Afrique* ont enregistré l'augmentation la plus forte en moyenne (2.1 points) entre 2010 et 2020, suivis des pays à faible revenu (1.7 point), tandis que le groupe des pays à revenu intermédiaire de la tranche supérieure et des pays à revenu élevé a connu une augmentation de 0.5 point en moyenne sur la même période. Dans tous les pays, indépendamment de la catégorie de revenu à laquelle ils appartiennent, l'augmentation des ratios impôts/PIB au cours de la dernière décennie a été inférieure à 5 points en moyenne, un niveau considéré par le FMI — avant la pandémie de COVID-19 — comme un objectif « ambitieux et approprié », nécessaire à de nombreux pays pour atteindre les ODD (Gaspar et al., 2019[21]). Il s'agit d'un objectif ambitieux pour les pays africains, si l'on tient compte des résultats obtenus au cours de la décennie précédente et des conséquences de la pandémie de COVID-19.

Graphique 1.14. **Ratios impôts/PIB (niveaux et variations annuelles) par groupes de revenu, 2020**

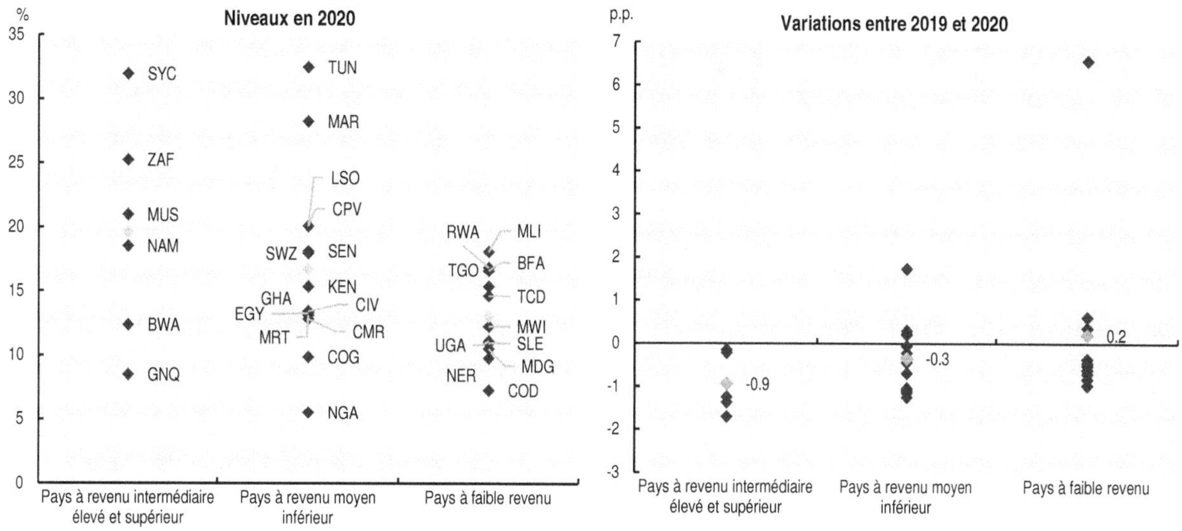

Notes : Les chiffres prennent en compte les recettes fiscales des administrations infranationales pour l'Afrique du Sud, l'Eswatini, le Maroc, Maurice et le Nigéria (recettes des États uniquement).

*Au Botswana, en Eswatini, au Lesotho et en Namibie, l'année fiscale court du mois d'avril au mois de mars. Les chiffres de 2020 pour ces pays incluent donc les recettes perçues jusqu'au 31 mars 2021.

Les Seychelles sont le seul pays du présent rapport qui est un pays à revenu élevé. C'est pourquoi les pays à revenu intermédiaire de la tranche supérieure (cinq pays) et les pays à revenu élevé (un pays) sont regroupés.

Source : Calculs des auteurs basés sur (OCDE/ATAF/CUA, 2022[4]), « Statistiques des recettes publiques en Afrique : Tableaux comparatifs », *Statistiques fiscales de l'OCDE* (base de données), *https://doi.org/10.1787/7f54581d-fr*. Classification des pays de la Banque mondiale en fonction de leurs revenus. (Banque mondiale, 2022[22])

StatLink *https://stat.link/4go8mz*

Les pays qui tirent des recettes substantielles des ressources naturelles affichent souvent un ratio impôts/PIB peu élevé. Le Graphique 1.15 montre la répartition des ratios impôts/PIB des pays riches en ressources naturelles par rapport aux pays pauvres en ressources naturelles. Cinq des pays étudiés sont considérés comme des pays riches en ressources (les pays dont plus de 10 % du PIB provenait de la production de pétrole, de gaz, de charbon et de minéraux pendant au moins cinq ans entre 2010 et 2019 ont été classés dans la catégorie des pays « riches en ressources » (CUA/OCDE, 2022[23])): le Tchad, la République du Congo, la Guinée équatoriale et le Nigéria sont riches en pétrole (Les pays dont plus de 10 % du PIB provenait de la production de pétrole pendant au moins cinq ans entre 2010 et 2019 ont été classés dans la catégorie des pays « riches en pétrole » (CUA/OCDE, 2022[23])), tandis que la Mauritanie possède d'importantes ressources minérales comme le minerai de fer, le cuivre, l'or et l'argent, et dépend également de l'agriculture, de l'élevage et de la pêche.

Graphique 1.15. **Ratios impôts/PIB (niveaux et variations annuelles) dans les pays riches en ressources et pauvres en ressources, 2020**

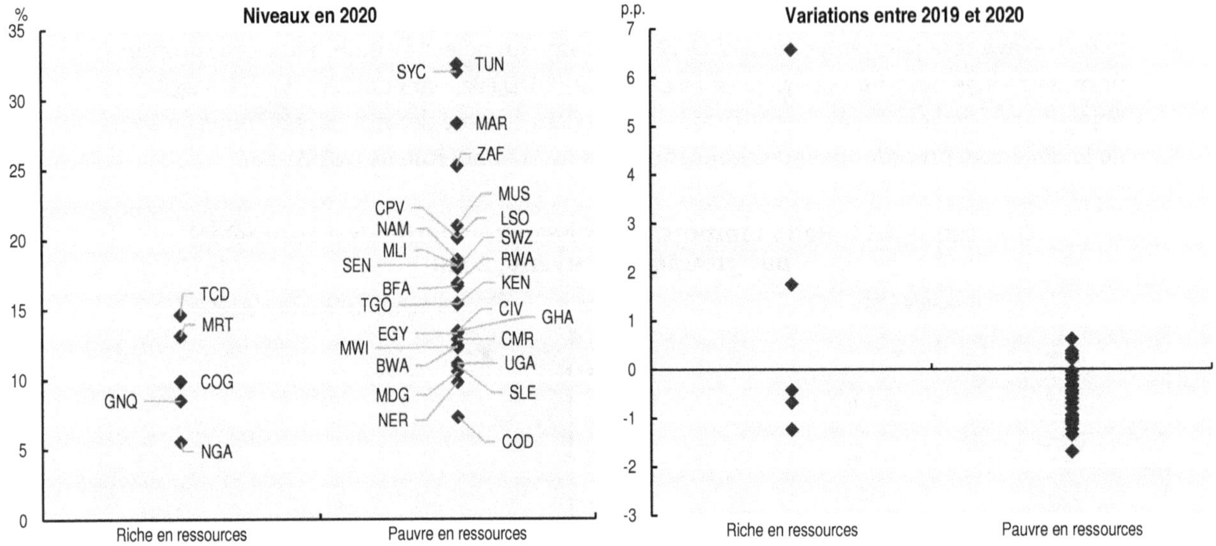

Notes : Les chiffres prennent en compte les recettes fiscales des administrations infranationales pour l'Afrique du Sud, l'Eswatini, le Maroc, Maurice et le Nigéria (recettes des États uniquement).

Source : Calculs des auteurs basés sur (OCDE/ATAF/CUA, 2022[4]), « Statistiques des recettes publiques en Afrique : Tableaux comparatifs », *Statistiques fiscales de l'OCDE* (base de données), *https://doi.org/10.1787/7f54581d-fr*. La classification des pays par niveau de ressources est basée sur (CUA/OCDE, 2022[23]).

StatLink *https://stat.link/dohp1y*

Le Graphique 1.15 confirme que les pays riches en ressources figurant dans cette publication affichent des ratios impôts/PIB inférieurs à ceux des pays pauvres en ressources naturelles. En 2020, tous les pays riches en ressources affichaient des ratios impôts/PIB inférieurs à 15 %. Les économies riches en pétrole, la République du Congo, la Guinée équatoriale, le Nigéria et le Tchad, affichaient des ratios impôts/PIB inférieurs à 10 %. Les recettes pétrolières proviennent pour l'essentiel des rentes et redevances pétrolières, qui ne sont pas considérées comme des recettes fiscales (voir chapitre 2). Les pays en développement ont beaucoup de mal à imposer les industries extractives en raison d'exonérations fiscales ou de contrats de longue date accordés aux industriels du secteur qui profitent aux élites locales (Gwaindepi, 2021[24]), (Brautigam, Fjeldstad et Moore, 2008[25]).

La crise liée au COVID-19 a eu un impact considérable sur les pays riches en ressources, en particulier les pays riches en pétrole. Le PIB des pays riches en pétrole a subi les effets des fortes fluctuations des cours du pétrole en 2020 ; trois des quatre pays concernés ont enregistré une baisse annuelle de leur PIB nominal comprise entre 4.3 % au Tchad et 20.3 % en République du Congo. La baisse des cours a pesé sur les recettes publiques, essentiellement en raison de ses effets sur les recettes non fiscales (voir chapitre 2). En ce qui concerne les recettes fiscales, le Graphique 1.15 montre que les variations annuelles des recettes fiscales en pourcentage du PIB entre 2019 et 2020 pour les pays riches en ressources étudiés dans cette publication n'ont pas été plus importantes que les variations des pays possédant peu de ressources naturelles.

Structures fiscales en Afrique

La structure fiscale d'un pays mesure la composition de ses recettes fiscales en fonction des différents types d'impôts. Il s'agit là d'un indicateur important, car différents impôts ont différents effets économiques et sociaux. La composition des impôts dans les 31 pays étudiés reflète des différences concernant leurs choix politiques, leurs structures et situations économiques, les capacités de leur administration fiscale, et d'autres facteurs historiques. Les pays peuvent être divisés en trois grands groupes en fonction de la source principale de leurs recettes : TVA, autres impôts sur les biens et services, et impôts sur le revenu.

Évolution des structures fiscales, 2010-2020

Depuis 2010, la part des recettes de l'IRPP et de la TVA dans la structure fiscale moyenne des pays étudiés dans cette publication a augmenté. Les hausses intervenues dans ces deux catégories d'impôts expliquent également pour beaucoup l'augmentation globale du ratio impôts/PIB moyen au cours de la période. Les recettes tirées de l'IRPP en pourcentage du PIB ont progressé de 0.8 point, tandis que celles issues de la TVA ont augmenté de 0.7 point entre 2010 et 2020, atteignant respectivement 3.1 % et 4.5 % du PIB en 2020 (Graphique 1.16).

La part de la TVA et de l'IRPP dans le total des recettes fiscales a également augmenté. La fraction des recettes fiscales provenant de la TVA a crû de 0.8 point pour s'établir à 27.8 % du total en 2020, ce qui traduit la poursuite d'une tendance durable à l'augmentation des recettes de TVA au détriment de celles d'autres impôts sur les biens et services. La part des recettes issues de l'IRPP a augmenté de 3.0 points au cours de cette période, atteignant 18.5 % des recettes fiscales totales en 2020, alors que la part des recettes provenant de l'IS a diminué de 2.0 points. Néanmoins, la part moyenne des recettes tirées de l'IRPP dans le total des recettes fiscales est restée inférieure à celle des recettes de l'IS en 2020, à 19.3 % du total.

Graphique 1.16. **Structure fiscale, moyenne Afrique (31) en pourcentage du total des recettes fiscales et en pourcentage du PIB, 2010 et 2020**

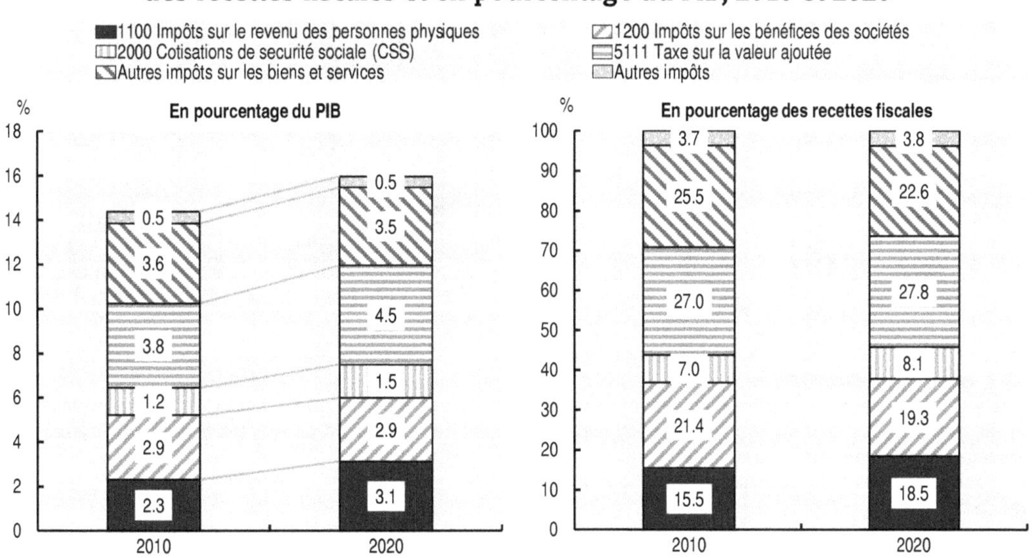

Note : La moyenne Afrique (31) n'est pas pondérée. La moyenne Afrique (31) doit être interprétée avec précaution, car des données relatives aux cotisations de sécurité sociale sont indisponibles ou incomplètes pour quelques pays. Voir les tableaux des pays au chapitre 5 pour plus d'informations.

Source : Calculs des auteurs basés sur des données figurant dans (OCDE/ATAF/CUA, 2022[4]), « Statistiques des recettes publiques en Afrique : Tableaux comparatifs », *Statistiques fiscales de l'OCDE* (base de données), *https://doi.org/10.1787/7f54581d-fr*.

StatLink *https://stat.link/94yxti*

Durant la pandémie de COVID-19, on observe que l'évolution de la structure fiscale moyenne des pays d'Afrique (31) s'est poursuivie en 2020 avec une hausse des recettes tirées de l'impôt sur le revenu par rapport aux recettes provenant des impôts sur les biens et services, en raison de la forte baisse de cette catégorie d'impôt et de la stabilité des recettes tirées de l'impôt sur le revenu en pourcentage du PIB. La part des recettes générées par les impôts sur la consommation dans le total des recettes fiscales a diminué de 1.5 point en moyenne entre 2019 et 2020, alors que la part des recettes de l'IRPP et de l'IS dans le total des recettes fiscales a augmenté de respectivement 0.7 et 0.8 point au cours de la période.

Structures fiscales en 2020

En 2020, les recettes de TVA ont généré la majeure partie des recettes fiscales dans les pays couverts par cette publication (Graphique 1.17). Elles ont représenté 27.8 % du total des recettes fiscales en moyenne, soit un pourcentage comparable à la moyenne ALC (27.5 %), mais 7.5 points de plus que la moyenne de l'OCDE (chiffre de 2019), et 4.7 points de plus que la moyenne des pays d'Asie-Pacifique (28). Toutefois, les recettes de TVA des pays d'Afrique (31) sont en moyenne inférieures aux moyennes ALC et OCDE lorsqu'elles sont mesurées en pourcentage du PIB (4.5 % du PIB en Afrique, contre 5.7 % dans la région ALC et 6.7 % dans la zone OCDE [chiffre de 2019]), mais supérieures à la moyenne Asie-Pacifique (28) (4.1 % du PIB).

Graphique 1.17. **Structure fiscale pour la moyenne Afrique (31), ALC, Asie-Pacifique et OCDE en pourcentage du total des recettes fiscales et du PIB, 2020**

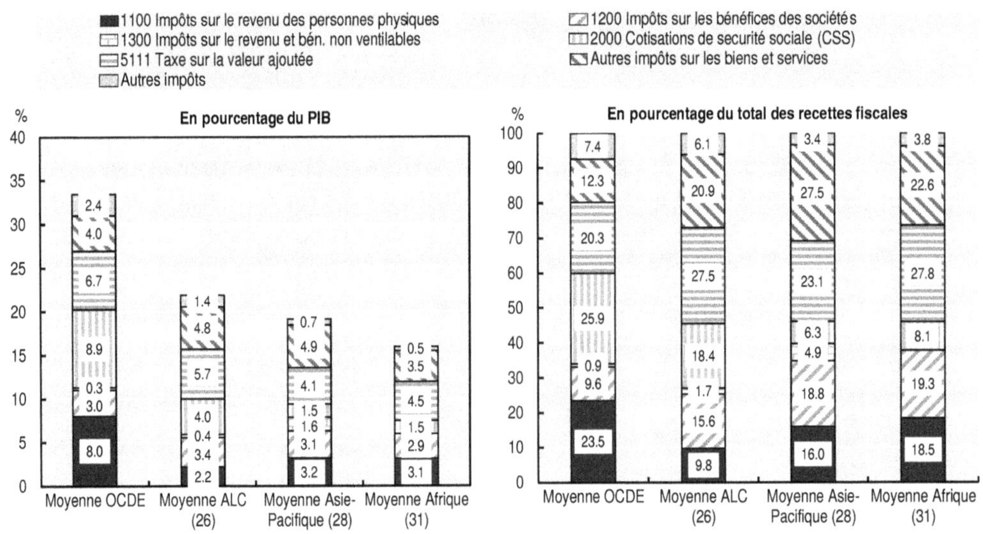

Note : La moyenne Afrique (31) et les moyennes Asie-Pacifique (28 économies), ALC (26 pays) et OCDE (38 pays) sont des moyennes non pondérées.

Il convient d'interpréter avec précaution la moyenne des pays d'Afrique (31), car les données relatives aux cotisations de sécurité sociale sont indisponibles ou incomplètes pour quelques pays. Pour plus de précisions, se reporter aux tableaux par pays présentés dans le chapitre 5.

Les données concernant l'OCDE portent sur l'année 2019, car les données définitives relatives à l'année 2020 ne sont pas disponibles.

Source : Calculs des auteurs basés sur des données figurant dans (OCDE/ATAF/CUA, 2022[4]), « Statistiques des recettes publiques en Afrique : Tableaux comparatifs », *Statistiques fiscales de l'OCDE* (base de données), *https://doi.org/10.1787/7f54581d-fr*.

StatLink *https://stat.link/8m17wi*

La part moyenne des recettes de l'IS dans le total des recettes fiscales en Afrique s'élevait à 19.3 % en 2020, soit davantage que dans les régions Asie-Pacifique (28) et ALC et dans la zone OCDE (respectivement 18.8 %, 15.6 % et 9.6 % [chiffre de 2019]). En pourcentage du PIB, les parts moyennes des recettes de l'IS pour les pays d'Afrique, d'Asie-Pacifique et pour l'OCDE étaient similaires (respectivement 2.9 %, 3.1 % et 3.0 % du PIB [chiffre de 2019]) ; ces pourcentages sont néanmoins inférieurs à la moyenne ALC (3.4 % du PIB en 2020 (Graphique 1.17).

En revanche, la part moyenne, dans les 31 pays d'Afrique, des recettes de l'IRPP (18.5 % du total des recettes) était inférieure à la moyenne de l'OCDE (23.5 % [chiffre de 2019]), mais supérieure aux moyennes ALC (9.8 %) et Asie-Pacifique (28) (16.0 %). En pourcentage du PIB, le niveau moyen des recettes issues de l'IRPP dans la zone OCDE était plus de deux fois supérieur à la moyenne des 31 pays d'Afrique.

Le Graphique 1.18 illustre, pour tous les pays étudiés dans cette publication, la ventilation des recettes fiscales entre impôts sur le revenu (personnes physiques et sociétés), cotisations de sécurité sociale et impôts sur les biens et services (y compris la TVA ainsi que d'autres impôts sur les biens et services).

Les impôts sur les biens et services constituaient la principale source de recettes fiscales pour 22 des 31 pays étudiés (les deux premiers groupes de pays représentés dans le Graphique 1.18). Dans ces pays, ils ont généré de 34.5 % des recettes fiscales en Tunisie à 77.0 % au Togo. La TVA y représentait le principal poste de recettes tirées des impôts sur les biens et services, sauf en République du Congo, en Côte d'Ivoire, au Ghana, au Kenya, en Mauritanie et en Ouganda.

Graphique 1.18. **Structure fiscale, par pays, 2020**

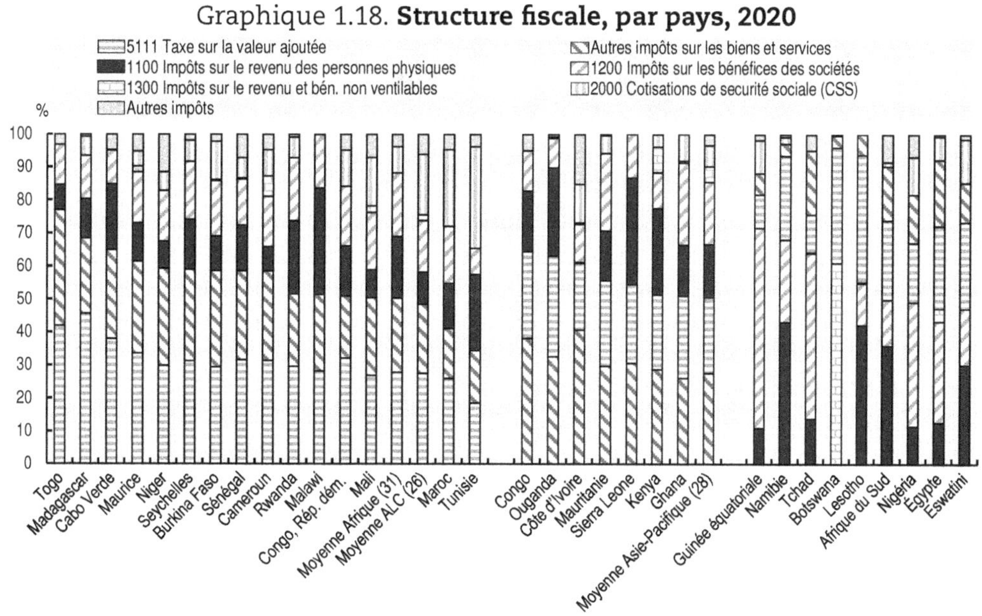

Notes : Les chiffres prennent en compte les recettes fiscales des administrations infranationales pour l'Afrique du Sud, l'Eswatini, le Maroc, Maurice et le Nigéria (recettes des États uniquement) pour l'année 2020. La moyenne Afrique (31) et les moyennes Asie-Pacifique (28 pays), ALC (26 pays) et OCDE (38 pays) sont des moyennes non pondérées.
Il convient d'interpréter avec précaution la moyenne des pays d'Afrique (31), car des données relatives aux cotisations de sécurité sociale sont indisponibles ou incomplètes pour quelques pays. Pour plus de précisions, se reporter aux tableaux par pays présentés dans le chapitre 5.
La ventilation des recettes tirées des impôts sur le revenu des personnes physiques et sur les bénéfices n'est pas disponible pour le Botswana.
Les données concernant l'OCDE portent sur l'année 2019, car les données définitives relatives à l'année 2020 ne sont pas disponibles.
Source : Calculs des auteurs basés sur des données figurant dans (OCDE/ATAF/CUA, 2022[4]), « Statistiques des recettes publiques en Afrique : Tableaux comparatifs », *Statistiques fiscales de l'OCDE* (base de données), *https://doi.org/10.1787/7f54581d-fr.*

StatLink *https://stat.link/h806ts*

Dans neuf pays (Afrique du Sud, Botswana, Égypte, Eswatini, Guinée équatoriale, Lesotho, Namibie, Nigéria, Tchad), la plus grande partie des recettes fiscales provient des impôts sur le revenu et les bénéfices. Ils représentaient dans ces pays une part plus importante des recettes fiscales totales que les moyennes OCDE et ALC : de 47.2 % des recettes totales en Égypte et Eswatini, à 71.6 % en Guinée équatoriale.

Dans 18 des 31 pays couverts par cette publication, la part des recettes fiscales tirées de l'IS était supérieure à celle provenant de l'IRPP. La part des recettes de l'IS était particulièrement importante au Tchad et en Guinée équatoriale, où elles représentaient respectivement 50.2 % et 60.6 % du total des recettes, tandis qu'au Lesotho et en Namibie, plus de 40 % des recettes totales provenaient de l'IRPP en 2020. Dans 23 pays, les recettes issues de la TVA représentaient une part plus importante des recettes totales que les recettes provenant d'autres taxes sur les biens et services. Dans huit pays, la Côte d'Ivoire, le Ghana, le Kenya, la Mauritanie, l'Ouganda, la République du Congo, la Sierra Leone et le Tchad, la part des recettes fiscales provenant d'autres taxes sur les biens et services était plus élevée. En revanche, le Botswana, le Lesotho et la Namibie, qui sont tous membres de la SACU[9], tirent moins de 7.0 % de leurs recettes fiscales totales d'autres taxes sur les biens et services. L'accord de partage des recettes entre les pays de la SACU explique cette part relativement faible par rapport aux autres pays.

L'importance des cotisations de sécurité sociale[10] dans le total des recettes fiscales varie considérablement entre les 31 pays étudiés. Leur part dans le total des recettes fiscales était la plus élevée au Maroc (23.3 %) et en Tunisie (30.9 %) ; dans les autres pays, elle s'échelonne entre moins de 0.2 % au Cabo Verde à environ 14.8 % au Mali. Cette hétérogénéité reflète la diversité des régimes de sécurité sociale et des taux de cotisation. Par exemple, les CSS en Afrique du Sud financent le Fonds d'assurance chômage, tandis que d'autres prestations, telles que les programmes d'aide sociale couvrant la vieillesse, la maladie et la maternité, sont financées par les recettes générales. À l'inverse, les régimes de sécurité sociale marocain et tunisien sont calqués sur le système français, et couvrent un large éventail de prestations financées par des cotisations, y compris la vieillesse, l'incapacité, la maladie, la maternité, les accidents du travail (Tunisie), le chômage (Maroc) et les allocations familiales (SSA, 2015[26]).

Recettes des taxes liées à l'environnement

En vertu de l'Accord de Paris de 2016, les pays se sont engagés à décarboner leurs économies d'ici au milieu du siècle, ce qui implique de se détourner des combustibles fossiles comme source d'énergie. Les taxes environnementales, et plus généralement les instruments fondés sur les prix, jouent un rôle croissant dans de nombreux pays. En intégrant un signal-prix dans les décisions des consommateurs, ces taxes mettent en application le principe du pollueur-payeur, et incitent les entreprises et les ménages à prendre en compte le coût environnemental de leurs choix.

Une taxe liée à l'environnement est une taxe dont l'assiette est une unité physique (ou une approximation d'une unité physique) de quelque chose qui a un impact négatif spécifique et avéré sur l'environnement, que la taxe vise à changer les comportements ou soit perçue dans un autre but (OCDE, 2005[27]). Les recettes tirées des taxes sur l'énergie peuvent augmenter à moyen terme si les pays relèvent les taux effectifs de la taxe sur la teneur en carbone des carburants (Marten et van Dender, 2019[28]). Une étude (OCDE/FIT, 2019[29]) conjointe du FIT et de l'OCDE montre comment les recettes tirées du transport routier peuvent être stabilisées à long terme en associant des taxes sur les distances parcourues, les véhicules et les carburants.

Bien que les recettes tirées des taxes liées à l'environnement ne ressortent pas de la classification type des recettes fiscales établie par l'OCDE, on peut les identifier en examinant la liste détaillée des taxes spécifiques fournies pour la plupart des pays, qui s'inscrivent dans la classification globale. C'est sur cette base qu'elles ont été intégrées dans la base de données de l'OCDE sur les instruments de la politique de l'environnement (PINE) (OCDE, 2022[30])[11].

Un examen détaillé des taxes prélevées par les 31 pays africains couverts montre qu'en moyenne, les recettes tirées des taxes liées à l'environnement s'élevaient à 1.1 % du PIB en 2020, un niveau supérieur aux moyennes des régions Asie-Pacifique[12] et ALC (respectivement 0.8 % et 1.0 % du PIB), mais inférieur à la moyenne non pondérée de l'OCDE (2.2 % du PIB). Les recettes générées par les taxes liées à l'environnement s'échelonnaient entre un peu moins de 0.1 % du PIB en République du Congo et au Nigéria, et 4.8 % aux Seychelles (Graphique 1.19). Ces chiffres doivent être interprétés avec prudence, car il n'est pas possible de déterminer précisément le niveau des recettes issues des taxes liées à l'environnement pour chaque pays ; aussi, le niveau des recettes indiqué dans le Graphique 1.19 varie en fonction de la granularité des données disponibles.

Graphique 1.19. **Recettes provenant des taxes liées à l'environnement par pays et par principales catégories de taxe, 2020**

Percentage of GDP

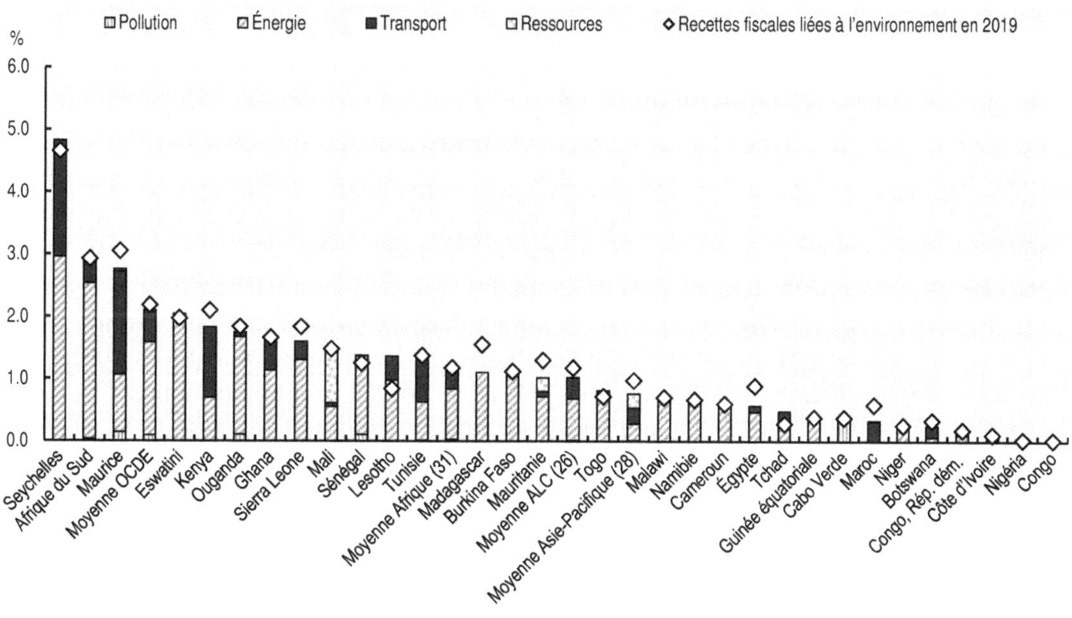

Note : Ces chiffres doivent être interprétés avec prudence, car il n'est pas possible de déterminer précisément le niveau des recettes fiscales issues des taxes liées à l'environnement pour chaque pays. Les chiffres concernant les recettes fiscales issues des taxes liées à l'environnement dépendent de la granularité des données sur les recettes fiscales fournies par les pays participants. Le Rwanda est exclu compte tenu de l'impossibilité d'identifier des recettes tirées de taxes liées à l'environnement.

Source : Calculs des auteurs basés sur des données figurant dans (OCDE/ATAF/CUA, 2022[4]), (OCDE, 2022[30]), sur la base de données PINE pour la moyenne de l'OCDE, dans (OCDE et al., 2022[2]) pour la moyenne ALC, et dans (OCDE, 2022[1]) pour la moyenne Asie-Pacifique.

StatLink https://stat.link/k6pgit

En 2020, les recettes provenant des taxes sur les produits énergétiques constituaient l'essentiel des recettes tirées des taxes liées à l'environnement dans les pays couverts par cette publication (0.8 % du PIB en moyenne). Les recettes issues des taxes sur les produits énergétiques, généralement sur le gazole et sur l'essence, représentaient environ les deux tiers des recettes générées par les taxes liées à l'environnement en moyenne. Les recettes tirées des taxes sur les transports et sur les véhicules à moteur constituaient l'essentiel du solde, tandis que celles générées par d'autres catégories étaient négligeables, de l'ordre de

0.02 % du total en moyenne. Cette structure est très similaire à la ventilation de ces recettes observée dans les pays de l'OCDE et de la région ALC. En 2020, en revanche, les économies de la région Asie-Pacifique ont davantage recouru aux taxes sur les ressources et les transports qu'aux taxes sur l'énergie.

Les taxes sur les produits énergétiques représentaient la majeure partie des recettes des taxes liées à l'environnement dans tous les pays sauf huit. Les taxes sur les véhicules à moteur et sur les transports constituaient la principale source de recettes issues des taxes liées à l'environnement au Botswana, en Côte d'Ivoire, au Kenya, au Maroc, à Maurice, au Nigéria et en Tunisie. Les recettes provenant des taxes sur les ressources et sur la pollution arrivaient en tête au Cabo Verde, en Guinée équatoriale et au Mali.

Entre 2019 et 2020, les recettes tirées des taxes liées à l'environnement dans la région Afrique (31) sont restées inchangées. La zone OCDE a enregistré une baisse de 0.1 point, une baisse inférieure à celles des moyennes ALC et Asie-Pacifique sur la même période (0.2 point dans les deux cas). En Afrique, la baisse des recettes provenant des taxes liées à l'environnement s'explique principalement par la diminution des recettes tirées des taxes sur l'énergie, suivie d'une diminution des recettes tirées des taxes sur les ressources naturelles. Ces baisses sont dues pour l'essentiel au recul des recettes générées par les accises sur les carburants en raison des restrictions à la mobilité, des confinements, et du télétravail imposés pendant la pandémie de COVID-19.

L'Afrique du Sud affiche l'un des plus hauts niveaux de recettes liées aux taxes liées à l'environnement, soit l'équivalent de 2.9 % du PIB en 2020, la taxe sur les carburants occupant la première place (1.4 % du PIB). Au cours de la dernière décennie, l'Afrique du Sud a mis en place une taxe sur les ampoules incandescentes (2009/10), une taxe sur l'électricité (2009/10), une taxe sur les émissions de CO_2 des véhicules (2010/11), et une taxe sur les pneus (2016/17). Plus récemment, le pays a instauré en 2019 une taxe carbone qui s'élève à 120 rands (8.34 USD) par tonne d'équivalent dioxyde de carbone (SARS, 2020[31]), (Reuters, 2019[32]), (OCDE, 2020[33]). Depuis le 1er janvier 2022, le montant de la taxe carbone en Afrique du Sud est passé à 144 rands (environ 9 USD). L'Afrique du Sud prévoit de relever progressivement ce tarif pour le porter à 20 USD en 2026, afin de respecter ses engagements pris à la COP26. À compter de 2026, l'Afrique du Sud entend relever le montant de la taxe carbone à un rythme plus soutenu pour atteindre au moins 30 USD d'ici à 2030 et 120 USD au-delà de 2050 (The conversation, 2022[34]). Dans quatre autres pays, une taxe carbone est en cours de finalisation ou d'examen (Botswana, Côte d'Ivoire, Maroc et Sénégal) (News Ghana, 2022[35]), (Institut de Recherches économiques et Fiscales (IREF), 2021[36]), (Coalition pour le leadership en matière de tarification du carbone, 2018[37]), (CCNUCC, 2021[38]).

Dans le contexte de la mise en place d'un mécanisme d'ajustement carbone aux frontières (MACF) par l'Union européenne (UE) à partir de 2023, qui s'inscrit dans un ensemble de mesures visant à réduire les émissions de gaz à effet de serre de 55 % dans l'UE à l'horizon 2030, les pays africains devront faire face à de nouvelles taxes sur certaines de leurs exportations vers l'UE. Le MACF fixe un prix du carbone visant les importations dans l'UE d'après les émissions nécessaires à leur production. Le MACF vise à limiter le risque de fuite de carbone en incitant les producteurs des pays non membres de l'UE à verdir leurs processus de production, c'est-à-dire à taxer le carbone dans leurs propres industries. Le MACF s'appliquera dans un premier temps aux secteurs les plus émetteurs (fer et acier, ciment, engrais, aluminium et production d'électricité), et d'autres produits seront inclus ultérieurement. Le Mozambique sera particulièrement touché, car on estime que 54.1 % des exportations d'aluminium de ce pays couvertes par le MACF sont destinées à l'UE

(Commission européenne, 2021[39]). En Afrique, certains responsables de l'action publique ont déjà commencé à mettre en œuvre de nouvelles mesures afin d'atténuer les effets du MACF sur leurs économies. Le Maroc travaille par exemple à obtenir la certification de l'empreinte carbone des produits marocains, et à assurer l'accès des industries exportatrices marocaines aux énergies renouvelables (Telquel, 2022[40]).

D'une manière générale, le recours à la fiscalité pour remédier aux problèmes environnementaux est faible dans la région, et il est possible de mobiliser bien davantage ces formes de prélèvements. La sous-utilisation des taxes liées à l'environnement en Afrique doit également s'appréhender dans le contexte de l'utilisation généralisée des subventions aux combustibles fossiles. On estime que les subventions aux combustibles fossiles en Afrique représentaient 3.8 % du PIB en 2020 (AIE, 2021[41]). Parmi les pays couverts par cette publication, l'Égypte, le Ghana et le Nigéria ont accordé des subventions aux combustibles fossiles pour un montant d'environ 7.9 milliards USD, 200 millions USD et 400 millions USD en 2020. La pandémie de COVID-19 a eu un impact significatif sur ces subventions ; en Égypte et au Nigéria, elles ont diminué de plus de 50 % entre 2019 et 2020. Selon les estimations de l'Agence internationale de l'énergie, les subventions aux combustibles fossiles s'élevaient à 27.7 milliards USD en Afrique et à 180 milliards USD dans le monde en 2020, ce qui représente une baisse de 40 % par rapport à 2019, et le niveau le plus bas depuis 14 ans (AIE, 2021[42]), (Chuku et Ajayi, 2021[43]).

La réforme des subventions à l'énergie, parallèlement à la mise en place d'une fiscalité environnementale, pourrait permettre de mobiliser d'importantes recettes publiques, contribuant à la réalisation de l'Agenda 2063 et des Objectifs de développement durable (ODD).

Impôts par niveaux d'administration

L'analyse de la répartition des impôts par niveaux d'administration dans les pays couverts par cette publication est limitée par le fait que les données sur les recettes fiscales perçues par les administrations infranationales étaient disponibles pour cinq pays seulement : l'Afrique du Sud, l'Eswatini[13], le Maroc, Maurice, et le Nigéria[14]. En 2020, les recettes des administrations infranationales représentaient 0.3 % du total des recettes fiscales à Maurice, 1.0 % en Eswatini, 2.9 % au Maroc et 6.9 % en Afrique du Sud. Elles s'élevaient en revanche à 15.3 % du total des recettes fiscales au Nigéria. Les recettes fiscales des administrations infranationales sont considérées comme faibles dans la région.

La pandémie de COVID-19 a provoqué une baisse sensible des recettes fiscales infranationales dans le monde entier, et l'Afrique ne fait pas exception. Elles ont diminué en Eswatini (0.2 point), au Maroc (0.1 point) et au Nigéria (0.1 point), alors qu'elles ont légèrement augmenté en Afrique du Sud (0.1 point), et sont restées inchangées à Maurice.

En général, les compétences fiscales dévolues aux administrations infranationales en Afrique sont limitées. De nombreuses administrations locales perçoivent une fraction importante de leurs recettes totales grâce aux transferts opérés par l'administration centrale. Les collectivités locales dans la plupart des pays d'Afrique se heurtent à des contraintes de ressources, et les outils dont disposent leurs administrations fiscales sont inadaptés pour recouvrer les impôts et les imputer correctement en comptabilité. Cette situation entraîne des coûts de recouvrement élevés et un grand nombre d'impôts peu productifs. En outre, le traitement des données relatives aux recettes collectées et l'échange de renseignements avec d'autres institutions publiques sont peu développés, et les administrations locales coopèrent généralement peu avec l'administration centrale. Cela se traduit par des impôts en double ou qui vont à l'encontre des objectifs nationaux (comme des taxes locales sur les cultures d'exportation).

Les impôts sur le patrimoine constituent la plus importante source de revenus pour les administrations infranationales en Afrique du Sud, en Eswatini, au Maroc et à Maurice. Ils représentent la totalité des recettes fiscales locales recouvrées en Afrique du Sud, en Eswatini et à Maurice, et plus de 80 % au Maroc. Le solde se compose principalement des impôts sur les biens et services. À l'inverse, les recettes des administrations infranationales au Nigéria proviennent principalement des impôts sur le revenu.

On observe de grandes disparités en matière de fiscalité locale, et de nombreux pays africains ne lèvent aucune taxe locale sur le foncier bâti et non bâti, ni même sur les activités économiques (BAfD/OCDE/PNUD, 2015[44]). À l'exception de l'Afrique du Sud, les registres fonciers font défaut ou sont incomplets, ce qui entrave la collecte des impôts fonciers (Fjeldstad, O.-H., G. Chambas et J.-F. Brun, 2014[45]). À Maurice, par exemple, la taxe foncière est peu productive en partie à cause de cadastres périmés et de valeurs de biens qui ne sont plus à jour (FMI, 2014[46]).

Certains pays s'emploient à améliorer leur régime des impôts sur le patrimoine, avec une mise à jour des registres fonciers, et des outils administratifs plus efficaces. En 2007, le Maroc a lancé une réforme du système fiscal et des administrations fiscales locales en vue d'augmenter les recettes générées par les impôts locaux (Boisard, S., C. de Freitas et G. Hidouci, 2014[47]). La Côte d'Ivoire a déployé un logiciel SIG pour mieux gérer ses registres fonciers. L'Afrique du Sud a décentralisé avec succès le processus de recouvrement de la taxe foncière urbaine, et a élaboré un système moderne de collecte de cette taxe en utilisant des techniques statistiques afin de réaliser des évaluations de masse assistées par ordinateur (Monkam et Moore, 2015[48]).

Notes

1 Il convient d'interpréter la moyenne Afrique (31) avec précaution, car des données relatives aux cotisations de sécurité sociale sont indisponibles pour la République du Congo, la République démocratique du Congo (avant 2012), la Guinée Équatoriale (avant 2013), Madagascar (avant 2011), la Namibie (avant 2009), l'Ouganda, la Sierra Leone, le Tchad et le Togo, et sont incomplètes pour le Cameroun et le Sénégal. Les cotisations de sécurité sociale pour le Botswana, le Lesotho et le Malawi sont égales à zéro dans la mesure où elles ne remplissent pas les critères retenus pour être considérées comme des cotisations de sécurité sociale, selon la classification des impôts de l'OCDE figurant dans le Guide d'interprétation. Pour plus de précisions, se reporter aux tableaux par pays présentés dans le chapitre 5.

2 Au Botswana, en Eswatini, au Lesotho et en Namibie, l'année fiscale court du mois d'avril au mois de mars. Cela signifie que l'année fiscale 2020 correspond à la période T2/2020-T1/2021. En Égypte, au Kenya, au Malawi, à Maurice (années antérieures à 2010 et à partir de 2016) et en Ouganda, l'année fiscale se termine le 30 juin. L'année fiscale 2020 correspond à la période T2/2019-T2/2020. Certains pays communiquent certains éléments des recettes fiscales sur une base différente en fonction de la nature des recettes. Par exemple, les recettes au Rwanda sont déclarées sur la base de l'année civile, sauf pour les CSS, qui sont déclarées sur la base de l'année fiscale se terminant le 30 juin depuis 2008. Un autre exemple est l'Afrique du Sud, où les données se basent sur une année civile, sauf pour les CSS et les impôts à l'échelon provincial et local (communiquées sur la base d'une année fiscale se terminant le 30 mars).

3 Le Burundi, le Soudan du Sud, la Tanzanie, le Kenya, le Rwanda et l'Ouganda font partie de la Communauté d'Afrique de l'Est (CAE).

4 Le Burkina Faso, le Bénin, la Côte d'Ivoire, la Guinée Bissau, le Mali, le Niger, le Sénégal et le Togo font partie de l'Union économique et monétaire ouest-africaine (UEMOA).

5 Dans la présente publication, les recettes issues des droits de douane et d'accise sont incluses dans les recettes fiscales du pays de la SACU qui les a collectées (Afrique du Sud), et les montants redistribués par le fonds commun des recettes de la SACU sont classés dans les tableaux des recettes non fiscales, sous la rubrique des recettes diverses (Botswana, Eswatini, Lesotho, Namibie).

6 Les informations figurant dans cette section ont été communiquées par les points de contact dans chaque pays participant (Burkina Faso, Cabo Verde, Égypte, Eswatini, Lesotho, Mali, Namibia et Rwanda) ou proviennent de (OCDE, 2021[49]) (Afrique du Sud, Maurice, Nigéria et Seychelles).

7 À la suite de la création de la Communauté d'Afrique de l'Est (CAE) en 2010, le Rwanda a adopté le cadre relatif aux tarifs extérieurs communs, ce qui s'est traduit par une baisse des recettes tirées des taxes sur les échanges commerciaux de 0.3 point en 2010.

8 Les Seychelles sont le seul pays à revenu élevé du présent rapport. C'est pourquoi les pays à revenu intermédiaire de la tranche supérieure (5 pays) et les pays à revenu élevé (1 pays) sont regroupés.

9 Les cinq pays membres de la SACU sont liés par un accord de partage des recettes qui prévoit l'application de droits de douane extérieurs communs et une répartition des droits de douane et d'accise perçus par les pays membres. Dans la présente publication, les recettes issues des droits de douane et d'accise sont incluses dans les recettes fiscales du pays de la SACU qui les a collectées (Afrique du Sud), et les montants redistribués par le fonds commun des recettes de la SACU sont classés dans les tableaux des recettes non fiscales, sous la rubrique des recettes diverses (Botswana, Eswatini, Lesotho, Namibie).

10 Les données concernant les cotisations de sécurité sociale ne sont pas disponibles pour la République du Congo, la République démocratique du Congo (avant 2012), Madagascar (avant 2011), la Namibie, l'Ouganda, la Sierra Leone, le Tchad et le Togo, et ne sont que partiellement disponibles au Cameroun et au Sénégal. Pour plus de précisions, se reporter aux tableaux par pays présentés dans le chapitre 5.

11 La base de données PINE ventile les taxes liées à l'environnement entre les quatre catégories suivantes :

- Énergie : cette catégorie couvre l'imposition des produits énergétiques tels que les combustibles fossiles et l'électricité, y compris les carburants utilisés pour les transports comme l'essence et le gazole. Toutes les taxes sur les émissions de CO_2 font partie de cette catégorie.
- Véhicules à moteur et services de transport : cette catégorie englobe les taxes sur les importations ou les ventes de matériel de transport, les taxes périodiques sur la propriété, l'immatriculation ou l'usage routier de véhicules à moteur et d'autres taxes liées aux transports.
- Ressources : cette catégorie inclut les taxes sur les industries extractives, l'exploitation forestière, la protection de la vie sauvage et les produits de la pêche.
- Pollution : cette catégorie comprend les taxes sur les substances appauvrissant la couche d'ozone, l'eau et les eaux usées, et la gestion des déchets.

12 La moyenne Asie-Pacifique est calculée pour 22 pays et non 28, car il n'a pas été possible d'identifier les recettes fiscales liées à l'environnement pour six pays faute de données.

13 Les données concernant Maurice proviennent des états financiers établis par le Bureau des statistiques de Maurice.

14 Les recettes fiscales infranationales intègrent les recettes de l'État, mais excluent celles des collectivités locales.

Références

AIE (2021), *Fossil Fuel Database*, *https://www.iea.org/data-and-statistics/data-product/fossil-fuel-subsidies-database* (consulté le 13 Septemeber 2022). [41]

AIE (2021), *Tracking the impact of fossil-fuel subsidies*, *https://www.iea.org/topics/energy-subsidies* (consulté le 13 September 2022). [42]

Akitoby, B. et al. (2019), *Case Studies in Tax Revenue Mobilization in Low-Income Countries*, *https://www.imf.org/en/Publications/WP/Issues/2019/05/14/Case-Studies-in-Tax-Revenue-Mobilization-in-Low-Income-Countries-46719* (consulté le 20 septembre 2021). [11]

BAfD/OCDE/PNUD (2015), *Perspectives économiques en Afrique 2015 : Développement territorial et inclusion spatiale*, Éditions OCDE, Paris, *https://doi.org/10.1787/aeo-2015-fr*. [44]

Banque mondiale (2022), *World Bank Country and Lending Groups*, *https://datahelpdesk.worldbank.org/knowledgebase/articles/906519* (consulté le 20 septembre 2021). [22]

Boisard, S., C. de Freitas et G. Hidouci (2014), *Renforcer les recettes fiscales locales pour financer le développement urbain en Afrique*, Fonds mondial pour le développement des villes (FMDV), Paris, *http://resolutionstofundcities.fmdv.net/Files/pub_afrique_fr.pdf*. [47]

Brautigam, D., O. Fjeldstad et M. Moore (2008), *Taxation and State-Building in Developing Countries: Capacity and Consent – ICTD, CMI*, *https://www.ictd.ac/publication/taxation-and-state-building-in-developing-countries-capacity-and-consent/* (consulté le 20 septembre 2021). [25]

CCNUCC (2021), *Stakeholders consultation in Senegal under the consultancy study on carbon tax*, *https://unfccc.int/about-us/regional-collaboration-centres/rcc-lome/stakeholders-consultation-in-senegal-under-the-consultancy-study-on-carbon-tax*. [38]

Chuku, C. et V. Ajayi (2021), *Accelerating Africa's green economy transition*, *https://www.brookings.edu/blog/africa-in-focus/2021/11/04/accelerating-africas-green-economy-transition/*. [43]

Coalition pour le leadership en matière de tarification du carbone (2018), *Launch of the PMR project on carbon taxation in côte d'ivoire*, *https://www.carbonpricingleadership.org/calendar/2018/7/12/launch-of-the-pmr-project-on-carbon-taxation-in-cte-divoire*. [37]

Commission européenne (2021), *Proposal for a regulation of the European Parliament and of the Council establishing a carbon border adjustment mechanism*, *https://ec.europa.eu/info/sites/default/files/carbon_border_adjustment_mechanism_0.pdf#page=194*. [39]

CUA/OCDE (2022), *Dynamiques du développement en Afrique 2022 : Des chaînes de valeur régionales pour une reprise durable*, Éditions OCDE, Paris/Commission de l'Union Africaine, Addis-Abeba, *https://doi.org/10.1787/f92ecd72-fr*. [23]

Economist Intelligence Unit (2018), *New income tax law comes into force*, *http://country.eiu.com/article.aspx?articleid=1636776147&Country=Rwanda&topic=Economy&subtopic=Fo_2* (consulté le 20 septembre 2021). [14]

EY (2020), *Namibia announces Economic Stimulus and Relief Package to mitigate impact of COVID-19*, *https://taxnews.ey.com/news/2020-0884-namibia-announces-economic-stimulus-and-relief-package-to-mitigate-impact-of-covid-19?uAlertID=Sd%2FG8rua1oj6%2Fl58EZ2AiA%3D%3D* (consulté le 29 August 2022). [7]

Fjeldstad, O.-H., G. Chambas et J.-F. Brun (2014), *Local government taxation in Sub-Saharan Africa: a review and an agenda for research*, n° 2 Chr. Michelsen Institute, Bergen, *http://www.cmi.no/publications/file/5098-local-government-taxation-in-sub-saharan-africa.pdf*. [45]

FMI (2022), *Base de données des Perspectives de l'économie mondiale, avril 2022*, *https://www.imf.org/en/Publications/WEO/weo-database/2022/April* (consulté le 20 septembre 2021). [6]

FMI (2022), « Inflation rate, average consumer prices », *Perspectives de l'économie mondiale*, *https://www.imf.org/external/datamapper/PCPIPCH@WEO/OEMDC/ADVEC/WEOWORLD* (consulté le 19 September 2022). [5]

FMI (2020), *The Development Path Less Travelled-The Experience of Rwanda*, *https://www.imf.org/en/Publications/Departmental-Papers-Policy-Papers/Issues/2020/08/17/The-Development-Path-Less-Travelled-The-Experience-of-Rwanda-49609*. [13]

FMI (2019), *World Economic Outlook - Frequently Asked Questions*, *https://www.imf.org/external/pubs/ft/weo/faq.htm#q4d* (consulté le 6 septembre 2019). [19]

FMI (2014), *Mauritius: 2014 Article IV Consultation - Staff Report*, FMI, *http://www.imf.org/external/pubs/ft/scr/2014/cr14107.pdf*. [46]

Gaspar, V. et al. (2019), *Fiscal Policy and Development: Human, Social, and Physical Investments for the SDGs*, *https://www.imf.org/en/Publications/Staff-Discussion-Notes/Issues/2019/01/18/Fiscal-Policy-and-Development-Human-Social-and-Physical-Investments-for-the-SDGs-46444* (consulté le 20 septembre 2021). [21]

Gwaindepi, A. (2021), « Domestic revenue mobilisation in developing countries: An exploratory analysis of sub-Saharan Africa and Latin America », *Journal of International Development*, vol. vol. 33/n° 2, pp. pp. 396-421, *https://doi.org/10.1002/JID.3528*. [24]

Institut de Recherches économiques et Fiscales (IREF) (2021), *Morocco's tax policy: the urgent need for tax system reform*, *https://en.irefeurope.org/publications/online-articles/article/morocco-s-tax-policy-the-urgent-need-for-tax-system-reform/*. [36]

Marten, M. et K. van Dender (2019), « The use of revenues from carbon pricing », *Documents de travail de l'OCDE sur la fiscalité*, n° 43, Éditions OCDE, Paris, *https://doi.org/10.1787/3cb265e4-en*. [28]

Ministère des Finances et du Budget du Tchad (2021), *Note de conjoncture sur le secteur pétrole au Quatrième trimestre 2020*, *https://observatoire.td/upload/publications/2021/NCSP%20Q4%202020%20%20VF.pdf* (consulté le 30 August 2022). [8]

Monkam, N. et M. Moore (2015), *How Property Tax Would Benefit Africa*, Africa Research Institute, *http://www.africaresearchinstitute.org/publications/property-tax-benefit-africa.* [48]

Moore, M., W. Prichard et O. Fjeldstad (2018), *Taxing Africa: Coercion, Reform and Development – ICTD*, Zed Books, *https://www.ictd.ac/publication/taxing-africa-coercion-reform-and-development/* (consulté le 20 septembre 2021). [9]

News Ghana (2022), *Botswana finalizing plans for introduction of carbon tax*, *https://newsghana.com.gh/botswana-finalizing-plans-for-introduction-of-carbon-tax/.* [35]

OCDE (2022), *base de données PINE*, *https://www.oecd.org/fr/environnement/outils-evaluation/environmental taxation.htm.* [30]

OCDE (2022), *Revenue Statistics in Asia and the Pacific 2022 : Strengthening Tax Revenues in Developing Asia*, Éditions OCDE, Paris, *https://doi.org/10.1787/db29f89a-en.* [1]

OCDE (2021), *Country tax measures in response to COVID-19 pandemic*, *https://www.oecd.org/tax/covid-19-tax-policy-and-other-measures.xlsm.* [49]

OCDE (2021), *Statistiques des recettes publiques 2021 : L'impact initial du COVID-19 sur les recettes fiscales de l'OCDE*, Éditions OCDE, Paris, *https://doi.org/10.1787/ed5596c6-fr.* [3]

OCDE (2020), « OECD analysis of budgetary support and tax expenditures 2020 country notes », *Inventory of Support Measures for Fossil Fuels database*, *http://www.oecd.org/fossil-fuels/data/.* [33]

OCDE (2020), *OECD Tax Policy Reviews: Seychelles 2020*, OECD Tax Policy Reviews, Éditions OCDE, Paris, *https://doi.org/10.1787/cba38d19-en.* [15]

OCDE (2019), *Tax Morale: What Drives People and Businesses to Pay Tax?*, Éditions OCDE, Paris, *https://doi.org/10.1787/f3d8ea10-en.* [18]

OCDE (2014), *Coopération pour le développement 2014 : Mobiliser les ressources au service du développement durable*, Éditions OCDE, Paris, *https://doi.org/10.1787/dcr-2014-fr.* [17]

OCDE (2005), *Glossary of statistical terms*, *https://stats.oecd.org/glossary/detail.asp?ID=6437.* [27]

OCDE/ATAF/CUA (2022), *Recettes fiscales en Afrique : Tableaux comparatifs*, Éditions OCDE, Paris. [4]

OCDE et al. (2022), *Revenue Statistics in Latin America and the Caribbean 2022*, Éditions OCDE, Paris, *https://doi.org/10.1787/58a2dc35-en-es.* [2]

OCDE/CUA/ATAF (2020), *Statistiques des recettes publiques en Afrique 2020 : 1990-2018*, Éditions OCDE, Paris, *https://doi.org/10.1787/14e1edb1-en-fr.* [10]

OCDE/FIT (2019), *Tax Revenue Implications of Decarbonising Road Transport: Scenarios for Slovenia*, Éditions OCDE, Paris, *https://doi.org/10.1787/87b39a2f-en.* [29]

OMS (2015), *Purchasing Power Parity 2005*, Organisation mondiale de la santé, *http://www.who.int/choice/costs/ppp/en/.* [20]

PwC (2019), *Sustaining the momemtum. Rwanda's 2019/20 National Budget Bulletin*, *https://www.pwc.com/rw/en/pdf/rwanda-budget-analysis-2019-20.pdf.* [12]

Reuters (2019), *South African carbon tax finally becomes law*, *https://www.reuters.com/article/us-safrica-carbontax/south-african-carbon-tax-finally-becomes-law-idUSKCN1SW0K6* (consulté le 6 septembre 2019). [32]

SACU (2020), *What is SACU?*, *http://www.sacu.int/about/what_is.html* (consulté le 10 septembre 2020). [16]

SARS (2020), *Tax statistics 2020*, *https://www.sars.gov.za/wp-content/uploads/Docs/TaxStats/2020/Tax-Statistics-2020.pdf.* [31]

SSA (2015), *Social Security Throughout the World: Africa*, SSA Publication Social Security Administration, Washington, D.C., *http://www.ssa.gov/policy/docs/progdesc/ssptw/2014-2015/africa/ssptw15africa.pdf.*[26]

Telquel (2022), *Maroc-UE : Ryad Mezzour dévoile ses mesures d'adaptation à la nouvelle taxe carbone*, *https://telquel.ma/instant-t/2022/06/03/maroc-ue-ryad-mezzour-devoile-ses-mesures-dadaptation-a-la-nouvelle-taxe-carbone_1770177/.* [40]

The conversation (2022), *South Africa's carbon tax rate goes up but emitters get more time to clean up*, *https://theconversation.com/south-africas-carbon-tax-rate-goes-up-but-emitters-get-more-time-to-clean-up-177834#:~:text=Carbon%20tax%20rate%20increase%3A%20The,until%20it%20reaches%20US%2420.* [34]

Chapter 2

Non-tax revenue trends, 2010-20

Chapitre 2

Tendances des recettes non fiscales, 2010-20

Chapter 2

Non-tax revenue trends, 2010-20

Introduction

A complete picture of public finances requires statistics that go beyond taxation, especially for many African countries that obtain substantial revenues in the form of grants or royalties from oil and minerals. *Revenue Statistics in Africa* collects statistics on both tax and non-tax revenues, non-tax revenues being government revenues that do not meet the OECD definition of taxation. Although there are some important methodological difference between tax and non-tax revenues, they need to be included in any accounting of a country's total financial resources.[1] This chapter provides cross-country comparisons of non-tax revenues for the countries in this publication.[2]

The main categories of non-tax revenues[3] reported as part of this project are:[4]

- grants from foreign governments or international organisations (budget aid, food aid, capital transfers, current transfers, project grants, programme grants, international debt relief, etc.);
- rents and royalties (such as oil or mining royalties);
- other property income (interest, dividends and other returns on government investment);
- sales of goods and services (which include some administrative fees);
- fines and penalties (including fines and penalties due to tax violations);
- miscellaneous and unidentified revenues (non-tax revenues that cannot be classified according to the other categories).

This edition of *Revenue Statistics in Africa* is the first to show revenue data from the period of the COVID-19 pandemic. The interpretation of non-tax revenue data in this chapter therefore requires some understanding of the extraordinary factors at play during this period, which have caused major fluctuation in many relevant indicators. Although COVID-19 has had a major impact on many social and economic indicators, this chapter will focus on those factors that have the clearest connection to the main sources of non-tax revenues for African countries, such as international grants and natural resource extraction.

Non-tax revenues as a percentage of GDP

In 2020, non-tax revenues as a percentage of GDP tended to be lower than tax revenues, but varied significantly among the 31 countries included in this publication. On average, the amount of non-tax revenue collected in each country was 48.4% of the amount collected in tax revenues. The non-tax revenues ranged from 35.1% of GDP in Lesotho to 0.5% of GDP in South Africa. Botswana, Lesotho, and the Republic of the Congo were the only countries for which non-tax revenues was higher than tax revenues in 2020 (Figure 2.1). This was also true for these three countries in most previous years thanks to high SACU revenues in Botswana and Lesotho, and high oil revenues in the Republic of the Congo. Equatorial Guinea's oil revenues in most years lead it to collect more non-tax revenues than tax revenues, but due to low oil prices, this wasn't true in 2015, 2019 and 2020.

Figure 2.1. **Total tax and non-tax revenue by country, 2020**

Percentage of GDP

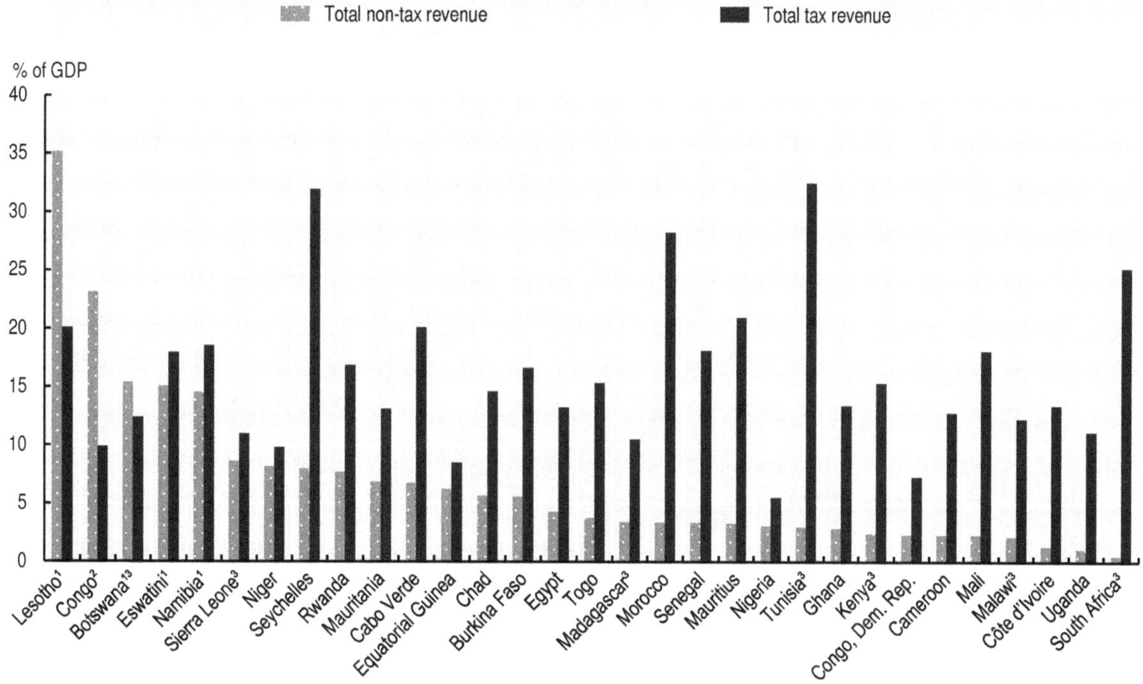

Notes: Non-tax revenue includes sub-national non-tax government revenues for Eswatini, Kenya, Mauritius and Morocco, the only countries for which such revenues are reported. In 2020, these represented, respectively, 2%, 14%, 4% and 38% of all non-tax revenue collected for each country. Mauritania, Nigeria and South Africa reported some local and regional taxes, but no local and regional non-tax revenues.

1. Non-tax revenues for Botswana, Eswatini, Lesotho and Namibia include funds from excises and customs duties collected by South Africa and then transferred to them through the Southern African Customs Union (SACU) revenue-sharing agreement.
2. Figures for grant revenues and oil revenues for the Republic of the Congo are those reported by the IMF in its April 2022 *World Economic Outlook* (IMF, 2022$_{[1]}$).
3. The GDP figures used to calculate the revenue-to-GDP ratios reported here were taken from the April 2022 edition of the World Economic Outlook (IMF, 2022$_{[1]}$). In the cases of Botswana, Equatorial Guinea, Kenya, Madagascar, Malawi, Seychelles, Tunisia and South Africa, these GDP differed from the figures used to calculate revenue-to-GDP ratios in the previous edition of *Revenue Statistics in Africa* by 3% or more.

The tax-to-GDP ratios and non-tax-to-GDP ratios need to be interpreted with caution for some countries due to incomplete data. See the country tables in Chapters 5 and 6 for further information.

Source: Table 4.1 in Chapter 4 and Table 6.1 in Chapter 6 and (OECD/ATAF/AUC, 2022$_{[2]}$), "Revenue Statistics in Africa: Comparative tables", *OECD Tax Statistics* (database), *http://dx.doi.org/10.1787/be755711-en.*

StatLink *https://stat.link/rt46wc*

While the Africa (31) average tax-to-GDP ratio rose between 2010 and 2020, average non-tax revenues have gone down substantially (Figure 2.2). After peaking in 2012 at 8.5% of GDP, average non-tax revenues dropped to 5.8% in 2016 before reaching 6.3% in 2019, and then rising by 0.6 percentage points to 6.8% in 2020. Much of the decline between 2012 and 2016 was driven by a drop in grant revenues and rents and royalties, which declined by 0.4 and 1.4 percentage points (p.p.) of GDP, respectively. Since 2016, both grants and rents and royalties have increased slightly, both rising by 0.3 p.p, but an even greater impact on non-tax revenues was caused by an increase in Southern African Customs Union (SACU) revenues in countries such as Lesotho and Eswatini.

Trends in non-tax revenues and tax revenues have generally been uncorrelated. During the period 2010-19, average tax revenues increased 1.8 p.p. of GDP, while non-tax revenues decreased by 1.7 p.p. yielding a net increase in all government revenues of 0.2 p.p. Between 2019 and 2020, the first year of the COVID-19 pandemic, these trajectories reversed. While tax revenues declined by 0.3 p.p., non-tax revenues increased by 0.6 p.p, yielding an average increase in government revenues during the pandemic of 0.3 p.p.

Figure 2.2. **Africa (31) average non-tax revenues, 2010-20**

Percentage of GDP

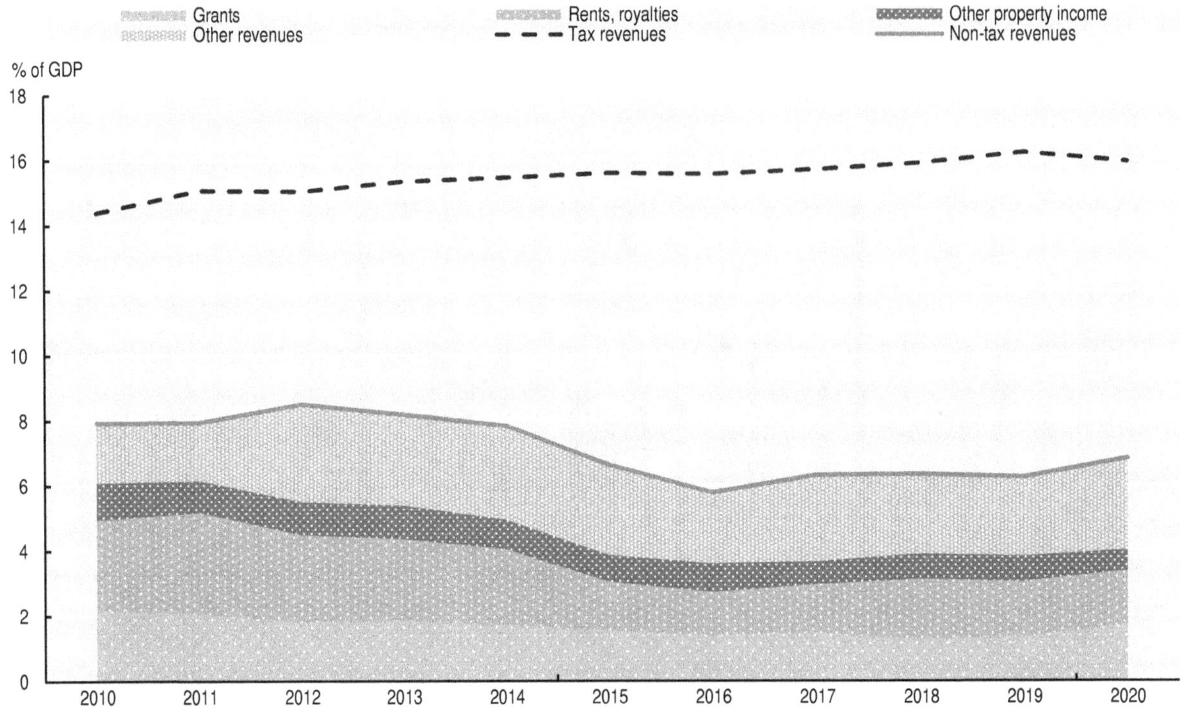

Source: Authors' calculations based on data from (OECD/ATAF/AUC, 2022[2]), "Revenue Statistics in Africa: Comparative tables", *OECD Tax Statistics* (database), *https://doi.org/10.1787/be755711-en*.

StatLink *https://stat.link/db7eay*

Figure 2.3 shows the contribution of each sub-category to total non-tax revenues for each country. Four distinct groups are apparent in the data:

- Eleven countries received a majority of their non-tax revenue in the form of grants in 2020 (in descending order, Sierra Leone, Niger, Rwanda, Chad, Burkina Faso, Togo, Madagascar, Senegal, Mali, Malawi, and Uganda). On average, these countries received grants revenue equivalent to 3.3% of GDP.
- Five countries received most of their non-tax revenues from rents and royalties (in descending order, the Republic of the Congo, Mauritania, Equatorial Guinea, Nigeria and Cameroon). For all these countries, oil royalties provided the majority of non-tax revenues. On average, rents and royalties for these countries was equivalent to 6.4% of GDP.
- Botswana, Eswatini, Lesotho and Namibia, the four neighbours of South Africa that belong to SACU, received substantial non-tax revenues in terms of transfers from the SACU Common Revenue Pool (Box 2.2). On average, these countries collected non-tax revenues outside of grants and rents and royalties equivalent to 15.7% of GDP.
- For the remaining 11 countries, neither grants, rents and royalties nor SACU revenues constituted a majority of revenues. The main alternative sources of non-tax revenues for these countries included: interest and dividends for Kenya and Tunisia; fees for goods and services for Ghana; and miscellaneous and unallocated revenues for Egypt and Morocco. Grants were the largest source of non-tax revenues for Cabo Verde, Côte d'Ivoire, the Democratic Republic of the Congo, Mauritius, and Seychelles, but were less than 50% of non-tax revenues. Similarly, rents and royalties were the largest source of non-tax revenues for South Africa, but were less than half of its non-tax revenues.

Figure 2.3. **Structure of non-tax revenues by country, 2020**

Percentage of GDP

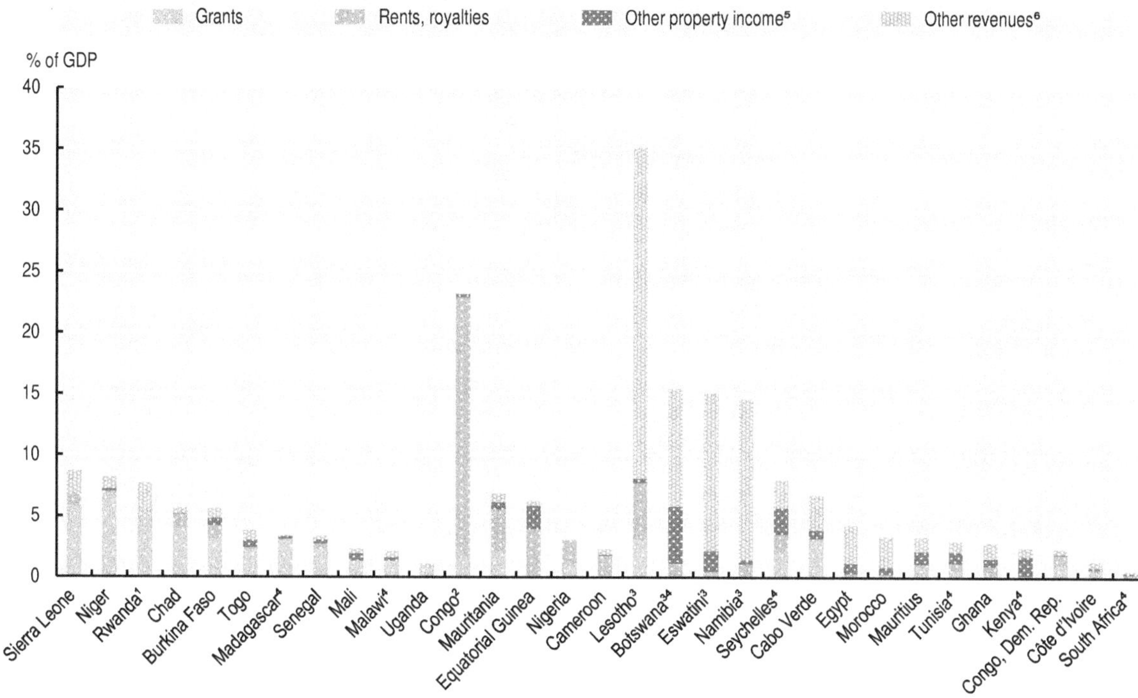

Note: Data include sub-national government non-tax revenues for Eswatini, Kenya, Mauritius and Morocco.

1. For Rwanda, non-tax revenues aside from grants were not disaggregated in the data and are therefore classified as miscellaneous and unidentified revenues.
2. Figures reported here represent mainly grant revenue and oil revenue obtained from the IMF's April 2022 *World Economic Outlook* (IMF, 2022[1]) classified as rents and royalties.
3. For Botswana, Eswatini, Lesotho and Namibia, "Other revenues" include funds from excises and customs duties collected by South Africa and then transferred to these countries through the Southern African Customs Union (SACU) revenue-sharing agreement.
4. The GDP figures used to calculate the revenue-to-GDP ratios reported here were taken from the April 2022 edition of the World Economic Outlook (IMF, 2022[1]). In the cases of Botswana, Kenya, Madagascar, Malawi, Seychelles, Tunisia and South Africa, these GDP differed from the figures used to calculate revenue-to-GDP ratios in the previous edition of *Revenue Statistics in Africa* by 3% or more.
5. Interest, dividends, etc.
6. Sales, fines, SACU revenues, etc.

See the footnotes to Figure 2.1 and country tables in Chapters 5 and 6 for further information.

Source: Table 6.2 in Chapter 6 and (OECD/ATAF/AUC, 2022[2]), "Revenue Statistics in Africa: Comparative tables", *OECD Tax Statistics* (database), *http://dx.doi.org/10.1787/be755711-en*.

StatLink https://stat.link/0v63ho

COVID-19 and non-tax revenues in 2020

The economic impact of the COVID-19 crisis made 2020 an exceptional year for the African countries in the publication. Figure 2.4 shows the changes in the non-tax revenues and other indicators between 2019 and 2020, in comparison with the highest and lowest annual changes recorded over the previous ten years. Real GDP declined by 3.3% on average in 2020, whereas since 2000 the average real GDP growth for these countries never went below 2.4%. For 24 of the countries in this publication, real GDP declined more than in any year over the previous decade.

Despite the unprecedented nature of the COVID-19 crisis, Africa's non-tax revenues remained more in line with recent history than tax revenues and other macro-economic indicators. Among the 31 African countries, 19 recorded an increase in non-tax revenues between 2019 and 2020 (in local currency) and 12 recorded a decrease; in all but four cases, these changes were within the range of annual changes recorded over the previous decade.

The fact that 2020 was less of an outlier in terms of non-tax revenues reflects not only the high variability of these revenues but also the consequences of the pandemic. Lower fuel prices reduced petroleum royalties but the health crisis inspired an increase in foreign aid. Eleven African countries received a larger increase in ODA in 2020 than in any other year since 2010. Three of the four biggest oil and gas exporters among the countries in this publication over the last decade – the Republic of the Congo, Equatorial Guinea, and Nigeria – all saw major declines in revenues from oil and gas exports in 2020 but none of these declines were larger than they had experienced in the previous decade, which included a major drop of almost 50% in oil prices between 2014 and 2015.

Revenue-to-GDP ratios should be treated with caution in light of the major shocks to both volumes and prices in 2020. The revenue-to-GDP ratio is an indicator of choice for international and annual comparisons of public revenues, since it accounts for inflation and the differences in the size of economies. However, as explained in Box 1.1 in Chapter One, major fluctuations in the numerator of this ratio are not always aligned with fluctuations in the denominator. Between 2019 and 2020, the average GDP for African countries increased by 0.2% in nominal terms. This change in GDP accounts for 27% of the change of 0.6 p.p. in the non-tax revenue-to-GDP ratios between 2019 and 2020.

Figure 2.4. **Change in selected indicators 2019-20, compared to range of annual changes between 2010 and 2019, by country**

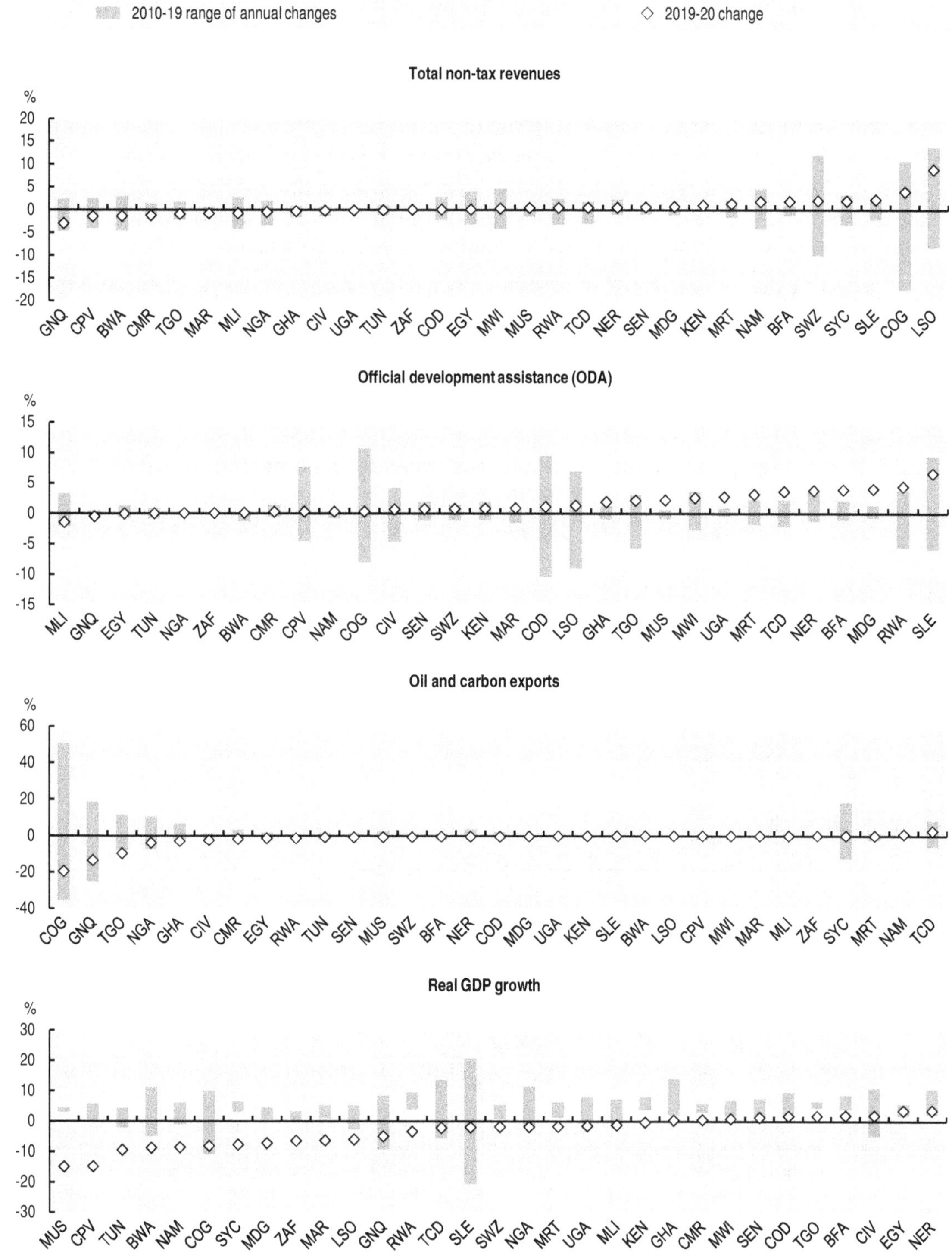

Note: The top of the green bars correspond to the maximum annual value, and the bottom of the green bars correspond to the minimum annual values attained between the years 2010 and 2019, inclusive.

Source: Authors' calculations based on data from (OECD/ATAF/AUC, 2022[2]), "Revenue Statistics in Africa: Comparative tables", *OECD Tax Statistics* (database), *https://doi.org/10.1787/be755711-en*; OECD Development Assistance Committee (OECD-DAC, 2022[3]) for Official Development Assistance figures; BACI International Trade Database at the Product-Level from (CEPII, 2022[4]) for figures on oil and carbon exports; and the April 2022 edition of the World Economic Outlook (IMF, 2022[1]).

StatLink *https://stat.link/s7q9ba*

Figure 2.5 shows changes in non-tax revenues between 2019 and 2020 for grants, rents and royalties, and other non-tax revenues. For comparison, the change in non-tax revenues as a percentage of GDP is charted alongside the nominal change in total non-tax revenues as percentage of 2019 GDP (the white diamonds on the chart). Using the same denominator for both years allows for the correct identification of the direction of change in revenues. For example, in the Republic of the Congo, non-tax revenue as a percentage of GDP was higher in 2020 than in 2019, but this was mostly due to a decrease of 21% in its GDP. Due to a drop in oil prices, non-tax revenues for the Republic of the Congo in nominal terms were actually lower in 2020 than they were in 2019. For 18 of the countries in this publication, calculating the change in non-tax revenues as a percentage of 2019 GDP results in a higher number than calculating the percentage point change in non-tax revenue to GDP between 2019 and 2020.

Reflecting the increased level of international aid in response to the pandemic and the reduced demand for fuel, grant revenues tended to increase between 2019 and 2020 while rents and royalties decreased in a number of countries. On average, grants increased by an amount equivalent to 0.4% of GDP in 2020, while property income decreased an amount equivalent to 0.2% of GDP in 2020, due to lower revenues from natural resources.

Figure 2.5. **Percentage point increases in non-tax revenues as a percentage of GDP, 2019-20**

Percentage of GDP

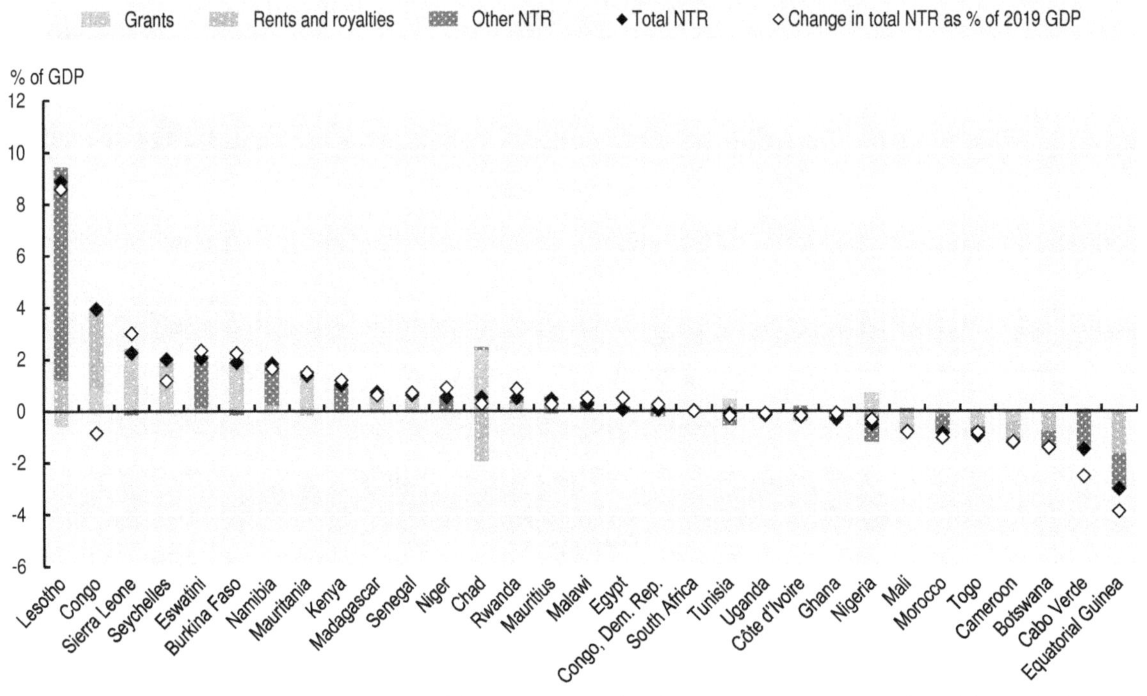

Note: The black diamonds correspond to the sum of the percentage point changes in grants, rents and royalties and other non-tax revenues between 2019 and 2020. The white diamonds show the ratio of the total non-tax revenues between 2019 and 2020 over the 2019 GDP. The white diamonds the change between 2019 and 2020 revenue-to-GDP ratios when the effect of GDP change is removed.

Source: Authors' calculations based on data from (OECD/ATAF/AUC, 2022[2]), "Revenue Statistics in Africa: Comparative tables", *OECD Tax Statistics* (database), *https://doi.org/10.1787/be755711-en*.

StatLink *https://stat.link/zh7812*

Between 2019 and 2020, the biggest driver of change in non-tax revenues for 10 countries was an increase in grants. In Chad, a 2.4 p.p. increase in grants revenue as a percentage of GDP was almost entirely offset by a concurrent decrease in rents and royalties of 2 p.p. of GDP. For 14 countries, the biggest driver of change in non-tax revenues was changes in non-tax revenues other than grants, rents and royalties. This includes increases in SACU revenues for Lesotho, Eswatini and Namibia. The increase in SACU revenues for Lesotho of 8.3 p.p alone accounted for almost half of the average increase in the average non-tax revenue in Africa. As shown later in the chapter, such a large fluctuation in SACU payments is not out of line with what has been experienced by Lesotho and Eswatini in the past.

Grants

Revenue Statistics in Africa includes countries that receive substantial grant revenues alongside some for which grants are negligible. On average, grant revenues for the 31 African countries in this publication amounted to 1.7% of GDP in 2020, up from 1.4% of GDP the previous year, an increase of 0.4 p.p. of GDP. In 2020, 10 countries received grant revenues amounting to less than 0.5% of GDP (Figure 2.6). All of these countries were middle income countries, according to the World Bank's classification based on gross national incomes (World Bank, 2022[5]). On the other hand, all but one low income country covered by this report (Uganda) received grants amounting to more than 1% of GDP.

Figure 2.6. **Grants by country, 2020 and 2019**

Percentage of GDP

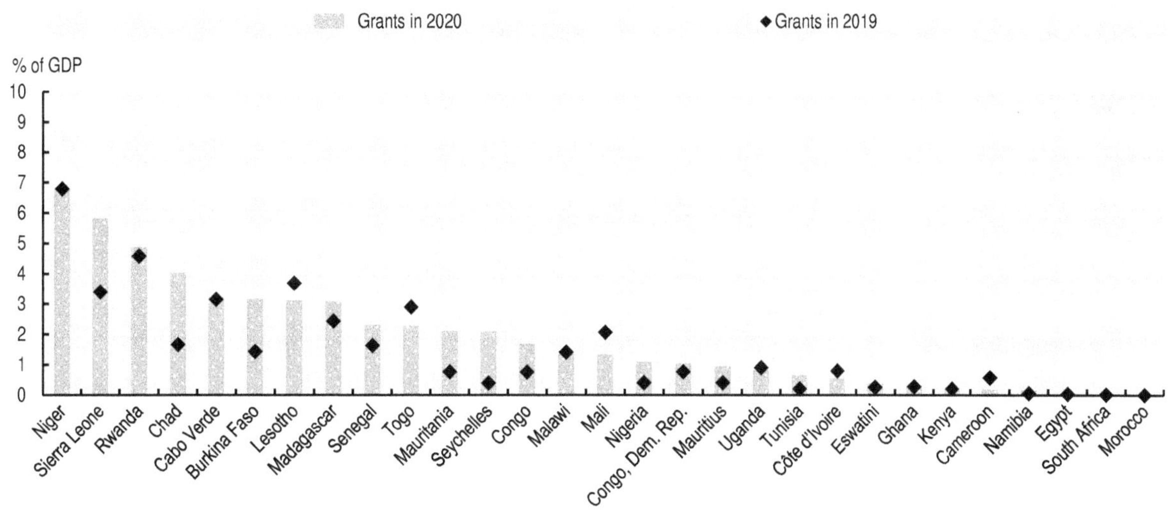

Source: Tables 6.2 and 6.3 in Chapter 6 and (OECD/ATAF/AUC, 2022[2]), "Revenue Statistics in Africa: Comparative tables", *OECD Tax Statistics* (database), *http://dx.doi.org/10.1787/be755711-en*.

StatLink *https://stat.link/mjvqsz*

Figure 2.7 presents grants as a percentage of GDP received by countries in this publication and their gross national income (GNI) per capita. The figure has an empty upper right-hand quadrant as higher income African countries receive proportionately lower grant revenues. However, many countries occupy the bottom left quadrant of the graph, as there are countries that receive relatively low levels of grant income despite having lower incomes. For example, Burkina Faso, Rwanda and Uganda had GNI per capita in 2020 between USD 770 and USD 830 but they reported grants as a percentage of GDP in that year ranging from 0.8% (Uganda) and 1.4% (Burkina Faso) to 4.9% (Rwanda).

Figure 2.7. **Grants as a percentage of GDP and GNI per capita by country, 2020**

Percentage of GDP

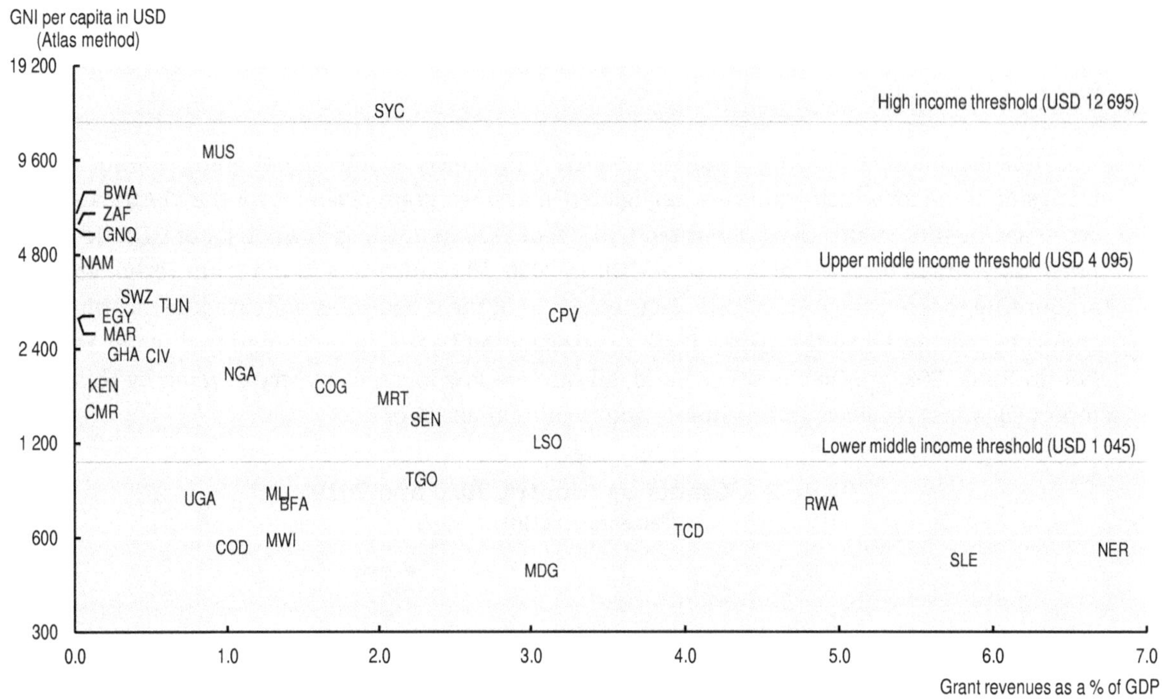

Note: GNI figures are converted to USD using the World Bank Atlas Method.

Source: Table 6.2 in Chapter 6, and World Bank *World Development Indicators* (database) (World Bank, 2022[6]) and (OECD/ATAF/AUC, 2022[2]), "Revenue Statistics in Africa: Comparative tables", *OECD Tax Statistics* (database), *http://dx.doi.org/10.1787/be755711-en.*

StatLink *https://stat.link/la9dhm*

Grant revenues and foreign aid are similar concepts, although in practice it is difficult to align aid statistics, as reported by donor countries, with the grant revenues reported by recipient countries, due to data, methodological and conceptual issues.

- Grant revenues have some overlap with official development assistance (ODA), as defined by the OECD Development Assistance Committee (DAC).[5] Grants covered by this publication focus on revenues received by countries from foreign governments and international organisations. ODA is a measure of donor countries' efforts to support development in low and middle income countries. ODA not only covers flows captured under "grants" in this publication (budget aid, food aid, capital transfers, current transfers, project grants, programme grants, international debt relief, etc.), but also encompasses concessional loans, in-kind technical assistance, in-donor administrative costs, in-donor refugee costs and scholarships, as well as other activities that do not generate a (net) revenue flow to the country. The volume of ODA provided by a donor to a given country will thus be different from – and usually higher than – the volume of grants reported by the recipient country in *Revenue Statistics*.
- Statistics collected by the DAC on ODA flows to African countries include public flows from all members of the DAC and some countries outside the DAC, as well as multilateral organisations such as the World Bank, the IMF and the UN. Statistics on development co-operation provided by some large non-OECD economies, such as Brazil, China, India, Indonesia and Russia, are not included (OECD, 2022[7]).

Figure 2.8 shows that ODA payments to Africa are far greater than the amount that is paid directly to African governments, due in part to the presence of development programmes that receive international funds that are not intermediated by African governments. Although the countries receiving the most net ODA tend to receive the most grant revenues, the relationship is not linear and there are notable outliers, such as Malawi, whose net ODA as a percentage of GDP of 13.8% far exceeds all other African countries, but whose grant revenues as a percentage of GDP trail behind 13 African countries.

Figure 2.8. **Grants and net official development assistance received, 2020**

Percentage of GDP

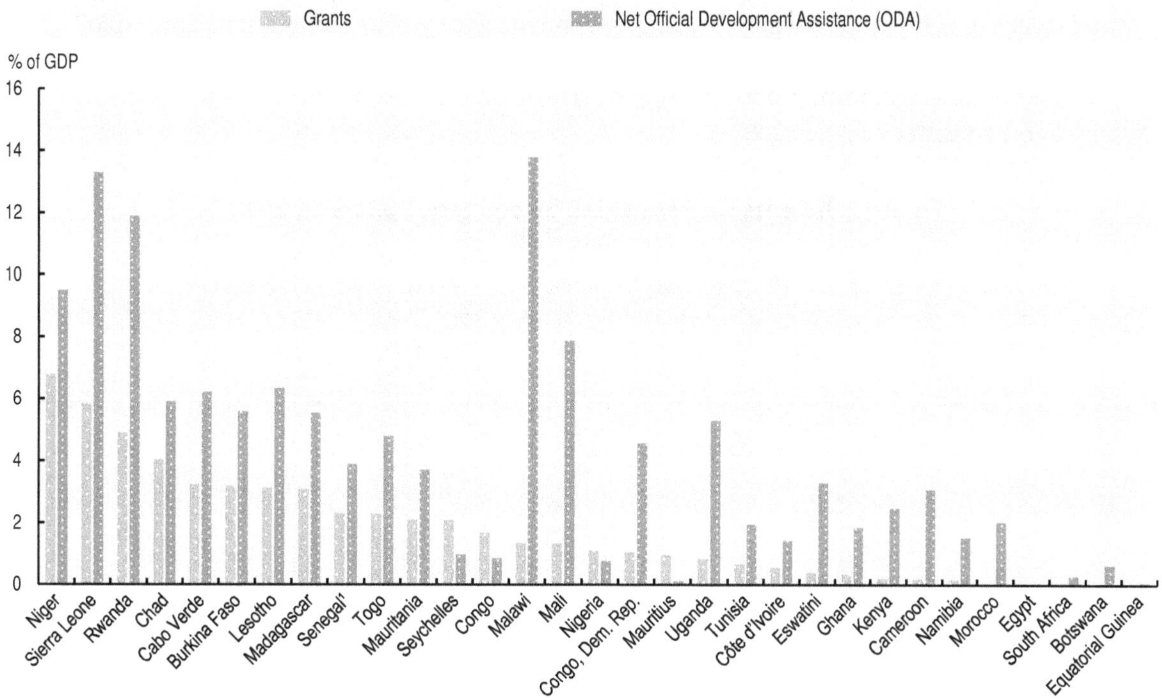

Note: Figures for net ODA include donations from the 31 member countries of the OECD Development Assistance Committee (DAC), the 20 non-DAC countries, as well as multilateral institutions, and private donations. Some major donor countries, such as Brazil, China, India, Indonesia, and Russia and are not yet accounted for in these data.

Source: Table 6.2 in Chapter 6 and OECD Development Assistance Committee (OECD-DAC, 2022[3]) for the ODA data and (OECD/ATAF/AUC, 2022[2]), "Revenue Statistics in Africa: Comparative tables", *OECD Tax Statistics* (database), *http://dx.doi.org/10.1787/be755711-en.*

StatLink *https://stat.link/w6x4rt*

Countries relying on grant revenues often face sudden drops in grants from one year to the next. Nine countries in this publication faced a single-year drop in grant revenues of at least 2 p.p. of GDP in at least one year between 2010 and 2020; for six of these, it was over 3 p.p. Malawi had grants amounting to over 7.1% of GDP in 2013. They dropped by 65% in US dollar terms in 2014, the year of the CashGate Scandal (VOANews, 2013[8]). In total, 13 countries among the 31 participating in this publication registered a one-year drop in grant revenues equivalent to at least 1.0% of GDP over the decade.

Average grant revenues for the countries in this publication declined from 2.2% of GDP in 2010 to 1.3% in 2018, but have since rebounded to 1.7% in 2020. Changes in grant revenues often depend on circumstances unique to the country. Egypt, for example, saw a spike in grant revenues in 2014 following the normalisation of international relations after its internal political crisis, while Mali saw its grant revenues disappear in 2012 with the outbreak of the Mali War before resuming the following year.

Resource revenues and other property income

One of the most important sources of non-tax revenues for governments originates from their status as the owner of property, especially land. Such revenues are reported as property income in *Revenue Statistics in Africa* and encompass various forms of income (Figure 2.9).

Rents and royalties are revenues generated from property the government owns, usually by prospecting and extracting non-renewable resources from government land or from harvesting government-owned farms and forests. Interest and dividends are returns on government-owned investments in corporations. In general, royalties from oil and minerals are kept distinct from other forms of investment income, but the issue can become complicated. Many African governments create public corporations that manage oil revenues or maintain revenue-sharing agreements with private corporations that exploit these natural resources. The classification of such funds is not always clear. For example, in Botswana, a significant proportion of property income comes from companies investing in diamond extraction (Box 2.2).

Figure 2.9. **Rents and royalties by country, 2020 and 2019**

Percentage of GDP

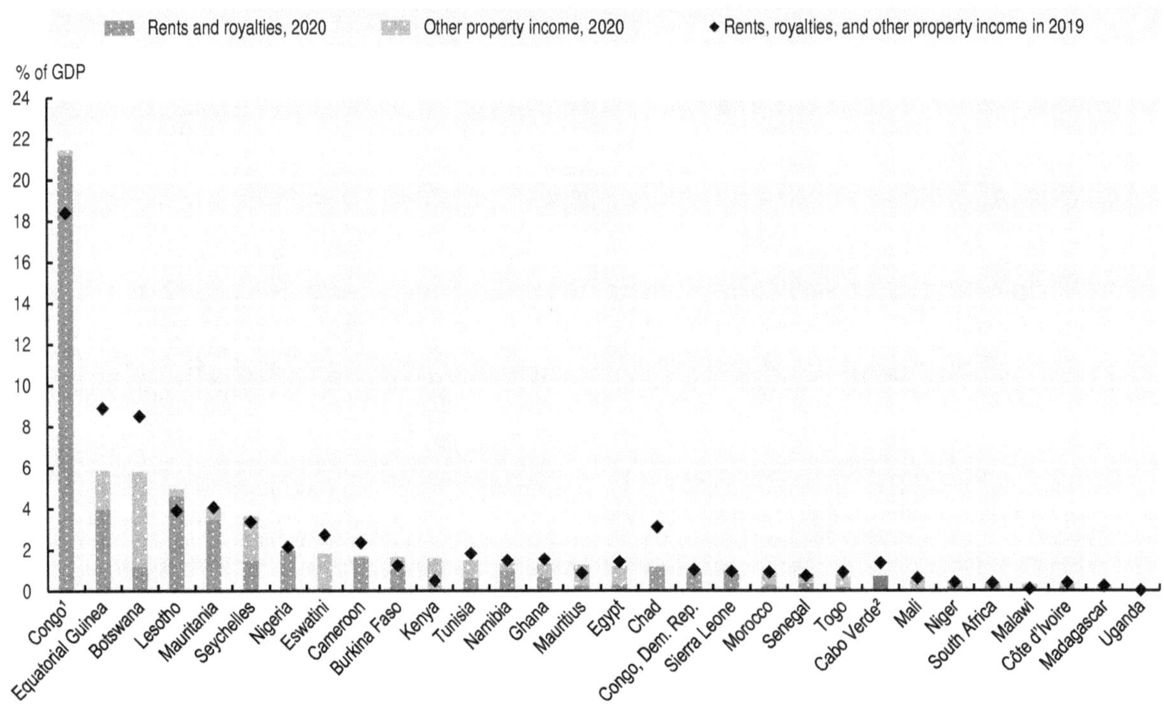

Note: Rwanda is excluded as the data are not available.

1. Property income for Congo was lower in 2020 than it was in 2019. However, due to the decrease of 21% in the Republic of the Congo's GDP, the ratio of property income to GDP was higher in 2020 than 2019.
2. Cabo Verde property income is not disaggregated.

Source: Authors' calculations based on Tables 6.5-6.35 and Table 4.17 and (OECD/ATAF/AUC, 2022[2]), "Revenue Statistics in Africa: Comparative tables", *OECD Tax Statistics* (database), *http://dx.doi.org/10.1787/be755711-en*.

StatLink *https://stat.link/qhbpda*

Revenues from natural resources

Rents and royalties among the 29 countries for which this information was available was equivalent to 1.7% of GDP in 2020, only 0.04 p.p. lower than the ratio for rents and royalties to GDP in 2019. Most of these revenues consisted of oil revenues. In 2020, 61.9% of total rents and royalties in USD were specifically reported as oil revenues (royalties and revenues from revenue-sharing agreements with oil companies), which accounted for a majority of rents and royalties for Cameroon, Chad, the Republic of the Congo, Egypt, Equatorial Guinea and Nigeria. Meanwhile, minerals were the source of most rents and royalties for Botswana, Burkina Faso, the Democratic Republic of the Congo, Ghana, Namibia, Niger, Sierra Leone and Uganda. Fishing accounted for 65% of all revenue recorded as rents and royalties in Seychelles and for 63% in Mauritania in 2020. In Mauritania in 2020, fishing rents were USD 192 million or 2.4% of GDP. Nearly all rents and royalties recorded here were resource-related, whether it was from mining, fishing or forestry. Only 0.1% of rents and royalties came from land rent.

Natural resource revenues tend to be a highly volatile source of financing. Five countries (Chad, the Republic of the Congo, Equatorial Guinea, Mauritania and Nigeria) generated rents and royalties equivalent to more than 5% of GDP in at least one of the most recent ten years and they all registered at least one year-on-year decrease in rents and royalties as a percentage of GDP of over 33%. Chad and the Republic of the Congo both saw at least one year with a decrease of over 64%.

Box 2.1. **Natural resources and public finances**

There are various mechanisms[6] by which natural resources generate revenues or savings for government. Rents and royalties are the most direct means of deriving revenue from natural resource wealth. The government charges fees to companies and individuals in exchange for the right to access government lands. It does this in its capacity as landowner and these fees are generally decided through negotiation. These are recorded under property income. Payment for services provided by the government is another source of non-tax revenue paid for by businesses in the primary sector. This can include, for example, payments for environmental inspections or for the construction of infrastructure, or, in the case of Mauritius, payment for weather data and maps. These are recorded under sales of goods and services.

- Public ownership (full or partial) of a corporation that exploits natural resources on the government's behalf results in government revenues in the form of profits and dividends. These are recorded under property income. For example, the revenues collected by the government of Botswana from dividends it receives from its 50% stake in Debswana, the company that operates the main diamond mines in Botswana, are recorded under property income (MiningTechnology, 2020[9]).
- Taxes targeting natural resource exploitation could be introduced, such as an excise tax on the sale of materials extracted from public lands or a tax on mining that targets the activity, rather than the individual or company exploiting natural resources. These, too, will be recorded as taxes. Such taxes on mining exist in Niger and Senegal, which impose taxes on mining activities that are classified in *Revenue Statistics* under other taxes on goods and services.
- Companies and individuals exploiting natural resources are generally subject to the same taxes (such as income taxes and value-added taxes) as other economic entities. Revenues from these general taxes will be included in government financial statements but not necessarily attributed to sectors exploiting natural resources.
- Companies and individuals may use some of the wealth they obtain from natural resource extraction to build infrastructure or provide services. Where this satisfies demand for public investment or services, it could result in savings on government expenditure, but it would not be recorded as revenue. In some cases, as a condition for access to publicly-owned natural resources, governments may demand that companies and individuals provide certain services, for example paying for at least part of the cost of constructing and maintaining roads to mines. An example of this was mining companies participating in a proposed 3 000 km rail link between Benin, Burkina Faso, Niger, Côte d'Ivoire, Ghana, Nigeria and Togo (CNN, 2015[10]).

The total value of oil, coal and gas exports from *Revenue Statistics in Africa* countries has been mainly determined by changes in the price of the commodities rather than in the volume of exports. With or without Nigerian rents and royalties, which, since 2010, have amounted to between 45% and 70% of total rents and royalties collected by African governments, the evolution of African rents and royalties tracks the international crude oil price.

The sudden drop in oil prices in 2015 led to a fall in the value of oil exports from Africa, which translated directly into a decline in revenues (Figure 2.10). At the same time, exports of ore, raw metals, diamonds and other minerals have grown steadily over the past decade and have surpassed the value of coal, oil and gas exports. However, African countries have not been generating rents and royalties from these other minerals to the same extent as they have been able to collect rents from the oil and gas industry.

Figure 2.10. **Rents and royalties and commodity exports for *Revenue Statistics in Africa* countries, 2010-20**

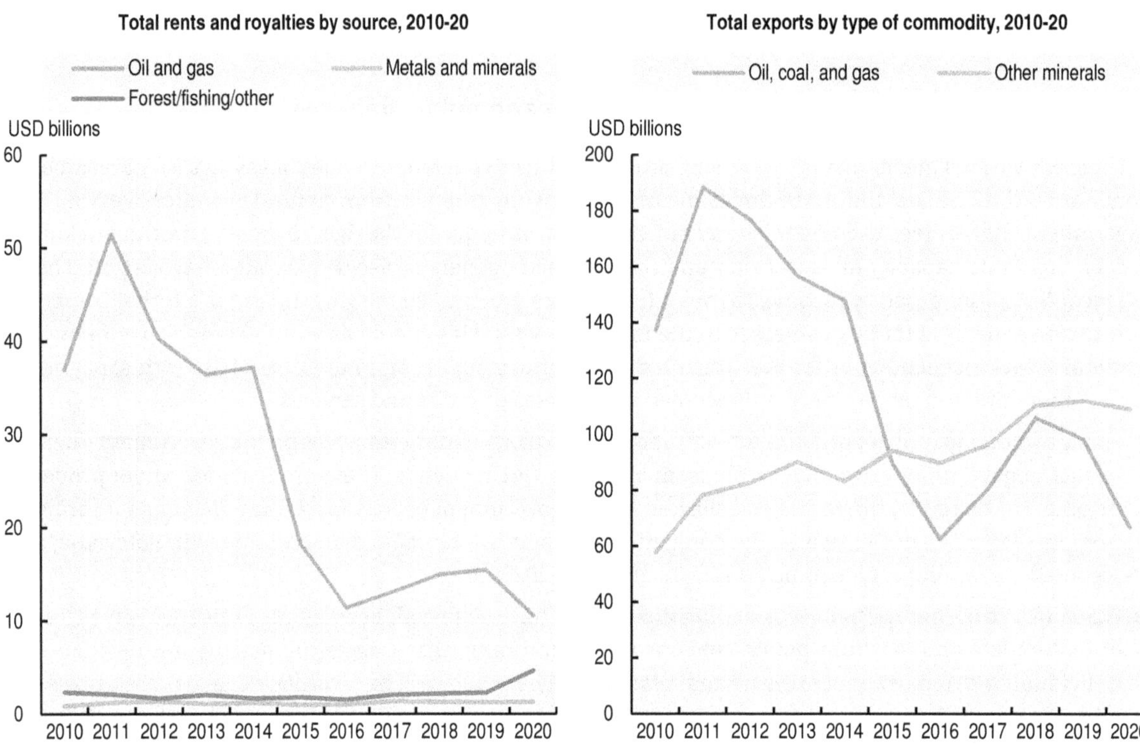

Source: Authors' calculations based on data from BACI International Trade Database at the Product-Level from (CEPII, 2022[4]) for figures on oil and carbon exports; and the April 2022 edition of the World Economic Outlook (IMF, 2022[1]) and (OECD/ATAF/AUC, 2022[2]), "Revenue Statistics in Africa: Comparative tables", *OECD Tax Statistics* (database), *http://dx.doi.org/10.1787/be755711-en*.

StatLink *https://stat.link/vcf48s*

The COVID-19 pandemic introduced both supply and demand shocks, which impacted the prices of basic commodities. Oil prices were particularly affected (Figure 2.11). Crude oil dropped to USD 23 per barrel in April 2020, the lowest price recorded since 2002, but quickly stabilised, yielding an annual oil price in 2020 of USD 42.3 per barrel that was 34% lower than the price in 2019 and equivalent to oil prices in 2016. However, many commodities increased in price during the pandemic. The price index for non-energy commodities increased between 2019 and 2020, reflecting higher prices for agricultural commodities and metals. Among the metals that increased in price were copper and gold, the main metals produced by the countries in *Revenue Statistics in Africa*, as well as platinum, silver and iron ore. Minerals that decreased in price were aluminium, lead, tin, nickel, zinc and potassium chloride.

Figure 2.11. **Prices of key commodities, before and during the COVID-19 pandemic**

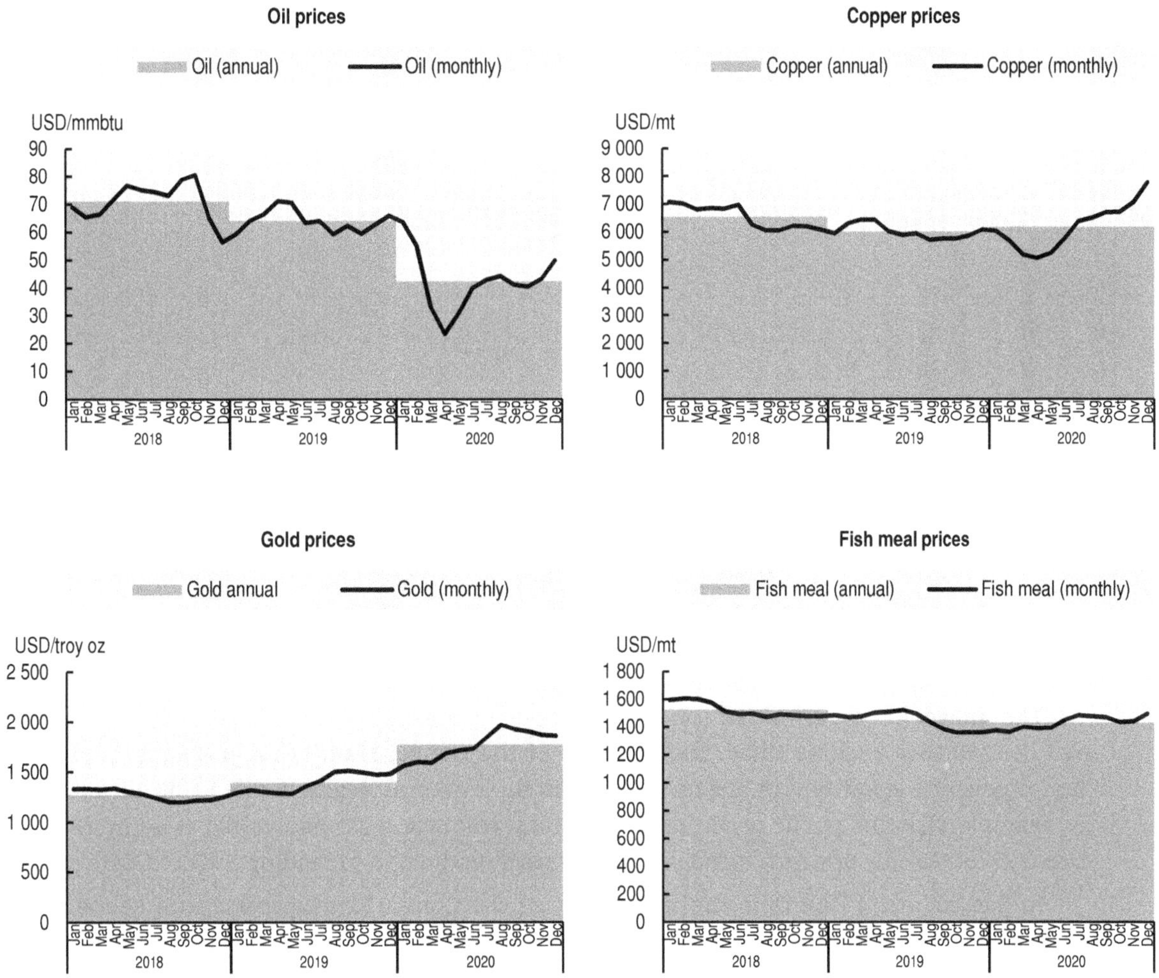

Note: The oil price reported here is the price of Brent, Dubai, and West Texas Intermediate Crude.
Source: World Bank Commodity Price Data (The Pink Sheet) (World Bank, 2022[11]).

StatLink https://stat.link/8zno6s

There is a great deal of variation in the size and type of natural resource endowments in African countries. The contribution of this natural wealth to countries' GDP also varies, as does its impact on government budgets. For example, according to World Bank estimates of the contribution of natural resources to economic output (Figure 2.12), the Republic of the Congo (mostly oil), the Democratic Republic of the Congo (mostly minerals), and Equatorial Guinea (mostly oil) were the three countries for which underground natural resources contributed at least 17% of GDP to economic output in 2020 (World Bank, 2022[6]).[7]

Figure 2.12. **Estimated natural resource extraction, 2020**

Percentage of GDP

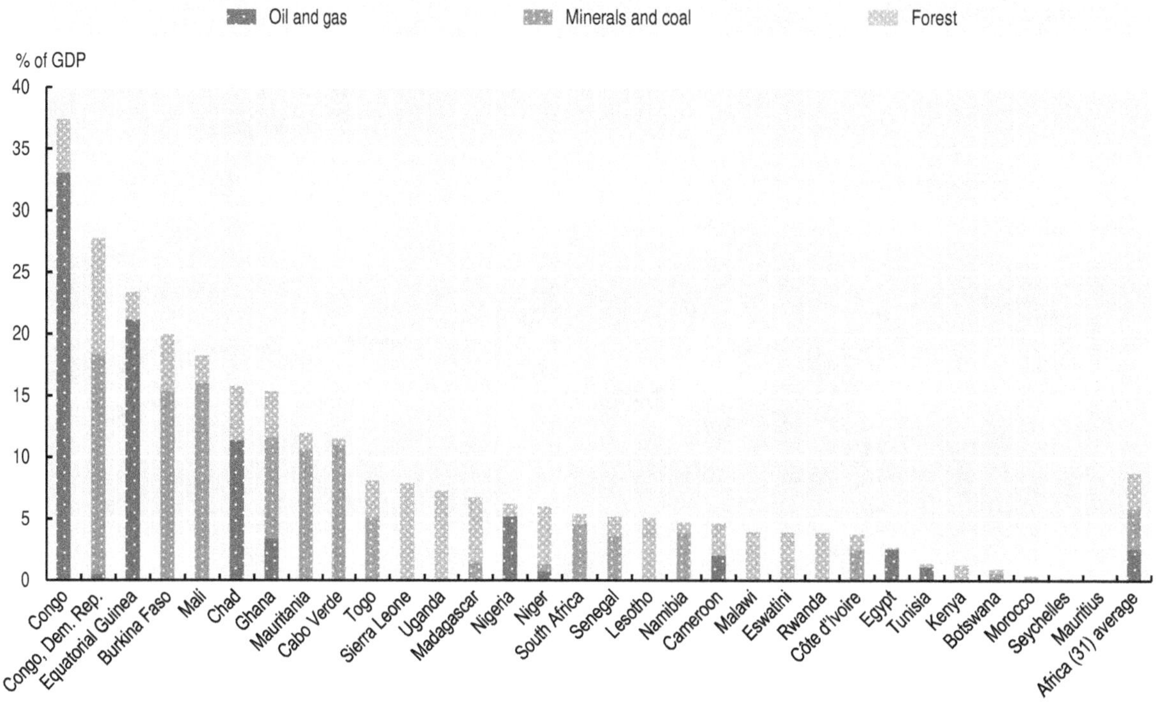

Source: (World Bank, 2022[6]), *World Development Indicators* (database) for estimates of the total value of natural resource production in each country.

StatLink https://stat.link/98rud7

The impact of countries' natural resource endowment on public finances also varies greatly. Countries such as Chad, the Republic of the Congo, Mauritania and Equatorial Guinea generate significant public revenues from their natural wealth, while South Africa, for example, reported public revenues from natural resource rents equivalent to no more than 0.3% of GDP despite its natural resource wealth production exceeding 5.4% of GDP.

In five countries (the Democratic Republic of the Congo, Madagascar, Sierra Leone, Uganda and Lesotho), wealth generated by forests exceeded 5% of GDP but did not contribute significantly to national revenues. Although countries such as Cameroon and Niger collected some royalties from logging, forest revenues were a small part of the non-tax revenues for the countries in question.

Other non-tax revenues

Certain countries generate substantial non-tax revenues from the normal operations of government. These revenues can be divided into sales of goods and services, fines and penalties, and miscellaneous and unidentified non-tax revenues. The challenges in compiling non-tax revenues outlined in Box 2.1 are often encountered in these kinds of revenues, since they are typically not collected by tax administrations and are often not defined by legislation. They might not even be captured by government budgets.

For all these categories of revenues, there can be arguments about the degree to which they are unrequited or compulsory, and therefore whether they are more properly classified as taxes. The question of which administrative fees are taxes and which are not is discussed in Annexes A and B. However, this is not always clear for the question of fines and penalties.

Institutions and governments that have less authority, and thus less power to collect taxes, may rely more on these kinds of non-tax revenues. This means that non-tax revenues collected by local government may be underestimated.

Sales of goods and services and administrative fees

Governments produce goods and services both as a market- and as a non-market participant. As a market participant, governments sometimes provide goods and services that can also be obtained from private companies (such as food or transportation). At the same time, they also provide services in the course of administering programmes and executing laws that are unique to the function of government. Fees charged for these non-market services are generally classified as administrative fees.

Administrative fees are often difficult to classify since they occupy a grey area between payments for services (which are non-tax revenues) and compulsory unrequited payments collected during government operations (which are taxes).[8] Court fees and fees for driver's licences, passports, patent registrations and marriage certificates tend to be classified as non-tax revenues. When administrative fees are classified as taxes, they are typically assigned to one of the following categories:

- 4400 Taxes on financial and capital transactions (for example, taxes on sales of land);
- 5200 Taxes on use of goods and performing activities (for example hunting licences, vehicle registrations);
- 6000 Other taxes (for example, sales of fiscal stamps, where stamps are used to pay for taxes and administrative fees).

Five countries generated non-tax revenues from sales of goods and services and administrative fees equivalent to at least 1% of GDP in 2020 (Figure 2.13): Cabo Verde (2.3% of GDP), Egypt (1.3% of GDP), Ghana (1.2% of GDP), Morocco (1.2% of GDP) and Seychelles (2.0% of GDP). With the addition of the three tax categories listed above, these revenues rise to more than 2.5% of GDP for Cabo Verde and the Seychelles.

Figure 2.13. **Sales of goods and services and administrative fees and other revenues related to administration, 2020**

Percentage of GDP

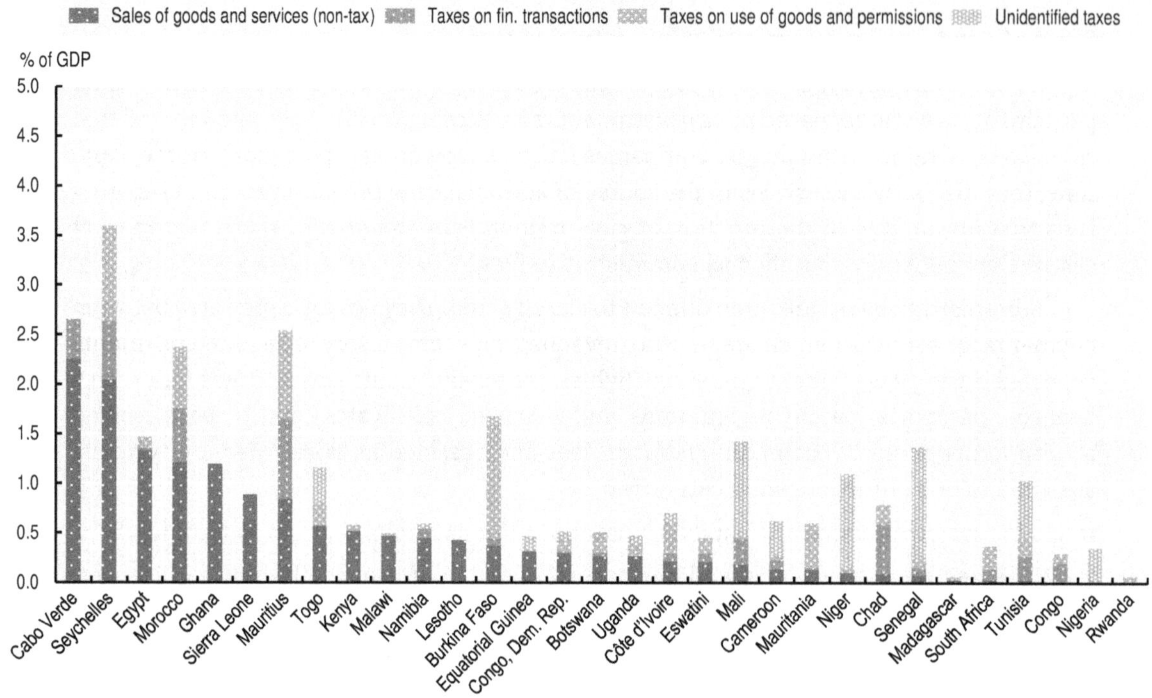

Note: Figures reported here include sub-national tax revenues for Mauritius, Morocco, Nigeria, and South Africa and sub-national non-tax revenues for Eswatini, Kenya, Mauritius, and Morocco, the only countries for which such revenues were reported for 2020.

Source: Authors' calculations based on data from (OECD/ATAF/AUC, 2022[2]), "Revenue Statistics in Africa: Comparative tables", *OECD Tax Statistics* (database), *https://doi.org/10.1787/be755711-en*.

StatLink *https://stat.link/jmnwyh*

The composition of these revenues varied by country. In Cabo Verde, 98% of revenues listed under "sales of goods and services" were fees. In Ghana, most revenues listed as sales of goods and services were collected by Municipalities, Departments and Agencies or by Metropolitan, Municipal and District Assemblies. In Morocco, 55% of revenues from government sales of goods and services were collected at the local level.

Miscellaneous or unidentified revenue

Some notable categories of non-tax revenue do not fit within any of the categories listed above. These include:

- capital transfers not included elsewhere;
- voluntary donations to government agencies from individuals or private corporations (not including donations from international organisations, which are classified as grants);
- private payments to government made as a result of major court settlements or insurance claims (such as the EUR 100 million payment Arcelor Mittal agreed to pay to the government of Senegal after a court case following the cancelation of an iron mine (RFI, 2014[12]));
- payments covering different categories in the classification list where a breakdown is not available;
- payments whose proper classification is unknown due to a lack of data. Rwanda did not disaggregate non-tax revenue outside of grants, so these were included in this category;
- SACU revenues to Botswana, Eswatini, Lesotho and Namibia (see Box 2.2).

Miscellaneous and unidentified revenues can be a significant component of non-tax revenues in certain countries. These include exceptional voluntary contributions to government in Tunisia, capital transfers from special statutory funds in Mauritius and, in Morocco, payments made to government in exchange for the right to compete with state institutions in the provision of services.

The volatility of miscellaneous and unidentified revenues may be due to large capital transfers, revenue streams that are short-lived or funds that are reclassified as unidentified due to lack of information. The higher values for this category could reflect uncertainty as to the true amount of revenue within other non-tax revenue classifications.

Box 2.2. **SACU revenues**

The Southern African Customs Union (SACU) incorporates Botswana, Eswatini, Lesotho, Namibia and South Africa. It is headquartered in Windhoek, Namibia. Its vision is "an economic community with equitable and sustainable development, dedicated to the welfare of its people for a common future".

SACU is the oldest customs union in the world, having been founded in 1899 between the British colony of Cape of Good Hope and the Orange Free State Boer Republic. Subsequent agreements in 1910 and 1969 included Botswana, Eswatini and Lesotho. Following Namibia's independence in 1990 and the end of apartheid in South Africa in 1994, new negotiations led to the current SACU agreement, which was signed in 2002.

The SACU agreement provides for free movement of SACU manufactured products within the union, without application of tariffs or duties. It also provides for common external tariffs and for the payment of customs and excise duties into a common pool to be shared between the SACU countries under the revenue-sharing formula set out in the Annex to the agreement.

The revenue-sharing agreement includes three components:

- A customs component, which divides the gross amount of customs duties according to the value of goods each country imports from other SACU countries in a given year (as a percentage of intra-SACU imports).
- An excise component, which divides the gross amount of excise duties according to each country's GDP as a percentage of SACU's combined GDP.
- A development component, which is funded from 15% of the excise component and is weighted toward less developed SACU countries using a formula based on GDP per capita.

In this publication, revenue from excises, tariffs and customs duties are included as tax revenues in the SACU country that collected the revenue. They are included under headings 5121 (Excises) and 5123 (Customs and import duties) in the tax revenue tables. Revenues received from the SACU Common Revenue Pool are included as miscellaneous revenue in the non-tax revenue tables, as seen in Table 6.13 for Eswatini. In the case of South Africa, where payments exceed the revenue share received from the Pool, the payments net of the share received are recorded as a memorandum item in the non-tax revenue table (Table 6.23).

Sources: (SACU, 2017[13]), (SACU, 2014[14]).

Southern African Customs Union revenues

All five members of SACU collect customs and excise taxes under a unified tax regime and then transfer those funds to the SACU Common Revenue Pool. The SACU Revenue Pool in turn redistributes the tax moneys collected under a complex revenue-sharing formula. In practice, however, South Africa possesses the main ports of entry into Southern Africa and ends up collecting almost all the customs duties and excises allocated to the SACU Common

Revenue Pool. South Africa therefore ends up making net payments into the SACU Revenue Pool, while the other SACU countries are net recipients of funds.

SACU revenues to South Africa are negligible but they have a strong impact on the finances of the other members of the customs union (Figure 2.14). In 2020, these revenues boosted the revenues of Botswana, Eswatini, Lesotho and Namibia by 9.3%, 12.6%, 26.6% and 12.6% of GDP, respectively. Besides exogenous economic shocks, member countries also saw their SACU revenues rise and fall due to changes in the parameters used in the SACU revenue-sharing formula. The economic shock of the global financial crisis rendered many economic forecasts of the time inaccurate; because SACU payments were calculated based on these forecasts, major adjustments to SACU payments were required in 2010 and 2011 to compensate for years of overpayments into the SACU pool (Mongardini et al., 2011[15]). A similar situation occurred in 2014, when a slowdown in South Africa's economy caused forecasts to be revised downward; Eswatini, Lesotho and Namibia's SACU revenues declined as a percentage of GDP in 2015 and 2016, although this trend was reversed in 2017.

Figure 2.14. **Total SACU and other non-tax revenues by country**

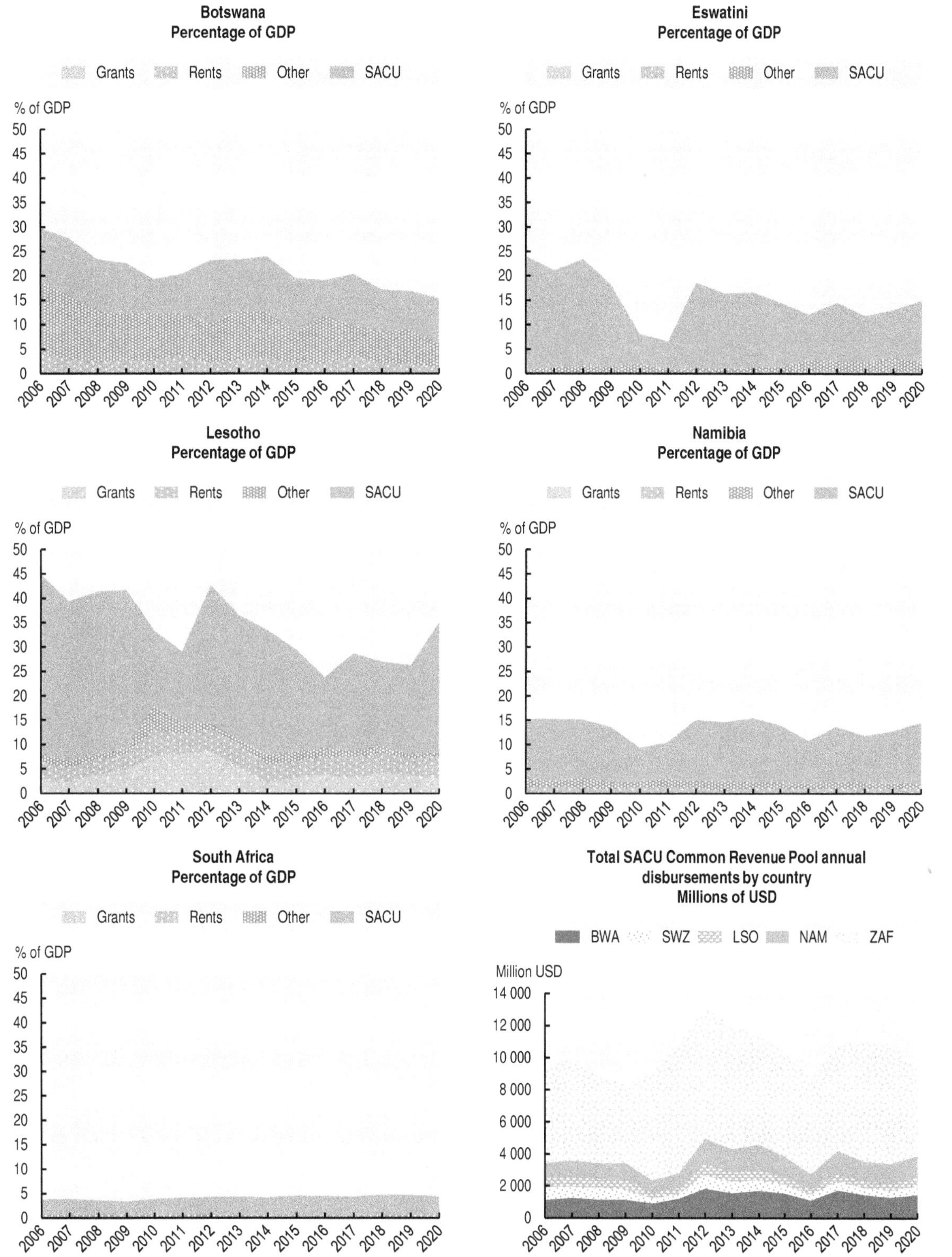

Note: SACU revenues reported here are classified as non-tax revenues for all countries presented here except for South Africa. For South Africa, SACU revenues received by the government of South Africa are classified under customs duties and excise taxes, and not non-tax revenues.

Source: Authors' calculations based on data from and (OECD/ATAF/AUC, 2022[2]), "Revenue Statistics in Africa: Comparative tables", *OECD Tax Statistics* (database), *https://doi.org/10.1787/be755711-en.*

StatLink *https://stat.link/kvm5nf*

Notes

1 Several methodological issues are present in non-tax revenues which do not necessarily arise in tax statistics. Some revenues, such as administrative fees, might be used as cost-recovery mechanisms and subtracted from cost figures rather than reported as revenues. This could be the case for local governments or other public institutions for which data only exists on net transfers of funds to the central government. If sales of goods and services are reported without deduction of costs, this could overstate a government's revenues. Grants, legal settlements and mining and oil contracts involve large payments by external entities such as multinational corporations and foreign governments who may be subject to different national oversight mechanisms. Some resource-rich countries may negotiate large payments from resource extraction payments as a lump sum that bundles together many categories of both tax and non-tax revenue, making detailed breakdowns less feasible. Finally, non-tax revenues are often under the responsibility of different authorities than tax revenues, and sometimes there is not necessarily a separation made between revenues and expenses, so these revenues might not necessarily follow the same reporting standard. Please see Annex B for more details on the methodology used for non-tax revenues.

2 There is no comparison with the averages of the 28 Latin American and Caribbean (LAC) countries (see (OECD et al., 2022[17])) and the 38 OECD countries (see (OECD, 2021[18])), as these publications do not cover non-tax revenues.

3 Please see the Interpretative Guide to non-tax revenue in Annex B of this report for the definitions of these revenue categories.

4 Please see also Annex B.

5 The official definition of ODA is: "flows to countries and territories on the Development Assistance Committee List of ODA Recipients and to multilateral institutions which are provided by official agencies, including state and local governments, or by their executive agencies. In addition, each transaction must be administered with the promotion of the economic development and welfare of developing countries as its main objective; and be concessional in character and conveys a grant element of at least 25% (calculated at a rate of discount of 10%)". Further information is available at: *www.oecd.org/dac/financing-sustainable-development/index-terms.htm#ODA*.

6 Note that taxes on oil extraction can include corporate income tax, excise taxes on energy products, un-refunded sales taxes such as VATs and non-tax revenue can include royalties, profit sharing, dividends received from state enterprises, and other investment income received from government direct participation in extractive enterprises (Mansour and Rota-Graziosi, 2013[16]).

7 The World Bank refers to "natural resource rents". This is calculated as the difference between the value of natural resource production in the countries according to commodity prices and the estimated cost of resource extraction. It is not to be confused with the definition of resource rent used by the OECD, for which it is defined as a form of government revenue. Please see the documentation of resource rents in the World Bank World Development Indicators dataset (see *https://databank.worldbank.org/metadataglossary/adjusted-net-savings/series/NY.GDP.TOTL.RT.ZS*) and the Interpretative Guide for more details."

8 See paragraphs 12-15 of the OECD Interpretative Guide in Annex A for an explanation of how administrative fees are classified in this publication.

References

CEPII (2022), *BACI International Trade Database at the Product-Level*, *http://www.cepii.fr/CEPII/en/bdd_modele/bdd_modele_item.asp?id=37* (accessed on 22 February 2022). [4]

CNN (2015), *Mammoth rail network to put West African economies on the right track*, *https://edition.cnn.com/2015/03/05/africa/west-africa-minerals-railway/index.html* (accessed on 21 September 2020).[10]

IMF (2022), *World Economic Outlook, April 2022 Edition (database)*, *https://www.imf.org/en/Publications/WEO/weo-database/2022/April.* [1]

Mansour, M. and G. Rota-Graziosi (2013), "Tax Coordination, Tax Competition, and Revenue Mobilization in the West African Economic and Monetary Union", *IMF Working Paper*, Vol. 13/163, *https://www.imf.org/en/Publications/WP/Issues/2016/12/31/Tax-Coordination-Tax-Competition-and-Revenue-Mobilization-in-the-West-African-Economic-and-40756.* [16]

MiningTechnology (2020), *Debswana diamond mines*, *https://www.mining-technology.com/projects/debswana/* (accessed on 20 September 2020). [9]

Mongardini, J. et al. (2011), *In the wake of the global economic crisis: adjusting to lower revenue of the Southern African Customs*, International Monetary Fund, *https://www.imf.org/external/pubs/ft/dp/2011/afr1101.pdf.* [15]

OECD (2022), *DAC Data submitters*, *http://www.oecd.org/dac/financing-sustainable-development/development-finance-standards/dacdatasubmitters.htm* (accessed on 8 September 2022). [7]

OECD (2021), *Revenue Statistics 2021*, OECD Publishing, Paris, *https://doi.org/10.1787/6e87f932-en.* [18]

OECD/ATAF/AUC (2022), *Revenue Statistics in Africa: Comparative tables*, OECD Publishing, Paris. [2]

OECD et al. (2022), *Revenue Statistics in Latin America and the Caribbean 2022*, OECD Publishing, Paris, *https://doi.org/10.1787/58a2dc35-en-es.* [17]

OECD-DAC (2022), *International Development Statistics (IDS) online databases*, *http://www.oecd.org/dac/stats/idsonline* (accessed on 10 September). [3]

RFI (2014), *Le gros chèque d'Arcelor Mittal au Sénégal*, *http://www.rfi.fr/economie/20140605-le-gros-cheque-arcelor-mittal-senegal.* [12]

SACU (2017), *Southern African Customs Union Agreement 2002 (As amended on 12 April 2013)*, *http://www.sacu.int/list.php?type=Agreements.* [13]

SACU (2014), *Implementing a Common Agenda Towards Regional Integration: 2014 Annual Report*, *http://www.sacu.int/docs/reports_annual/2014/annual_report.pdf.* [14]

VOANews (2013), *Malawi: Donors Withhold Aid Over Cashgate Scandal*, *https://www.voanews.com/africa/malawi-donors-withhold-aid-over-cashgate-scandal* (accessed on 21 September 2020). [8]

World Bank (2022), *World Bank Commodity Price Data (The Pink Sheet)*, *https://www.worldbank.org/en/research/commodity-markets* (accessed on September 2022). [11]

World Bank (2022), *World Bank Country and Lending Groups*, *https://datahelpdesk.worldbank.org/knowledgebase/articles/906519* (accessed on June 2022). [5]

World Bank (2022), *World Development Indicators*, *https://data.worldbank.org/* (accessed on 9 September 2022). [6]

Revenue Statistics in Africa 1990-2020/Statistiques des recettes publiques en Afrique 1990-2020

Chapitre 2

Tendances des recettes non fiscales, 2010-20

Introduction

Les statistiques relatives à la fiscalité ne sauraient suffire pour dresser le panorama complet des finances publiques, notamment celui de nombreux pays africains, qui perçoivent d'importantes recettes sous la forme de dons ou de redevances pétrolières et minières. Les *Statistiques des recettes publiques en Afrique* présentent des données sur les recettes fiscales et non fiscales, ces dernières étant les recettes des administrations publiques qui ne correspondent pas à la définition des recettes fiscales établie par l'OCDE. En dépit de différences méthodologiques importantes entre les recettes fiscales et non fiscales, celles-ci doivent être prises en compte dans la comptabilité des ressources financières totales d'un pays[1]. Le présent chapitre livre des comparaisons des recettes non fiscales entre les pays couverts par la présente publication[2].

Les principales catégories de recettes non fiscales[3] examinées dans le cadre de ce projet sont les suivantes[4] :

- dons émanant de pays étrangers ou d'organisations internationales (aide budgétaire, aide alimentaire, transferts de capitaux, transferts courants, subventions de projets, bourses de programme, allégement de la dette internationale, etc.) ;
- loyers et redevances (comme les redevances pétrolières ou minières) ;
- autres revenus de la propriété (intérêts, dividendes et autres rémunérations d'investissements publics) ;
- ventes de biens et de services (dont certains frais administratifs) ;
- amendes et pénalités (notamment pour infraction à la législation fiscale) ;
- recettes diverses non identifiées (recettes non fiscales qui ne peuvent être classées dans les autres catégories).

La présente édition des *Statistiques des recettes publiques en Afrique* est la première à présenter des données portant sur la période de la pandémie du COVID-19. L'interprétation des données relatives aux recettes non fiscales dans ce chapitre requiert donc une certaine compréhension des facteurs exceptionnels qui ont joué au cours de cette période et qui ont été à l'origine de fluctuations importantes de nombreux indicateurs pertinents. Bien que la pandémie ait eu des retombées majeures sur de nombreux indicateurs sociaux et économiques, le chapitre se concentrera sur les éléments les plus étroitement liés aux principales sources de recettes non fiscales des pays africains, comme les dons internationaux et l'extraction des ressources naturelles.

Recettes non fiscales exprimées en pourcentage du PIB

En 2020, les recettes non fiscales exprimées en pourcentage du PIB ont de manière générale été inférieures aux recettes fiscales, mais avec des variations importantes selon les 31 pays couverts dans ce rapport. En moyenne, les recettes non fiscales perçues dans chacun de ces pays ont représenté 48.4 % du montant des recettes fiscales recouvrées. Elles s'inscrivent dans une fourchette comprise entre 35.1 % du PIB au Lesotho et 0.5 % du PIB en

Afrique du Sud. Le Botswana, le Lesotho et la République du Congo sont les seuls pays où les recettes non fiscales ont été supérieures aux recettes fiscales en 2020 (Graphique 2.1). C'était également le cas au cours de la plupart des années précédentes grâce aux recettes importantes de la SACU au Botswana et au Lesotho, et aux recettes pétrolières élevées en République du Congo. Grâce à ses revenus pétroliers, la Guinée équatoriale encaisse d'ordinaire des recettes non fiscales supérieures aux recettes fiscales mais, étant donné la faiblesse des cours du pétrole, cela n'a pas été le cas en 2015, 2019 et 2020.

Graphique 2.1. **Recettes fiscales et non fiscales totales par pays, 2020**

Pourcentage du PIB

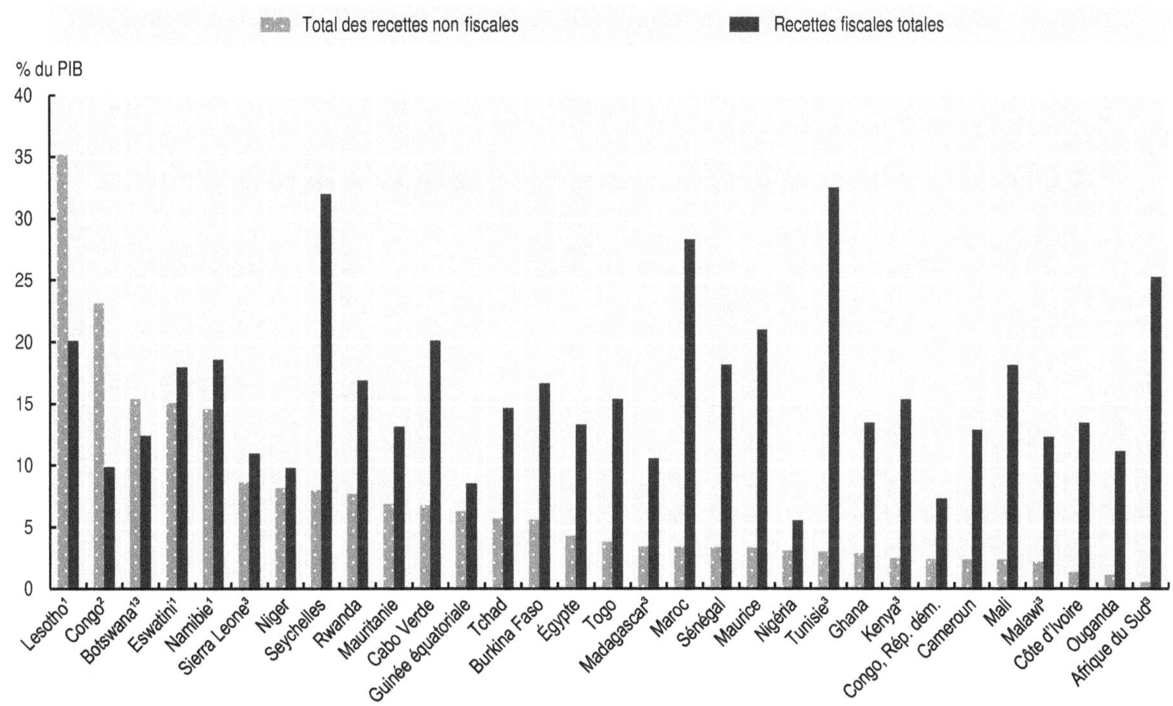

Notes : Les données relatives aux recettes non fiscales prennent en compte les recettes non fiscales perçues par les administrations infranationales pour l'Eswatini, le Kenya, le Maroc et Maurice, seuls pays pour lesquels les données correspondantes sont disponibles. En 2020, les recettes non fiscales perçues par les administrations infranationales représentaient, pour chacun de ces pays, respectivement 2 %, 14 %, 4 % et 38 % des recettes non fiscales totales. L'Afrique du Sud, la Mauritanie et le Nigéria ont déclaré percevoir des taxes locales et régionales, mais n'ont pas fait état de recettes non fiscales à ces niveaux.

1. Dans les cas du Botswana, de l'Eswatini, du Lesotho et de la Namibie, les recettes non fiscales comprennent les fonds qui leur sont transférés en vertu de l'accord de partage des recettes de l'Union douanière d'Afrique australe (SACU) après perception des droits de douane et d'accise par l'Afrique du Sud.

2. Les montants indiqués ici pour les dons et recettes pétrolières de la République du Congo sont ceux publiés en avril 2022 dans les *Perspectives de l'économie mondiale* du FMI (FMI, 2022[1]).

3. Les chiffres relatifs au PIB utilisés pour calculer les ratios impôts/PIB indiqués ici sont tirés de l'édition d'avril 2022 des *Perspectives de l'économie mondiale* (FMI, 2022[1]). S'agissant de l'Afrique du Sud, du Botswana, de la Guinée équatoriale, du Kenya, de Madagascar, du Malawi, des Seychelles et de la Tunisie, ces chiffres s'écartaient de 3 % ou plus de ceux utilisés pour calculer les ratios recettes/PIB dans l'édition précédente de *Statistiques des recettes publiques en Afrique*.

Pour certains pays, les valeurs des ratios recettes fiscales/PIB et recettes non fiscales/PIB sont à interpréter avec prudence, car elles reposent sur des données incomplètes. Pour plus d'informations, se reporter aux tableaux par pays présentés aux chapitres 5 et 6.

Source : Tableaux 4.1 (chapitre 4) et 6.1 (chapitre 6), et (OCDE/ATAF/CUA, 2022[2]), « Statistiques des recettes publiques en Afrique : Tableaux comparatifs », *Statistiques fiscales de l'OCDE* (base de données), *http://dx.doi.org/10.1787/be755711-en.*

StatLink *https://stat.link/lk8vd3*

En Afrique (31 pays), le ratio moyen recettes fiscales/PIB a progressé entre 2010 et 2020, celui des recettes non fiscales ayant en revanche accusé une baisse sensible (Graphique 2.2). Après le pic enregistré en 2012 (8.5 % du PIB), ce dernier a chuté à 5.8 % en 2016 avant de remonter à 6.3 % en 2019, puis de gagner encore 0.6 point de pourcentage pour atteindre

6.8 % en 2020. Une bonne part du recul observé entre 2012 et 2016 a été dû à une baisse des recettes sous forme de dons et de loyers et redevances, qui ont respectivement fléchi de 0.4 point et 1.4 point de pourcentage du PIB. Depuis 2016, ces deux catégories de recettes ont légèrement augmenté, toutes deux de 0.3 point, mais la hausse des recettes issues de la SACU enregistrée dans des pays comme le Lesotho et l'Eswatini a eu un effet encore plus prononcé sur les recettes non fiscales.

Il n'y a généralement pas de corrélation entre l'évolution des recettes non fiscales et celle des recettes fiscales. Au cours de la période 2010-19, les recettes fiscales moyennes ont progressé de 1.8 point de PIB, les recettes non fiscales diminuant pour leur part de 1.7 point, ce qui s'est traduit par une augmentation nette de 0.2 point du total des recettes publiques. Entre 2019 et 2020, première année de la pandémie du COVID-19, ces évolutions se sont inversées. Alors que les recettes fiscales ont reculé de 0.3 point, les recettes non fiscales ont crû de 0.6 point, d'où une hausse moyenne de 0.3 point des recettes publiques pendant la pandémie.

Graphique 2.2. **Niveau moyen des recettes non fiscales en Afrique (31), 2010-20**

Pourcentage du PIB

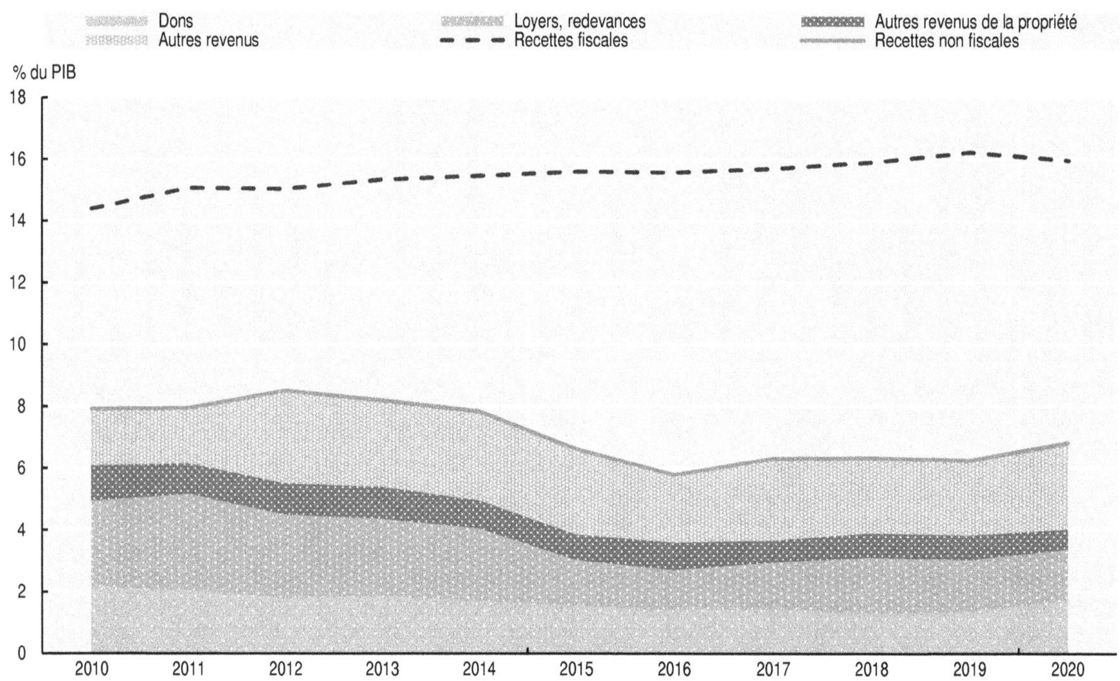

Source : Calculs des auteurs basés sur des données figurant dans (OCDE/ATAF/CUA, 2022[2]), « Statistiques des recettes publiques en Afrique : Tableaux comparatifs », *Statistiques fiscales de l'OCDE* (base de données), *https://doi.org/10.1787/7f54581d-fr*.

StatLink *https://stat.link/bx2mj5*

Le Graphique 2.3 montre la part de chaque sous-catégorie dans le total des recettes non fiscales des pays. Les données font apparaître quatre groupes distincts :

- Onze pays ont perçu la majeure partie de leurs recettes non fiscales sous forme de dons en 2020 (par ordre décroissant : Sierra Leone, Niger, Rwanda, Tchad, Burkina Faso, Togo, Madagascar, Sénégal, Mali, Malawi et Ouganda). Celles-ci se montent en moyenne à 3.3 % du PIB.
- Cinq pays ont perçu l'essentiel de leurs recettes non fiscales sous forme de loyers et redevances (par ordre décroissant : République du Congo, Mauritanie, Guinée équatoriale, Nigéria et Cameroun), dont les redevances pétrolières ont représenté la majeure partie. Dans ces pays, les loyers et redevances correspondent en moyenne à 6.4 % du PIB.

- Les quatre pays voisins de l'Afrique du Sud membres de la SACU, à savoir le Botswana, l'Eswatini, le Lesotho et la Namibie, ont perçu une partie substantielle de leurs recettes non fiscales sous la forme de revenus transférés par la SACU (encadré 2.2). Globalement, les recettes non fiscales hors dons et loyers et redevances ont représenté pour eux l'équivalent de 15.7 % du PIB.
- Dans les 11 pays restants, la majeure partie des recettes non fiscales ne provient ni des dons, loyers et redevances, ni des recettes de la SACU. Les principales sources de recettes non fiscales sont les suivantes : les intérêts et dividendes au Kenya et en Tunisie ; les produits de la vente de biens et services au Ghana ; des recettes diverses et non affectées en Égypte et au Maroc. Pour le Cabo Verde, la Côte d'Ivoire, Maurice, la République démocratique du Congo et les Seychelles, les dons ont été la première source de recettes non fiscales mais en ont représenté moins de 50 %. De la même manière, les loyers et redevances ont été la principale source de recettes non fiscales de l'Afrique du Sud, mais en ont constitué moins de la moitié.

Graphique 2.3. **Structure des recettes non fiscales par pays, 2020**

Pourcentage du PIB

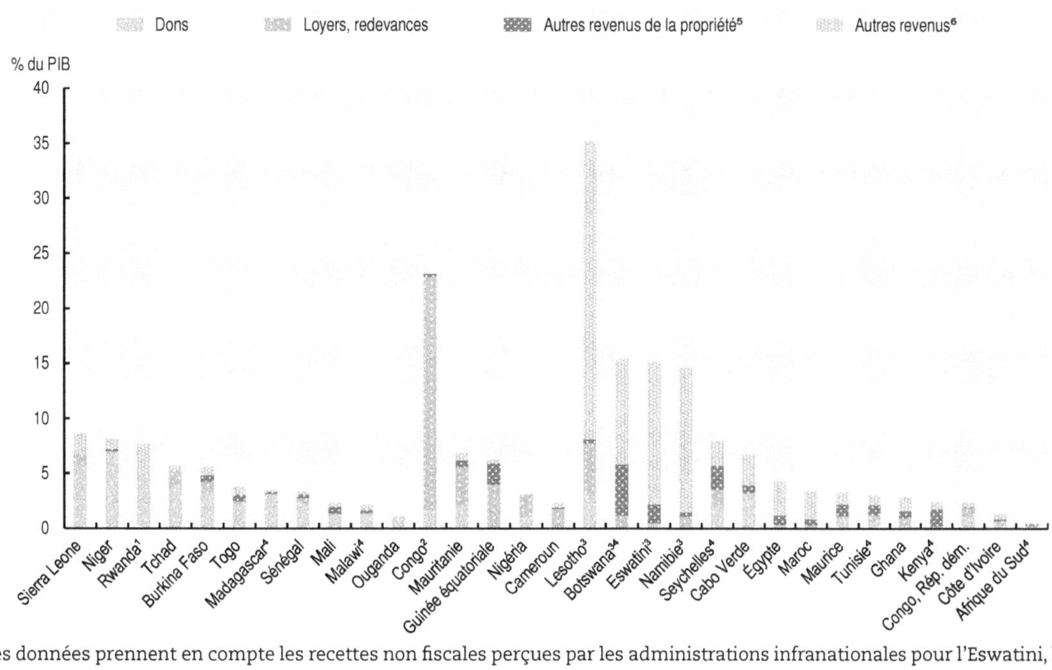

Note : Les données prennent en compte les recettes non fiscales perçues par les administrations infranationales pour l'Eswatini, le Kenya, le Maroc et Maurice.

1. Dans le cas du Rwanda, les recettes non fiscales autres que les dons ne sont pas ventilées par sous-catégorie et sont donc assimilées aux recettes diverses et non identifiées.
2. Les chiffres présentés ici correspondent principalement aux dons et recettes pétrolières recensés dans les *Perspectives de l'économie mondiale* du FMI d'avril 2022 (FMI, 2022[1]) au titre des loyers et redevances.
3. Dans les cas du Botswana, de l'Eswatini, du Lesotho et de la Namibie, les « autres recettes » incluent les fonds qui leur sont transférés en vertu de l'accord de partage des recettes de l'Union douanière d'Afrique australe (SACU) après perception des droits de douane et d'accise par l'Afrique du Sud.
4. Les chiffres relatifs au PIB utilisés pour calculer les ratios recettes/PIB indiqués ici sont tirés de l'édition d'avril 2022 des *Perspectives de l'économie mondiale* (FMI, 2022[1]). S'agissant de l'Afrique du Sud, du Botswana, du Kenya, de Madagascar, du Malawi, des Seychelles et de la Tunisie, ces chiffres s'écartaient de 3 % ou plus de ceux utilisés pour calculer les ratios recettes/PIB dans l'édition précédente de *Statistiques des recettes publiques en Afrique*.
5. Intérêts, dividendes, etc.
6. Ventes, amendes, recettes de la SACU, etc.

Pour plus de précisions, se reporter aux notes du graphique 2.1 et aux tableaux par pays présentés dans les chapitres 5 et 6.

Source : Tableau 6.2 (chapitre 6) et (OCDE/ATAF/CUA, 2022[2]), « Statistiques des recettes publiques en Afrique : Tableaux comparatifs », *Statistiques fiscales de l'OCDE* (base de données), *https://doi.org/10.1787/7f54581d-fr*.

StatLink *https://stat.link/28j3ud*

COVID-19 et recettes non fiscales en 2020

Les retombées économiques de la crise du COVID-19 ont fait de 2020 une année exceptionnelle pour les pays africains considérés ici. Le Graphique 2.4 montre l'évolution des recettes non fiscales et d'autres indicateurs entre 2019 et 2020 en regard des variations annuelles les plus fortes et les plus faibles enregistrées au cours des dix années précédentes. Le PIB réel a globalement reculé de 3.3 % en 2020, alors qu'il n'avait jamais progressé de moins de 2.4 % en moyenne dans ces pays depuis 2000. Pour 24 des pays couverts, c'est la plus forte baisse enregistrée depuis dix ans.

Malgré le caractère inédit de la crise du COVID-19, l'évolution des recettes non fiscales de l'Afrique correspond davantage aux orientations récentes que celle des recettes fiscales et des autres indicateurs macroéconomiques. Parmi les 31 pays africains, 19 ont enregistré une hausse des recettes non fiscales entre 2019 et 2020 (en monnaie locale), et 12 les ont vues reculer ; à quatre exceptions près, ces variations se situent dans la fourchette des variations annuelles enregistrées au cours de la décennie précédente.

Si, sur ce plan, l'année 2020 a été moins atypique que les autres, cela tient à la forte variabilité de ces recettes, mais aussi aux répercussions de la pandémie. Les redevances pétrolières ont diminué sous l'effet de la baisse des prix du carburant, mais la crise sanitaire a entraîné une augmentation de l'aide extérieure internationale. Onze pays africains ont bénéficié d'une hausse plus importante de l'APD en 2020 qu'au cours de toute autre année depuis 2010. Trois des quatre plus grands exportateurs de pétrole et de gaz sur la dernière décennie parmi les pays de cette publication - République du Congo, Guinée équatoriale, et Nigéria - ont enregistré des baisses considérables de leurs recettes pétrolières et gazières mais aucune de ces baisses n'a été plus forte que celles enregistrées au cours de la décennie précédente, marquée par une chute importante, de près de 50 %, des prix du pétrole entre 2014 et 2015.

Graphique 2.4. **Variation de certains indicateurs 2019-20, par rapport à la fourchette de variations annuelles entre 2010 et 2019, par pays**

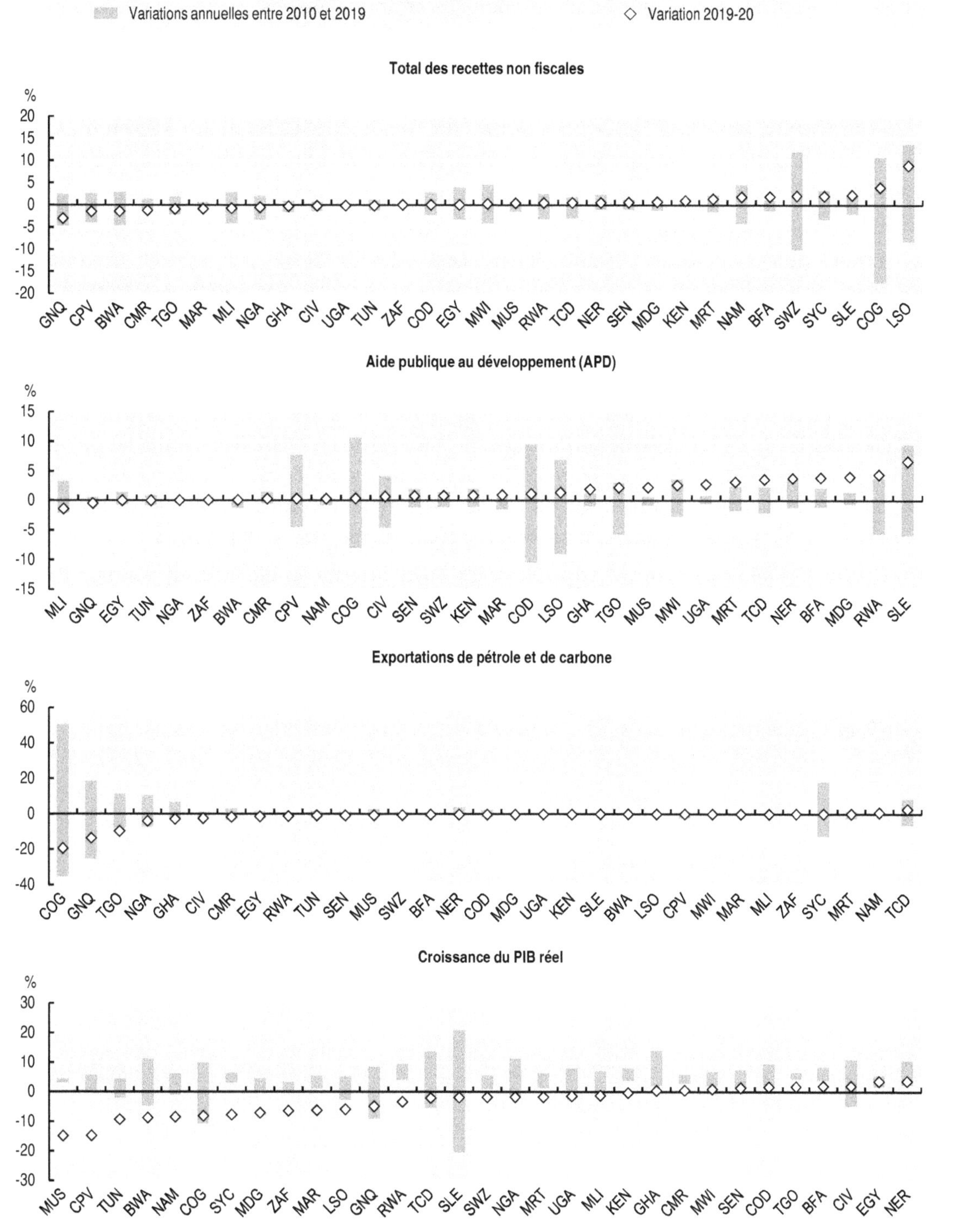

Note : La partie supérieure des barres vertes correspond à la valeur annuelle maximale, la partie inférieure aux valeurs annuelles minimales atteintes entre les années 2010 et 2019 comprises.

Source : Calculs des auteurs basés sur des données figurant dans (OCDE/ATAF/CUA, 2022[2]), « Statistiques des recettes publiques en Afrique : Tableaux comparatifs », *Statistiques fiscales de l'OCDE* (base de données), *https://doi.org/10.1787/7f54581d-fr* ; OCDE, Comité d'aide au développement (OCDE-CAD, 2022[3]) pour les données relatives à l'APD et (OCDE/ATAF/CUA, 2022[2]) pour les chiffres de l'aide publique au développement ; base de données de commerce international au niveau des produits de BACI (CEPII, 2022[4]) pour les chiffres relatifs aux exportations de pétrole et d'hydrocarbures ; édition d'avril 2022 des *Perspectives de l'économie mondiale* (FMI, 2022[1]).

StatLink https://stat.link/xpjmto

Les ratios recettes/PIB doivent être considérés avec prudence compte tenu des chocs majeurs intervenus sur les volumes et les prix en 2020. Le ratio recettes/PIB est un indicateur privilégié pour les comparaisons internationales et annuelles des recettes publiques car il tient compte de l'inflation et des différences de taille entre les économies. Néanmoins, comme expliqué à l'encadré 1.1 du chapitre 1, les fortes fluctuations de son numérateur ne concordent pas toujours avec celles du dénominateur. Entre 2019 et 2020, le PIB moyen des pays africains a progressé de 0.2 % en termes nominaux. Cette évolution représente 27 % de la variation de 0.6 point de pourcentage des ratios des recettes non fiscales au PIB entre 2019 et 2020.

Le graphique 2.5 illustre l'évolution des recettes non fiscales entre 2019 et 2020 (dons, loyers et redevances, et autres recettes non fiscales). À des fins de comparaison, leur évolution en pourcentage du PIB est représentée graphiquement aux côtés de l'évolution nominale de leur total en pourcentage du PIB 2019 (losanges blancs). L'utilisation du même dénominateur pour les deux années permet de définir correctement le sens de la variation. En République du Congo, par exemple, les recettes non fiscales, en pourcentage du PIB, ont été plus élevées en 2020 qu'en 2019, mais cette hausse tient essentiellement à la baisse de 21 % du PIB national. En réalité, du fait de la baisse des prix du pétrole, les recettes non fiscales nominales ont été plus faibles en 2020 qu'en 2019. Pour 18 des pays couverts ici, le calcul de la variation des recettes non fiscales en pourcentage du PIB 2019 aboutit à un chiffre plus élevé que celui de la variation en points de pourcentage du rapport de ces recettes au PIB entre 2019 et 2020.

Étant donné l'accroissement du volume de l'aide internationale face à la pandémie et le recul de la demande de carburant, les recettes sous forme de dons ont dans l'ensemble augmenté entre 2019 et 2020, alors que les loyers et les redevances ont plutôt diminué. Les dons ont globalement progressé d'un montant équivalent à 0.4 % du PIB en 2020, les revenus de la propriété reculant pour leur part d'un montant équivalent à 0.2 % du PIB en 2020, principalement en raison de la baisse des revenus tirés des ressources naturelles.

Graphique 2.5. **Augmentation, en points de pourcentage, des recettes non fiscales exprimées en pourcentage du PIB, 2019-20**

Pourcentage du PIB

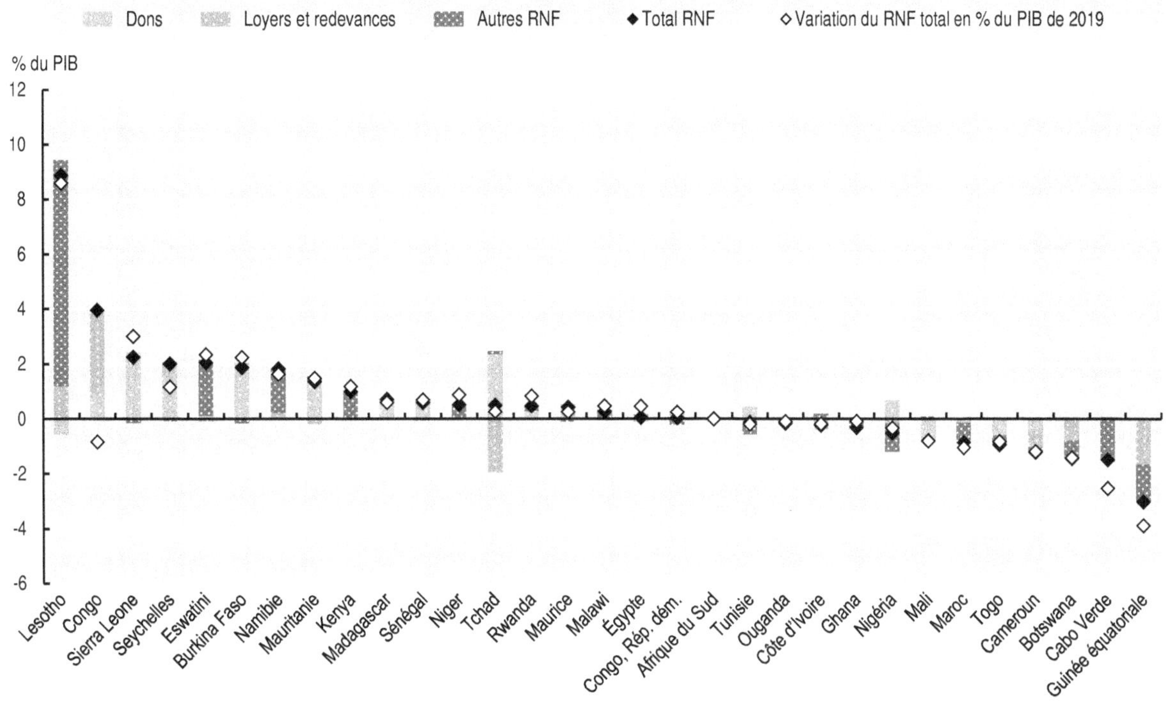

Note : Les losanges noirs correspondent à la somme des variations en points de pourcentage des dons, loyers et redevances et autres recettes non fiscales entre 2019 et 2020. Les losanges blancs indiquent le ratio du total des recettes non fiscales entre 2019 et 2020 au PIB de 2019. Ils illustrent la fluctuation des ratios recettes/PIB entre 2019 et 2020 lorsque l'effet de la variation du PIB est neutralisé.

Source : Calculs des auteurs basés sur les données figurant dans (OCDE/ATAF/CUA, 2022[2]), « Statistiques des recettes publiques en Afrique : Tableaux comparatifs », *Statistiques fiscales de l'OCDE* (base de données), *https://doi.org/10.1787/7f54581d-fr*.

StatLink *https://stat.link/om054l*

Entre 2019 et 2020, l'augmentation des dons a été le principal facteur de variation des recettes non fiscales dans dix pays. Au Tchad, la hausse de 2.4 points des recettes sous forme de dons en pourcentage du PIB a été presque entièrement contrebalancée par la baisse concomitante de 2 points des loyers et redevances. Dans 14 pays, la variation a été essentiellement due à celle des recettes non fiscales autres que les dons, loyers et redevances. Dans le cas du Lesotho, de l'Eswatini et de la Namibie, cela comprend la hausse des recettes issues de la SACU. Au Lesotho, l'augmentation des recettes de la SACU (8.3 points) a représenté à elle seule près de la moitié de la hausse moyenne des recettes non fiscales en Afrique. Comme indiqué plus loin dans ce chapitre, une telle fluctuation des paiements de la SACU n'est pas sans rapport avec ce que le Lesotho et l'Eswatini ont déjà connu par le passé.

Dons

Les dons constituent une source de recettes plus ou moins importante selon les pays étudiés dans les *Statistiques des recettes publiques en Afrique*. En 2020, ils se sont montés en moyenne à 1.7 % du PIB des 31 pays couverts, contre 1.4 % l'année précédente, ce qui correspond à une hausse de 0.4 point. Ils ont représenté cette même année moins de 0.5 % du PIB de dix pays (Graphique 2.6), dont tous sont des pays à revenu intermédiaire, d'après la classification de la Banque mondiale fondée sur le revenu national brut (Banque mondiale, 2022[5]). À l'inverse, le volume de dons s'est monté à plus de 1 % du PIB de tous les pays à faible revenu considérés dans la présente étude, hormis l'Ouganda.

Graphique 2.6. **Dons par pays, 2020 et 2019**

Pourcentage du PIB

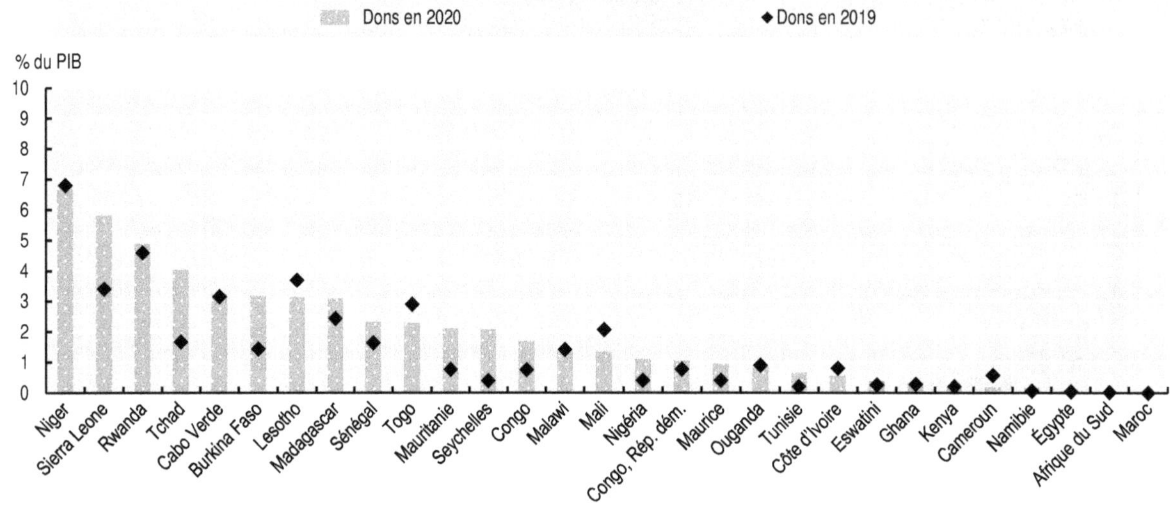

Source : Tableaux 6.2 et 6.3 (chapitre 6) et (OCDE/ATAF/CUA, 2022[2]), « Statistiques des recettes publiques en Afrique : Tableaux comparatifs », *Statistiques fiscales de l'OCDE* (base de données), *https://doi.org/10.1787/7f54581d-fr*.

StatLink *https://stat.link/ta4rew*

Le Graphique 2.7 indique le volume des dons perçus par les pays étudiés dans la présente publication (en pourcentage du PIB) ainsi que le montant de leur revenu national brut (PNB) par habitant. Si la partie supérieure droite est vide, c'est parce que les dons constituent, en proportion, une source de recettes moins importante pour les pays africains dont le revenu est plus élevé. De nombreux pays figurent toutefois dans la partie inférieure gauche car il en est qui, malgré un revenu faible, perçoivent proportionnellement peu de recettes sous forme de dons. Le Burkina Faso, l'Ouganda et le Rwanda, par exemple, ont enregistré un RNB par habitant compris entre 770 USD et 830 USD en 2020, alors que les dons qu'ils ont déclaré avoir perçus cette même année ont représenté 0.8 % (Ouganda), 1.4 % (Burkina Faso) et 4.9 % (Rwanda) de leur PIB.

Graphique 2.7. **Dons en pourcentage du PIB et du PNB par habitant et par pays, 2020**

Pourcentage du PIB

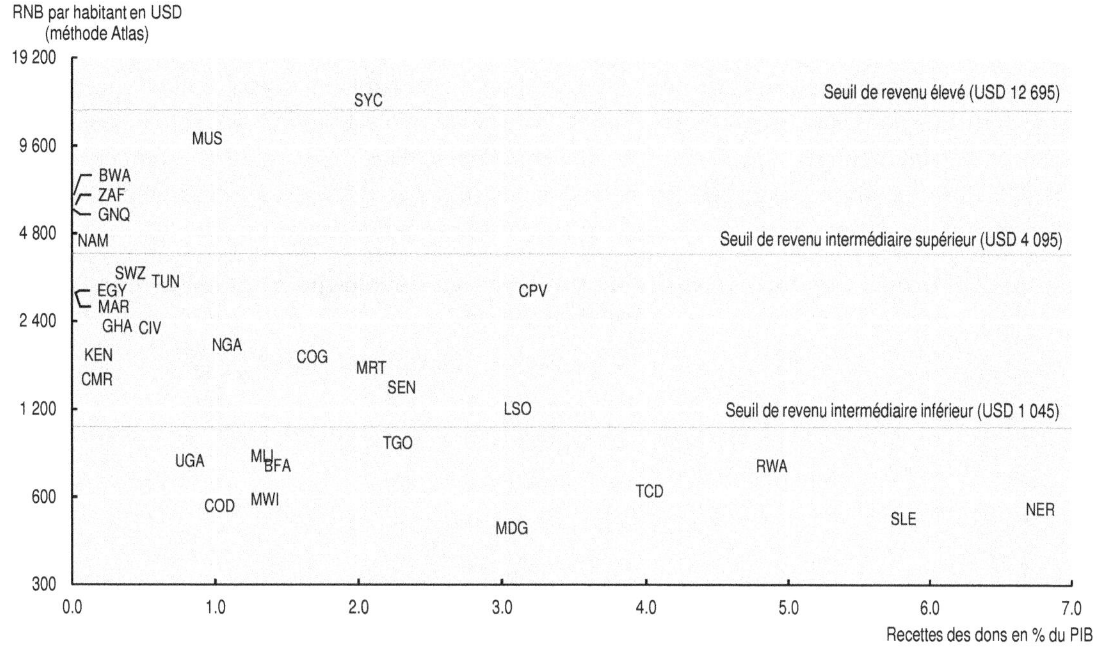

Note : Les chiffres du PNB ont été convertis en USD suivant la méthode Atlas de la Banque mondiale.

Source : Tableau 6.2 (chapitre 6), et les Indicateurs du développement dans le monde (base de données) (Banque mondiale, 2022[6]) et (OCDE/ATAF/CUA, 2022[2]), « Statistiques des recettes publiques en Afrique : Tableaux comparatifs », *Statistiques fiscales de l'OCDE* (base de données), *https://doi.org/10.1787/7f54581d-fr*.

StatLink https://stat.link/zvp74t

Si les recettes sous forme de dons et l'aide extérieure recouvrent des notions similaires, la diversité des données, méthodes et concepts employés fait qu'il difficile dans la pratique, d'accorder les statistiques de l'aide tirées des déclarations des pays donneurs avec les revenus issus de dons dont les pays récipiendaires font état.

- Les recettes sous forme de dons présentent des éléments communs avec l'aide publique au développement (APD), telle que définie par le Comité d'aide au développement (CAD) de l'OCDE[5]. Les dons considérés ici correspondent principalement à des recettes perçues d'autres États et d'organisations internationales. L'APD mesure les efforts déployés par les pays donneurs en faveur du développement dans les pays à faible revenu et à revenu intermédiaire. L'APD recouvre les apports considérés comme des « dons » dans la présente publication (aide budgétaire, aide alimentaire, transferts de capitaux, transferts courants, subventions de projets, bourses de programme, allègement de la dette internationale, etc.), mais elle englobe également les prêts concessionnels, l'assistance technique en nature, les dépenses administratives supportées par les donneurs, le coût des réfugiés dans les pays donneurs et les bourses d'étude, ainsi que d'autres activités ne générant pas d'entrées de recettes (nettes) dans le pays. C'est pourquoi le volume de l'APD fournie par un pays donneur à un pays diffère du montant des dons indiqué dans les *Statistiques des recettes publiques*, et lui est généralement plus élevé.
- Les statistiques relatives aux apports d'APD à destination de l'Afrique qui sont recueillies par le CAD englobent les apports publics provenant de l'ensemble des membres du CAD et de certains pays non membres du CAD, ainsi que des organisations multilatérales comme la Banque mondiale, le FMI et l'ONU. En sont exclues les statistiques relatives à la coopération pour le développement de grandes économies non membres de l'OCDE, comme le Brésil, la Chine, l'Inde, l'Indonésie et la Russie (OCDE, 2022[7]).

Le Graphique 2.8 montre que le montant de l'APD versé aux pays africains est nettement supérieur aux sommes qui sont versées directement aux autorités nationales, ce qui s'explique en partie par la présence de programmes de développement qui bénéficient de financements internationaux qui ne passent par l'intermédiaire des autorités nationales. Si, en règle générale, les pays qui perçoivent les apports nets d'APD les plus élevés sont aussi ceux dont les recettes sous forme de dons sont les plus importantes, la corrélation n'est pas linéaire et l'on observe des cas notablement atypiques, comme celui du Malawi, dont l'APD nette en pourcentage du PIB (13.8 %) le place loin en tête des pays africains, alors qu'il arrive en treizième place du classement des recettes sous forme de dons exprimées en pourcentage du PIB.

Graphique 2.8. **Dons et apports nets d'aide publique au développement (APD) perçus, 2020**

Pourcentage du PIB

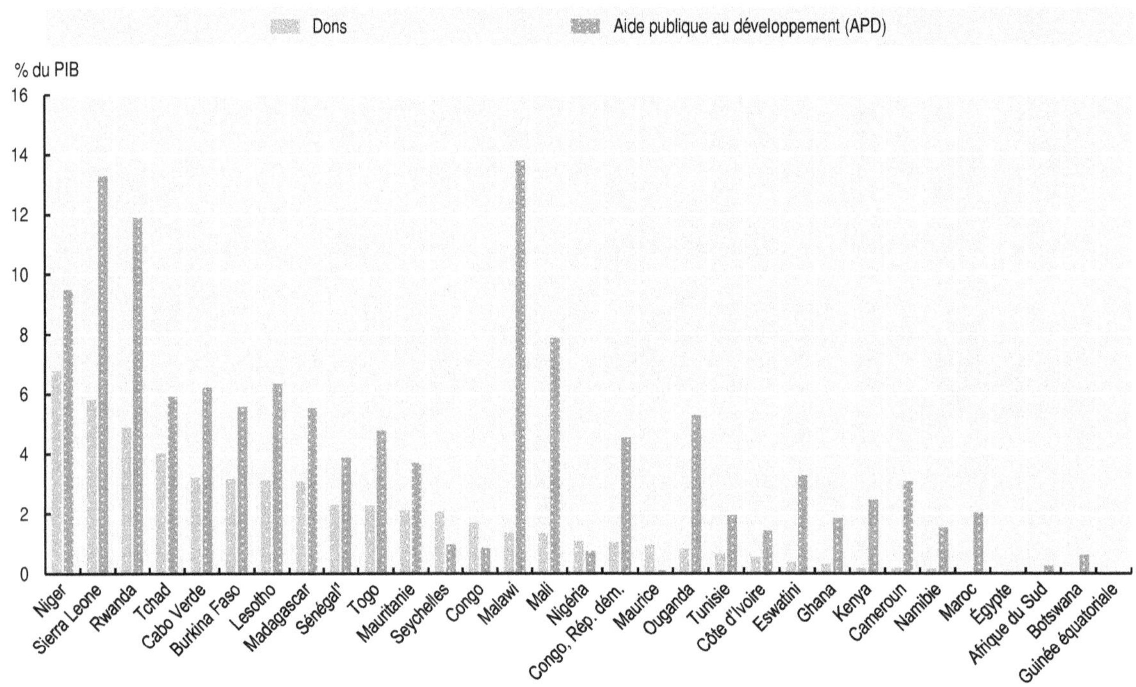

Note : Les valeurs de l'APD nette incluent les dons versés par les 31 pays membres du Comité d'aide au développement (CAD) de l'OCDE, 20 pays non membres du CAD ainsi que des organisations multilatérales et des organismes privés. Ces chiffres ne prennent pas encore en compte certains grands pays donneurs comme le Brésil, la Chine, l'Inde, l'Indonésie et la Russie.

Source : Tableau 6.2 3 (chapitre 6), Comité d'aide au développement (OCDE-CAD, 2022[3]) pour les chiffres de l'APD, et (OCDE/ATAF/CUA, 2022[2]), « Statistiques des recettes publiques en Afrique : Tableaux comparatifs », *Statistiques fiscales de l'OCDE* (base de données), *https://doi.org/10.1787/7f54581d-fr*.

StatLink *https://stat.link/k0z97x*

Les pays tributaires des dons se trouvent souvent confrontés à des baisses annuelles soudaines de cette source de recettes. Neuf en ont enregistré une d'au moins 2 points de pourcentage entre 2010 et 2020 ; pour six d'entre eux, elle a même été de plus de 3 points. Au Malawi, les dons, qui représentaient plus de 7.1 % du PIB en 2013, ont chuté de 65 %, en USD, l'année suivante, marquée par le scandale du Cashgate (VOANews, 2013[8]). Au total, 13 pays parmi les 31 considérés ont enregistré une baisse de leurs recettes annuelles sous forme de dons équivalant à 1.0 % au moins du PIB au cours de la décennie écoulée.

Dans l'ensemble, les recettes sous forme de dons perçues par les pays considérés ici ont diminué, passant de 2.2 % du PIB en 2010 à 1.3 % du PIB en 2018, mais elles ont depuis rebondi à 1.7 % en 2020. Leurs fluctuations sont souvent liées à des circonstances propres à chaque pays. L'Égypte, par exemple, a vu ses recettes sous forme de dons augmenter brusquement en 2014, dans le contexte de la normalisation des relations internationales qui a suivi sa crise politique interne ; au Mali, en revanche, cette source s'est tarie en 2012, lorsque la guerre a éclaté, avant de réapparaître l'année suivante.

Recettes tirées des ressources et autres revenus de la propriété

C'est en leur qualité de propriétaire, et en particulier de propriétaire terrien, que les États tirent une grande partie de leurs recettes non fiscales. Ces recettes sont comptabilisées comme revenus de la propriété dans les *Statistiques des recettes publiques en Afrique* et englobent différents types de revenus (Graphique 2.9).

Les loyers et redevances sont des recettes tirées de l'utilisation de terres appartenant à l'État, généralement dans le cadre d'activités de prospection et d'exploitation de ressources naturelles non renouvelables sur des terres appartenant au domaine de l'État, ou de l'exploitation de fermes et de forêts détenues par l'État. Les intérêts et dividendes sont la rémunération d'investissements réalisés par l'État dans des sociétés. En règle générale, les redevances pétrolières et minières ne sont pas comptabilisées avec les autres catégories de revenus d'investissement, mais la question peut se révéler complexe. De nombreux pays africains créent des entreprises publiques chargées de gérer les recettes pétrolières ou nouent des accords de répartition des recettes avec des entreprises privées qui exploitent ces ressources naturelles. La classification de ces fonds n'est pas toujours claire. Au Botswana, par exemple, une part importante des revenus de la propriété provient des entreprises qui investissent dans l'extraction du diamant (encadré 2.2).

Graphique 2.9. **Loyers et redevances par pays, 2020 et 2019**

Pourcentage du PIB

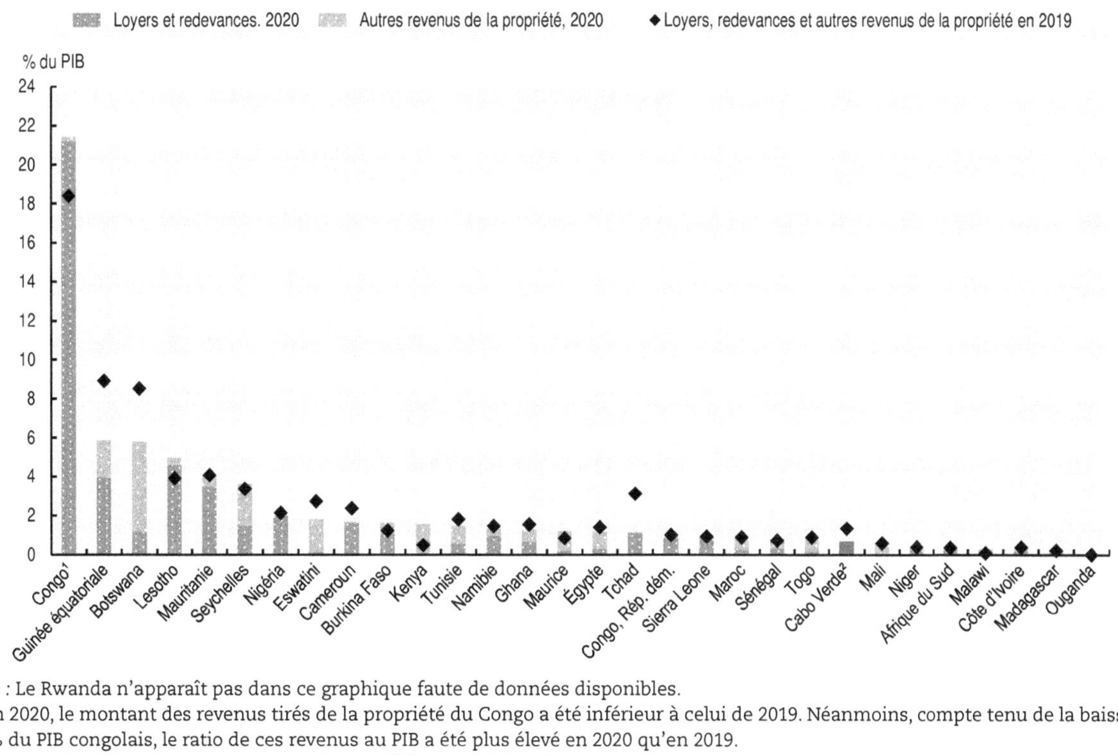

Note : Le Rwanda n'apparaît pas dans ce graphique faute de données disponibles.

1. En 2020, le montant des revenus tirés de la propriété du Congo a été inférieur à celui de 2019. Néanmoins, compte tenu de la baisse de 21 % du PIB congolais, le ratio de ces revenus au PIB a été plus élevé en 2020 qu'en 2019.
2. Les données relatives aux revenus de la propriété pour le Cabo Verde ne sont pas ventilées.

Source : Calculs des auteurs basés sur des données figurant aux tableaux 6.5 à 6.35 et au tableau 4.17, et (OCDE/ATAF/CUA, 2022[2]), « Statistiques des recettes publiques en Afrique : Tableaux comparatifs », *Statistiques fiscales de l'OCDE* (base de données), *https://doi.org/10.1787/7f54581d-fr*.

StatLink *https://stat.link/cligh8*

Recettes tirées des ressources naturelles

Les loyers et redevances des 29 pays pour lesquels ces informations sont disponibles ont représenté 1.7 % du PIB en 2020, marquant un recul de 0.04 point seulement par rapport à 2019. Ces recettes sont dans leur majorité tirées du pétrole. En 2020, 61.9 % du total des loyers et redevances, exprimé en USD, ont été spécifiquement déclarés comme recettes pétrolières (redevances et recettes perçues au titre d'accords de partage des recettes conclus avec des compagnies pétrolières), celles-ci représentant l'essentiel des loyers et redevances perçus par le Cameroun, l'Égypte, la Guinée équatoriale, le Nigéria, la République du Congo et le Tchad. Parallèlement, les ressources minières étaient à l'origine de la majeure partie des loyers et redevances perçus par le Botswana, le Burkina Faso, le Ghana, la Namibie, le Niger, l'Ouganda, la Sierra Leone et la République démocratique du Congo. En 2020, la pêche a représenté 65 % de l'ensemble des recettes comptabilisées en loyers et redevances aux Seychelles, et 63 % en Mauritanie. Cette même année, en Mauritanie, les rentes de la pêche ont rapporté 192 millions USD, soit 2.4 % du PIB. La quasi-totalité des loyers et redevances enregistrés ici proviennent des ressources naturelles, qu'il s'agisse des industries extractives, de la pêche ou de la sylviculture. Les revenus de la propriété n'en constituent que 0.1 %.

Les recettes issues de ressources naturelles sont une source de financement souvent marquée par une forte volatilité. Cinq pays (Guinée équatoriale, Mauritanie, Nigéria, République du Congo et Tchad) ont perçu des loyers et redevances équivalant à plus de 5 % du PIB une année au moins au cours de la décennie écoulée, et tous ont enregistré une fois au moins une baisse annuelle en pourcentage du PIB de plus de 33 % de ces recettes. Celles de la République du Congo et du Tchad ont diminué au moins une fois de plus de 64 %.

Encadré 2.1. **Ressources naturelles et finances publiques**

Divers mécanismes[6] permettent aux États de dégager des recettes ou des économies à partir des ressources naturelles, les loyers et redevances étant le plus direct. L'État impose des redevances aux entreprises et aux particuliers en contrepartie du droit d'accéder aux terres appartenant au domaine public. Il agit en sa qualité de propriétaire des terrains concernés et les montants à verser sont généralement fixés par voie de négociations. Ces redevances sont comptabilisées au titre de revenus de la propriété. Le paiement des services fournis par les administrations publiques est une autre source de recettes non fiscales émanant d'entreprises du secteur primaire. Il s'agit par exemple de paiements au titre des contrôles environnementaux, de la construction d'infrastructures ou, dans le cas de Maurice, de la fourniture de données météorologiques et de cartes. Les recettes correspondantes sont comptabilisées comme produits de la vente de biens et de services.

- Le fait, pour l'État, de détenir une partie ou la totalité du capital d'une société exploitant en son nom des ressources naturelles peut lui procurer des recettes sous forme de bénéfices et de dividendes. Celles-ci sont comptabilisées comme revenus de la propriété. C'est par exemple à ce poste que sont comptabilisées les recettes que le gouvernement du Botswana dégage des dividendes que lui rapporte sa participation de 50 % au capital de la société Debswana, qui exploite les principales mines de diamants du pays (Mining Technology, 2020[9]).
- Il est possible de taxer l'exploitation des ressources naturelles, notamment sous la forme de droits d'accise sur les matières premières extraites de terres appartenant au domaine public ou de taxes minières qui ciblent non pas la personne physique ou morale qui exploite les ressources naturelles, mais l'activité d'exploitation proprement dite. Les revenus correspondants sont alors également

Encadré 2.1. **Ressources naturelles et finances publiques** *(suite)*

comptabilisés dans les recettes fiscales. Le Niger et le Sénégal appliquent des taxes de cette nature aux activités d'extraction, qui relèvent de la catégorie « autres impôts sur les biens et services » dans les *Statistiques des recettes publiques.*

- Les sociétés et les particuliers qui exploitent des ressources naturelles sont généralement assujettis aux mêmes impôts et taxes (impôts sur le revenu et taxe sur la valeur ajoutée par exemple) que les autres entités économiques. Les recettes correspondantes figurent dans les comptes publics, mais ne sont pas nécessairement imputées aux secteurs qui exploitent les ressources naturelles.
- Il arrive que des sociétés et des particuliers consacrent une partie de leur richesse issue de l'extraction de ressources naturelles à la construction d'infrastructures ou à la fourniture de services. Ces infrastructures ou services, lorsqu'ils répondent à une demande d'investissements ou de services publics, peuvent se traduire par une économie sur les dépenses publiques, qui ne sera cependant pas comptabilisée comme une recette pour l'État. Dans certains cas, l'État impose, comme condition à l'accès aux ressources naturelles dont il est propriétaire, que les entreprises et particuliers concernés fournissent certains services, par exemple en prenant à leur charge une partie au moins du coût de la construction et de l'entretien des routes desservant les mines. Des entreprises minières ont ainsi été mises à contribution dans le financement d'un réseau ferroviaire qui reliera sur 3 000 km le Bénin, le Burkina Faso, le Niger, la Côte d'Ivoire, le Ghana, le Nigéria et le Togo (CNN, 2015[10]).

Le montant total des exportations de pétrole, de charbon et de gaz des pays considérés dans les *Statistiques des recettes publiques en Afrique* a été essentiellement déterminé par les fluctuations du prix des produits de base, et non par celles du volume de ces exportations. Le montant total des rentes et redevances perçues par les États africains – que l'on compte ou non celles du Nigéria qui, depuis 2010, représentent entre 45 % et 70 % de ce total – évolue au même rythme que les cours internationaux du pétrole brut.

La chute soudaine des cours du pétrole en 2015 a entraîné une baisse du montant des exportations pétrolières en provenance d'Afrique qui s'est directement traduite par un fléchissement des recettes (Graphique 2.10). En même temps, les exportations de minerais, de métaux bruts, de diamants et autres minéraux ont régulièrement progressé tout au long de la décennie, et leur montant a dépassé celui des exportations de pétrole, de charbon et de gaz. Les loyers et redevances que les pays africains ont dégagées de ces autres minéraux n'ont cependant pas atteint le niveau des rentes tirées de l'industrie pétrolière et gazière.

Graphique 2.10. **Loyers et redevances et exportations de produits de base des pays considérés dans les *Statistiques des recettes publiques en Afrique*, 2010-20**

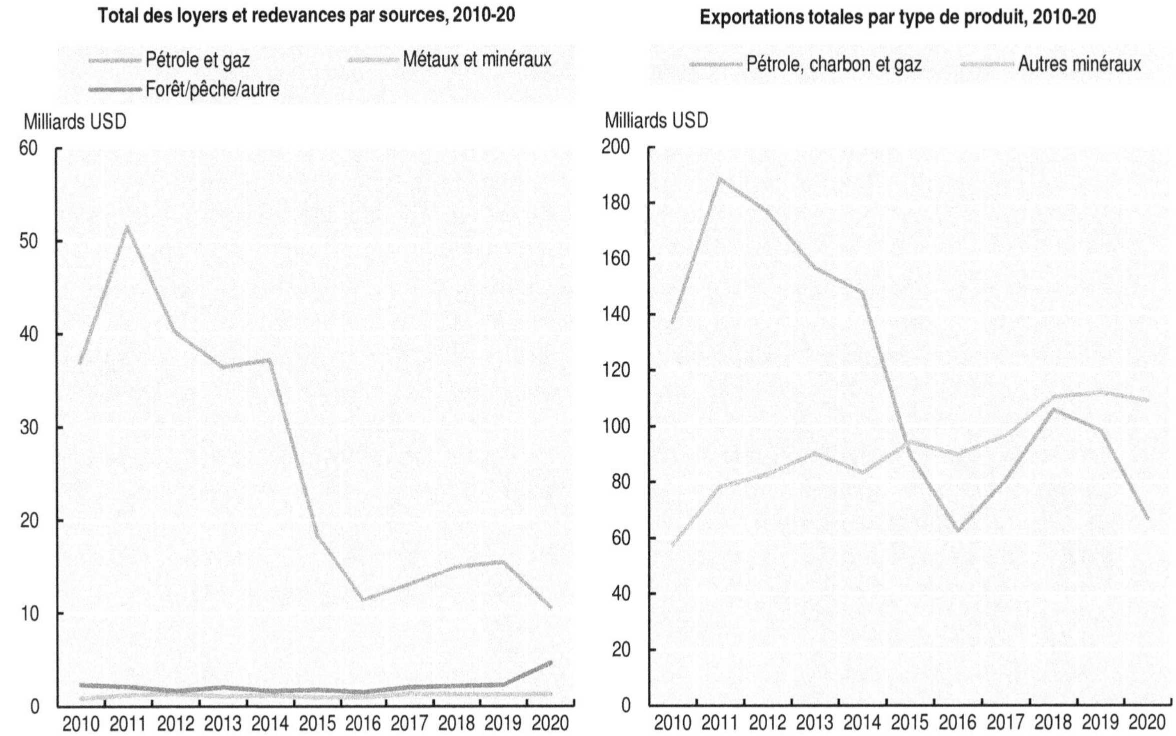

Source : Calculs des auteurs fondés sur les données de la base de données de commerce international au niveau des produits de BACI (CEPII, 2022[4]) pour les chiffres relatifs aux exportations de pétrole et de charbon ; édition d'avril 2022 des *Perspectives de l'économie mondiale* (FMI, 2022[1]) et (OCDE/ATAF/CUA, 2022[2]), « Statistiques des recettes publiques en Afrique : Tableaux comparatifs », *Statistiques fiscales de l'OCDE* (base de données), *https://doi.org/10.1787/7f54581d-fr*.

StatLink *https://stat.link/uh9bkx*

Les chocs que la pandémie de COVID-19 a provoqués au niveau de l'offre et de la demande ont eu des répercussions sur les prix des produits de base, tout particulièrement sur ceux du pétrole (Graphique 2.11). Le cours du pétrole brut a chuté à 23 USD par baril en avril 2020, son plus bas niveau depuis 2002, mais s'est rapidement stabilisé, le cours annuel s'établissant en 2020 à 42.3 USD par baril, soit un niveau inférieur de 34 % à celui enregistré en 2019 et équivalent à celui de 2016. En revanche, le prix de nombreux produits de base a augmenté pendant la pandémie. L'indice des prix des produits de base non énergétiques a progressé entre 2019 et 2020 sous l'effet de la hausse des prix des produits agricoles et des métaux. Figurent parmi les métaux dont le prix a augmenté le cuivre et l'or, qui sont les principaux métaux produits par les pays considérés ici, ainsi que le platine, l'argent et le minerai de fer. Les prix de l'aluminium, du plomb, de l'étain, du nickel, du zinc et du chlorure de potassium ont pour leur part diminué.

Graphique 2.11. **Prix des principaux produits de base, avant et pendant la pandémie du COVID-19**

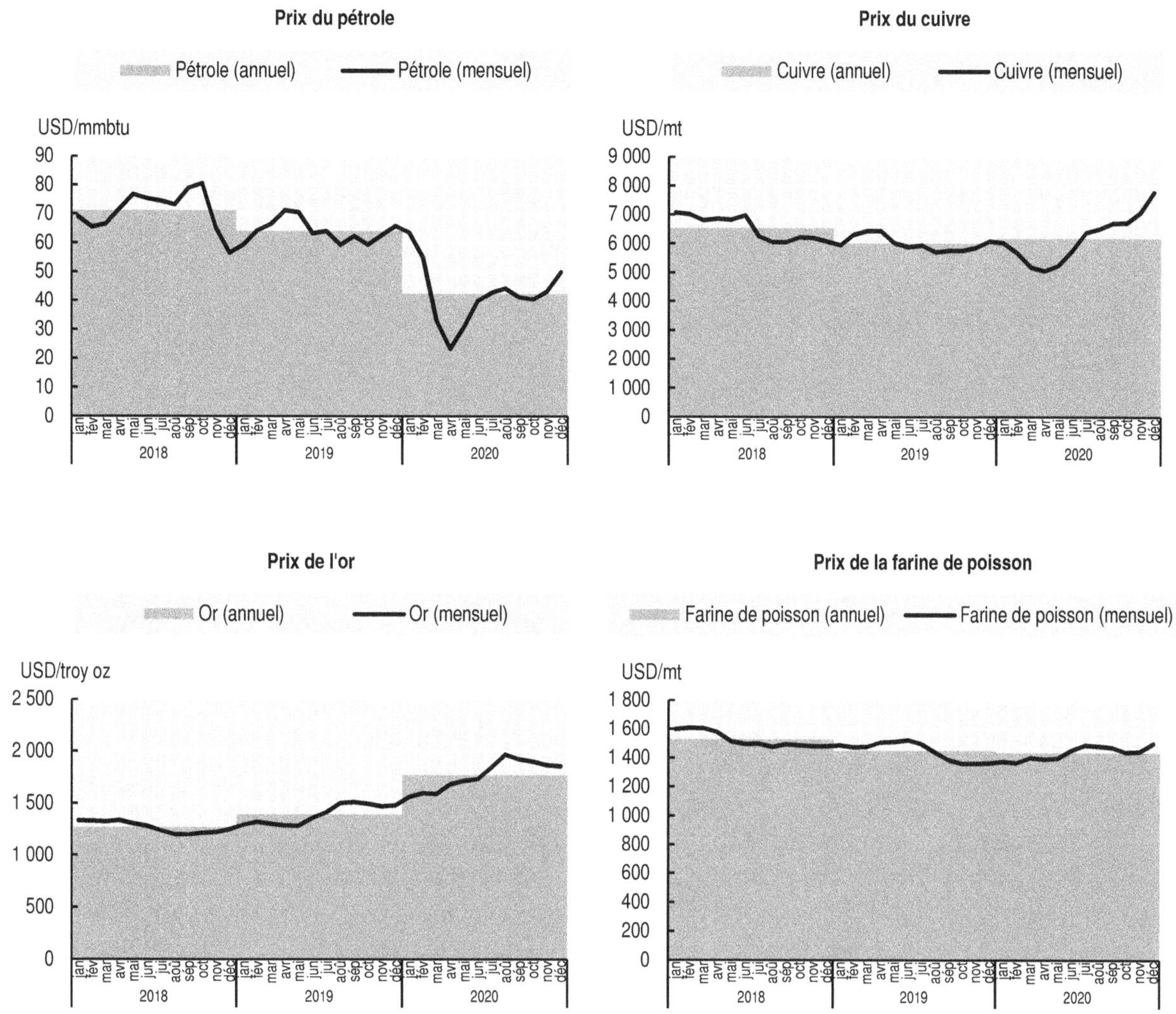

Note : Le prix du pétrole indiqué ici est le prix du Brent Crude.
Source : Données sur les prix des matières premières (« The Pink Sheet ») (Banque mondiale, 2022[11]).

StatLink https://stat.link/fyj654

La nature et l'ampleur des richesses naturelles des pays africains varient considérablement. La contribution de ces richesses au PIB est également variable selon les pays, de même que leur incidence sur les budgets publics. Ainsi, d'après les estimations de la Banque mondiale concernant la contribution des ressources naturelles souterraines à la production économique (Graphique 2.12), cette contribution s'est montée en 2020 à 17 % du PIB au moins dans trois pays : la République du Congo (pétrole principalement), la République démocratique du Congo (essentiellement les minerais) et la Guinée équatoriale (pétrole essentiellement) (Banque mondiale, 2022[6])[7].

Graphique 2.12. **Extraction de ressources naturelles, estimations, 2020**

Pourcentage du PIB

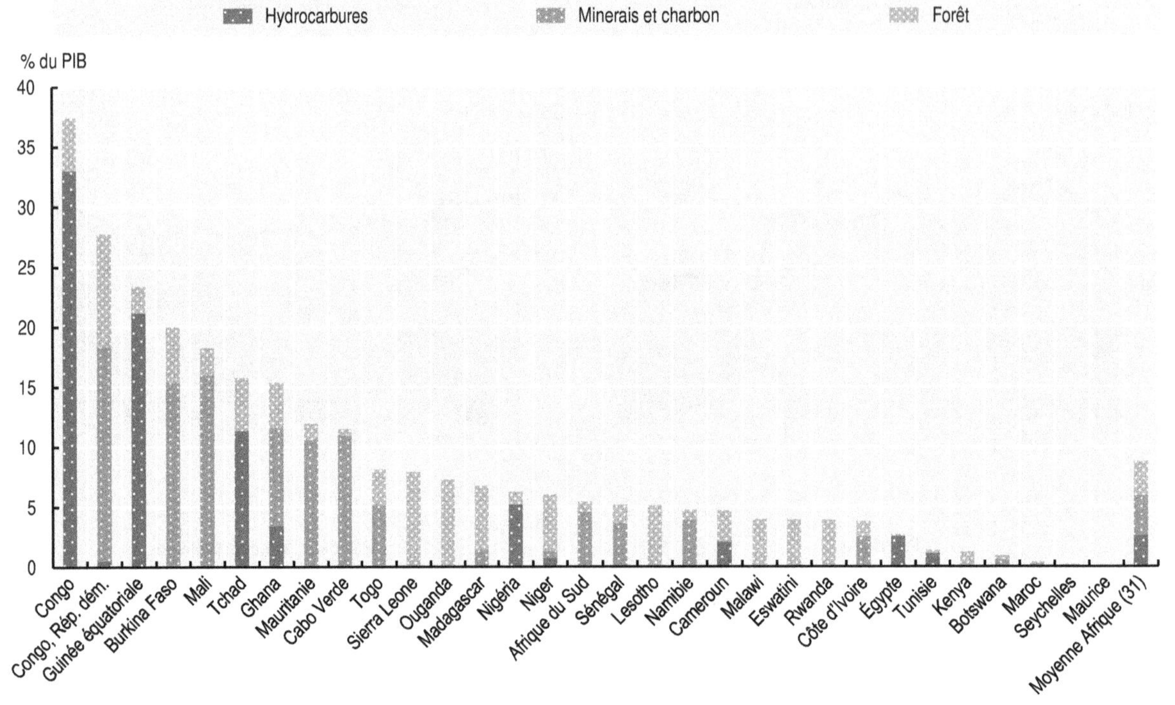

Source : (Banque mondiale, 2022[6]), *Indicateurs du développement dans le monde* (base de données), pour les estimations de la valeur totale de la production de ressources naturelles de chaque pays.

StatLink https://stat.link/mnpifq

L'incidence des ressources naturelles de chaque pays sur les finances publiques varie aussi considérablement. Des pays comme la Guinée équatoriale, la Mauritanie, la République du Congo et le Tchad tirent des recettes publiques substantielles de ces ressources alors que l'Afrique du Sud, par exemple, dont la richesse issue de leur exploitation représente pourtant plus de 5.4 % du PIB, a déclaré un montant de recettes publiques au titre des rentes correspondantes équivalent à 0.3 % du PIB.

Dans cinq pays (Lesotho, Madagascar, Ouganda, République démocratique du Congo et Sierra Leone), la richesse provenant des forêts équivaut à plus de 5 % du PIB mais ne contribue guère aux recettes publiques. Bien que certains pays, comme le Cameroun et le Niger, aient perçu quelques redevances au titre de l'exploitation de leurs forêts, les recettes forestières n'ont représenté qu'une faible part de leurs recettes non fiscales.

Autres recettes non fiscales

Certains pays dégagent d'importantes recettes non fiscales du fonctionnement courant des administrations publiques. Ces recettes peuvent être regroupées en trois catégories : ventes de biens et services, amendes et pénalités, et recettes diverses et non identifiées. Leur collecte présente souvent les difficultés posées par le recouvrement des recettes non fiscales exposées à l'encadré 2.1 ; en effet, elles ne sont généralement pas perçues par les administrations fiscales et, souvent, ne sont pas définies par la législation. Parfois, elles ne figurent même pas dans les comptes publics.

Pour toutes ces catégories de recettes, la question peut se poser de savoir s'il s'agit de prélèvements obligatoires ou sans contrepartie et, par conséquent, s'il ne serait pas plus approprié de les classer dans les recettes fiscales. La question de savoir quels frais administratifs doivent être ou non considérés comme des impôts est examinée aux annexes A et B. Le problème de la classification des amendes et des pénalités n'est cependant pas toujours facile à trancher.

Il se peut que les institutions et administrations publiques qui ont moins de pouvoir, et donc moins d'autorité pour prélever l'impôt, recourent davantage à ce type de recettes non fiscales. Autrement dit, les recettes non fiscales perçues par les administrations locales risquent d'être sous-estimées.

Produits de la vente de biens et de services et frais administratifs

Les administrations publiques peuvent produire des biens et des services relevant aussi bien du secteur marchand que non marchand. Dans le secteur marchand, elles fournissent parfois des biens et services qui peuvent également être obtenus auprès d'entreprises privées (produits alimentaires ou services de transport par exemple). En parallèle, elles assurent, lorsqu'elles gèrent des programmes ou garantissent le respect de la loi, différents services qui sont du seul ressort de l'État. Les frais facturés pour ces services non marchands sont le plus souvent considérés comme des frais administratifs.

Les frais administratifs sont souvent difficiles à classer, car ils se situent dans une zone grise, à mi-chemin entre les rémunérations de services (qui sont des recettes non fiscales) et les prélèvements obligatoires effectués sans contrepartie au profit d'administrations publiques (qui sont des recettes fiscales)[8]. Les frais de justice, ainsi que les frais de dossiers pour les permis de conduire, passeports, enregistrements de brevets et certificats de mariage sont généralement classés dans les recettes non fiscales. Lorsqu'ils sont considérés comme des recettes fiscales, ils sont en principe rattachés à l'une des catégories suivantes :

- 4400 - Impôts sur les transactions mobilières et immobilières (taxes sur les transactions foncières par exemple) ;
- 5200 - Impôts sur l'utilisation des biens et l'autorisation d'exercer des activités (permis de chasse, enregistrement des véhicules, etc.) ;
- 6000 - Autres impôts (comme la vente de timbres fiscaux, dans les cas où ces timbres sont utilisés pour le paiement des taxes et frais administratifs).

Dans cinq des pays étudiés, les recettes tirées de la vente de biens et de services et de la perception de frais administratifs ont représenté au moins 1 % du PIB en 2020 (Graphique 2.13) : Cabo Verde (2.3 % du PIB), Égypte (1.3 %), Ghana (1.2 %), Maroc (1.2 %) et Seychelles (2.0 %). Avec l'ajout de ces trois catégories de taxes énumérées ci-dessus, ces recettes s'élèvent à plus de 2.5% du PIB pour Cabo Verde et les Seychelles.

Graphique 2.13. **Ventes de biens et services, frais administratifs et autres recettes liées à l'administration, 2020**

Pourcentage du PIB

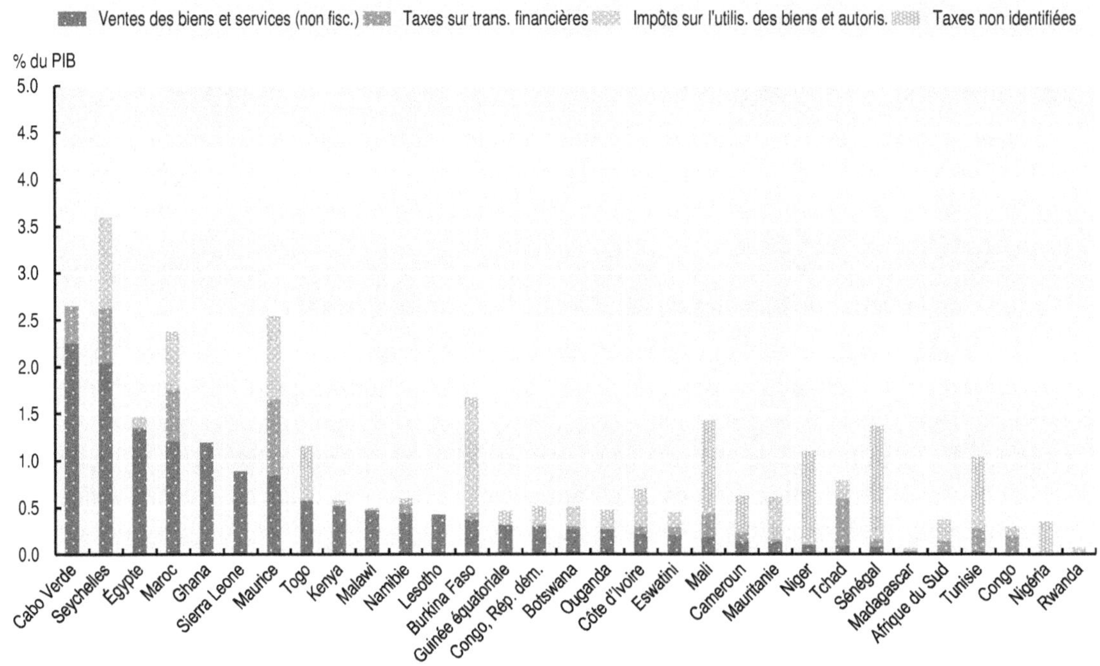

Note : Les montants indiqués ici incluent les recettes fiscales perçues par les administrations infranationales dans les cas de l'Afrique du Sud, du Maroc, de Maurice et du Nigéria, et les recettes non fiscales perçues par ces mêmes administrations dans les cas de l'Eswatini, du Kenya, du Maroc, et de Maurice, seuls pays pour lesquels les données correspondantes sont disponibles pour 2020.

Source : Calculs des auteurs basés sur des données figurant dans (OCDE/ATAF/CUA, 2022[2]), « Statistiques des recettes publiques en Afrique : Tableaux comparatifs », *Statistiques fiscales de l'OCDE* (base de données), *https://doi.org/10.1787/7f54581d-fr*.

StatLink *https://stat.link/mjwqg8*

La composition de ces recettes varie selon les pays. Au Cabo Verde, 98 % des recettes enregistrées au titre de la vente de biens et de services étaient des frais administratifs. Au Ghana, elles ont dans leur majeure partie été perçues au niveau des communes et services et organismes administratifs, ou bien au niveau des districts, assemblées municipales et métropolitaines. Au Maroc, 55 % de ces recettes ont été recouvrées au niveau local.

Recettes diverses ou non identifiées

Certaines recettes non fiscales représentent des montants significatifs, mais ne relèvent d'aucune des catégories citées ci-dessus. Il s'agit des suivantes :

- transferts en capital non compris ailleurs ;
- dons versés par des particuliers ou sociétés à des organismes publics (à l'exception des dons émanant d'organisations internationales, qui relèvent de la catégorie des dons) ;
- sommes versées par des entités privées aux administrations publiques à l'issue d'importants règlements judiciaires ou au titre d'indemnités d'assurance (comme les 100 millions EUR d'indemnités qu'Arcelor Mittal a dû payer à l'État sénégalais en application de la décision de justice rendue suite à l'annulation d'un projet de mine de fer (RFI, 2014[12]) ;
- versements relevant de différentes catégories de la classification pour lesquels aucune ventilation n'est disponible ;
- versements inclassables faute de données pertinentes. Le Rwanda n'ayant pas donné le détail de ses recettes non fiscales, sauf en ce qui concerne les dons, celles-ci ont été classées dans cette catégorie ;

- revenus transférés par la SACU au Botswana, à l'Eswatini, au Lesotho et à la Namibie (voir encadré 2.2).

Les recettes diverses et non identifiées peuvent représenter une composante non négligeable des recettes non fiscales de certains pays. Elles recouvrent notamment les contributions volontaires exceptionnelles versées à l'administration en Tunisie, les transferts en capital depuis des fonds statutaires spéciaux à Maurice et, au Maroc, les versements effectués au bénéfice de l'administration en contrepartie du droit à entrer en concurrence avec des institutions publiques pour la prestation de services.

La variabilité des recettes diverses et non identifiées peut être imputable à des transferts de capitaux importants, à des entrées de recettes éphémères ou à la reclassification de fonds dans la catégorie des recettes non identifiées en raison de l'absence de données. La présence de montants élevés dans cette rubrique pourrait conduire à s'interroger sur la précision des montants inscrits dans les autres catégories de recettes non fiscales.

Encadré 2.2. **Recettes issues de la SACU**

L'Union douanière d'Afrique australe (South African Customs Union, SACU) réunit l'Afrique du Sud, le Botswana, l'Eswatini, le Lesotho et la Namibie. Son siège se trouve à Windhoek (Namibie). Elle a pour objectif d'établir « une communauté économique qui favorise un développement équitable et durable, au service du bien-être des peuples, pour construire un avenir commun ».

La SACU, qui est la plus ancienne union douanière au monde, a été créée en 1899 entre la colonie britannique du Cap de Bonne-Espérance et la République boer de l'État libre d'Orange. Des accords conclus ultérieurement, en 1910 puis en 1969, ont marqué l'adhésion du Botswana, de l'Eswatini et du Lesotho. Après l'accession à l'indépendance de la Namibie, en 1990, et la fin de l'apartheid en Afrique du Sud, en 1994, de nouvelles négociations ont été ouvertes pour aboutir, en 2002, à la conclusion de l'accord en vigueur aujourd'hui.

Celui-ci prévoit la libre circulation entre les pays membres de la SACU de tous les produits manufacturés fabriqués dans ces pays, en franchise de droits et taxes. Il définit également des tarifs extérieurs communs et la mise en commun des recettes perçues au titre des droits de douane et d'accise en vue de leur répartition entre les pays membres de la SACU suivant la formule exposée en annexe à l'Accord.

L'accord de partage des recettes comporte trois composantes :

- Une composante douanière, qui divise le montant brut des droits de douane en fonction de la valeur des marchandises importées par chaque pays depuis les autres pays membres de la SACU au cours de l'année considérée (en pourcentage des importations totales intra-SACU).
- Une composante portant sur les droits d'accise, qui divise le montant brut de ces droits selon le ratio correspondant au PIB de chaque pays rapporté au PIB total de la SACU.
- Une composante de développement, financée par 15 % de la composante liée aux droits d'accise et pondérée en faveur des pays moins développés de la SACU selon une formule fondée sur le PIB par habitant.

Dans la présente publication, les recettes issues des droits de douane et d'accise sont incluses dans les recettes fiscales du pays de la SACU qui les a collectées. Elles sont rapportées dans les rubriques 5121 (accises) et 5123 (droits de douane et droits à l'importation) des tableaux des recettes fiscales. Les montants redistribués par le fonds commun des recettes de la SACU sont classés dans les tableaux des recettes non fiscales, sous la rubrique des recettes diverses et non identifiées, comme indiqué dans le tableau 6.13 à propos de l'Eswatini. En ce qui concerne l'Afrique du Sud, contributeur net au mécanisme de la SACU, les contributions, nettes des reversements perçus, sont indiquées pour mémoire dans le tableau des recettes non fiscales (tableau 6.23).

Source : (SACU, 2017[13]), (SACU, 2014[14]).

Recettes issues de l'Union douanière d'Afrique australe

Les cinq membres de la SACU prélèvent des droits de douane et d'accise dans le cadre d'un régime fiscal uniforme, puis transfèrent les sommes collectées dans le fonds commun de recettes de la SACU. Ce dernier les redistribue ensuite selon une formule complexe de répartition des recettes. En pratique, toutefois, comme l'Afrique du Sud détient les principaux ports d'entrée de l'Afrique australe, elle recouvre la quasi-totalité des droits de douane et d'accise destinés à ce fonds. Elle en est par conséquent un contributeur net, les autres pays membres en étant en revanche des bénéficiaires nets.

Si les recettes issues de la SACU sont négligeables pour l'Afrique du Sud, elles ont en revanche une incidence majeure sur les finances des autres membres de l'Union douanière (Graphique 2.14). En 2020, elles ont augmenté les recettes du Botswana, de l'Eswatini, du Lesotho et de la Namibie de 9.3 %, 12.6 %, 26.6 % et 12.6 % de leur PIB respectivement. Indépendamment des chocs économiques exogènes, le montant des recettes ainsi redistribuées a fluctué au gré de l'évolution des paramètres employés dans la formule de répartition des recettes. Le choc économique provoqué par la crise financière mondiale a rendu caduques bon nombre des prévisions économiques d'alors ; les paiements de la SACU étant calculés à partir de ces prévisions, il a fallu procéder à d'importants ajustements en 2010 et 2011 pour compenser les versements excessifs effectués pendant plusieurs années au titre du système de regroupement et de redistribution des recettes de la SACU (Mongardini et al., 2011[15]). Une situation similaire s'est produite en 2014, le ralentissement de l'économie sud-africaine ayant de nouveau contraint à corriger les prévisions à la baisse. Les recettes redistribuées par la SACU à l'Eswatini, au Lesotho et à la Namibie ont diminué, en pourcentage du PIB, en 2015 et 2016, mais la tendance s'est inversée en 2017.

Graphique 2.14. **Total des recettes issues de la SACU et autres recettes non fiscales, par pays**

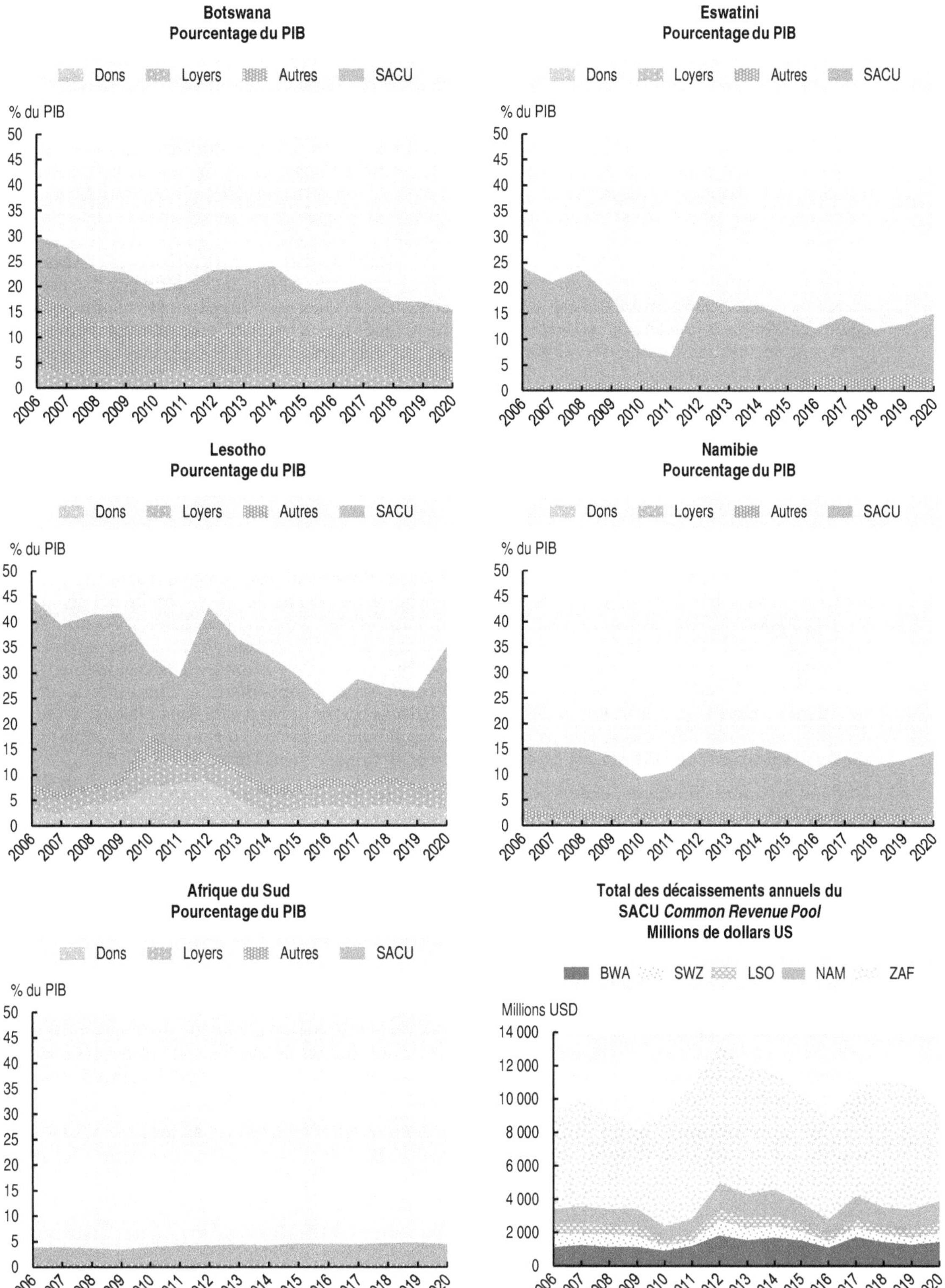

Note : Les recettes issues de la SACU indiquées ici sont classées dans la catégorie des recettes non fiscales pour tous les pays considérés ici à l'exception de l'Afrique du Sud. Pour ce pays, elles sont classées dans celle des droits de douane et d'accise.

Source : Calculs des auteurs basés sur les données figurant dans (OCDE/ATAF/CUA, 2022[2]), « Statistiques des recettes publiques en Afrique : Tableaux comparatifs », *Statistiques fiscales de l'OCDE* (base de données), *https://doi.org/10.1787/7f54581d-fr*.

StatLink *https://stat.link/e7lygp*

Notes

1 Les recettes non fiscales soulèvent plusieurs problèmes méthodologiques que ne posent pas nécessairement les statistiques fiscales. Il est possible que certaines recettes, comme les frais administratifs, servent de mécanismes d'amortissement et viennent minorer les coûts au lieu d'être comptabilisées comme recettes. Ce cas de figure peut concerner les collectivités locales et autres institutions publiques pour lesquelles les données disponibles concernent uniquement les transferts nets de fonds à destination de l'administration centrale. La comptabilisation des ventes de biens et de services sans déduction des coûts peut entraîner une surestimation des recettes d'un gouvernement. Les dons, les règlements juridiques, les contrats d'exploitation minière ou pétrolière donnent lieu à des versements importants de la part d'entités extérieures telles que des entreprises multinationales ou des administrations étrangères parfois soumises à des mécanismes de contrôle nationaux distincts. Il est plus difficile d'établir des ventilations détaillées dès lors qu'un pays riche en ressources négocie en contrepartie de leur extraction le versement de sommes forfaitaires élevées, qui regroupent plusieurs catégories de recettes, fiscales et non fiscales. Enfin, les recettes non fiscales relèvent souvent d'autres autorités que les recettes fiscales, les recettes et les dépenses n'étant par ailleurs pas toujours présentées séparément, de sorte qu'elles ne suivent pas forcément les mêmes normes de déclaration. Se reporter à l'annexe B pour une description détaillée de la méthodologie utilisée pour les recettes non fiscales.

2 Il n'y a pas de comparaison possible avec les moyennes des 28 pays d'Amérique latine et des Caraïbes (ALC) (voir (OCDE et al., 2022[17])) et des 38 pays de l'OCDE (voir (OCDE, 2021[18])), car les publications correspondantes ne couvrent pas les recettes non fiscales.

3 Voir le Guide d'interprétation sur les recettes non fiscales dans l'annexe B du présent rapport pour la définition de ces catégories de revenus.

4 Voir également l'annexe B.

5 La définition officielle de l'APD est la suivante : « tous les apports de ressources qui sont fournis aux pays et territoires figurant sur la Liste des bénéficiaires d'APD établie par le Comité d'aide au développement ou à des institutions multilatérales et qui émanent d'organismes publics, y compris des États et des collectivités locales, ou d'organismes agissant pour le compte d'organismes publics, sachant que chaque opération doit en outre avoir pour but essentiel de favoriser le développement économique et l'amélioration du niveau de vie des pays en développement, et être assortie de conditions favorables et comporter un élément de libéralité au moins égal à 25 % (sur la base d'un taux d'actualisation de 10 %) ». Des informations supplémentaires sont disponibles à l'adresse suivante : *www.oecd.org/dac/financing-sustainable-development/index-terms.htm#ODA*.

6 La Banque mondiale utilise l'expression « bénéfices tirés des ressources naturelles ». Ceux-ci correspondent à la différence entre la valeur des ressources naturelles produites dans les pays, qui est fonction des prix des matières premières, et le coût estimé de l'extraction des ressources. À ne pas confondre avec la rente de ressources, que l'OCDE définit comme étant une catégorie de recette publique. Se reporter à la documentation sur les rentes de ressources dans l'ensemble de données des indicateurs de développement mondial de la Banque mondiale (voir *https://databank.worldbank.org/metadataglossary/adjusted-net-savings/series/NY.GDP.TOTL.RT.ZS*) et au guide d'interprétation pour de plus amples détails.

7 Il convient de noter que les recettes fiscales tirées de l'extraction pétrolière peuvent englober l'impôt sur les bénéfices des sociétés, les droits indirects sur des produits énergétiques et des taxes sur les ventes non remboursables, comme la TVA ; les recettes non fiscales peuvent inclure les redevances, les transferts de bénéfices, les dividendes versés par les entreprises publiques et d'autres revenus d'investissements perçus au titre de la participation directe de l'État dans le capital d'entreprises du secteur extractif (Mansour et Rota-Graziosi, 2013[16]).

8 Pour de plus amples informations sur la classification des frais administratifs, consulter, à l'annexe A, les paragraphes 12 à 15 du Guide d'interprétation de l'OCDE.

Références

Banque mondiale (2022), *Indicateurs du développement dans le monde*, *https://data.worldbank.org/* (consulté le 9 September 2022). [6]

Banque mondiale (2022), *World Bank Commodity Price Data (The Pink Sheet)*, *https://www.worldbank.org/en/research/commodity-markets* (consulté le September 2022). [11]

Banque mondiale (2022), *World Bank Country and Lending Groups*, *https://datahelpdesk.worldbank.org/knowledgebase/articles/906519* (consulté le June 2022). [5]

CEPII (2022), *BACI Base de données de commerce international au niveau des produits, http://www.cepii.fr/CEPII/fr/bdd_modele/bdd_modele_item.asp?id=37* (consulté le 22 février). [4]

CNN (2015), *Mammoth rail network to put West African economies on the right track, https://edition.cnn.com/2015/03/05/africa/west-africa-minerals-railway/index.html* (consulté le 21 September 2020). [10]

FMI (2022), *Perspectives de l'économie mondiale, édition avril 2022 (base de données), https://www.imf.org/fr/Publications/WEO/Issues/2022/04/19/world-economic-outlook-april-2022.* [1]

Mansour, M. et G. Rota-Graziosi (2013), « Tax Coordination, Tax Competition, and Revenue Mobilization in the West African Economic and Monetary Union », *Document de travail du FMI*, vol. 13/vol. 163, *https://www.imf.org/en/Publications/WP/Issues/2016/12/31/Tax-Coordination-Tax-Competition-and-Revenue-Mobilization-in-the-West-African-Economic-and-40756.* [16]

Mining Technology (2020), *Debswana diamond mines, https://www.mining-technology.com/projects/debswana/* (consulté le 20 September 2020). [9]

Mongardini, J. et al. (2011), *In the wake of the global economic crisis: adjusting to lower revenue of the Southern African Customs*, Fonds monétaire international, *https://www.imf.org/external/pubs/ft/dp/2011/afr1101.pdf.* [15]

OCDE (2022), *DAC Data submitters, http://www.oecd.org/dac/financing-sustainable-development/development-finance-standards/dacdatasubmitters.htm* (consulté le 8 September 2022). [7]

OCDE (2021), *Statistiques des recettes publiques 2021 : l'impact initial du COVID-19 sur les recettes fiscales de l'OCDE*, Éditions OCDE, Paris, *https://doi.org/10.1787/ed5596c6-fr.* [18]

OCDE/ATAF/CUA (2022), « Recettes fiscales en Afrique : Tableaux comparatifs », *Statistiques fiscales de l'OCDE, https://doi.org/10.1787/7f54581d-fr* (consulté le 21 septembre 2022). [2]

OCDE et al. (2022), *Revenue Statistics in Latin America and the Caribbean 2022*, Éditions OCDE, Paris, *https://doi.org/10.1787/58a2dc35-en-es.* [17]

OCDE-CAD (2022), *Statistiques en ligne sur le développement international (SDI), https://www.oecd.org/fr/cad/comite-d-aide-au-developpement/* (consulté le 10 Septembre). [3]

RFI (2014), *Le gros chèque d'Arcelor Mittal au Sénégal, http://www.rfi.fr/economie/20140605-le-gros-cheque-arcelor-mittal-senegal.* [12]

SACU (2017), *Southern African Customs Union Agreement 2002 (tel qu'amendé le 12 avril 2013), http://www.sacu.int/list.php?type=Agreements.* [13]

SACU (2014), *Implementing a Common Agenda Towards Regional Integration: 2014 Annual Report, http://www.sacu.int/docs/reports_annual/2014/annual_report.pdf.* [14]

VOANews (2013), *Malawi: Donors Withhold Aid Over Cashgate Scandal, https://www.voanews.com/a/malawi-donors-withhold-aid-over-cashgate-scandal/1786120.html* (consulté le 21 September 2020). [8]

Chapter 3

Efficient taxation of the informal sector in Africa

Chapitre 3

Imposer efficacement le secteur informel en Afrique

Revenue Statistics in Africa 1990-2020/Statistiques des recettes publiques en Afrique 1990-2020

Chapter 3

Efficient taxation of the informal sector in Africa

Introduction

This chapter[1] is based on the Guidebook on the Efficient Taxation of the Informal Sector in Africa (hereafter, the Guidebook, (ATAF, 2021[1]))[2] produced by the African Tax Administration Forum (ATAF) and on ATAF's presentation and discussions during the *Revenue Statistics in Africa* Webinar 2022 (2-3 June 2022).[3] The chapter articulates the rationale for taxing the informal sector in Africa and provides an overview of good practices and African experiences in this area. It includes short case studies from three countries – Ghana, Kenya and Nigeria – that are based on interventions during the same Webinar.

Over the years, numerous attempts have been made to find a suitable definition and scope of the term "informal sector". The International Labour Organisation defines the informal sector as including 'all economic activities by workers and economic units that are – in law or practice – not covered or insufficiently covered by formal arrangements' (ILO, 2015[2]). On the other hand, (Buehn, Karmann and Schneider, 2009[3]) consider the informal sector to include all market-based legal production of goods and services that are intentionally concealed (hidden) from public authorities.

In light of the various definitions, (ATAF, 2021[1]) defines the informal sector as follows: "All economic activities by workers and economic entities which are not covered or insufficiently covered by formal arrangements including underground production activities, and not registered with revenue authorities or tax administrations."[4] This definition explicitly includes informal sector activities which are not registered by revenue authorities, thus not paying (direct) taxes. It is worth noting that informal sector economic activities are prevalent in both developing and developed economies, where they are not a temporary, marginal or peripheral phenomenon but rather a permanent feature.

The informal sector remains the main source of livelihoods for a majority of African citizens, with eight out of ten workers in Africa in informal employment (ILO, 2018[4]). The high incidence of informality is a major challenge for the respect of workers' rights and the quality of working conditions in Africa, and is a constraint on growth. Ensuring an empowered, competitive and productive informal economy for the well-being of all workers in Africa is a priority of the African Union. A joint AUC/ILO programme is currently working to establish a legal and policy framework and other measures to recognise, regulate and promote the transformative development of the informal economy (AUC/ILO, 2019[5]).

The informal sector has not been contributing significantly to domestic resource mobilisation (DRM) as far as payment of taxes to respective national revenue authorities is concerned. In an effort to boost DRM and tax-to-GDP ratios in African countries, ATAF, through the support of the African Development Bank, embarked on a research project to assess the effective and efficient ways to tax the informal sector in Africa. The project commenced in 2019 and was concluded in 2021. The main objectives of the project were as follows:

1. Provide a description of the informal sector in Africa based on country questionnaires, focus group discussions with relevant stakeholders as well as good practices, success stories, and lessons learnt from country experiences;

2. Propose a framework or model for the effective taxation of the informal sector in Africa;
3. Describe how this proposed framework/model for the effective taxation of the informal sector should be administered;
4. Present a monitoring and evaluation (M&E) framework aimed at ensuring successful and sustainable implementation of the informal sector taxation model;
5. Provide key recommendations for optimal informal sector taxation in the continent.

The outcomes of this project include, among others, a Guidebook which provides a pragmatic set of options rooted in African experiences for taxing the informal sector on the continent. Other outcomes include a booklet of good practices, success stories and lessons learnt in the sector.

This chapter outlines the objectives and major findings of the study, and it presents a framework for efficient taxation of the informal sector in Africa. Among the most important findings is that policy makers should institute a culture of good governance, promote the benefits of tax compliance, specify robust technical requirements for implementation of the taxation model, adopt a simplified tax system, introduce binding taxes, and recognise the heterogeneity of the informal sector in Africa.

The study provides a model for the taxation of the informal sector that was designed around a consultative approach with key players in the fiscal management of the informal sector in Africa (tax administrations, informal sector actors and policy makers). This inclusive approach ensured that the outcomes from the project were relevant to the African continent as regards the improvement of DRM through optimally taxing the informal sector.

Box 3.1. **Using technology and tax policy to bring informal operators into Kenya's tax net**

Over 83% of employment in Kenya is in the informal sector, and informal workers are distributed across the economy (Kenya National Bureau of Statistics, 2022[6]). More than 61% of informal workers are engaged in the wholesale and retail trade, hotels and restaurant sectors, while 21% of informal workers are in manufacturing, and 10% in community social and personal services, with the rest in transport, communications and construction.

There is no special treatment for informal workers in Kenya. The government expects workers to file returns for personal income tax and VAT when they reach certain income thresholds; however, workers in the informal sector rarely comply. Part of the reason why compliance is so low is that mobility is so high: Kenya's use of block management approaches to track informal enterprises proved ineffective because informal sector operators move frequently – even on an hourly basis – to find the greatest volume of potential customers. Informal enterprises are frequently unwilling to pay tax or unable to do so because they do not keep proper records. The prevalence of cash transactions in the informal sector means there is not an electronic paper trail of business activities.

Kenya has adopted a range of measures to ensure informal sector operators account and pay taxes, with certain measures being in place for decades. For example, since 1996, operators of *matatus* (minibus taxis) and other forms of transport have been required to pay an advance tax each year when they renew their operations licence; although compliance is high, the disadvantage is that these operators rarely file a return at the end of the year due to poor record-keeping.

Box 3.1. **Using technology and tax policy to bring informal operators into Kenya's tax net** *(cont.)*

There is also a turnover tax, which requires people earning between KES 1 million and KES 50 million to pay 1% of their gross income. This was used interchangeably with a presumptive tax that was introduced in 2018, which local governments levied on business operators in exchange for their operational certificates (at a rate of 15% of renewal fees) to bring them into the tax net. However, the presumptive tax was not widely used. Lastly, Kenya has made it possible for informal workers to register voluntarily for VAT payments even if their turnover was below the minimum threshold. To improve access to third-party information about the activities of the informal sector, the Kenya Revenue Authority (KRA) has signed memoranda of understanding with local governments and business registries.

The KRA is taking active steps to make it easier for actors in the informal sector to pay taxes, not only by harnessing technology but also by investing in taxpayer education. Many taxpayers find the process of registering for and paying taxes to be complex and they often lack the required documents. The KRA has fully automated its tax system and put all its services online. The M-Service app, for example, simplifies filing and payment of the turnover tax, monthly rental income, and property registration as well as the application for a tax clearance certificate. The KRA has also set up tax clinics to educate informal sector operators.

Source: Based on country experiences shared during the *Revenue Statistics in Africa* Webinar 2022 (2-3 June 2022).

Major findings

The study used questionnaires and focus groups to collect data from African countries[5]. According to the survey, major reasons motivating taxpayers to operate in the informal sector were poor relations with tax administrations, insufficient tax information, and difficulties in computing tax, filing, and reporting, which would force them to hire a tax consultant. Poor relations with tax administrations and insufficient tax information were the two main reasons given by interviewees for operating in the informal sector (Figure 3.1). The major constraints and challenges to formalising business enterprises are costly registration processes, excessive requirements in terms of documentation/paperwork, high tax rates and a multiplicity of tax types, lack of credit lines and a challenging business environment.

The various taxation initiatives covering the informal sector that have been implemented by African countries over the years include the introduction of personal income tax and value-added tax as the leading tax types (mentioned by 64.9% and 63.2% of interviewees respectively), as well as turnover tax and withholding tax (Figure 3.2). Studies of the impact of tax regimes on tax compliance and additional revenue are lacking in most tax administrations, to the extent that about 66% of tax authorities claim that they have not assessed the impact of tax regimes targeted at operators in the informal sector.

Feedback from focus groups and questionnaires highlighted major weaknesses in the established tax rules for the informal sector. These include: (i) unfair presumptive taxation focused on the nature of business; (ii) the arbitrary nature of turnover-based taxation; (iii) progressive taxation based on various turnover thresholds, which can be a source of vertical injustice if the variation in the amount of tax payable is not proportional to turnover; (iv) the negative impact of the presumptive minimum profit on investment by micro and small enterprises; (v) the rapid graduation of micro-enterprises to taxable business regimes, which can create an unmanageable tax burden; (vi) the negative impact of import-based down payments on cashflow; (vii) the ineffectiveness of tax amnesty programmes; (viii) the multiplicity of taxes for informal sector operators; (ix) ineffective tax management of the informal sector within tax administrations and (x) low volume of tax returns from the informal sector.

Figure 3.1. **Reasons and motivation for operating in the informal sector**

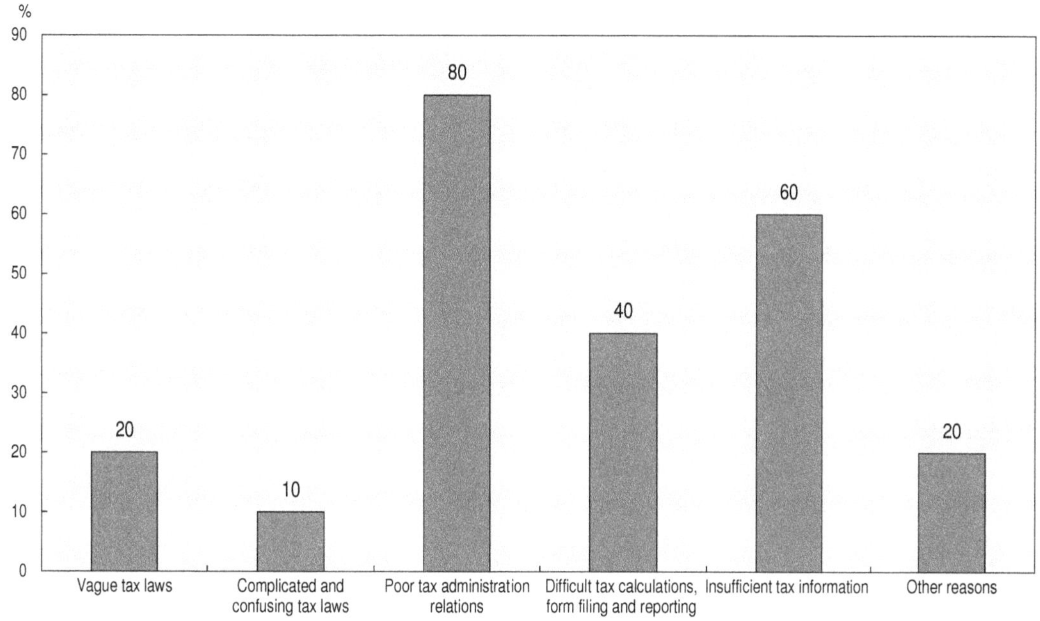

Note: Respondents were asked to indicate as many reasons as possible, thus the reasons sum to more than 100%.
Source: Informal sector taxation project, ATAF's survey (country questionnaire), September 2020.

StatLink *https://stat.link/sk6wqp*

Figure 3.2. **Tax regimes applied to informal sector**

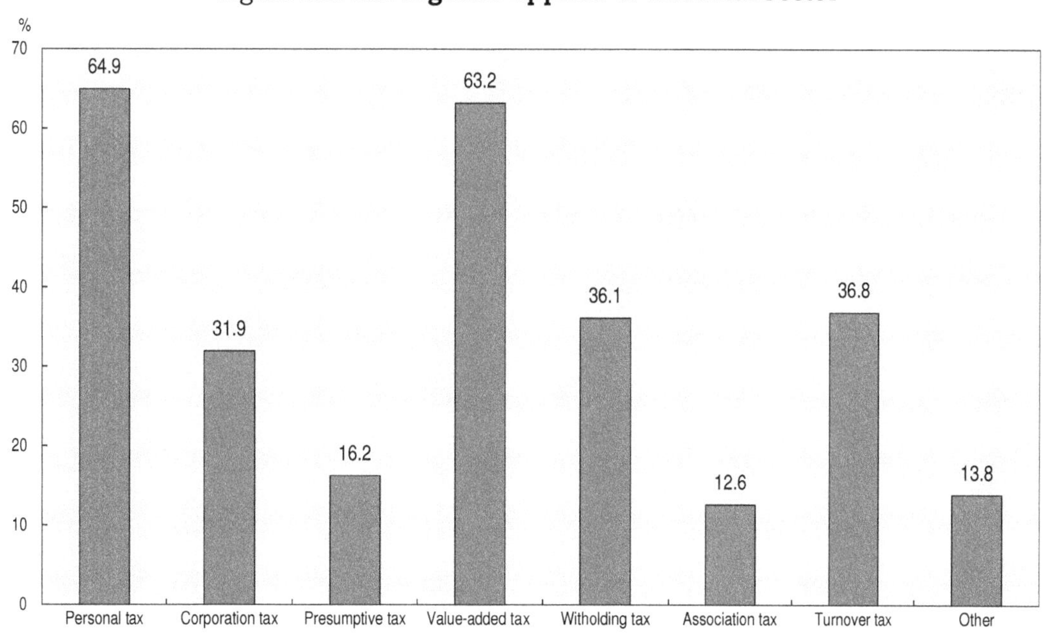

Note: Respondents were asked to indicate as many reasons as possible, thus the reasons sum to more than 100%.
Source: Informal sector taxation project, ATAF's survey (country questionnaire), September 2020.

StatLink *https://stat.link/wuenkj*

Despite the shortcomings and weaknesses detected in the existing programmes established by tax authorities, there are various successful experiences in taxation of the informal sector in some African countries. The most successful programme is represented by the simplification of tax procedures (this programme was judged successful to extremely successful by 69.6% of interviewees) while amnesties on tax liabilities were considered «unsuccessful» by 55.6% of interviewees, suggesting this to be the least effective approach (Table 3.1).

Table 3.1. **Results of implemented reforms**

REFORMS IMPLEMENTED	Extremely successful	Very successful	Successful	Not successful
Legal reforms	5.8%	11.6%	39.1%	43.5%
Creation of specialised tax units on informal sector	6.1%	16.7%	34.8%	42.4%
Adoption of a strategic plan for informal sector taxation	6.1%	15.1%	30.3%	48.5%
Amnesty on the tax liabilities of informal sector players	9.5%	11.1%	23.8%	55.6%
Tracking of players and sanctions strengthening	7.9%	12.7%	25.4%	54.0%
Simplified tax compliance procedures for SMEs	8.7%	18.8%	42.0%	30.4%

Source: Informal sector taxation project, ATAF's survey (country questionnaire), September 2020.

Along with the initiatives described in the boxes in this chapter, these include measures adopted in:

- **Madagascar:** The Anjarahetrako programme uses mobile tax unit teams to promote formalisation. Heterogeneous teams comprising tax administration staff and other government agencies are sent into the field to conduct campaigns, address taxpayer questions, register taxpayers and issue tax cards. As of 2021, the programme had not yet been evaluated but positive results were witnessed as revenues increased as more tax cards were issued.
- **Rwanda:** The country implemented a trading license enforcement initiative to identify businesses operating without a trading license through hiring a private company, which received a percentage of the amount paid for each trading license as an incentive. This programme helped, through an available database, to identify taxpayers who pay trading licenses and are not registered for income tax.
- **Zambia:** The Block Management System was introduced to identify areas in the informal sector with a high potential for non-compliance and map them onto blocks according to street, landmark buildings and business type. Tax administration officers visit each block and have a one-on-one engagement with potential taxpayers. This facilitates registration of new taxpayers and enhances tax compliance. Indeed, by the end of 2020, a total of 2 265 new taxpayers had been registered and there was a noticeable increase in compliance on return filing.

Detailed case studies for these countries and others can be accessed in the booklet of good practices (ATAF, 2021[1]), success stories and lessons learnt in the taxation of the informal sector.

Box 3.2. **Overcoming information gaps and institutional fragmentation in Nigeria**

Nigeria's informal sector represents a major challenge to the country's ambitions to enhance domestic resource mobilisation. It is estimated that the informal sector accounts for a significant proportion of economic activity and employs approximately 80% of the

Box 3.2. **Overcoming information gaps and institutional fragmentation in Nigeria** *(cont.)*

labour force. A majority of the country's estimated 42 million micro, small and medium-sized enterprises (MSMEs) are not registered.

At present, responsibility for taxing the informal sector rests primarily with state and local governments. Some states have created a directorate for the informal sector that is responsible for collecting income taxes. Others operate a presumptive tax regime, a measure that Nigeria hopes to roll out nationally, with standard rates across different states. In certain cases, the presumptive tax applies different tax rates for different income categories and imposes an income threshold below which enterprises are not required to pay tax. This has encouraged MSMEs to register, at which point they receive a tax identification number that allows them to open a bank account.

There are nonetheless numerous challenges to taxing the informal sector. With only a small proportion of informal enterprises registered for tax purposes and visible to the government, large gaps still exist in official databases and documentation. It can be very difficult to obtain accurate information on informal enterprises: many do not maintain proper records of their transactions or use personal bank accounts or social media for professional transactions. Enterprises are also deterred from complying when confronted by a multiplicity of taxes at the local, state and federal level.

Nigeria is taking steps to enhance taxation of the informal sector. The Federal Inland Revenue Service (FIRS) has established memoranda of understanding on data sharing with the Nigeria Customs Service, the Nigerian Communications Commission and the Securities and Exchange Commission. The Finance Act 2021 has empowered FIRS to leverage technology to increase tax revenues, and the agency is developing a mobile app to help informal enterprises register and comply with their tax obligations. The country is looking at further technological solutions, with a particular focus on acquiring data from unions and associations. Lastly, Nigeria is considering a single entity for tax administration that would simplify compliance, improve efficiency and eliminate loopholes.

Source: Based on country experiences shared during the *Revenue Statistics in Africa* Webinar 2022 (2-3 June 2022).

Considerations for an informal sector taxation model

The informal sector taxation model proposed in the guidebook was developed through a consultative and inclusive process with the aim of aligning it with the specific context of the informal sector, thus facilitating its ownership by ATAF members. Stakeholder consensus and views from the survey indicate that the optimal taxation system for taxing the activities of the informal sector in African countries should take into account the following:

- Heterogeneity of Africa's informal sector
- Holistic approach to the taxation of the informal sector
- Availability of financial information as a base for optimal taxation
- Simplification of the tax system focused on its rationalisation
- Permanent culture of good governance, especially at the local level (AfDB/OECD/UNDP, 2016[7])
- Promotion of tax compliance benefits such as special rewards through taxpayer appreciation programmes and social protection coverage.

- Technical requirements in the implementation of the taxation model, for instance expertise is needed in developing a model that is based on realistic segmentation of the informal sector.
- Introduction of binding taxation for 'opportunists and free riders' in the informal sector.

The study proposes a taxation model for the informal sector, based on a standard fiscal policy model centred on realistic segmentation of informal sector entities into micro, small and medium-sized enterprises. The model requires the incorporation of indicators that can help detect opportunists and free riders hiding in the informal sector.

The administration of the proposed taxation model would require collaboration with actors in the informal sector, creation of specific structures for the taxation of the informal sector, strengthening the automation and digitalisation of tax administration, coordination/collaboration at the institutional policy level, creation of a robust database on the informal sector, and strengthening partnerships with local and regional authorities.

Additionally, the promotion of voluntary compliance must lie at the heart of informal sector taxation strategies. That is, authorities and policy makers should set an example of tax compliance for informal sector actors through good financial governance and by using collected revenues for productive and sustainable public investments.

Other initiatives include incorporating voluntary tax compliance courses in basic training curricula; broadcasting adverts during peak hours on public and private radio and television stations to promote voluntary compliance; issuing tax declaration and payment deadline reminders; disseminating tax news; and using decentralised government channels to encourage tax compliance as a duty. Furthermore, it would be beneficial to institutionalise consultation sessions, exchanges, and direct and continuous dialogue between tax administration and taxpayers in the informal sector so that they can effectively engage in self-assessment of their taxes.

The implementation of a taxation system should be accompanied by a monitoring system to ensure its stability and an evaluation system is needed to bring it closer to the objectives pursued. The two important aspects to be taken into consideration are: (i) identifying monitoring indicators, and (ii) the use of impact indicators. The impact indicators should show the impact of the model on revenues, broadening of the tax base, and the behaviour of informal sector actors. Ultimately, the tax administration should assess the profitability of the taxation model, taking into account the revenues collected and the costs incurred by the tax administration.

Box 3.3. **Understanding the revenue potential of Ghana's informal sector**

Ghana's informal sector accounts for some 40% of the country's GDP, but a detailed understanding of the sector is difficult because informal establishments are small and scattered across the country. Better information about the sector is a crucial first step towards increasing tax revenues and financing Ghana's development.

In 2015, Ghana organised a census to collect employment and other operational data on all establishments. A registry was created on the basis of this census, classifying establishments by size – micro, small, medium-sized and large. However, the census did not collect information on enterprises' value added.

Box 3.3. **Understanding the revenue potential of Ghana's informal sector** *(cont.)*

In 2022, Ghana will carry out a second census, which will gather information on inputs and output and thus the value that establishments add. This will allow the government to classify establishments more accurately and estimate how much tax these enterprises should be paying. The tax agency will also address challenges in updating its registry by working with local governments to ensure it has access to up-to-date information.

Meanwhile, Ghana is exploring ways in which it can persuade informal enterprises to come into the tax net. One approach is to allow informal sector operators to pay social security contributions, so that they receive some kind of compensation if their business fails. Another approach is looking at the possibility of offering a small financial incentive to businesses that register for tax purposes.

Source: Based on country experiences shared during the *Revenue Statistics in Africa* Webinar 2022 (2-3 June 2022).

Recommendations

Based on a literature review, survey findings, and data/secondary analysis undertaken during this project, key recommendations for successful and effective taxation of the informal sector in African countries include:

1. Adopt an inclusive approach to the taxation of the informal sector by institutionalising or formalising the framework for exchanges between tax authorities and taxpayers in the informal sector.
2. Use a holistic approach to better understand and adapt to the changing realities of informal sector actors, for example by simplifying and rationalising business registration, where registration processes include registering with the registrar of companies, relevant local authorities, tax registration (that is, registering with tax authorities to declare and pay taxes effectively), along with formalisation procedures for informal sector actors.
3. Establish a robust database of informal sector actors that can serve as a decision-making tool in the fiscal management of the sector is necessary. Furthermore, it is essential to establish a taxation model that is simple in its application by informal sector actors and flexible in its governance by the tax authorities.
4. Establish appropriate units to deal with the informal sector's fiscal governance and strengthening the human resources ready to promote formalisation.
5. Rationalise, consolidate and simplify the multiplicity of taxes and contributions required of informal sector actors by local, provincial, and national administrative authorities.
6. Ensure the gradual transfer of the fiscal management of microenterprises to local governments, given their low fiscal yield compared to the high costs of governance borne by the tax authorities.
7. Establish Approved Management Centres to help informal sector participants to enhance their productivity in addition to the expected fiscal and accounting assistance.
8. Introduce restrictive tax measures for profiteers or free riders in the informal sector whose actions are motivated by fraud and tax avoidance strategies.
9. Strengthen withholding tax provisions through use of instalments, compliance levies, or limitation of the right to deductions for informal sector players who do not have a tax identification number and a tax clearance certificate,

10. Establish a requirement for all economic actors to hold a tax identification number as a prerequisite for carrying out administrative procedures.
11. Use indicators to monitor the established informal sector taxation model and its impact on well-controlled governance of the model; the advent of a culture of evaluation of the informal sector taxation model through the establishment of impact indicators on revenues; the rate of tax compliance; the broadening of the tax base and on the behaviour of actors through the prism of observed readjustments; and the promotion of good governance in the management of public resources.

Notes

1 This special feature was written by Michael Masiya and Ezera Madzivanyika (ATAF). The boxes on country experiences are based on interventions by Asuo Afram (Ghana), Alex Muhanji (Kenya) and Cephas Tiye (Nigeria).

2 The Guidebook can be downloaded at the following link: *https://events.ataftax.org/index.php?page=documents&func=view&document_id=128*

3 All documentation related to the *Revenue Statistics in Africa* Webinar 2022 is available at *https://www.oecd.org/tax/tax-policy/revenue-statistics-in-africa-webinar-2022.htm*

4 The terms 'revenue administration' and 'tax administration' are used interchangeably in the context of the Guidebook to refer to integrated revenue authorities (domestic tax and customs) and non-integrated tax departments within the Ministry of Finance, respectively.

5 A total of 27 African countries replied to the questionnaire while six countries participated in the focus group discussions.

References

AfDB/OECD/UNDP (2016), *African Economic Outlook 2016: Sustainable Cities and Structural Transformation*, OECD Publishing, Paris, *https://doi.org/10.1787/aeo-2016-en.* [7]

ATAF (2021), *The efficient taxation of the informal sector in Africa - ATAF Guidebook*, African Tax Administration Forum, *https://events.ataftax.org/index.php?page=documents&func=view&document_id=128.* [1]

AUC/ILO (2019), *Decent Work for Transformation of Informal Economy in Africa, https://au.int/sites/default/files/newsevents/workingdocuments/37691-wd-flyer_au_ilo_joint_programme_on_dwtransformation_of_ie_in_africa_prodoc_v5_final_budget_and_published_for_the_event_fridaynov8.pdf.* [5]

Buehn, A., A. Karmann and F. Schneider (2009), "Shadow economy and do-it-yourself activities: the German case", *Journal of Institutional and Theoretical Economics (JITE) / Zeitschrift für die gesamte Staatswissenschaft*, Vol. 165/4, pp. 701-722, *www.researchgate.net/publication/227458165_Shadow_Economy_and_Do-it-Yourself_Activities_The_German_Case.* [3]

ILO (2018), *Women and men in the informal economy: a statistical picture (third edition)*, International Labour Office, Geneva, *www.ilo.org/wcmsp5/groups/public/---dgreports/---dcomm/documents/publication/wcms_626831.pdf.* [4]

ILO (2015), *Recommendation No. 204 concerning the Transition from the Informal to the Formal Economy*, International Labour Organization, Geneva, *www.ilo.org/ilc/ILCSessions/previous-sessions/104/texts-adopted/WCMS_377774/lang--en/index.htm.* [2]

Kenya National Bureau of Statistics (2022), *Economic Survey 2022*, Kenya National Bureau of Statistics, *www.knbs.or.ke/wp-content/uploads/2022/05/2022-Economic-Survey1.pdf.* [6]

Revenue Statistics in Africa 1990-2020/Statistiques des recettes publiques en Afrique 1990-2020

Chapitre 3

Imposer efficacement le secteur informel en Afrique

Introduction

Ce chapitre[1] s'appuie sur le Manuel sur l'imposition efficace du secteur informel en Afrique (ci-après dénommé le « Manuel »)[2] (ATAF, 2021[1]), rédigé par le Forum sur l'administration fiscale africaine (ATAF), ainsi que sur les exposés et les débats de l'ATAF lors du webinaire 2022 sur les *Statistiques des recettes publiques en Afrique* (2-3 juin 2022)[3]. Ce chapitre expose les raisons qui justifient d'imposer le secteur informel en Afrique et passe en revue les bonnes pratiques et certains exemples africains dans ce domaine. Il présente trois brèves études de cas — le Ghana, le Kenya et le Nigéria — fondées sur des interventions données lors de ce même webinaire.

Au fil des années, on a tenté à maintes reprises de définir l'expression « secteur informel » et de circonscrire le champ qu'elle recouvre. L'Organisation internationale du travail définit le secteur informel comme « toutes les activités économiques des travailleurs et des unités économiques qui — en droit ou en pratique — ne sont pas couvertes ou sont insuffisamment couvertes par des dispositions formelles » (OIT, 2015[2]). En revanche, (Buehn, Karmann et Schneider, 2009[3]) considèrent que le secteur informel comprend toute production légale de biens et de services fondée sur le marché qui est volontairement dissimulée (cachée) aux autorités publiques.

À la lumière de ces différentes définitions, (ATAF, 2021[1]) définit le secteur informel comme suit : « Toutes les activités économiques des travailleurs et des entités économiques qui ne sont pas ou ne sont pas suffisamment couvertes par des dispositions formelles, y compris les activités de production clandestines, et qui ne sont pas déclarées aux autorités ou aux administrations fiscales »[4]. Cette définition englobe expressément les activités du secteur informel qui ne sont pas déclarées aux autorités fiscales et qui ne donnent donc pas lieu au versement d'impôts (directs). Il convient de noter que les activités économiques du secteur informel sont très répandues tant dans les économies en développement que dans économiques développées, où elles ne constituent pas un phénomène temporaire, marginal ou périphérique, mais plutôt un état de fait permanent.

Le secteur informel demeure la principale source de moyens de subsistance pour la majorité des citoyens africains : en Afrique, huit travailleurs sur dix appartiennent à l'économie informelle (OIT, 2020[4]). L'incidence élevée de l'informalité est un défi majeur pour le respect des droits des travailleurs et la qualité des conditions de travail en Afrique, et constitue un frein à la croissance. Garantir une économie informelle autonome, compétitive et productive pour le bien-être de tous les travailleurs en Afrique est une priorité de l'Union africaine. Un programme conjoint CUA/BIT travaille actuellement à l'établissement d'un cadre juridique et politique et d'autres mesures visant à reconnaître, réglementer et promouvoir le développement transformateur de l'économie informelle les (CUA /OIT, 2019[5])

Le secteur informel ne contribue pas de manière significative à la mobilisation des ressources intérieures s'agissant du versement d'impôts aux autorités fiscales nationales concernées.

Dans le souci d'accroître la mobilisation des ressources intérieures et d'augmenter le ratio de l'impôt rapporté au PIB dans les pays d'Afrique, l'ATAF, avec l'aide de la Banque africaine de développement (BAfD), a lancé un projet de recherche visant à déterminer les moyens de taxer le secteur informel en Afrique de manière efficace et efficiente. Le projet, qui a débuté en 2019 et s'est achevé en 2021, poursuivait les principaux objectifs suivants :

1. Brosser un tableau du secteur informel en Afrique sur la base de questionnaires adressés aux pays, de débats avec les parties prenantes concernées au sein de groupes de réflexion, ainsi que de bonnes pratiques, de réussites et d'enseignements tirés des expériences nationales.
2. Proposer un cadre ou un modèle pour imposer efficacement le secteur informel en Afrique.
3. Décrire la manière dont il conviendrait d'administrer le cadre ou le modèle proposé.
4. Présenter un cadre de suivi et d'évaluation destiné à garantir que le modèle d'imposition du secteur informel soit mis en œuvre de façon efficace et pérenne.
5. Formuler de grandes recommandations visant à optimiser l'imposition du secteur informel à l'échelle du continent.

Ce projet a notamment débouché sur la rédaction d'un Manuel proposant, pour imposer le secteur informel à l'échelle du continent, une série d'options pragmatiques inspirées par la réalité africaine, ainsi que sur la publication d'un livret recensant des bonnes pratiques, des exemples de réussite et des enseignements tirés du secteur informel.

Ce chapitre présente les objectifs et les principales conclusions de l'étude, ainsi que le cadre d'imposition efficace du secteur informel en Afrique. L'une des conclusions les plus importantes est que les responsables de l'action publique devraient instituer une culture de la bonne gouvernance, promouvoir les avantages de la discipline fiscale, définir des critères techniques stricts pour la mise en œuvre du modèle d'imposition, adopter un système fiscal simplifié, mettre en place des impôts contraignants et reconnaître l'hétérogénéité du secteur informel en Afrique.

L'étude propose un modèle d'imposition du secteur informel né d'une démarche consultative : l'ensemble des intervenants majeurs impliqués dans la gestion budgétaire du secteur informel en Afrique — administrations fiscales, acteurs du secteur informel et responsables de l'action publique — ont été réunis. Cette démarche inclusive a permis de faire en sorte que les résultats du projet, en ce qui concerne l'amélioration de la mobilisation des ressources internes par une imposition optimale du secteur informel, présentent de l'intérêt pour le continent africain dans la pratique.

Encadré 3.1. **Au Kenya, fiscaliser les revenus des opérateurs du secteur informel à travers les technologies et la politique fiscale**

Au Kenya, plus de 83 % des emplois relèvent du secteur informel (Bureau national des statistiques du Kenya, n° 2022[6]), qui concerne tous les pans de l'économie. Plus de 61 % des travailleurs informels sont employés dans le commerce de gros et de détail, l'hôtellerie et la restauration, tandis qu'ils sont 20.6 % à travailler dans le secteur manufacturier et 10.2 % dans les services collectifs, sociaux et personnels, le reste se partageant entre les transports, les communications et la construction.

Encadré 3.1. **Au Kenya, fiscaliser les revenus des opérateurs du secteur informel à travers les technologies et la politique fiscale** *(suite)*

Le Kenya n'accorde aucun traitement particulier aux travailleurs informels. Les autorités attendent des travailleurs qu'ils remplissent des déclarations d'impôt sur le revenu et de TVA au-delà de certains seuils, mais les travailleurs du secteur informel se conforment rarement à ces obligations. Cette absence de respect des obligations fiscales s'explique en partie par l'importante mobilité qui caractérise le secteur : les méthodes de gestion par blocs appliquées par le Kenya pour dépister les entreprises informelles se sont révélées inefficaces, car les opérateurs du secteur informel se déplacent souvent — parfois toutes les heures — afin de trouver un maximum de clients potentiels. Les entreprises informelles sont souvent réticentes à payer des impôts, ou ne sont pas en mesure de le faire, parce qu'elles ne tiennent pas de registres en bonne et due forme. Du fait de la prédominance des transactions en espèces dans le secteur informel, les activités commerciales ne sont pas consignées sur papier ou par voie électronique.

Le Kenya a adopté une série de mesures — il y a des dizaines d'années pour certaines d'entre elles — visant à faire en sorte que les opérateurs du secteur informel rendent des comptes et s'acquittent de l'impôt. Par exemple, depuis 1996, les chauffeurs de *matatus* (minibus qui font taxi) et d'autres moyens de transport sont tenus de verser un acompte d'impôt chaque année lors du renouvellement de leur licence d'exploitation. Cette règle est largement respectée, mais il subsiste un inconvénient : faute de registres tenus en bonne et due forme, rares sont les chauffeurs à introduire une déclaration à la fin de l'année.

Le pays applique aussi une taxe sur le chiffre d'affaires au titre de laquelle les contribuables percevant entre 1 et 50 millions KES sont tenus de verser un impôt équivalant à 1 % de leur revenu brut. Celui-ci a été utilisé de manière interchangeable avec un impôt forfaitaire mis en place en 2018, que les administrations locales prélèvent sur les opérateurs économiques en contrepartie de leur certificat d'exploitation (au taux de 15 % des frais de renouvellement) afin de les soumettre à l'impôt. Cette taxe forfaitaire n'a toutefois pas été appliquée à grande échelle. Enfin, le Kenya a permis aux travailleurs informels de s'enregistrer volontairement aux fins du paiement de la TVA, même si leur chiffre d'affaires était inférieur au seuil minimum. Pour améliorer l'accès aux informations sur les activités du secteur informel détenues par des tiers, la Kenya Revenue Authority (KRA) a signé des protocoles d'accord avec les administrations locales et les registres des entreprises.

La KRA s'emploie activement à faciliter le paiement des impôts par les acteurs du secteur informel, non seulement en mettant à profit les technologies, mais aussi en investissant dans l'éducation des contribuables. De nombreux contribuables estiment que le processus d'enregistrement et de paiement des impôts est complexe, sans compter que, souvent, ils ne disposent pas des documents nécessaires. La KRA a entièrement automatisé son système fiscal et l'ensemble de ses services sont accessibles en ligne. L'application M-Service, par exemple, permet de simplifier la déclaration et le paiement de la taxe sur le chiffre d'affaires, des revenus locatifs mensuels et de l'inscription au registre foncier, ainsi que l'introduction de la demande d'attestation de paiement de l'impôt. Par ailleurs, la KRA a mis sur pied des guichets d'information fiscale destinés à renseigner les opérateurs du secteur informel.

Source : Basé sur les expériences des pays partagées lors du Webinaire 2022 sur les *Statistiques des recettes publiques en Afrique* (2-3 juin 2022).

Principales conclusions

L'étude s'est appuyée sur des questionnaires et des groupes de réflexion pour recueillir des données provenant de pays d'Afrique. Il en ressort que les principales raisons qui poussent les contribuables à travailler dans le secteur informel sont les suivantes : piètres relations avec l'administration fiscale, information insuffisante, difficultés à calculer et à déclarer l'impôt qui imposent de faire appel à un conseiller fiscal. Les mauvaises relations avec l'administration fiscale et l'insuffisance des informations fiscales sont les deux principales raisons invoquées par les personnes interrogées pour justifier leur activité dans le secteur informel (Graphique 3.1). En outre, les principaux éléments qui font obstacle à la régularisation des entreprises sont le coût des procédures d'enregistrement, le nombre excessif de documents demandés, le niveau élevé des taux d'imposition et la multiplicité des types d'impôts, l'absence de facilités de crédit et les difficultés liées au climat des affaires.

Graphique 3.1. **Raisons et motivation pour opérer dans le secteur informel**

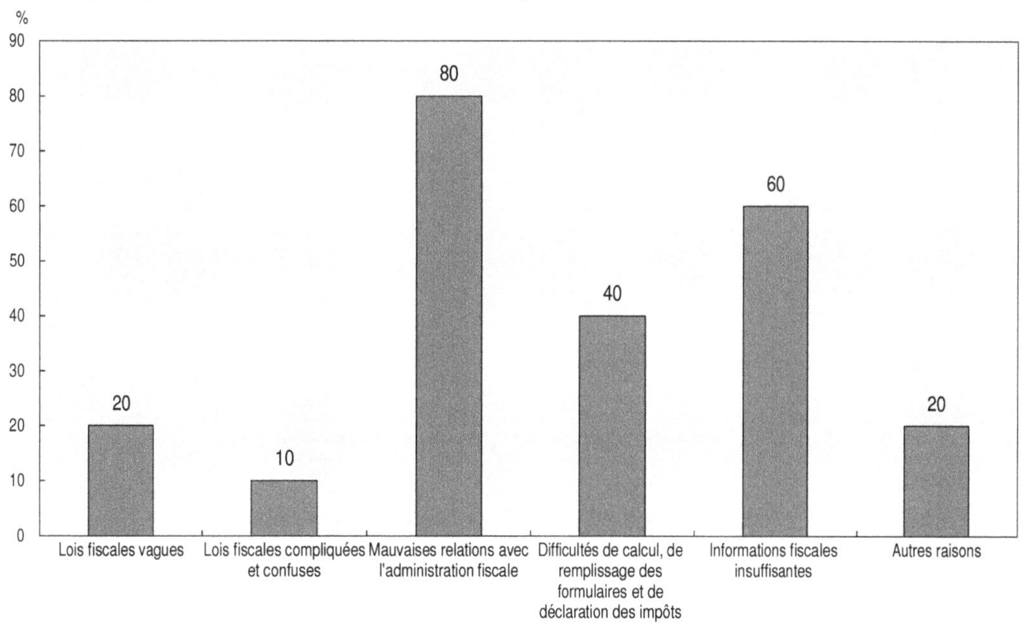

Note : Les répondants ont indiqué autant de raisons possibles, donc leur somme est supérieure à 100%.
Source : Projet de taxation du secteur informel, enquête de l'ATAF (questionnaire national), septembre 2020.

StatLink https://stat.link/xcz87o

Au chapitre des initiatives fiscales ciblant le secteur informel, les pays africains ont notamment mis en place, au fil des ans, l'impôt sur le revenu des personnes physiques et la taxe sur la valeur ajoutée, qui constituent les principaux prélèvements (mentionné respectivement par 64.9% et 63.2% des personnes interrogées), ainsi que la taxe sur le chiffre d'affaires et la retenue à la source (Graphique 3.2). Les études sur les retombées des régimes fiscaux sur le respect des obligations fiscales et l'augmentation des recettes font défaut dans la plupart des administrations : environ 66 % des autorités fiscales déclarent ne pas avoir analysé les effets des régimes fiscaux ciblant les opérateurs du secteur informel.

Les observations formulées par les groupes de réflexion et les réponses aux questionnaires ont mis en lumière d'importantes faiblesses dans les règles fiscales qui s'appliquent au secteur informel, notamment : (i) le caractère inéquitable des taxes forfaitaires axées sur la nature des activités ; (ii) le caractère arbitraire de l'imposition fondée sur le chiffre d'affaires ; (iii) le fait que la progressivité de l'imposition fondée sur différents seuils de chiffre d'affaires peut entraîner des injustices verticales si la variation du montant de l'impôt dû n'est pas proportionnelle à celle du chiffre d'affaires ; (iv) l'impact négatif du bénéfice minimum forfaitaire sur les investissements réalisés par les micro et les petites entreprises ; (v) l'intégration rapide des microentreprises à des régimes d'imposition, susceptible de créer une charge fiscale ingérable ; (vi) les effets négatifs sur la trésorerie des acomptes versés au titre des importations ; (vii) l'inefficacité des programmes d'amnistie fiscale ; (viii) la multiplicité des impôts frappant les opérateurs du secteur informel ; (ix) la gestion inefficace de la fiscalité du secteur informel au sein des administrations fiscales et (x) le faible volume de déclarations fiscales émanant du secteur informel.

Graphique 3.2. **Régimes fiscaux appliqués au secteur informel**

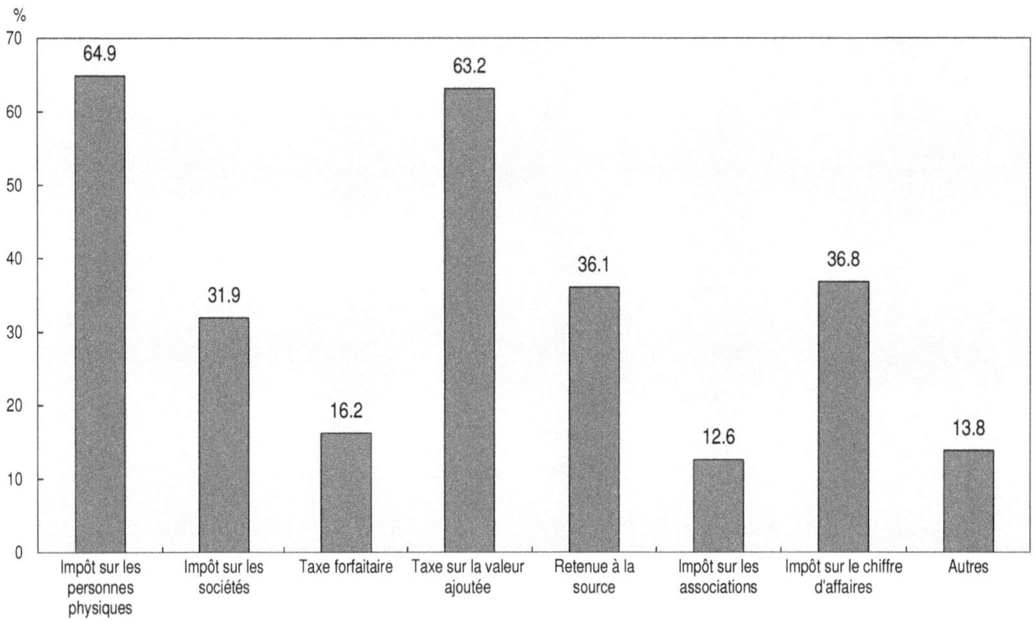

Note : Les répondants ont indiqué autant de raisons possibles, donc leur somme est supérieure à 100 %.
Source : Projet de taxation du secteur informel, enquête de l'ATAF (questionnaire national), septembre 2020.

StatLink https://stat.link/6drgoh

Malgré les défaillances et les faiblesses décelées dans les programmes qu'appliquent actuellement les autorités fiscales, certains pays africains affichent des réussites en matière d'imposition du secteur informel. Le programme le plus fructueux est la simplification des procédures de conformité fiscale (ce programme a été jugé réussi à extrêmement réussi par 69.6% des personnes interrogées), tandis que les amnisties sur les dettes fiscales ont été considérées comme un progamme qui n'a "pas réussi" par 55.6 % des personnes interrogées, ce qui suggère qu'il s'agit de l'approche la moins efficace. (Tableau 3.1).

Tableau 3.1. **Résultats des réformes mises en œuvre**

RÉFORMES MISES EN ŒUVRE	Extrêmement Réussi	Très Réussi	Réussi	Pas Réussi
Réformes juridiques	5.8%	11.6%	39.1%	43.5%
Création d'unités fiscales spécialisées dans le secteur informel	6.1%	16.7%	34.9%	42.4%
Adoption d'un plan stratégique pour la taxation du secteur informel	6.1%	15.2%	30.3%	48.5%
Amnistie sur les dettes fiscales des acteurs du secteur informel	9.5%	11.1%	23.8%	55.6%
Suivi des acteurs et renforcement des sanctions	7.9%	12.7%	25.4%	54.0%
Simplification des procédures de conformité fiscale pour les PME	8.7%	18.8%	42.0%	30.4%
Autres stratégies ou politiques (non décrites ci-dessus)	7.0%	22.8%	22.8%	47.4%

Source : Projet de taxation du secteur informel, enquête de l'ATAF (questionnaire national), septembre 2020.

Outre les initiatives présentées dans les encadrés de ce chapitre, il s'agit notamment des exemples suivants :

- **Madagascar** – Dans le cadre du programme Anjarahetrako, l'administration recourt à des unités fiscales mobiles dans le but d'encourager la régularisation. Des équipes hétéroclites, composées d'agents de l'administration fiscale et d'autres organismes publics, sont envoyées sur le terrain pour y mener des campagnes d'information, répondre aux questions des contribuables, enregistrer les contribuables et délivrer des cartes fiscales. En 2021, le programme n'avait pas encore fait l'objet d'une évaluation, mais des résultats positifs ont été constatés : les recettes se sont accrues à mesure que le nombre de cartes fiscales délivrées a augmenté.
- **Rwanda** – Le pays a lancé une initiative de contrôle des autorisations d'exercer afin de recenser toutes les entreprises qui opèrent sans autorisation d'exercer par recours à une société privée qui perçoit un pourcentage du montant payé pour chaque autorisation d'exercer. Grâce à une base de données, ce programme a permis d'identifier des contribuables qui achètent des autorisations d'exercer, mais qui ne sont pas inscrits à l'impôt sur le revenu.
- **Zambie** – Le système de gestion par blocs a été mis en place pour repérer les segments du secteur informel présentant un potentiel élevé de fraude et les cartographier en blocs selon les rues, les principaux bâtiments et le type d'entreprise. Les agents de l'administration fiscale se rendent dans chaque bloc et ont un entretien en personne avec les contribuables potentiels. Cette démarche permet de faciliter l'enregistrement des nouveaux contribuables et d'améliorer la discipline fiscale. Fin 2020, 2 265 nouveaux contribuables avaient ainsi été enregistrés au total et le respect des obligations déclaratives s'était sensiblement amélioré.

Des études de cas détaillées, concernant ces pays et d'autres, figurent dans le Manuel sur les bonnes pratiques (ATAF, 2021[1]), les exemples de réussite et les enseignements tirés de l'imposition du secteur informel.

Encadré 3.2. **Combler les lacunes d'information et surmonter l'éclatement institutionnel au Nigéria**

Au Nigéria, le secteur informel représente un obstacle majeur à l'ambition affichée par le pays : accroître la mobilisation de ses ressources intérieures. On estime en effet qu'il recouvre une part importante de l'activité économique et emploie environ 80 % de la population active. La plupart des quelque 42 millions de micro, petites et moyennes entreprises (MPME) du pays ne sont pas enregistrées auprès de l'administration.

Actuellement, c'est aux autorités des États et des collectivités locales qu'incombe pour l'essentiel la responsabilité d'imposer le secteur informel. Certains États ont créé une direction chargée du secteur informel qui est responsable de la perception des impôts sur le revenu. D'autres appliquent un régime d'imposition forfaitaire, une mesure que le Nigéria espère étendre à l'échelle nationale, en fixant des taux standard dans les différents États. Dans certains cas, ce régime forfaitaire prévoit différents taux en fonction des catégories de revenus et impose un seuil en deçà duquel les entreprises ne sont pas tenues d'acquitter l'impôt. Les MPME ont ainsi été encouragées à s'enregistrer auprès de l'administration, formalité à l'issue de laquelle elles se voient délivrer un numéro d'identification fiscale leur permettant d'ouvrir de compte bancaire.

Encadré 3.2. **Combler les lacunes d'information et surmonter l'éclatement institutionnel au Nigéria** *(suite)*

L'imposition du secteur informel comporte toutefois son lot de difficultés. Comme seule une petite partie des entreprises informelles sont enregistrées auprès des autorités fiscales et sont donc connues de l'administration, les bases de données et les dossiers officiels demeurent très fragmentaires. Il peut s'avérer très difficile d'obtenir des informations précises sur les entreprises informelles : nombre d'entre elles ne tiennent pas de registres de leurs opérations en bonne et due forme, ou recourent à des comptes bancaires personnels ou aux réseaux sociaux pour effectuer des transactions d'ordre professionnel. Par ailleurs, les entreprises sont dissuadées de se conformer à la législation du fait des multiples impôts auxquels elles sont confrontées au niveau local et fédéral ainsi qu'à l'échelon des États.

Le Nigéria engage des efforts pour mieux imposer le secteur informel. L'administration fiscale fédérale (*Federal Inland Revenue Service* ou FIRS) a conclu des protocoles d'accord avec l'administration des douanes, la commission des communications et l'autorité des marchés financiers du pays. La loi de finances 2021 a donné à la FIRS les moyens de tirer profit des technologies pour accroître les recettes fiscales et l'administration travaille à la mise au point d'une application mobile ayant pour vocation d'aider les entreprises informelles à s'enregistrer auprès des autorités et à s'acquitter de leurs obligations fiscales. Le pays cherche à adopter d'autres solutions technologiques, en particulier dans le but d'obtenir des données provenant de syndicats et d'associations professionnelles. Enfin, le Nigéria envisage de créer, pour l'administration de l'impôt, une entité unique qui permettrait de faciliter le respect des obligations, d'améliorer l'efficience du système et d'en corriger les failles.

Source : Basé sur les expériences des pays partagées lors du Webinaire 2022 sur les *Statistiques des recettes publiques en Afrique* (2-3 juin 2022).

Considérations relatives au modèle d'imposition du secteur informel

Le modèle d'imposition du secteur informel proposé dans le manuel a été élaboré au travers d'un processus consultatif et inclusif dans le but de l'adapter au contexte spécifique du secteur informel afin que les membres de l'ATAF puissent se l'approprier plus aisément. Le consensus des parties prenantes et les avis recueillis lors de l'enquête indiquent que pour être optimal, le système d'imposition des activités du secteur informel dans les pays africains devrait tenir compte des éléments suivants :

- L'hétérogénéité du secteur informel en Afrique
- Une approche globale de l'imposition du secteur informel
- L'accès aux informations financières comme base d'une imposition optimale
- La simplification du système fiscal axée sur sa rationalisation
- Une culture permanente de la bonne gouvernance, notamment au niveau local. (BAD/OCDE/PNUD, 2016[7]).
- La mise en avant des avantages liés au respect des obligations fiscales, tels que des récompenses spéciales par le biais de programmes d'appréciation des contribuables et de programmes de protection sociale
- Les critères techniques de la mise en œuvre du modèle d'imposition, par exemple une expertise est nécessaire pour développer un modèle qui repose sur une segmentation réaliste du secteur informel

- La mise en place d'une imposition contraignante pour les « opportunistes et les profiteurs » du secteur informel

Le modèle d'imposition du secteur informel proposé par l'étude s'appuie sur un modèle de politique budgétaire standard axé sur une segmentation réaliste des entités du secteur informel en micro, petites et moyennes entreprises. Ce modèle nécessite l'intégration d'indicateurs facilitant la détection des « opportunistes et profiteurs » dissimulés au sein du secteur informel.

L'administration du modèle proposé nécessiterait de collaborer avec les acteurs du secteur informel, de créer des structures spécifiques pour l'imposition du secteur informel, d'automatiser et de numériser davantage l'administration fiscale, de mettre en place des mécanismes de coordination ou de coopération au niveau de la politique institutionnelle, de mettre sur pied une base de données solide sur le secteur informel et de renforcer les partenariats avec les autorités locales et régionales.

En outre, la promotion du respect volontaire des obligations fiscales doit être au cœur des stratégies adoptées dans le cadre de l'imposition du secteur informel. Pour le dire autrement, les autorités et les responsables de l'action publique devraient donner l'exemple, en matière de discipline fiscale, par la mise en place d'une bonne gouvernance financière et par l'affectation des recettes perçues à la réalisation d'investissements publics productifs et durables.

Parmi les autres initiatives, citons l'intégration de cours sur le respect volontaire des obligations fiscales dans les programmes de formation de base, la diffusion d'annonces publicitaires, pendant les heures de grande écoute, sur les chaînes de radio et de télévision publiques et privées, afin d'encourager la discipline fiscale volontaire, l'envoi de rappels pour le dépôt des déclarations et les dates limites de paiement, la diffusion d'informations ayant trait à l'actualité fiscale, et l'utilisation des canaux d'information des administrations décentralisées pour présenter la discipline fiscale comme un devoir. Il serait en outre bénéfique d'institutionnaliser les sessions de consultation, les échanges ainsi que le dialogue direct et continu entre les administrations fiscales et les contribuables du secteur informel afin qu'ils puissent procéder effectivement à l'auto-évaluation des impôts dont ils sont redevables.

La mise en œuvre d'un système d'imposition devrait s'accompagner de la mise en place d'un système de suivi destiné à assurer sa stabilité, ainsi que d'un système d'évaluation pour le rapprocher des objectifs poursuivis. Les deux aspects importants à prendre en considération sont les suivants : (i) définir des indicateurs de suivi et (ii) utiliser des indicateurs d'impact. Les indicateurs d'impact devraient mettre en évidence l'incidence du modèle sur les recettes, l'élargissement de la base d'imposition et le comportement des acteurs du secteur informel. Enfin, l'administration fiscale devrait évaluer la rentabilité du modèle d'imposition en tenant compte des recettes qu'elle perçoit et des coûts qu'elle supporte.

Encadré 3.3. **Mesurer le potentiel du secteur informel du Ghana en termes de recettes fiscales**

Le secteur informel du Ghana représente quelque 40 % du PIB national, mais il est difficile de mesurer la situation dans le détail tant les établissements informels sont petits et dispersés à travers tout le pays. Pour accroître les recettes fiscales et financer le développement du Ghana, il est indispensable de commencer, avant toute chose, par obtenir des informations plus précises.

Encadré 3.3. **Mesurer le potentiel du secteur informel du Ghana en termes de recettes fiscales** *(suite)*

En 2015, le Ghana a organisé un recensement visant à recueillir des données sur l'emploi et d'autres renseignements sur les activités de l'ensemble des établissements du pays. Un registre a été créé sur cette base, en classant les établissements par taille : micro, petit, moyen et grand. Toutefois, aucune information sur la valeur ajoutée des entreprises n'a été collectée dans le cadre du recensement.

En 2022, le Ghana effectuera un deuxième recensement qui portera aussi sur les intrants et les extrants et donc sur la valeur créée par les établissements, ce qui permettra aux autorités de classer ces derniers avec plus de précision et d'estimer le montant de la taxe dont devraient s'acquitter ces entreprises. L'administration fiscale s'attaquera aussi aux problèmes de mise à jour de son registre, en collaborant avec les autorités locales, pour s'assurer que les informations à sa disposition sont actualisées.

Dans l'intervalle, le Ghana étudie les moyens de persuader les entreprises informelles de régulariser leur situation au regard de la fiscalité. Une des solutions envisagées consiste à permettre aux opérateurs du secteur informel de verser des cotisations de sécurité sociale de manière à pouvoir bénéficier de certains types de prestations en cas de faillite. Une autre porte sur la possibilité d'encourager les entreprises à s'enregistrer auprès de l'administration fiscale par une petite incitation financière.

Source : Basé sur les expériences des pays partagées lors du Webinaire 2022 sur les *Statistiques des recettes publiques en Afrique* (2-3 juin 2022).

Recommandations

Sur la base des travaux consacrés à ce sujet, ainsi que de l'analyse des données et de l'analyse secondaire réalisées dans le cadre de ce projet, les recommandations formulées en vue d'aboutir à une imposition fructueuse et efficace du secteur informel dans les pays d'Afrique sont notamment les suivantes :

1. Adopter une approche inclusive en institutionnalisant ou en formalisant le cadre d'échange entre les autorités fiscales et les contribuables du secteur informel.
2. Procéder de manière globale afin de mieux comprendre les réalités changeantes des acteurs du secteur informel, et de s'y adapter, par exemple par la simplification et la rationalisation de l'enregistrement des entreprises, lorsque le processus impose l'inscription au registre des sociétés, l'enregistrement auprès des autorités locales compétentes, l'identification auprès de l'administration fiscale (c'est-à-dire l'enregistrement en vue de la déclaration et du paiement effectifs des impôts), ainsi que par la formalisation des procédures que doivent suivre les acteurs du secteur informel.
3. Il est nécessaire de constituer une base de données solide des acteurs du secteur informel qui pourra servir d'outil d'aide à la décision dans le cadre de la gestion budgétaire du secteur. En outre, il est essentiel d'établir un modèle d'imposition que les acteurs du secteur informel puissent appliquer avec simplicité et les autorités fiscales gérer avec souplesse.
4. Établir des unités appropriées appelées à assurer la gouvernance budgétaire du secteur informel et renforcer les ressources humaines chargées de favoriser la formalisation.
5. Rationaliser, consolider et simplifier les multiples taxes et contributions imposées aux acteurs du secteur informel par les autorités locales, régionales et nationales.

6. Assurer le transfert graduel de la gestion budgétaire des microentreprises vers les autorités locales, étant donné leur faible rendement par rapport aux coûts de gouvernance élevés supportés par les autorités fiscales.
7. Mettre en place des centres de gestion agréés pour aider les participants du secteur informel à améliorer leur productivité en plus de l'assistance fiscale et comptable attendue.
8. Mettre en place des mesures fiscales restrictives pour les profiteurs du secteur informel dont les agissements sont motivés par des stratégies de fraude et d'évasion fiscale.
9. Renforcer l'utilisation de dispositions relatives à la retenue à la source au moyen de paiements échelonnés, de prélèvements obligatoires ou de la limitation du droit à déduction pour, les acteurs du secteur informel qui ne disposent pas d'un numéro d'identification fiscale et d'une attestation de paiement de l'impôt.
10. Faire de l'obligation pour tous les acteurs économiques de détenir un numéro d'identification fiscale une condition préalable à l'accomplissement des procédures administratives.
11. Utiliser des indicateurs pour permettre le suivi du modèle d'imposition établi pour le secteur informel et de ses effets sur une gouvernance bien contrôlée du modèle ; faire advenir une culture de l'évaluation du modèle d'imposition du secteur informel par la mise en place d'indicateurs d'impact sur les recettes, le niveau de discipline fiscale, l'élargissement de la base d'imposition et le comportement des acteurs à travers le prisme des réajustements observés ; et promouvoir la bonne gouvernance des ressources publiques.

Notes

1 Ce document spécial a été rédigé par Michael Masiya et Ezera Madzivanyika du Forum sur l'administration fiscale africaine. Les encadrés présentant des exemples nationaux s'appuient sur les interventions d'Asuo Afram (Ghana), d'Alex Muhanji (Kenya) et de Cephas Tiye (Nigéria) lors du webinaire 2022 sur les *Statistiques des recettes publiques en Afrique* (2-3 juin 2022).

2 Le Manuel peut être téléchargé en cliquant sur le lien suivant : *https://events.ataftax.org/index.php?page=documents&func=view&document_id=128&language=fr_FR*

3 Tous les documents se rapportant au webinaire 2022 sur les *Statistiques des recettes publiques en Afrique* sont accessibles à l'adresse suivante : *https://www.oecd.org/fr/fiscalite/politiques-fiscales/statistiques-recettes-publiques-afrique-webinaire-2022.htm*

4 Les expressions « autorité fiscale » et « administration fiscale » sont utilisées indifféremment l'une pour l'autre, dans le cadre du Manuel, pour désigner respectivement les autorités intégrées (impôts nationaux et douanes) et les services fiscaux non intégrés au sein du ministère des Finances.

Références

ATAF (2021), *L'imposition efficace du secteur informel en Afrique - Manuel de l'ATAF*, Forum sur l'administration fiscale africaine, *https://events.ataftax.org/index.php?page=documents&func=view&document_id=128&function=changelangpost&language=fr_FR*. [1]

BAD/OCDE/PNUD (2016), *Perspectives économiques en Afrique 2016: Villes durables et transformation structurelle*, OECD Publishing, *https://doi.org/10.1787/aeo-2016-fr*. [7]

Buehn, A., A. Karmann et F. Schneider (2009), « Shadow economy and do-it-yourself activities: the German case », *Journal of Institutional and Theoretical Economics (JITE) / Zeitschrift für die gesamte Staatswissenschaft*, vol. vol. 165/n° 4, pp. pp. 701-722, *www.researchgate.net/publication/227458165_Shadow_Economy_and_Do-it-Yourself_Activities_The_German_Case*. [3]

Bureau national des statistiques du Kenya (n° 2022), *Economic Survey 2022*, Bureau national des statistiques du Kenya, *www.knbs.or.ke/wp-content/uploads/2022/05/2022-Economic-Survey1.pdf*. [6]

CUA /OIT (2019), *Decent Work for Transformation of Informal Economy in Africa*, *https://au.int/sites/default/files/newsevents/workingdocuments/37691-wd-flyer_au_ilo_joint_programme_on_dwtransformation_of_ie_in_africa_prodoc_v5_final_budget_and_published_for_the_event_fridaynov8.pdf*. [5]

OIT (2020), *Femmes et hommes dans l'économie informelle : Un panorama statistique (troisième édition)*, Organisation internationale du Travail, Genève, *www.ilo.org/global/publications/books/WCMS_734075/lang--fr/index.htm*. [4]

OIT (2015), *Recommendation n°204 concernant la transition de l'économie informelle vers l'économie formelle*, Organisation ternationale du Travail, Genève, *www.ilo.org/ilc/ILCSessions/previous-sessions/104/texts-adopted/WCMS_377776/lang--fr/index.htm*. [2]

Chapter 4

Tax levels and tax structures, 1990-2020

Chapitre 4

Niveaux et structures des impôts, 1990-2020

Chapter 4 / Chapitre 4

Comparative tables, 1990-2020

In all of the following tables a ("..") indicates not available. The main series in this volume cover the years 1990 to 2020.

Figures referring to 1991-99 and 2011 in Table 4.1 and 4.2 and figures relating to 1990-94, 1996-1999, 2001-04, 2006-09 and 2011-14 in Tables 4.5 to 4.19 have been omitted because of lack of space. Complete series are, however, available on line at OECD/ATAF/AUC (2022), "Revenue Statistics in Africa: Comparative tables", *OECD Tax Statistics* (database), *http://dx.doi.org/10.1787/be755711-en.*

Tableaux comparatifs, 1990-2020

Dans tous les tableaux suivants le symbole («..») signifie que l'information n'est pas disponible. La principale série dans ce volume couvre les années 1990 à 2020.

Les données pour les années 1991 à 1999 et 2011 dans le tableau 4.1 et 4.2 et pour les années 1990-94, 1996-99, 2001-04, 2006-09 et 2011-14 dans les tableaux 4.5 à 4.19 ont été omises en raison du manque d'espace. Les séries complètes sont cependant disponibles en ligne sur OCDE/ATAF/CUA (2022), « Statistiques des recettes publiques en Afrique : Tableaux comparatifs », *Statistiques fiscales de l'OCDE* (base de données), *http://dx.doi.org/10.1787/7f54581d-fr.*

Table 4.1. **Total tax revenue as percentage of GDP, 1990-2020**
Tableau 4.1. **Total des recettes fiscales en pourcentage du PIB, 1990-2020**

	1990	2000	2003	2004	2005	2006	2007	2008	2009	2010
Botswana	..	..	..	15.7	15.4	15.6	14.1	17.4	16.0	15.8
Burkina Faso	..	10.2	11.3	12.4	11.7	12.1	12.6	11.9	12.6	14.0
Cabo Verde	10.5	15.6	17.7	18.7	19.5	20.9	20.8	21.6	18.8	19.0
Cameroon / Cameroun	..	10.8	11.2	10.5	11.0	11.5	12.0	12.0	12.3	11.5
Chad / Tchad	..	..	..	..	..	..	..	..	..	14.6
Congo	..	3.8	7.9	7.5	5.9	5.6	5.9	6.0	8.0	7.0
Congo, Dem. Rep. / Congo, Rép. dém.[1]	..	1.1	3.4	4.8	5.3	6.0	7.1	8.7	8.0	8.6
Côte d'Ivoire	15.6	11.1	10.6	11.5	11.3	11.7	12.4	12.2	12.2	11.9
Egypt / Égypte	..	..	15.7	15.9	15.7	17.4	16.5	16.4	16.5	15.2
Equatorial Guinea / Guinée équatoriale	..	..	..	..	8.2	9.7	7.5	7.8	12.8	7.6
Eswatini	..	10.7	11.8	11.4	11.6	11.7	11.8	12.9	12.9	13.9
Ghana	..	7.8	9.7	10.4	10.5	9.9	10.0	10.5	10.4	10.8
Kenya	..	..	9.0	9.7	10.8	10.5	11.4	13.0	14.7	15.7
Lesotho	..	..	..	16.7	15.4	14.4	14.6	15.2	17.1	17.3
Madagascar[2]	..	9.6	8.8	9.6	8.9	9.4	10.0	11.4	9.5	9.5
Malawi	..	..	..	..	9.0	9.0	9.7	10.3	10.9	11.3
Mali	..	11.4	13.9	14.9	14.5	14.1	14.3	13.3	14.4	14.1
Mauritania / Mauritanie	..	..	..	..	..	..	10.0	10.2	10.4	9.8
Mauritius / Maurice[3]	22.3	18.3	17.3	17.4	17.9	17.8	17.0	18.7	19.2	19.0
Morocco / Maroc[2,4]	..	22.0	22.4	22.7	24.9	26.2	28.6	31.1	27.7	27.6
Namibia / Namibie	..	..	..	..	..	16.2	17.2	17.7	17.9	18.6
Niger	..	7.3	8.2	8.8	8.3	8.6	9.0	9.0	10.4	9.6
Nigeria / Nigéria	..	..	..	..	..	..	..	..	..	7.3
Rwanda[2]	..	8.5	10.5	10.6	10.7	11.3	11.5	12.5	12.1	12.3
Senegal / Sénégal[5]	..	13.1	13.9	14.5	15.3	15.7	16.2	15.2	15.0	15.9
Seychelles	..	..	..	..	..	..	..	27.9	28.8	30.7
Sierra Leone	..	..	8.5	8.6	7.8	8.2	7.6	8.1	8.2	9.1
South Africa / Afrique du Sud[6]	..	20.1	20.2	21.2	22.8	24.0	25.3	25.3	23.2	23.1
Togo	..	7.0	8.8	9.8	9.9	10.7	11.3	10.7	10.8	10.9
Tunisia / Tunisie[2]	..	23.3	23.1	23.0	23.1	23.2	24.0	25.6	25.5	25.9
Uganda / Ouganda	..	8.3	8.8	9.0	9.3	9.4	9.5	9.3	8.5	8.3
Africa (31) average / Moyenne Afrique (31)[7]	..	..	..	..	..	..	..	..	**14.2**	**14.4**
Asia-Pacific (28) average / Moyenne Asie-Pacifique (28)[8]	..	..	..	..	..	..	..	..	..	**18.2**
LAC average / Moyenne ALC[9]	**15.6**	**18.0**	**18.7**	**19.1**	**19.9**	**20.5**	**21.2**	**21.2**	**20.5**	**20.9**
OECD average / Moyenne OCDE[10]	**30.8**	**33.0**	**32.2**	**32.2**	**32.7**	**32.8**	**32.9**	**32.3**	**31.6**	**31.6**

	2011	2012	2013	2014	2015	2016	2017	2018	2019	2020
Botswana	16.0	14.3	15.3	16.0	13.4	14.6	13.3	13.3	13.7	12.4
Burkina Faso	13.4	14.9	15.9	14.3	14.6	15.3	16.2	16.6	17.3	16.6
Cabo Verde	20.2	18.3	18.4	17.5	19.3	19.4	20.5	22.0	21.2	20.1
Cameroon / Cameroun	12.5	13.0	13.6	13.8	14.1	13.7	14.0	14.2	13.9	12.8
Chad / Tchad	17.9	14.6	15.4	10.6	5.8	4.7	6.2	7.9	8.1	14.6
Congo	7.4	6.9	8.7	9.7	12.9	13.3	10.8	7.5	8.1	9.9
Congo, Dem. Rep. / Congo, Rép. dém.[1]	8.9	10.8	10.2	9.7	9.9	8.6	7.0	7.7	7.7	7.3
Côte d'Ivoire	11.1	12.8	12.7	12.2	12.6	13.1	13.3	13.0	13.2	13.4
Egypt / Égypte	15.0	14.1	15.5	14.3	14.7	14.5	15.3	15.0	14.4	13.3
Equatorial Guinea / Guinée équatoriale	7.0	8.8	8.9	9.8	12.0	7.1	6.6	6.6	9.7	8.5
Eswatini	13.9	12.8	13.7	14.9	15.0	16.1	17.0	17.4	18.3	18.0
Ghana	11.8	12.0	11.3	11.9	12.9	13.1	13.4	13.7	13.2	13.4
Kenya	16.5	16.1	16.1	17.3	16.8	17.0	17.4	16.6	16.4	15.3
Lesotho	17.7	16.9	18.6	18.9	19.3	19.2	19.9	22.6	21.3	20.1
Madagascar[2]	9.9	9.2	9.3	9.0	9.5	10.0	10.9	11.5	11.5	10.5
Malawi	11.6	10.3	11.5	12.7	12.0	12.0	13.2	12.8	12.8	12.3
Mali	13.7	14.0	14.2	13.9	15.2	16.5	16.7	13.3	17.5	18.1
Mauritania / Mauritanie	10.6	13.5	13.3	15.1	14.5	14.2	14.4	15.4	13.8	13.1
Mauritius / Maurice[3]	19.0	19.5	19.2	19.3	19.3	19.5	19.9	20.4	21.1	21.0
Morocco / Maroc[2,4]	28.4	29.5	28.1	27.8	26.8	27.5	28.0	28.2	28.3	28.3
Namibia / Namibie	21.5	19.9	20.0	21.1	21.5	21.1	20.4	19.4	20.2	18.5
Niger	10.2	10.6	12.7	12.4	12.6	10.5	9.5	11.2	10.4	9.8
Nigeria / Nigéria	9.6	9.4	8.3	7.6	6.1	5.3	5.7	6.3	6.0	5.5
Rwanda[2]	13.0	13.7	15.0	15.4	16.2	16.3	16.2	16.9	17.3	16.9
Senegal / Sénégal[5]	16.0	16.1	15.4	16.2	16.4	17.0	16.4	17.0	18.4	18.1
Seychelles	32.8	31.2	29.3	29.5	29.0	30.8	31.3	32.8	32.2	32.0
Sierra Leone	9.1	9.7	8.3	8.7	9.9	10.6	10.8	10.9	11.8	11.0
South Africa / Afrique du Sud[6]	24.0	24.4	24.8	25.4	26.5	26.1	26.1	26.6	26.2	25.2
Togo	12.0	12.5	14.5	15.5	16.0	16.4	15.8	14.6	15.0	15.4
Tunisia / Tunisie[2]	27.7	27.7	28.3	29.3	28.5	27.9	29.2	29.9	32.2	32.5
Uganda / Ouganda	8.4	8.5	9.0	9.3	10.5	11.0	11.4	11.7	12.1	11.1
Africa (31) average / Moyenne Afrique (31)[7]	**15.1**	**15.0**	**15.3**	**15.5**	**15.6**	**15.6**	**15.7**	**15.9**	**16.2**	**16.0**
Asia-Pacific (28) average / Moyenne Asie-Pacifique (28)[8]	**18.5**	**19.1**	**19.2**	**18.6**	**19.0**	**18.4**	**19.4**	**20.0**	**20.3**	**19.1**
LAC average / Moyenne ALC[9]	**21.3**	**21.6**	**21.6**	**21.8**	**22.3**	**22.2**	**22.3**	**22.5**	**22.7**	**21.9**
OECD average / Moyenne OCDE[10]	**31.9**	**32.4**	**32.7**	**32.9**	**32.9**	**33.6**	**33.4**	**33.5**	**33.4**	**33.5**

Table 4.1. **Total tax revenue as percentage of GDP, 1990-2020** *(cont.)*
Tableau 4.1. **Total des recettes fiscales en pourcentage du PIB, 1990-2020** *(suite)*

.. Not available

Note: The figures include sub-national government tax revenues for Eswatini, Mauritania (since 2009), Mauritius, Morocco, Nigeria (only state revenues) and South Africa (since 2002). Sub-national government tax revenues are not available in other countries.

Data on social security contributions are not available for Chad, the Republic of the Congo, the Democratic Republic of the Congo (prior to 2012), Equatorial Guinea (prior to 2013), Madagascar (prior to 2011), Namibia (prior to 2009), Sierra Leone, Togo and Uganda; and are only partially available in Cameroon and Senegal. Social security contributions for Botswana, Lesotho and Malawi are deemed to be null as they do not meet the criteria to be classified as social security contributions set out in the OECD classification of taxes in the *OECD Interpretative Guide*.

In Ghana, Lesotho, Malawi, Nigeria, Sierra Leone and Uganda, revenues from property taxes are mainly levied by local governments for which data on revenue are not available. In the Democratic Republic of the Congo only data for property taxes levied by the Direction Générale des Recettes Administratives, Judiciaires, Domaniales et de Participation (DGRAD) are available since 2010.

See the country tables in Chapter 5 for further information on data issues for individual countries.

1. The figures should be interpreted with caution as they are affected by macroeconomic instability in the early 2000s. For the years prior to 2010, the figures exclude some revenues collected by the Direction Générale des Recettes Administratives, Judiciaires, Domaniales et de Participation (DGRAD), which are estimated to be less than 1% of total tax revenue. See Table 5.6 in Chapter 5 for further information.
2. Madagascar, Morocco, Rwanda and Tunisia do not include social security contributions in the tax-to-GDP ratio in their official publications as these countries do not consider them to be taxes. They are included as tax revenue in this publication, following the classification set out in the *OECD Interpretative Guide*.
3. The fiscal year for Mauritius changed in 2010 and in 2015. Figures for 2015 needed to be estimated as a result.
4. Social security contributions in Morocco are estimated for years prior to 2002.
5. These figures include contributions to the Senegalese Pension Institute (IPRES) (estimated prior to 2006) and contributions to the social security fund (CSS) (from 2012 as data for previous years are not available). Social security contributions in Senegal are estimated since 2018.
6. Includes payments made by South Africa to the Southern African Customs Union (SACU) Common Revenue Pool.
7. Represents an unweighted average of the 31 African countries in this publication. In 2009, the Africa (31) average is calculated based on estimated tax-to-GDP ratios for Chad and Nigeria in that year, as data were not available prior to 2010 in these countries. The estimations in 2009 for these two countries are based on data for later years and on IMF figures from the World Economic Outlook April 2022. Details of the estimations are available in the metadata. The Africa (31) should be interpreted with caution as data for social security contributions (category 2000) and property taxes (category 4000) are not available or are partial in a few countries. See the country tables in Chapter 5 for further information.
8. Represents an unweighted average for 28 Asian and Pacific economies included in the publication *Revenue Statistics in Asia and the Pacific 2022*.
9. Represents an unweighted average for 26 Latin American and Caribbean (LAC) countries included in the publication *Revenue Statistics in Latin America and the Caribbean 2022*.
10. Represents an unweighted average for 38 OECD countries.

.. Non disponible

Note : Les chiffres incluent les recettes fiscales collectées par les administrations infranationales pour l'Afrique du Sud (à partir de 2002), Eswatini, le Maroc, Maurice, la Mauritanie (à partir de 2009) et le Nigéria (recettes des administrations régionales). Les données des recettes fiscales collectées par les administrations infranationales ne sont pas disponibles pour les autres pays.

Les données des cotisations de sécurité sociale ne sont pas disponibles pour la République du Congo, la République démocratique du Congo (avant 2012), la Guinée Équatoriale, (avant 2013), Madagascar (avant 2011), la Namibie (avant 2009), l'Ouganda, la Sierra Leone, le Tchad et le Togo et ne sont que partiellement disponibles au Cameroun et au Sénégal. Les cotisations de sécurité sociale pour le Botswana, le Lesotho et le Malawi sont nulles car elles ne répondent pas aux critères de classification des cotisations de sécurité sociale de la classification des impôts établie dans le *guide d'interprétation de l'OCDE*.

Au Ghana, au Lesotho, au Malawi, au Nigéria, en Ouganda et en Sierra Leone, les recettes provenant des impôts sur le patrimoine sont principalement perçues par les administrations locales pour lesquelles les données ne sont pas disponibles. En République démocratique du Congo, seules les données des impôts sur le patrimoine qui sont prélevées par la Direction Générale des Recettes Administratives, Judiciaires, Domaniales et de Participation (DGRAD) sont disponibles à partir de 2010.

Voir les tableaux par pays au chapitre 5 pour plus d'informations sur les problèmes de données pour chaque pays.

1. Les chiffres doivent être interprétés avec prudence car ils sont affectés par une instabilité macroéconomique au début des années 2000. Pour les années antérieures à 2010, les chiffres excluent certaines recettes perçues par la Direction Générale des Recettes Administratives, Judiciaires, Domaniales et de Participation (DGRAD) estimées inférieures à 1 % du total des recettes fiscales. Voir le tableau 5.6 du chapitre 5 pour plus d'informations.
2. Madagascar, le Maroc, le Rwanda et la Tunisie n'incluent pas les cotisations de sécurité sociale dans le ratio impôts/PIB dans leurs publications officielles car ces pays ne les considèrent pas comme des impôts. Elles sont incluses dans les recettes fiscales de cette publication en accordance avec la classification des impôts établie dans le *guide d'interprétation de l'OCDE*.
3. L'année fiscale pour Maurice a changé en 2010 et en 2015. Les chiffres pour 2015 ont dû être estimés en conséquence.
4. Les cotisations de sécurité sociale au Maroc antérieures à 2002 sont estimées.
5. Les chiffres comprennent les cotisations de sécurité sociale de l'Institution de prévoyance retraite du Sénégal (IPRES) (estimées pour les années antérieures à 2006) et les cotisations de sécurité sociale de la Caisse de Sécurité Sociale (CSS) (à partir de 2012 car les données pour les années précédentes ne sont pas disponibles). Les cotisations de sécurité sociale à partir de 2018 sont estimées.
6. Comprend les paiements effectués par l'Afrique du Sud au fond collectif de l'Union douanière d'Afrique australe (SACU).
7. Représente une moyenne non pondérée des 31 pays africains inclus dans cette publication. En 2009, la moyenne de l'Afrique (31) est calculée sur la base des ratios impôts/PIB estimés pour le Nigéria et le Tchad car les données n'étaient pas disponibles avant 2010 dans ces pays. Les estimations en 2009 pour ces deux pays sont basées sur des données des années ultérieures et sur les chiffres du FMI tirés des *Perspectives de l'économie mondiale* d'avril 2022. Les détails des estimations sont disponibles dans les métadonnées. Il convient d'interpréter cette moyenne avec prudence à cause de valeurs manquantes ou incomplètes pour la rubrique 2000 (cotisations de sécurité sociale) et la rubrique 4000 (taxes sur le patrimoine). Voir les tableaux de pays au chapitre 5 pour plus d'informations.
8. Représente la moyenne non pondérée pour 28 économies de l'Asie et du Pacifique incluses dans la publication *Revenue Statistics in Asia and the Pacific 2022*.
9. Représente la moyenne non pondérée pour 26 pays d'Amérique latine et des Caraïbes (ALC) inclus dans la publication *Revenue Statistics in Latin America and the Caribbean 2022*.
10. Représente la moyenne non pondérée pour 38 pays de l'OCDE.

StatLink https://stat.link/n5kxos

Table 4.2. **Total tax revenue (excluding social security) as percentage of GDP**
Tableau 4.2. **Total des recettes fiscales (sécurité sociale non comprise) en pourcentage du PIB**

	1990	2000	2003	2004	2005	2006	2007	2008	2009	2010
Botswana	..	..	..	15.7	15.4	15.6	14.1	17.4	16.0	15.8
Burkina Faso	..	8.6	9.7	10.7	10.2	10.5	11.0	10.4	11.1	12.4
Cabo Verde	10.5	14.8	17.2	18.2	18.9	20.4	20.7	21.6	18.8	18.9
Cameroon / Cameroun	..	9.9	10.3	9.6	10.2	10.7	11.2	11.2	11.4	10.6
Chad / Tchad	..	..	..	..	..	..	..	..	..	14.6
Congo	..	3.8	7.9	7.5	5.9	5.6	5.9	6.0	8.0	7.0
Congo, Dem. Rep. / Congo, Rép. dém.[1]	..	1.1	3.4	4.8	5.3	6.0	7.1	8.7	8.0	8.6
Côte d'Ivoire	14.6	10.1	9.7	10.5	10.4	10.8	11.4	11.3	11.2	11.0
Egypt / Égypte	..	..	12.3	12.7	12.8	14.6	14.0	14.0	14.5	13.0
Equatorial Guinea / Guinée équatoriale	..	..	..	..	8.2	9.7	7.5	7.8	12.8	7.6
Eswatini	..	9.5	10.6	10.1	10.2	10.2	10.2	11.4	11.1	12.0
Ghana	..	7.1	8.8	9.5	9.7	8.8	8.9	9.5	9.1	9.9
Kenya	..	..	8.9	9.6	10.6	10.4	11.2	12.9	14.5	15.5
Lesotho	..	..	..	16.7	15.4	14.4	14.6	15.2	17.1	17.3
Madagascar	..	9.6	8.8	9.6	8.9	9.4	10.0	11.4	9.5	9.5
Malawi	..	..	..	..	9.0	9.0	9.7	10.3	10.9	11.3
Mali	..	10.5	12.8	13.6	13.1	12.7	12.8	11.9	12.9	12.8
Mauritania / Mauritanie	..	..	..	..	..	..	9.4	9.5	9.8	9.1
Mauritius / Maurice[2]	21.4	17.5	16.6	16.7	17.2	17.2	16.4	18.1	18.6	18.3
Morocco / Maroc	..	19.6	19.0	19.2	20.7	21.5	23.8	26.5	23.0	22.8
Namibia / Namibie	..	..	..	..	..	16.2	17.2	17.7	17.6	18.3
Niger	..	6.9	7.8	8.4	7.9	8.3	8.7	8.6	9.9	9.1
Nigeria / Nigéria	..	..	..	..	..	..	..	..	..	6.7
Rwanda	..	8.1	10.0	9.8	9.9	10.6	10.8	11.6	11.3	11.6
Senegal / Sénégal	..	12.6	13.3	13.9	14.7	15.1	15.5	14.5	14.3	15.0
Seychelles	..	..	..	..	..	..	..	22.6	23.9	27.9
Sierra Leone	..	..	8.5	8.6	7.8	8.2	7.6	8.1	8.2	9.1
South Africa / Afrique du Sud[3]	..	20.1	19.9	20.9	22.4	23.6	24.9	24.9	22.8	22.8
Togo	..	7.0	8.8	9.8	9.9	10.7	11.3	10.7	10.8	10.9
Tunisia / Tunisie	..	18.3	17.8	17.7	17.8	17.5	18.1	19.4	18.9	18.9
Uganda / Ouganda	..	8.3	8.8	9.0	9.3	9.4	9.5	9.3	8.5	8.3
Africa (31) average / Moyenne Afrique (31)[4]	..	..	..	..	..	..	..	..	..	**13.2**
Asia-Pacific (28) average / Moyenne Asie-Pacifique (28)[5]	..	..	..	..	..	..	..	..	..	**17.1**
LAC average / Moyenne ALC[6]	**13.3**	**15.3**	**16.0**	**16.4**	**17.1**	**17.7**	**18.3**	**18.3**	**17.3**	**17.6**
OECD average / Moyenne OCDE[7]	**23.7**	**24.6**	**23.7**	**23.8**	**24.4**	**24.6**	**24.7**	**23.9**	**22.9**	**23.0**

	2011	2012	2013	2014	2015	2016	2017	2018	2019	2020
Botswana	16.0	14.3	15.3	16.0	13.4	14.6	13.3	13.3	13.7	12.4
Burkina Faso	12.0	13.5	14.3	12.7	12.8	13.5	14.4	14.8	15.4	14.7
Cabo Verde	20.2	18.3	18.3	17.5	19.3	19.4	20.5	21.9	21.2	20.0
Cameroon / Cameroun	11.5	12.0	12.6	13.0	13.3	12.7	13.0	13.2	12.8	11.8
Chad / Tchad	17.9	14.6	15.4	10.6	5.8	4.7	6.2	7.9	8.1	14.6
Congo	7.4	6.9	8.7	9.7	12.9	13.3	10.8	7.5	8.1	9.9
Congo, Dem. Rep. / Congo, Rép. dém.[1]	8.9	10.3	9.6	9.1	9.4	8.1	6.5	7.3	6.9	6.5
Côte d'Ivoire	10.3	11.6	11.3	10.8	11.2	11.6	11.8	11.5	11.7	11.9
Egypt / Égypte	13.0	12.1	13.2	11.9	12.2	12.7	13.0	13.8	13.4	12.3
Equatorial Guinea / Guinée équatoriale	7.0	8.8	8.4	9.2	11.3	6.3	5.9	5.9	9.0	7.6
Eswatini	12.2	11.3	12.3	13.1	13.0	14.1	14.7	15.0	15.9	15.6
Ghana	10.8	11.1	10.3	10.8	11.7	12.3	12.5	13.0	12.5	12.4
Kenya	16.4	15.8	15.9	17.0	16.6	16.6	17.0	16.1	15.8	14.8
Lesotho	17.7	16.9	18.6	18.9	19.3	19.2	19.9	22.6	21.3	20.1
Madagascar	9.6	8.9	8.9	8.6	9.1	9.7	10.5	10.9	11.0	9.9
Malawi	11.6	10.3	11.5	12.7	12.0	12.0	13.2	12.8	12.8	12.3
Mali	12.3	12.5	12.8	12.4	13.7	14.7	15.0	11.7	15.2	15.4
Mauritania / Mauritanie	10.0	12.8	12.7	14.2	13.6	13.4	13.7	14.6	13.1	12.4
Mauritius / Maurice[2]	18.3	18.8	18.5	18.6	18.5	18.7	19.0	19.6	20.2	20.0
Morocco / Maroc	23.2	24.1	22.8	22.4	21.5	22.0	22.3	22.4	22.1	21.7
Namibia / Namibie	21.1	19.5	19.7	20.8	21.1	20.8	20.0	19.1	19.9	18.2
Niger	9.6	10.1	12.1	11.8	12.0	9.9	8.9	10.6	9.8	9.2
Nigeria / Nigéria	9.0	8.7	7.6	6.9	5.5	4.7	5.1	5.8	5.3	4.9
Rwanda	12.1	12.8	14.0	14.4	15.3	15.2	15.2	15.9	16.3	15.8
Senegal / Sénégal	15.3	15.1	14.4	15.2	15.3	15.9	15.2	15.8	17.2	17.0
Seychelles	32.2	30.6	28.5	28.5	27.8	29.7	30.1	30.4	30.5	29.9
Sierra Leone	9.1	9.7	8.3	8.7	9.9	10.6	10.8	10.9	11.8	11.0
South Africa / Afrique du Sud[3]	23.6	24.0	24.4	25.0	26.1	25.7	25.8	26.2	25.8	24.9
Togo	12.0	12.5	14.5	15.5	16.0	16.4	15.8	14.6	15.0	15.4
Tunisia / Tunisie	20.1	19.8	20.1	21.2	20.1	19.1	20.1	21.2	23.1	22.5
Uganda / Ouganda	8.4	8.5	9.0	9.3	10.5	11.0	11.4	11.7	12.1	11.1
Africa (31) average / Moyenne Afrique (31)[4]	**13.9**	**13.9**	**14.1**	**14.2**	**14.3**	**14.3**	**14.3**	**14.6**	**14.8**	**14.5**
Asia-Pacific (28) average / Moyenne Asie-Pacifique (28)[5]	**17.4**	**17.9**	**18.0**	**17.4**	**17.8**	**17.2**	**18.2**	**18.7**	**18.8**	**17.6**
LAC average / Moyenne ALC[6]	**17.9**	**18.1**	**18.0**	**18.2**	**18.5**	**18.5**	**18.4**	**18.7**	**18.8**	**17.9**
OECD average / Moyenne OCDE[7]	**23.3**	**23.7**	**23.9**	**24.1**	**24.1**	**24.7**	**24.5**	**24.5**	**24.5**	..

Table 4.2. **Total tax revenue (excluding social security) as percentage of GDP** *(cont.)*
Tableau 4.2. **Total des recettes fiscales (sécurité sociale non comprise) en pourcentage du PIB** *(suite)*

Note: The figures include sub-national government tax revenues for Eswatini, Mauritania (since 2009), Mauritius, Morocco, Nigeria (only state revenues) and South Africa (since 2002). Sub-national government tax revenues are not available in other countries.

In Ghana, Lesotho, Malawi, Nigeria, Sierra Leone and Uganda, revenues from property taxes are mainly levied by local governments for which data on revenue are not available. In the Democratic Republic of the Congo only data for property taxes levied by the Direction Générale des Recettes Administratives, Judiciaires, Domaniales et de Participation (DGRAD) are available since 2010.

See the country tables in Chapter 5 for further information on data issues for individual countries.

1. The figures should be interpreted with caution as they are affected by macroeconomic instability in the early 2000s. For the years prior to 2010, the figures exclude some revenues collected by the Direction Générale des Recettes Administratives, Judiciaires, Domaniales et de Participation (DGRAD), which are estimated to be less than 1% of total tax revenue. See Table 5.6 in Chapter 5 for further information.
2. The fiscal year for Mauritius changed in 2010 and in 2015. Figures for 2015 needed to be estimated as a result.
3. Includes payments made by South Africa to the Southern African Customs Union (SACU) Common Revenue Pool.
4. Represents an unweighted average of the 31 African countries in this publication. In 2009, the Africa (31) average is calculated based on estimated tax-to-GDP ratios for Chad and Nigeria in that year, as data were not available prior to 2010 in these countries. The estimations in 2009 for these two countries are based on data for later years and on IMF figures from the *World Economic Outlook* April 2022. Details of the estimations are available in the metadata. The Africa (31) should be interpreted with caution as data for social security contributions (category 2000) and property taxes (category 4000) are not available or are partial in a few countries. See the country tables in Chapter 5 for further information.
5. Represents an unweighted average for 28 Asian and Pacific economies included in the publication *Revenue Statistics in Asia and the Pacific 2022*.
6. Represents an unweighted average for 26 Latin American and Caribbean (LAC) countries included in the publication *Revenue Statistics in Latin America and the Caribbean 2022*.
7. Represents an unweighted average for 38 OECD countries.

.. Non disponible

Note : Les chiffres incluent les recettes fiscales collectées par les administrations infranationales pour l'Afrique du Sud (à partir de 2002), Eswatini, le Maroc, Maurice, la Mauritanie (à partir de 2009) et le Nigéria (recettes des administrations régionales). Les données des recettes fiscales collectées par les administrations infranationales ne sont pas disponibles pour les autres pays. Au Ghana, au Lesotho, au Malawi, au Nigéria, en Ouganda et en Sierra Leone, les recettes provenant des impôts sur le patrimoine sont principalement perçues par les administrations locales pour lesquelles les données ne sont pas disponibles. En République démocratique du Congo, seules les données des impôts sur le patrimoine qui sont prélevées par la Direction Générale des Recettes Administratives, Judiciaires, Domaniales et de Participation (DGRAD) sont disponibles pour 2010-19.Voir les tableaux par pays au chapitre 5 pour plus d'informations sur les problèmes de données pour chaque pays.

1. Les chiffres doivent être interprétés avec prudence car ils sont affectés par une instabilité macroéconomique au début des années 2000. Pour les années antérieures à 2010, les chiffres excluent certaines recettes perçues par la Direction Générale des Recettes Administratives, Judiciaires, Domaniales et de Participation (DGRAD) estimées inférieures à 1 % du total des recettes fiscales. Voir le tableau 5.6 du chapitre 5 pour plus d'informations.
2. L'année fiscale pour Maurice a changé en 2010 et en 2015. Les chiffres pour 2015 ont dû être estimés en conséquence.
3. Comprend les paiements effectués par l'Afrique du Sud au fond collectif de l'Union douanière d'Afrique australe (SACU).
4. Représente une moyenne non pondérée des 31 pays africains inclus dans cette publication. En 2009, la moyenne de l'Afrique (31) est calculée sur la base des ratios impôts/PIB estimés pour le Nigéria et le Tchad car les données n'étaient pas disponibles avant 2010 dans ces pays. Les estimations en 2009 pour ces deux pays sont basées sur des données des années ultérieures et sur les chiffres du FMI tirés des *Perspectives de l'économie mondiale* d'avril 2022. Les détails des estimations sont disponibles dans les métadonnées. Il convient d'interpréter cette moyenne avec prudence à cause de valeurs manquantes ou incomplètes pour la rubrique 2000 (cotisations de sécurité sociale) et la rubrique 4000 (taxes sur le patrimoine). Voir les tableaux de pays au chapitre 5 pour plus d'informations.
5. Représente la moyenne non pondérée pour 28 économies de l'Asie et du Pacifique incluses dans la publication *Revenue Statistics in Asia and the Pacific 2022*.
6. Représente la moyenne non pondérée pour 26 pays d'Amérique latine et des Caraïbes (ALC) inclus dans la publication *Revenue Statistics in Latin America and the Caribbean 2022*.
7. Représente la moyenne non pondérée pour 38 pays de l'OCDE.

StatLink https://stat.link/v9pt6d

Table 4.3. **Tax revenue of the main headings as percentage of GDP, 2020**
Tableau 4.3. **Recettes fiscales des principales rubriques en pourcentage du PIB, 2020**

	1000 Income & profits / Impôts & profits	2000 Social security / Sécurité sociale	3000 Payroll / Salaires	4000 Property / Patrimoine	5000 Goods and services / Biens et services	6000 Other taxes / Autres impôts
Botswana	7.6	0.0	0.0	0.0	4.8	0.0
Burkina Faso	4.6	1.9	0.1	0.1	9.7	0.1
Cabo Verde	6.1	0.0	0.0	0.9	13.0	0.0
Cameroon / Cameroun	3.7	1.0	0.2	0.1	7.5	0.3
Chad / Tchad	9.4	..	0.2	0.5	4.5	0.0
Congo	3.0	..	0.3	0.2	6.4	0.0
Congo, Dem. Rep. / Congo, Rép. dém.	2.4	0.8	0.2	0.1	3.7	0.1
Côte d'Ivoire	1.6	1.6	1.6	0.4	8.2	0.1
Egypt / Égypte	6.3	0.9	0.0	0.1	6.0	0.0
Equatorial Guinea / Guinée équatoriale	6.1	0.9	0.0	0.0	1.4	0.1
Eswatini	8.5	2.4	0.0	0.3	6.8	0.0
Ghana	5.5	1.1	0.0	..	6.9	0.0
Kenya	6.9	0.6	0.0	0.0	7.9	0.0
Lesotho	11.1	0.0	0.0	..	9.0	0.0
Madagascar[1]	2.6	0.6	0.0	0.1	7.2	0.0
Malawi	5.9	0.0	0.0	..	6.3	0.0
Mali	5.0	2.7	0.1	0.3	9.1	1.0
Mauritania / Mauritanie[2]	5.1	0.7	0.0	0.0	7.3	0.0
Mauritius / Maurice	6.0	1.0	0.2	0.9	12.9	0.0
Morocco / Maroc[1]	8.8	6.6	0.0	1.2	11.6	0.1
Namibia / Namibie	12.6	0.4	0.0	0.1	5.4	0.1
Niger	2.3	0.5	0.0	0.2	5.8	0.9
Nigeria / Nigéria	2.7	0.6	0.0	..	1.8	0.3
Rwanda[1]	7.0	1.0	0.0	0.2	8.7	0.0
Senegal / Sénégal[3]	5.1	1.1	0.1	0.1	10.6	1.1
Seychelles	10.5	2.1	0.0	0.6	18.8	0.0
Sierra Leone	5.0	..	0.0	..	6.0	0.0
South Africa / Afrique du Sud[4]	12.6	0.3	0.3	1.8	10.2	0.0
Togo	3.0	..	0.0	0.1	11.8	0.3
Tunisia / Tunisie[1]	10.0	10.0	0.4	0.3	11.2	0.6
Uganda / Ouganda	4.0	..	0.0	..	7.0	0.1
Africa (31) average / Moyenne Afrique (31)[5]	**6.2**	**1.5**	**0.1**	**0.3**	**8.0**	**0.2**
Asia-Pacific (28) average / Moyenne Asie-Pacifique (28)[6]	**7.7**	**1.5**	**0.1**	**0.7**	**9.0**	**0.2**
LAC average / Moyenne ALC[7]	**5.9**	**4.0**	**0.3**	**0.8**	**10.5**	**0.4**
OECD average / Moyenne OCDE[8]	**11.3**	**8.9**	**0.5**	**1.8**	**10.8**	**0.2**

Table 4.3. **Tax revenue of the main headings as percentage of GDP, 2020** *(cont.)*
Tableau 4.3. **Recettes fiscales des principales rubriques en pourcentage du PIB, 2020** *(suite)*

.. Not available

Note: The figures include sub-national government tax revenues for Eswatini, Mauritania (since 2009), Mauritius, Morocco, Nigeria (only state revenues) and South Africa (since 2002). Sub-national government tax revenues are not available in other countries.

Data on social security contributions are not available for Chad, the Republic of the Congo, the Democratic Republic of the Congo (prior to 2012), Equatorial Guinea (prior to 2013), Madagascar (prior to 2011), Namibia (prior to 2009), Sierra Leone, Togo and Uganda; and are only partially available in Cameroon and Senegal. Social security contributions for Botswana, Lesotho and Malawi are deemed to be null as they do not meet the criteria to be classified as social security contributions set out in the OECD classification of taxes in the *OECD Interpretative Guide.*

In Ghana, Lesotho, Malawi, Nigeria, Sierra Leone and Uganda, revenues from property taxes are mainly levied by local governments for which data on revenue are not available. In the Democratic Republic of the Congo only data for property taxes levied by the Direction Générale des Recettes Administratives, Judiciaires, Domaniales et de Participation (DGRAD) are available since 2010.

1. Madagascar, Morocco, Rwanda and Tunisia do not include social security contributions in the tax-to-GDP ratio in their official publications as these countries do not consider them to be taxes. They are included as tax revenue in this publication, following the classification set out in the *OECD Interpretative Guide.*
2. Social security contributions from the Caisse Nationale de Sécurité Sociale are estimated since 2018.
3. Social security contributions are estimated since 2018.
4. The figures for heading 5000 goods and services should be interpreted with caution as they include payments made by South Africa to the Southern African Customs Union (SACU) Common Revenue Pool.
5. Represents an unweighted average of the 31 African countries in this publication. The Africa (31) should be interpreted with caution as data for social security contributions (category 2000) and property taxes (category 4000) are not available or are partial in a few countries. See the country tables in Chapter 5 for further information.
6. Represents an unweighted average for 28 Asian and Pacific economies included in the publication *Revenue Statistics in Asia and the Pacific 2022.*
7. Represents an unweighted average for 26 Latin American and Caribbean (LAC) countries included in the publication *Revenue Statistics in Latin America and the Caribbean 2022.*
8. Represents an unweighted average for 38 OECD countries. Data are for 2019 as data for 2020 were not available at the date of publication.

.. Non disponible

Note : Les chiffres incluent les recettes fiscales collectées par les administrations infranationales pour l'Afrique du Sud (à partir de 2002), Eswatini, le Maroc, Maurice, la Mauritanie (à partir de 2009) et le Nigéria (recettes des administrations régionales). Les données des recettes fiscales collectées par les administrations infranationales ne sont pas disponibles pour les autres pays.

Les données des cotisations de sécurité sociale ne sont pas disponibles pour la République du Congo, la République démocratique du Congo (avant 2012), la Guinée Équatoriale, (avant 2013), Madagascar (avant 2011), la Namibie (avant 2009), l'Ouganda, la Sierra Leone, le Tchad et le Togo et ne sont que partiellement disponibles au Cameroun et au Sénégal. Les cotisations de sécurité sociale pour le Botswana, le Lesotho et le Malawi sont nulles car elles ne répondent pas aux critères de classification des cotisations de sécurité sociale de la classification des impôts établie dans le *guide d'interprétation de l'OCDE.*

Au Ghana, au Lesotho, au Malawi, au Nigéria, en Ouganda et en Sierra Leone, les recettes provenant des impôts sur le patrimoine sont principalement perçues par les administrations locales pour lesquelles les données ne sont pas disponibles. En République démocratique du Congo, seules les données des impôts sur le patrimoine qui sont prélevées par la Direction Générale des Recettes Administratives, Judiciaires, Domaniales et de Participation (DGRAD) sont disponibles pour 2010-19.

1. Madagascar, le Maroc, le Rwanda et la Tunisie n'incluent pas les cotisations de sécurité sociale dans le ratio impôts/PIB dans leurs publications officielles car ces pays ne les considèrent pas comme des impôts. Elles sont incluses dans les recettes fiscales de cette publication en accordance avec la classification des impôts établie dans le *guide d'interprétation de l'OCDE.*
2. Les cotisations de sécurité sociale de la Caisse Nationale de Sécurité Sociale sont estimées à partir de 2018.
3. Les cotisations de sécurité sociale sont estimées à partir de 2018.
4. Les chiffres relatifs à la rubrique 5000 produits et services doivent être interprétés avec prudence car ils incluent les paiements effectués par l'Afrique du Sud au fonds commun des recettes de l'Union douanière d'Afrique australe (SACU).
5. Représente une moyenne non pondérée des 31 pays africains inclus dans cette publication. Il convient d'interpréter cette moyenne avec prudence à cause de valeurs manquantes ou incomplètes pour la rubrique 2000 (cotisations de sécurité sociale) et la rubrique 4000 (taxes sur le patrimoine). Veuillez voir les tableaux de pays au chapitre 5 pour plus d'informations.
6. Représente la moyenne non pondérée pour 28 économies de l'Asie et du Pacifique incluses dans la publication *Revenue Statistics in Asia and the Pacific 2022.*
7. Représente la moyenne non pondérée pour 26 pays d'Amérique latine et des Caraïbes (ALC) inclus dans la publication *Revenue Statistics in Latin America and the Caribbean 2022.*
8. Représente la moyenne non pondérée pour 38 pays de l'OCDE. Les données sont pour 2019 car les données pour 2020 n'étaient pas disponibles à la date de la publication.

StatLink https://stat.link/oriqg3

Table 4.4. **Tax revenue of the main headings as percentage of total taxes, 2020**
Tableau 4.4. **Recettes fiscales des principales rubriques en pourcentage du total des recettes fiscales, 2020**

	1000 Income & profits / Impôts & profits	2000 Social security / Sécurité sociale	3000 Payroll / Salaires	4000 Property / Patrimoine	5000 Goods and services / Biens et services	6000 Other taxes / Autres impôts
Botswana	61.1	0.0	0.0	0.3	38.7	0.0
Burkina Faso	27.5	11.7	0.9	0.8	58.6	0.5
Cabo Verde	30.2	0.2	0.0	4.7	64.9	0.0
Cameroon / Cameroun	28.7	8.1	1.2	0.9	58.5	2.7
Chad / Tchad	64.2	..	1.4	3.5	30.9	0.0
Congo	30.6	..	2.8	2.0	64.4	0.1
Congo, Dem. Rep. / Congo, Rép. dém.	33.1	11.1	2.7	0.8	51.0	1.2
Côte d'Ivoire	12.3	11.6	11.6	2.9	60.9	0.7
Egypt / Égypte	47.2	7.1	0.0	0.6	45.0	0.0
Equatorial Guinea / Guinée équatoriale	71.6	10.2	0.0	0.0	16.4	1.7
Eswatini	47.2	13.3	0.0	1.5	38.0	0.0
Ghana	40.9	8.0	0.0	..	51.1	0.0
Kenya	44.7	3.8	0.0	0.0	51.4	0.0
Lesotho	55.3	0.0	0.0	..	44.7	0.0
Madagascar[1]	25.1	5.9	0.0	0.6	68.4	0.1
Malawi	48.5	0.0	0.0	..	51.4	0.1
Mali	27.7	14.8	0.3	1.5	50.5	5.3
Mauritania / Mauritanie[2]	38.6	5.4	0.1	0.2	55.6	0.1
Mauritius / Maurice	28.7	4.7	0.8	4.2	61.5	0.1
Morocco / Maroc[1]	31.0	23.3	0.0	4.4	41.1	0.3
Namibia / Namibie	68.1	2.0	0.0	0.5	29.1	0.3
Niger	23.5	5.6	0.2	1.8	59.3	9.6
Nigeria / Nigéria	49.1	11.5	0.8	..	32.5	6.0
Rwanda[1]	41.3	6.2	0.0	0.9	51.6	0.0
Senegal / Sénégal[3]	28.1	6.2	0.3	0.7	58.5	6.2
Seychelles	32.8	6.4	0.0	1.8	58.9	0.0
Sierra Leone	45.5	..	0.0	..	54.5	0.0
South Africa / Afrique du Sud[4]	49.9	1.4	1.3	7.1	40.4	0.0
Togo	19.8	..	0.1	0.8	77.0	2.3
Tunisia / Tunisie[1]	30.9	30.9	1.1	0.8	34.5	1.8
Uganda / Ouganda	36.2	..	0.0	..	63.1	0.7
Africa (31) average / Moyenne Afrique (31)[5]	**39.3**	**8.1**	**0.8**	**1.7**	**50.4**	**1.3**
Asia-Pacific (28) average / Moyenne Asie-Pacifique (28)[6]	**38.4**	**6.3**	**0.5**	**3.0**	**50.6**	**1.1**
LAC average / Moyenne ALC[7]	**26.9**	**18.4**	**1.0**	**3.5**	**48.4**	**1.6**
OECD average / Moyenne OCDE[8]	**34.0**	**25.9**	**1.3**	**5.5**	**32.6**	**0.5**

Table 4.4. **Tax revenue of the main headings as percentage of total taxes, 2020** *(cont.)*
Tableau 4.4. **Recettes fiscales des principales rubriques en pourcentage du total des recettes fiscales, 2020** *(suite)*

.. Not available

Note: The figures include sub-national government tax revenues for Eswatini, Mauritania (since 2009), Mauritius, Morocco, Nigeria (only state revenues) and South Africa (since 2002). Sub-national government tax revenues are not available in other countries.

Data on social security contributions are not available for Chad, the Republic of the Congo, the Democratic Republic of the Congo (prior to 2012), Equatorial Guinea (prior to 2013), Madagascar (prior to 2011), Namibia (prior to 2009), Sierra Leone, Togo and Uganda; and are only partially available in Cameroon and Senegal. Social security contributions for Botswana, Lesotho and Malawi are deemed to be null as they do not meet the criteria to be classified as social security contributions set out in the OECD classification of taxes in the *OECD Interpretative Guide.*

In Ghana, Lesotho, Malawi, Nigeria, Sierra Leone and Uganda, revenues from property taxes are mainly levied by local governments for which data on revenue are not available. In the Democratic Republic of the Congo only data for property taxes levied by the Direction Générale des Recettes Administratives, Judiciaires, Domaniales et de Participation (DGRAD) are available since 2010.

1. Madagascar, Morocco, Rwanda and Tunisia do not include social security contributions in the tax-to-GDP ratio in their official publications as these countries do not consider them to be taxes. They are included as tax revenue in this publication, following the classification set out in the *OECD Interpretative Guide.*
2. Social security contributions from the Caisse Nationale de Sécurité Sociale are estimated since 2018.
3. Social security contributions are estimated since 2018.
4. The figures for heading 5000 goods and services should be interpreted with caution as they include payments made by South Africa to the Southern African Customs Union (SACU) Common Revenue Pool.
5. Represents an unweighted average of the 31 African countries in this publication. The Africa (31) should be interpreted with caution as data for social security contributions (category 2000) and property taxes (category 4000) are not available or are partial in a few countries. See the country tables in Chapter 5 for further information.
6. Represents an unweighted average for 28 Asian and Pacific economies included in the publication *Revenue Statistics in Asia and the Pacific 2022.*
7. Represents an unweighted average for 26 Latin American and Caribbean (LAC) countries included in the publication *Revenue Statistics in Latin America and the Caribbean 2022.*
8. Represents an unweighted average for 38 OECD countries. Data are for 2019 as data for 2020 were not available at the date of publication.

.. Non disponible

Note : Les chiffres incluent les recettes fiscales collectées par les administrations infranationales pour l'Afrique du Sud (à partir de 2002), Eswatini, le Maroc, Maurice, la Mauritanie (à partir de 2009) et le Nigéria (recettes des administrations régionales). Les données des recettes fiscales collectées par les administrations infranationales ne sont pas disponibles pour les autres pays.

Les données des cotisations de sécurité sociale ne sont pas disponibles pour la République du Congo, la République démocratique du Congo (avant 2012), la Guinée Équatoriale, (avant 2013), Madagascar (avant 2011), la Namibie (avant 2009), l'Ouganda, la Sierra Leone, le Tchad et le Togo et ne sont que partiellement disponibles au Cameroun et au Sénégal. Les cotisations de sécurité sociale pour le Botswana, le Lesotho et le Malawi sont nulles car elles ne répondent pas aux critères de classification des cotisations de sécurité sociale de la classification des impôts établie dans le *guide d'interprétation de l'OCDE.*

Au Ghana, au Lesotho, au Malawi, au Nigéria, en Ouganda et en Sierra Leone, les recettes provenant des impôts sur le patrimoine sont principalement perçues par les administrations locales pour lesquelles les données ne sont pas disponibles. En République démocratique du Congo, seules les données des impôts sur le patrimoine qui sont prélevées par la Direction Générale des Recettes Administratives, Judiciaires, Domaniales et de Participation (DGRAD) sont disponibles pour 2010-19.

1. Madagascar, le Maroc, le Rwanda et la Tunisie n'incluent pas les cotisations de sécurité sociale dans le ratio impôts/PIB dans leurs publications officielles car ces pays ne les considèrent pas comme des impôts. Elles sont incluses dans les recettes fiscales de cette publication en accordance avec la classification des impôts établie dans le *guide d'interprétation de l'OCDE.*
2. Les cotisations de sécurité sociale de la Caisse Nationale de Sécurité Sociale sont estimées à partir de 2018.
3. Les cotisations de sécurité sociale sont estimées à partir de 2018.
4. Les chiffres relatifs à la rubrique 5000 produits et services doivent être interprétés avec prudence car ils incluent les paiements effectués par l'Afrique du Sud au fonds commun des recettes de l'Union douanière d'Afrique australe (SACU).
5. Représente une moyenne non pondérée des 31 pays africains inclus dans cette publication. Il convient d'interpréter cette moyenne avec prudence à cause de valeurs manquantes ou incomplètes pour la rubrique 2000 (cotisations de sécurité sociale) et la rubrique 4000 (taxes sur le patrimoine). Veuillez voir les tableaux de pays au chapitre 5 pour plus d'informations.
6. Représente la moyenne non pondérée pour 28 économies de l'Asie et du Pacifique incluses dans la publication *Revenue Statistics in Asia and the Pacific 2022.*
7. Représente la moyenne non pondérée pour 26 pays d'Amérique latine et des Caraïbes (ALC) inclus dans la publication *Revenue Statistics in Latin America and the Caribbean 2022.*
8. Représente la moyenne non pondérée pour 38 pays de l'OCDE. Les données sont pour 2019 car les données pour 2020 n'étaient pas disponibles à la date de la publication.

StatLink *https://stat.link/3f90sv*

Table 4.5. **Taxes on income and profits (1000) as percentage of GDP**
Tableau 4.5. **Impôts sur le revenu et les bénéfices (1000) en pourcentage du PIB**

	1995	2000	2005	2010	2015	2016	2017	2018	2019	2020
Botswana	..	..	11.3	10.4	9.1	10.2	8.2	8.6	8.6	7.6
Burkina Faso	..	2.5	2.4	2.7	3.4	3.8	4.0	4.2	4.8	4.6
Cabo Verde	5.1	5.5	6.0	5.7	6.1	6.1	6.5	6.7	6.6	6.1
Cameroon / Cameroun	2.2	3.0	3.2	3.1	4.6	3.8	3.5	3.8	3.8	3.7
Chad / Tchad	..	..	..	11.3	3.3	2.1	3.0	4.2	3.9	9.4
Congo	..	1.8	1.8	2.3	5.0	5.2	4.3	1.8	2.5	3.0
Congo, Dem. Rep. / Congo, Rép. dém.	..	0.2	1.0	2.3	3.5	2.6	2.5	3.4	3.2	2.4
Côte d'Ivoire	1.8	1.8	1.5	1.5	1.5	1.5	1.6	1.8	1.6	1.6
Egypt / Égypte	..	..	6.3	6.8	6.4	6.6	6.2	6.5	6.2	6.3
Equatorial Guinea / Guinée équatoriale	..	..	7.5	6.8	9.9	4.8	4.6	4.4	7.4	6.1
Eswatini	5.4	5.5	6.2	7.2	7.3	8.1	8.2	8.4	8.8	8.5
Ghana	..	2.3	2.9	3.9	4.1	3.7	4.5	5.3	5.6	5.5
Kenya	..	..	3.9	6.4	7.8	7.8	7.8	7.3	7.0	6.9
Lesotho	..	..	8.5	9.7	12.0	12.0	11.7	12.7	11.9	11.1
Madagascar	1.1	1.6	2.1	2.4	2.1	2.3	2.4	2.6	2.8	2.6
Malawi	..	..	3.8	5.0	5.8	5.8	6.4	6.1	6.0	5.9
Mali	1.6	1.6	2.4	3.5	3.8	3.9	4.4	3.3	4.0	5.0
Mauritania / Mauritanie	..	..	..	3.4	4.9	4.4	4.5	4.5	4.3	5.1
Mauritius / Maurice[1]	2.5	2.4	3.0	4.9	4.8	4.8	5.1	5.2	5.7	6.0
Morocco / Maroc	..	5.7	7.7	8.0	8.0	8.3	8.7	8.7	8.5	8.8
Namibia / Namibie	..	..	..	11.7	12.8	12.8	12.6	12.1	12.6	12.6
Niger	..	1.3	1.5	2.4	3.1	2.8	2.6	2.4	2.3	2.3
Nigeria / Nigéria	..	..	..	4.6	3.6	2.9	3.2	3.8	3.4	2.7
Rwanda	..	2.2	3.1	4.5	6.2	6.3	6.3	6.8	6.9	7.0
Senegal / Sénégal	..	2.9	3.5	4.1	4.1	4.6	4.5	4.7	5.2	5.1
Seychelles	..	..	..	9.1	9.0	9.9	10.5	10.2	10.0	10.5
Sierra Leone	..	..	2.3	2.8	4.1	5.2	4.3	4.9	5.1	5.0
South Africa / Afrique du Sud	10.5	11.4	12.0	12.0	13.8	13.5	13.8	13.8	13.4	12.6
Togo	..	1.5	2.3	1.8	2.7	3.2	2.7	3.0	3.2	3.0
Tunisia / Tunisie	..	5.3	6.7	7.7	8.5	7.7	8.3	7.9	10.2	10.0
Uganda / Ouganda	1.2	1.5	2.7	2.6	3.6	3.8	3.9	4.0	4.3	4.0
Africa (31) average / Moyenne Afrique (31)[2]	**..**	**..**	**..**	**5.5**	**6.0**	**5.8**	**5.8**	**5.9**	**6.1**	**6.2**
Asia-Pacific (28) average / Moyenne Asie-Pacifique (28)[3]	**..**	**..**	**..**	**6.9**	**6.9**	**6.7**	**7.2**	**7.5**	**7.9**	**7.7**
LAC average / Moyenne ALC[4]	**3.6**	**4.1**	**5.1**	**5.5**	**5.9**	**5.7**	**5.7**	**6.0**	**6.0**	**5.9**
OECD average / Moyenne OCDE[5]	**10.8**	**11.5**	**11.3**	**10.2**	**10.9**	**10.9**	**11.2**	**11.3**	**11.3**	**..**

.. Not available

Note: The figures include sub-national government tax revenues for Eswatini, Mauritania (since 2009), Mauritius, Morocco, Nigeria (only state revenues) and South Africa (since 2002). Sub-national government tax revenues are not available in other countries.

1. The fiscal year for Mauritius changed in 2010 and in 2015. Figures for 2015 needed to be estimated as a result.
2. Represents an unweighted average of the 31 African countries in this publication.
3. Represents an unweighted average for 28 Asian and Pacific economies included in the publication *Revenue Statistics in Asia and the Pacific 2022*.
4. Represents an unweighted average for 26 Latin American and Caribbean (LAC) countries included in the publication *Revenue Statistics in Latin America and the Caribbean 2022*.
5. Represents an unweighted average for 38 OECD countries.

.. Non disponible

Note : Les chiffres incluent les recettes fiscales collectées par les administrations infranationales pour l'Afrique du Sud (à partir de 2002), Eswatini, le Maroc, Maurice, la Mauritanie (à partir de 2009) et le Nigéria (recettes des administrations régionales). Les données des recettes fiscales collectées par les administrations infranationales ne sont pas disponibles pour les autres pays.

1. L'année fiscale pour Maurice a changé en 2010 et en 2015. Les chiffres pour 2015 ont dû être estimés en conséquence.
2. Représente une moyenne non pondérée des 31 pays africains inclus dans cette publication.
3. Représente la moyenne non pondérée pour 28 économies de l'Asie et du Pacifique incluses dans la publication *Revenue Statistics in Asia and the Pacific 2022*.
4. Représente la moyenne non pondérée pour 26 pays d'Amérique latine et des Caraïbes (ALC) inclus dans la publication *Revenue Statistics in Latin America and the Caribbean 2022*.
5. Représente la moyenne non pondérée pour 38 pays de l'OCDE.

StatLink https://stat.link/2u3ctw

Table 4.6. **Taxes on income and profits (1000) as percentage of total taxation**
Tableau 4.6. **Impôts sur le revenu et les bénéfices (1000) en pourcentage du total des recettes fiscales**

	1995	2000	2005	2010	2015	2016	2017	2018	2019	2020
Botswana	..	..	73.2	65.3	67.9	69.5	61.3	64.7	63.0	61.1
Burkina Faso	..	24.7	20.9	19.3	23.2	24.8	24.5	25.4	27.8	27.5
Cabo Verde	33.5	35.7	30.9	30.0	31.5	31.2	31.8	30.5	30.9	30.2
Cameroon / Cameroun	24.0	28.1	28.7	27.1	32.3	28.1	25.3	27.0	27.4	28.7
Chad / Tchad	..	..	..	77.6	56.3	45.6	48.0	53.0	48.5	64.2
Congo	..	48.2	30.3	33.3	38.5	39.0	39.9	24.5	30.2	30.6
Congo, Dem. Rep. / Congo, Rép. dém.	..	18.4	18.1	26.7	35.1	30.2	36.3	43.5	42.5	33.1
Côte d'Ivoire	15.0	16.4	13.7	12.8	12.0	11.2	12.2	13.7	12.3	12.3
Egypt / Égypte	..	..	40.0	44.4	43.8	45.6	40.4	43.6	43.5	47.2
Equatorial Guinea / Guinée équatoriale	..	..	91.3	89.1	82.5	67.1	69.4	66.8	76.3	71.6
Eswatini	52.6	51.0	53.6	51.7	48.7	50.2	48.5	48.3	48.2	47.2
Ghana	..	28.9	27.4	36.1	32.1	28.1	33.1	38.7	42.2	40.9
Kenya	..	..	35.9	40.6	46.4	45.6	44.9	44.2	42.8	44.7
Lesotho	..	..	55.2	56.3	62.2	62.3	58.7	56.3	56.0	55.3
Madagascar	16.9	17.0	23.4	24.8	22.5	23.4	22.4	22.3	24.5	25.1
Malawi	..	..	42.7	44.2	48.7	48.4	48.5	48.0	46.7	48.5
Mali	21.3	14.5	16.6	24.7	25.2	23.9	26.2	24.8	23.2	27.7
Mauritania / Mauritanie	..	..	..	34.8	33.4	31.2	31.2	29.4	31.5	38.6
Mauritius / Maurice[1]	14.7	13.0	16.7	25.7	25.0	24.8	25.9	25.4	26.9	28.7
Morocco / Maroc	..	26.0	31.0	28.9	29.8	30.2	31.1	30.7	30.1	31.0
Namibia / Namibie	..	..	..	63.0	59.4	60.5	61.8	62.1	62.4	68.1
Niger	..	18.0	18.3	25.4	24.7	26.4	27.0	21.1	21.9	23.5
Nigeria / Nigéria	..	..	..	63.5	59.9	55.8	55.7	60.1	56.6	49.1
Rwanda	..	26.0	28.6	36.2	38.1	38.6	39.1	40.3	39.8	41.3
Senegal / Sénégal	..	22.1	23.1	25.9	25.3	26.9	27.2	27.7	28.2	28.1
Seychelles	..	..	..	29.5	31.0	32.2	33.6	31.2	31.0	32.8
Sierra Leone	..	..	29.4	31.4	41.9	48.7	40.1	45.0	43.1	45.5
South Africa / Afrique du Sud	53.8	56.7	52.6	52.1	51.9	51.8	52.8	51.8	51.2	49.9
Togo	..	20.9	23.6	16.5	16.6	19.2	17.1	20.3	21.4	19.8
Tunisia / Tunisie	..	22.6	28.9	29.7	30.0	27.8	28.5	26.5	31.7	30.9
Uganda / Ouganda	14.8	18.2	29.0	31.5	34.7	34.9	34.7	34.3	35.2	36.2
Africa (31) average / Moyenne Afrique (31)[2]	**..**	**..**	**..**	**38.6**	**39.1**	**38.2**	**38.0**	**38.1**	**38.6**	**39.3**
Asia-Pacific (28) average / Moyenne Asie-Pacifique (28)[3]	**..**	**..**	**..**	**36.9**	**36.9**	**36.7**	**37.1**	**37.2**	**37.3**	**38.4**
LAC average / Moyenne ALC[4]	**20.5**	**22.1**	**24.6**	**26.0**	**26.3**	**26.0**	**25.9**	**26.5**	**26.6**	**26.9**
OECD average / Moyenne OCDE[5]	**33.0**	**33.9**	**33.8**	**32.2**	**33.2**	**32.8**	**33.6**	**34.0**	**34.0**	**..**

.. Not available

Note: The figures include sub-national government tax revenues for Eswatini, Mauritania (since 2009), Mauritius, Morocco, Nigeria (only state revenues) and South Africa (since 2002). Sub-national government tax revenues are not available in other countries.

1. The fiscal year for Mauritius changed in 2010 and in 2015. Figures for 2015 needed to be estimated as a result.
2. Represents an unweighted average of the 31 African countries in this publication.
3. Represents an unweighted average for 28 Asian and Pacific economies included in the publication *Revenue Statistics in Asia and the Pacific 2022*.
4. Represents an unweighted average for 26 Latin American and Caribbean (LAC) countries included in the publication *Revenue Statistics in Latin America and the Caribbean 2022*.
5. Represents an unweighted average for 38 OECD countries.

.. Non disponible

Note : Les chiffres incluent les recettes fiscales collectées par les administrations infranationales pour l'Afrique du Sud (à partir de 2002), Eswatini, le Maroc, Maurice, la Mauritanie (à partir de 2009) et le Nigéria (recettes des administrations régionales). Les données des recettes fiscales collectées par les administrations infranationales ne sont pas disponibles pour les autres pays.

1. L'année fiscale pour Maurice a changé en 2010 et en 2015. Les chiffres pour 2015 ont dû être estimés en conséquence.
2. Représente une moyenne non pondérée des 31 pays africains inclus dans cette publication.
3. Représente la moyenne non pondérée pour 28 économies de l'Asie et du Pacifique incluses dans la publication *Revenue Statistics in Asia and the Pacific 2022*.
4. Représente la moyenne non pondérée pour 26 pays d'Amérique latine et des Caraïbes (ALC) inclus dans la publication *Revenue Statistics in Latin America and the Caribbean 2022*.
5. Représente la moyenne non pondérée pour 38 pays de l'OCDE.

StatLink *https://stat.link/xjdpyt*

Table 4.7. **Social security contributions (2000) as percentage of GDP**
Tableau 4.7. **Cotisations de sécurité sociale (2000) en pourcentage du PIB**

	1995	2000	2005	2010	2015	2016	2017	2018	2019	2020
Botswana	..	..	0.0	0.0	0.0	0.0	0.0	0.0	0.0	0.0
Burkina Faso	..	1.6	1.5	1.5	1.7	1.8	1.8	1.8	1.9	1.9
Cabo Verde	0.0	0.8	0.6	0.0	0.0	0.0	0.0	0.0	0.0	0.0
Cameroon / Cameroun	0.8	0.9	0.8	1.0	0.8	1.0	1.0	1.0	1.0	1.0
Chad / Tchad	..	..	..	..	..	..	..	..	..	..
Congo	..	..	..	..	..	..	..	..	..	..
Congo, Dem. Rep. / Congo, Rép. dém.	..	..	..	..	0.6	0.5	0.5	0.5	0.8	0.8
Côte d'Ivoire	0.7	1.0	0.9	1.0	1.4	1.6	1.5	1.5	1.5	1.6
Egypt / Égypte	..	..	2.9	2.2	2.5	1.8	2.3	1.2	0.9	0.9
Equatorial Guinea / Guinée équatoriale	..	..	0.0	0.0	0.8	0.7	0.7	0.7	0.7	0.9
Eswatini	1.6	1.2	1.4	1.9	1.9	2.0	2.3	2.5	2.4	2.4
Ghana	..	0.7	0.9	0.9	1.2	0.8	0.9	0.7	0.7	1.1
Kenya	..	..	0.1	0.2	0.2	0.4	0.4	0.5	0.6	0.6
Lesotho	..	..	0.0	0.0	0.0	0.0	0.0	0.0	0.0	0.0
Madagascar[1]	..	..	..	..	0.4	0.4	0.4	0.6	0.5	0.6
Malawi	..	..	0.0	0.0	0.0	0.0	0.0	0.0	0.0	0.0
Mali	0.8	0.9	1.4	1.4	1.5	1.8	1.8	1.7	2.3	2.7
Mauritania / Mauritanie[2]	..	..	..	0.7	0.9	0.8	0.8	0.8	0.7	0.7
Mauritius / Maurice[3]	1.0	0.8	0.7	0.7	0.8	0.8	0.8	0.8	0.9	1.0
Morocco / Maroc[1,4]	..	2.4	4.2	4.8	5.3	5.5	5.7	5.8	6.2	6.6
Namibia / Namibie	..	..	..	0.4	0.4	0.3	0.4	0.3	0.3	0.4
Niger	..	0.4	0.3	0.5	0.6	0.6	0.6	0.5	0.6	0.5
Nigeria / Nigéria	..	..	..	0.6	0.6	0.5	0.6	0.5	0.6	0.6
Rwanda[1]	..	0.4	0.7	0.8	1.0	1.1	1.0	1.0	1.0	1.0
Senegal / Sénégal[5]	..	0.5	0.6	0.9	1.1	1.1	1.2	1.2	1.2	1.1
Seychelles	..	..	..	2.8	1.1	1.1	1.2	2.4	1.7	2.1
Sierra Leone	..	..	..	..	..	..	..	..	..	..
South Africa / Afrique du Sud	0.0	0.0	0.4	0.4	0.4	0.4	0.4	0.4	0.4	0.3
Togo	..	..	..	..	..	..	..	..	..	..
Tunisia / Tunisie[1]	..	5.0	5.3	7.0	8.4	8.8	9.1	8.7	9.1	10.0
Uganda / Ouganda	..	..	..	..	..	..	..	..	..	..
Africa (31) average / Moyenne Afrique (31)[6]	..	..	..	**1.2**	**1.3**	**1.3**	**1.4**	**1.4**	**1.4**	**1.5**
Asia-Pacific (28) average / Moyenne Asie-Pacifique (28)[7]	..	..	..	**1.1**	**1.2**	**1.2**	**1.2**	**1.3**	**1.5**	**1.5**
LAC average / Moyenne ALC[8]	**2.6**	**2.8**	**2.8**	**3.3**	**3.8**	**3.8**	**3.8**	**3.8**	**3.9**	**4.0**
OECD average / Moyenne OCDE[9]	**8.5**	**8.4**	**8.3**	**8.6**	**8.8**	**8.9**	**8.9**	**9.0**	**8.9**	..

Table 4.7. **Social security contributions (2000) as percentage of GDP** *(cont.)*
Tableau 4.7. **Cotisations de sécurité sociale (2000) en pourcentage du PIB** *(suite)*

.. Not available

Note: The figures include sub-national government tax revenues for Eswatini, Mauritania (since 2009), Mauritius, Morocco, Nigeria (only state revenues) and South Africa (since 2002). Sub-national government tax revenues are not available in other countries.

Data on social security contributions are not available for Chad, the Republic of the Congo, the Democratic Republic of the Congo (prior to 2012), Equatorial Guinea (prior to 2013), Madagascar (prior to 2011), Namibia (prior to 2009), Sierra Leone, Togo and Uganda; and are only partially available in Cameroon and Senegal. Social security contributions for Botswana, Lesotho and Malawi are deemed to be null as they do not meet the criteria to be classified as social security contributions set out in the OECD classification of taxes in the *OECD Interpretative Guide.*

1. Madagascar, Morocco, Rwanda and Tunisia do not include social security contributions in the tax-to-GDP ratio in their official publications as these countries do not consider them to be taxes. They are included as tax revenue in this publication, following the classification set out in the OECD *Interpretative Guide.*
2. Social security contributions from the Caisse Nationale de Sécurité Sociale are estimated since 2018.
3. The fiscal year for Mauritius changed in 2010 and in 2015. Figures for 2015 needed to be estimated as a result.
4. Social security contributions in Morocco are estimated for years prior to 2002.
5. These figures include contributions to the Senegalese Pension Institute (IPRES) (estimated prior to 2006) and contributions to the social security fund (CSS) (from 2012 as data for previous years are not available). Social security contributions in Senegal are estimated since 2018.
6. Represents an unweighted average of the 31 African countries in this publication. The Africa (31) should be interpreted with caution as data for social security contributions (category 2000) are not available or are partial in a few countries. See the country tables in Chapter 5 for further information.
7. Represents an unweighted average for 28 Asian and Pacific economies included in the publication *Revenue Statistics in Asia and the Pacific 2022.*
8. Represents an unweighted average for 26 Latin American and Caribbean (LAC) countries included in the publication *Revenue Statistics in Latin America and the Caribbean 2022.*
9. Represents an unweighted average for 38 OECD countries.

.. Non disponible

Note : Les chiffres incluent les recettes fiscales collectées par les administrations infranationales pour l'Afrique du Sud (à partir de 2002), Eswatini, le Maroc, Maurice, la Mauritanie (à partir de 2009) et le Nigéria (recettes des administrations régionales). Les données des recettes fiscales collectées par les administrations infranationales ne sont pas disponibles pour les autres pays. Les données des cotisations de sécurité sociale ne sont pas disponibles pour la République du Congo, la République démocratique du Congo (avant 2012), la Guinée Équatoriale, (avant 2013), Madagascar (avant 2011), la Namibie (avant 2009), l'Ouganda, la Sierra Leone, le Tchad et le Togo et ne sont que partiellement disponibles au Cameroun et au Sénégal. Les cotisations de sécurité sociale pour le Botswana, le Lesotho et le Malawi sont nulles car elles ne répondent pas aux critères de classification des cotisations de sécurité sociale de la classification des impôts établie dans le *guide d'interprétation de l'OCDE.*

1. Madagascar, le Maroc, le Rwanda et la Tunisie n'incluent pas les cotisations de sécurité sociale dans le ratio impôts/PIB dans leurs publications officielles car ces pays ne les considèrent pas comme des impôts. Elles sont incluses dans les recettes fiscales de cette publication en accordance avec la classification des impôts établie dans le *guide d'interprétation de l'OCDE.*
2. Les cotisations de sécurité sociale de la Caisse Nationale de Sécurité Sociale sont estimées à partir de 2018.
3. L'année fiscale pour Maurice a changé en 2010 et en 2015. Les chiffres pour 2015 ont dû être estimés en conséquence.
4. Les cotisations de sécurité sociale au Maroc antérieures à 2002 sont estimées.
5. Les chiffres comprennent les cotisations de sécurité sociale de l'Institution de prévoyance retraite du Sénégal (IPRES) (estimées pour les années antérieures à 2006) et les cotisations de sécurité sociale de la Caisse de Sécurité Sociale (CSS) (à partir de 2012 car les données pour les années précédentes ne sont pas disponibles). Les cotisations de sécurité sociale à partir de 2018 sont estimées.
6. Représente une moyenne non pondérée des 31 pays africains inclus dans cette publication. Il convient d'interpréter cette moyenne avec prudence à cause de valeurs manquantes ou incomplètes pour la rubrique 2000 (cotisations de sécurité sociale). Veuillez voir les tableaux de pays au chapitre 5 pour plus d'informations.
7. Représente la moyenne non pondérée pour 28 économies de l'Asie et du Pacifique incluses dans la publication *Revenue Statistics in Asia and the Pacific 2022.*
8. Représente la moyenne non pondérée pour 26 pays d'Amérique latine et des Caraïbes (ALC) inclus dans la publication *Revenue Statistics in Latin America and the Caribbean 2022.*
9. Représente la moyenne non pondérée pour 38 pays de l'OCDE.

StatLink https://stat.link/eh3agm

Table 4.8. **Social security contributions (2000) as percentage of total taxation**

Tableau 4.8. **Cotisations de sécurité sociale (2000) en pourcentage du total des recettes fiscales**

	1995	2000	2005	2010	2015	2016	2017	2018	2019	2020
Botswana	..	..	0.0	0.0	0.0	0.0	0.0	0.0	0.0	0.0
Burkina Faso	..	15.9	13.2	11.0	11.8	11.5	11.0	11.1	10.9	11.7
Cabo Verde	0.0	5.2	2.8	0.2	0.1	0.2	0.2	0.2	0.2	0.2
Cameroon / Cameroun	8.3	8.1	7.4	8.6	6.0	7.3	7.3	7.2	7.3	8.1
Chad / Tchad	..	..	..	..	..	..	..	..	..	..
Congo	..	..	..	..	..	..	..	..	..	..
Congo, Dem. Rep. / Congo, Rép. dém.	..	..	..	..	5.8	5.9	7.4	6.0	9.9	11.1
Côte d'Ivoire	5.6	8.8	8.3	8.0	11.2	11.9	11.4	11.4	11.3	11.6
Egypt / Égypte	..	..	18.2	14.5	16.9	12.5	15.0	7.9	6.3	7.1
Equatorial Guinea / Guinée équatoriale	..	..	0.0	0.0	6.3	10.5	10.8	9.9	7.5	10.2
Eswatini	15.5	11.6	11.9	13.6	13.0	12.3	13.4	14.1	13.0	13.3
Ghana	..	9.4	8.1	8.6	9.0	6.4	6.7	5.2	5.2	8.0
Kenya	..	..	1.3	1.1	1.5	2.6	2.5	3.2	3.6	3.8
Lesotho	..	..	0.0	0.0	0.0	0.0	0.0	0.0	0.0	0.0
Madagascar[1]	..	..	..	..	4.2	3.5	3.6	5.6	4.5	5.9
Malawi	..	..	0.0	0.0	0.0	0.0	0.0	0.0	0.0	0.0
Mali	10.6	7.7	9.5	9.8	9.9	11.2	10.5	12.5	13.3	14.8
Mauritania / Mauritanie[2]	..	..	..	6.8	6.2	5.5	5.4	5.1	5.0	5.4
Mauritius / Maurice[3]	5.6	4.5	3.8	3.6	4.1	4.1	4.1	3.8	4.1	4.7
Morocco / Maroc[1,4]	..	11.0	16.7	17.5	19.8	20.1	20.2	20.7	21.9	23.3
Namibia / Namibie	..	..	..	1.9	1.7	1.6	1.8	1.8	1.7	2.0
Niger	..	5.4	3.8	5.3	4.7	5.5	6.1	4.7	5.4	5.6
Nigeria / Nigéria	..	..	..	7.6	9.9	10.2	10.9	8.4	10.7	11.5
Rwanda[1]	..	5.0	6.9	6.4	6.0	6.7	6.0	5.9	5.9	6.2
Senegal / Sénégal[5]	..	4.0	4.1	5.8	6.7	6.7	7.1	6.9	6.3	6.2
Seychelles	..	..	..	9.1	3.9	3.5	3.8	7.2	5.2	6.4
Sierra Leone	..	..	..	..	..	..	..	..	..	..
South Africa / Afrique du Sud	0.0	0.0	1.5	1.6	1.5	1.4	1.4	1.3	1.3	1.4
Togo	..	..	..	..	..	..	..	..	..	..
Tunisia / Tunisie[1]	..	21.6	22.7	27.0	29.5	31.6	31.1	29.1	28.3	30.9
Uganda / Ouganda	..	..	..	..	..	..	..	..	..	..
Africa (31) average / Moyenne Afrique (31)[6]	**..**	**..**	**..**	**7.0**	**7.3**	**7.4**	**7.6**	**7.3**	**7.3**	**8.1**
Asia-Pacific (28) average / Moyenne Asie-Pacifique (28)[7]	**..**	**..**	**..**	**4.8**	**5.1**	**5.3**	**5.2**	**5.2**	**6.2**	**6.3**
LAC average / Moyenne ALC[8]	**15.3**	**15.3**	**14.3**	**15.7**	**16.7**	**16.7**	**17.1**	**16.9**	**17.3**	**18.4**
OECD average / Moyenne OCDE[9]	**25.5**	**24.9**	**25.0**	**26.6**	**25.9**	**25.9**	**25.8**	**25.9**	**25.9**	**..**

Table 4.8. **Social security contributions (2000) as percentage of total taxation** *(cont.)*
Tableau 4.8. **Cotisations de sécurité sociale (2000) en pourcentage du total des recettes fiscales** *(suite)*

.. Not available

Note: The figures include sub-national government tax revenues for Eswatini, Mauritania (since 2009), Mauritius, Morocco, Nigeria (only state revenues) and South Africa (since 2002). Sub-national government tax revenues are not available in other countries.

Data on social security contributions are not available for Chad, the Republic of the Congo, the Democratic Republic of the Congo (prior to 2012), Equatorial Guinea (prior to 2013), Madagascar (prior to 2011), Namibia (prior to 2009), Sierra Leone, Togo and Uganda; and are only partially available in Cameroon and Senegal. Social security contributions for Botswana, Lesotho and Malawi are deemed to be null as they do not meet the criteria to be classified as social security contributions set out in the OECD classification of taxes in the *OECD Interpretative Guide.*

1. Madagascar, Morocco, Rwanda and Tunisia do not include social security contributions in the tax-to-GDP ratio in their official publications as these countries do not consider them to be taxes. They are included as tax revenue in this publication, following the classification set out in the *OECD Interpretative Guide.*
2. Social security contributions from the Caisse Nationale de Sécurité Sociale are estimated since 2018.
3. The fiscal year for Mauritius changed in 2010 and in 2015. Figures for 2015 needed to be estimated as a result.
4. Social security contributions in Morocco are estimated for years prior to 2002.
5. These figures include contributions to the Senegalese Pension Institute (IPRES) (estimated prior to 2006) and contributions to the social security fund (CSS) (from 2012 as data for previous years are not available). Social security contributions in Senegal are estimated since 2018.
6. Represents an unweighted average of the 31 African countries in this publication. The Africa (31) should be interpreted with caution as data for social security contributions (category 2000) are not available or are partial in a few countries. See the country tables in Chapter 5 for further information.
7. Represents an unweighted average for 28 Asian and Pacific economies included in the publication *Revenue Statistics in Asia and the Pacific 2022.*
8. Represents an unweighted average for 26 Latin American and Caribbean (LAC) countries included in the publication *Revenue Statistics in Latin America and the Caribbean 2022.*
9. Represents an unweighted average for 38 OECD countries.

.. Non disponible

Note : Les chiffres incluent les recettes fiscales collectées par les administrations infranationales pour l'Afrique du Sud (à partir de 2002), Eswatini, le Maroc, Maurice, la Mauritanie (à partir de 2009) et le Nigéria (recettes des administrations régionales). Les données des recettes fiscales collectées par les administrations infranationales ne sont pas disponibles pour les autres pays. Les données des cotisations de sécurité sociale ne sont pas disponibles pour la République du Congo, la République démocratique du Congo (avant 2012), la Guinée Équatoriale, (avant 2013), Madagascar (avant 2011), la Namibie (avant 2009), l'Ouganda, la Sierra Leone, le Tchad et le Togo et ne sont que partiellement disponibles au Cameroun et au Sénégal. Les cotisations de sécurité sociale pour le Botswana, le Lesotho et le Malawi sont nulles car elles ne répondent pas aux critères de classification des cotisations de sécurité sociale de la classification des impôts établie dans le *guide d'interprétation de l'OCDE.*

1. Madagascar, le Maroc, le Rwanda et la Tunisie n'incluent pas les cotisations de sécurité sociale dans le ratio impôts/PIB dans leurs publications officielles car ces pays ne les considèrent pas comme des impôts. Elles sont incluses dans les recettes fiscales de cette publication en accordance avec la classification des impôts établie dans le *guide d'interprétation de l'OCDE.*
2. Les cotisations de sécurité sociale de la Caisse Nationale de Sécurité Sociale sont estimées à partir de 2018.
3. L'année fiscale pour Maurice a changé en 2010 et en 2015. Les chiffres pour 2015 ont dû être estimés en conséquence.
4. Les cotisations de sécurité sociale au Maroc antérieures à 2002 sont estimées.
5. Les chiffres comprennent les cotisations de sécurité sociale de l'Institution de prévoyance retraite du Sénégal (IPRES) (estimées pour les années antérieures à 2006) et les cotisations de sécurité sociale de la Caisse de Sécurité Sociale (CSS) (à partir de 2012 car les données pour les années précédentes ne sont pas disponibles). Les cotisations de sécurité sociale à partir de 2018 sont estimées.
6. Représente une moyenne non pondérée des 31 pays africains inclus dans cette publication. Il convient d'interpréter cette moyenne avec prudence à cause de valeurs manquantes ou incomplètes pour la rubrique 2000 (cotisations de sécurité sociale). Veuillez voir les tableaux de pays au chapitre 5 pour plus d'informations.
7. Représente la moyenne non pondérée pour 28 économies de l'Asie et du Pacifique incluses dans la publication *Revenue Statistics in Asia and the Pacific 2022.*
8. Représente la moyenne non pondérée pour 26 pays d'Amérique latine et des Caraïbes (ALC) inclus dans la publication *Revenue Statistics in Latin America and the Caribbean 2022.*
9. Représente la moyenne non pondérée pour 38 pays de l'OCDE.

StatLink https://stat.link/wzkn1h

Table 4.9. **Taxes on property (4000) as percentage of GDP**
Tableau 4.9. **Impôts sur le patrimoine (4000) en pourcentage du PIB**

	1995	2000	2005	2010	2015	2016	2017	2018	2019	2020
Botswana	..	..	0.0	0.1	0.0	0.0	0.0	0.0	0.0	0.0
Burkina Faso	..	0.0	0.1	0.1	0.1	0.2	0.1	0.1	0.1	0.1
Cabo Verde	0.8	0.8	0.8	1.0	1.0	1.0	0.7	1.0	1.0	0.9
Cameroon / Cameroun	0.2	0.2	0.1	0.1	0.1	0.2	0.2	0.1	0.1	0.1
Chad / Tchad	..	..	..	0.5	0.2	0.1	0.1	0.1	0.4	0.5
Congo	..	0.1	0.0	0.0	0.2	0.1	0.1	0.1	0.2	0.2
Congo, Dem. Rep. / Congo, Rép. dém.[1]	..	..	..	0.0	0.0	0.0	0.0	0.1	0.1	0.1
Côte d'Ivoire	0.2	0.3	0.4	0.3	0.3	0.4	0.3	0.4	0.4	0.4
Egypt / Égypte	..	..	0.1	0.1	0.1	0.1	0.1	0.1	0.1	0.1
Equatorial Guinea / Guinée équatoriale	..	..	0.0	0.0	0.0	0.0	0.0	0.0	0.0	0.0
Eswatini	0.2	0.3	0.3	0.3	0.3	0.3	0.4	0.5	0.5	0.3
Ghana[1]	..	..	..	..	..	..	..	..	..	..
Kenya	..	..	0.0	0.0	0.0	0.0	0.0	0.0	0.0	0.0
Lesotho[1]	..	..	..	..	..	..	..	..	..	..
Madagascar	0.1	0.1	0.1	0.1	0.1	0.1	0.1	0.1	0.1	0.1
Malawi[1]	..	..	..	..	..	..	..	..	..	..
Mali	0.2	0.1	0.2	0.2	0.2	0.3	0.4	0.3	0.3	0.3
Mauritania / Mauritanie[2]	..	..	..	0.4	0.7	0.6	0.5	0.4	0.0	0.0
Mauritius / Maurice[3]	1.3	1.2	1.0	1.1	1.0	1.1	1.1	1.0	1.0	0.9
Morocco / Maroc	..	1.3	1.5	1.6	2.0	2.0	1.6	1.5	1.4	1.2
Namibia / Namibie	..	..	..	0.2	0.2	0.2	0.2	0.1	0.1	0.1
Niger	..	0.1	0.1	0.1	0.0	0.0	0.0	0.1	0.1	0.2
Nigeria / Nigéria[1]	..	..	..	..	..	..	..	..	..	..
Rwanda	..	0.0	0.0	0.0	0.0	0.0	0.0	0.0	0.0	0.2
Senegal / Sénégal	..	0.3	0.4	0.5	0.4	0.5	0.1	0.1	0.1	0.1
Seychelles	..	..	..	1.1	0.7	0.5	0.5	0.6	0.7	0.6
Sierra Leone[1]	..	..	..	..	..	..	..	..	..	..
South Africa / Afrique du Sud	0.3	0.4	1.3	1.3	1.3	1.4	1.6	1.6	1.7	1.8
Togo	..	0.0	0.0	0.1	0.1	0.1	0.1	0.1	0.1	0.1
Tunisia / Tunisie	..	0.3	0.2	0.3	0.3	0.3	0.3	0.3	0.3	0.3
Uganda / Ouganda[1]	..	..	..	..	..	..	..	..	..	..
Africa (31) average / Moyenne Afrique (31)[4]	**..**	**..**	**..**	**0.4**	**0.4**	**0.4**	**0.3**	**0.3**	**0.4**	**0.3**
Asia-Pacific (28) average / Moyenne Asie-Pacifique (28)[5]	**..**	**..**	**..**	**0.7**	**0.7**	**0.6**	**0.7**	**0.7**	**0.7**	**0.7**
LAC average / Moyenne ALC[6]	**0.8**	**0.7**	**1.0**	**0.8**	**0.9**	**0.8**	**0.9**	**0.8**	**0.9**	**0.8**
OECD average / Moyenne OCDE[7]	**1.5**	**1.7**	**1.7**	**1.6**	**1.8**	**2.2**	**1.9**	**1.8**	**1.8**	**..**

.. Not available

Note: The figures include sub-national government tax revenues for Eswatini, Mauritania (since 2009), Mauritius, Morocco, Nigeria (only state revenues) and South Africa (since 2002). Sub-national government tax revenues are not available in other countries.

1. In Ghana, Lesotho, Malawi, Nigeria, Sierra Leone and Uganda, revenues from property taxes are mainly levied by local governments, for which data are not available. In the Democratic Republic of the Congo, only data for property tax revenues levied by the Direction Générale des Recettes Administratives, Judiciaires, Domaniales et de Participation (DGRAD) are available since 2010. See the country tables in Chapter 5 for further information.
2. Local government revenue data are missing for 2019 and 2020.
3. The fiscal year for Mauritius changed in 2010 and in 2015. Figures for 2015 needed to be estimated as a result.
4. Represents an unweighted average of the 31 African countries in this publication. The Africa (31) should be interpreted with caution as data for property taxes (category 4000) are not available or are partial in a few countries. See the country tables in Chapter 5 for further information.
5. Represents an unweighted average for 28 Asian and Pacific economies included in the publication *Revenue Statistics in Asia and the Pacific 2022.*
6. Represents an unweighted average for 26 Latin American and Caribbean (LAC) countries included in the publication *Revenue Statistics in Latin America and the Caribbean 2022.*
7. Represents an unweighted average for 38 OECD countries.

.. Non disponible

Note : Les chiffres incluent les recettes fiscales collectées par les administrations infranationales pour l'Afrique du Sud (à partir de 2002), Eswatini, le Maroc, Maurice, la Mauritanie (à partir de 2009) et le Nigéria (recettes des administrations régionales). Les données des recettes fiscales collectées par les administrations infranationales ne sont pas disponibles pour les autres pays.

1. Au Ghana, au Lesotho, au Malawi, au Nigéria, en Ouganda et en Sierra Leone, les recettes provenant des impôts sur le patrimoine sont principalement perçues par les administrations locales pour lesquelles les données ne sont pas disponibles. En République démocratique du Congo, seules les données des recettes relatives aux impôts sur le patrimoine qui sont prélevées par la Direction Générale des Recettes Administratives, Judiciaires, Domaniales et de Participation (DGRAD) sont disponibles à partir de 2010. Voir les tableaux des pays au chapitre 5 pour plus d'informations.
2. Les données des recettes des collectivités sont manquantes en 2019 et 2020.
3. L'année fiscale pour Maurice a changé en 2010 et en 2015. Les chiffres pour 2015 ont dû être estimés en conséquence.
4. Représente une moyenne non pondérée des 31 pays africains inclus dans cette publication. Il convient d'interpréter cette moyenne avec prudence à cause de valeurs manquantes ou incomplètes pour la rubrique 4000 (taxes sur le patrimoine). Veuillez voir les tableaux de pays au chapitre 5 pour plus d'informations.
5. Représente la moyenne non pondérée pour 28 économies de l'Asie et du Pacifique incluses dans la publication *Revenue Statistics in Asia and the Pacific 2022.*
6. Représente la moyenne non pondérée pour 26 pays d'Amérique latine et des Caraïbes (ALC) inclus dans la publication *Revenue Statistics in Latin America and the Caribbean 2022.*
7. Représente la moyenne non pondérée pour 38 pays de l'OCDE.

StatLink https://stat.link/1poc6a

Table 4.10. **Taxes on property (4000) as percentage of total taxation**
Tableau 4.10. **Impôts sur le patrimoine (4000) en pourcentage du total des recettes fiscales**

	1995	2000	2005	2010	2015	2016	2017	2018	2019	2020
Botswana	..	..	0.2	0.4	0.3	0.3	0.3	0.3	0.3	0.3
Burkina Faso	..	0.4	0.5	0.7	0.8	1.0	0.7	0.7	0.7	0.8
Cabo Verde	5.3	5.3	4.3	5.5	5.2	5.0	3.2	4.7	4.5	4.7
Cameroon / Cameroun	1.6	1.6	1.2	1.1	0.9	1.1	1.1	0.8	0.8	0.9
Chad / Tchad	..	..	..	3.1	3.2	2.8	1.6	1.5	4.5	3.5
Congo	..	1.3	0.8	0.7	1.7	0.5	0.7	1.8	2.3	2.0
Congo, Dem. Rep. / Congo, Rép. dém.[1]	..	..	..	0.6	0.4	0.5	0.5	0.7	0.7	0.8
Côte d'Ivoire	1.7	2.8	3.1	2.4	2.6	2.9	2.6	2.9	3.1	2.9
Egypt / Égypte	..	..	0.7	0.6	0.6	0.6	0.6	0.6	0.8	0.6
Equatorial Guinea / Guinée équatoriale	..	..	0.0	0.0	0.0	0.1	0.0	0.1	0.0	0.0
Eswatini	2.0	2.6	2.3	2.0	1.7	1.6	2.3	2.6	2.6	1.5
Ghana[1]	..	..	..	..	..	..	..	..	..	..
Kenya	..	..	0.1	0.2	0.1	0.1	0.1	0.0	0.0	0.0
Lesotho[1]	..	..	..	..	..	..	..	..	..	..
Madagascar	1.1	0.7	0.8	0.5	0.8	0.7	0.6	0.8	0.5	0.6
Malawi[1]	..	..	..	..	..	..	..	..	..	..
Mali	2.2	1.3	1.7	1.6	1.5	2.1	2.2	2.1	1.7	1.5
Mauritania / Mauritanie[2]	..	..	..	4.3	4.8	4.0	3.3	2.9	0.1	0.2
Mauritius / Maurice[3]	7.7	6.4	5.5	5.7	5.2	5.7	5.5	4.9	4.6	4.2
Morocco / Maroc	..	5.9	6.1	5.9	7.4	7.2	5.6	5.3	5.1	4.4
Namibia / Namibie	..	..	..	0.9	1.0	0.8	0.8	0.6	0.5	0.5
Niger	..	1.1	0.8	0.8	0.4	0.3	0.4	0.7	1.2	1.8
Nigeria / Nigéria[1]	..	..	..	..	..	..	..	..	..	..
Rwanda	..	0.2	0.0	0.0	0.1	0.1	0.1	0.1	0.1	0.9
Senegal / Sénégal	..	2.0	2.6	3.1	2.4	2.7	0.7	0.7	0.6	0.7
Seychelles	..	..	..	3.5	2.6	1.6	1.5	1.7	2.2	1.8
Sierra Leone[1]	..	..	..	..	..	..	..	..	..	..
South Africa / Afrique du Sud	1.7	1.8	5.6	5.7	5.0	5.4	6.0	5.9	6.3	7.1
Togo	..	0.4	0.4	0.8	0.8	0.8	0.7	0.8	0.8	0.8
Tunisia / Tunisie	..	1.1	1.0	1.0	1.1	1.1	1.0	0.9	0.9	0.8
Uganda / Ouganda[1]	..	..	..	..	..	..	..	..	..	..
Africa (31) average / Moyenne Afrique (31)[4]	..	..	..	**2.0**	**2.0**	**2.0**	**1.7**	**1.8**	**1.8**	**1.7**
Asia-Pacific (28) average / Moyenne Asie-Pacifique (28)[5]	..	..	..	**3.2**	**3.0**	**2.9**	**2.9**	**2.9**	**3.0**	**3.0**
LAC average / Moyenne ALC[6]	**4.6**	**3.7**	**5.2**	**4.0**	**4.0**	**3.8**	**3.9**	**3.7**	**3.8**	**3.5**
OECD average / Moyenne OCDE[7]	**5.0**	**5.3**	**5.5**	**5.4**	**5.7**	**6.5**	**5.8**	**5.5**	**5.5**	..

.. Not available

Note: The figures include sub-national government tax revenues for Eswatini, Mauritania (since 2009), Mauritius, Morocco, Nigeria (only state revenues) and South Africa (since 2002). Sub-national government tax revenues are not available in other countries.

1. In Ghana, Lesotho, Malawi, Nigeria, Sierra Leone and Uganda, revenues from property taxes are mainly levied by local governments, for which data are not available. In the Democratic Republic of the Congo, only data for property tax revenues levied by the Direction Générale des Recettes Administratives, Judiciaires, Domaniales et de Participation (DGRAD) are available since 2010. See the country tables in Chapter 5 for further information.
2. Local government revenue data are missing for 2019 and 2020.
3. The fiscal year for Mauritius changed in 2010 and in 2015. Figures for 2015 needed to be estimated as a result.
4. Represents an unweighted average of the 31 African countries in this publication. The Africa (31) should be interpreted with caution as data for property taxes (category 4000) are not available or are partial in a few countries. See the country tables in Chapter 5 for further information.
5. Represents an unweighted average for 28 Asian and Pacific economies included in the publication *Revenue Statistics in Asia and the Pacific 2022*.
6. Represents an unweighted average for 26 Latin American and Caribbean (LAC) countries included in the publication *Revenue Statistics in Latin America and the Caribbean 2022*.
7. Represents an unweighted average for 38 OECD countries.

.. Non disponible

Note : Les chiffres incluent les recettes fiscales collectées par les administrations infranationales pour l'Afrique du Sud (à partir de 2002), Eswatini, le Maroc, Maurice, la Mauritanie (à partir de 2009) et le Nigéria (recettes des administrations régionales). Les données des recettes fiscales collectées par les administrations infranationales ne sont pas disponibles pour les autres pays.

1. Au Ghana, au Lesotho, au Malawi, au Nigéria, en Ouganda et en Sierra Leone, les recettes provenant des impôts sur le patrimoine sont principalement perçues par les administrations locales pour lesquelles les données ne sont pas disponibles. En République démocratique du Congo, seules les données des recettes relatives aux impôts sur le patrimoine qui sont prélevées par la Direction Générale des Recettes Administratives, Judiciaires, Domaniales et de Participation (DGRAD) sont disponibles à partir de 2010. Voir les tableaux des pays au chapitre 5 pour plus d'informations.
2. Les données des recettes des collectivités sont manquantes en 2019 et 2020.
3. L'année fiscale pour Maurice a changé en 2010 et en 2015. Les chiffres pour 2015 ont dû être estimés en conséquence.
4. Représente une moyenne non pondérée des 31 pays africains inclus dans cette publication. Il convient d'interpréter cette moyenne avec prudence à cause de valeurs manquantes ou incomplètes pour la rubrique 4000 (taxes sur le patrimoine). Veuillez voir les tableaux de pays au chapitre 5 pour plus d'informations.
5. Représente la moyenne non pondérée pour 28 économies de l'Asie et du Pacifique incluses dans la publication *Revenue Statistics in Asia and the Pacific 2022*.
6. Représente la moyenne non pondérée pour 26 pays d'Amérique latine et des Caraïbes (ALC) inclus dans la publication *Revenue Statistics in Latin America and the Caribbean 2022*.
7. Représente la moyenne non pondérée pour 38 pays de l'OCDE.

StatLink https://stat.link/6j9qls

Table 4.11. **Taxes on goods and services (5000) as percentage of GDP**
Tableau 4.11. **Impôts sur les biens et services (5000) en pourcentage du PIB**

	1995	2000	2005	2010	2015	2016	2017	2018	2019	2020
Botswana	..	..	4.1	5.4	4.3	4.4	5.1	4.6	5.0	4.8
Burkina Faso	..	5.8	7.5	9.4	9.1	9.3	10.1	10.2	10.2	9.7
Cabo Verde	9.3	8.4	12.1	12.2	12.2	12.4	13.3	14.2	13.7	13.0
Cameroon / Cameroun	6.1	6.7	6.7	6.9	8.0	8.2	8.8	8.8	8.4	7.5
Chad / Tchad	..	..	..	2.7	2.2	2.3	3.0	3.6	3.7	4.5
Congo	..	1.7	4.0	4.3	7.3	7.6	6.0	5.2	5.2	6.4
Congo, Dem. Rep. / Congo, Rép. dém.	..	0.9	3.6	5.6	5.4	5.2	3.6	3.4	3.2	3.7
Côte d'Ivoire	8.4	6.6	7.2	7.9	7.9	8.2	8.2	7.8	8.0	8.2
Egypt / Égypte	..	..	6.5	6.2	5.7	6.0	6.7	7.2	7.1	6.0
Equatorial Guinea / Guinée équatoriale	..	..	0.7	0.7	1.2	1.4	1.2	1.3	1.5	1.4
Eswatini	3.1	3.7	3.7	4.5	5.5	5.8	6.1	6.1	6.6	6.8
Ghana	..	4.8	6.8	6.0	7.6	8.6	8.1	7.7	6.9	6.9
Kenya	..	..	6.7	9.1	8.8	8.8	9.1	8.7	8.8	7.9
Lesotho	..	..	6.9	7.6	7.3	7.2	8.2	9.9	9.4	9.0
Madagascar	5.4	7.8	6.6	7.1	6.8	7.2	8.0	8.2	8.0	7.2
Malawi	..	..	5.1	6.3	6.1	6.2	6.8	6.6	6.8	6.3
Mali	4.5	8.2	10.0	8.5	8.9	9.8	9.8	7.7	9.8	9.1
Mauritania / Mauritanie	..	..	..	5.3	8.1	8.4	8.7	9.6	8.7	7.3
Mauritius / Maurice[1]	11.9	13.6	13.0	12.2	12.5	12.6	12.6	13.3	13.4	12.9
Morocco / Maroc	..	12.3	11.2	12.9	11.3	11.3	11.7	12.1	12.1	11.6
Namibia / Namibie	..	..	..	6.1	8.0	7.7	7.2	6.8	7.1	5.4
Niger	..	5.3	6.0	6.1	7.5	6.4	5.7	7.4	6.6	5.8
Nigeria / Nigéria	..	..	..	1.9	1.6	1.5	1.6	1.6	1.6	1.8
Rwanda	..	5.9	6.9	7.1	9.1	8.9	8.9	9.1	9.4	8.7
Senegal / Sénégal	..	9.1	10.4	10.1	10.3	10.5	10.1	10.2	11.3	10.6
Seychelles	..	..	..	17.8	18.1	19.3	19.1	19.6	19.8	18.8
Sierra Leone	..	..	5.5	6.2	5.7	5.5	6.4	6.0	6.7	6.0
South Africa / Afrique du Sud	8.5	8.0	8.9	9.1	10.7	10.5	10.1	10.6	10.4	10.2
Togo	..	5.2	7.2	8.6	12.8	12.7	12.4	11.1	11.4	11.8
Tunisia / Tunisie	..	12.1	10.4	10.2	10.2	10.0	10.5	11.9	11.4	11.2
Uganda / Ouganda	6.4	6.8	6.6	5.6	6.8	7.2	7.4	7.6	7.8	7.0
Africa (31) average / Moyenne Afrique (31)[2]	..	..	..	**7.4**	**8.0**	**8.1**	**8.2**	**8.3**	**8.4**	**8.0**
Asia-Pacific (28) average / Moyenne Asie-Pacifique (28)[3]	..	..	..	**9.4**	**10.0**	**9.7**	**10.1**	**10.3**	**10.0**	**9.0**
LAC average / Moyenne ALC[4]	**9.7**	**10.1**	**10.4**	**10.5**	**11.1**	**11.2**	**11.3**	**11.3**	**11.2**	**10.5**
OECD average / Moyenne OCDE[5]	**10.8**	**10.8**	**10.8**	**10.5**	**10.8**	**10.9**	**10.9**	**10.8**	**10.8**	..

.. Not available

Note: The figures include sub-national government tax revenues for Eswatini, Mauritania (since 2009), Mauritius, Morocco, Nigeria (only state revenues) and South Africa (since 2002). Sub-national government tax revenues are not available in other countries.

1. The fiscal year for Mauritius changed in 2010 and in 2015. Figures for 2015 needed to be estimated as a result.
2. Represents an unweighted average of the 31 African countries in this publication.
3. Represents an unweighted average for 28 Asian and Pacific economies included in the publication *Revenue Statistics in Asia and the Pacific 2022*.
4. Represents an unweighted average for 26 Latin American and Caribbean (LAC) countries included in the publication *Revenue Statistics in Latin America and the Caribbean 2022*.
5. Represents an unweighted average for 38 OECD countries.

.. Non disponible

Note : Les chiffres incluent les recettes fiscales collectées par les administrations infranationales pour l'Afrique du Sud (à partir de 2002), Eswatini, le Maroc, Maurice, la Mauritanie (à partir de 2009) et le Nigéria (recettes des administrations régionales). Les données des recettes fiscales collectées par les administrations infranationales ne sont pas disponibles pour les autres pays.

1. L'année fiscale pour Maurice a changé en 2010 et en 2015. Les chiffres pour 2015 ont dû être estimés en conséquence.
2. Représente une moyenne non pondérée des 31 pays africains inclus dans cette publication.
3. Représente la moyenne non pondérée pour 28 économies de l'Asie et du Pacifique incluses dans la publication *Revenue Statistics in Asia and the Pacific 2022*.
4. Représente la moyenne non pondérée pour 26 pays d'Amérique latine et des Caraïbes (ALC) inclus dans la publication *Revenue Statistics in Latin America and the Caribbean 2022*.
5. Représente la moyenne non pondérée pour 38 pays de l'OCDE.

StatLink https://stat.link/tm0w7s

Table 4.12. **Taxes on goods and services (5000) as percentage of total taxation**
Tableau 4.12. **Impôts sur les biens et services (5000) en pourcentage du total des recettes fiscales**

	1995	2000	2005	2010	2015	2016	2017	2018	2019	2020
Botswana	..	..	26.6	34.3	31.7	30.2	38.4	35.0	36.7	38.7
Burkina Faso	..	57.0	63.6	67.3	62.8	61.2	62.2	61.4	59.1	58.6
Cabo Verde	61.3	53.8	62.0	64.3	63.1	63.6	64.8	64.7	64.4	64.9
Cameroon / Cameroun	66.1	62.2	60.5	60.1	57.0	59.9	62.8	62.2	60.9	58.5
Chad / Tchad	..	..	..	18.3	37.6	49.2	48.5	45.2	45.4	30.9
Congo	..	45.5	67.3	61.9	57.0	57.4	55.9	69.9	64.4	64.4
Congo, Dem. Rep. / Congo, Rép. dém.	..	81.2	68.2	65.3	54.2	60.1	51.5	44.1	42.3	51.0
Côte d'Ivoire	68.6	59.8	63.9	66.0	62.7	62.1	62.0	59.6	61.0	60.9
Egypt / Égypte	..	..	41.1	40.5	38.7	41.2	44.0	47.9	49.4	45.0
Equatorial Guinea / Guinée équatoriale	..	..	8.5	9.4	10.3	20.0	18.7	19.2	15.2	16.4
Eswatini	29.9	34.8	32.2	32.6	36.6	35.8	35.7	35.0	36.3	38.0
Ghana	..	61.7	64.4	55.3	58.9	65.5	60.1	56.0	52.6	51.1
Kenya	..	..	62.7	58.1	52.0	51.7	52.5	52.6	53.6	51.4
Lesotho	..	..	44.8	43.7	37.8	37.7	41.3	43.7	44.0	44.7
Madagascar	80.2	81.3	74.6	74.3	72.4	72.0	73.1	71.0	70.0	68.4
Malawi	..	..	57.2	55.6	51.2	51.5	51.3	51.9	53.2	51.4
Mali	59.3	72.0	68.9	60.4	58.7	59.2	58.6	57.7	55.9	50.5
Mauritania / Mauritanie	..	..	..	54.0	55.4	59.1	60.0	62.5	63.2	55.6
Mauritius / Maurice[1]	70.3	74.6	72.6	64.4	64.9	64.6	63.6	65.2	63.6	61.5
Morocco / Maroc	..	55.7	45.2	46.8	42.2	41.2	41.9	42.9	42.7	41.1
Namibia / Namibie	..	..	..	32.9	37.2	36.4	35.1	34.9	35.1	29.1
Niger	..	72.0	72.7	62.9	59.8	60.9	60.2	65.9	63.4	59.3
Nigeria / Nigéria	..	..	..	25.8	26.4	29.0	27.8	25.4	26.7	32.5
Rwanda	..	68.8	64.5	57.4	55.9	54.7	54.8	53.6	54.2	51.6
Senegal / Sénégal	..	69.2	67.8	63.4	63.1	61.9	61.3	60.1	61.5	58.5
Seychelles	..	..	..	57.8	62.4	62.7	61.1	59.9	61.5	58.9
Sierra Leone	..	..	70.6	68.6	58.1	51.3	59.9	55.0	56.9	54.5
South Africa / Afrique du Sud	43.4	39.9	38.9	39.5	40.3	40.1	38.5	39.8	39.9	40.4
Togo	..	74.8	73.0	78.4	80.1	77.5	78.5	76.3	75.9	77.0
Tunisia / Tunisie	..	51.8	45.0	39.5	35.8	35.8	35.8	39.7	35.6	34.5
Uganda / Ouganda	82.2	81.6	70.9	67.3	65.1	65.1	64.9	65.5	64.8	63.1
Africa (31) average / Moyenne Afrique (31)[2]	..	..	..	**52.5**	**51.3**	**52.2**	**52.4**	**52.4**	**51.9**	**50.4**
Asia-Pacific (28) average / Moyenne Asie-Pacifique (28)[3]	..	..	..	**53.9**	**53.3**	**53.5**	**53.2**	**53.0**	**51.8**	**50.6**
LAC average / Moyenne ALC[4]	**58.3**	**57.0**	**53.5**	**51.1**	**50.4**	**50.6**	**50.6**	**50.3**	**49.7**	**48.4**
OECD average / Moyenne OCDE[5]	**34.4**	**33.9**	**33.8**	**34.0**	**33.3**	**33.1**	**33.1**	**32.8**	**32.6**	..

.. Not available

Note: The figures include sub-national government tax revenues for Eswatini, Mauritania (since 2009), Mauritius, Morocco, Nigeria (only state revenues) and South Africa (since 2002). Sub-national government tax revenues are not available in other countries.

1. The fiscal year for Mauritius changed in 2010 and in 2015. Figures for 2015 needed to be estimated as a result.
2. Represents an unweighted average of the 31 African countries in this publication.
3. Represents an unweighted average for 28 Asian and Pacific economies included in the publication *Revenue Statistics in Asia and the Pacific 2022*.
4. Represents an unweighted average for 26 Latin American and Caribbean (LAC) countries included in the publication *Revenue Statistics in Latin America and the Caribbean 2022*.
5. Represents an unweighted average for 38 OECD countries.

.. Non disponible

Note : Les chiffres incluent les recettes fiscales collectées par les administrations infranationales pour l'Afrique du Sud (à partir de 2002), Eswatini, le Maroc, Maurice, la Mauritanie (à partir de 2009) et le Nigéria (recettes des administrations régionales). Les données des recettes fiscales collectées par les administrations infranationales ne sont pas disponibles pour les autres pays.

1. L'année fiscale pour Maurice a changé en 2010 et en 2015. Les chiffres pour 2015 ont dû être estimés en conséquence.
2. Représente une moyenne non pondérée des 31 pays africains inclus dans cette publication.
3. Représente la moyenne non pondérée pour 28 économies de l'Asie et du Pacifique incluses dans la publication *Revenue Statistics in Asia and the Pacific 2022*.
4. Représente la moyenne non pondérée pour 26 pays d'Amérique latine et des Caraïbes (ALC) inclus dans la publication *Revenue Statistics in Latin America and the Caribbean 2022*.
5. Représente la moyenne non pondérée pour 38 pays de l'OCDE.

StatLink https://stat.link/z4ubdm

Table 4.13. **Taxes on general consumption (5110) as percentage of GDP**
Tableau 4.13. **Impôts généraux sur la consommation (5110) en pourcentage du PIB**

	1995	2000	2005	2010	2015	2016	2017	2018	2019	2020
Botswana	..	..	3.6	5.0	3.8	4.0	4.5	4.1	4.5	4.3
Burkina Faso	..	2.9	4.1	4.6	4.9	5.0	5.4	5.5	5.7	4.9
Cabo Verde	0.0	0.0	6.6	7.2	6.8	6.6	7.3	8.2	7.7	7.6
Cameroon / Cameroun	2.7	3.5	3.5	3.6	4.6	4.6	5.1	5.2	4.9	4.0
Chad / Tchad	..	..	..	1.4	1.0	1.4	1.7	1.2	1.5	1.7
Congo	..	1.5	2.2	2.4	4.0	4.2	3.5	3.2	3.1	3.7
Congo, Dem. Rep. / Congo, Rép. dém.	..	0.1	1.9	3.0	2.5	2.8	2.0	1.9	1.7	2.3
Côte d'Ivoire	2.7	2.4	2.3	2.9	2.6	2.5	2.7	2.8	2.9	2.8
Egypt / Égypte	..	..	3.3	3.1	2.7	2.6	3.2	3.5	3.7	3.3
Equatorial Guinea / Guinée équatoriale	..	..	0.5	0.6	0.8	0.8	0.7	0.7	0.9	0.9
Eswatini	2.4	3.0	3.2	3.8	4.0	4.2	4.2	4.3	4.6	4.7
Ghana	..	2.0	2.7	3.2	4.1	3.9	3.9	3.7	3.5	3.4
Kenya	..	..	2.8	4.1	4.1	4.0	4.2	4.0	4.0	3.5
Lesotho	..	..	6.9	7.6	7.3	7.2	7.9	8.9	8.6	7.7
Madagascar	3.2	4.5	3.9	4.8	4.7	4.9	5.5	5.6	5.5	4.8
Malawi	..	..	2.5	2.9	3.4	3.3	3.6	3.6	3.7	3.5
Mali	1.7	3.8	5.8	4.9	4.2	4.7	4.9	3.9	5.3	4.9
Mauritania / Mauritanie	..	..	..	3.3	4.7	4.3	4.3	4.8	4.5	3.4
Mauritius / Maurice[1]	0.1	4.6	6.4	6.8	6.8	6.8	6.8	7.0	7.1	7.0
Morocco / Maroc	..	5.2	5.9	8.3	7.6	7.5	7.7	7.8	7.4	7.3
Namibia / Namibie	..	..	..	6.0	7.8	7.4	6.9	6.3	6.4	4.7
Niger	..	2.0	3.5	3.5	4.5	3.7	3.2	5.0	3.8	3.2
Nigeria / Nigéria	..	..	..	1.0	0.8	0.8	0.8	0.9	0.8	1.0
Rwanda	..	1.7	3.5	3.7	5.0	4.8	5.0	5.1	5.5	5.0
Senegal / Sénégal	..	5.2	6.1	6.0	5.9	5.8	5.7	5.7	6.4	5.7
Seychelles	..	..	..	4.0	10.0	10.5	10.5	11.4	11.4	10.5
Sierra Leone	..	..	0.0	2.4	2.7	2.7	2.6	2.7	2.8	2.6
South Africa / Afrique du Sud	5.1	4.9	5.9	5.6	6.3	6.2	5.8	6.1	5.9	6.0
Togo	..	2.6	4.0	5.0	7.5	7.6	7.3	6.5	6.7	6.7
Tunisia / Tunisie	..	5.9	5.3	5.8	5.8	5.5	5.8	6.8	6.6	6.2
Uganda / Ouganda	2.4	2.7	3.1	2.7	3.4	3.6	3.6	3.7	3.7	3.4
Africa (31) average / Moyenne Afrique (31)[2]	..	..	..	**4.2**	**4.7**	**4.7**	**4.7**	**4.8**	**4.9**	**4.5**
Asia-Pacific (28) average / Moyenne Asie-Pacifique (28)[3]	..	..	..	**4.6**	**5.2**	**5.1**	**5.2**	**5.3**	**5.2**	**4.6**
LAC average / Moyenne ALC[4]	**4.7**	**5.5**	**6.1**	**6.4**	**7.1**	**7.2**	**7.2**	**7.2**	**7.1**	**6.8**
OECD average / Moyenne OCDE[5]	**6.4**	**6.6**	**6.7**	**6.6**	**6.8**	**6.9**	**6.9**	**7.0**	**6.9**	..

.. Not available

Note: The figures include sub-national government tax revenues for Eswatini, Mauritania (since 2009), Mauritius, Morocco, Nigeria (only state revenues) and South Africa (since 2002). Sub-national government tax revenues are not available in other countries.

1. The fiscal year for Mauritius changed in 2010 and in 2015. Figures for 2015 needed to be estimated as a result.
2. Represents an unweighted average of the 31 African countries in this publication.
3. Represents an unweighted average for 28 Asian and Pacific economies included in the publication *Revenue Statistics in Asia and the Pacific 2022*.
4. Represents an unweighted average for 26 Latin American and Caribbean (LAC) countries included in the publication *Revenue Statistics in Latin America and the Caribbean 2022*.
5. Represents an unweighted average for 38 OECD countries.

.. Non disponible

Note : Les chiffres incluent les recettes fiscales collectées par les administrations infranationales pour l'Afrique du Sud (à partir de 2002), Eswatini, le Maroc, Maurice, la Mauritanie (à partir de 2009) et le Nigéria (recettes des administrations régionales). Les données des recettes fiscales collectées par les administrations infranationales ne sont pas disponibles pour les autres pays.

1. L'année fiscale pour Maurice a changé en 2010 et en 2015. Les chiffres pour 2015 ont dû être estimés en conséquence.
2. Représente une moyenne non pondérée des 31 pays africains inclus dans cette publication.
3. Représente la moyenne non pondérée pour 28 économies de l'Asie et du Pacifique incluses dans la publication *Revenue Statistics in Asia and the Pacific 2022*.
4. Représente la moyenne non pondérée pour 26 pays d'Amérique latine et des Caraïbes (ALC) inclus dans la publication *Revenue Statistics in Latin America and the Caribbean 2022*.
5. Représente la moyenne non pondérée pour 38 pays de l'OCDE.

StatLink https://stat.link/a25s3n

Table 4.14. **Taxes on general consumption (5110) as percentage of total taxation**
Tableau 4.14. **Impôts généraux sur la consommation (5110) en pourcentage du total des recettes fiscales**

	1995	2000	2005	2010	2015	2016	2017	2018	2019	2020
Botswana	..	..	23.2	31.3	28.2	27.1	34.0	31.1	32.6	35.0
Burkina Faso	..	28.7	34.7	32.8	33.7	32.8	33.3	32.9	33.1	29.4
Cabo Verde	0.0	0.0	34.0	38.2	35.3	34.2	35.6	37.5	36.3	38.0
Cameroon / Cameroun	29.0	32.2	31.7	31.2	32.9	33.8	36.3	36.8	35.3	31.2
Chad / Tchad	..	..	..	9.9	17.8	30.5	27.9	14.9	18.9	11.5
Congo	..	40.2	37.9	34.9	31.5	31.4	32.0	42.9	37.6	37.3
Congo, Dem. Rep. / Congo, Rép. dém.	..	10.0	36.2	35.2	25.6	32.6	29.0	24.7	22.3	32.1
Côte d'Ivoire	22.4	21.8	20.5	24.1	20.3	19.2	20.3	21.4	21.7	21.0
Egypt / Égypte	..	..	21.1	20.6	18.3	18.2	21.3	23.5	25.9	24.9
Equatorial Guinea / Guinée équatoriale	..	..	6.2	7.4	6.3	11.1	11.0	11.3	8.9	10.1
Eswatini	23.2	28.0	27.5	27.4	26.7	26.4	25.0	24.5	25.0	26.2
Ghana	..	26.1	25.4	30.0	32.1	29.7	29.3	26.8	26.6	25.0
Kenya	..	..	26.2	26.1	24.5	23.6	24.1	24.1	24.6	22.7
Lesotho	..	..	44.8	43.7	37.6	37.6	39.6	39.5	40.1	38.5
Madagascar	47.7	46.5	43.6	50.7	49.2	48.7	50.6	48.6	47.9	45.5
Malawi	..	..	27.8	25.4	28.3	27.6	27.7	28.1	29.2	28.2
Mali	22.3	33.7	40.2	34.8	27.9	28.8	29.4	29.4	30.4	26.9
Mauritania / Mauritanie	..	..	..	33.4	32.5	30.3	29.7	31.2	32.4	25.9
Mauritius / Maurice[1]	0.5	25.3	36.0	36.1	35.4	35.0	34.1	34.5	33.8	33.6
Morocco / Maroc	..	23.6	23.7	30.1	28.4	27.2	27.4	27.5	26.2	25.9
Namibia / Namibie	..	..	..	32.1	36.5	35.2	33.9	32.6	31.8	25.4
Niger	..	27.4	42.0	36.7	35.6	35.2	34.2	45.1	36.8	32.2
Nigeria / Nigéria	..	..	..	14.0	13.3	15.3	14.9	13.6	13.7	18.0
Rwanda	..	20.0	33.1	29.9	30.6	29.5	31.0	30.2	31.5	29.6
Senegal / Sénégal	..	39.6	40.0	37.7	35.8	33.9	35.0	33.7	35.1	31.5
Seychelles	..	..	..	13.0	34.5	34.1	33.4	34.9	35.5	32.7
Sierra Leone	..	..	0.0	26.5	27.8	25.7	24.2	25.0	23.8	23.9
South Africa / Afrique du Sud	26.0	24.6	26.1	24.1	23.7	23.7	22.2	22.8	22.5	23.9
Togo	..	36.9	40.1	45.9	46.9	46.2	46.0	44.6	44.5	43.6
Tunisia / Tunisie	..	25.2	23.1	22.3	20.3	19.9	19.9	22.8	20.4	19.1
Uganda / Ouganda	30.4	33.0	33.0	32.3	32.3	32.4	31.6	32.0	30.8	30.5
Africa (31) average / Moyenne Afrique (31)[2]	..	..	..	**29.6**	**29.3**	**29.6**	**29.8**	**30.0**	**29.5**	**28.4**
Asia-Pacific (28) average / Moyenne Asie-Pacifique (28)[3]	..	..	..	**24.1**	**27.1**	**26.7**	**26.8**	**26.6**	**26.8**	**25.9**
LAC average / Moyenne ALC[4]	**27.2**	**28.9**	**29.5**	**30.1**	**31.5**	**32.0**	**31.7**	**31.9**	**31.3**	**31.0**
OECD average / Moyenne OCDE[5]	**20.3**	**20.4**	**21.1**	**21.3**	**21.0**	**20.8**	**21.1**	**21.1**	**21.0**	..

.. Not available

Note: The figures include sub-national government tax revenues for Eswatini, Mauritania (since 2009), Mauritius, Morocco, Nigeria (only state revenues) and South Africa (since 2002). Sub-national government tax revenues are not available in other countries.

1. The fiscal year for Mauritius changed in 2010 and in 2015. Figures for 2015 needed to be estimated as a result.
2. Represents an unweighted average of the 31 African countries in this publication.
3. Represents an unweighted average for 28 Asian and Pacific economies included in the publication *Revenue Statistics in Asia and the Pacific 2022*.
4. Represents an unweighted average for 26 Latin American and Caribbean (LAC) countries included in the publication *Revenue Statistics in Latin America and the Caribbean 2022*.
5. Represents an unweighted average for 38 OECD countries.

.. Non disponible

Note : Les chiffres incluent les recettes fiscales collectées par les administrations infranationales pour l'Afrique du Sud (à partir de 2002), Eswatini, le Maroc, Maurice, la Mauritanie (à partir de 2009) et le Nigéria (recettes des administrations régionales). Les données des recettes fiscales collectées par les administrations infranationales ne sont pas disponibles pour les autres pays.

1. L'année fiscale pour Maurice a changé en 2010 et en 2015. Les chiffres pour 2015 ont dû être estimés en conséquence.
2. Représente une moyenne non pondérée des 31 pays africains inclus dans cette publication.
3. Représente la moyenne non pondérée pour 28 économies de l'Asie et du Pacifique incluses dans la publication *Revenue Statistics in Asia and the Pacific 2022*.
4. Représente la moyenne non pondérée pour 26 pays d'Amérique latine et des Caraïbes (ALC) inclus dans la publication *Revenue Statistics in Latin America and the Caribbean 2022*.
5. Représente la moyenne non pondérée pour 38 pays de l'OCDE.

StatLink https://stat.link/fv6krj

Table 4.15. **Taxes on specific goods and services (5120) as percentage of GDP**
Tableau 4.15. **Impôts sur les biens et services déterminés (5120) en pourcentage du PIB**

	1995	2000	2005	2010	2015	2016	2017	2018	2019	2020
Botswana	..	..	0.3	0.2	0.3	0.3	0.3	0.2	0.3	0.3
Burkina Faso	..	2.2	2.8	2.8	3.6	3.7	4.0	4.1	3.8	3.7
Cabo Verde	9.3	8.4	5.4	5.0	5.4	5.7	6.0	6.0	6.0	5.4
Cameroon / Cameroun	3.4	3.2	3.1	3.3	3.4	3.5	3.7	3.6	3.5	3.5
Chad / Tchad	..	..	..	1.2	1.1	0.9	1.3	2.2	2.1	2.7
Congo	..	0.2	1.7	1.9	3.3	3.4	2.6	2.0	2.1	2.6
Congo, Dem. Rep. / Congo, Rép. dém.	..	0.7	1.7	2.4	2.8	2.3	1.5	1.4	1.5	1.3
Côte d'Ivoire	5.5	4.0	4.7	4.7	5.0	5.3	5.2	4.7	4.9	5.0
Egypt / Égypte	..	..	3.0	2.9	2.9	3.2	3.4	3.6	3.3	2.6
Equatorial Guinea / Guinée équatoriale	..	..	0.2	0.2	0.5	0.6	0.5	0.5	0.6	0.5
Eswatini	0.6	0.6	0.5	0.6	1.4	1.4	1.7	1.7	1.9	2.0
Ghana	..	2.8	4.1	2.7	3.5	4.7	4.1	4.0	3.4	3.5
Kenya	..	..	3.8	4.9	4.5	4.7	4.9	4.6	4.7	4.4
Lesotho	..	..	0.0	0.0	0.0	0.0	0.3	0.9	0.8	1.2
Madagascar	2.2	3.3	2.7	2.2	2.2	2.3	2.4	2.5	2.5	2.4
Malawi	..	..	2.6	3.4	2.7	2.9	3.1	3.0	3.1	2.8
Mali	2.7	4.3	4.1	3.6	4.6	5.0	4.8	3.7	4.4	4.2
Mauritania / Mauritanie	..	..	..	1.9	3.2	3.6	3.9	4.3	3.8	3.4
Mauritius / Maurice[1]	11.6	8.8	5.6	4.4	4.7	4.8	4.9	5.3	5.3	5.0
Morocco / Maroc	..	6.8	5.1	4.3	3.4	3.5	3.7	3.8	4.1	3.8
Namibia / Namibie	..	..	..	0.1	0.1	0.3	0.2	0.4	0.7	0.7
Niger	..	3.1	2.5	2.5	3.0	2.7	2.4	2.3	2.7	2.6
Nigeria / Nigéria	..	..	..	0.8	0.8	0.7	0.7	0.7	0.8	0.8
Rwanda	..	4.1	3.3	3.3	4.0	4.0	3.8	3.9	3.9	3.6
Senegal / Sénégal	..	3.8	4.2	4.0	4.4	4.6	4.2	4.4	4.8	4.8
Seychelles	..	..	..	12.7	7.1	7.8	7.7	7.3	7.5	7.4
Sierra Leone	..	..	5.5	3.8	3.0	2.7	3.8	3.3	3.9	3.4
South Africa / Afrique du Sud	3.4	3.1	2.7	3.4	4.2	4.1	4.1	4.3	4.4	3.9
Togo	..	2.6	3.2	3.5	5.2	5.1	5.1	4.6	4.5	4.9
Tunisia / Tunisie	..	6.0	4.8	4.2	4.2	4.2	4.4	4.9	4.7	4.8
Uganda / Ouganda	3.8	3.8	3.2	2.7	3.3	3.5	3.6	3.8	4.0	3.5
Africa (31) average / Moyenne Afrique (31)[2]	**..**	**..**	**..**	**3.0**	**3.2**	**3.3**	**3.3**	**3.3**	**3.3**	**3.2**
Asia-Pacific (28) average / Moyenne Asie-Pacifique (28)[3]	**..**	**..**	**..**	**4.3**	**4.3**	**4.2**	**4.4**	**4.6**	**4.4**	**4.0**
LAC average / Moyenne ALC[4]	**4.7**	**4.3**	**4.0**	**3.7**	**3.6**	**3.6**	**3.7**	**3.7**	**3.7**	**3.5**
OECD average / Moyenne OCDE[5]	**3.8**	**3.7**	**3.5**	**3.3**	**3.3**	**3.4**	**3.3**	**3.2**	**3.1**	**..**

.. Not available

Note: The figures include sub-national government tax revenues for Eswatini, Mauritania (since 2009), Mauritius, Morocco, Nigeria (only state revenues) and South Africa (since 2002). Sub-national government tax revenues are not available in other countries.

1. The fiscal year for Mauritius changed in 2010 and in 2015. Figures for 2015 needed to be estimated as a result.
2. Represents an unweighted average of the 31 African countries in this publication.
3. Represents an unweighted average for 28 Asian and Pacific economies included in the publication *Revenue Statistics in Asia and the Pacific 2022*.
4. Represents an unweighted average for 26 Latin American and Caribbean (LAC) countries included in the publication *Revenue Statistics in Latin America and the Caribbean 2022*.
5. Represents an unweighted average for 38 OECD countries.

.. Non disponible

Note : Les chiffres incluent les recettes fiscales collectées par les administrations infranationales pour l'Afrique du Sud (à partir de 2002), Eswatini, le Maroc, Maurice, la Mauritanie (à partir de 2009) et le Nigéria (recettes des administrations régionales). Les données des recettes fiscales collectées par les administrations infranationales ne sont pas disponibles pour les autres pays.

1. L'année fiscale pour Maurice a changé en 2010 et en 2015. Les chiffres pour 2015 ont dû être estimés en conséquence.
2. Représente une moyenne non pondérée des 31 pays africains inclus dans cette publication.
3. Représente la moyenne non pondérée pour 28 économies de l'Asie et du Pacifique incluses dans la publication *Revenue Statistics in Asia and the Pacific 2022*.
4. Représente la moyenne non pondérée pour 26 pays d'Amérique latine et des Caraïbes (ALC) inclus dans la publication *Revenue Statistics in Latin America and the Caribbean 2022*.
5. Représente la moyenne non pondérée pour 38 pays de l'OCDE.

StatLink https://stat.link/14vpzf

Table 4.16. **Taxes on specific goods and services (5120) as percentage of total taxation**

Tableau 4.16. **Impôts sur les biens et services déterminés (5120) en pourcentage du total des recettes fiscales**

	1995	2000	2005	2010	2015	2016	2017	2018	2019	2020
Botswana	..	..	1.8	1.3	2.2	1.8	2.5	1.8	2.2	2.0
Burkina Faso	..	21.7	24.0	20.3	25.0	24.3	24.7	24.6	22.1	22.2
Cabo Verde	61.3	53.8	27.9	26.2	27.8	29.4	29.3	27.1	28.1	26.9
Cameroon / Cameroun	36.5	29.6	28.1	28.4	23.8	25.7	26.2	25.1	25.3	27.0
Chad / Tchad	..	..	..	8.1	19.1	18.2	20.3	28.4	26.1	18.2
Congo	..	5.1	29.3	26.9	25.4	25.8	23.8	26.4	26.2	26.3
Congo, Dem. Rep. / Congo, Rép. dém.	..	70.5	31.8	28.5	28.1	26.9	21.8	18.1	19.0	17.4
Côte d'Ivoire	45.3	35.8	41.3	39.5	40.0	40.5	39.3	35.7	36.9	37.7
Egypt / Égypte	..	..	19.1	18.8	19.6	22.3	22.2	23.8	22.6	19.3
Equatorial Guinea / Guinée équatoriale	..	..	2.3	2.0	4.0	8.8	7.7	7.9	6.3	6.3
Eswatini	5.6	5.9	4.0	4.1	9.0	8.7	10.0	9.7	10.4	11.0
Ghana	..	35.6	39.0	25.3	26.9	35.8	30.8	29.1	25.9	26.1
Kenya	..	..	35.2	31.2	26.9	27.5	28.0	27.9	28.6	28.4
Lesotho	..	..	0.0	0.0	0.2	0.1	1.7	4.2	3.9	6.2
Madagascar	32.5	34.4	30.8	23.4	23.0	23.1	22.4	22.1	21.9	22.7
Malawi	..	..	29.4	30.2	22.9	23.9	23.6	23.8	24.0	23.1
Mali	36.5	37.9	28.4	25.3	30.6	30.1	29.0	27.9	25.3	23.4
Mauritania / Mauritanie	..	..	..	19.2	21.8	25.7	26.7	27.8	27.5	26.3
Mauritius / Maurice[1]	68.8	48.3	31.3	23.4	24.3	24.5	24.8	26.2	25.2	23.8
Morocco / Maroc	..	30.9	20.4	15.6	12.7	12.8	13.3	13.5	14.5	13.3
Namibia / Namibie	..	..	..	0.7	0.7	1.2	1.1	2.3	3.4	3.7
Niger	..	42.9	30.4	25.8	23.9	25.3	25.5	20.4	26.1	26.6
Nigeria / Nigéria	..	..	..	11.6	12.7	13.3	12.6	11.5	12.6	14.2
Rwanda	..	47.9	31.0	26.9	24.4	24.4	23.3	22.9	22.3	21.6
Senegal / Sénégal	..	29.2	27.4	25.4	26.8	27.3	25.8	25.8	25.9	26.5
Seychelles	..	..	..	41.4	24.4	25.3	24.6	22.3	23.3	23.2
Sierra Leone	..	..	70.6	42.1	30.3	25.5	35.8	30.0	33.1	30.6
South Africa / Afrique du Sud	17.4	15.3	12.0	14.6	15.9	15.7	15.6	16.2	16.6	15.6
Togo	..	37.7	32.7	32.2	32.8	30.9	32.1	31.2	30.3	31.9
Tunisia / Tunisie	..	25.7	20.8	16.3	14.7	15.1	15.2	16.3	14.6	14.8
Uganda / Ouganda	49.2	46.4	34.6	32.9	31.2	31.4	32.1	32.3	32.9	31.5
Africa (31) average / Moyenne Afrique (31)[2]	**..**	**..**	**..**	**21.5**	**21.0**	**21.7**	**21.7**	**21.4**	**21.4**	**20.9**
Asia-Pacific (28) average / Moyenne Asie-Pacifique (28)[3]	**..**	**..**	**..**	**26.3**	**23.7**	**24.2**	**23.9**	**24.2**	**22.8**	**22.3**
LAC average / Moyenne ALC[4]	**29.6**	**26.5**	**22.5**	**19.2**	**17.0**	**16.8**	**17.1**	**16.7**	**16.7**	**16.0**
OECD average / Moyenne OCDE[5]	**12.4**	**11.6**	**10.9**	**10.8**	**10.2**	**10.2**	**10.0**	**9.7**	**9.5**	**..**

.. Not available

Note: The figures include sub-national government tax revenues for Eswatini, Mauritania (since 2009), Mauritius, Morocco, Nigeria (only state revenues) and South Africa (since 2002). Sub-national government tax revenues are not available in other countries.

1. The fiscal year for Mauritius changed in 2010 and in 2015. Figures for 2015 needed to be estimated as a result.
2. Represents an unweighted average of the 31 African countries in this publication.
3. Represents an unweighted average for 28 Asian and Pacific economies included in the publication *Revenue Statistics in Asia and the Pacific 2022*.
4. Represents an unweighted average for 26 Latin American and Caribbean (LAC) countries included in the publication *Revenue Statistics in Latin America and the Caribbean 2022*.
5. Represents an unweighted average for 38 OECD countries.

.. Non disponible

Note : Les chiffres incluent les recettes fiscales collectées par les administrations infranationales pour l'Afrique du Sud (à partir de 2002), Eswatini, le Maroc, Maurice, la Mauritanie (à partir de 2009) et le Nigéria (recettes des administrations régionales). Les données des recettes fiscales collectées par les administrations infranationales ne sont pas disponibles pour les autres pays.

1. L'année fiscale pour Maurice a changé en 2010 et en 2015. Les chiffres pour 2015 ont dû être estimés en conséquence.
2. Représente une moyenne non pondérée des 31 pays africains inclus dans cette publication.
3. Représente la moyenne non pondérée pour 28 économies de l'Asie et du Pacifique incluses dans la publication *Revenue Statistics in Asia and the Pacific 2022*.
4. Représente la moyenne non pondérée pour 26 pays d'Amérique latine et des Caraïbes (ALC) inclus dans la publication *Revenue Statistics in Latin America and the Caribbean 2022*.
5. Représente la moyenne non pondérée pour 38 pays de l'OCDE.

StatLink https://stat.link/3jyv1p

Table 4.17. **Gross domestic product for tax reporting years at current prices, in national currency units**

Tableau 4.17. **Produit intérieur brut pour les années de déclaration fiscale à prix courants, en monnaie nationale**

	1995	2000	2005	2010	2015	2016	2017	2018	2019	2020
Botswana[1]	14 054	29 719	52 191	90 222	143 894	164 975	168 416	175 189	177 445	177 631
Burkina Faso	1 335 831	2 108 160	3 240 716	5 002 182	6 995 311	7 605 123	8 191 299	8 920 421	9 369 188	9 988 366
Cabo Verde	41 215	70 536	96 690	138 569	158 699	165 782	173 097	183 698	195 202	164 911
Cameroon / Cameroun	5 225 059	7 504 469	10 286 733	13 610 554	19 043 067	20 038 566	20 960 865	22 203 329	23 243 662	23 486 470
Chad / Tchad	816 756	1 115 969	3 518 122	5 290 608	6 474 073	6 047 146	5 854 572	6 130 689	6 440 466	6 165 754
Congo	1 226 473	2 580 266	3 506 269	6 505 751	7 029 660	6 021 964	6 453 235	7 577 813	7 493 800	5 936 500
Congo, Dem. Rep. / Congo, Rép. dém.	1 758	1 317 075	5 670 065	19 536 677	35 111 226	37 517 392	55 676 093	76 495 500	83 048 340	90 181 048
Côte d'Ivoire	7 589 595	10 547 104	12 456 698	17 036 122	27 086 150	28 423 874	29 955 010	32 222 266	34 298 893	35 311 383
Egypt / Égypte[2]	214 501	357 607	566 220	1 268 711	2 443 900	2 709 400	3 470 000	4 437 400	5 322 100	5 855 000
Equatorial Guinea / Guinée équatoriale	84 131	822 850	4 316 629	8 072 293	7 795 420	6 661 366	7 084 543	7 274 689	6 689 510	5 768 440
Eswatini[1]	7 221	12 366	20 730	33 123	52 877	56 771	59 459	62 569	65 080	66 371
Ghana	1 752	6 250	22 294	62 001	183 526	219 595	262 798	308 587	356 544	383 486
Kenya[2]	1 160 509	1 989 658	2 574 753	3 436 636	6 444 076	7 239 191	8 038 730	8 911 852	9 797 981	10 504 323
Lesotho[1]	3 501	5 876	9 497	16 950	30 419	31 197	30 627	32 207	33 990	33 718
Madagascar	3 274 385	6 265 668	11 736 269	20 863 367	33 216 184	37 637 590	41 058 841	45 886 302	51 035 217	49 453 220
Malawi[2]	38 871	222 319	571 292	1 352 608	4 060 849	5 027 820	6 041 645	6 883 582	7 727 897	8 517 596
Mali	1 650 181	2 103 270	3 294 055	5 288 939	7 747 730	8 311 926	8 922 038	9 481 959	10 124 715	10 052 782
Mauritania / Mauritanie	27 144	42 517	77 981	155 297	200 221	225 473	243 407	262 320	289 478	294 389
Mauritius / Maurice[2]	72 518	121 023	194 372	307 957	409 893	422 329	445 983	469 229	489 755	463 974
Morocco / Maroc	333 319	412 897	552 671	784 624	987 950	1 013 229	1 063 045	1 108 463	1 152 806	1 089 521
Namibia / Namibie[1]	13 282	27 979	48 139	84 476	148 941	161 173	173 944	180 940	179 126	176 745
Niger	1 145 340	1 586 921	2 304 126	3 875 000	5 724 873	6 135 410	6 497 014	7 134 254	7 564 953	7 907 391
Nigeria / Nigéria	2 895 201	6 897 482	22 269 978	55 469 351	95 177 736	102 575 419	114 899 251	129 086 908	145 639 140	154 252 320
Rwanda	385 387	806 000	1 636 000	3 569 000	6 147 000	6 842 000	7 694 000	8 302 000	9 315 000	9 746 000
Senegal / Sénégal	3 007 532	4 270 612	5 804 605	7 976 735	10 508 650	11 283 396	12 191 796	12 840 090	13 712 800	14 101 000
Seychelles	2 420	3 513	5 055	11 705	18 852	19 848	21 474	22 763	23 635	21 151
Sierra Leone	959 634	1 941 321	4 769 788	10 255 614	21 583 301	24 296 286	27 465 429	32 401 626	36 730 872	39 938 072
South Africa / Afrique du Sud	622 901	1 053 138	1 837 001	3 055 613	4 420 793	4 759 555	5 078 190	5 357 640	5 605 034	5 521 075
Togo	1 118 314	1 429 225	1 622 674	2 289 158	3 334 957	3 574 400	3 713 574	3 950 447	4 230 509	4 359 854
Tunisia / Tunisie	19 497	30 874	43 920	66 140	89 802	95 287	102 012	112 985	122 578	119 526
Uganda / Ouganda[2]	6 676 316	12 067 688	20 823 563	51 348 000	93 210 500	100 300 500	109 307 500	120 558 500	133 477 000	140 597 000

1. The GDP for Botswana, Eswatini and Namibia are adjusted using the following formula: GDP(n)*3/4+GDP(n+1))/4 in order to make them correspond more closely to an April(n)-to-March(n+1) fiscal year. The GDP for Lesotho is not adjusted because it is already reported on an April-March fiscal year basis in the IMF *World Economic Outlook*.
2. The GDP for Kenya, Malawi and Uganda in all years and for Mauritius in the years preceding 2010 and for 2016 are adjusted using the formula GDP(n)/2+GDP(n-1)/2. This is done in order to make the value of the GDP correspond more closely to a July(n-1)-to-June(n) fiscal year. The GDP for Egypt is not adjusted because it is already reported on a July-June fiscal year basis in the IMF *World Economic Outlook*. The GDP for Mauritius is not adjusted from 2010 to 2015 because public finance data are reported on a calendar year for those years.

Source: IMF, *World Economic Outlook*, April 2022.

1. Le PIB pour Botswana, Eswatini, et la Namibie est ajusté selon la formule PIB(n)*3/4+PIB(n+1))/4 afin de le faire correspondre le mieux possible à une année fiscale de avril (n) à mars (n+1). Le PIB du Lesotho n'est pas ajusté car il est déjà publié sur la base d'un exercice fiscal avril-mars dans les *Perspectives de l'économie mondiale* du FMI.
2. Le PIB pour le Kenya, le Malawi et l'Ouganda, pour toutes les années et pour Maurice dans les années antérieures à 2010 et pour l'année 2016, est ajusté selon la formule suivante : PIB(n)/2+PIB(n-1)/2 afin de le faire correspondre le mieux possible à une année fiscale de juillet (n-1) à juin (n). Le PIB de l'Égypte n'est pas ajusté car il est déjà publié sur la base de l'exercice juillet-juin dans les *Perspectives de l'économie mondiale* du FMI. Le PIB de Maurice n'est pas ajusté de 2010 à 2015 car les données de finances publiques sont reportées sur une année civile pour ces années.

Source : FMI, *Perspectives de l'économie mondiale, avril 2022.*

StatLink https://stat.link/0gfe41

Table 4.18. Gross domestic product for tax reporting years at current prices, in millions of US dollars at market exchange rates

Tableau 4.18. Produit intérieur brut pour les années de déclaration fiscale à prix courants, en millions de dollars US aux taux de change du marché

	1995	2000	2005	2010	2015	2016	2017	2018	2019	2020
Botswana[1]	4 835	5 627	9 854	13 256	13 919	15 338	16 337	16 948	16 254	15 649
Burkina Faso	2 676	2 961	6 150	10 118	11 833	12 830	14 102	16 067	15 991	17 378
Cabo Verde	536	609	1 091	1 664	1 597	1 663	1 770	1 967	1 982	1 707
Cameroon / Cameroun	10 075	10 245	19 534	27 530	32 213	33 805	36 086	39 992	39 673	40 863
Chad / Tchad	1 636	1 572	6 676	10 701	10 952	10 202	10 079	11 042	10 993	10 728
Congo	2 457	3 624	6 654	13 159	11 891	10 159	11 110	13 649	12 791	10 329
Congo, Dem. Rep. / Congo, Rép. dém.	25 021	19 077	12 069	21 541	37 915	36 640	37 981	47 146	50 399	48 707
Côte d'Ivoire	15 205	14 851	23 625	34 431	45 815	47 964	51 588	58 011	58 539	61 437
Egypt / Égypte[2]	63 250	104 752	94 127	230 024	332 075	332 484	236 528	250 253	302 335	364 023
Equatorial Guinea / Guinée équatoriale	169	1 159	8 187	16 314	13 185	11 241	12 201	13 097	11 417	10 022
Eswatini[1]	1 907	1 690	3 206	4 535	4 000	3 963	4 472	4 623	4 365	4 151
Ghana	14 610	11 470	24 600	43 326	49 437	56 144	60 385	67 259	68 353	68 498
Kenya[2]	21 705	27 191	33 337	43 877	69 382	72 593	78 391	87 088	96 357	100 891
Lesotho[1]	965	847	1 484	2 356	2 207	2 219	2 356	2 342	2 299	2 061
Madagascar	3 838	4 629	5 859	9 983	11 323	11 849	13 176	13 760	14 105	13 056
Malawi[2]	3 171	4 296	5 022	9 260	8 770	8 373	8 338	9 413	10 457	11 439
Mali	3 337	2 963	6 251	10 698	13 106	14 022	15 360	17 079	17 281	17 491
Mauritania / Mauritanie	2 092	1 780	2 936	5 637	6 182	6 414	6 826	7 351	7 889	8 110
Mauritius / Maurice[2]	4 108	4 702	6 822	10 004	11 692	11 962	12 746	13 721	14 114	12 483
Morocco / Maroc	39 029	38 859	62 343	93 217	101 179	103 312	109 683	118 096	119 871	114 724
Namibia / Namibie[1]	3 501	3 821	7 440	11 566	11 267	11 260	13 081	13 381	12 025	11 051
Niger	2 296	2 235	4 372	7 838	9 684	10 350	11 185	12 850	12 912	13 758
Nigeria / Nigéria	132 230	67 824	169 645	369 062	492 437	404 649	375 745	421 737	448 120	429 423
Rwanda	1 470	2 049	2 943	6 121	8 542	8 691	9 253	9 641	10 356	10 332
Senegal / Sénégal	6 026	6 016	11 015	16 134	17 777	19 035	20 989	23 127	23 405	24 534
Seychelles	508	615	919	970	1 416	1 490	1 573	1 629	1 683	1 202
Sierra Leone	1 273	941	1 610	2 578	4 252	3 855	3 713	4 085	4 074	4 059
South Africa / Afrique du Sud	171 736	151 855	288 750	417 315	346 663	323 493	381 317	404 673	387 849	335 344
Togo	2 240	2 014	3 080	4 630	5 641	6 030	6 393	7 115	7 221	7 586
Tunisia / Tunisie	20 616	22 524	33 851	46 210	45 779	44 360	42 167	42 687	41 772	42 502
Uganda / Ouganda[2]	6 857	7 789	11 605	24 395	30 381	28 619	30 499	32 801	36 131	37 751

1. The GDP for Botswana, Eswatini and Namibia are adjusted using the following formula: GDP(n)*3/4+GDP(n+1))/4 in order to make them correspond more closely to an April(n)-to-March(n+1) fiscal year. The GDP for Lesotho is not adjusted because it is already reported on an April-March fiscal year basis in the IMF *World Economic Outlook*.
2. The GDP for Kenya, Malawi and Uganda in all years and for Mauritius in the years preceding 2010 and for 2016 are adjusted using the formula GDP(n)/2+GDP(n-1)/2. This is done in order to make the value of the GDP correspond more closely to a July(n-1)-to-June(n) fiscal year. The GDP for Egypt is not adjusted because it is already reported on a July-June fiscal year basis in the IMF *World Economic Outlook*. The GDP for Mauritius is not adjusted from 2010 to 2015 because public finance data are reported on a calendar year for those years.

Source: IMF, *World Economic Outlook*, April 2022.

1. Le PIB pour Botswana, Eswatini, et la Namibie est ajusté selon la formule PIB(n)*3/4+PIB(n+1))/4 afin de le faire correspondre le mieux possible à une année fiscale de avril (n) à mars (n+1). Le PIB du Lesotho n'est pas ajusté car il est déjà publié sur la base d'un exercice fiscal avril-mars dans les *Perspectives de l'économie mondiale* du FMI.
2. Le PIB pour le Kenya, le Malawi et l'Ouganda, pour toutes les années et pour Maurice dans les années antérieures à 2010 et pour l'année 2016, est ajusté selon la formule suivante : PIB(n)/2+PIB(n-1)/2 afin de le faire correspondre le mieux possible à une année fiscale de juillet (n-1) à juin (n). Le PIB de l'Égypte n'est pas ajusté car il est déjà publié sur la base de l'exercice juillet-juin dans les *Perspectives de l'économie mondiale* du FMI. Le PIB de Maurice n'est pas ajusté de 2010 à 2015 car les données de finances publiques sont reportées sur une année civile pour ces années.

Source : FMI, *Perspectives de l'économie mondiale, avril 2022.*

StatLink https://stat.link/1e5oq0

Table 4.19. **Exchange rates used, national currency per US dollar**
Tableau 4.19. **Taux de change utilisés, unités de monnaie nationale par dollar US**

	1995	2000	2005	2010	2015	2016	2017	2018	2019	2020
Botswana	2.91	5.28	5.30	6.81	10.34	10.76	10.31	10.34	10.92	11.35
Burkina Faso	499.15	711.98	526.97	494.39	591.15	592.77	580.86	555.19	585.89	574.75
Cabo Verde	76.85	115.88	88.65	83.28	99.39	99.69	97.81	93.41	98.50	96.62
Cameroon / Cameroun	518.63	732.49	526.60	494.39	591.15	592.77	580.86	555.19	585.89	574.75
Chad / Tchad	499.15	709.89	526.97	494.39	591.15	592.77	580.86	555.19	585.89	574.75
Congo	499.15	711.98	526.97	494.39	591.15	592.77	580.86	555.19	585.89	574.75
Congo, Dem. Rep. / Congo, Rép. dém.	0.07	69.04	469.81	906.96	926.06	1 023.96	1 465.91	1 622.51	1 647.82	1 851.52
Côte d'Ivoire	499.15	710.21	527.26	494.79	591.21	592.61	580.66	555.45	585.91	574.75
Egypt / Égypte	3.39	3.41	6.02	5.52	7.36	8.15	14.67	17.73	17.60	16.08
Equatorial Guinea / Guinée équatoriale	499.15	710.21	527.26	494.79	591.21	592.61	580.66	555.45	585.91	575.59
Eswatini	3.79	7.32	6.47	7.30	13.22	14.33	13.30	13.53	14.91	15.99
Ghana	0.12	0.54	0.91	1.43	3.71	3.91	4.35	4.59	5.22	5.60
Kenya	53.47	73.17	77.24	78.32	92.88	99.72	102.55	102.33	101.68	104.12
Lesotho	3.63	6.94	6.40	7.19	13.78	14.06	13.00	13.75	14.79	16.36
Madagascar	853.13	1 353.50	2 003.03	2 089.95	2 933.51	3 176.54	3 116.11	3 334.75	3 618.32	3 787.75
Malawi	12.26	51.75	113.77	146.08	463.04	600.45	724.59	731.30	739.05	744.61
Mali	494.45	709.89	526.97	494.39	591.15	592.77	580.86	555.19	585.89	574.75
Mauritania / Mauritanie	12.98	23.89	26.56	27.55	32.39	35.15	35.66	35.68	36.69	36.30
Mauritius / Maurice	17.65	25.74	28.49	30.78	35.06	35.30	34.99	34.20	34.70	37.17
Morocco / Maroc	8.54	10.63	8.87	8.42	9.76	9.81	9.69	9.39	9.62	9.50
Namibia / Namibie	3.79	7.32	6.47	7.30	13.22	14.31	13.30	13.52	14.90	15.99
Niger	498.80	709.89	526.97	494.39	591.15	592.77	580.86	555.20	585.89	574.76
Nigeria / Nigéria	21.90	101.70	131.27	150.30	193.28	253.49	305.79	306.08	325.00	359.21
Rwanda	262.21	393.44	555.94	583.12	719.60	787.25	831.53	861.08	899.45	943.26
Senegal / Sénégal	499.10	709.89	526.97	494.39	591.15	592.77	580.86	555.19	585.89	574.75
Seychelles	4.76	5.71	5.50	12.07	13.32	13.32	13.65	13.97	14.05	17.60
Sierra Leone	754.00	2 063.07	2 963.34	3 978.09	5 075.74	6 303.21	7 397.39	7 931.91	9 016.42	9 839.91
South Africa / Afrique du Sud	3.63	6.94	6.36	7.32	12.75	14.71	13.32	13.24	14.45	16.46
Togo	499.15	709.60	526.90	494.39	591.15	592.77	580.86	555.19	585.89	574.75
Tunisia / Tunisie	0.95	1.37	1.30	1.43	1.96	2.15	2.42	2.65	2.93	2.81
Uganda / Ouganda	973.71	1 549.25	1 794.39	2 104.89	3 068.09	3 504.65	3 583.94	3 675.46	3 694.30	3 724.30

Note: The exchange rate is calculated by taking the ratio of the estimated fiscal year GDP in national currency for Table 4.17 to the estimated fiscal year GDP in US dollars in Table 4.18.

Note : Le taux de change est calculé en prenant le rapport entre le PIB estimé de l'année fiscale en monnaie nationale du tableau 4.17 et le PIB estimé de l'année fiscale en dollars US du tableau 4.18.

StatLink https://stat.link/gnsb81

Chapter 5

Country tables, 1995-2020 – Tax revenues

Chapitre 5

Tableaux pays, 1995-2020 – Recettes fiscales

Chapter 5 / Chapitre 5

Country tables, 1995-2020

In all of the following tables a ("..") indicates not available or not applicable. The main series in this volume cover the years 1995 to 2020.

Figures referring to 1990-94, 1996-99, 2001-04, 2006-09 and 2011-14 in Tables 5.1 to 5.31 have been omitted because of lack of space. Complete series are, however, available on line at *http://dx.doi.org/10.1787/93add7a4-en*.

Tableaux pays, 1995-2020

Dans tous les tableaux suivants le symbole («..») signifie que l'information n'est pas disponible ou qu'elle n'est pas applicable. La principale série dans ce volume couvre les années 1999 à 2020.

Les données pour les années 1990-94, 1996-99, 2001-04, 2006-09 et 2011-14 dans les tableaux 5.1 à 5.31 ont été omises en raison du manque d'espace. Les séries complètes sont cependant disponibles en ligne sur *http://dx.doi.org/10.1787/ef1bbbc4-fr*..

Table 5.1. **Botswana**

Details of tax revenue / Recettes fiscales détaillées

Million BWP

	1995	2000	2005	2010	2015	2016	2017	2018	2019	2020
Total tax revenue	..	..	**8 039**	**14 300**	**19 332**	**24 139**	**22 470**	**23 287**	**24 357**	**21 973**
1000 Taxes on income, profits and capital gains	..	..	**5 887**	**9 345**	**13 134**	**16 777**	**13 772**	**15 069**	**15 341**	**13 418**
1100 Of individuals	..	..	..	..	..	..	..	..	..	..
1110 On income and profits	..	..	..	..	..	..	..	..	..	..
1120 On capital gains	..	..	..	..	..	..	..	..	..	..
1200 Corporate	..	..	..	..	..	..	..	..	..	..
1210 On profits	..	..	..	..	..	..	..	..	..	..
1220 On capital gains	..	..	..	..	..	..	..	..	..	..
1300 Unallocable between 1100 and 1200	..	..	5 887	9 345	13 134	16 777	13 772	15 069	15 341	13 418
Assessed income tax	..	..	3 877	5 168	6 825	9 454	6 894	7 661	6 501	4 836
Income tax arrears and deductions	..	..	1 171	3 114	5 259	5 172	4 948	5 349	7 187	7 287
Withholding tax	..	..	840	1 062	1 050	2 152	1 930	2 059	1 653	1 295
PAYE taxes	..	..	0	0	0	0	0	0	0	0
2000 Social security contributions	..	..	**0**	**0**	**0**	**0**	**0**	**0**	**0**	**0**
2100 Employees	..	..	..	..	..	..	..	..	..	..
2110 On a payroll basis	..	..	..	..	..	..	..	..	..	..
2120 On an income tax basis	..	..	..	..	..	..	..	..	..	..
2200 Employers	..	..	..	..	..	..	..	..	..	..
2210 On a payroll basis	..	..	..	..	..	..	..	..	..	..
2220 On an income tax basis	..	..	..	..	..	..	..	..	..	..
2300 Self-employed or non-employed	..	..	..	..	..	..	..	..	..	..
2310 On a payroll basis	..	..	..	..	..	..	..	..	..	..
2320 On an income tax basis	..	..	..	..	..	..	..	..	..	..
2400 Unallocable between 2100, 2200 and 2300	..	..	..	..	..	..	..	..	..	..
2410 On a payroll basis	..	..	..	..	..	..	..	..	..	..
2420 On an income tax basis	..	..	..	..	..	..	..	..	..	..
3000 Taxes on payroll and workforce	..	..	**0**	**0**	**0**	**0**	**0**	**0**	**0**	**0**
4000 Taxes on property	..	..	**13**	**52**	**66**	**62**	**63**	**78**	**71**	**63**
4100 Recurrent taxes on immovable property	..	..	0	0	0	0	0	0	0	0
4110 Households	..	..	..	..	..	..	..	..	..	..
4120 Others	..	..	..	..	..	..	..	..	..	..
4200 Recurrent taxes on net wealth	..	..	0	0	0	0	0	0	0	0
4210 Individual	..	..	..	..	..	..	..	..	..	..
4220 Corporate	..	..	..	..	..	..	..	..	..	..
4300 Estate, inheritance and gift taxes	..	..	0	0	0	0	0	0	0	0
4310 Estate and inheritance taxes	..	..	..	..	..	..	..	..	..	..
4320 Gift taxes	..	..	..	..	..	..	..	..	..	..
4400 Taxes on financial and capital transactions	..	..	13	52	66	62	63	78	71	63
4500 Non-recurrent taxes	..	..	0	0	0	0	0	0	0	0
4510 On net wealth	..	..	..	..	..	..	..	..	..	..
4520 Other non-recurrent taxes	..	..	..	..	..	..	..	..	..	..
4600 Other recurrent taxes on property	..	..	0	0	0	0	0	0	0	0
5000 Taxes on goods and services	..	..	**2 138**	**4 903**	**6 132**	**7 300**	**8 635**	**8 140**	**8 944**	**8 493**
5100 Taxes on production, sale, transfer, etc.	..	..	2 008	4 669	5 870	6 981	8 207	7 661	8 475	8 131
5110 General taxes	..	..	1 864	4 481	5 448	6 535	7 650	7 253	7 939	7 687
5111 Value added taxes	..	..	1 864	4 481	5 448	6 535	7 650	7 253	7 939	7 687
VAT revenues (gross)	..	..	1 832	4 481	5 448	6 535	7 650	7 253	7 939	7 687
VAT accrued interest	..	..	31	0	0	0	0	0	0	0
VAT refunds	..	..	1	0	0	0	0	0	0	0
5112 Sales tax	..	..	0	0	0	0	0	0	0	0
5113 Other	..	..	0	0	0	0	0	0	0	0
5120 Taxes on specific goods and services	..	..	144	188	422	446	557	408	536	445
5121 Excises	..	..	115	157	393	435	553	405	531	353
Alcohol levy	..	..	0	0	284	327	427	284	401	236
Fuel levy	..	..	115	157	109	107	126	121	130	117
5122 Profits of fiscal monopolies	..	..	0	0	0	0	0	0	0	0
5123 Customs and import duties	..	..	2	9	4	6	2	1	1	2
5124 Taxes on exports	..	..	0	2	2	3	2	2	3	1
5125 Taxes on investment goods	..	..	0	0	0	0	0	0	0	0
5126 Taxes on specific services	..	..	27	20	23	2	0	0	1	88
5127 Other taxes on internat. trade and transactions	..	..	0	0	0	0	0	0	0	0
5128 Other taxes	..	..	0	0	0	0	0	0	0	0
5130 Unallocable between 5110 and 5120	..	..	0	0	0	0	0	0	0	0
5200 Taxes on use of goods and perform activities	..	..	131	234	262	319	428	479	469	361

Table 5.1. **Botswana** *(cont.)*

Details of tax revenue / Recettes fiscales détaillées

Million BWP

	1995	2000	2005	2010	2015	2016	2017	2018	2019	2020
5210 Recurrent taxes	..	..	131	234	262	319	428	479	469	361
5211 Paid by households: motor vehicles	..	..	41	62	77	85	110	115	118	120
5212 Paid by others: motor vehicles	..	..	74	144	180	193	270	317	346	196
5213 Paid in respect of other goods	..	..	15	29	5	40	48	46	5	45
5220 Non-recurrent taxes	..	..	0	0	0	0	0	0	0	0
5300 Unallocable between 5100 and 5200	..	..	0	0	0	0	0	0	0	0
6000 Other taxes	**..**	**..**	**0**	**0**	**0**	**0**	**0**	**0**	**0**	**0**
6100 Paid solely by business	..	..	..	..	..	..	..	..	..	..
6200 Other	..	..	..	..	..	..	..	..	..	..

.. Not available

Note: Data are on a fiscal year basis beginning 1st April. For example, the data for 2020 represent April 2020 to March 2021.

The data are on a cash basis.

Figures exclude tax revenues collected by sub-national governments as the data are not available.

Heading 2000: Social security contributions for Botswana are deemed to be null as they do not meet the criteria to be classified as social security contributions set out in the OECD classification of taxes in the *OECD Interpretative Guide*.

Source: Botswana Ministry of Finance and Economic Development, and Statistics Botswana.

StatLink https://stat.link/t1g5si

Table 5.2. **Burkina Faso**

Details of tax revenue / Recettes fiscales détaillées

Million XOF

	1995	2000	2005	2010	2015	2016	2017	2018	2019	2020
Recettes fiscales totales	..	**214 601**	**380 161**	**698 853**	**1 018 759**	**1 161 369**	**1 326 065**	**1 484 685**	**1 622 546**	**1 660 178**
1000 Impôts sur revenu, bénéfices et gains en capital	..	**53 109**	**79 290**	**135 056**	**236 193**	**287 770**	**325 403**	**377 120**	**450 579**	**456 645**
1100 Des personnes physiques	..	15 371	27 639	56 429	75 300	88 707	102 422	125 405	149 467	172 403
1110 Sur le revenu et les bénéfices	..	15 371	27 639	56 429	75 300	88 707	102 422	125 405	149 467	172 403
Impôt sur les revenus	..	0	16	84	18	14	49	1	0	0
Impôt sur les bénéfices industriels, commerciaux et agricoles (pers. phys.)	..	1 235	1 640	3 133	4 828	4 884	6 888	16 128	26 249	30 086
Impôt sur les bénéfices non commerciaux (pers. phys.)	..	754	5 996	2 404	4 809	5 492	5 821	8 008	9 479	7 537
Impôt unique sur les traitements et salaires	..	13 382	19 987	50 809	65 646	78 317	89 665	101 268	113 738	134 780
1120 Sur les gains en capital	..	..	..	..	..	..	..	..	..	..
1200 Des sociétés	..	36 190	48 829	76 008	157 319	194 665	217 472	246 558	295 436	278 203
1210 Sur les bénéfices	..	36 190	48 829	76 008	157 319	194 665	217 472	246 558	295 436	278 203
Impôt sur les sociétés	..	0	0	67 027	132 050	163 454	186 641	209 595	249 434	225 534
Contribution du secteur informel et des micro-entreprises	..	0	0	1 475	1 638	1 938	1 926	2 244	2 082	1 611
Impôt sur les bénéfices industriels, commerciaux et agricoles (pers. mor.)	..	32 221	43 991	0	0	0	0	0	0	0
Impôts sur le revenu des créances	..	548	1 033	1 622	4 698	5 463	6 155	0	0	0
Impôts sur le revenu des valeurs mobilières	..	3 420	3 805	5 884	18 932	23 810	22 750	0	0	0
Impôts sur le revenu des capitaux mobiliers	..	0	0	0	0	0	0	34 719	43 920	51 058
1220 Sur les gains en capital	..	..	..	..	..	..	..	..	..	..
1300 Non ventilables entre 1100 et 1200	..	1 549	2 821	2 619	3 574	4 399	5 509	5 157	5 675	6 039
Impôts sur les revenus fonciers	..	1 402	1 425	2 337	3 206	3 668	4 175	4 813	4 874	4 956
Reversement des honoraires	..	91	249	19	0	0	0	0	0	0
Taxes sur les plus-values	..	56	1 147	263	367	731	1 334	345	801	1 084
2000 Cotisations de sécurité sociale	..	**34 142**	**50 081**	**76 584**	**120 046**	**133 708**	**145 635**	**164 195**	**177 435**	**194 360**
2100 A la charge des salariés	..	10 332	15 753	23 424	35 064	34 204	37 255	42 003	45 391	58 694
2110 Sur la base du salaire	..	10 332	15 753	23 424	35 064	34 204	37 255	42 003	45 391	58 694
2120 Sur la base de l'impôt sur le revenu	..	0	0	0	0	0	0	0	0	0
2200 A la charge des employeurs	..	23 810	34 329	53 160	84 983	99 504	108 380	122 192	132 044	135 666
2210 Sur la base du salaire	..	23 810	34 329	53 160	84 983	99 504	108 380	122 192	132 044	135 666
2220 Sur la base de l'impôt sur le revenu	..	0	0	0	0	0	0	0	0	0
2300 A charge des travailleurs indép. ou sans emploi	..	0	0	0	0	0	0	0	0	0
2310 Sur la base du salaire	..	..	..	..	..	..	..	..	..	..
2320 Sur la base de l'impôt sur le revenu	..	..	..	..	..	..	..	..	..	..
2400 Non ventilables entre 2100, 2200 et 2300	..	0	0	0	0	0	0	0	0	0
2410 Sur la base du salaire	..	..	..	..	..	..	..	..	..	..
2420 Sur la base de l'impôt sur le revenu	..	..	..	..	..	..	..	..	..	..
3000 Sur salaires ou main-d'œuvre	..	**2 678**	**4 370**	**5 479**	**7 889**	**8 762**	**10 813**	**12 331**	**13 210**	**14 647**
Taxe patronale et d'apprentissage	..	2 678	4 370	5 479	7 889	8 762	10 813	12 331	13 210	14 647
4000 Impôts sur le patrimoine	..	**938**	**2 076**	**4 778**	**8 529**	**12 061**	**9 784**	**9 982**	**11 025**	**13 012**
4100 Impôts périodiques sur la propriété immobilière	..	54	0	615	1 011	1 366	1 359	2 013	2 438	2 775
Contribution foncière	..	0	..	0	0	0	75	169	232	280
Taxe de résidence	..	8	..	460	469	749	624	681	781	681
Taxe sur les biens de mainmorte	..	45	..	155	542	617	659	1 163	1 425	1 814
4110 Ménages	..	0	..	0	0	0	0	0	0	0
4120 Autres agents	..	0	..	0	0	0	0	0	0	0
4200 Impôts périodiques sur l'actif net	..	0	0	0	0	0	0	0	0	0
4210 Personnes physiques	..	..	..	..	..	..	..	..	..	..
4220 Sociétés	..	..	..	..	..	..	..	..	..	..
4300 Impôts sur mut. par décès, succ. et donations	..	73	56	41	200	188	101	170	317	306
4310 Impôts sur mut. par décès et successions	..	66	38	28	179	169	95	156	265	251
Droits de succession	..	66	38	28	179	169	95	156	265	251
4320 Impôts sur les donations	..	7	18	13	21	19	5	13	52	55
4400 Impôts sur transact. mobilières et immob.	..	646	1 481	2 803	6 160	8 836	6 702	5 818	5 778	7 241
Droits de mutation	..	646	1 481	2 803	6 160	8 836	6 702	5 818	5 778	7 241
4500 Impôts non-périodiques	..	165	539	1 318	1 158	1 671	1 621	1 981	2 492	2 690
4510 Sur l'actif net	..	0	0	0	0	0	0	0	0	0
4520 Autres non-périodiques	..	165	539	1 318	1 158	1 671	1 621	1 981	2 492	2 690
Droits d'immatriculation et d'inscription foncières	..	165	539	1 318	1 158	1 671	1 621	1 981	2 492	2 690
4600 Autres impôts périodiques sur patrimoine	..	0	0	0	0	0	0	0	0	0
5000 Impôts sur les biens et services	..	**122 232**	**241 776**	**470 504**	**639 524**	**710 978**	**824 168**	**911 247**	**959 602**	**973 051**
5100 Impôts sur production, vente, transfert, etc.	..	108 003	222 923	370 927	598 102	662 383	769 064	852 880	895 777	856 840
5110 Impôts généraux	..	61 497	131 867	229 176	343 378	380 664	441 791	487 799	536 770	488 599

Table 5.2. **Burkina Faso** *(cont.)*

Details of tax revenue / Recettes fiscales détaillées

Million XOF

	1995	2000	2005	2010	2015	2016	2017	2018	2019	2020
5111 Taxes sur la valeur ajoutée	..	61 497	131 005	228 498	342 660	379 986	440 983	486 929	535 895	488 276
Recettes TVA (brute)	..	62 566	132 010	236 198	393 160	440 486	511 508	537 954	586 658	528 254
Remboursements de la TVA	..	-1 068	-1 004	-7 700	-50 500	-60 500	-70 525	-51 025	-50 763	-39 977
5112 Impôts sur les ventes	..	0	0	0	0	0	0	0	0	0
5113 Autres impôts	..	0	862	678	719	678	808	870	874	322
Taxe sur chiffre d'affaires	..	..	0	0	0	0	0	0	0	0
Taxe de développement touristique	..	..	862	678	719	678	808	870	874	322
5120 Impôts sur biens et services déterminés	..	46 506	91 056	141 750	254 723	281 719	327 273	365 080	359 007	368 242
5121 Accises	..	16 129	31 956	46 912	94 105	105 434	129 214	141 049	138 068	145 014
Boissons	..	4 954	8 120	13 887	26 202	30 596	35 726	36 685	30 097	33 626
Taxes sur le café, le thé et les noix de cola	..	549	525	938	1 603	1 417	1 380	1 500	1 832	1 653
Taxe sur les produits pétroliers	..	10 515	23 169	31 710	65 266	71 818	90 167	100 432	102 918	106 863
Taxe sur les tabacs et allumettes	..	111	141	139	789	1 187	1 279	1 839	1 712	1 499
Taxe sur les emballages et sachets plastiques non biodégradables	..	..	..	..	..	..	..	119	563	487
Autres accises	..	0	0	239	246	415	662	474	947	887
5122 Bénéfices des monopoles fiscaux	..	2 912	5 344	7 234	15 212	17 668	18 360	22 259	24 158	22 646
Monopole des tabacs	..	2 912	5 344	7 234	15 212	17 668	18 360	22 259	24 158	22 646
5123 Droits de douane et droits à l'importation	..	25 242	52 066	85 075	128 465	140 632	161 095	182 180	176 799	167 212
Redevance informatique et statistique	..	3 574	5 502	10 030	16 218	17 484	20 852	22 277	22 581	23 054
Droits de douanes	..	21 589	46 092	75 045	112 247	123 148	140 243	159 903	154 217	144 158
Taxe dégressive de protection	..	79	472	0	0	0	0	0	0	0
5124 Taxes à l'exportation	..	572	322	434	601	416	455	454	422	345
Contribution du secteur élevage	..	572	322	434	601	416	455	454	422	345
5125 Impôts sur biens d'équipement	..	0	0	0	0	0	0	0	0	0
5126 Impôts sur services déterminés	..	1 651	1 369	2 096	16 339	17 570	18 149	19 139	19 560	33 026
Taxe sur billets avions	..	3	176	349	563	671	697	645	509	160
Taxe spécifique sur les entreprises de télécommunication	..	0	0	0	11 970	11 965	12 268	13 152	13 796	27 259
Taxe sur les contrats d'assurance	..	1 648	1 192	1 748	3 806	4 373	4 338	4 007	4 404	4 971
Taxe sur les jeux de hasard	..	0	0	0	0	561	847	1 335	851	636
5127 Autres impôts sur commerce et transact. internat.	..	0	0	0	0	0	0	0	0	0
5128 Autres impôts	..	0	0	0	0	0	0	0	0	0
5130 Non ventilables entre 5110 et 5120	..	0	0	0	0	0	0	0	0	0
5200 Impôts sur utilisation des biens et exerc. activites	..	10 503	15 876	98 077	38 970	45 082	52 634	53 794	58 412	114 498
5210 Impôts périodiques	..	3 837	648	70 529	12 022	14 361	16 270	19 339	21 043	73 348
5211 A la charge des ménages: véhicules à moteur	..	0	0	0	0	0	0	0	942	900
Taxe sur les véhicules à moteur	..	..	..	..	..	..	..	..	942	900
5212 A la charge autres agents: véhicules à moteur	..	0	0	0	0	0	0	0	0	0
5213 Autres impôts périodiques	..	3 837	648	70 529	12 022	14 361	16 270	19 339	20 101	72 448
Taxe sur les armes	..	0	0	32	30	34	36	38	41	56
Contribution des patentes	..	3 347	0	7 218	10 736	13 087	13 557	18 186	19 128	20 065
Taxe de visionnnement et de vérification	..	9	26	82	0	0	0	0	0	0
Matière forestière, faune sauvage et pêche	..	461	605	1 215	1 239	1 183	1 159	1 093	874	798
Recettes en matière d'hydraulique	..	0	0	0	0	0	0	0	0	0
Autorisation d'exploiter les hôtels et les restaurants	..	0	0	0	0	0	1	4	1	6
Licence de téléphonie mobile	..	0	0	61 793	0	0	1 500	0	0	51 500
Licence - vente à la consommation	..	20	17	190	18	56	16	17	56	23
5220 Impôts non-périodiques	..	6 666	15 228	27 547	26 948	30 721	36 365	34 456	37 369	41 150
Autres droits d'enregistrement	..	4 418	14 105	22 202	21 309	24 410	31 001	29 372	32 219	35 135
Taxe de jouissance	..	2 241	1 118	5 327	5 637	6 302	5 339	5 066	5 132	5 996
Licences d'agences et de guides touristiques	..	0	0	3	0	3	17	17	12	12
Agrément armes à feu	..	0	0	0	0	2	0	1	0	0
Agréments au code des investissements	..	7	5	14	2	3	8	0	6	7
5300 Non ventilables entre 5100 et 5200	..	3 726	2 977	1 501	2 452	3 514	2 470	4 573	5 413	1 713
Autres impôts non ventilables	..	74	84	169	264	668	641	734	1 323	638
Taxe préférentielle communautaire	..	3 154	1 890	0	0	0	0	0	0	0
Taxe pour le développement de la télévision	..	498	1 002	1 332	2 188	2 846	1 829	3 839	4 090	1 075
6000 Autres impôts	**..**	**1 502**	**2 568**	**6 452**	**6 579**	**8 089**	**10 262**	**9 810**	**10 695**	**8 462**
Droits de timbre	..	1 436	2 557	5 678	6 538	7 995	10 191	9 770	9 963	7 973
Autres recettes fiscales	..	66	11	774	41	94	71	39	732	490
6100 A la charge exclusive des entreprises	..	..	..	..	..	..	..	..	..	..
6200 A la charge d'autres agents	..	..	..	..	..	..	..	..	..	..
Pour mémoire :										
Prélèvement communautaire de solidarité (UEMOA)	..	1	6	6	9 855	11 433	11 884	11 035	10 394	10 635
Prélèvement communautaire (CEDEAO)	..	1 144	2 249	4 243	7 018	7 504	8 705	9 504	9 325	9 066

Table 5.2. **Burkina Faso** *(cont.)*

Details of tax revenue / Recettes fiscales détaillées

.. Non disponible

Note : Année civile se terminant le 31 décembre.

Les données sont sur la base des encaissements.

Les chiffres n'incluent pas les recettes fiscales collectées par les collectivités locales car elles ne sont pas disponibles. Cependant, ils incluent des recettes collectées par l'administration centrale au profit des collectivités locales.

Les recettes provenant de la taxe de location de biens, des droits sur les titres miniers, des redevances minières et des frais administratifs sont incluses dans les recettes non fiscales comme le préconise la classification OCDE (voir le *Guide d'interprétation* en Annexe A). La classification nationale du Burkina Faso les comptabilise comme des recettes fiscales.

À partir de 2018, les impôts sur le revenu des créances et les impôts sur le revenu des valeurs mobilières sont rapportés ensemble sous la rubrique des impôts sur le revenu des capitaux mobiliers.

Les recettes des licences de téléphonie mobile ont été majoritairement collectées en 2010 et 2020, car ces licences se renouvèlent tous les 10 ans.

Source : Ministère de l'Économie, des Finances et du Développement du Burkina Faso.

StatLink https://stat.link/2nyx4g

Table 5.3. **Cabo Verde**

Details of tax revenue / Recettes fiscales détaillées

Million CVE

	1995	2000	2005	2010	2015	2016	2017	2018	2019	2020
Recettes fiscales totales	**6 290**	**10 974**	**18 828**	**26 290**	**30 692**	**32 205**	**35 554**	**40 338**	**41 447**	**33 130**
1000 Impôts sur revenu, bénéfices et gains en capital	**2 105**	**3 913**	**5 815**	**7 892**	**9 669**	**10 050**	**11 292**	**12 300**	**12 806**	**9 990**
1100 Des personnes physiques	1 579	2 958	3 516	4 645	5 327	6 317	7 062	6 927	7 334	6 581
1110 Sur le revenu et les bénéfices	..	..	..	..	..	..	..	..	..	..
1120 Sur les gains en capital	..	..	..	..	..	..	..	..	..	..
1200 Des sociétés	526	955	2 299	3 247	4 342	3 733	4 230	5 374	5 472	3 410
1210 Sur les bénéfices	..	..	..	..	..	..	..	..	..	..
1220 Sur les gains en capital	..	..	..	..	..	..	..	..	..	..
1300 Non ventilables entre 1100 et 1200	0	0	0	0	0	0	0	0	0	0
2000 Cotisations de sécurité sociale	**0**	**569**	**533**	**42**	**46**	**56**	**60**	**77**	**76**	**77**
2100 A la charge des salariés	..	..	..	..	..	..	..	..	..	..
2110 Sur la base du salaire	..	..	..	..	..	..	..	..	..	..
2120 Sur la base de l'impôt sur le revenu	..	..	..	..	..	..	..	..	..	..
2200 A la charge des employeurs	..	..	..	..	..	..	..	..	..	..
2210 Sur la base du salaire	..	..	..	..	..	..	..	..	..	..
2220 Sur la base de l'impôt sur le revenu	..	..	..	..	..	..	..	..	..	..
2300 A charge des travailleurs indép. ou sans emploi	..	..	..	..	..	..	..	..	..	..
2310 Sur la base du salaire	..	..	..	..	..	..	..	..	..	..
2320 Sur la base de l'impôt sur le revenu	..	..	..	..	..	..	..	..	..	..
2400 Non ventilables entre 2100, 2200 et 2300	..	569	533	42	46	56	60	77	76	77
2410 Sur la base du salaire	..	569	533	42	46	56	60	77	76	77
Contributions pour la sécurité sociale	..	11	1	28	40	56	60	77	76	77
Taxe sociale unique	..	558	532	14	5	0	0	0	0	0
2420 Sur la base de l'impôt sur le revenu	..	0	0	0	0	0	0	0	0	0
3000 Sur salaires ou main-d'œuvre	**0**	**0**	**0**	**0**	**0**	**0**	**0**	**0**	**0**	**0**
4000 Impôts sur le patrimoine	**332**	**584**	**810**	**1 439**	**1 606**	**1 621**	**1 147**	**1 882**	**1 884**	**1 556**
4100 Impôts périodiques sur la propriété immobilière	..	..	..	738	1 024	1 149	637	1 140	1 250	905
Taxe unique sur le patrimoine	..	..	..	738	1 024	1 149	637	1 140	1 250	905
4110 Ménages	..	..	..	..	..	..	..	..	..	..
4120 Autres agents	..	..	..	..	..	..	..	..	..	..
4200 Impôts périodiques sur l'actif net	0	0	0	0	0	0	0	0	0	0
4210 Personnes physiques	..	..	..	..	..	..	..	..	..	..
4220 Sociétés	..	..	..	..	..	..	..	..	..	..
4300 Impôts sur mut. par décès, succ. et donations	0	0	0	0	0	0	0	0	0	0
4310 Impôts sur mut. par décès et successions	..	..	..	..	..	..	..	..	..	..
4320 Impôts sur les donations	..	..	..	..	..	..	..	..	..	..
4400 Impôts sur transact. mobilières et immob.	332	584	810	701	582	472	509	742	634	651
4500 Impôts non-périodiques	0	0	0	0	0	0	0	0	0	0
4510 Sur l'actif net	..	..	..	..	..	..	..	..	..	..
4520 Autres non-périodiques	..	..	..	..	..	..	..	..	..	..
4600 Autres impôts périodiques sur patrimoine	0	0	0	0	0	0	0	0	0	0
5000 Impôts sur les biens et services	**3 853**	**5 908**	**11 670**	**16 917**	**19 370**	**20 479**	**23 055**	**26 079**	**26 681**	**21 507**
5100 Impôts sur production, vente, transfert, etc.	3 853	5 908	11 670	16 917	19 370	20 479	23 055	26 079	26 681	21 507
5110 Impôts généraux	0	0	6 409	10 035	10 824	11 017	12 646	15 139	15 048	12 589
5111 Taxes sur la valeur ajoutée	..	..	6 409	10 035	10 824	11 017	12 646	15 139	15 048	12 589
TVA à l'importation (brute) - DGA	..	..	4 192	6 180	6 358	6 601	7 260	7 801	8 260	6 670
TVA intérieure (brute) - DGCI	..	..	2 359	4 341	4 935	5 385	6 046	8 412	8 468	6 371
Remboursements de la TVA	..	..	-143	-486	-469	-969	-661	-1 074	-1 679	-452
5112 Impôts sur les ventes	..	..	0	0	0	0	0	0	0	0
5113 Autres impôts	..	..	0	0	0	0	0	0	0	0
5120 Impôts sur biens et services déterminés	3 853	5 908	5 261	6 882	8 546	9 462	10 409	10 940	11 633	8 918
5121 Accises	1 197	1 938	1 030	1 494	2 073	2 228	2 621	2 680	2 931	2 295
Taxe spéciale sur la consommation	1 197	1 812	838	1 227	1 478	1 550	1 937	1 963	2 192	1 702
Taxe écologique	0	126	192	267	595	678	684	717	739	593
5122 Bénéfices des monopoles fiscaux	0	0	0	0	0	0	0	0	0	0
5123 Droits de douane et droits à l'importation	2 656	3 971	4 231	5 388	5 827	6 523	6 906	7 409	7 672	6 296
5124 Taxes à l'exportation	0	0	0	0	0	0	0	0	0	0
5125 Impôts sur biens d'équipement	0	0	0	0	0	0	0	0	0	0
5126 Impôts sur services déterminés	0	0	0	0	645	711	881	851	1 030	327
Contribution touristique	..	..	..	..	645	711	849	811	992	297
Autres (taxe incendie, taxe touristique)	..	..	..	..	0	0	32	40	38	30
5127 Autres impôts sur commerce et transact. internat.	0	0	0	0	0	0	0	0	0	0
5128 Autres impôts	0	0	0	0	0	0	0	0	0	0
5130 Non ventilables entre 5110 et 5120	0	0	0	0	0	0	0	0	0	0

Table 5.3. **Cabo Verde** *(cont.)*

Details of tax revenue / Recettes fiscales détaillées

Million CVE

	1995	2000	2005	2010	2015	2016	2017	2018	2019	2020
5200 Impôts sur utilisation des biens et exerc. activites	0	0	0	0	0	0	0	0	0	0
5210 Impôts périodiques	..	..	..	..	..	..	..	..	..	..
5211 A la charge des ménages: véhicules à moteur	..	..	..	..	..	..	..	..	..	..
5212 A la charge autres agents: véhicules à moteur	..	..	..	..	..	..	..	..	..	..
5213 Autres impôts périodiques	..	..	..	..	..	..	..	..	..	..
5220 Impôts non-périodiques	..	..	..	..	..	..	..	..	..	..
5300 Non ventilables entre 5100 et 5200	0	0	0	0	0	0	0	0	0	0
6000 Autres impôts	**0**	**0**	**0**	**0**	**0**	**0**	**0**	**0**	**0**	**0**
6100 A la charge exclusive des entreprises	..	..	..	..	..	..	..	..	..	..
6200 A la charge d'autres agents	..	..	..	..	..	..	..	..	..	..
Pour mémoire : *Prélèvement communautaire de la CEDEAO*	0	67	156	245	254	290	317	324	339	297

.. Non disponible

Note : Année civile se terminant le 31 décembre.

Les données sont sur la base des encaissements.

Rubrique 4100 : Cette rubrique comprend les recettes provenant de la taxe unique sur le patrimoine (Imposto Único sobre o Património), recettes collectées par les municipalités de Cabo Verde.

Rubrique 4400 : Cette rubrique comprend les droits de timbre, classifiés au Cabo Verde dans la rubrique « autres impôts ».

Rubrique 5126 : La taxe incendie et la taxe touristique sont classifiées dans la rubrique « autres impôts » au Cabo Verde.

Le prélèvement communautaire de la CEDEAO (Communauté économique des États de l'Afrique de l'Ouest) n'est pas compris parmi les impôts selon le *Guide d'interprétation de l'OCDE* (voir § 4). La classification nationale du Cabo Verde le compte comme une recette fiscale. Cette recette qui n'est pas comprise dans le total des recettes fiscales ou des recettes non fiscales est présentée à titre de rubrique « Pour mémoire » dans le tableau 6.7 du chapitre 6.

Source : Ministère des Finances et du Plan du Cabo Verde.

StatLink *https://stat.link/r0gbus*

Table 5.4. **Cameroon / Cameroun**

Details of tax revenue / Recettes fiscales détaillées

Million XAF

	1995	2000	2005	2010	2015	2016	2017	2018	2019	2020
Recettes fiscales totales	**481 383**	**810 500**	**1 135 257**	**1 571 695**	**2 687 926**	**2 743 908**	**2 935 179**	**3 146 494**	**3 222 162**	**3 014 088**
1000 Impôts sur revenu, bénéfices et gains en capital	**115 300**	**228 100**	**325 764**	**425 741**	**867 834**	**771 155**	**741 551**	**848 398**	**882 190**	**863 643**
1100 Des personnes physiques	55 400	87 100	66 598	102 793	185 512	179 475	200 845	247 546	226 293	221 249
1110 Sur le revenu et les bénéfices	55 400	87 100	66 548	102 728	184 213	177 669	199 386	246 321	225 213	219 377
Traitements, salaires, pensions et rentes viagères	37 100	60 800	17 722	86 440	135 738	131 524	139 280	165 187	150 396	152 945
Revenus fonciers	0	0	2 225	2 402	12 405	12 716	13 058	14 401	12 442	12 865
Bénéfices artisanaux, industriels et commerciaux	0	0	3 904	5 342	21 010	15 689	26 107	29 610	35 745	28 826
Bénéfices agricoles	0	0	77	47	56	31	30	161	253	23
Bénéfices des professions non commerciales	0	0	249	295	2 875	5 687	9 750	24 643	14 865	13 387
Autres impôts sur le revenu	18 300	26 300	42 372	8 202	12 130	12 022	11 162	12 319	11 511	11 332
1120 Sur les gains en capital	..	..	50	65	1 299	1 806	1 459	1 225	1 079	1 872
Impôts sur plus-values sur cession immobilière	..	..	46	46	1 297	1 803	1 440	1 223	1 079	1 871
Impôts sur les autres gains en capital	..	..	3	19	2	3	19	2	0	1
1200 Des sociétés	58 800	119 400	217 495	256 404	538 969	460 785	385 971	441 882	457 428	459 160
1210 Sur les bénéfices	58 800	119 400	217 495	256 404	538 969	460 785	385 971	441 882	457 428	459 160
Bénéfices des sociétés pétrolières	28 600	39 000	76 523	83 764	171 891	108 966	66 471	86 948	113 018	106 845
Bénéfices des sociétés non pétrolières	30 200	80 400	140 972	172 639	367 078	351 818	319 500	354 934	344 410	352 315
1220 Sur les gains en capital	..	..	..	..	..	..	..	..	..	..
1300 Non ventilables entre 1100 et 1200	1 100	21 600	41 671	66 544	143 352	130 896	154 735	158 970	198 470	183 234
Taxe spéciale sur les revenus payés à l'étranger	0	12 400	19 198	38 877	84 412	68 691	62 806	67 809	91 879	85 517
Impôts sur les revenus des capitaux mobiliers	1 100	9 200	21 619	27 629	48 774	39 350	42 155	42 715	47 612	54 227
Centimes communaux sur l'impôt sur le revenu	0	0	854	39	10 166	22 855	49 774	48 446	58 978	43 490
2000 Cotisations de sécurité sociale	**40 183**	**65 500**	**83 903**	**135 747**	**160 992**	**200 960**	**213 796**	**226 610**	**235 937**	**243 702**
2100 A la charge des salariés	11 294	19 747	24 123	33 297	44 669	44 655	45 763	48 105	45 565	55 342
2110 Sur la base du salaire	11 294	19 747	24 123	33 297	44 669	44 655	45 763	48 105	45 565	55 342
2120 Sur la base de l'impôt sur le revenu	0	0	0	0	0	0	0	0	0	0
2200 A la charge des employeurs	..	..	..	..	..	..	..	..	..	..
2210 Sur la base du salaire	..	..	..	..	..	..	..	..	..	..
2220 Sur la base de l'impôt sur le revenu	..	..	..	..	..	..	..	..	..	..
2300 A charge des travailleurs indép. ou sans emploi	..	..	..	..	..	..	..	..	..	..
2310 Sur la base du salaire	..	..	..	..	..	..	..	..	..	..
2320 Sur la base de l'impôt sur le revenu	..	..	..	..	..	..	..	..	..	..
2400 Non ventilables entre 2100, 2200 et 2300	28 889	45 753	59 780	102 450	116 323	156 305	168 033	178 505	190 372	188 360
2410 Sur la base du salaire	28 889	45 753	59 780	102 450	116 323	156 305	168 033	178 505	190 372	188 360
2420 Sur la base de l'impôt sur le revenu	0	0	0	0	0	0	0	0	0	0
3000 Sur salaires ou main-d'œuvre	**0**	**0**	**8 644**	**17 860**	**53 572**	**52 826**	**54 350**	**32 131**	**36 046**	**35 521**
4000 Impôts sur le patrimoine	**7 900**	**13 100**	**13 361**	**18 003**	**25 437**	**30 471**	**33 393**	**25 311**	**27 113**	**25 639**
4100 Impôts périodiques sur la propriété immobilière	500	500	1 318	1 552	1 743	3 905	3 652	2 443	2 249	2 044
4110 Ménages	..	..	..	..	..	..	..	..	..	..
4120 Autres agents	..	..	..	..	..	..	..	..	..	..
4200 Impôts périodiques sur l'actif net	0	0	0	0	0	0	0	0	0	0
4210 Personnes physiques	..	..	..	..	..	..	..	..	..	..
4220 Sociétés	..	..	..	..	..	..	..	..	..	..
4300 Impôts sur mut. par décès, succ. et donations	0	0	33	39	62	160	60	86	38	180
4310 Impôts sur mut. par décès et successions	..	..	33	39	62	160	60	86	38	180
4320 Impôts sur les donations	..	..	0	0	0	0	0	0	0	0
4400 Impôts sur transact. mobilières et immob.	7 400	12 600	12 010	16 412	23 632	26 406	29 681	22 782	24 827	23 415
Droits d'enregistrement sur les mutations entre vifs	..	..	82	32	391	376	577	76	301	46
Droits d'enrgmnt. sur les mutations immob.	..	..	1 909	2 747	3 080	2 921	3 107	3 924	4 991	5 005
Droits de bail	..	..	3 976	4 602	2 364	2 425	2 452	2 395	2 802	2 517
Droits autres mutations et transactions	..	..	6 043	9 031	17 797	20 685	23 545	16 388	16 733	15 847
4500 Impôts non-périodiques	0	0	0	0	0	0	0	0	0	0
4510 Sur l'actif net	..	..	..	..	..	..	..	..	..	..
4520 Autres non-périodiques	..	..	..	..	..	..	..	..	..	..
4600 Autres impôts périodiques sur patrimoine	0	0	0	0	0	0	0	0	0	0
5000 Impôts sur les biens et services	**318 000**	**503 800**	**686 416**	**944 412**	**1 532 668**	**1 642 804**	**1 844 728**	**1 958 026**	**1 963 031**	**1 763 852**
5100 Impôts sur production, vente, transfert, etc.	315 100	501 100	679 379	936 564	1 522 834	1 632 420	1 834 787	1 948 068	1 952 839	1 754 298
5110 Impôts généraux	139 600	260 900	360 218	490 521	883 618	928 368	1 066 216	1 158 458	1 138 354	941 804
5111 Taxes sur la valeur ajoutée	0	260 900	360 218	490 513	883 580	928 368	1 066 216	1 158 458	1 138 354	941 804
TVA intérieure (brute)	..	186 500	251 019	299 504	604 046	629 355	803 903	846 136	810 285	700 919
TVA à la porte (brute)	..	107 300	157 799	259 343	354 701	355 033	344 389	384 310	394 070	319 879
Remboursements de la TVA	..	-32 900	-48 600	-68 333	-75 167	-56 020	-82 076	-71 988	-66 002	-78 995
5112 Impôts sur les ventes	0	0	0	0	0	0	0	0	0	0
5113 Autres impôts	139 600	0	0	8	39	0	0	0	0	0

Table 5.4. **Cameroon / Cameroun** *(cont.)*

Details of tax revenue / Recettes fiscales détaillées

Million XAF

	1995	2000	2005	2010	2015	2016	2017	2018	2019	2020
5120 Impôts sur biens et services déterminés	175 500	240 200	319 161	446 043	639 216	704 052	768 571	789 609	814 485	812 494
5121 Accises	55 800	84 000	114 306	164 943	289 280	323 562	334 313	337 533	380 616	430 287
Droits d'accises intérieure	18 300	26 500	42 754	68 414	170 164	204 785	193 857	192 954	217 381	255 610
Droits d'accises à la porte	800	1 900	2 198	12 936	14 608	12 662	17 872	16 655	33 798	38 440
Taxe spéciale sur les produits pétroliers	36 700	55 600	69 345	82 962	103 773	105 579	122 036	127 456	128 709	135 652
Vignette sur tabac et produits manufacturés	0	0	8	632	736	537	548	469	728	585
5122 Bénéfices des monopoles fiscaux	0	0	0	0	0	0	0	0	0	0
5123 Droits de douane et droits à l'importation	62 400	119 900	189 364	261 731	320 314	350 705	397 478	394 169	386 778	336 729
5124 Taxes à l'exportation	56 400	24 300	1 725	8 793	17 133	16 330	22 654	36 581	31 799	38 440
5125 Impôts sur biens d'équipement	0	0	0	0	0	0	0	0	0	0
5126 Impôts sur services déterminés	900	1 100	3 108	3 600	5 035	6 387	6 059	12 271	13 889	6 387
5127 Autres impôts sur commerce et transact. internat.	0	0	0	0	0	0	0	0	0	0
5128 Autres impôts	0	10 900	10 658	6 977	7 454	7 068	8 068	9 054	1 403	650
5130 Non ventilables entre 5110 et 5120	0	0	0	0	0	0	0	0	0	0
5200 Impôts sur utilisation des biens et exerc. activités	2 900	2 700	7 037	7 848	9 835	10 385	9 940	9 959	10 193	9 553
5210 Impôts périodiques	2 900	2 700	7 037	7 848	9 835	10 385	9 940	9 959	10 193	9 553
5211 A la charge des ménages: véhicules à moteur	2 200	1 600	4 987	6 111	7 539	8 050	7 386	7 000	7 000	7 000
5212 A la charge autres agents: véhicules à moteur	700	1 100	1 902	1 663	2 213	2 205	2 451	2 710	2 859	2 418
5213 Autres impôts périodiques	0	0	149	74	83	130	103	248	334	136
5220 Impôts non-périodiques	0	0	0	0	0	0	0	0	0	0
5300 Non ventilables entre 5100 et 5200	0	0	0	0	0	0	0	0	0	0
6000 Autres impôts	**0**	**0**	**17 169**	**29 932**	**47 424**	**45 692**	**47 360**	**56 018**	**77 845**	**81 731**
6100 A la charge exclusive des entreprises	..	..	..	..	..	..	..	..	..	..
6200 A la charge d'autres agents	..	..	..	..	..	..	..	..	..	..

.. Non disponible

Note : Année civile se terminant le 31 décembre.

Les données sont sur la base des encaissements.

Les chiffres n'incluent pas les recettes fiscales collectées par les collectivités locales car elles ne sont pas disponibles.

Rubrique 2000 : Les cotisations de sécurité sociale du secteur public (APU) incluent uniquement les cotisations pour les retraites et ne couvrent pas les prestations familiales et d'invalidité.

Rubrique 5111 : Les données antérieures à 1999 correspondent aux recettes de la taxe sur le chiffre d'affaire (TCA) et ont été reclassées dans la rubrique « 5113 Autres impôts généraux sur les biens et services » La TVA a été introduite au Cameroun en 1999. Dans cette édition, les données des recettes TVA sont présentées nettes des remboursements TVA comme le préconise la classification OCDE (voir le Guide d'interprétation en Annexe A).

Source : Ministère des Finances du Cameroun.

StatLink https://stat.link/invs32

Table 5.5. **Chad / Tchad**

Details of tax revenue / Recettes fiscales détaillées

Million XAF

	1995	2000	2005	2010	2015	2016	2017	2018	2019	2020
Recettes fiscales totales	..	..	..	**773 265**	**374 178**	**284 409**	**361 952**	**482 781**	**519 374**	**901 890**
1000 Impôts sur revenu, bénéfices et gains en capital	..	..	..	**599 849**	**210 813**	**129 769**	**173 818**	**255 820**	**251 862**	**578 849**
1100 Des personnes physiques	..	..	..	55 020	94 216	86 497	88 590	88 445	105 077	124 911
1110 Sur le revenu et les bénéfices	..	..	..	55 020	94 216	86 497	88 590	88 445	105 077	124 911
Salariés, Bénéficiaires des pensions et rentes viagères	..	..	..	45 127	62 041	61 862	62 232	45 048	75 996	66 857
Bénéfice des proféssions libérales (non commerciales)	..	..	..	4 877	21 221	14 983	13 095	18 587	19 740	48 205
Bénéfice industriel et commercial	..	..	..	0	82	1 093	1 644	1 059	96	1 908
Propriétaires fonciers	..	..	..	1 470	2 434	281	1 094	7 077	2 098	1 337
Revenus des capitaux et valeurs mobilières	..	..	..	3 546	8 438	8 278	10 526	16 674	7 147	6 604
1120 Sur les gains en capital	..	..	..	0	0	0	0	0	0	0
1200 Des sociétés	..	..	..	539 410	114 480	41 350	83 464	165 042	140 200	452 400
1210 Sur les bénéfices	..	..	..	539 410	114 480	41 350	83 464	165 042	140 200	452 400
Impots sur les bénéfices des sociétés pétrolières	..	..	..	464 428	41 797	4 620	32 339	115 930	93 866	415 990
Impots sur les bénéfices des sociétés non-pétrolières	..	..	..	53 381	60 901	29 937	43 741	39 784	30 091	13 907
Autres impôts sur les sociétés	..	..	..	21 601	11 782	6 794	7 384	9 329	16 243	22 504
1220 Sur les gains en capital	..	..	..	0	0	0	0	0	0	0
1300 Non ventilables entre 1100 et 1200	..	..	..	5 418	2 118	1 921	1 763	2 333	6 585	1 538
2000 Cotisations de sécurité sociale	..	..	..	..	..	..	..	..	..	..
2100 A la charge des salariés	..	..	..	..	..	..	..	..	..	..
2110 Sur la base du salaire	..	..	..	..	..	..	..	..	..	..
2120 Sur la base de l'impôt sur les revenus	..	..	..	..	..	..	..	..	..	..
2200 A la charge des employeurs	..	..	..	..	..	..	..	..	..	..
2210 Sur la base du salaire	..	..	..	..	..	..	..	..	..	..
2220 Sur la base de l'impôt sur le revenu	..	..	..	..	..	..	..	..	..	..
2300 A charge des travailleurs indép. ou sans emploi	..	..	..	..	..	..	..	..	..	..
2310 Sur la base du salaire	..	..	..	..	..	..	..	..	..	..
2320 Sur la base de l'impôt sur le revenu	..	..	..	..	..	..	..	..	..	..
2400 Non ventilables entre 2100, 2200 et 2300	..	..	..	..	..	..	..	..	..	..
2410 Sur la base du salaire	..	..	..	..	..	..	..	..	..	..
2420 Sur la base de l'impôt sur le revenu	..	..	..	..	..	..	..	..	..	..
3000 Sur salaires ou main-d'œuvre	..	..	..	**8 304**	**10 856**	**6 703**	**6 860**	**1 512**	**8 058**	**12 397**
4000 Impôts sur le patrimoine	..	..	..	**23 875**	**11 922**	**7 909**	**5 740**	**7 041**	**23 620**	**31 309**
4100 Impôts périodiques sur la propriété immobilière	..	..	..	0	0	0	0	0	0	0
4110 Ménages	..	..	..	..	..	..	..	..	..	..
4120 Autres agents	..	..	..	..	..	..	..	..	..	..
4200 Impôts périodiques sur l'actif net	..	..	..	0	0	0	0	0	0	0
4210 Personnes physiques	..	..	..	..	..	..	..	..	..	..
4220 Sociétés	..	..	..	..	..	..	..	..	..	..
4300 Impôts sur mut. par décès, succ. et donations	..	..	..	71	0	0	1	12	1	0
4310 Impôts sur mut. par décès et successions	..	..	..	8	0	0	0	1	0	0
4320 Impôts sur les donations	..	..	..	63	0	0	1	12	1	0
4400 Impôts sur transact. mobilières et immob.	..	..	..	23 651	11 473	7 713	5 630	6 911	23 386	31 022
4500 Impôts non-périodiques	..	..	..	153	449	197	109	118	233	288
4510 Sur l'actif net	..	..	..	0	0	0	0	0	0	0
4520 Autres non-périodiques	..	..	..	153	449	197	109	118	233	288
4600 Autres impôts périodiques sur patrimoine	..	..	..	0	0	0	0	0	0	0
5000 Impôts sur les biens et services	..	..	..	**141 171**	**140 525**	**139 995**	**175 473**	**218 349**	**235 751**	**279 105**
5100 Impôts sur production, vente, transfert, etc.	..	..	..	139 026	138 375	138 379	174 252	209 235	233 597	267 313
5110 Impôts généraux	..	..	..	76 549	66 730	86 646	100 815	72 160	98 038	103 449
5111 Taxes sur la valeur ajoutée	..	..	..	76 549	66 730	86 646	100 815	72 160	98 038	103 449
Taxe sur la valeur ajoutée intérieure	..	..	..	46 148	45 476	56 619	69 912	39 374	55 598	59 254
TVA a l'importation	..	..	..	30 401	21 254	30 027	30 903	32 786	42 440	44 195
5112 Impôts sur les ventes	..	..	..	0	0	0	0	0	0	0
5113 Autres impôts	..	..	..	0	0	0	0	0	0	0
5120 Impôts sur biens et services déterminés	..	..	..	62 477	71 644	51 733	73 437	137 075	135 559	163 865
5121 Accises	..	..	..	9 387	10 161	11 436	22 541	31 307	34 947	30 234
Droit d'accises intérieurs	..	..	..	2 356	7 045	7 921	15 678	7 111	11 575	5 412
Droit d'accises importation	..	..	..	243	125	733	2 460	1 261	3 917	1 808
Carburants et lubrifiants	..	..	..	6 168	1 814	1 538	2 544	16 888	13 751	21 692
Taxe sur vente de bétail	..	..	..	621	1 177	1 243	1 859	1 581	1 734	1 322
Taxe intérieure sur les produits pétroliers	..	..	..	0	0	1	0	4 466	3 970	0
5122 Bénéfices de monopoles fiscaux	..	..	..	0	0	0	0	0	0	0

Table 5.5. **Chad / Tchad** *(cont.)*

Details of tax revenue / Recettes fiscales détaillées

Million XAF

	1995	2000	2005	2010	2015	2016	2017	2018	2019	2020
5123 Droits de douane et droits à l'importation	..	..	..	33 151	48 642	35 700	44 570	79 650	82 129	89 397
Droits de douane	..	..	..	26 441	44 056	31 167	31 229	51 448	54 869	67 357
Redevance statistique	..	..	..	6 709	4 586	4 533	13 341	28 202	27 260	22 040
5124 Taxes à l'exportation	..	..	..	19 078	12 375	3 832	5 683	8 152	5 224	24 960
Redevance statistique consortium	..	..	..	16 821	9 611	2 052	1 860	3 816	2 505	23 220
Droits de sortie	..	..	..	2 257	2 764	1 780	3 823	4 336	2 719	1 740
5125 Impôts sur biens d'équipement	..	..	..	0	0	0	0	0	0	0
5126 Impôts sur services déterminés	..	..	..	775	431	535	614	17 851	13 126	19 142
5127 Autres impôts sur commerce et transact. internat.	..	..	..	0	0	0	0	0	0	0
5128 Autres impôts	..	..	..	86	35	230	30	115	133	131
5130 Non ventilables entre 5110 et 5120	..	..	..	0	0	0	0	0	0	0
5200 Impôts sur utilisation des biens et exerc. activites	..	..	..	2 145	2 150	1 617	1 221	9 114	2 154	11 792
5210 Impôts périodiques	..	..	..	2 145	2 150	1 617	1 221	9 114	2 154	11 792
5211 A la charge des ménages: véhicules à moteur	..	..	..	1 567	1 929	1 355	694	8 829	519	8 317
5212 A la charge autres agents: véhicules à moteur	..	..	..	204	144	135	395	74	313	35
5213 Autres impôts périodiques	..	..	..	374	77	127	132	211	1 322	3 440
5220 Impôts non-périodiques	..	..	..	0	0	0	0	0	0	0
5300 Non ventilables entre 5100 et 5200	..	..	..	0	0	0	0	0	0	0
6000 Autres impôts	**..**	**..**	**..**	**67**	**62**	**33**	**61**	**59**	**83**	**230**
6100 A la charge exclusive des entreprises	..	..	..	..	..	..	..	..	..	..
6200 A la charge d'autres agents	..	..	..	..	..	..	..	..	..	..

.. Non disponible

Note : Année civile se terminant le 31 décembre.

Les données sont sur la base des encaissements.

Les chiffres n'incluent pas les recettes fiscales collectées par les collectivités locales car elles ne sont pas disponibles.

Les recettes provenant des amendes fiscales, des recettes des valeurs mobilières de l'État et de la redevance audiovisuelle sont incluses dans les recettes non fiscales comme le préconise la classification OCDE (voir le *Guide d'interprétation* en Annexe A). La classification nationale du Tchad les comptabilise comme des recettes fiscales.

Source : Ministère des Finances et du Budget du Tchad.

StatLink https://stat.link/l860mw

Table 5.6. **Congo**

Details of tax revenue / Recettes fiscales détaillées

Million XAF

	1995	2000	2005	2010	2015	2016	2017	2018	2019	2020
Recettes fiscales totales	..	**98 684**	**206 416**	**454 298**	**904 335**	**800 746**	**697 009**	**566 420**	**609 101**	**585 818**
1000 Impôts sur revenu, bénéfices et gains en capital	..	**47 544**	**62 458**	**151 128**	**348 011**	**312 146**	**278 082**	**138 956**	**183 900**	**179 210**
1100 Des personnes physiques	..	22 850	28 265	64 700	150 869	152 392	154 434	114 722	111 996	107 221
1110 Sur le revenu et les bénéfices	..	22 850	28 265	64 700	150 869	152 392	154 434	114 722	111 996	107 221
Traitements et salaires	..	21 836	22 581	54 763	103 818	99 671	113 244	103 858	101 282	94 784
Revenus fonciers	..	549	1 079	2 259	5 531	6 020	3 534	3 658	3 433	3 582
Bénéfices non commerciaux (BNC)	..	0	62	112	50	19	37	1 377	2 098	7 881
Bénéfices industriels et commerciaux (BIC)	..	0	468	25	152	307	143	175	1 119	339
Revenu des valeurs mobilières (IRVM)	..	466	4 075	7 176	35 441	41 625	35 517	5 427	0	0
Retenues à la source	..	0	0	0	471	407	313	221	1 817	633
Autres recettes sur le revenu des personnes physiques	..	0	0	365	5 406	4 345	1 646	6	2 247	2
1120 Sur les gains en capital	..	0	0	0	0	0	0	0	0	0
1200 Des sociétés	..	24 694	34 193	86 428	197 141	159 753	123 648	24 233	71 904	71 990
1210 Sur les bénéfices	..	24 694	34 193	86 428	197 141	159 753	123 648	24 233	71 904	71 990
1220 Sur les gains en capital	..	0	0	0	0	0	0	0	0	0
1300 Non ventilables entre 1100 et 1200	..	0	0	0	0	0	0	0	0	0
2000 Cotisations de sécurité sociale	..	..	..	..	..	..	..	..	..	..
2100 A la charge des salariés	..	..	..	..	..	..	..	..	..	..
2110 Sur la base du salaire	..	..	..	..	..	..	..	..	..	..
2120 Sur la base de l'impôt sur le revenu	..	..	..	..	..	..	..	..	..	..
2200 A la charge des employeurs	..	..	..	..	..	..	..	..	..	..
2210 Sur la base du salaire	..	..	..	..	..	..	..	..	..	..
2220 Sur la base de l'impôt sur le revenu	..	..	..	..	..	..	..	..	..	..
2300 A charge des travailleurs indép. ou sans emploi	..	..	..	..	..	..	..	..	..	..
2310 Sur la base du salaire	..	..	..	..	..	..	..	..	..	..
2320 Sur la base de l'impôt sur le revenu	..	..	..	..	..	..	..	..	..	..
2400 Non ventilables entre 2100, 2200 et 2300	..	..	..	..	..	..	..	..	..	..
2410 Sur la base du salaire	..	..	..	..	..	..	..	..	..	..
2420 Sur la base de l'impôt sur le revenu	..	..	..	..	..	..	..	..	..	..
3000 Sur salaires ou main-d'œuvre	..	**4 965**	**3 455**	**16 585**	**24 528**	**22 754**	**22 962**	**20 436**	**17 356**	**16 466**
4000 Impôts sur le patrimoine	..	**1 299**	**1 571**	**3 052**	**15 070**	**4 145**	**5 021**	**10 110**	**14 265**	**12 004**
4100 Impôts périodiques sur la propriété immobilière	..	0	0	0	0	0	0	0	0	0
4110 Ménages	..	..	..	..	..	..	..	..	..	..
4120 Autres agents	..	..	..	..	..	..	..	..	..	..
4200 Impôts périodiques sur l'actif net	..	0	0	0	0	0	0	0	0	0
4210 Personnes physiques	..	..	..	..	..	..	..	..	..	..
4220 Sociétés	..	..	..	..	..	..	..	..	..	..
4300 Impôts sur mut. par décès, succ. et donations	..	0	0	0	0	0	0	0	0	0
4310 Impôts sur mut. par décès et successions	..	..	..	..	..	..	..	..	..	..
4320 Impôts sur les donations	..	..	..	..	..	..	..	..	..	..
4400 Impôts sur transact. mobilières et immob.	..	1 299	1 571	3 052	15 070	4 145	5 021	10 110	14 265	12 004
4500 Impôts non-périodiques	..	0	0	0	0	0	0	0	0	0
4510 Sur l'actif net	..	..	..	..	..	..	..	..	..	..
4520 Autres non-périodiques	..	..	..	..	..	..	..	..	..	..
4600 Autres impôts périodiques sur patrimoine	..	0	0	0	0	0	0	0	0	0
5000 Impôts sur les biens et services	..	**44 876**	**138 932**	**281 274**	**515 385**	**459 867**	**389 929**	**396 133**	**391 993**	**377 294**
5100 Impôts sur production, vente, transfert, etc.	..	44 809	138 834	280 869	513 854	458 170	388 864	394 360	389 284	372 668
5110 Impôts généraux	..	39 641	78 187	158 512	284 586	251 308	222 924	242 924	228 784	218 280
5111 Taxes sur la valeur ajoutée	..	36 889	75 247	147 032	253 875	221 768	191 438	149 926	156 262	154 519
TVA Intérieure (brute)	..	38 962	54 294	92 054	163 875	140 255	125 630	95 165	93 529	93 963
TVA Douane (brute)	..	0	23 744	57 110	90 000	81 512	67 756	54 761	62 733	60 556
Remboursements de la TVA	..	-2 073	-2 791	-2 132	0	0	-1 948	0	0	0
5112 Impôts sur les ventes	..	0	0	1 742	2 214	2 175	2 145	2 568	1 980	2 146
ASDI (Acompte sur divers impôts)	..	0	0	1 742	2 214	2 175	2 145	2 568	1 980	2 146
5113 Autres impôts	..	2 753	2 940	9 738	28 497	27 366	29 340	90 430	70 542	61 616
Taxe spéciale sur les societés (TSS)	..	2 753	2 940	9 738	26 248	25 999	28 288	23 758	24 907	25 107
Impôt global forfaitaire	..	0	0	0	2 250	1 366	1 052	830	850	899
Impôt forfaitaire sur les sociétés	..	0	0	0	0	0	0	57 916	36 860	31 097
Impôt forfaitaire sur le revenu des valeurs mobilières	..	0	0	0	0	0	0	7 925	7 925	4 513
5120 Impôts sur biens et services déterminés	..	5 059	60 506	122 357	229 268	206 862	165 940	149 746	159 863	154 155
5121 Accises	..	4 966	8 313	17 603	24 337	24 112	24 311	22 207	21 356	15 214
Taxe speciale sur les boissons alcoolisées et le tabac	..	0	0	0	11 140	11 320	10 114	9 351	8 649	2 073
Droits d'accises	..	4 966	8 313	17 603	13 197	12 792	14 197	12 855	12 566	12 955

Table 5.6. **Congo** *(cont.)*

Details of tax revenue / Recettes fiscales détaillées

Million XAF

	1995	2000	2005	2010	2015	2016	2017	2018	2019	2020
Taxe spécif. sur les boissons (TSB) - douanes	..	0	0	0	0	0	0	0	140	186
Taxe spécifique sur le tabac (TST) - douanes	..	0	0	0	0	0	0	0	1	0
5122 Bénéfices des monopoles fiscaux	..	0	0	0	0	0	0	0	0	0
5123 Droits de douane et droits à l'importation	..	0	44 446	85 775	166 613	139 716	106 503	91 286	104 670	106 173
Recettes importation	..	0	41 022	77 852	148 444	125 944	94 833	80 210	92 640	93 544
Recettes douanes hors budget	..	0	3 424	7 923	18 169	13 771	11 670	11 076	12 030	12 629
5124 Taxes à l'exportation	..	0	0	0	0	0	617	5 380	3 220	1 502
5125 Impôts sur biens d'équipement	..	0	0	0	0	0	0	0	0	0
5126 Impôts sur services déterminés	..	93	7 746	18 979	38 318	43 034	34 509	30 873	30 618	31 266
Taxe sur les billets d'avion	..	0	0	597	849	791	721	634	624	256
Taxe sur les télécommunications électroniques	..	0	0	0	0	3 596	4 306	5 564	6 378	6 947
Taxe sur les assurances	..	93	687	1 526	2 703	2 250	2 418	2 741	3 639	3 567
Taxe sur le transfert de fonds	..	0	7 060	16 856	34 766	36 394	27 049	21 906	19 912	20 474
Taxe sur les jeux de hasard	..	0	0	0	0	3	14	27	64	21
5127 Autres impôts sur commerce et transact. internat.	..	0	0	0	0	0	0	0	0	0
5128 Autres impôts	..	0	0	0	0	0	0	0	0	0
5130 Non ventilables entre 5110 et 5120	..	109	141	0	0	0	0	1 690	637	232
5200 Impôts sur utilisation des biens et exerc. activites	..	67	98	405	1 531	1 697	1 065	1 774	2 709	4 626
5210 Impôts périodiques	..	67	98	405	1 531	1 697	1 065	1 598	2 368	4 288
5211 A la charge des ménages: véhicules à moteur	..	0	0	0	0	0	0	0	0	0
5212 A la charge autres agents: véhicules à moteur	..	67	98	343	1 405	1 006	887	814	746	1 174
5213 Autres impôts périodiques	..	0	0	62	126	691	178	784	1 622	3 114
Taxe sur abonnements et réabonnements télévisuelles	..	..	..	0	0	0	0	0	1 495	2 966
Redevance audiovisuelle	..	..	..	52	126	83	178	764	127	148
Droits de Chasse	..	..	..	10	0	608	0	20	0	0
5220 Impôts non-périodiques	..	0	0	0	0	0	0	176	341	339
Timbres sur les véhicules automobiles	..	..	..	..	..	..	..	176	341	339
5300 Non ventilables entre 5100 et 5200	..	0	0	0	0	0	0	0	0	0
6000 Autres impôts	**..**	**0**	**0**	**2 259**	**1 340**	**1 834**	**1 015**	**785**	**1 587**	**844**
6100 A la charge exclusive des entreprises	..	..	..	..	..	..	..	..	..	..
6200 A la charge d'autres agents	..	..	..	..	..	..	..	..	..	..

.. Non disponible

Note : Année civile se terminant le 31 décembre.

Les données sont sur la base des encaissements.

Les chiffres n'incluent pas les recettes fiscales collectées par les collectivités locales car elles ne sont pas disponibles.

Rubrique 1210 : Cette rubrique inclut les recettes de l'impôt forfaitaire sur les sociétés et de l'impôt forfaitaire sur le revenu des valeurs mobilières des sociétés pour les années à partir de 1998 à 2017 car il n'a pas été possible de les distinguer des recettes de l'impôt sur les sociétés.

Rubrique 5113 : Cette rubrique inclut les recettes de l'impôt forfaitaire sur les sociétés et de l'impôt forfaitaire sur le revenu des valeurs mobilières des sociétés à partir de 2018 comme le préconise la classification OCDE (voir le *Guide d'interprétation* en Annexe A). La classification nationale de la république du Congo les comptabilise comme des recettes sur les bénéfices des sociétés.

Rubrique 5123 : Les droits d'exportation et des accises perçues à la douane sont inclus dans les données pour la période 2002-2016 car il n'a pas été possible de ventiler ces recettes.

Rubrique 5123 : Les droits d'exportation pour la période 2002-2016 sont inclus dans la rubrique 5123 car il n'a pas été possible de ventiler ces recettes.

Source : Ministère des Finances de la République du Congo.

StatLink https://stat.link/48rwph

Table 5.7. **Congo, Dem. Rep. / Congo, Rép. dém.**

Details of tax revenue / Recettes fiscales détaillées

Million CDF

	1995	2000	2005	2010	2015	2016	2017	2018	2019	2020
Recettes fiscales totales	..	**13 951**	**303 088**	**1 677 170**	**3 486 346**	**3 237 755**	**3 893 729**	**5 901 005**	**6 353 269**	**6 577 357**
1000 Impôts sur revenu, bénéfices et gains en capital	..	**2 565**	**54 761**	**447 039**	**1 225 021**	**976 671**	**1 411 916**	**2 564 782**	**2 697 780**	**2 179 654**
1100 Des personnes physiques	..	996	24 243	208 715	515 851	509 354	660 669	821 801	834 587	993 999
1110 Sur le revenu et les bénéfices	..	996	24 243	208 715	515 851	509 354	660 669	821 801	834 587	993 999
Impôt sur les revenus des nationaux	..	899	15 444	162 931	417 442	409 977	507 845	589 377	631 366	629 181
Impôt sur les revenus - Institutions politiques	..	0	0	1 842	16 698	18 828	17 190	21 901	27 224	44 541
Impôt sur les revenus - Fonctionnaires et agents publics	..	0	0	0	12 825	12 789	9 632	10 968	8 855	156 720
Impôt sur les revenus - Régies financières	..	0	0	0	8 186	5 094	5 022	27 654	18 094	21 965
Impôt sur les revenus - Expatriés	..	81	7 513	43 779	59 921	62 241	119 707	170 926	148 489	140 484
Impôt sur les revenus - Proféssions libérales	..	15	1 286	44	0	0	0	0	0	0
Taxe ad valorem sur les gains des parieurs (DGRAD)	..	0	0	119	779	424	1 274	975	558	1 108
1120 Sur les gains en capital	..	..	..	..	..	..	..	..	..	..
1200 Des sociétés	..	1 569	30 518	237 937	709 095	467 230	751 074	1 742 853	1 862 769	1 185 045
Impôts sur les revenus des capitaux mobiliers	..	30	2 065	23 356	53 212	53 445	65 017	164 586	130 849	117 911
1210 Sur les bénéfices	..	1 539	28 453	214 582	655 884	413 785	686 057	1 578 267	1 731 920	804 482
Impôt sur les bénéfices - Sociétés non pétrolières	..	1 061	22 942	194 758	607 004	365 466	604 456	1 466 176	1 603 430	695 141
Impôt sur les bénéfices - Non résidents	..	0	0	0	46 124	45 450	75 010	102 597	97 818	100 534
Impôt sur les bénéfices - Entreprises individuelles	..	410	3 523	19 823	2 756	2 869	6 590	9 494	6 747	8 807
Impôts sur les revenus locatifs	..	69	1 988	0	0	0	0	0	0	0
Impôt spécial sur les profits excédentaires miniers	..	0	0	0	0	0	0	0	23 925	0
1220 Sur les gains en capital	..	..	..	..	..	..	..	..	..	262 652
1300 Non ventilables entre 1100 et 1200	..	..	..	386	75	87	173	128	424	610
2000 Cotisations de sécurité sociale	..	..	..	..	**201 761**	**192 308**	**286 819**	**352 934**	**629 162**	**729 838**
2100 A la charge des salariés	..	..	..	..	56 493	77 021	114 904	117 412	176 369	202 733
2110 Sur la base du salaire	..	..	..	..	56 493	77 021	114 904	117 412	176 369	202 733
2120 Sur la base de l'impôt sur le revenu	..	..	..	..	0	0	0	0	0	0
2200 A la charge des employeurs	..	..	..	..	145 268	115 287	171 915	235 521	452 793	527 105
2210 Sur la base du salaire	..	..	..	..	145 268	115 287	171 915	235 521	452 793	527 105
2220 Sur la base de l'impôt sur le revenu	..	..	..	..	0	0	0	0	0	0
2300 A charge des travailleurs indép. ou sans emploi	..	..	..	..	0	0	0	0	0	0
2310 Sur la base du salaire	..	..	..	..	..	..	..	..	..	..
2320 Sur la base de l'impôt sur le revenu	..	..	..	..	..	..	..	..	..	..
2400 Non ventilables entre 2100, 2200 et 2300	..	..	..	..	0	0	0	0	0	0
2410 Sur la base du salaire	..	..	..	..	..	..	..	..	..	..
2420 Sur la base de l'impôt sur le revenu	..	..	..	..	..	..	..	..	..	..
3000 Sur salaires ou main-d'œuvre	..	**56**	**4 266**	**25 904**	**79 248**	**71 507**	**96 035**	**143 254**	**172 187**	**180 583**
Impôt sur les rémunérations des expatriés (IERE)	..	56	2 630	15 370	48 503	43 343	59 173	91 777	121 128	125 228
Contributions pour l'Institut National de Préparation Professionnelle (INPP)	..	0	1 636	10 534	28 447	24 780	32 464	46 030	44 570	48 254
Contributions pour l'Office National de l'Emploi (ONEM)	..	..	..	..	2 298	3 385	4 398	5 447	6 488	7 102
4000 Impôts sur le patrimoine	..	..	..	**9 644**	**12 968**	**14 854**	**19 593**	**38 796**	**44 567**	**55 764**
4100 Impôts périodiques sur la propriété immobilière	..	..	..	3 695	8 817	9 254	10 546	28 719	31 985	38 687
4110 Ménages	..	..	..	..	..	..	..	..	..	..
4120 Autres agents	..	..	..	..	..	..	..	..	..	..
4200 Impôts périodiques sur l'actif net	..	..	..	..	..	..	..	..	..	..
4210 Personnes physiques	..	..	..	..	..	..	..	..	..	..
4220 Sociétés	..	..	..	..	..	..	..	..	..	..
4300 Impôts sur mut. par décès, succ. et donations	..	..	..	..	..	..	..	..	..	..
4310 Impôts sur mut. par décès et successions	..	..	..	..	..	..	..	..	..	..
4320 Impôts sur les donations	..	..	..	..	..	..	..	..	..	..
4400 Impôts sur transact. mobilières et immob.	..	..	..	5 949	4 151	5 600	9 047	10 078	12 582	17 077
4500 Impôts non-périodiques	..	..	..	..	..	..	..	..	..	..
4510 Sur l'actif net	..	..	..	..	..	..	..	..	..	..
4520 Autres non-périodiques	..	..	..	..	..	..	..	..	..	..
4600 Autres impôts périodiques sur patrimoine	..	..	..	..	..	..	..	..	..	..
5000 Impôts sur les biens et services	..	**11 331**	**206 583**	**1 095 498**	**1 888 533**	**1 945 072**	**2 004 065**	**2 600 730**	**2 686 857**	**3 352 114**
5100 Impôts sur production, vente, transfert, etc.	..	11 233	206 005	1 068 789	1 870 291	1 925 628	1 977 784	2 525 463	2 622 648	3 254 464
5110 Impôts généraux	..	1 390	109 602	590 594	891 546	1 056 005	1 127 384	1 456 884	1 417 107	2 110 083
5111 Taxes sur la valeur ajoutée	..	0	0	0	891 404	1 055 955	1 127 186	1 456 766	1 417 090	2 109 867
TVA intérieure	..	..	..	..	639 995	619 212	705 628	939 202	1 055 667	1 227 594
TVA à l'importation	..	..	..	..	879 549	561 978	538 173	766 232	803 860	882 273
Remboursements TVA	..	..	..	..	-628 140	-125 234	-116 616	-248 668	-442 438	0

Table 5.7. **Congo, Dem. Rep. / Congo, Rép. dém.** *(cont.)*

Details of tax revenue / Recettes fiscales détaillées

Million CDF

	1995	2000	2005	2010	2015	2016	2017	2018	2019	2020
5112 Impôts sur les ventes	..	..	..	110	0	0	0	0	0	215
5113 Autres impôts	..	1 390	109 602	590 484	143	49	199	119	18	1
Impôt sur le chiffre d'affaires (ICA)/ ventes locales	..	194	20 440	110 004	143	47	196	118	14	0
Impôt sur le chiffre d'affaires (ICA) - Prestations de services	..	409	28 534	181 338	0	0	0	0	0	0
Impôt sur le chiffre d'affaires (ICA) - Travaux immobiliers	..	14	3 971	5 969	0	0	0	0	0	0
Impôt sur le chiffre d'affaires (ICA) - Exportation produits miniers	..	0	2	0	0	0	0	0	0	0
Impôt sur le chiffre d'affaires (ICA) - Exportation hors produits miniers	..	6	0	0	0	0	0	0	0	0
Impôt sur le chiffre d'affaires ICA à l'importation	..	768	56 654	291 557	0	0	0	0	0	0
Autres impôts géneraux sur les biens et services (DGRAD)	..	0	0	1 616	0	2	3	0	3	1
5120 Impôts sur biens et services déterminés	..	9 842	96 403	478 194	978 745	869 623	850 400	1 068 579	1 205 541	1 144 381
5121 Accises	..	7 817	33 864	195 837	409 441	440 387	414 521	482 304	526 419	583 713
Redevances sur produits spécifiques (DGRAD)	..	..	..	12 259	3 256	1 303	502	563	630	560
Accises intérieures - Bières	..	..	..	57 301	131 359	117 612	147 107	169 694	172 880	183 894
Accises intérieures - Eaux de table et limonades	..	..	..	5 336	13 457	12 705	16 196	21 246	21 593	24 015
Accises intérieures - Alcools et boissons alcooliques	..	..	..	147	3 363	2 919	15 040	7 818	9 530	7 823
Accises intérieures - Tabacs et allumettes fabriqués	..	..	..	40 034	2 643	9 149	3 875	4 901	10 448	14 546
Accises intérieures - Télécommunication	..	..	..	49 338	86 315	88 198	116 686	145 710	168 852	194 138
Accises intérieures - Autres produits	..	..	..	848	4 339	5 605	2 501	2 875	4 245	6 185
Accises à l'importation - Bières	..	..	..	483	3 545	7 368	2 602	10 751	5 504	3 707
Accises à l'importation - Eaux de table et limonades	..	..	..	467	4 631	1 464	1 478	1 384	1 315	2 429
Accises à l'importation - Alcools et boissons alcooliques	..	..	..	1 481	5 380	5 015	7 616	8 577	5 168	3 824
Accises à l'importation - Tabacs et allumettes fabriqués	..	..	..	4 739	59 422	46 449	60 476	54 475	66 304	66 184
Accises à l'importation - Produits pétroliers	..	..	..	9 257	53 350	102 829	0	0	0	10 535
Accises à l'importation - Véhicules	..	..	..	9 901	15 878	12 022	15 444	23 427	22 940	38 355
Accises à l'importation - Autres produits	..	..	..	4 246	22 504	27 749	24 997	30 883	37 011	27 517
5122 Bénéfices des monopoles fiscaux	..	0	0	0	0	0	0	0	0	0
5123 Droits de douane et droits à l'importation	..	1 942	56 349	270 089	560 340	420 432	423 341	569 751	670 378	549 396
5124 Taxes à l'exportation	..	83	6 190	7 725	5 446	4 529	7 413	9 505	7 984	10 216
Droits de sortie sur les minerais	..	82	5 623	3 850	3 238	2 774	5 391	4 780	2 713	1 933
Droits de sortie sur les produits agricoles	..	1	567	3 046	2 208	1 755	2 022	4 725	5 271	8 283
Droits de sortie sur les autres produits	..	0	0	829	0	0	0	0	0	0
5125 Impôts sur biens d'équipement	..	0	0	0	0	0	0	0	0	0
5126 Impôts sur services déterminés	..	0	0	4 543	3 518	4 275	5 126	7 019	759	1 056
5127 Autres impôts sur commerce et transact. internat.	..	0	0	0	0	0	0	0	0	0
5128 Autres impôts	..	0	0	0	0	0	0	0	0	0
5130 Non ventilables entre 5110 et 5120	..	0	0	0	0	0	0	0	0	0
5200 Impôts sur utilisation des biens et exerc. activites	..	98	579	26 710	18 242	19 445	26 281	75 267	64 209	97 650
5210 Impôts périodiques	..	0	0	822	619	812	506	1 448	887	6 620
5211 A la charge des ménages: véhicules à moteur	..	..	..	0	0	0	0	0	0	0
5212 A la charge autres agents: véhicules à moteur	..	..	..	0	0	0	0	0	0	0
5213 Autres impôts périodiques	..	..	..	822	619	812	506	1 448	887	6 620
5220 Impôts non-périodiques	..	98	579	25 888	17 622	18 632	25 774	73 819	63 322	91 030
Immatriculation des véhicules routiers (plaques)	..	98	579	2 681	1 366	1 373	2 425	3 734	3 476	3 032
Autorisations d'exportation et d'importation	..	0	0	2 909	3 567	2 642	4 013	9 299	9 137	14 802
Taxe d'implantation établisssements dangeureux, insalubres et incommodes	..	0	0	1 225	2 939	3 616	3 353	46 159	32 995	49 963
Autres autorisations	..	0	0	19 073	9 751	11 001	15 983	14 627	17 713	23 233
5300 Non ventilables entre 5100 et 5200	..	0	0	0	0	0	0	0	0	0
6000 Autres impôts	**..**	**0**	**37 477**	**99 085**	**78 815**	**37 342**	**75 301**	**200 509**	**122 716**	**79 405**
Recettes des produits pétroliers	..	..	37 477	98 431	78 417	35 540	74 389	106 245	121 703	77 670
Droits proportionnels sur les S.A.R.L. (DGRAD)	..	..	0	654	398	1 803	912	94 264	1 013	1 734
6100 A la charge exclusive des entreprises	..	..	..	..	..	..	..	..	..	..
6200 A la charge d'autres agents	..	..	..	..	..	..	..	..	..	..

Table 5.7. **Congo, Dem. Rep. / Congo, Rép. dém.** *(cont.)*

Details of tax revenue / Recettes fiscales détaillées

.. Non disponible

Note : Année civile se terminant le 31 décembre.

Les données sont sur la base des encaissements.

Les chiffres n'incluent pas les données des recettes fiscales collectées par les collectivités locales car elles ne sont pas disponibles.

Les données entre 2000 à 2003 doivent être interprétées avec prudence car elles sont largement affectées par des taux d'inflation élevés.

La classification des données de la DGRAD a été révisée et affinée suite à la provision d'un nouvel ensemble de données couvrant 2008 à 2020. La révision de la classification a résulté à un plus grand nombre de recettes de la DGRAD classifié comme des recettes fiscales par rapport aux années précédentes.

Les recettes provenant de la vente des imprimés sont incluses dans les recettes non fiscales (Ventes de biens et services) comme le préconise la classification OCDE (voir le *Guide d'interprétation* en Annexe A). Elles sont considérées comme des recettes fiscales en République Démocratique du Congo.

Rubrique 3000 : Cette rubrique inclut les contributions pour l'Institut National de Préparation Professionnelle (INPP) pour la première fois dans cette édition.

Rubriques 1110, 5113, 5121, 5220, 6000 : Pour 2008 et les années qui suivent, ces rubriques contiennent des recettes provenant de la Direction Générale des Recettes Administratives, Judiciaires, Domaniales et de Participation (DGRAD) et sont annotées comme telles.

Rubriques 1300, 4100, 4400, 5112, 5126, 5128 : Pour 2008 et les années qui suivent, ces rubriques contiennent des recettes provenant exclusivement de la DGRAD.

Source : Ministère des Finances de la République démocratique du Congo.

StatLink *https://stat.link/itk3s4*

Table 5.8. **Côte d'Ivoire**

Details of tax revenue / Recettes fiscales détaillées

Million XOF

	1995	2000	2005	2010	2015	2016	2017	2018	2019	2020
Recettes fiscales totales	**924 472**	**1 169 607**	**1 407 277**	**2 035 468**	**3 414 418**	**3 736 455**	**3 983 683**	**4 194 689**	**4 527 842**	**4 734 486**
1000 Impôts sur revenu, bénéfices et gains en capital	**138 299**	**192 282**	**192 895**	**260 799**	**408 880**	**419 405**	**484 103**	**574 179**	**557 445**	**580 534**
1100 Des personnes physiques	3 397	5 108	6 184	6 970	10 054	10 762	12 199	13 894	13 089	14 508
1110 Sur le revenu et les bénéfices	3 397	5 093	6 164	6 937	10 011	10 711	12 147	13 822	13 023	14 435
Impôt général sur le revenu	0	0	323	1 420	817	663	283	114	57	12
Impôt BIC hors pétrole-gaz (personnes physiques)	3 397	5 045	5 770	5 431	9 008	9 859	11 660	13 457	12 760	14 141
IR des valeurs mobilières (pers. physiques)	0	48	71	86	186	189	204	252	206	282
1120 Sur les gains en capital	0	16	20	33	42	51	52	72	67	73
IR des capitaux (pers. physiques)	..	16	20	33	42	51	52	72	67	73
1200 Des sociétés	86 005	148 900	176 272	240 768	375 893	384 251	444 595	534 279	517 653	541 288
1210 Sur les bénéfices	86 005	143 602	169 683	229 732	361 782	367 300	427 439	510 483	495 535	517 177
Impôt BIC pétrole-gaz	0	0	0	63 649	71 985	54 962	64 392	86 071	104 181	65 361
Impôt BIC hors pétrole-gaz (personnes morales)	86 005	127 710	146 074	137 500	228 043	249 588	295 180	340 667	323 022	357 997
IR des valeurs mobilieres (pers. morales)	0	15 892	23 609	28 583	61 753	62 750	67 868	83 745	68 332	93 819
1220 Sur les gains en capital	0	5 297	6 589	11 036	14 111	16 951	17 155	23 796	22 118	24 112
Impôt sur le revenu des capitaux (personnes morales)	..	5 297	6 589	11 036	14 111	16 951	17 155	23 796	22 118	24 112
1300 Non ventilables entre 1100 et 1200	48 897	38 274	10 439	13 061	22 934	24 392	27 310	26 006	26 703	24 738
L'acompte d'impôt sur le revenu du secteur informel (ex ASDI)	45 763	33 983	5 882	7 624	14 637	16 380	18 567	15 845	16 023	16 124
Impôt synthétique	3 134	4 291	4 557	5 437	8 296	8 011	8 744	10 162	10 680	8 614
2000 Cotisations de sécurité sociale	**52 200**	**102 700**	**116 818**	**162 754**	**383 540**	**443 310**	**455 744**	**479 197**	**509 592**	**549 890**
2100 A la charge des salariés	..	..	..	64 364	151 728	177 045	180 368	189 616	201 522	218 051
CNPS	..	..	..	39 044	92 206	113 016	109 856	115 381	122 230	134 183
CGRAE	..	..	..	25 320	59 522	64 029	70 512	74 235	79 292	83 868
2110 Sur la base du salaire	..	..	..	0	0	0	0	0	0	0
2120 Sur la base de l'impôt sur le revenu	..	..	..	0	0	0	0	0	0	0
2200 A la charge des employeurs	..	..	..	98 390	231 812	266 265	275 376	289 581	308 070	331 839
CNPS	..	..	..	47 721	112 697	138 130	134 268	141 022	149 392	164 002
CGRAE	..	..	..	50 669	119 115	128 135	141 108	148 559	158 678	167 837
2210 Sur la base du salaire	..	..	..	0	0	0	0	0	0	0
2220 Sur la base de l'impôt sur le revenu	..	..	..	0	0	0	0	0	0	0
2300 A charge des travailleurs indép. ou sans emploi	..	..	..	0	0	0	0	0	0	0
2310 Sur la base du salaire	..	..	..	..	..	..	..	..	..	..
2320 Sur la base de l'impôt sur le revenu	..	..	..	..	..	..	..	..	..	..
2400 Non ventilables entre 2100, 2200 et 2300	52 200	102 700	116 818	0	0	0	0	0	0	0
2410 Sur la base du salaire	..	..	..	..	..	..	..	..	..	..
2420 Sur la base de l'impôt sur le revenu	..	..	..	..	..	..	..	..	..	..
3000 Sur salaires ou main-d'œuvre	**84 393**	**138 023**	**148 912**	**207 243**	**372 524**	**424 516**	**448 740**	**497 124**	**527 045**	**549 630**
Fonds de formation professionnelle	0	6 990	7 473	9 776	11 805	13 336	18 439	22 674	23 966	25 144
Impôt sur traitements et salaires (ITS), solde	84 393	131 033	141 439	197 467	360 719	411 180	430 301	474 449	503 079	524 487
4000 Impôts sur le patrimoine	**15 825**	**32 732**	**43 879**	**49 706**	**89 040**	**106 691**	**102 450**	**120 153**	**139 654**	**135 324**
4100 Impôts périodiques sur la propriété immobilière	15 825	24 664	34 032	38 009	72 299	79 627	83 394	99 417	113 362	106 889
4110 Ménages	..	..	..	..	..	..	..	..	..	..
4120 Autres agents	..	..	..	..	..	..	..	..	..	..
4200 Impôts périodiques sur l'actif net	0	0	0	0	0	0	0	0	0	0
4210 Personnes physiques	..	..	..	..	..	..	..	..	..	..
4220 Sociétés	..	..	..	..	..	..	..	..	..	..
4300 Impôts sur mut. par décès, succ. et donations	0	0	0	0	0	0	0	0	0	0
4310 Impôts sur mut. par décès et successions	..	..	..	..	..	..	..	..	..	..
4320 Impôts sur les donations	..	..	..	..	..	..	..	..	..	..
4400 Impôts sur transact. mobilières et immob.	0	8 068	9 847	11 697	16 741	27 064	19 055	20 735	26 292	28 435
4500 Impôts non-périodiques	0	0	0	0	0	0	0	0	0	0
4510 Sur l'actif net	..	..	..	..	..	..	..	..	..	..
4520 Autres non-périodiques	..	..	..	..	..	..	..	..	..	..
4600 Autres impôts périodiques sur patrimoine	0	0	0	0	0	0	0	0	0	0
5000 Impôts sur les biens et services	**633 755**	**699 518**	**899 720**	**1 344 201**	**2 139 379**	**2 319 981**	**2 470 069**	**2 499 839**	**2 760 029**	**2 885 098**
5100 Impôts sur production, vente, transfert, etc.	625 607	674 206	870 745	1 294 835	2 057 991	2 229 495	2 375 614	2 396 326	2 650 639	2 776 423
5110 Impôts généraux	206 914	255 297	288 886	490 521	692 417	717 607	809 711	897 334	982 115	993 540
5111 Taxes sur la valeur ajoutée	206 914	255 297	267 107	473 712	680 081	703 826	795 366	883 175	963 541	960 051
Recettes TVA (brute) - DGI	67 614	106 797	112 304	194 241	327 995	354 521	422 679	471 327	516 161	505 522
Remboursements credits de TVA (DGI)	0	0	-8 100	-15 480	-41 825	-38 159	-43 107	-42 599	-49 349	-44 080
Recettes TVA (brute) - DGD	139 300	148 500	172 802	313 870	445 028	446 235	469 599	504 893	547 827	544 935
Remboursements credits de TVA (DGD)	0	0	-9 899	-18 919	-51 118	-58 771	-53 805	-50 446	-51 099	-46 326
5112 Impôts sur les ventes	0	0	0	0	0	0	0	0	0	0

Table 5.8. **Côte d'Ivoire** *(cont.)*

Details of tax revenue / Recettes fiscales détaillées

Million XOF

	1995	2000	2005	2010	2015	2016	2017	2018	2019	2020
Recettes fiscales totales	**924 472**	**1 169 607**	**1 407 277**	**2 035 468**	**3 414 418**	**3 736 455**	**3 983 683**	**4 194 689**	**4 527 842**	**4 734 486**
1000 Impôts sur revenu, bénéfices et gains en capital	**138 299**	**192 282**	**192 895**	**260 799**	**408 880**	**419 405**	**484 103**	**574 179**	**557 445**	**580 534**
1100 Des personnes physiques	3 397	5 108	6 184	6 970	10 054	10 762	12 199	13 894	13 089	14 508
1110 Sur le revenu et les bénéfices	3 397	5 093	6 164	6 937	10 011	10 711	12 147	13 822	13 023	14 435
Impôt général sur le revenu	0	0	323	1 420	817	663	283	114	57	12
Impôt BIC hors pétrole-gaz (personnes physiques)	3 397	5 045	5 770	5 431	9 008	9 859	11 660	13 457	12 760	14 141
IR des valeurs mobilières (pers. physiques)	0	48	71	86	186	189	204	252	206	282
1120 Sur les gains en capital	0	16	20	33	42	51	52	72	67	73
IR des capitaux (pers. physiques)	..	16	20	33	42	51	52	72	67	73
1200 Des sociétés	86 005	148 900	176 272	240 768	375 893	384 251	444 595	534 279	517 653	541 288
1210 Sur les bénéfices	86 005	143 602	169 683	229 732	361 782	367 300	427 439	510 483	495 535	517 177
Impôt BIC pétrole-gaz	0	0	0	63 649	71 985	54 962	64 392	86 071	104 181	65 361
Impôt BIC hors pétrole-gaz (personnes morales)	86 005	127 710	146 074	137 500	228 043	249 588	295 180	340 667	323 022	357 997
IR des valeurs mobilieres (pers. morales)	0	15 892	23 609	28 583	61 753	62 750	67 868	83 745	68 332	93 819
1220 Sur les gains en capital	0	5 297	6 589	11 036	14 111	16 951	17 155	23 796	22 118	24 112
Impôt sur le revenu des capitaux (personnes morales)	..	5 297	6 589	11 036	14 111	16 951	17 155	23 796	22 118	24 112
1300 Non ventilables entre 1100 et 1200	48 897	38 274	10 439	13 061	22 934	24 392	27 310	26 006	26 703	24 738
L'acompte d'impôt sur le revenu du secteur informel (ex ASDI)	45 763	33 983	5 882	7 624	14 637	16 380	18 567	15 845	16 023	16 124
Impôt synthétique	3 134	4 291	4 557	5 437	8 296	8 011	8 744	10 162	10 680	8 614
2000 Cotisations de sécurité sociale	**52 200**	**102 700**	**116 818**	**162 754**	**383 540**	**443 310**	**455 744**	**479 197**	**509 592**	**549 890**
2100 A la charge des salariés	..	..	..	64 364	151 728	177 045	180 368	189 616	201 522	218 051
CNPS	..	..	..	39 044	92 206	113 016	109 856	115 381	122 230	134 183
CGRAE	..	..	..	25 320	59 522	64 029	70 512	74 235	79 292	83 868
2110 Sur la base du salaire	..	..	..	0	0	0	0	0	0	0
2120 Sur la base de l'impôt sur le revenu	..	..	..	0	0	0	0	0	0	0
2200 A la charge des employeurs	..	..	..	98 390	231 812	266 265	275 376	289 581	308 070	331 839
CNPS	..	..	..	47 721	112 697	138 130	134 268	141 022	149 392	164 002
CGRAE	..	..	..	50 669	119 115	128 135	141 108	148 559	158 678	167 837
2210 Sur la base du salaire	..	..	..	0	0	0	0	0	0	0
2220 Sur la base de l'impôt sur le revenu	..	..	..	0	0	0	0	0	0	0
2300 A charge des travailleurs indép. ou sans emploi	..	..	..	0	0	0	0	0	0	0
2310 Sur la base du salaire	..	..	..	..	..	..	..	..	..	..
2320 Sur la base de l'impôt sur le revenu	..	..	..	..	..	..	..	..	..	..
2400 Non ventilables entre 2100, 2200 et 2300	52 200	102 700	116 818	0	0	0	0	0	0	0
2410 Sur la base du salaire	..	..	..	..	..	..	..	..	..	..
2420 Sur la base de l'impôt sur le revenu	..	..	..	..	..	..	..	..	..	..
3000 Sur salaires ou main-d'œuvre	**84 393**	**138 023**	**148 912**	**207 243**	**372 524**	**424 516**	**448 740**	**497 124**	**527 045**	**549 630**
Fonds de formation professionnelle	0	6 990	7 473	9 776	11 805	13 336	18 439	22 674	23 966	25 144
Impôt sur traitements et salaires (ITS), solde	84 393	131 033	141 439	197 467	360 719	411 180	430 301	474 449	503 079	524 487
4000 Impôts sur le patrimoine	**15 825**	**32 732**	**43 879**	**49 706**	**89 040**	**106 691**	**102 450**	**120 153**	**139 654**	**135 324**
4100 Impôts périodiques sur la propriété immobilière	15 825	24 664	34 032	38 009	72 299	79 627	83 394	99 417	113 362	106 889
4110 Ménages	..	..	..	..	..	..	..	..	..	..
4120 Autres agents	..	..	..	..	..	..	..	..	..	..
4200 Impôts périodiques sur l'actif net	0	0	0	0	0	0	0	0	0	0
4210 Personnes physiques	..	..	..	..	..	..	..	..	..	..
4220 Sociétés	..	..	..	..	..	..	..	..	..	..
4300 Impôts sur mut. par décès, succ. et donations	0	0	0	0	0	0	0	0	0	0
4310 Impôts sur mut. par décès et successions	..	..	..	..	..	..	..	..	..	..
4320 Impôts sur les donations	..	..	..	..	..	..	..	..	..	..
4400 Impôts sur transact. mobilières et immob.	0	8 068	9 847	11 697	16 741	27 064	19 055	20 735	26 292	28 435
4500 Impôts non-périodiques	0	0	0	0	0	0	0	0	0	0
4510 Sur l'actif net	..	..	..	..	..	..	..	..	..	..
4520 Autres non-périodiques	..	..	..	..	..	..	..	..	..	..
4600 Autres impôts périodiques sur patrimoine	0	0	0	0	0	0	0	0	0	0
5000 Impôts sur les biens et services	**633 755**	**699 518**	**899 720**	**1 344 201**	**2 139 379**	**2 319 981**	**2 470 069**	**2 499 839**	**2 760 029**	**2 885 098**
5100 Impôts sur production, vente, transfert, etc.	625 607	674 206	870 745	1 294 835	2 057 991	2 229 495	2 375 614	2 396 326	2 650 639	2 776 423
5110 Impôts généraux	206 914	255 297	288 886	490 521	692 417	717 607	809 711	897 334	982 115	993 540
5111 Taxes sur la valeur ajoutée	206 914	255 297	267 107	473 712	680 081	703 826	795 366	883 175	963 541	960 051
Recettes TVA (brute) - DGI	67 614	106 797	112 304	194 241	327 995	354 521	422 679	471 327	516 161	505 522
Remboursements credits de TVA (DGI)	0	0	-8 100	-15 480	-41 825	-38 159	-43 107	-42 599	-49 349	-44 080
Recettes TVA (brute) - DGD	139 300	148 500	172 802	313 870	445 028	446 235	469 599	504 893	547 827	544 935
Remboursements credits de TVA (DGD)	0	0	-9 899	-18 919	-51 118	-58 771	-53 805	-50 446	-51 099	-46 326
5112 Impôts sur les ventes	0	0	0	0	0	0	0	0	0	0

Table 5.8. **Côte d'Ivoire** *(cont.)*

Details of tax revenue / Recettes fiscales détaillées

.. Non disponible

Note : Année civile se terminant le 31 décembre.

Les données sont sur la base des encaissements.

Les chiffres n'incluent pas les recettes fiscales collectées par les collectivités locales.

Rubrique 2000 : Des données plus détaillées sont disponibles pour la première fois pour cette édition.

La rubrique 5113 comprend la taxe ad-valorem, une taxe domaniale. Les recettes autres que celles de la taxe ad-valorem sont considérées comme des recettes non fiscales selon la classification OCDE (voir le *Guide d'interprétation* en Annexe A). La classification nationale de la Côte d'Ivoire les comptabilise comme des recettes fiscales.

La rubrique 5113 comprend la Contribution à la reconstruction nationale (CRN) instituée en 2004 pour cinq ans et arrivée à expiration en 2009. Elle a été remplacée par la Contribution pour la sortie de crise. Celle-ci était basée sur les charges d'exploitation des entreprises réalisant un chiffre d'affaire annuel supérieur ou égal à 1 milliard de francs, au titre de l'exercice clos au 31 décembre 2009.

La rubrique 6100 comprend le Fonds de soutien à l'habitat (FSH) alimenté par des recettes fiscales affectées (contribution patronale sur la masse salariale, taxes sur services déterminés et taxe sur le carburant). Il n'est pas possible de distinguer ces différents éléments d'où sa classification dans la rubrique 6100. Cette taxe a été supprimée en 2010.

Les recettes de la taxe audiovisuelle et la redevance radiodiffusion télévision ivoirienne (RTI) sont considérées comme des recettes non fiscales selon la classification OCDE (voir le *Guide d'interprétation* en Annexe A) et ont été classifiées dans la rubrique « vente de biens et services». La classification nationale de la Côte d'Ivoire les comptabilise comme des recettes fiscales.

Source : Ministère de l'Économie et des Finances.

StatLink https://stat.link/zl2kjo

Table 5.9. **Egypt / Égypte**

Details of tax revenue / Recettes fiscales détaillées

Million EGP

	1995	2000	2005	2010	2015	2016	2017	2018	2019	2020
Total tax revenue	..	..	**88 858**	**193 429**	**358 947**	**393 785**	**529 232**	**665 089**	**764 117**	**776 473**
1000 Taxes on income, profits and capital gains	..	..	**35 551**	**85 867**	**157 041**	**179 543**	**213 748**	**289 904**	**332 239**	**366 875**
1100 Of individuals	..	..	9 315	16 403	38 215	42 356	51 014	64 578	87 306	98 032
1110 On income and profits	..	..	9 310	16 319	37 936	42 013	50 630	64 128	86 382	96 978
Tax on domestic salaries	..	..	3 997	9 623	23 803	28 098	34 189	40 976	56 938	64 022
Taxes on industrial & commercial profits	..	..	3 715	4 570	10 589	9 247	11 508	16 815	24 657	28 672
Stamp duty on salaries	..	..	1 180	1 778	2 998	3 933	3 776	4 683	2 243	1 486
Tax on professionals income	..	..	150	314	544	731	1 154	1 650	2 506	2 798
Other taxes on activity other than employment	..	..	268	35	2	5	3	3	37	0
1120 On capital gains	..	..	5	84	279	343	384	450	924	1 054
1200 Corporate	..	..	22 257	66 022	108 285	125 457	146 747	186 374	209 702	237 846
1210 On profits	..	..	22 257	66 022	108 285	125 457	146 747	186 374	209 702	237 846
Egyptian General Petroleum Corporation (EGPC) & foreign partner	..	..	4 030	32 181	36 000	37 313	42 464	51 976	42 532	26 337
Suez Canal Authority (SCA)	..	..	7 343	9 443	13 400	14 903	22 300	29 900	34 480	42 913
Central Bank of Egypt (C.B.E)	..	..	212	0	3 691	13 245	3 860	0	0	0
Other companies	..	..	10 672	18 591	38 512	36 926	47 259	60 776	85 763	119 625
Interest income from T-Bills and Bonds	..	..	0	5 808	16 682	23 069	30 864	43 722	46 928	48 972
1220 On capital gains	..	..	..	..	..	..	..	..	..	..
1300 Unallocable between 1100 and 1200	..	..	3 979	3 442	10 542	11 730	15 987	38 952	35 231	30 996
Tax on movable capital revenues from C.B.E & other entities	..	..	3 979	3 309	10 235	10 966	15 691	38 497	34 538	30 579
Delayed tax income	..	..	0	134	306	765	296	455	693	417
2000 Social security contributions	..	..	**16 141**	**28 032**	**60 693**	**49 331**	**79 454**	**52 500**	**48 500**	**55 001**
2100 Employees	..	..	0	0	0	0	0	0	0	0
2110 On a payroll basis	..	..	..	..	..	..	..	..	..	..
2120 On an income tax basis	..	..	..	..	..	..	..	..	..	..
2200 Employers	..	..	0	0	0	0	0	0	0	0
2210 On a payroll basis	..	..	..	..	..	..	..	..	..	..
2220 On an income tax basis	..	..	..	..	..	..	..	..	..	..
2300 Self-employed or non-employed	..	..	0	0	0	0	0	0	0	0
2310 On a payroll basis	..	..	..	..	..	..	..	..	..	..
2320 On an income tax basis	..	..	..	..	..	..	..	..	..	..
2400 Unallocable between 2100, 2200 and 2300	..	..	16 141	28 032	60 693	49 331	79 454	52 500	48 500	55 001
2410 On a payroll basis	..	..	..	..	..	..	..	..	..	..
2420 On an income tax basis	..	..	..	..	..	..	..	..	..	..
3000 Taxes on payroll and workforce	..	..	**0**	**0**	**0**	**0**	**0**	**0**	**0**	**0**
4000 Taxes on property	..	..	**640**	**1 128**	**2 224**	**2 484**	**3 237**	**4 214**	**6 281**	**4 836**
4100 Recurrent taxes on immovable property	..	..	327	518	637	1 172	2 055	2 976	4 871	3 393
4110 Households	..	..	..	..	..	..	..	..	..	..
4120 Others	..	..	..	..	..	..	..	..	..	..
4200 Recurrent taxes on net wealth	..	..	0	0	0	0	0	0	0	0
4210 Individual	..	..	..	..	..	..	..	..	..	..
4220 Corporate	..	..	..	..	..	..	..	..	..	..
4300 Estate, inheritance and gift taxes	..	..	0	0	0	0	0	0	0	0
4310 Estate and inheritance taxes	..	..	..	..	..	..	..	..	..	..
4320 Gift taxes	..	..	..	..	..	..	..	..	..	..
4400 Taxes on financial and capital transactions	..	..	312	610	1 588	1 312	1 182	1 238	1 410	1 443
Property transferring fees	..	..	312	607	948	1 002	1 134	1 235	1 407	1 443
Stamps taxes	..	..	0	3	640	310	49	3	3	0
4500 Non-recurrent taxes	..	..	..	..	..	..	..	..	..	..
4510 On net wealth	..	..	..	..	..	..	..	..	..	..
4520 Other non-recurrent taxes	..	..	..	..	..	..	..	..	..	..
4600 Other recurrent taxes on property	..	..	0	0	0	0	0	0	0	0
5000 Taxes on goods and services	..	..	**36 527**	**78 401**	**138 988**	**162 427**	**232 793**	**318 471**	**377 097**	**349 762**
5100 Taxes on production, sale, transfer, etc.	..	..	35 697	76 232	135 761	159 187	229 874	314 484	370 724	343 523
5110 General taxes	..	..	18 725	39 864	65 523	71 527	112 523	156 276	197 679	193 730
5111 Value added taxes	..	..	18 725	39 864	65 523	71 527	112 523	156 276	197 679	193 730
Local commodities	..	..	5 257	11 735	18 415	21 102	32 690	43 100	50 351	53 017
Imported goods	..	..	8 548	18 977	35 010	36 352	61 694	83 939	105 000	95 249
Hotel and restaurant services for tourists	..	..	1 126	2 172	2 334	2 157	3 061	5 894	7 127	5 478
Operating services for others	..	..	1 555	2 936	4 844	6 845	9 563	15 819	24 048	28 190
International and local communication services	..	..	1 911	3 700	4 393	4 559	4 599	6 065	8 915	10 393
Other services	..	..	328	345	527	512	916	1 460	2 238	1 403
5112 Sales tax	..	..	0	0	0	0	0	0	0	0

Table 5.9. **Egypt / Égypte** *(cont.)*

Details of tax revenue / Recettes fiscales détaillées

Million EGP

	1995	2000	2005	2010	2015	2016	2017	2018	2019	2020
5113 Other	..	..	0	0	0	0	0	0	0	0
5120 Taxes on specific goods and services	..	..	16 971	36 369	70 238	87 660	117 351	158 208	173 045	149 793
5121 Excises	..	..	6 539	17 170	41 207	49 468	72 730	106 447	114 977	100 726
Tobacco & cigarettes	..	..	3 987	6 997	26 463	33 584	35 412	51 654	56 389	61 141
Petroleum products	..	..	818	7 563	12 004	13 181	33 072	40 470	41 484	27 599
Alcohol	..	..	95	198	181	144	138	218	315	250
Beer	..	..	170	241	499	614	750	960	1 113	1 602
Fizz water	..	..	510	0	0	0	608	1 550	2 128	2 836
Stamp taxes on specific goods	..	..	536	1 603	1 198	948	1 782	1 214	3 687	443
Other excises	..	..	422	567	864	998	968	10 381	9 861	6 857
5122 Profits of fiscal monopolies	..	..	80	0	0	0	0	0	0	0
5123 Customs and import duties	..	..	7 664	13 733	21 460	27 534	33 411	36 848	40 995	31 644
Valued customs taxes	..	..	7 285	13 242	20 955	26 933	32 777	36 246	40 344	31 106
Customs taxes on imported cigarettes and tobacco	..	..	379	491	506	601	634	603	651	538
5124 Taxes on exports	..	..	1	819	180	216	258	429	427	354
5125 Taxes on investment goods	..	..	0	0	0	0	0	0	0	0
5126 Taxes on specific services	..	..	1 952	2 729	3 699	4 866	4 739	7 414	5 261	6 948
Stamp taxes on specific services	..	..	1 114	1 950	2 700	3 361	3 286	5 487	3 517	5 517
Other taxes on specific services	..	..	838	779	999	1 505	1 453	1 927	1 744	1 431
5127 Other taxes on internat. trade and transactions	..	..	0	0	0	0	0	0	0	0
5128 Other taxes	..	..	736	1 919	3 690	5 576	6 213	7 070	11 386	10 121
5130 Unallocable between 5110 and 5120	..	..	0	0	0	0	0	0	0	0
5200 Taxes on use of goods and perform activities	..	..	830	2 169	3 227	3 241	2 919	3 987	6 373	6 239
5210 Recurrent taxes	..	..	830	2 169	3 227	3 241	2 919	3 987	6 373	6 239
5211 Paid by households: motor vehicles	..	..	394	1 837	2 841	2 747	2 487	3 477	5 702	5 789
5212 Paid by others: motor vehicles	..	..	0	0	0	0	0	0	0	0
5213 Paid in respect of other goods	..	..	436	332	386	494	432	509	672	450
5220 Non-recurrent taxes	..	..	0	0	0	0	0	0	0	0
5300 Unallocable between 5100 and 5200	..	..	0	0	0	0	0	0	0	0
6000 Other taxes	**..**	**..**	**0**	**0**	**0**	**0**	**0**	**0**	**0**	**0**
6100 Paid solely by business	..	..	..	..	..	..	..	..	..	..
6200 Other	..	..	..	..	..	..	..	..	..	..
Memo items:										
VAT revenues	..	..	18 397	39 519	64 996	71 015	111 607	154 816	195 441	192 327
VAT revenues (gross)	..	..	19 215	40 142	65 708	71 785	112 323	155 565	196 638	193 167
VAT refunds	..	..	-819	-623	-712	-770	-716	-749	-1 197	-840

.. Not available

Note: Fiscal year ends on 30 June. For example, the data for 2020 represent July 2019 to June 2020.

The data are on a cash basis.

Figures exclude tax revenues collected by sub-national governments as the data are not available. They are estimated to be unsignificant.

Heading 2000: Egypt does not include social security contributions in its tax revenue data as the Egyptian authorities do not consider them as taxes.

Royalties on the Suez Canal as well as other royalties and administrative fees are reported as taxes in Egypt. These revenues are considered as non-tax revenues according to the OECD classification, described in the *OECD Interpretative Guide* in Annex A.

Source: Ministry of Finance.

StatLink https://stat.link/35k7fz

Table 5.10. **Equatorial Guinea / Guinée équatoriale**

Details of tax revenue / Recettes fiscales détaillées

Million XAF

	1995	2000	2005	2010	2015	2016	2017	2018	2019	2020
Total tax revenue	..	..	**356 040**	**612 377**	**935 907**	**472 214**	**471 096**	**480 100**	**651 421**	**490 389**
1000 Taxes on income, profits and capital gains	..	..	**324 934**	**545 376**	**772 421**	**316 872**	**326 993**	**320 639**	**497 079**	**351 160**
1100 Of individuals	..	..	18 417	59 938	85 021	67 146	48 799	57 188	60 285	53 978
1110 On income and profits	..	..	18 417	59 938	85 021	67 146	48 799	57 188	60 285	53 978
Petroleum tax on physical persons	..	..	25 926	44 339	64 217	48 186	33 101	39 652	41 720	39 403
Personal income tax	..	..	7 390	15 325	20 421	18 581	15 456	17 201	18 245	14 299
Taxes on urban farms	..	..	101	129	379	369	235	305	297	272
Taxes on rural farms	..	..	-15 000	145	4	10	7	30	22	5
1120 On capital gains	..	..	0	0	0	0	0	0	0	0
1200 Corporate	..	..	306 517	485 438	687 400	249 726	278 194	263 451	436 794	297 182
1210 On profits	..	..	306 517	485 438	687 400	249 726	278 194	263 451	436 794	297 182
Oil companies - Contractors	..	..	32 454	406 163	546 181	175 230	167 822	184 343	331 801	216 081
Oil companies - Subcontractors	..	..	218 977	29 619	51 317	31 498	13 841	36 969	52 261	52 375
Non-Oil companies - Taxes on companies	..	..	18 251	38 659	86 658	38 744	34 795	36 571	51 395	26 796
Oil companies - Year end (PNT)	..	..	34 763	9 765	573	1 180	58 081	609	172	1 777
OCIPEF Tax on wood exporters	..	..	2 072	1 233	2 671	3 074	3 655	4 958	1 166	153
1220 On capital gains	..	..	0	0	0	0	0	0	0	0
1300 Unallocable between 1100 and 1200	..	..	0	0	0	0	0	0	0	0
2000 Social security contributions	..	..	**0**	**0**	**58 868**	**49 766**	**51 009**	**47 725**	**48 881**	**49 925**
2100 Employees	..	..	..	..	7 935	6 481	6 575	7 054	7 612	7 806
2110 On a payroll basis	..	..	..	..	0	0	0	0	0	0
2120 On an income tax basis	..	..	..	..	7 935	6 481	6 575	7 054	7 612	7 806
2200 Employers	..	..	..	..	41 793	33 954	34 339	36 711	36 370	37 294
2210 On a payroll basis	..	..	..	..	0	0	0	0	0	0
2220 On an income tax basis	..	..	..	..	41 793	33 954	34 339	36 711	36 370	37 294
2300 Self-employed or non-employed	..	..	..	..	0	0	0	0	0	0
2310 On a payroll basis	..	..	..	..	..	..	..	..	..	..
2320 On an income tax basis	..	..	..	..	..	..	..	..	..	..
2400 Unallocable between 2100, 2200 and 2300	..	..	..	..	9 140	9 331	10 094	3 960	4 900	4 826
2410 On a payroll basis	..	..	..	..	0	0	0	0	0	0
2420 On an income tax basis	..	..	..	..	9 140	9 331	10 094	3 960	4 900	4 826
3000 Taxes on payroll and workforce	..	..	**0**	**0**	**0**	**0**	**0**	**0**	**0**	**0**
4000 Taxes on property	..	..	**27**	**160**	**211**	**352**	**192**	**278**	**227**	**139**
4100 Recurrent taxes on immovable property	..	..	0	0	0	0	0	0	0	0
4110 Households	..	..	..	..	..	..	..	..	..	..
4120 Others	..	..	..	..	..	..	..	..	..	..
4200 Recurrent taxes on net wealth	..	..	0	0	0	0	0	0	0	0
4210 Individual	..	..	..	..	..	..	..	..	..	..
4220 Corporate	..	..	..	..	..	..	..	..	..	..
4300 Estate, inheritance and gift taxes	..	..	0	0	0	0	0	0	0	0
4310 Estate and inheritance taxes	..	..	..	..	..	..	..	..	..	..
4320 Gift taxes	..	..	..	..	..	..	..	..	..	..
4400 Taxes on financial and capital transactions	..	..	27	160	211	352	192	278	227	139
4500 Non-recurrent taxes	..	..	0	0	0	0	0	0	0	0
4510 On net wealth	..	..	..	..	..	..	..	..	..	..
4520 Other non-recurrent taxes	..	..	..	..	..	..	..	..	..	..
4600 Other recurrent taxes on property	..	..	0	0	0	0	0	0	0	0
5000 Taxes on goods and services	..	..	**30 243**	**57 852**	**96 353**	**94 252**	**88 168**	**92 399**	**98 695**	**80 589**
5100 Taxes on production, sale, transfer, etc.	..	..	30 243	57 852	96 353	94 252	88 168	92 399	98 695	80 589
5110 General taxes	..	..	22 122	45 607	58 761	52 501	51 978	54 466	57 859	49 509
5111 Value added taxes	..	..	22 122	45 607	58 761	52 501	51 978	54 466	57 859	49 509
VAT revenues on petroleum products	..	..	7 132	15 066	6 799	4 705	3 826	2 355	2 160	2 129
VAT revenues other products and services	..	..	14 990	30 541	51 962	47 796	48 152	52 111	55 699	47 381
5112 Sales tax	..	..	0	0	0	0	0	0	0	0
5113 Other	..	..	0	0	0	0	0	0	0	0
5120 Taxes on specific goods and services	..	..	8 121	12 245	37 592	41 751	36 190	37 933	40 836	31 079
5121 Excises	..	..	0	0	19 961	21 041	15 824	18 570	20 904	19 155
Taxes on petroleum products	..	..	0	0	19 961	21 041	15 824	18 570	17 604	17 504
Taxes on alcoholic beverages and others drinks	..	..	0	0	0	0	0	0	3 300	1 515
Other excise taxes	..	..	0	0	0	0	0	0	0	136
5122 Profits of fiscal monopolies	..	..	0	0	0	0	0	0	0	0
5123 Customs and import duties	..	..	3 974	9 667	13 434	15 854	12 292	13 015	15 438	9 952
Imports of petroleum products	..	..	618	1 446	2 009	1 865	1 309	1 448	1 297	1 245
Imports of other products	..	..	3 356	8 221	11 425	13 989	10 983	11 567	14 141	8 707

Table 5.10. **Equatorial Guinea / Guinée équatoriale** *(cont.)*

Details of tax revenue / Recettes fiscales détaillées

Million XAF

	1995	2000	2005	2010	2015	2016	2017	2018	2019	2020
5124 Taxes on exports	..	..	4 147	2 578	4 197	4 856	8 074	6 348	4 494	1 972
Wood exports	..	..	3 916	2 517	4 088	4 772	7 956	6 253	4 294	1 906
Exports of other products	..	..	91	21	91	84	116	89	193	64
Re-exports	..	..	140	40	18	0	3	6	6	2
5125 Taxes on investment goods	..	..	0	0	0	0	0	0	0	0
5126 Taxes on specific services	..	..	0	0	0	0	0	0	0	0
5127 Other taxes on internat. trade and transactions	..	..	0	0	0	0	0	0	0	0
5128 Other taxes	..	..	0	0	0	0	0	0	0	0
5130 Unallocable between 5110 and 5120	..	..	0	0	0	0	0	0	0	0
5200 Taxes on use of goods and perform activities	..	..	0	0	0	0	0	0	0	0
5210 Recurrent taxes	..	..	..	..	..	..	..	..	..	..
5211 Paid by households: motor vehicles	..	..	..	..	..	..	..	..	..	..
5212 Paid by others: motor vehicles	..	..	..	..	..	..	..	..	..	..
5213 Paid in respect of other goods	..	..	..	..	..	..	..	..	..	..
5220 Non-recurrent taxes	..	..	..	..	..	..	..	..	..	..
5300 Unallocable between 5100 and 5200	..	..	0	0	0	0	0	0	0	0
6000 Other taxes	**..**	**..**	**836**	**8 989**	**8 054**	**10 972**	**4 733**	**19 060**	**6 538**	**8 575**
6100 Paid solely by business	..	..	..	..	..	..	..	..	..	..
6200 Other	..	..	..	..	..	..	..	..	..	..

.. Not available

Note: Year ending 31st December.

The data are on a cash basis.

Heading 2000: Social security contributions to the Instituto Nacional de Seguridad Social de Guinea Ecuatorial (INSESO) are reported under this heading for the years 2013-20.

Source: Ministry of Finance, Economy and Planning; Instituto Nacional de Seguridad Social de Guinea Ecuatorial (INSESO).

StatLink *https://stat.link/46f5dh*

Table 5.11. **Eswatini**

Details of tax revenue / Recettes fiscales détaillées

Million SZL

	1995	2000	2005	2010	2015	2016	2017	2018	2019	2020
Total tax revenue	**745**	**1 327**	**2 406**	**4 588**	**7 907**	**9 140**	**10 101**	**10 891**	**11 893**	**11 916**
1000 Taxes on income, profits and capital gains	**392**	**677**	**1 289**	**2 373**	**3 854**	**4 590**	**4 897**	**5 259**	**5 732**	**5 624**
1100 Of individuals	165	428	804	1 449	2 278	2 766	3 071	3 289	3 513	3 586
1110 On income and profits	165	428	804	1 449	2 278	2 766	3 071	3 289	3 513	3 586
Pay-as-you-earn tax (PAYE)	162	421	733	1 321	2 176	2 662	2 976	3 181	3 407	3 466
Provisional income tax (farmers, directors, individuals)	0	2	16	75	24	31	32	44	38	40
Taxes on interest, dividends and trust income	0	0	8	35	1	1	0	0	0	0
Personal income tax on non-residents	0	0	0	3	1	2	0	0	0	0
Tax on benefits	0	0	5	11	15	15	17	18	18	19
Withholding tax on resident suppliers of goods and services	0	0	40	0	0	0	0	0	0	0
Personal income tax on the self employed	2	4	0	1	59	52	43	43	47	56
Lottery levy	0	1	1	2	2	3	4	3	3	5
1120 On capital gains	0	0	0	0	0	0	0	0	0	0
1200 Corporate	202	236	461	905	1 507	1 730	1 825	1 969	2 218	2 036
1210 On profits	202	236	461	905	1 507	1 730	1 825	1 969	2 218	2 036
Corporate income tax on resident companies	201	233	394	739	1 358	1 527	1 388	1 479	1 734	1 462
Taxes on royalties	0	0	54	144	42	58	0	0	0	0
Corporate income tax on non-resident companies	0	3	13	22	107	145	438	490	483	574
1220 On capital gains	0	0	0	0	0	0	0	0	0	0
1300 Unallocable between 1100 and 1200	26	14	23	20	68	95	1	1	1	2
Income taxes on non-residents	23	11	20	15	67	93	0	0	0	0
Other taxes on income	2	3	3	4	2	2	1	1	1	2
2000 Social security contributions	**115**	**154**	**287**	**626**	**1 028**	**1 126**	**1 357**	**1 536**	**1 542**	**1 589**
2100 Employees	29	38	72	157	309	342	407	472	475	495
2110 On a payroll basis	..	..	..	..	..	..	..	..	..	..
2120 On an income tax basis	..	..	..	..	..	..	..	..	..	..
2200 Employers	87	115	215	469	719	785	950	1 065	1 067	1 094
2210 On a payroll basis	..	..	..	..	..	..	..	..	..	..
2220 On an income tax basis	..	..	..	..	..	..	..	..	..	..
2300 Self-employed or non-employed	0	0	0	0	0	0	0	0	0	0
2310 On a payroll basis	..	..	..	..	..	..	..	..	..	..
2320 On an income tax basis	..	..	..	..	..	..	..	..	..	..
2400 Unallocable between 2100, 2200 and 2300	0	0	0	0	0	0	0	0	0	0
2410 On a payroll basis	..	..	..	..	..	..	..	..	..	..
2420 On an income tax basis	..	..	..	..	..	..	..	..	..	..
3000 Taxes on payroll and workforce	**0**	**0**	**0**	**0**	**0**	**0**	**0**	**0**	**0**	**0**
4000 Taxes on property	**15**	**34**	**55**	**92**	**133**	**147**	**237**	**285**	**306**	**174**
4100 Recurrent taxes on immovable property	8	24	30	54	78	77	165	212	236	118
Local property taxes	8	24	30	54	78	77	165	212	236	118
4110 Households	0	0	0	0	0	0	0	0	0	0
4120 Others	0	0	0	0	0	0	0	0	0	0
4200 Recurrent taxes on net wealth	0	0	0	0	0	0	0	0	0	0
4210 Individual	..	..	..	..	..	..	..	..	..	..
4220 Corporate	..	..	..	..	..	..	..	..	..	..
4300 Estate, inheritance and gift taxes	0	0	0	0	0	0	0	0	0	0
4310 Estate and inheritance taxes	..	..	..	..	..	..	..	..	..	..
Tax on trust beneficiaries	..	..	..	..	..	..	..	..	..	..
4320 Gift taxes	..	..	..	..	..	..	..	..	..	..
4400 Taxes on financial and capital transactions	7	10	25	39	56	70	72	73	70	56
Transfer duties	3	5	13	26	30	46	42	49	37	30
Stamp duties	4	5	12	12	25	24	30	23	34	27
4500 Non-recurrent taxes	0	0	0	0	0	0	0	0	0	0
4510 On net wealth	..	..	..	..	..	..	..	..	..	..
4520 Other non-recurrent taxes	..	..	..	..	..	..	..	..	..	..
4600 Other recurrent taxes on property	0	0	0	0	0	0	0	0	0	0
5000 Taxes on goods and services	**223**	**462**	**776**	**1 496**	**2 892**	**3 276**	**3 609**	**3 811**	**4 313**	**4 529**
5100 Taxes on production, sale, transfer, etc.	214	449	758	1 442	2 823	3 202	3 532	3 729	4 205	4 429
5110 General taxes	173	372	661	1 255	2 109	2 409	2 521	2 668	2 972	3 123
5111 Value added taxes	0	0	0	0	2 107	2 407	2 520	2 668	2 965	3 119
VAT revenues (gross)	..	..	..	..	3 048	3 337	3 584	3 753	4 349	4 595
VAT refunds	..	..	..	..	-941	-929	-1 063	-1 085	-1 384	-1 475
5112 Sales tax	173	372	661	1 255	2	1	1	0	7	4
5113 Other	0	0	0	0	0	0	0	0	0	0

Table 5.11. **Eswatini** *(cont.)*

Details of tax revenue / Recettes fiscales détaillées

Million SZL

	1995	2000	2005	2010	2015	2016	2017	2018	2019	2020
5120 Taxes on specific goods and services	41	78	97	186	714	793	1 011	1 061	1 232	1 306
5121 Excises	40	75	73	148	667	732	1 005	1 050	1 218	1 291
Fuel taxes	40	75	73	148	667	732	1 005	1 050	1 202	1 261
Levy on alcohol and tobacco	0	0	0	0	0	0	0	0	16	29
5122 Profits of fiscal monopolies	0	0	0	0	0	0	0	0	0	0
5123 Customs and import duties	0	0	0	0	0	0	0	5	9	12
5124 Taxes on exports	0	0	0	0	0	0	0	0	0	0
Cattle export tax	0	0	0	0	0	0	0	0	0	0
5125 Taxes on investment goods	0	0	0	0	0	0	0	0	0	0
5126 Taxes on specific services	1	2	23	39	47	61	6	5	6	3
Tax on management fees	0	0	17	37	42	58	0	0	0	0
Taxes on lotteries, gaming and betting	1	2	7	2	5	3	6	5	6	3
Other taxes on services and hospitality	0	0	0	0	0	0	0	0	0	0
5127 Other taxes on internat. trade and transactions	0	0	0	0	0	0	0	0	0	0
5128 Other taxes	0	0	0	0	0	0	0	0	0	0
5130 Unallocable between 5110 and 5120	0	0	0	0	0	0	0	0	0	0
5200 Taxes on use of goods and perform activities	8	12	18	54	68	74	77	82	108	100
5210 Recurrent taxes	4	8	13	30	38	43	45	48	51	51
5211 Paid by households: motor vehicles	2	4	1	11	16	18	19	20	22	25
5212 Paid by others: motor vehicles	0	0	0	0	0	0	0	0	0	0
5213 Paid in respect of other goods	2	3	11	19	22	25	26	28	29	26
Trading licences	1	1	8	11	14	16	16	18	19	20
Company licences	1	1	2	7	7	8	8	9	9	5
Special activities licences (gaming, casino, labor agents, cattle slaughter)	0	1	1	1	1	1	1	1	1	1
5220 Non-recurrent taxes	4	5	5	25	31	31	32	34	57	49
Road tolls	4	4	4	24	30	30	32	33	56	48
Firearm registration fees	0	0	1	1	1	1	1	1	1	1
5300 Unallocable between 5100 and 5200	0	0	0	0	0	0	0	0	0	0
6000 Other taxes	**0**	**0**	**0**	**0**	**0**	**0**	**0**	**0**	**0**	**0**
6100 Paid solely by business	..	..	..	..	..	..	..	..	..	..
6200 Other	..	..	..	..	..	..	..	..	..	..

.. Not available

Note: Data are reported on a fiscal year basis beginning 1st April. For example, the data for 2020 represent April 2020 to March 2021.

The data are on a cash basis.

Heading 5211: This heading includes revenue from motor vehicle licences, the change of ownership fees and the registration of new motor vehicles. These revenues are considered as tax revenue according to the OECD classification, described in the *OECD Interpretative Guide* in Annex A. The national classification of Eswatini classifies these revenues as non-tax revenues.

Heading 5213: This heading includes revenue from business and sundry licences. These revenues are considered as tax revenues according to the OECD classification, described in the *OECD Interpretative Guide* in Annex A. The national classification of Eswatini classifies them as non tax revenues.

Heading 5220: This heading includes revenue from the registrations of specific goods (e.g firearms). These revenues are considered as tax revenues under the OECD classification, as set out in the *OECD Interpretative Guide* in Annex A. The national classification of Eswatini classifies these revenues as non-tax revenues. Revenue from PAYE Penalties, tax interest and penalties on taxes are considered as non-tax revenue under the OECD classification, as set out in the *OECD Interpretative Guide* in Annex A. The national classification of Eswatini classifies these revenues as tax revenues.

Source: Eswatini Revenue Authority; Local Government; Eswatini National Provident Fund and Public Service Pension Fund; Ministry of Economic Planning and Development; Central Government.

StatLink https://stat.link/rzlvx8

Table 5.12. **Ghana**

Details of tax revenue / Recettes fiscales détaillées

Million GHS

	1995	2000	2005	2010	2015	2016	2017	2018	2019	2020
Total tax revenue	..	**487**	**2 342**	**6 695**	**23 592**	**28 750**	**35 343**	**42 184**	**47 039**	**51 467**
1000 Taxes on income, profits and capital gains	..	**141**	**642**	**2 417**	**7 570**	**8 084**	**11 712**	**16 344**	**19 853**	**21 075**
1100 Of individuals	..	56	269	1 115	3 570	3 702	5 191	6 649	7 734	7 901
1110 On income and profits	..	56	269	1 115	3 570	3 702	5 191	6 649	7 734	7 901
Employees income tax	..	48	232	1 015	3 310	3 466	4 859	6 270	7 313	7 507
Self employers income/profit tax	..	8	37	100	260	237	332	379	421	394
1120 On capital gains	..	..	..	..	..	..	..	..	..	..
1200 Corporate	..	70	303	1 080	3 837	4 233	6 214	9 563	11 833	12 860
1210 On profits	..	70	303	1 080	3 837	4 233	6 214	9 563	11 833	12 860
Income/profit tax on companies (excl. oil)	..	70	303	988	3 620	4 052	5 793	8 528	10 567	11 426
Income/profit tax on oil companies	..	0	0	0	45	42	225	736	926	951
National Fiscal Stabilisation Levy (NFSL)	..	0	0	85	172	139	196	299	340	483
National Reconstruction Levy (NRL)	..	0	0	7	0	0	0	0	0	0
1220 On capital gains	..	..	..	..	..	..	..	..	..	..
1300 Unallocable between 1100 and 1200	..	15	70	222	163	148	307	132	286	314
Other direct taxes aside from oil and mineral royalties	..	15	70	222	163	148	307	132	286	314
2000 Social security contributions	..	**46**	**191**	**577**	**2 122**	**1 849**	**2 374**	**2 213**	**2 466**	**4 107**
2100 Employees	..	..	..	..	..	..	..	..	..	..
2110 On a payroll basis	..	..	..	..	..	..	..	..	..	..
2120 On an income tax basis	..	..	..	..	..	..	..	..	..	..
2200 Employers	..	..	..	..	..	..	..	..	..	..
2210 On a payroll basis	..	..	..	..	..	..	..	..	..	..
2220 On an income tax basis	..	..	..	..	..	..	..	..	..	..
2300 Self-employed or non-employed	..	..	..	..	..	..	..	..	..	..
2310 On a payroll basis	..	..	..	..	..	..	..	..	..	..
2320 On an income tax basis	..	..	..	..	..	..	..	..	..	..
2400 Unallocable between 2100, 2200 and 2300	..	46	191	577	2 122	1 849	2 374	2 213	2 466	4 107
SSNIT revenue - Social security contributions	..	46	191	577	2 122	1 849	2 374	2 213	2 466	4 107
2410 On a payroll basis	..	..	..	..	..	..	..	..	..	..
2420 On an income tax basis	..	..	..	..	..	..	..	..	..	..
3000 Taxes on payroll and workforce	..	**0**	**0**	**0**	**0**	**0**	**0**	**0**	**0**	**0**
4000 Taxes on property	..	..	..	..	..	..	..	..	..	..
4100 Recurrent taxes on immovable property	..	..	..	..	..	..	..	..	..	..
4110 Households	..	..	..	..	..	..	..	..	..	..
4120 Others	..	..	..	..	..	..	..	..	..	..
4200 Recurrent taxes on net wealth	..	..	..	..	..	..	..	..	..	..
4210 Individual	..	..	..	..	..	..	..	..	..	..
4220 Corporate	..	..	..	..	..	..	..	..	..	..
4300 Estate, inheritance and gift taxes	..	..	..	..	..	..	..	..	..	..
4310 Estate and inheritance taxes	..	..	..	..	..	..	..	..	..	..
4320 Gift taxes	..	..	..	..	..	..	..	..	..	..
4400 Taxes on financial and capital transactions	..	..	..	..	..	..	..	..	..	..
4500 Non-recurrent taxes	..	..	..	..	..	..	..	..	..	..
4510 On net wealth	..	..	..	..	..	..	..	..	..	..
4520 Other non-recurrent taxes	..	..	..	..	..	..	..	..	..	..
4600 Other recurrent taxes on property	..	..	..	..	..	..	..	..	..	..
5000 Taxes on goods and services	..	**301**	**1 509**	**3 701**	**13 900**	**18 817**	**21 256**	**23 627**	**24 720**	**26 286**
5100 Taxes on production, sale, transfer, etc.	..	301	1 509	3 701	13 900	18 817	21 256	23 606	24 659	26 286
5110 General taxes	..	127	595	2 006	7 562	8 530	10 366	11 326	12 498	12 875
5111 Value added taxes	..	127	595	2 006	7 562	8 530	10 366	11 326	12 498	12 875
VAT revenues (external collection)	..	89	399	970	3 489	4 108	4 992	4 912	4 121	3 906
VAT revenues (domestic)	..	39	196	649	2 766	3 022	3 557	3 980	5 209	5 302
National Health Insurance Levy (NHIL - customs collection)	..	0	0	183	558	613	778	810	715	744
National Health Insurance Levy (NHIL - domestic)	..	0	0	133	461	506	598	691	1 030	1 060
Social Security and National Insurance Trust (SSNIT) contributions to the National Health Insurance Scheme (NHIS)	..	0	0	72	289	280	440	377	153	46
GETFund Levy (external collection)	..	0	0	0	0	0	0	289	834	757
GETFund Levy (domestic)	..	0	0	0	0	0	0	267	435	1 060
5112 Sales tax	..	0	0	0	0	0	0	0	0	0
5113 Other	..	0	0	0	0	0	0	0	0	0
5120 Taxes on specific goods and services	..	173	915	1 695	6 337	10 287	10 890	12 279	12 161	13 411

Table 5.12. **Ghana** *(cont.)*

Details of tax revenue / Recettes fiscales détaillées

Million GHS

	1995	2000	2005	2010	2015	2016	2017	2018	2019	2020
5121 Excises	..	75	477	374	2 402	5 289	4 729	5 282	5 817	7 153
Petroleum taxes aside from EFL and RFL	..	53	403	221	2 163	2 319	1 665	1 975	1 952	2 170
Energy Fund Levy (EFL)	..	0	0	36	0	25	28	35	39	38
Road Fund Levy (RFL)	..	0	0	0	0	1 002	1 058	1 331	1 541	1 780
Energy Debt Recovery Levy (EDRL)	..	0	0	0	0	1 264	962	876	1 665	2 040
Price Stabilisation and Recovery Levy	..	0	0	0	0	326	346	548	125	484
Public Lighting Levy (PLL)	..	0	0	0	0	23	180	119	63	134
National Electrification Scheme Levy (NESL)	..	0	0	0	0	33	151	78	44	90
Other excise duties	..	21	74	118	239	297	339	319	387	415
5122 Profits of fiscal monopolies	..	0	0	0	0	0	0	0	0	0
5123 Customs and import duties	..	81	377	1 051	3 078	4 122	5 485	6 102	5 410	5 514
5124 Taxes on exports	..	18	61	95	371	269	0	0	0	0
Levies on cocoa exports	..	18	61	95	371	269	..	..	..	..
5125 Taxes on investment goods	..	0	0	0	0	0	0	0	0	0
5126 Taxes on specific services	..	0	0	174	486	608	676	896	934	745
Communication service tax	..	..	..	137	252	339	329	420	412	559
Airport tax	..	..	..	37	235	269	347	476	521	185
5127 Other taxes on internat. trade and transactions	..	0	0	0	0	0	0	0	0	0
5128 Other taxes	..	0	0	0	0	0	0	0	0	0
5130 Unallocable between 5110 and 5120	..	0	0	0	0	0	0	0	0	0
5200 Taxes on use of goods and perform activities	..	0	0	0	0	0	0	21	61	0
5210 Recurrent taxes	..	..	..	..	..	..	..	21	61	..
5211 Paid by households: motor vehicles	..	..	..	..	..	..	..	21	61	..
Luxury Vehicle Levy	..	..	..	..	..	..	..	21	61	..
5212 Paid by others: motor vehicles	..	..	..	..	..	..	..	0	0	..
5213 Paid in respect of other goods	..	..	..	..	..	..	..	0	0	..
5220 Non-recurrent taxes	..	..	..	..	..	..	..	0	0	..
5300 Unallocable between 5100 and 5200	..	0	0	0	0	0	0	0	0	0
6000 Other taxes	**..**	**0**	**0**	**0**	**0**	**0**	**0**	**0**	**0**	**0**
6100 Paid solely by business	..	..	..	..	..	..	..	..	..	..
6200 Other	..	..	..	..	..	..	..	..	..	..
Memo items: *VAT refunds*	..	0	12	45	627	1 445	1 803	2 125	2 470	2 587

.. Not available

Note: Year ending 31st December.

The data are on a cash basis.

Figures exclude tax revenues collected by sub-national governments as the data are not available.

Heading 2000: The data are not available from 2000 to 2007.

Heading 4000: Property tax is levied annually by local authorities and is not available for this report.

Heading 5111: The national health insurance levy is a tax on goods and services whose funds are allocated to the National Health Insurance Scheme (NHIS). The division of GETFund Levy revenues between domestic and external collections are estimates based on programmed budget figures for 2019.

Heading 5121: In previous editions, revenues under the Public Lighting Levy (PLL) and the National Electrification Scheme Levy (NESL) were grouped together with the Energy Debt Recovery Levy (EDRL). These are now reported as separate revenues.

Heading 5211: The Luxury Vehicle Levy has been added to the classification in this edition.

Source: Ghana Statistical Service.

StatLink https://stat.link/8w0x9k

Table 5.13. **Kenya**

Details of tax revenue / Recettes fiscales détaillées

Million KES

	1995	2000	2005	2010	2015	2016	2017	2018	2019	2020
Total tax revenue	..	..	**277 202**	**540 164**	**1 085 219**	**1 231 771**	**1 399 657**	**1 482 598**	**1 607 445**	**1 611 601**
1000 Taxes on income, profits and capital gains	..	..	**99 557**	**219 227**	**504 077**	**561 792**	**628 373**	**654 675**	**687 183**	**721 164**
1100 Of individuals	..	..	55 818	124 392	284 222	322 885	348 783	377 353	410 193	419 325
1110 On income and profits	..	..	55 818	124 392	284 222	322 885	348 783	377 353	410 193	419 325
Paye As You Earn (PAYE)	..	..	52 767	120 593	277 068	312 032	336 596	364 104	392 693	400 508
Individual income tax	..	..	3 051	3 799	7 154	8 821	8 179	7 191	8 916	8 672
Tax on rental income	..	..	0	0	0	2 033	4 007	6 058	8 584	10 145
1120 On capital gains	..	..	..	..	..	..	..	..	..	..
1200 Corporate	..	..	31 947	67 661	126 541	152 407	180 162	160 059	168 783	175 843
1210 On profits	..	..	31 947	67 661	126 541	152 407	180 162	160 059	168 783	175 843
Corporation tax	..	..	31 947	67 661	126 541	152 407	180 162	160 059	168 783	175 843
1220 On capital gains	..	..	..	..	..	..	..	..	..	..
1300 Unallocable between 1100 and 1200	..	..	11 792	27 174	93 313	86 500	99 427	117 263	108 207	125 995
Withholding tax	..	..	11 792	27 174	92 678	82 690	97 009	100 623	105 256	121 511
Capital gains tax	..	..	0	0	636	3 811	2 419	16 640	2 951	4 484
2000 Social security contributions	..	..	**3 675**	**6 026**	**15 826**	**31 996**	**34 978**	**47 889**	**58 081**	**60 815**
2100 Employees	..	..	558	..	..	..	..	..	..	..
Women and children's pension	..	..	558	..	..	..	..	..	..	..
2110 On a payroll basis	..	..	..	..	..	..	..	..	..	..
2120 On an income tax basis	..	..	..	..	..	..	..	..	..	..
2200 Employers	..	..	..	..	..	..	..	..	..	..
2210 On a payroll basis	..	..	..	..	..	..	..	..	..	..
2220 On an income tax basis	..	..	..	..	..	..	..	..	..	..
2300 Self-employed or non-employed	..	..	..	..	..	..	..	..	..	..
2310 On a payroll basis	..	..	..	..	..	..	..	..	..	..
2320 On an income tax basis	..	..	..	..	..	..	..	..	..	..
2400 Unallocable between 2100, 2200 and 2300	..	..	3 117	6 026	15 826	31 996	34 978	47 889	58 081	60 815
2410 On a payroll basis	..	..	..	..	..	..	..	..	..	..
2420 On an income tax basis	..	..	..	..	..	..	..	..	..	..
3000 Taxes on payroll and workforce	..	..	**0**	**0**	**0**	**0**	**0**	**0**	**0**	**0**
4000 Taxes on property	..	..	**185**	**1 133**	**1 051**	**1 237**	**940**	**629**	**682**	**567**
4100 Recurrent taxes on immovable property	..	..	185	1 133	1 051	1 237	940	629	682	567
Immovable property (Stand premia on town plots)	..	..	7	86	6	36	79	28	94	93
Land rates	..	..	178	0	0	0	0	0	0	0
Land rent	..	..	0	1 047	1 045	1 201	861	601	588	474
4110 Households	..	..	..	..	..	..	..	..	..	..
4120 Others	..	..	..	..	..	..	..	..	..	..
4200 Recurrent taxes on net wealth	..	..	0	0	0	0	0	0	0	0
4210 Individual	..	..	..	..	..	..	..	..	..	..
4220 Corporate	..	..	..	..	..	..	..	..	..	..
4300 Estate, inheritance and gift taxes	..	..	0	0	0	0	0	0	0	0
4310 Estate and inheritance taxes	..	..	..	..	..	..	..	..	..	..
4320 Gift taxes	..	..	..	..	..	..	..	..	..	..
4400 Taxes on financial and capital transactions	..	..	0	0	0	0	0	0	0	0
4500 Non-recurrent taxes	..	..	0	0	0	0	0	0	0	0
4510 On net wealth	..	..	..	..	..	..	..	..	..	..
4520 Other non-recurrent taxes	..	..	..	..	..	..	..	..	..	..
4600 Other recurrent taxes on property	..	..	0	0	0	0	0	0	0	0
5000 Taxes on goods and services	..	..	**173 785**	**313 615**	**564 115**	**636 585**	**735 283**	**779 319**	**861 433**	**829 049**
5100 Taxes on production, sale, transfer, etc.	..	..	170 235	309 829	557 630	629 546	728 596	771 150	855 448	823 249
5110 General taxes	..	..	72 656	141 152	265 501	291 229	336 674	356 881	395 215	366 127
5111 Value added taxes	..	..	72 656	141 041	264 872	290 843	336 572	356 777	395 127	366 103
VAT - Ordinary imports	..	..	28 287	57 594	127 744	125 105	137 232	144 035	157 496	146 482
VAT - Oil imports	..	..	4 186	5 352	7 894	6 368	6 260	7 643	21 683	5 506
VAT - Domestic (Gross)	..	..	48 583	92 255	143 922	174 051	206 545	219 499	230 348	228 515
VAT - Domestic (Refunds)	..	..	-8 400	-14 160	-14 688	-14 681	-13 464	-14 400	-14 400	-14 400
5112 Sales tax	..	..	0	0	0	0	0	0	0	0
5113 Other	..	..	0	111	630	385	102	103	88	24
Turnover tax	..	..	0	111	630	385	102	103	88	24
5120 Taxes on specific goods and services	..	..	97 579	168 677	292 129	338 317	391 923	414 270	460 233	457 122

Table 5.13. **Kenya** *(cont.)*

Details of tax revenue / Recettes fiscales détaillées

Million KES

	1995	2000	2005	2010	2015	2016	2017	2018	2019	2020
5121 Excises	..	..	58 254	99 135	142 489	178 703	215 753	225 319	239 516	231 392
Excise duty - Oil	..	..	24 876	35 780	42 687	51 611	59 502	61 216	63 834	65 065
Excise duty - Domestic	..	..	15 744	23 755	38 246	48 986	55 499	53 011	59 509	55 721
Road maintenance levy	..	..	9 645	23 780	30 890	45 407	69 557	73 668	78 159	74 458
Excise duty - Imports	..	..	4 235	6 994	15 175	18 096	19 696	22 311	24 622	23 739
Sugar levy	..	..	1 587	1 590	1 329	1 357	115	16	0	0
Petroleum development levy	..	..	1 041	1 585	1 817	1 974	2 168	2 262	2 165	2 044
Petroleum regulatory levy	..	..	0	134	301	485	498	521	1 087	1 073
Second hand motor vehicles purchase tax	..	..	186	183	466	369	166	171	192	186
Stamp duty - Domestic taxes	..	..	940	5 332	11 579	10 417	8 553	12 143	9 947	9 105
5122 Profits of fiscal monopolies	..	..	0	0	0	0	0	0	0	0
5123 Customs and import duties	..	..	32 992	57 047	120 612	125 025	131 577	142 194	154 748	156 503
Import duty - Ordinary	..	..	22 722	40 382	72 346	79 372	85 532	92 076	103 511	96 494
Import declaration fees	..	..	9 724	15 836	27 119	25 851	24 486	26 189	26 782	33 560
Railway development levy	..	..	0	0	18 940	17 273	18 903	20 780	21 303	23 258
Import duty - Oil	..	..	427	797	1 387	1 595	1 329	1 638	1 698	1 656
Merchant superintendent shipping levy	..	..	0	32	820	934	1 328	1 512	1 454	1 535
Stamp duty - Customs services	..	..	119	0	0	0	0	0	0	0
5124 Taxes on exports	..	..	0	0	0	0	0	0	0	0
5125 Taxes on investment goods	..	..	0	0	0	0	0	0	0	0
5126 Taxes on specific services	..	..	6 333	12 495	29 028	34 589	44 592	46 756	65 969	69 227
Excise on air time	..	..	2 982	7 893	13 122	14 884	15 964	15 626	25 120	28 841
Airport revenue	..	..	1 846	2 464	6 619	6 570	11 199	10 414	12 291	11 176
Aviation revenue	..	..	1 505	2 138	3 565	4 122	4 854	4 819	5 912	4 860
Excise on financial services	..	..	0	0	5 722	9 013	12 575	15 898	22 646	24 351
5127 Other taxes on internat. trade and transactions	..	..	0	0	0	0	0	0	0	0
5128 Other taxes	..	..	0	0	0	0	0	0	0	0
5130 Unallocable between 5110 and 5120	..	..	0	0	0	0	0	0	0	0
5200 Taxes on use of goods and perform activities	..	..	3 550	3 786	6 485	7 039	6 687	8 169	5 985	5 800
5210 Recurrent taxes	..	..	3 550	3 786	6 485	7 039	6 687	8 169	5 985	5 800
5211 Paid by households: motor vehicles	..	..	3 266	3 367	6 010	6 564	6 185	7 678	5 474	5 284
Road transport fees	..	..	2 793	2 499	3 947	3 911	4 100	3 366	4 302	4 010
Foreign motor vehicles tax	..	..	0	0	0	0	93	69	0	0
Advance and other taxes	..	..	473	868	2 064	2 653	1 993	4 243	1 172	1 274
5212 Paid by others: motor vehicles	..	..	0	0	0	0	0	0	0	0
5213 Paid in respect of other goods	..	..	284	419	475	475	501	491	511	516
Kenya Bureau of Standards (KEBS) tax	..	..	284	419	475	475	501	491	511	516
5220 Non-recurrent taxes	..	..	0	0	0	0	0	0	0	0
5300 Unallocable between 5100 and 5200	..	..	0	0	0	0	0	0	0	0
6000 Other taxes	**..**	**..**	**0**	**164**	**150**	**161**	**83**	**86**	**66**	**6**
Other taxes	..	..	..	164	150	161	83	86	66	6
6100 Paid solely by business	..	..	..	..	..	..	..	..	..	..
6200 Other	..	..	..	..	..	..	..	..	..	..

.. Not available

Note: Data are reported on a fiscal year basis beginning 1st July. For example, the data for 2020 represent July 2019 to June 2020.

The data are on a cash basis.

Figures exclude tax revenues collected by sub-national governments as the data are not available.

Heading 2000: Data on social security contributions are not readily available but are deemed to be minimal.

Heading 4100: The data for the immovable property (Stand premia on town plots) tax are not readily available for the years 2001-04 and 2006. No estimation was undertaken given the magnitude of the figures.

Heading 5121: Data for the second hand motor vehicles purchase tax are not readily available for the years 2001-04, 2006, 2013 and 2014. No estimation was undertaken given the magnitude of the figures. Stamp duties on domestic taxes are classified under this heading in this editon; In the previous edition they were classified under 4400 taxes on financial and capital transactions.

Heading 5123: Stamp duties - customs services are classified under this heading in this editon; In the previous edition they were classified under 4400 taxes on financial and capital transactions.

Source: Kenya Revenue Authority (KRA).

StatLink https://stat.link/s9yvap

Table 5.14. **Lesotho**

Details of tax revenue / Recettes fiscales détaillées

Million LSL

	1995	2000	2005	2010	2015	2016	2017	2018	2019	2020
Total tax revenue	..	..	**1 462**	**2 933**	**5 872**	**5 995**	**6 095**	**7 289**	**7 248**	**6 771**
1000 Taxes on income, profits and capital gains	..	..	**807**	**1 652**	**3 651**	**3 734**	**3 576**	**4 103**	**4 056**	**3 743**
1100 Of individuals	..	..	618	1 180	2 484	2 695	2 751	3 112	3 142	2 851
1110 On income and profits	..	..	618	1 180	2 484	2 695	2 751	3 112	3 142	2 851
Personal income tax	..	..	618	1 180	1 737	1 965	1 977	2 212	2 296	2 023
Withholding tax	..	..	0	0	748	730	774	900	847	828
1120 On capital gains	..	..	0	0	0	0	0	0	0	0
1200 Corporate	..	..	189	472	1 133	991	791	959	884	862
1210 On profits	..	..	189	472	1 133	991	791	959	884	862
Corporate income tax	..	..	189	472	1 126	983	784	955	877	858
Gambling levy	..	..	0	0	8	8	7	4	7	3
1220 On capital gains of corporates	..	..	0	0	0	0	0	0	0	0
1300 Unallocable between 1100 and 1200	..	..	0	0	34	48	33	33	29	31
2000 Social security contributions	..	..	**0**	**0**	**0**	**0**	**0**	**0**	**0**	**0**
2100 Employees	..	..	..	..	..	..	..	..	..	..
2110 On a payroll basis	..	..	..	..	..	..	..	..	..	..
2120 On an income tax basis	..	..	..	..	..	..	..	..	..	..
2200 Employers	..	..	..	..	..	..	..	..	..	..
2210 On a payroll basis	..	..	..	..	..	..	..	..	..	..
2220 On an income tax basis	..	..	..	..	..	..	..	..	..	..
2300 Self-employed or non-employed	..	..	..	..	..	..	..	..	..	..
2310 On a payroll basis	..	..	..	..	..	..	..	..	..	..
2320 On an income tax basis	..	..	..	..	..	..	..	..	..	..
2400 Unallocable between 2100, 2200 and 2300	..	..	..	..	..	..	..	..	..	..
2410 On a payroll basis	..	..	..	..	..	..	..	..	..	..
2420 On an income tax basis	..	..	..	..	..	..	..	..	..	..
3000 Taxes on payroll and workforce	..	..	**0**	**0**	**0**	**0**	**0**	**0**	**0**	**0**
4000 Taxes on property	..	..	..	..	..	..	..	..	..	..
4100 Recurrent taxes on immovable property	..	..	..	..	..	..	..	..	..	..
4110 Households	..	..	..	..	..	..	..	..	..	..
4120 Others	..	..	..	..	..	..	..	..	..	..
4200 Recurrent taxes on net wealth	..	..	..	..	..	..	..	..	..	..
4210 Individual	..	..	..	..	..	..	..	..	..	..
4220 Corporate	..	..	..	..	..	..	..	..	..	..
4300 Estate, inheritance and gift taxes	..	..	..	..	..	..	..	..	..	..
4310 Estate and inheritance taxes	..	..	..	..	..	..	..	..	..	..
4320 Gift taxes	..	..	..	..	..	..	..	..	..	..
4400 Taxes on financial and capital transactions	..	..	..	..	..	..	..	..	..	..
4500 Other non-reccurrent taxes on property	..	..	..	..	..	..	..	..	..	..
4510 On net wealth	..	..	..	..	..	..	..	..	..	..
4520 Other non-recurrent taxes	..	..	..	..	..	..	..	..	..	..
4600 Other recurrent taxes on property	..	..	..	..	..	..	..	..	..	..
5000 Taxes on goods and services	..	..	**656**	**1 281**	**2 221**	**2 261**	**2 519**	**3 185**	**3 192**	**3 028**
5100 Taxes on production, sale, transfer, etc	..	..	656	1 281	2 221	2 261	2 519	3 185	3 192	3 028
5110 General taxes on goods and services	..	..	656	1 281	2 210	2 254	2 414	2 880	2 907	2 608
5111 Value added taxes	..	..	656	1 281	2 210	2 254	2 414	2 880	2 907	2 608
VAT on imports	..	..	252	473	780	798	795	880	896	662
VAT - Domestic (Net)	..	..	403	808	1 430	1 456	1 619	2 000	2 011	1 946
VAT - Domestic (Gross)	..	..	463	1 046	1 996	2 131	2 250	2 681	2 877	2 668
VAT - Domestic (Refunds)	..	..	-59	-238	-566	-675	-632	-682	-867	-722
5112 Sales tax	..	..	0	0	0	0	0	0	0	0
5113 Other	..	..	0	0	0	0	0	0	0	0
5120 Taxes on specific goods and services	..	..	0	0	11	7	105	305	285	420
5121 Excises	..	..	..	..	11	7	105	305	285	420
Oil levy	..	..	..	..	11	7	7	17	22	229
Motor vehicle assurance	..	..	..	..	..	..	51	189	147	8
Petroleum levy	..	..	..	..	..	..	47	61	22	72
Road maintenance levy	..	..	..	..	..	..	..	39	93	111
5122 Profits of fiscal monopolies	..	..	..	..	..	..	..	..	..	..
5123 Customs and import duties	..	..	..	..	..	..	..	..	..	..
5124 Taxes on exports	..	..	..	..	..	..	..	..	..	..
5125 Taxes on investment goods	..	..	..	..	..	..	..	..	..	..
5126 Taxes on specific services	..	..	..	..	..	..	..	..	..	..
5127 Other taxes on internat. trade and transactions	..	..	..	..	..	..	..	..	..	..

Table 5.14. **Lesotho** *(cont.)*

Details of tax revenue / Recettes fiscales détaillées

Million LSL

	1995	2000	2005	2010	2015	2016	2017	2018	2019	2020
5128 Other taxes	..	..	..	..	..	..	..	..	..	..
5130 Unallocable between 5110 and 5120	..	..	0	0	0	0	0	0	0	0
5200 Taxes on use of goods and to perform activities	..	..	0	0	0	0	0	0	0	0
5210 Recurrent taxes	..	..	..	..	..	..	..	..	..	..
5211 Paid by households: motor vehicles	..	..	..	..	..	..	..	..	..	..
5212 Paid by others: motor vehicles	..	..	..	..	..	..	..	..	..	..
5213 Paid in respect of other goods	..	..	..	..	..	..	..	..	..	..
5220 Non-recurrent taxes	..	..	..	..	..	..	..	..	..	..
5300 Unallocable between 5100 and 5200	..	..	0	0	0	0	0	0	0	0
6000 Other taxes	**..**	**..**	**0**	**0**	**0**	**0**	**0**	**0**	**0**	**0**
6100 Paid solely by business	..	..	..	..	..	..	..	..	..	..
6200 Other	..	..	..	..	..	..	..	..	..	..
Memo items:										
Excise taxes collected on behalf of the SACU Common Revenue Pool	..	..	53	110	102	128	191	212	215	82
Import duties collected on behalf of the SACU Common Revenue Pool	..	..	18	32	145	108	121	145	147	107

.. Not available

Note: Data are on a fiscal year basis beginning 1st April. For example, the data for 2020 represent April 2020 to March 2021.

Data are reported on a cash basis.

Heading 2000: Social security contributions for Lesotho are deemed to be null as they do not meet the criteria to be classified as social security contributions set out in the OECD classification of taxes in the OECD *Interpretative Guide*.

Heading 5121: this heading includes for the first time extra-budgetary revenues. The oil levy, road maintenance levy, motor vehicle assurance and petroleum levy do not form part of the SACU Common Revenue Pool. Revenue from the road maintenance levy, motor vehicle assurance and petroleum levy are transferred to the Road fund and Petroleum Fund.

Source: Revenue Services Lesotho.

StatLink https://stat.link/frxbz6

Table 5.15. **Madagascar**

Details of tax revenue / Recettes fiscales détaillées

Million MGA

	1995	2000	2005	2010	2015	2016	2017	2018	2019	2020
Recettes fiscales totales	**219 280**	**603 200**	**1 043 558**	**1 980 849**	**3 141 695**	**3 771 945**	**4 473 868**	**5 277 348**	**5 862 561**	**5 202 842**
1000 Impôts sur revenu, bénéfices et gains en capital	**36 960**	**102 580**	**244 707**	**490 294**	**706 750**	**882 598**	**1 002 793**	**1 174 764**	**1 437 601**	**1 305 413**
1100 Des personnes physiques	12 600	36 080	77 147	253 868	366 600	429 165	474 685	547 816	687 985	620 915
1110 Sur le revenu et les bénéfices	9 660	25 800	60 645	216 415	338 560	387 703	430 830	492 008	626 286	567 759
Traitements et salaires	9 180	25 260	56 673	201 077	315 570	359 334	398 027	446 571	549 317	490 419
Bénéfices non commerciaux (BNC)	480	540	1 893	1 841	3 850	5 994	6 874	6 094	7 802	8 336
Bénéfices industriels et commerciaux (BIC)	0	0	2 079	13 497	19 140	22 376	25 930	39 344	69 167	69 004
1120 Sur les gains en capital	2 940	10 280	16 502	37 453	28 040	41 461	43 855	55 807	61 699	53 156
1200 Des sociétés	23 040	62 240	159 183	236 426	340 150	453 433	528 108	626 948	749 616	684 499
1210 Sur les bénéfices	20 500	56 880	142 797	236 426	340 150	453 433	528 108	626 948	749 616	684 499
1220 Sur les gains en capital	2 540	5 360	16 386	0	0	0	0	0	0	0
1300 Non ventilables entre 1100 et 1200	1 320	4 260	8 377	0	0	0	0	0	0	0
2000 Cotisations de sécurité sociale	..	..	..	..	**133 072**	**132 033**	**159 300**	**295 800**	**260 981**	**304 656**
2100 A la charge des salariés	..	..	..	..	0	0	0	0	0	0
2110 Sur la base du salaire	..	..	..	..	..	..	..	..	..	..
2120 Sur la base de l'impôt sur le revenu	..	..	..	..	..	..	..	..	..	..
2200 A la charge des employeurs	..	..	..	..	0	0	0	0	0	0
2210 Sur la base du salaire	..	..	..	..	..	..	..	..	..	..
2220 Sur la base de l'impôt sur le revenu	..	..	..	..	..	..	..	..	..	..
2300 A charge des travailleurs indép. ou sans emploi	..	..	..	..	0	0	0	0	0	0
2310 Sur la base du salaire	..	..	..	..	..	..	..	..	..	..
2320 Sur la base de l'impôt sur le revenu	..	..	..	..	..	..	..	..	..	..
2400 Non ventilables entre 2100, 2200 et 2300	..	..	..	..	133 072	132 033	159 300	295 800	260 981	304 656
2410 Sur la base du salaire	..	..	..	..	..	..	..	..	..	..
2420 Sur la base de l'impôt sur le revenu	..	..	..	..	..	..	..	..	..	..
3000 Sur salaires ou main-d'œuvre	**0**	**0**	**0**	**0**	**0**	**0**	**0**	**0**	**0**	**0**
4000 Impôts sur le patrimoine	**2 380**	**4 340**	**8 514**	**10 560**	**24 150**	**25 056**	**25 784**	**41 045**	**31 454**	**30 321**
4100 Impôts périodiques sur la propriété immobilière	0	0	0	0	0	0	0	0	0	0
4110 Ménages	..	..	..	..	..	..	..	..	..	..
4120 Autres agents	..	..	..	..	..	..	..	..	..	..
4200 Impôts périodiques sur l'actif net	0	0	0	0	0	0	0	0	0	0
4210 Personnes physiques	..	..	..	..	..	..	..	..	..	..
4220 Sociétés	..	..	..	..	..	..	..	..	..	..
4300 Impôts sur mut. par décès, succ. et donations	0	0	0	0	0	0	0	0	0	0
4310 Impôts sur mut. par décès et successions	..	..	..	..	..	..	..	..	..	..
4320 Impôts sur les donations	..	..	..	..	..	..	..	..	..	..
4400 Impôts sur transact. mobilières et immob.	0	0	0	0	0	0	0	0	0	0
4500 Impôts non-périodiques	0	0	0	0	0	0	0	0	0	0
4510 Sur l'actif net	..	..	..	..	..	..	..	..	..	..
4520 Autres non-périodiques	..	..	..	..	..	..	..	..	..	..
4600 Autres impôts périodiques sur patrimoine	2 380	4 340	8 514	10 560	24 150	25 056	25 784	41 045	31 454	30 321
5000 Impôts sur les biens et services	**175 880**	**490 160**	**778 937**	**1 472 696**	**2 274 573**	**2 717 568**	**3 270 758**	**3 744 286**	**4 106 225**	**3 556 468**
5100 Impôts sur production, vente, transfert, etc.	175 880	488 480	776 544	1 468 130	2 267 473	2 709 818	3 263 032	3 735 594	4 096 746	3 546 289
5110 Impôts généraux	104 600	280 700	455 232	1 004 032	1 545 130	1 837 385	2 262 049	2 566 967	2 811 054	2 367 393
5111 Taxes sur la valeur ajoutée	104 600	244 860	410 256	1 004 032	1 545 130	1 837 385	2 262 049	2 566 967	2 811 054	2 367 393
TVA Intérieure	48 460	102 560	196 922	437 348	544 130	693 241	843 911	906 711	953 565	911 289
TVA Douane import	56 140	142 300	213 334	387 092	728 300	881 624	1 088 765	1 232 623	1 346 233	1 135 945
TVA Douane sur les produits pétroliers	0	0	0	179 592	272 700	262 520	329 373	427 632	511 256	320 159
5112 Impôts sur les ventes	0	0	0	0	0	0	0	0	0	0
5113 Autres impôts	0	35 840	44 976	0	0	0	0	0	0	0
5120 Impôts sur biens et services déterminés	71 280	207 780	321 312	464 098	722 343	872 433	1 000 982	1 168 628	1 285 693	1 178 896
5121 Accises	180	43 700	54 139	201 039	249 470	304 817	319 036	343 817	360 581	389 869
Accises domestiques	160	31 920	43 610	201 039	..	..	..	..	..	..
Accises domestiques - intermittents	..	..	..	..	25 923	44 547	45 799	54 128	51 978	70 782
Accises domestiques - Alcools	..	..	..	..	37 975	53 142	57 465	62 773	57 150	71 274
Accises domestiques - Boissons hygieniques	..	..	..	..	0	2 520	2 919	2 803	2 758	2 864
Accises domestiques - Tabacs	..	..	..	..	185 571	204 607	212 852	224 113	248 696	244 949
Accises à la douane	20	11 780	10 529	0	0	0	0	0	0	0
5122 Bénéfices des monopoles fiscaux	9 280	0	0	0	0	0	0	0	0	0
5123 Droits de douane et droits à l'importation	61 820	152 380	266 588	262 726	458 100	538 485	628 505	767 173	890 053	730 087
Droit de douanes	16 260	24 700	112 160	172 369	331 400	412 085	493 156	535 458	604 739	498 342
Taxe d'importation	29 780	48 140	0	0	0	0	0	0	0	0
Taxes s/ prod. Pétroliers (total)	15 780	79 540	154 428	90 357	126 700	126 400	135 349	231 715	285 314	231 745
5124 Taxes à l'exportation	0	0	0	0	0	0	0	0	0	0

Table 5.15. **Madagascar** *(cont.)*

Details of tax revenue / Recettes fiscales détaillées

Million MGA

	1995	2000	2005	2010	2015	2016	2017	2018	2019	2020
5125 Impôts sur biens d'équipement	0	0	0	0	0	0	0	0	0	0
5126 Impôts sur services déterminés	0	0	0	0	14 673	29 088	52 969	57 127	34 260	57 748
Télécommunications	..	..	..	..	14 673	29 088	52 969	57 127	34 260	57 748
5127 Autres impôts sur commerce et transact. internat.	0	11 700	585	333	100	44	473	510	799	1 192
Taxe statistique s/ import	..	8 040	0	0	0	0	0	0	0	0
Autres	..	3 660	585	333	100	44	473	510	799	1 192
5128 Autres impôts	0	0	0	0	0	0	0	0	0	0
5130 Non ventilables entre 5110 et 5120	0	0	0	0	0	0	0	0	0	0
5200 Impôts sur utilisation des biens et exerc. activités	0	1 680	2 393	4 566	7 100	7 750	7 727	8 692	9 479	10 179
5210 Impôts périodiques	0	1 680	2 393	4 566	7 100	7 750	7 727	8 692	9 479	10 179
5211 A la charge des ménages: véhicules à moteur	..	0	0	0	0	0	0	0	0	0
5212 A la charge autres agents: véhicules à moteur	..	0	0	0	0	0	0	0	0	0
5213 Autres impôts périodiques	..	1 680	2 393	4 566	7 100	7 750	7 727	8 692	9 479	10 179
5220 Impôts non-périodiques	0	0	0	0	0	0	0	0	0	0
5300 Non ventilables entre 5100 et 5200	0	0	0	0	0	0	0	0	0	0
6000 Autres impôts	**4 060**	**6 120**	**11 400**	**7 299**	**3 150**	**14 690**	**15 233**	**21 453**	**26 300**	**5 984**
6100 A la charge exclusive des entreprises	2 720	2 540	4 349	3 739	650	1 004	944	687	1 178	872
6200 A la charge d'autres agents	1 340	3 580	7 051	3 560	2 500	13 686	14 289	20 766	25 123	5 112

.. Non disponible

Note : Année civile se terminant le 31 décembre.

Les données sont sur la base des encaissements.

Les chiffres n'incluent pas les recettes fiscales collectées par les collectivités locales car elles ne sont pas disponibles.

Les cotisations de sécurité sociale sous la rubrique 2000 ne sont pas considérées comme des recettes fiscales au Madagascar.

Rubrique 5121 : la ventilation des accises domestiques est presentée à partir de 2013. Les accises domestiques sur les télécommunications sont classifiées dans la rubrique 5126 Impôts sur des services déterminés comme préconisé dans le guide d'interprétation des *Statistiques des recettes publiques en Afrique* en Annexe A. A partir de 2009, les droits d'accises à la douane sont inclus dans les catégories de droits d'accises intermittents ou les autres catégories de droits d'accises collectés par l'administration fiscale, c'est-à-dire qu' ils sont compris dans les recettes fiscales intérieures.

Source : Ministère de l'économie et des Finances de Madagascar.

StatLink *https://stat.link/qxnsu4*

Table 5.16. **Malawi**

Details of tax revenue / Recettes fiscales détaillées

Million MWK

	1995	2000	2005	2010	2015	2016	2017	2018	2019	2020
Total tax revenue	**..**	**..**	**51 183**	**152 744**	**485 326**	**604 221**	**795 784**	**880 895**	**986 710**	**1 044 516**
1000 Taxes on income, profits and capital gains	**..**	**..**	**21 837**	**67 576**	**236 126**	**292 729**	**386 078**	**423 259**	**460 724**	**506 568**
1100 Of individuals	..	..	12 152	36 525	139 074	186 751	224 334	256 576	302 061	335 991
1110 On income and profits	..	..	12 152	36 525	139 074	186 751	224 334	256 576	302 061	335 991
Pay as you earn tax (PAYE)	..	..	11 098	32 849	126 367	166 855	199 315	228 697	269 244	296 370
Fringe benefits	..	..	844	1 675	5 350	7 506	8 981	10 749	12 111	11 947
Non-resident tax	..	..	196	835	4 585	8 488	13 153	13 116	16 350	22 479
Dividends	..	..	14	1 165	2 772	3 901	2 885	4 013	4 355	5 195
1120 On capital gains	..	..	0	0	0	0	0	0	0	0
1200 Corporate	..	..	9 685	31 051	97 052	105 978	161 744	166 683	158 664	170 577
1210 On profits	..	..	9 685	31 051	97 052	105 978	161 744	166 683	158 664	170 577
Company assessments	..	..	1 984	6 981	14 186	14 753	21 125	28 858	19 619	16 369
Provisional corporate income tax	..	..	3 957	16 253	43 723	42 897	64 656	64 987	55 936	65 470
Withholding tax on corporations	..	..	3 745	7 817	39 143	48 328	64 041	72 839	83 109	88 738
Capital gains tax	..	..	0	0	0	0	11 923	0	0	0
1220 On capital gains of corporates	..	..	0	0	0	0	0	0	0	0
1300 Unallocable between 1100 and 1200	..	..	0	0	0	0	0	0	0	0
2000 Social security contributions	**..**	**..**	**0**	**0**	**0**	**0**	**0**	**0**	**0**	**0**
2100 Employees	..	..	..	..	..	..	..	..	..	..
2110 On a payroll basis	..	..	..	..	..	..	..	..	..	..
2120 On an income tax basis	..	..	..	..	..	..	..	..	..	..
2200 Employers	..	..	..	..	..	..	..	..	..	..
2210 On a payroll basis	..	..	..	..	..	..	..	..	..	..
2220 On an income tax basis	..	..	..	..	..	..	..	..	..	..
2300 Self-employed or non-employed	..	..	..	..	..	..	..	..	..	..
2310 On a payroll basis	..	..	..	..	..	..	..	..	..	..
2320 On an income tax basis	..	..	..	..	..	..	..	..	..	..
2400 Unallocable between 2100, 2200 and 2300	..	..	..	..	..	..	..	..	..	..
2410 On a payroll basis	..	..	..	..	..	..	..	..	..	..
2420 On an income tax basis	..	..	..	..	..	..	..	..	..	..
3000 Taxes on payroll and workforce	**..**	**..**	**0**	**0**	**0**	**0**	**0**	**0**	**0**	**0**
4000 Taxes on property	**..**	**..**	**..**	**..**	**..**	**..**	**..**	**..**	**..**	**..**
4100 Recurrent taxes on immovable property	..	..	..	..	..	..	..	..	..	..
4110 Households	..	..	..	..	..	..	..	..	..	..
4120 Others	..	..	..	..	..	..	..	..	..	..
4200 Recurrent taxes on net wealth	..	..	..	..	..	..	..	..	..	..
4210 Individual	..	..	..	..	..	..	..	..	..	..
4220 Corporate	..	..	..	..	..	..	..	..	..	..
4300 Estate, inheritance and gift taxes	..	..	..	..	..	..	..	..	..	..
4310 Estate and inheritance taxes	..	..	..	..	..	..	..	..	..	..
4320 Gift taxes	..	..	..	..	..	..	..	..	..	..
4400 Taxes on financial and capital transactions	..	..	..	..	..	..	..	..	..	..
4500 Other non-reccurrent taxes on property	..	..	..	..	..	..	..	..	..	..
4510 On net wealth	..	..	..	..	..	..	..	..	..	..
4520 Other non-recurrent taxes	..	..	..	..	..	..	..	..	..	..
4600 Other recurrent taxes on property	..	..	..	..	..	..	..	..	..	..
5000 Taxes on goods and services	**..**	**..**	**29 263**	**84 865**	**248 646**	**310 922**	**408 050**	**457 223**	**525 273**	**537 055**
5100 Taxes on production, sale, transfer, etc	..	..	29 263	84 865	248 646	310 922	408 050	457 223	525 273	535 785
5110 General taxes on goods and services	..	..	14 216	38 751	137 551	166 781	220 278	247 658	287 974	294 434
5111 Value added taxes	..	..	14 216	38 751	137 539	166 761	220 266	247 632	287 926	294 408
VAT revenues (domestic)	..	..	6 880	21 932	67 149	75 727	108 064	132 750	163 852	176 801
VAT on imports	..	..	8 279	22 482	80 007	99 900	129 668	139 080	152 835	138 453
VAT refunds	..	..	-942	-5 663	-9 618	-8 866	-17 466	-24 199	-28 761	-20 847
5112 Sales tax	..	..	0	0	0	0	0	0	0	0
5113 Other	..	..	0	0	12	20	13	26	48	27
Turnover tax	..	..	..	..	12	20	13	26	48	27
5120 Taxes on specific goods and services	..	..	15 047	46 115	111 094	144 141	187 771	209 565	237 299	241 350
5121 Excises	..	..	8 097	31 122	64 856	91 580	117 941	133 326	149 006	156 678
Local excise taxes	..	..	1 294	5 805	15 368	19 860	28 389	32 208	36 215	40 042
Excise taxes on imports	..	..	5 401	14 233	26 419	29 981	41 714	48 544	55 172	52 302
Road Levy (fuel tax)	..	..	1 402	7 507	9 312	19 619	24 002	26 277	31 218	38 465
Road tax (fuel tax)	..	..	0	0	3 837	4 425	4 717	5 580	6 662	7 048
Rural Electrification Levy (fuel tax)	..	..	0	3 577	8 681	16 255	17 530	18 950	17 781	16 588
Storage Levy (fuel tax)	..	..	0	0	1 240	1 441	1 590	1 768	1 958	2 233

Table 5.16. **Malawi** *(cont.)*

Details of tax revenue / Recettes fiscales détaillées

Million MWK

	1995	2000	2005	2010	2015	2016	2017	2018	2019	2020
5122 Profits of fiscal monopolies	..	..	0	0	0	0	0	0	0	0
5123 Customs and import duties	..	..	6 950	14 993	46 238	52 562	69 830	76 239	88 292	84 672
Import duty	..	..	6 229	15 775	46 121	52 197	69 773	76 179	88 213	82 528
Prepayments collected on import duties	..	..	721	-783	117	365	57	60	79	33
Surcharges on import duties	..	..	0	0	0	0	0	0	0	2 112
5124 Taxes on exports	..	..	0	0	0	0	0	0	0	0
5125 Taxes on investment goods	..	..	0	0	0	0	0	0	0	0
5126 Taxes on specific services	..	..	0	0	0	0	0	0	0	0
5127 Other taxes on internat. trade and transactions	..	..	0	0	0	0	0	0	0	0
5128 Other taxes	..	..	0	0	0	0	0	0	0	0
5130 Unallocable between 5110 and 5120	..	..	0	0	0	0	0	0	0	0
5200 Taxes on use of goods and to perform activities	..	..	0	0	0	0	0	0	0	1 271
5210 Recurrent taxes	..	..	..	..	..	..	..	..	..	1 271
5211 Paid by households: motor vehicles	..	..	..	..	..	..	..	..	..	0
5212 Paid by others: motor vehicles	..	..	..	..	..	..	..	..	..	1 271
Carbon tax on vehicle ownership	..	..	..	..	..	..	..	..	..	1 271
5213 Paid in respect of other goods	..	..	..	..	..	..	..	..	..	0
5220 Non-recurrent taxes	..	..	..	..	..	..	..	..	..	0
5300 Unallocable between 5100 and 5200	..	..	0	0	0	0	0	0	0	0
6000 Other taxes	**..**	**..**	**82**	**303**	**554**	**570**	**1 656**	**413**	**714**	**893**
6100 Paid solely by business	..	..	82	303	554	570	1 656	413	714	893
6200 Other	..	..	0	0	0	0	0	0	0	0

.. Not available

Note: Data are on a fiscal year basis beginning 1st July. For example, the data for 2020 represent July 1, 2019 to June 30, 2020.

The data are on a cash basis.

Figures exclude revenues from business licenses and permits collected by city and district councils from business entities within their jurisdictions.

Heading 2000: Social security contributions for Malawi are deemed to be null as they do not meet the criteria to be classified as social security contributions set out in the OECD classification of taxes in the *OECD Interpretative Guide*.

Heading 4000: Revenues from property taxes are mainly levied by local governments for which data on revenue are not available.

Source: Ministry of Finance, Economic Planning and Development of Malawi.

StatLink https://stat.link/4wk8ol

Table 5.17. **Mali**

Details of tax revenue / Recettes fiscales détaillées

Million XOF

	1995	2000	2005	2010	2015	2016	2017	2018	2019	2020
Recettes fiscales totales	**124 203**	**239 362**	**476 775**	**748 245**	**1 174 860**	**1 371 149**	**1 491 790**	**1 263 918**	**1 770 989**	**1 820 348**
1000 Impôts sur revenu, bénéfices et gains en capital	**26 399**	**34 698**	**78 979**	**184 760**	**296 284**	**327 103**	**391 107**	**313 752**	**410 014**	**504 543**
1100 Des personnes physiques	10 053	16 061	33 283	50 375	88 233	94 711	111 698	90 875	125 158	152 980
1110 Sur le revenu et les bénéfices	10 053	16 061	33 283	50 375	88 233	94 711	111 698	90 875	125 158	152 980
ITS retenue, secteur privé	5 853	12 374	25 119	39 859	71 153	76 734	91 859	74 395	101 950	128 979
ITS retenue, secteur public	2 723	3 311	7 125	8 624	13 904	13 882	15 677	12 004	18 066	19 624
Taxe sur les plus-values de cession	0	0	0	0	862	1 042	1 137	1 371	1 599	989
Impôts sur les revenus fonciers	1 477	376	1 039	1 892	2 314	3 053	3 025	3 105	3 543	3 388
1120 Sur les gains en capital	0	0	0	0	0	0	0	0	0	0
1200 Des sociétés	10 840	16 034	38 386	118 346	179 458	206 698	250 612	201 763	253 131	315 366
1210 Sur les bénéfices	10 840	16 034	38 386	118 346	179 458	206 698	250 612	201 763	253 131	315 366
Impôt sur les societés (IS privé)	..	..	31 767	107 582	174 433	199 055	246 446	197 499	249 245	311 333
Impôt sur les societés (IS état)	..	..	0	121	1	0	3	157	26	108
BIC secteur privé	10 840	15 996	6 589	10 643	5 024	7 643	4 163	4 107	3 859	3 925
BIC secteur état	0	38	30	0	0	0	0	0	0	0
1220 Sur les gains en capital	..	..	..	..	..	..	..	..	..	..
1300 Non ventilables entre 1100 et 1200	5 506	2 603	7 310	16 039	28 593	25 694	28 797	21 115	31 725	36 197
Taxe synthétique	0	480	1 449	1 212	1 441	1 503	1 503	1 469	1 486	1 399
Impôt sur le revenu des valeurs mobilières	5 506	2 123	5 861	14 827	27 152	24 191	27 294	19 646	30 239	34 798
2000 Cotisations de sécurité sociale	**13 169**	**18 442**	**45 497**	**73 600**	**116 702**	**153 398**	**156 268**	**158 559**	**235 011**	**268 659**
2100 A la charge des salariés	..	..	..	..	..	..	..	..	..	..
2110 Sur la base du salaire	..	..	..	..	..	..	..	..	..	..
2120 Sur la base de l'impôt sur le revenu	..	..	..	..	..	..	..	..	..	..
2200 A la charge des employeurs	..	..	..	..	..	..	..	..	..	..
2210 Sur la base du salaire	..	..	..	..	..	..	..	..	..	..
2220 Sur la base de l'impôt sur le revenu	..	..	..	..	..	..	..	..	..	..
2300 A charge des travailleurs indép. ou sans emploi	..	..	..	..	..	..	..	..	..	..
2310 Sur la base du salaire	..	..	..	..	..	..	..	..	..	..
2320 Sur la base de l'impôt sur le revenu	..	..	..	..	..	..	..	..	..	..
2400 Non ventilables entre 2100, 2200 et 2300	13 169	18 442	45 497	73 600	116 702	153 398	156 268	158 559	235 011	268 659
Cotisations sécurité sociale (CMSS)	..	..	9 259	12 834	26 550	45 311	41 985	34 758	98 520	114 470
Cotisations sécurité sociale (INPS)	13 169	18 442	36 238	60 766	90 152	108 086	114 283	123 801	136 492	154 189
2410 Sur la base du salaire	..	..	..	..	..	..	..	..	..	..
2420 Sur la base de l'impôt sur le revenu	..	..	..	..	..	..	..	..	..	..
3000 Sur salaires ou main-d'œuvre	**2 470**	**4 671**	**8 381**	**6 278**	**11 567**	**13 192**	**13 685**	**11 938**	**14 737**	**5 724**
4000 Impôts sur le patrimoine	**2 724**	**3 149**	**7 909**	**12 062**	**17 933**	**28 489**	**32 171**	**26 353**	**30 862**	**26 729**
4100 Impôts périodiques sur la propriété immobilière	54	119	930	979	1 561	1 590	2 156	1 779	1 957	1 365
Droits de conservation de la propriété	54	119	930	979	1 549	1 572	2 139	1 764	1 914	1 316
Taxe sur les locations des particuliers	0	0	0	0	12	18	17	15	42	49
4110 Ménages	..	..	..	..	..	..	..	..	..	..
4120 Autres agents	..	..	..	..	..	..	..	..	..	..
4200 Impôts périodiques sur l'actif net	0	0	0	0	0	0	0	0	0	0
4210 Personnes physiques	..	..	..	..	..	..	..	..	..	..
4220 Sociétés	..	..	..	..	..	..	..	..	..	..
4300 Impôts sur mut. par décès, succ. et donations	0	0	0	0	0	0	0	0	0	0
4310 Impôts sur mut. par décès et successions	..	..	..	..	..	..	..	..	..	..
4320 Impôts sur les donations	..	..	..	..	..	..	..	..	..	..
4400 Impôts sur transact. mobilières et immob.	2 670	3 030	6 979	11 083	16 372	26 899	30 015	24 573	28 905	25 363
Droits d'enregistrements (DGI)	2 600	2 934	3 414	6 928	11 023	18 390	19 941	16 754	13 027	12 155
Droits d'enregistrements (DND)	0	0	3 055	4 107	5 321	8 436	9 815	7 499	15 583	13 174
Transfert lettre et permis OCC en TF	70	96	510	0	0	0	0	0	0	0
Taxe sur les frais d'édilité	0	0	0	48	28	73	259	320	295	35
4500 Impôts non-périodiques	0	0	0	0	0	0	0	0	0	0
4510 Sur l'actif net	..	..	..	..	..	..	..	..	..	..
4520 Autres non-périodiques	..	..	..	..	..	..	..	..	..	..
4600 Autres impôts périodiques sur patrimoine	0	0	0	0	0	0	0	0	0	0
5000 Impôts sur les biens et services	**73 710**	**172 271**	**328 545**	**451 942**	**689 931**	**811 118**	**874 248**	**728 932**	**989 465**	**919 030**
5100 Impôts sur production, vente, transfert, etc.	73 011	171 443	327 388	450 213	687 273	807 832	871 041	724 619	985 878	915 450
5110 Impôts généraux	27 647	80 633	191 827	260 599	328 157	394 552	438 914	371 539	537 907	489 239
5111 Taxes sur la valeur ajoutée	27 647	80 633	191 827	260 599	328 157	394 552	438 914	371 539	537 907	489 239
TVA à l'importation	13 863	46 622	119 548	161 656	210 431	232 434	282 199	268 881	316 487	329 261
Recettes TVA (privé)	9 332	31 218	67 629	95 383	113 512	150 102	153 442	100 982	220 473	159 455
Recettes TVA (gouvernement)	4 452	2 793	4 650	3 560	4 214	12 016	3 273	1 677	947	522
5112 Impôts sur les ventes	0	0	0	0	0	0	0	0	0	0

Table 5.17. **Mali** *(cont.)*

Details of tax revenue / Recettes fiscales détaillées

Million XOF

	1995	2000	2005	2010	2015	2016	2017	2018	2019	2020
5113 Autres impôts	0	0	0	0	0	0	0	0	0	0
5120 Impôts sur biens et services déterminés	45 364	90 810	135 561	189 614	359 116	413 280	432 127	353 080	447 970	426 212
5121 Accises	23 257	45 791	42 725	56 909	136 898	159 013	148 200	103 676	118 607	127 509
Taxes intérieures sur produits petroliers (TIPP)	9 133	33 694	26 389	25 660	93 264	100 648	87 789	48 611	43 626	55 356
Taxe Ad Valorem (entreprises minières) (DNDC)	439	4 233	9 811	20 479	25 253	30 605	30 681	27 246	45 845	40 165
Taxes locales sur les tabacs	981	816	3 285	5 385	8 264	12 787	14 725	14 405	13 420	14 571
Taxes sur les boissons alcoolisés	867	1 169	1 317	1 777	3 611	3 672	4 806	4 750	6 037	4 430
Impôt spécial sur les boissons	133	1 519	708	2 088	4 237	5 431	6 755	5 459	5 144	5 670
Taxe sur autres produits	11 704	4 360	1 215	1 520	2 269	5 870	3 444	3 205	4 535	7 319
5122 Bénéfices des monopoles fiscaux	0	0	0	0	0	0	0	0	0	0
5123 Droits de douane et droits à l'importation	19 055	30 734	67 175	86 853	124 049	139 263	161 928	147 355	173 683	173 712
Droits de douanes	19 029	29 328	60 305	76 287	111 062	124 320	144 024	129 869	154 469	153 707
Redevance Statistique	0	315	6 485	9 702	12 940	14 803	17 804	16 939	19 148	19 967
Taxe degréssive de protection (TDP)	0	6	373	831	0	0	0	0	0	0
Taxe conjoncturelle à l'importation	26	1 085	12	33	47	140	100	547	67	38
5124 Taxes à l'exportation	102	4 046	9 922	20 503	30 243	29 288	37 421	33 887	53 055	42 532
CPS sur l'or	102	4 046	9 922	20 503	30 243	29 288	37 421	33 887	53 055	42 532
5125 Impôts sur biens d'équipement	0	0	0	0	0	0	0	0	0	0
5126 Impôts sur services déterminés	2 950	10 239	15 739	25 349	67 926	85 716	84 578	68 162	102 625	82 458
Taxes sur les Activités Financières	0	5 785	9 995	17 828	39 608	41 562	43 886	32 993	59 838	44 939
Ristournes sur PMU et CASINO	1 497	1 515	1 955	3 061	5 966	6 821	6 832	7 069	7 478	3 968
Taxes sur les transporteurs routiers	620	1 676	2 287	2 659	3 499	4 890	4 072	4 212	3 505	2 712
Taxes sur les contrats d'assurances	830	1 261	1 475	1 787	3 321	4 783	4 454	4 066	4 852	5 149
Autres taxes sur les services déterminés	3	2	27	14	2	10	1	1	3	1
Taxe sur Accès au Reseau de Télécom Ouvert au Public (TARTOP)	0	0	0	0	15 530	27 650	25 333	19 822	26 950	25 688
5127 Autres impôts sur commerce et transact. internat.	0	0	0	0	0	0	0	0	0	0
5128 Autres impôts	0	0	0	0	0	0	0	0	0	0
5130 Non ventilables entre 5110 et 5120	0	0	0	0	0	0	0	0	0	0
5200 Impôts sur utilisation des biens et exerc. activites	699	828	1 157	1 729	2 658	3 286	3 207	4 313	3 588	3 579
5210 Impôts périodiques	699	828	1 157	1 729	2 658	3 286	3 207	4 313	3 588	3 579
5211 A la charge des ménages: véhicules à moteur	583	716	1 140	1 715	2 658	3 286	3 207	3 389	3 588	3 579
5212 A la charge autres agents: véhicules à moteur	0	0	0	0	0	0	0	0	..	..
5213 Autres impôts périodiques	116	112	17	14	0	0	0	924	..	..
5220 Impôts non-périodiques	0	0	0	0	0	0	0	0	0	0
5300 Non ventilables entre 5100 et 5200	0	0	0	0	0	0	0	0	0	0
6000 Autres impôts	**5 731**	**6 131**	**7 464**	**19 603**	**42 443**	**37 849**	**24 311**	**24 385**	**90 899**	**95 664**
Droits de Timbres (DGI)	4 839	4 188	6 172	10 797	16 840	18 821	16 502	17 702	20 027	19 495
Droits de timbres (DND)	0	0	911	143	235	277	455	406	550	509
Recettes sur exercices antérieurs	892	1 943	381	8 663	25 368	18 751	7 354	6 277	70 323	75 660
6100 A la charge exclusive des entreprises	..	..	..	..	..	..	..	..	..	..
6200 A la charge d'autres agents	..	..	..	..	..	..	..	..	..	..
Pour mémoire : *Prélevement communautaire (PC) (taxe UEMOA)*	1 978	1 394	0	0	0	0	0	0	0	0

.. Non disponible

Note : Année civile se terminant le 31 décembre.

Les données sont sur la base des encaissements.

Les chiffres n'incluent pas les recettes fiscales collectées par les collectivités locales car elles ne sont pas disponibles.

Les recettes de la Caisse Nationale d'Assurance Maladie (CANAM) ne sont pas disponibles. Les données sur les cotisations de la Caisse Malienne de Sécurité Sociale (CMSS) et les données de l'Institut National de Prévoyance Sociale (INPS) ne sont disponibles qu'à partir de 2004 et 2006 respectivement. Ces recettes ne sont pas incluses dans les recettes de l'État du Mali.

Rubrique 5123 : Les recettes de la CEDEAO (Communauté économique des États de l'Afrique de l'Ouest), y compris les redevances statistiques, le prélèvement communautaire, et la taxe dégressive de protection, ne sont pas considérées comme des recettes fiscales ou des recettes non fiscales selon le *Guide d'interprétation de l'OCDE* (voir § 4).

Rubrique 5126 : Les recettes de TARTOP étaient incluses dans les recettes non fiscales (Ventes de biens et services) dans les éditions précédentes.

Rubriques 5212 et 5213 : Les chiffres sur les recettes du Mali ne sont pas disponibles pour 2019 et 2020.

Source : Ministère de l'Économie et des Finances et la Direction Nationale du Trésor et de la Comptabilité Publique du Mali.

StatLink *https://stat.link/x9tynd*

Table 5.18. **Mauritania / Mauritanie**

Details of tax revenue / Recettes fiscales détaillées

Million MRU

	1995	2000	2005	2010	2015	2016	2017	2018	2019	2020
Recettes fiscales totales	..	..	..	**15 182**	**29 093**	**31 957**	**35 153**	**40 366**	**39 933**	**38 601**
1000 Impôts sur revenu, bénéfices et gains en capital	..	..	..	**5 282**	**9 722**	**9 980**	**10 971**	**11 853**	**12 566**	**14 906**
1100 Des personnes physiques	..	..	..	2 266	4 324	4 088	4 110	4 586	5 081	5 812
1110 Sur le revenu et les bénéfices	..	..	..	2 266	4 324	4 088	4 110	4 586	5 081	5 812
Impôt sur le traitement de salaires	..	..	..	1 396	3 819	3 588	3 635	3 936	4 325	4 865
Dont: ITS Pétrole	..	..	..	94	129	196	258	342	..	..
impot sur le revenu des capitaux mobiliers	..	..	..	777	400	379	352	526	635	834
Impôt sur les revenus fonciers	..	..	..	45	101	121	119	124	121	112
Impôt général sur le revenu	..	..	..	48	4	0	4	0	0	0
1120 Sur les gains en capital	..	..	..	0	0	0	0	0	0	0
1200 Des sociétés	..	..	..	3 015	5 398	5 892	6 861	7 267	7 485	9 094
1210 Sur les bénéfices	..	..	..	3 015	5 398	5 892	6 861	7 267	7 485	9 094
Bénéfices industriels et commerciaux (BIC), non commerciaux (BNC) et impôt minimum forfaitaire (IMF)	..	..	..	1 400	3 400	3 324	3 025	3 398	3 759	3 909
Dont: BIC Pétrole	..	..	..	144	43	103	238	296	..	..
Taxe unique de la SNIM (Société Nationale Industrielle et Minière de Mauritanie)	..	..	..	921	223	430	1 249	408	1 196	1 890
IMF Douanes	..	..	..	695	1 452	1 378	1 590	1 850	1 946	1 504
Régime simplifié d'imposition	..	..	..	0	323	760	998	1 610	585	1 792
1220 Sur les gains en capital	..	..	..	0	0	0	0	0	0	0
1300 Non ventilables entre 1100 et 1200	..	..	..	0	0	0	0	0	0	0
2000 Cotisations de sécurité sociale	..	..	..	**1 026**	**1 818**	**1 756**	**1 890**	**2 061**	**2 015**	**2 100**
2100 A la charge des salariés	..	..	..	..	..	..	..	..	..	..
2110 Sur la base du salaire	..	..	..	..	..	..	..	..	..	..
2120 Sur la base de l'impôt sur le revenu	..	..	..	..	..	..	..	..	..	..
2200 A la charge des employeurs	..	..	..	..	..	..	..	..	..	..
2210 Sur la base du salaire	..	..	..	..	..	..	..	..	..	..
2220 Sur la base de l'impôt sur le revenu	..	..	..	..	..	..	..	..	..	..
2300 A charge des travailleurs indép. ou sans emploi	..	..	..	..	..	..	..	..	..	..
2310 Sur la base du salaire	..	..	..	..	..	..	..	..	..	..
2320 Sur la base de l'impôt sur le revenu	..	..	..	..	..	..	..	..	..	..
2400 Non ventilables entre 2100, 2200 et 2300	..	..	..	1 026	1 818	1 756	1 890	2 061	2 015	2 100
Cotisations CNSS	..	..	..	424	592	622	646	650	686	707
Cotisations CNAM	..	..	..	602	1 227	1 134	1 244	1 411	1 329	1 393
2410 Sur la base du salaire	..	..	..	..	..	..	..	..	..	..
2420 Sur la base de l'impôt sur le revenu	..	..	..	..	..	..	..	..	..	..
3000 Sur salaires ou main-d'oeuvre	..	..	..	**32**	**48**	**40**	**42**	**41**	**50**	**45**
4000 Impôts sur le patrimoine	..	..	..	**646**	**1 387**	**1 294**	**1 155**	**1 172**	**45**	**58**
4100 Impôts périodiques sur la propriété immobilière	..	..	..	622	1 346	1 251	1 097	1 113	..	..
4110 Ménages	..	..	..	..	..	..	..	..	..	..
4120 Autres agents	..	..	..	..	..	..	..	..	..	..
4200 Impôts périodiques sur l'actif net	..	..	..	0	0	0	0	0	0	0
4210 Personnes physiques	..	..	..	..	..	..	..	..	..	..
4220 Sociétés	..	..	..	..	..	..	..	..	..	..
4300 Impôts sur mut. par décès, succ. et donations	..	..	..	0	0	0	0	0	0	0
4310 Impôts sur mut. par décès et successions	..	..	..	..	..	..	..	..	..	..
4320 Impôts sur les donations	..	..	..	..	..	..	..	..	..	..
4400 Impôts sur transact. mobilières et immob.	..	..	..	25	41	43	58	59	45	58
Droits de conservation foncière	..	..	..	25	41	43	58	59	45	58
4500 Impôts non-périodiques	..	..	..	0	0	0	0	0	0	0
4510 Sur l'actif net	..	..	..	..	..	..	..	..	..	..
4520 Autres non-périodiques	..	..	..	..	..	..	..	..	..	..
4600 Autres impôts périodiques sur patrimoine	..	..	..	0	0	0	0	0	0	0
5000 Impôts sur les biens et services	..	..	..	**8 196**	**16 118**	**18 888**	**21 096**	**25 240**	**25 257**	**21 472**
5100 Impôts sur production, vente, transfert, etc.	..	..	..	7 983	15 785	17 916	19 822	23 826	23 925	20 160
5110 Impôts généraux	..	..	..	5 069	9 454	9 691	10 428	12 605	12 951	10 014
5111 Taxes sur la valeur ajoutée	..	..	..	5 069	9 454	9 691	10 428	12 605	12 951	10 014
Recettes TVA intérieure	..	..	..	1 290	3 500	3 481	3 264	3 643	3 937	3 339
Recettes TVA à l'importation	..	..	..	3 779	5 954	6 210	7 164	8 963	9 014	6 675
5112 Impôts sur les ventes	..	..	..	0	0	0	0	0	0	0
5113 Autres impôts	..	..	..	0	0	0	0	0	0	0
5120 Impôts sur biens et services déterminés	..	..	..	2 915	6 330	8 224	9 394	11 220	10 974	10 146
5121 Accises	..	..	..	188	586	982	1 047	1 256	1 027	983
5122 Bénéfices des monopoles fiscaux	..	..	..	0	0	0	0	0	0	0

Table 5.18. **Mauritania / Mauritanie** *(cont.)*

Details of tax revenue / Recettes fiscales détaillées

Million MRU

	1995	2000	2005	2010	2015	2016	2017	2018	2019	2020
5123 Droits de douane et droits à l'importation	..	..	..	2 463	5 145	6 565	7 721	9 250	9 150	8 363
Droit Fiscal à l'importation	..	..	..	1 631	3 313	4 143	4 716	5 502	5 381	4 827
Taxe sur les prod. pétroliers	..	..	..	494	1 042	1 653	1 735	2 277	2 369	2 103
Taxes de consommation	..	..	..	0	0	0	0	0	0	528
Taxe statistique	..	..	..	319	553	539	657	810	808	648
Taxe pour la promotion de la culture et du sport	..	..	..	0	199	186	203	266	264	229
Autres droits et charges à l'importation	..	..	..	20	39	45	410	395	328	29
5124 Taxes à l'exportation	..	..	..	0	0	0	0	0	0	1
5125 Impôts sur biens d'équipement	..	..	..	0	0	0	0	0	0	0
5126 Impôts sur services déterminés	..	..	..	264	599	677	626	714	798	799
Taxe sur les les opérations financières	..	..	..	208	538	611	561	642	722	749
Taxe d'aéroport et destination à l'étranger	..	..	..	56	61	66	65	72	76	33
Taxe de Consommation sur la carte à Gratter (TCG)	..	..	..	0	0	0	0	0	0	17
5127 Autres impôts sur commerce et transact. internat.	..	..	..	0	0	0	0	0	0	0
5128 Autres impôts	..	..	..	0	0	0	0	0	0	0
5130 Non ventilables entre 5110 et 5120	..	..	..	0	0	0	0	0	0	0
5200 Impôts sur utilisation des biens et exerc. activités	..	..	..	213	333	972	1 274	1 414	1 332	1 312
5210 Impôts périodiques	..	..	..	213	333	972	1 274	1 414	1 332	1 312
5211 A la charge des ménages: véhicules à moteur	..	..	..	153	236	245	247	235	231	205
5212 A la charge autres agents: véhicules à moteur	..	..	..	0	0	0	0	0	0	110
5213 Autres impôts périodiques	..	..	..	60	97	727	1 028	1 179	1 102	997
Patente	..	..	..	0	76	77	77	80	75	73
Droit de pêche	..	..	..	60	21	650	951	1 098	1 027	600
Redevance d'Exploitation (RE)	..	..	..	0	0	0	0	0	0	324
5220 Impôts non-périodiques	..	..	..	0	0	0	0	0	0	0
5300 Non ventilables entre 5100 et 5200	..	..	..	0	0	0	0	0	0	0
6000 Autres impôts	**..**	**..**	**..**	**0**	**0**	**0**	**0**	**0**	**0**	**20**
6100 A la charge exclusive des entreprises	..	..	..	..	..	..	..	..	..	..
6200 A la charge d'autres agents	..	..	..	..	..	..	..	..	..	..
Pour mémoire : *Prélèvement communautaire Cedeao (PC)*	..	..	..	..	..	..	..	..	..	283

.. Non disponible

Note : Année civile se terminant le 31 décembre.

Les données sont sur la base des encaissements.

Rubrique 4100 : cette rubrique inclut les recettes communales. Ces recettes proviennent des différents impôts communaux et taxes municipales qui comprennent notamment la contribution foncière sur les propriétés bâties, la contribution foncière sur les terrains agricoles affectés à des cultures, la taxe d'habitation, la contribution communale, la patente, la taxe communale et les redevances et les droits domaniaux sur l'occupation du domaine public. Il n'a pas été possible de distinguer chacune de ces recettes ainsi la totalité de ces recettes sont classifiées dans la présente rubrique compte tenu que la majorité proviennent des impôts sur la propriété immobilière; Ces recettes sont manquantes en 2019 et 2020.

Rubrique 4400 : cette rubrique inclut les recettes des droits de conservation foncière. Elles sont incluses dans les recettes fiscales comme le préconise la classification OCDE (voir le guide d'interprétation en Annexe A) mais considérées comme des recettes non fiscales en Mauritanie.

Source : Ministère des Finances de la Mauritanie.

StatLink https://stat.link/icbqsl

Table 5.19. **Mauritius / Maurice**

Details of tax revenue / Recettes fiscales détaillées

Million MUR

	1995	2000	2005	2010	2015	2016	2017	2018	2019	2020
Total tax revenue	**12 262**	**22 146**	**34 828**	**58 404**	**79 225**	**82 339**	**88 584**	**95 752**	**103 385**	**97 275**
1000 Taxes on income, profits and capital gains	**1 804**	**2 881**	**5 829**	**15 005**	**19 793**	**20 403**	**22 938**	**24 325**	**27 810**	**27 940**
1100 Of individuals	863	1 540	2 553	4 583	7 614	7 621	8 661	9 527	10 453	11 221
1110 On income and profits	..	..	..	..	..	..	..	..	..	..
1120 On capital gains	..	..	..	..	..	..	..	..	..	..
1200 Corporate	941	1 341	3 276	9 457	10 993	11 686	13 040	13 407	15 648	15 000
1210 On profits	941	1 341	3 276	9 457	10 993	11 686	13 040	13 407	15 648	15 000
Income tax - companies & corporate bodies	..	..	..	8 428	9 788	10 459	11 881	12 403	14 556	13 876
Special levy on banks	..	..	..	455	748	771	846	846	934	939
Solidarity levy on telecommunication companies	..	..	..	424	331	308	313	158	158	185
Corporate social responsibility	..	..	..	150	126	147	0	0	0	0
Special contribution from hotels	..	..	..	0	0	0	0	0	0	0
COVID -19 Levy	..	..	..	..	..	..	..	..	..	..
Other taxes on corporate profits	..	..	..	..	..	..	..	..	..	..
1220 On capital gains	..	..	..	..	..	..	..	..	..	..
1300 Unallocable between 1100 and 1200	..	..	..	965	1 186	1 096	1 236	1 392	1 709	1 720
Tax deduction at source	..	..	..	965	1 186	1 096	1 236	1 392	1 709	1 720
2000 Social security contributions	**689**	**986**	**1 314**	**2 113**	**3 252**	**3 380**	**3 648**	**3 630**	**4 239**	**4 560**
2100 Employees	230	329	438	704	1 084	1 127	1 216	1 210	1 413	1 520
2110 On a payroll basis	..	..	..	..	..	..	..	..	..	..
2120 On an income tax basis	..	..	..	..	..	..	..	..	..	..
2200 Employers	459	657	876	1 408	2 168	2 253	2 432	2 420	2 826	3 040
2210 On a payroll basis	..	..	..	..	..	..	..	..	..	..
2220 On an income tax basis	..	..	..	..	..	..	..	..	..	..
2300 Self-employed or non-employed	0	0	0	0	0	0	0	0	0	0
2310 On a payroll basis	..	..	..	..	..	..	..	..	..	..
2320 On an income tax basis	..	..	..	..	..	..	..	..	..	..
2400 Unallocable between 2100, 2200 and 2300	0	0	0	0	0	0	0	0	0	0
2410 On a payroll basis	..	..	..	..	..	..	..	..	..	..
2420 On an income tax basis	..	..	..	..	..	..	..	..	..	..
3000 Taxes on payroll and workforce	**77**	**140**	**204**	**176**	**474**	**592**	**638**	**549**	**777**	**798**
Extra-budgetary taxes on payroll and workforce	77	140	204	176	474	592	638	549	777	798
4000 Taxes on property	**945**	**1 411**	**1 920**	**3 328**	**4 095**	**4 680**	**4 894**	**4 711**	**4 706**	**4 084**
4100 Recurrent taxes on immovable property	135	205	240	417	146	296	318	306	294	321
4110 Households	0	0	0	0	0	0	0	0	0	0
4120 Others	135	205	240	417	146	296	318	306	294	321
Local taxes on immovable property	135	205	240	410	143	292	314	299	288	313
Campement taxes	..	..	..	6	3	4	4	7	6	8
4200 Recurrent taxes on net wealth	0	0	0	0	0	0	0	0	0	0
4210 Individual	..	..	..	..	..	..	..	..	..	..
4220 Corporate	..	..	..	..	..	..	..	..	..	..
4300 Estate, inheritance and gift taxes	0	0	0	0	0	0	0	0	0	0
4310 Estate and inheritance taxes	..	..	..	..	..	..	..	..	..	..
4320 Gift taxes	..	..	..	..	..	..	..	..	..	..
4400 Taxes on financial and capital transactions	809	1 206	1 680	2 902	3 907	4 337	4 543	4 385	4 376	3 754
Land transfer tax	..	..	409	1 190	1 650	1 831	2 016	1 971	1 964	1 693
Registration duty on transfer of immovable property	..	..	562	1 180	1 708	1 943	1 951	1 884	1 859	1 619
Tax on transfer of leasehold rights in state lands	..	..	0	175	157	119	258	168	164	144
Registration duty on transfer of shares	..	..	0	84	122	174	44	50	53	25
Registration duty on fixed and floating charges	..	..	116	180	157	164	162	204	220	181
Stamp duties	..	..	14	75	112	105	113	109	115	91
Registration duty on loans	..	..	0	9	0	0	0	0	0	0
Mortgages, inscriptions and transcriptions	..	..	10	11	0	0	0	0	0	0
Other taxes on financial and capital transactions	..	..	568	0	0	0	0	0	0	0
4500 Non-recurrent taxes	0	0	0	10	42	47	33	20	36	10
4510 On net wealth	..	..	..	0	0	0	0	0	0	0
4520 Other non-recurrent taxes	..	..	..	10	42	47	33	20	36	10
4600 Other recurrent taxes on property	0	0	0	0	0	0	0	0	0	0
5000 Taxes on goods and services	**8 617**	**16 514**	**25 300**	**37 618**	**51 422**	**53 173**	**56 355**	**62 410**	**65 719**	**59 781**
5100 Taxes on production, sale, transfer, etc.	8 499	16 312	23 445	34 755	47 254	48 943	52 228	58 041	61 018	55 784
5110 General taxes	64	5 604	12 529	21 094	28 036	28 805	30 231	32 989	34 941	32 658
5111 Value added taxes	0	5 604	12 529	21 094	28 036	28 805	30 231	32 989	34 941	32 658
VAT revenues (gross)	..	..	..	26 590	33 302	34 142	36 555	39 176	41 948	39 061
VAT refunds	..	..	..	-5 495	-5 267	-5 337	-6 324	-6 187	-7 007	-6 403

Table 5.19. **Mauritius / Maurice** *(cont.)*

Details of tax revenue / Recettes fiscales détaillées

Million MUR

	1995	2000	2005	2010	2015	2016	2017	2018	2019	2020
5112 Sales tax	64	0	0	0	0	0	0	0	0	0
5113 Other	0	0	0	0	0	0	0	0	0	0
Extra-budgetary taxes on goods and services	..	..	..	..	..	..	..	..	..	..
Local taxes on goods and services	..	..	..	..	..	..	..	..	..	..
5120 Taxes on specific goods and services	8 435	10 707	10 916	13 660	19 218	20 138	21 996	25 052	26 077	23 125
Unallocated budgetary taxes on goods and services	..	..	3 279	0	0	0	0	0	0	0
5121 Excises	..	..	2 840	9 331	14 834	15 633	17 277	20 109	20 871	18 925
Spirits, liquors and alcoholic beverages	..	..	1 220	2 351	4 448	4 603	4 900	5 349	5 221	5 307
Tobacco products	..	..	1 617	2 371	3 851	4 196	4 735	5 333	5 233	5 620
Motor vehicles and motor cycles	..	..	0	1 928	2 471	2 582	3 126	3 384	3 756	3 120
Petroleum products (incl. MIDL)	..	..	0	2 421	3 292	3 438	3 642	5 141	5 700	3 938
PET bottles and other plastic products	..	..	0	159	250	235	232	252	270	273
Sugar content of soft drinks	..	..	0	0	344	345	374	404	445	428
Energy inefficient products	..	..	0	0	3	2	12	4	4	19
Sugar brokerage	..	..	1	0	0	0	0	0	0	0
Extra-budgetary excise taxes	..	..	0	0	0	0	0	0	0	0
Other excises	..	..	1	101	175	231	255	241	242	219
5122 Profits of fiscal monopolies	..	..	0	0	0	0	0	0	0	0
5123 Customs and import duties	..	..	3 899	1 525	1 302	1 343	1 177	1 344	1 379	1 216
5124 Taxes on exports	..	..	0	0	0	0	0	0	0	0
5125 Taxes on investment goods	..	..	0	0	0	0	0	0	0	0
5126 Taxes on specific services	..	..	898	2 731	3 083	3 163	3 543	3 599	3 827	2 984
Taxes on the national lottery and other lotteries	..	..	14	693	436	387	242	221	309	285
Betting taxes on horse racing, football, etc.	..	..	269	658	837	887	944	971	1 047	740
Gaming taxes on casinos and gaming houses	..	..	614	818	591	652	706	778	797	695
Passenger fee on air tickets	..	..	0	561	1 173	1 230	1 652	1 630	1 673	1 264
Levy on messaging services	..	..	0	0	46	7	0	0	0	0
Hotel and restaurant tax	..	..	0	0	0	0	0	0	0	0
5127 Other taxes on internat. trade and transactions	..	..	0	0	0	0	0	0	0	0
5128 Other taxes	..	..	0	73	0	0	0	0	0	0
Temporary solidarity tax on hotels	..	..	..	0	..	..	..	..	..	..
Local government taxes on goods and services	..	..	..	73	..	..	..	..	..	..
5130 Unallocable between 5110 and 5120	..	..	0	0	0	0	0	0	0	0
5200 Taxes on use of goods and perform activities	118	203	1 750	2 765	4 168	4 230	4 128	4 369	4 701	3 998
5210 Recurrent taxes	118	203	1 287	1 934	2 702	2 795	2 762	2 922	3 019	2 770
5211 Paid by households: motor vehicles	0	0	652	1 117	1 362	1 430	1 463	1 526	1 604	1 587
5212 Paid by others: motor vehicles	0	0	0	0	0	0	0	0	0	0
5213 Paid in respect of other goods	118	203	635	816	1 341	1 366	1 299	1 396	1 415	1 183
Company licences	..	..	103	148	306	196	198	200	200	203
Incorporation & lodging fees, search duty, etc.	..	..	5	9	18	16	12	14	13	12
Tourist enterprise licences	..	..	33	74	91	110	99	104	112	73
Gambling licences	..	..	48	100	368	438	411	465	439	344
Liquor licences	..	..	10	10	25	23	23	23	23	22
Freeport licences	..	..	0	0	6	7	7	7	1	9
Pharmacy licences	..	..	0	1	2	1	1	1	1	1
Fishing vessel licences	..	..	38	52	43	53	59	63	82	85
Registration of factories	..	..	2	2	3	3	3	3	3	2
Registration of associations	..	..	1	2	1	1	1	1	1	1
Recruitment licences	..	..	0	2	0	1	0	0	0	0
Environment protection fee	..	..	132	141	391	403	383	400	424	330
Advertising structure fee	..	..	0	0	63	64	58	52	58	44
Regional taxes on permission to use goods	..	..	2	2	2	2	3	3	0	3
Local taxes on permission to use goods	118	203	244	255	0	0	0	21	21	18
Other recurrent taxes on goods and activities	..	..	16	20	23	48	42	39	36	34
5220 Non-recurrent taxes	0	0	463	832	1 466	1 434	1 366	1 447	1 682	1 228
Processing fee on acquisitions schemes	..	..	0	0	4	5	4	5	1	7
Registration duty on transfer of motor vehicles	..	..	463	794	1 277	1 266	1 335	1 378	1 462	1 175
Land conversion tax	..	..	0	38	185	163	26	64	219	45
5300 Unallocable between 5100 and 5200	0	0	105	98	0	0	0	0	0	0
Extra-budgetary taxes on goods and services	..	..	105	98	..	..	..	..	..	..
6000 Other taxes	**130**	**215**	**260**	**164**	**188**	**111**	**110**	**126**	**134**	**112**
Mauritius Revenue Authority penalties	0	0	0	0	74	22	24	24	36	31
Unidentified local government taxes	0	0	0	0	0	0	0	0	0	0
Unidentified taxes	130	215	260	164	114	89	86	102	98	80
6100 Paid solely by business	..	..	..	..	..	..	..	..	..	..
6200 Other	..	..	..	..	..	..	..	..	..	..

Table 5.19. **Mauritius / Maurice** *(cont.)*

Details of tax revenue / Recettes fiscales détaillées

.. Not available

Note: Data for 2016 onwards and for years prior to 2010 are on a fiscal year basis beginning 1st July. For example, the data for 2009 represent July 2008 to June 2009 and 2020 represents July 2019 to June 2020. The data for years 2010-15 are on a calendar year (January-December) basis.

Mauritius budget statements cover January-June 2015 and July 2015 to June 2016, but neither the fiscal nor the calendar year for 2015. Figures for 2015 are therefore estimated using quarterly revenue figures at the aggregate level and fiscal year revenue data.

Data for the central government budgetary tax prior to 2007 and all extra-budgetary, regional and local data were classified according to the IMF Government Finance Statistics Manual. The 1986 manual was used for data up to 2009 and the 2001 manual for data up to 2009 onwards. Data from 2007 onwards are classified under the OECD classification, as set out in the *OECD Interpretative Guide* in Annex A.

The data are on a cash basis.

Heading 2000: revenues under this heading refer to revenues reported as contributions to the National Pension Fund (NPF) in the Digest of Social Security Statistics. Employer contributions and employee contributions are calculated by taking respectively one third and two thirds of total NPF contributions since employer contributions rates are set at twice those of employees. Contributions to the National Savings Fund (NSF) are not included in *Revenue Statistics in Africa*, since they do not meet the definition of social security contributions. For the years 1989/1990 to 1993/94, the revenues reported as social security contributions in the Digest of Public Finance Statistics. Linear interpolation was used for the years 1997/98, 2003/04, 2004/05, 2012/13, 2014, and 2015 where social security contributions data was missing.

Heading 3000: revenues under this heading include revenues collected by the Ministry of Social Services under the Training Levy.

Heading 1210: the solidarity levy on telecommunications companies, the corporate social responsibility tax and the special contribution from hotels are classified as "other taxes" by the Mauritius Revenue Authority.

Heading 5213: the Environment protection fee and advertising structure fee are classified as other taxes by the Mauritius Revenue Authority.

Heading 5220: includes the registration duty on transfer of motor vehicles and the land conversion tax that are classified as taxes on property by the Mauritius Revenue Authority.

Source: Mauritius Revenue Authority for the central government budgetary tax data from 2007 to 2014. Statistics Mauritius for extra-budgetary, local government, regional government and social security revenues from 1990 to 2020, as well as for budgetary central government tax revenues up to 2006; Ministry of Finance budget estimates for detailed revenue figures for the periods July 2005-June 2008, for 2016-20, and for the figures used to estimate calendar year 2015 revenues.

StatLink https://stat.link/cx4g0a

Table 5.20. **Morocco / Maroc**

Details of tax revenue / Recettes fiscales détaillées

Million MAD

	1995	2000	2005	2010	2015	2016	2017	2018	2019	2020
Recettes fiscales totales	..	**90 900**	**137 440**	**216 769**	**265 069**	**278 423**	**297 181**	**312 696**	**326 526**	**308 009**
1000 Impôts sur revenu, bénéfices et gains en capital	..	**23 656**	**42 613**	**62 646**	**78 952**	**84 111**	**92 372**	**96 026**	**98 277**	**95 427**
1100 Des personnes physiques	..	14 540	23 661	26 598	37 214	39 792	40 686	43 889	44 353	42 206
1110 Sur le revenu et les bénéfices	..	12 473	21 009	22 391	32 797	35 082	40 135	43 462	42 823	41 568
Salaires	..	10 829	18 830	19 409	28 277	30 833	31 440	32 561	32 865	32 516
Revenus professionnels	..	1 645	2 179	2 982	4 519	4 249	3 296	6 374	6 112	5 251
Autres types d'impôts sur le revenu	..	0	0	0	0	0	5 398	4 527	3 846	3 801
1120 Sur les gains en capital	..	2 067	2 653	4 207	4 417	4 710	552	427	1 530	637
1200 Des sociétés	..	9 116	18 952	36 049	41 738	44 319	51 686	52 137	53 924	53 221
1210 Sur les bénéfices	..	8 330	16 962	31 164	32 693	44 319	51 607	52 130	53 920	53 221
Bénéfices	..	8 084	16 494	29 381	30 553	42 303	49 410	49 529	51 396	50 971
Produits bruts versés aux sociétés étrangères	..	246	468	1 783	2 140	2 016	2 197	2 601	2 524	2 250
1220 Sur les gains en capital	..	786	1 990	4 884	9 045	0	78	7	4	0
1300 Non ventilables entre 1100 et 1200	..	0	0	0	0	0	0	0	0	0
2000 Cotisations de sécurité sociale	..	**9 982**	**22 983**	**37 924**	**52 418**	**55 998**	**60 112**	**64 622**	**71 422**	**71 654**
2100 A la charge des salariés	..	2 803	8 313	13 208	17 730	18 799	20 298	21 880	24 228	24 797
2110 Sur la base du salaire	..	..	..	..	..	..	..	..	..	..
2120 Sur la base de l'impôt sur le revenu	..	..	..	..	..	..	..	..	..	..
2200 A la charge des employeurs	..	7 179	14 644	24 524	34 385	36 823	39 409	42 310	46 690	46 308
2210 Sur la base du salaire	..	..	..	..	..	..	..	..	..	..
2220 Sur la base de l'impôt sur le revenu	..	..	..	..	..	..	..	..	..	..
2300 A charge des travailleurs indép. ou sans emploi	..	0	0	0	0	0	0	0	0	0
2310 Sur la base du salaire	..	..	..	..	..	..	..	..	..	..
2320 Sur la base de l'impôt sur le revenu	..	..	..	..	..	..	..	..	..	..
2400 Non ventilables entre 2100, 2200 et 2300	..	0	25	192	302	377	405	432	505	549
2410 Sur la base du salaire	..	..	..	..	..	..	..	..	..	..
2420 Sur la base de l'impôt sur le revenu	..	..	..	..	..	..	..	..	..	..
3000 Sur salaires ou main-d'œuvre	..	**0**	**0**	**0**	**0**	**0**	**0**	**0**	**0**	**0**
4000 Impôts sur le patrimoine	..	**5 405**	**8 403**	**12 702**	**19 536**	**20 182**	**16 693**	**16 679**	**16 536**	**13 445**
4100 Impôts périodiques sur la propriété immobilière	..	3 340	4 415	5 740	6 859	7 477	7 712	7 947	8 182	7 487
4110 Ménages	..	1 989	2 866	3 898	4 414	4 781	4 962	5 143	5 324	4 855
Taxe d'habitation	..	517	696	382	364	320	361	402	443	292
Taxe sur les terrains non bâtis	..	135	236	839	1 113	1 163	1 301	1 439	1 577	1 342
Taxe de services communaux	..	1 337	1 934	2 677	2 937	3 298	3 300	3 302	3 304	3 221
4120 Autres agents	..	1 351	1 549	1 842	2 445	2 696	2 750	2 804	2 858	2 632
4200 Impôts périodiques sur l'actif net	..	0	0	0	0	0	0	0	0	0
4210 Personnes physiques	..	..	..	..	..	..	..	..	..	..
4220 Sociétés	..	..	..	..	..	..	..	..	..	..
4300 Impôts sur mut. par décès, succ. et donations	..	0	0	0	0	0	0	0	0	0
4310 Impôts sur mut. par décès et successions	..	..	..	..	..	..	..	..	..	..
4320 Impôts sur les donations	..	..	..	..	..	..	..	..	..	..
4400 Impôts sur transact. mobilières et immob.	..	2 065	3 988	6 962	12 677	12 705	8 981	8 732	8 354	5 958
4500 Impôts non-périodiques	..	0	0	0	0	0	0	0	0	0
4510 Sur l'actif net	..	..	..	..	..	..	..	..	..	..
4520 Autres non-périodiques	..	..	..	..	..	..	..	..	..	..
4600 Autres impôts périodiques sur patrimoine	..	0	0	0	0	0	0	0	0	0
5000 Impôts sur les biens et services	..	**50 655**	**62 100**	**101 384**	**111 766**	**114 743**	**124 441**	**134 189**	**139 319**	**126 572**
5100 Impôts sur production, vente, transfert, etc.	..	49 539	60 701	99 056	108 848	111 457	121 108	128 153	132 920	120 742
5110 Impôts généraux	..	21 476	32 607	65 247	75 271	75 735	81 479	86 024	85 707	79 781
5111 Taxes sur la valeur ajoutée	..	21 476	32 607	65 247	75 271	75 735	81 479	86 024	85 707	79 781
5112 Impôts sur les ventes	..	0	0	0	0	0	0	0	0	0
5113 Autres impôts	..	0	0	0	0	0	0	0	0	0
5120 Impôts sur biens et services déterminés	..	28 063	28 094	33 809	33 577	35 722	39 629	42 128	47 212	40 961
5121 Accises	..	15 223	15 631	21 382	25 661	26 451	27 720	28 674	30 276	27 633
Taxes intérieures de consommation	..	15 183	15 544	21 132	25 366	26 134	27 383	28 318	29 900	27 390
Taxe sur la vente de produits forestiers	..	4	18	26	29	29	18	8	-3	4
Taxe sur les débits de boissons	..	23	37	143	162	167	185	203	221	117
Taxe sur les eaux minerales et de table	..	13	31	81	104	121	133	145	157	122
5122 Bénéfices des monopoles fiscaux	..	0	0	0	0	0	0	0	0	0
5123 Droits de douane et droits à l'importation	..	12 810	12 386	12 242	7 715	9 074	8 610	9 693	9 768	9 488
5124 Taxes à l'exportation	..	0	0	0	0	0	0	0	0	0
5125 Impôts sur biens d'équipement	..	0	0	0	0	0	0	0	0	0

Table 5.20. **Morocco / Maroc** *(cont.)*

Details of tax revenue / Recettes fiscales détaillées

Million MAD

	1995	2000	2005	2010	2015	2016	2017	2018	2019	2020
5126 Impôts sur services déterminés	..	30	77	184	201	197	3 299	3 762	7 169	3 840
Taxe de séjour	..	26	67	160	173	168	198	228	258	109
Taxe sur le transport public de voyageurs	..	4	10	24	28	29	32	35	3 108	23
Droit de timbre sur les annonces publicitaires sur écran	..	0	0	0	0	0	3 070	3 499	3 803	3 708
5127 Autres impôts sur commerce et transact. internat.	..	0	0	0	0	0	0	0	0	0
5128 Autres impôts	..	0	0	0	0	0	0	0	0	0
5130 Non ventilables entre 5110 et 5120	..	0	0	0	0	0	0	0	0	0
5200 Impôts sur utilisation des biens et exerc. activites	..	1 116	1 398	2 328	2 918	3 286	3 333	6 036	6 399	5 830
5210 Impôts périodiques	..	964	1 134	1 385	1 955	2 348	2 360	3 158	3 459	3 470
5211 A la charge des ménages: véhicules à moteur	..	959	1 119	1 351	1 920	2 310	2 325	2 570	2 846	2 805
5212 A la charge autres agents: véhicules à moteur	..	0	0	0	0	0	0	556	583	629
5213 Autres impôts périodiques	..	5	15	33	35	38	35	32	29	36
Taxe sur les permis de chasse	..	5	15	33	35	38	35	32	29	36
5220 Impôts non-périodiques	..	152	265	943	963	938	973	2 878	2 941	2 359
Taxe sur les opérations de construction	..	113	230	703	709	709	716	723	730	618
Taxe sur les opérations de lotissement	..	39	35	240	254	229	257	285	313	215
Autres	..	0	0	0	0	0	0	1 870	1 898	1 526
5300 Non ventilables entre 5100 et 5200	..	0	0	0	0	0	0	0	0	0
6000 Autres impôts	**..**	**1 201**	**1 341**	**2 112**	**2 398**	**3 390**	**3 562**	**1 179**	**972**	**912**
Droits de timbres	..	1 132	1 260	1 683	2 092	3 090	3 305	965	801	733
Taxes locales	..	69	81	429	306	300	257	214	171	179
6100 A la charge exclusive des entreprises	..	..	..	..	..	..	..	..	..	..
6200 A la charge d'autres agents	..	..	..	..	..	..	..	..	..	..

.. Non disponible

Note : Année civile se terminant le 31 décembre.

Les données sont sur la base des encaissements.

Les impôts affectés aux Fonds Spéciaux du Trésor sont compris dans les données.

Rubrique 2000 : Les données de cotisations de sécurité sociales sont estimées pour les années 2000 et 2001. Les recettes des majorations et pénalités relatives aux impôts sont désormais considérées comme des recettes non fiscales. La classification nationale du Maroc les compte comme des recettes fiscales.

Source : Ministère de l'Économie et des Finances.

StatLink https://stat.link/1pwvyk

Table 5.21. **Namibia / Namibie**

Details of tax revenue / Recettes fiscales détaillées

Million NAD

	1995	2000	2005	2010	2015	2016	2017	2018	2019	2020
Total tax revenue	..	..	..	**15 734**	**31 974**	**34 043**	**35 494**	**35 168**	**36 247**	**32 762**
1000 Taxes on income, profits and capital gains	..	..	..	**9 912**	**19 006**	**20 607**	**21 946**	**21 855**	**22 611**	**22 295**
1100 Of individuals	..	..	..	6 156	10 982	12 355	13 546	13 923	14 557	14 077
1110 On income and profits	..	..	..	6 156	10 982	12 355	13 546	13 923	14 557	14 077
Income tax on individuals	..	..	..	5 945	10 794	12 002	13 267	13 588	14 147	13 768
Non-resident shareholders tax	..	..	..	189	147	266	183	265	307	207
Tax on royalty	..	..	..	21	41	87	96	70	103	102
1120 On capital gains	..	..	..	0	0	0	0	0	0	0
1200 Corporate	..	..	..	3 756	8 024	8 252	8 400	7 932	8 054	8 218
1210 On profits	..	..	..	3 756	8 024	8 252	8 400	7 932	8 054	8 218
Diamond mining companies	..	..	..	354	2 199	1 611	1 654	1 496	1 143	1 367
Other mining companies	..	..	..	213	99	92	256	445	187	849
Non-mining companies	..	..	..	3 018	5 425	6 006	5 950	5 384	5 927	5 342
Withholding taxes	..	..	..	156	280	522	510	607	797	653
Annual levy on gambling income	..	..	..	15	21	21	30	0	0	6
1220 On capital gains	..	..	..	0	0	0	0	0	0	0
1300 Unallocable between 1100 and 1200	..	..	..	0	0	0	0	0	0	0
2000 Social security contributions	..	..	..	**305**	**537**	**547**	**649**	**621**	**621**	**650**
2100 Employees	..	..	..	..	..	..	..	..	..	..
2110 On a payroll basis	..	..	..	..	..	..	..	..	..	..
2120 On an income tax basis	..	..	..	..	..	..	..	..	..	..
2200 Employers	..	..	..	..	..	..	..	..	..	..
2210 On a payroll basis	..	..	..	..	..	..	..	..	..	..
2220 On an income tax basis	..	..	..	..	..	..	..	..	..	..
2300 Self-employed or non-employed	..	..	..	..	..	..	..	..	..	..
2310 On a payroll basis	..	..	..	..	..	..	..	..	..	..
2320 On an income tax basis	..	..	..	..	..	..	..	..	..	..
2400 Unallocable between 2100, 2200 and 2300	..	..	..	305	537	547	649	621	621	650
2410 On a payroll basis	..	..	..	..	..	..	..	..	..	..
2420 On an income tax basis	..	..	..	..	..	..	..	..	..	..
3000 Taxes on payroll and workforce	..	..	..	**0**	**0**	**0**	**0**	**0**	**0**	**0**
4000 Taxes on property	..	..	..	**139**	**313**	**284**	**270**	**221**	**174**	**173**
4100 Recurrent taxes on immovable property	..	..	..	0	0	0	0	0	0	0
4110 Households	..	..	..	..	..	..	..	..	..	..
4120 Others	..	..	..	..	..	..	..	..	..	..
4200 Recurrent taxes on net wealth	..	..	..	0	0	0	0	0	0	0
4210 Individual	..	..	..	..	..	..	..	..	..	..
4220 Corporate	..	..	..	..	..	..	..	..	..	..
4300 Estate, inheritance and gift taxes	..	..	..	0	0	0	0	0	0	0
4310 Estate and inheritance taxes	..	..	..	..	..	..	..	..	..	..
4320 Gift taxes	..	..	..	..	..	..	..	..	..	..
4400 Taxes on financial and capital transactions	..	..	..	139	313	284	270	221	174	173
4500 Non-recurrent taxes	..	..	..	0	0	0	0	0	0	0
4510 On net wealth	..	..	..	..	..	..	..	..	..	..
4520 Other non-recurrent taxes	..	..	..	..	..	..	..	..	..	..
4600 Other recurrent taxes on property	..	..	..	0	0	0	0	0	0	0
5000 Taxes on goods and services	..	..	..	**5 169**	**11 902**	**12 389**	**12 458**	**12 274**	**12 732**	**9 547**
5100 Taxes on production, sale, transfer, etc.	..	..	..	5 169	11 901	12 387	12 454	12 274	12 732	9 544
5110 General taxes	..	..	..	5 057	11 678	11 978	12 049	11 461	11 516	8 326
5111 Value added taxes	..	..	..	5 057	11 678	11 978	12 049	11 461	11 516	8 326
5112 Sales tax	..	..	..	0	0	0	0	0	0	0
5113 Other	..	..	..	0	0	0	0	0	0	0
5120 Taxes on specific goods and services	..	..	..	113	223	409	405	813	1 216	1 218
5121 Excises	..	..	..	0	0	0	0	0	0	0
5122 Profits of fiscal monopolies	..	..	..	0	0	0	0	0	0	0
5123 Customs and import duties	..	..	..	102	209	382	342	813	1 201	1 207
Levy on fuel	..	..	..	102	209	315	342	730	1 107	1 152
Environmental levies and carbon emission taxes	..	..	..	0	0	67	0	83	94	55
5124 Taxes on exports	..	..	..	0	0	0	0	0	0	0
5125 Taxes on investment goods	..	..	..	0	0	0	0	0	0	0
5126 Taxes on specific services	..	..	..	0	0	0	0	0	0	0
5127 Other taxes on internat. trade and transactions	..	..	..	0	0	0	0	0	0	0
5128 Other taxes	..	..	..	11	14	27	63	0	15	11
5130 Unallocable between 5110 and 5120	..	..	..	0	0	0	0	0	0	0

Table 5.21. **Namibia / Namibie** *(cont.)*

Details of tax revenue / Recettes fiscales détaillées

Million NAD

	1995	2000	2005	2010	2015	2016	2017	2018	2019	2020
5200 Taxes on use of goods and perform activities	..	..	..	0	1	2	4	0	0	3
5210 Recurrent taxes	..	..	..	0	1	2	4	0	0	3
5211 Paid by households: motor vehicles	..	..	..	0	0	0	0	0	0	0
5212 Paid by others: motor vehicles	..	..	..	0	0	0	0	0	0	0
5213 Paid in respect of other goods	..	..	..	0	1	2	4	0	0	3
5220 Non-recurrent taxes	..	..	..	0	0	0	0	0	0	0
5300 Unallocable between 5100 and 5200	..	..	..	0	0	0	0	0	0	0
6000 Other taxes	**..**	**..**	**..**	**208**	**216**	**216**	**171**	**197**	**109**	**97**
6100 Paid solely by business	..	..	..	..	..	..	..	..	..	..
6200 Other	..	..	..	..	..	..	..	..	..	..

.. Not available

Note: Data are on a cash basis.

Data are on a fiscal year basis beginning 1st April. For example, the data for 2020 represent April 2020 to March 2021.

Figures exclude tax revenues collected by sub-national governments as the data are not available.

Heading 2000: Data are not available prior 2009.

Source: Namibia Revenue Agency.

StatLink https://stat.link/f7s0bd

Table 5.22. **Niger**

Details of tax revenue / Recettes fiscales détaillées

Million XOF

	1995	2000	2005	2010	2015	2016	2017	2018	2019	2020
Recettes fiscales totales	..	**115 819**	**190 218**	**373 461**	**720 540**	**644 899**	**615 444**	**796 671**	**786 351**	**773 976**
1000 Impôts sur revenu, bénéfices et gains en capital	..	**20 891**	**34 848**	**94 839**	**177 695**	**170 506**	**166 432**	**167 981**	**172 209**	**181 800**
1100 Des personnes physiques	..	9 634	12 268	19 756	45 501	50 942	55 054	55 069	61 154	62 628
1110 Sur le revenu et les bénéfices	..	9 634	12 217	19 623	45 294	50 508	54 667	54 567	60 807	62 342
Impôt sur les traitements et salaires	..	8 000	11 207	18 575	44 198	49 415	53 542	51 539	58 686	60 552
Impôt synthétique	..	1 530	803	974	1 030	1 047	1 079	2 775	2 060	1 741
Impôt général sur le revenu (IGR)	..	103	207	74	66	47	46	253	62	49
1120 Sur les gains en capital	..	0	51	133	208	434	387	502	347	285
Plus-values de cessions immobilières (IPVCI)	..	0	51	133	208	434	387	502	347	285
1200 Des sociétés	..	11 257	22 580	75 083	132 194	119 564	111 379	112 913	111 055	119 173
1210 Sur les bénéfices	..	11 257	22 580	75 083	132 194	119 564	111 379	112 913	111 055	119 173
Impôt sur les bénéfices (ISB)	..	10 933	21 605	67 863	121 448	109 509	101 156	102 484	102 851	110 263
Bénéfices non commerciaux (BNC) (arriérés)	..	126	239	0	0	0	0	140	217	77
Impôt sur le revenu des valeurs mobilières (IRVM)	..	198	736	5 695	7 900	7 966	8 357	8 665	7 776	6 927
Recettes portuaires	..	0	0	1 525	2 846	2 089	1 866	1 623	212	1 907
1220 Sur les gains en capital	..	0	0	0	0	0	0	0	0	0
1300 Non ventilables entre 1100 et 1200	..	0	0	0	0	0	0	0	0	0
2000 Cotisations de sécurité sociale	..	**6 216**	**7 305**	**19 950**	**34 117**	**35 453**	**37 261**	**37 840**	**42 272**	**43 370**
2100 A la charge des salariés	..	..	..	..	..	..	..	..	..	..
2110 Sur la base du salaire	..	..	..	..	..	..	..	..	..	..
2120 Sur la base de l'impôt sur le revenu	..	..	..	..	..	..	..	..	..	..
2200 A la charge des employeurs	..	..	..	..	..	..	..	..	..	..
2210 Sur la base du salaire	..	..	..	..	..	..	..	..	..	..
2220 Sur la base de l'impôt sur le revenu	..	..	..	..	..	..	..	..	..	..
2300 A charge des travailleurs indép. ou sans emploi	..	..	..	..	..	..	..	..	..	..
2310 Sur la base du salaire	..	..	..	..	..	..	..	..	..	..
2320 Sur la base de l'impôt sur le revenu	..	..	..	..	..	..	..	..	..	..
2400 Non ventilables entre 2100, 2200 et 2300	..	6 216	7 305	19 950	34 117	35 453	37 261	37 840	42 272	43 370
2410 Sur la base du salaire	..	..	..	..	..	..	..	..	..	..
2420 Sur la base de l'impôt sur le revenu	..	..	..	..	..	..	..	..	..	..
3000 Sur salaires ou main-d'œuvre	..	**401**	**533**	**1 121**	**3 978**	**3 472**	**3 223**	**3 726**	**4 348**	**1 927**
Taxe d'apprentissage (TAP)	..	401	533	1 121	3 978	3 472	3 223	3 726	4 348	1 927
4000 Impôts sur le patrimoine	..	**1 252**	**1 590**	**2 906**	**2 742**	**2 117**	**2 318**	**5 564**	**9 804**	**13 569**
4100 Impôts périodiques sur la propriété immobilière	..	1 252	1 590	2 906	2 742	2 117	2 318	5 564	9 804	13 569
Taxe immobilière	..	1 015	1 150	2 904	2 742	2 117	2 318	2 366	1 684	995
Taxe foncière	..	238	440	0	0	0	0	2	0	60
Impôt forfaitaire de droit de propriétés	..	0	0	2	0	0	0	25	5	35
Impôt sur le revenu des baux d'habitation	..	0	0	0	0	0	0	207	386	317
Impôt sur le revenu des baux professionnels	..	0	0	0	0	0	0	704	1 548	1 165
Taxe d'habitation	..	0	0	0	0	0	0	2 184	3 141	2 433
4110 Ménages	..	..	..	..	..	..	..	..	..	..
4120 Autres agents	..	0	0	0	0	0	0	77	3 040	8 563
Taxe immobilière des personnes morales	..	0	0	0	0	0	0	77	3 040	8 563
4200 Impôts périodiques sur l'actif net	..	0	0	0	0	0	0	0	0	0
4210 Personnes physiques	..	..	..	..	..	..	..	..	..	..
4220 Sociétés	..	..	..	..	..	..	..	..	..	..
4300 Impôts sur mut. par décès, succ. et donations	..	0	0	0	0	0	0	0	0	0
4310 Impôts sur mut. par décès et successions	..	..	..	..	..	..	..	..	..	..
4320 Impôts sur les donations	..	..	..	..	..	..	..	..	..	..
4400 Impôts sur transact. mobilières et immob.	..	0	0	0	0	0	0	0	0	0
4500 Impôts non-périodiques	..	0	0	0	0	0	0	0	0	0
4510 Sur l'actif net	..	..	..	..	..	..	..	..	..	..
4520 Autres non-périodiques	..	..	..	..	..	..	..	..	..	..
4600 Autres impôts périodiques sur patrimoine	..	0	0	0	0	0	0	0	0	0
5000 Impôts sur les biens et services	..	**83 383**	**138 312**	**234 839**	**431 233**	**392 894**	**370 521**	**525 172**	**498 790**	**459 045**
5100 Impôts sur production, vente, transfert, etc.	..	81 489	137 675	233 477	428 892	390 385	367 939	521 777	494 738	454 784
5110 Impôts généraux	..	31 766	79 938	136 966	256 546	227 121	210 787	359 611	289 733	249 180
5111 Taxes sur la valeur ajoutée	..	31 766	79 938	136 966	237 621	204 248	190 420	341 450	269 488	230 633
TVA intérieure (brute)	..	12 375	31 686	76 999	145 529	123 186	127 968	259 228	183 386	137 964
TVA à l'importation (brute)	..	19 391	48 252	59 967	92 092	81 062	62 453	82 222	86 103	92 669
5112 Impôts sur les ventes	..	..	..	..	0	0	0	0	0	0
5113 Autres impôts	..	0	0	0	18 925	22 873	20 367	18 161	20 245	18 547
Redevance ad valorem	..	0	0	0	18 925	22 873	20 367	18 161	20 245	18 547
5120 Impôts sur biens et services déterminés	..	49 722	57 737	96 511	172 345	163 263	157 152	162 166	205 004	205 605

Table 5.22. **Niger** *(cont.)*

Details of tax revenue / Recettes fiscales détaillées

Million XOF

	1995	2000	2005	2010	2015	2016	2017	2018	2019	2020
5121 Accises	..	13 754	17 716	28 505	51 081	46 307	29 660	41 203	36 661	41 827
Taxe intérieure sur les produits pétroliers (TIPP) (y compris DGD)	..	4 313	6 654	11 694	19 375	12 703	10 691	18 804	15 673	17 226
Taxe sur les tabacs et les cigarettes	..	4 600	4 862	11 279	17 926	20 295	10 177	11 451	10 795	4 133
Taxe sur les boissons alcoolisés (TBA)	..	882	1 033	1 263	2 684	2 345	1 097	1 074	1 036	3 254
Taxe d'exploitation artisanale (TEA)	..	0	0	0	22	44	29	182	390	1 042
Autres droits d'accises	..	3 959	5 166	4 269	11 074	10 919	7 665	9 693	8 767	16 172
5122 Bénéfices des monopoles fiscaux	..	0	0	0	0	0	0	0	0	0
5123 Droits de douane et droits à l'importation	..	22 930	26 854	36 286	59 517	53 482	51 104	62 450	72 842	87 045
Droits de douane	..	14 722	24 354	28 141	53 226	48 392	45 933	56 383	64 396	77 464
Redevance statistique à l'importation	..	1 652	2 493	8 144	6 283	5 087	5 167	6 026	8 255	9 456
Droits Divers (y compris T.C.I)	..	6 556	7	0	8	3	5	41	192	124
5124 Taxes à l'exportation	..	11 671	12 012	27 567	31 025	27 590	43 958	48 130	48 086	33 725
Taxes sur les réexportations	..	9 997	11 069	25 405	25 657	23 056	36 838	41 097	41 039	26 933
Redevance statistique à l'exportation	..	1 673	943	1 465	5 342	4 524	7 117	6 671	6 982	6 427
Taxe forfaitaire sur la réexportation et/ou transit de tabacs et cigarettes (TFEAR)	..	0	0	696	25	10	3	363	64	365
5125 Impôts sur biens d'équipement	..	0	0	0	0	0	0	0	0	0
5126 Impôts sur services déterminés	..	1 238	901	3 080	30 399	35 691	32 096	10 224	46 982	42 432
Taxe sur la terminaison du trafic international entrant (TATTIE)	..	0	0	0	18 666	25 706	22 101	1 452	18 419	10 866
Taxe sur l'utilisation du réseau de télécommunication (TURTEL)	..	0	0	0	5 349	4 973	5 417	4 220	5 853	4 076
Taxe sur les recettes des loteries	..	877	104	1 303	3 377	2 474	2 292	1 778	2 716	3 084
Taxe unique sur les assurances (TUA)	..	361	792	1 490	2 310	2 291	2 275	2 338	2 852	2 804
Impôt sur les gains des loteries	..	0	5	0	550	7	1	0	31	1
Taxe sur les jeux de hasard (TJH)	..	0	0	246	140	240	11	435	33	24
Taxe sur la publicité commerciale extérieure (TPCE)	..	0	0	41	8	0	0	1	0	2
Taxe sur les activités financières (TAFI)	..	0	0	0	0	0	0	0	17 078	21 575
5127 Autres impôts sur commerce et transact. internat.	..	0	0	0	0	0	0	0	0	0
5128 Autres impôts	..	130	254	1 074	324	193	333	158	433	576
Droits miniers	..	130	254	1 074	295	120	25	3	2	0
Droit fixe mine	..	0	0	0	28	67	307	155	428	572
Droit fixe pétrole	..	0	0	0	1	6	0	0	3	5
5130 Non ventilables entre 5110 et 5120	..	0	0	0	0	0	0	0	0	0
5200 Impôts sur utilisation des biens et exerc. activites	..	894	637	1 362	2 341	2 509	2 582	3 394	4 052	4 261
5210 Impôts périodiques	..	529	637	1 362	2 316	2 474	2 562	3 390	4 050	4 081
Vignette	..	520	625	1 354	2 310	2 471	2 558	2 918	3 072	3 225
5211 A la charge des ménages: véhicules à moteur	..	0	0	0	0	0	0	0	0	0
5212 A la charge autres agents: véhicules à moteur	..	0	0	0	0	0	0	0	0	0
5213 Autres impôts périodiques	..	9	12	8	6	3	4	472	977	855
Permis de chasse et visite	..	0	1	0	2	0	0	3	18	10
Taxe sur les armes à feu (TAF)	..	9	11	8	4	3	4	4	13	1
Taxe sur les abonnements audiovisuels	..	0	0	0	0	0	0	465	946	844
5220 Impôts non-périodiques	..	365	0	0	25	35	20	5	3	180
Péage routier	..	365	..	..	0	0	0	0	0	0
Redevance plaque d'immatriculation	..	0	..	..	25	35	20	5	3	180
5300 Non ventilables entre 5100 et 5200	..	1 000	0	0	0	0	0	0	0	0
6000 Autres impôts	**..**	**3 676**	**7 630**	**19 807**	**70 775**	**40 457**	**35 690**	**56 389**	**58 927**	**74 264**
Droits d'enregistrement	..	2 166	4 834	8 048	51 113	24 353	18 750	34 344	35 469	45 326
Prélèvement pour cpte des collectivités locales	..	0	0	6 512	11 727	8 577	9 283	12 312	12 304	17 064
Taxe sur certains frais généraux des entreprises (TCFGE)	..	310	776	1 963	4 132	4 045	4 314	4 729	5 788	5 955
Droits de timbre	..	1 201	2 019	3 283	3 803	3 481	3 343	5 003	5 366	5 920
6100 A la charge exclusive des entreprises	..	..	..	..	..	..	..	..	..	..
6200 A la charge d'autres agents	..	..	..	..	..	..	..	..	..	..
Pour mémoire :										
Prélèvement communautaire de la CEDEAO	..	448	1 479	5 302	4 893	3 961	0	0	7 651	4 191
Prélèvement communautaire UEMOA	..	866	0	0	0	4 518	0	0	6 540	7 041
Prélèvement communautaire UA	..	..	0	0	0	0	0	0	0	1 451

Table 5.22. **Niger** *(cont.)*

Details of tax revenue / Recettes fiscales détaillées

.. Non disponible

Note : Année civile se terminant le 31 décembre.

Les données sont sur la base des encaissements.

Les chiffres n'incluent pas les données des recettes fiscales collectées par les collectivités locales car elles ne sont pas disponibles.

Les recettes provenant du domaine public, des redevances minières, des redevances superficiaires des mines et du pétrole et des amendes et pénalités relatives aux impôts sont incluses dans les recettes non fiscales dans cette publication comme le préconise la classification OCDE (voir le guide d'interprétation en Annexe A). La classification du Niger compte ces recettes comme des recettes fiscales.

Rubriques 5111 et 5121 : Ces rubriques contiennent des recettes provenant de la Direction Générale des Douanes (DGD) et sont annotées comme telles.

Rubrique 5220 : Cette rubrique comprend les recettes de la redevance plaques d'immatriculation collectées par la Direction Générale du Trésor et de la Comptabilité Publique (DGTCP) entre 2005 et 2020 comme le préconise la classification OCDE (voir le *Guide d'interprétation* en Annexe A). La classification du Niger compte ces recettes comme des recettes non fiscales.

Source : Direction Générale des Impôts.

StatLink https://stat.link/i8b1sj

Table 5.23. **Nigeria / Nigéria**

Details of tax revenue / Recettes fiscales détaillées

Million NGN

	1995	2000	2005	2010	2015	2016	2017	2018	2019	2020
Total tax revenue	..	..	..	**4 023 597**	**5 761 425**	**5 413 912**	**6 547 014**	**8 167 037**	**8 679 676**	**8 526 116**
1000 Taxes on income, profits and capital gains	..	..	..	**2 555 738**	**3 453 159**	**3 018 256**	**3 649 715**	**4 910 261**	**4 910 410**	**4 189 703**
1100 Of individuals	..	..	..	320 771	543 561	604 759	711 067	798 630	927 297	982 157
1110 On income and profits	..	..	..	320 771	543 561	604 759	711 067	798 630	927 297	982 157
Personal Income Tax (Federal)	..	..	..	32 564	57 377	59 469	107 682	85 146	70 307	93 371
State PAYE ("Pay as You Earn") Tax	..	..	..	268 821	456 595	511 911	566 212	669 218	809 320	851 731
Personal Income Tax (State)	..	..	..	19 386	29 589	33 379	37 172	44 266	47 670	37 056
1120 On capital gains	..	..	..	0	0	0	0	0	0	0
1200 Corporate	..	..	..	2 234 967	2 909 598	2 413 498	2 938 649	4 111 631	3 983 113	3 207 545
1210 On profits	..	..	..	2 233 931	2 892 796	2 314 094	2 935 469	4 099 036	3 977 136	3 204 027
Petroleum Profits Tax	..	..	..	1 480 364	1 289 961	1 157 808	1 520 482	2 467 581	2 114 268	1 516 979
Companies Income Tax	..	..	..	658 503	1 268 977	933 537	1 215 057	1 340 329	1 604 699	1 275 370
Education Tax	..	..	..	89 178	206 040	130 123	154 957	203 285	221 058	259 563
Income tax on gas exploration companies	..	..	..	0	115 569	85 878	34 839	75 988	21 930	134 063
National Information Technology Development Fund	..	..	..	5 886	12 249	6 748	10 134	11 853	15 181	18 051
1220 On capital gains	..	..	..	1 037	16 802	99 403	3 180	12 595	5 977	3 519
1300 Unallocable between 1100 and 1200	..	..	..	0	0	0	0	0	0	0
2000 Social security contributions	..	..	..	**305 163**	**569 879**	**550 052**	**714 218**	**687 080**	**931 600**	**982 909**
2100 Employees	..	..	..	172 418	269 328	261 414	332 914	324 012	430 691	452 199
2110 On a payroll basis	..	..	..	172 418	269 328	261 414	332 914	324 012	430 691	452 199
National Pension Commission (employee-side)	..	..	..	132 745	226 596	216 978	291 111	270 022	378 511	403 606
National Health Insurance Scheme	..	..	..	39 673	42 732	44 437	41 803	53 990	52 180	48 593
2120 On an income tax basis	..	..	..	0	0	0	0	0	0	0
2200 Employers	..	..	..	132 745	300 551	288 637	381 304	363 068	500 909	530 710
2210 On a payroll basis	..	..	..	132 745	300 551	288 637	381 304	363 068	500 909	530 710
National Pension Commission (employer-side)	..	..	..	132 745	283 244	271 222	363 889	337 528	473 139	504 507
Nigerian Social Insurance Trust Fund	..	..	..	0	17 307	17 415	17 415	25 540	27 770	26 203
2220 On an income tax basis	..	..	..	0	0	0	0	0	0	0
2300 Self-employed or non-employed	..	..	..	0	0	0	0	0	0	0
2310 On a payroll basis	..	..	..	..	..	..	..	..	..	..
2320 On an income tax basis	..	..	..	..	..	..	..	..	..	..
2400 Unallocable between 2100, 2200 and 2300	..	..	..	0	0	0	0	0	0	0
2410 On a payroll basis	..	..	..	..	..	..	..	..	..	..
2420 On an income tax basis	..	..	..	..	..	..	..	..	..	..
3000 Taxes on payroll and workforce	..	..	..	**12 610**	**32 766**	**31 704**	**40 890**	**50 310**	**54 760**	**69 950**
4000 Taxes on property	..	..	..	..	..	..	..	..	..	..
4100 Recurrent taxes on immovable property	..	..	..	..	..	..	..	..	..	..
4110 Households	..	..	..	..	..	..	..	..	..	..
4120 Others	..	..	..	..	..	..	..	..	..	..
4200 Recurrent taxes on net wealth	..	..	..	..	..	..	..	..	..	..
4210 Individual	..	..	..	..	..	..	..	..	..	..
4220 Corporate	..	..	..	..	..	..	..	..	..	..
4300 Estate, inheritance and gift taxes	..	..	..	..	..	..	..	..	..	..
4310 Estate and inheritance taxes	..	..	..	..	..	..	..	..	..	..
4320 Gift taxes	..	..	..	..	..	..	..	..	..	..
4400 Taxes on financial and capital transactions	..	..	..	..	..	..	..	..	..	..
4500 Non-recurrent taxes	..	..	..	..	..	..	..	..	..	..
4510 On net wealth	..	..	..	..	..	..	..	..	..	..
4520 Other non-recurrent taxes	..	..	..	..	..	..	..	..	..	..
4600 Other recurrent taxes on property	..	..	..	..	..	..	..	..	..	..
5000 Taxes on goods and services	..	..	..	**1 036 386**	**1 520 489**	**1 569 281**	**1 821 381**	**2 072 094**	**2 317 754**	**2 774 503**
5100 Taxes on production, sale, transfer, etc.	..	..	..	1 029 896	1 501 713	1 548 943	1 799 838	2 047 860	2 287 161	2 746 109
5110 General taxes	..	..	..	564 892	767 334	828 199	972 348	1 108 040	1 189 981	1 531 171
5111 Value added taxes	..	..	..	564 892	767 334	828 199	972 348	1 108 040	1 189 981	1 531 171
VAT revenues (domestic)	..	..	..	436 610	597 412	650 344	770 348	859 018	945 464	1 183 446
VAT revenues (imports)	..	..	..	128 281	169 921	177 855	202 001	249 022	244 517	347 725
5112 Sales tax	..	..	..	0	0	0	0	0	0	0
5113 Other	..	..	..	0	0	0	0	0	0	0
5120 Taxes on specific goods and services	..	..	..	465 005	734 380	720 743	827 490	939 820	1 097 180	1 214 938
5121 Excises	..	..	..	35 449	39 784	41 258	41 600	55 060	91 690	120 854
5122 Profits of fiscal monopolies	..	..	..	0	0	0	0	0	0	0
5123 Customs and import duties	..	..	..	429 555	694 596	679 485	785 890	884 760	1 005 490	1 094 084
Import duties	..	..	..	272 248	468 382	462 058	533 560	604 990	693 490	746 154
Other customs taxes	..	..	..	157 307	226 214	217 428	252 330	279 770	312 000	347 930

Table 5.23. **Nigeria / Nigéria** *(cont.)*

Details of tax revenue / Recettes fiscales détaillées

Million NGN

	1995	2000	2005	2010	2015	2016	2017	2018	2019	2020
5124 Taxes on exports	..	..	..	0	0	0	0	0	0	0
5125 Taxes on investment goods	..	..	..	0	0	0	0	0	0	0
5126 Taxes on specific services	..	..	..	0	0	0	0	0	0	0
5127 Other taxes on internat. trade and transactions	..	..	..	0	0	0	0	0	0	0
5128 Other taxes	..	..	..	0	0	0	0	0	0	0
5130 Unallocable between 5110 and 5120	..	..	..	0	0	0	0	0	0	0
5200 Taxes on use of goods and perform activities	..	..	..	6 490	18 775	20 339	21 542	24 234	30 593	28 394
5210 Recurrent taxes	..	..	..	6 490	18 775	20 339	21 542	24 234	30 593	28 394
5211 Paid by households: motor vehicles	..	..	..	6 121	18 412	19 948	21 214	23 957	30 270	28 394
5212 Paid by others: motor vehicles	..	..	..	0	0	0	0	0	0	0
5213 Paid in respect of other goods	..	..	..	368	364	391	328	277	323	0
5220 Non-recurrent taxes	..	..	..	0	0	0	0	0	0	0
5300 Unallocable between 5100 and 5200	..	..	..	0	0	0	0	0	0	0
6000 Other taxes	**..**	**..**	**..**	**113 700**	**185 133**	**244 619**	**320 811**	**447 292**	**465 152**	**509 051**
6100 Paid solely by business	..	..	..	0	0	0	0	0	0	0
6200 Other	..	..	..	113 700	185 133	244 619	320 811	447 292	465 152	509 051
Other tax revenue from states	..	..	..	107 106	178 048	238 714	311 873	431 493	446 960	388 894
Stamp duties	..	..	..	6 593	7 085	5 905	8 938	15 798	18 192	120 157

Note: "Year ending 31st December.

The data are on a cash basis.

Some personal income taxes, capital gains taxes, road taxes, and other taxes are collected at the state level.

Statistics on state level revenues were not available in disaggregated form for 2017 and 2018. For these years, revenues for the categories State PAYE ("Pay as You Earn") Tax, Personal Income Tax (State), Other tax revenue from states were estimations.

Heading 1110: State level income taxes on individuals on paid employment are collected on a PAYE ("Pay as you earn") basis, while those who are self-employed or receive business income on a non-salary basis are charged under direct assessment. These are reported separately in this table, but the tax basis is the same for both cases.

Heading 1210: The Petroleum Profits Tax includes all tax revenue payments by oil exploration companies irrespective of the type of exploration arrangement (production sharing, joint ventures, etc) despite the fact that different types of arrangements could give rise to different tax rates. This heading does not include the government's share of company revenue arising from the revenue-sharing component of the exploration arrangements. These latter funds are reported as oil revenues in the non-tax revenue table.

Heading 1220: Capital gains tax for resident companies and non-residents is collected at the federal level while capital gains tax for individuals is collected at the state level.

Heading 2000: The Pension Reform Act was passed in 2004 and mandated both employees and employers to contribute 7.5% each to the pension retirement savings account. However, in 2014 there was an amendment after which the employee was mandated to contribute 8% while the employer contributed a minimum of 10% thereby bringing the total contribution to at leat 18%. For the years up to and including 2014, therefore, 50% of social security contributions are reported under heading 2110 and the other half under heading 2210. Starting in 2015, 4/9 of total pension contributions are reported under heading 2110 and 5/9 of total pension contributions are reported under heading 2210.

Heading 3000: This heading consists of a 2.5% payroll tax that is used to finance the National Housing Fund.

Heading 5211: Road Taxes, or taxes charged on the issuance of motor vehicle licenses, are collected at the state level.

Heading 5213: This heading contains taxes collected under the Pre-Operational Levy. This is a tax charged each year to companies that, more than 18 months after being registered, still have not commenced operations.

Heading 6000: Other state taxes include stamp duties, capital gains taxes, business premise registration, Land Use Charge, market taxes, and levies that are collected by state governments."

Source: Federal Inland Revenue Service.

StatLink https://stat.link/7285hv

Table 5.24. **Rwanda**

Details of tax revenue / Recettes fiscales détaillées

Million RWF

	1995	2000	2005	2010	2015	2016	2017	2018	2019	2020
Total tax revenue	**..**	**68 909**	**174 606**	**440 724**	**997 232**	**1 115 636**	**1 248 017**	**1 401 503**	**1 611 730**	**1 642 978**
1000 Taxes on income, profits and capital gains	**..**	**17 943**	**49 911**	**159 567**	**379 676**	**430 431**	**488 184**	**565 235**	**640 854**	**678 516**
1100 Of individuals	..	6 621	24 587	102 037	224 553	253 893	278 076	312 070	354 545	363 018
1110 On income and profits	..	6 621	24 587	102 037	224 553	253 893	278 076	312 070	354 545	363 018
Pay As You Earn	..	..	..	..	216 750	245 138	267 311	300 751	343 064	351 474
Rental income tax	..	..	..	..	7 803	8 754	10 765	11 319	11 481	11 544
1120 On capital gains	..	0	0	0	0	0	0	0	0	0
1200 Corporate	..	11 322	25 324	57 530	155 123	176 538	210 108	253 165	286 309	315 499
1210 On profits	..	11 322	25 324	57 530	155 123	176 538	210 108	253 165	286 309	315 499
Corporation income tax	..	3 603	11 606	26 459	49 571	58 645	70 053	94 656	95 881	118 183
Withholding tax	..	59	605	10 764	58 422	71 929	84 786	71 474	96 990	137 450
Personal income tax	..	868	2 210	7 316	7 358	8 752	10 012	10 991	10 291	10 042
Other taxes on profits	..	6 792	10 903	12 991	39 772	37 212	45 257	76 044	83 147	49 824
1220 On capital gains	..	0	0	0	0	0	0	0	0	0
1300 Unallocable between 1100 and 1200	..	0	0	0	0	0	0	0	0	0
2000 Social security contributions	**..**	**3 423**	**11 988**	**28 235**	**59 687**	**74 717**	**74 897**	**83 344**	**94 371**	**102 178**
2100 Employees	..	1 283	4 493	10 586	22 379	28 014	28 082	31 249	35 384	38 311
2110 On a payroll basis	..	1 283	4 493	10 586	22 379	28 014	28 082	31 249	35 384	38 311
2120 On an income tax basis	..	0	0	0	0	0	0	0	0	0
2200 Employers	..	2 138	7 488	17 644	37 299	46 691	46 803	52 082	58 973	63 851
2210 On a payroll basis	..	2 138	7 488	17 644	37 299	46 691	46 803	52 082	58 973	63 851
2220 On an income tax basis	..	0	0	0	0	0	0	0	0	0
2300 Self-employed or non-employed	..	3	6	4	9	11	11	13	14	16
2310 On a payroll basis	..	3	6	4	9	11	11	13	14	16
2320 On an income tax basis	..	0	0	0	0	0	0	0	0	0
2400 Unallocable between 2100, 2200 and 2300	..	0	0	0	0	0	0	0	0	0
2410 On a payroll basis	..	..	..	..	..	..	..	..	..	..
2420 On an income tax basis	..	..	..	..	..	..	..	..	..	..
3000 Taxes on payroll and workforce	**..**	**0**	**0**	**0**	**0**	**0**	**0**	**0**	**0**	**0**
4000 Taxes on property	**..**	**130**	**43**	**97**	**632**	**779**	**1 156**	**1 293**	**2 142**	**14 957**
4100 Recurrent taxes on immovable property	..	130	42	96	632	779	1 156	1 293	2 142	14 957
4110 Households	..	130	42	96	632	779	1 156	1 293	2 142	14 957
4120 Others	..	0	0	0	0	0	0	0	0	0
4200 Recurrent taxes on net wealth	..	0	0	0	0	0	0	0	0	0
4210 Individual	..	..	..	..	..	..	..	..	..	..
4220 Corporate	..	..	..	..	..	..	..	..	..	..
4300 Estate, inheritance and gift taxes	..	0	0	0	0	0	0	0	0	0
4310 Estate and inheritance taxes	..	..	..	..	..	..	..	..	..	..
4320 Gift taxes	..	..	..	..	..	..	..	..	..	..
4400 Taxes on financial and capital transactions	..	0	0	0	0	0	0	0	0	0
4500 Non-recurrent taxes	..	0	0	0	0	0	0	0	0	0
4510 On net wealth	..	..	..	..	..	..	..	..	..	..
4520 Other non-recurrent taxes	..	..	..	..	..	..	..	..	..	..
4600 Other recurrent taxes on property	..	0	1	0	0	0	0	0	0	0
5000 Taxes on goods and services	**..**	**47 413**	**112 664**	**252 826**	**557 238**	**609 709**	**683 780**	**751 631**	**874 363**	**847 327**
5100 Taxes on production, sale, transfer, etc.	..	46 777	111 848	250 214	549 277	601 651	676 883	744 296	867 102	840 735
5110 General taxes	..	13 777	57 747	131 665	305 544	329 331	386 484	422 903	507 719	486 043
5111 Value added taxes	..	13 777	57 747	131 665	305 544	329 331	386 484	422 903	507 719	486 043
VAT revenues (gross)	..	..	64 163	146 295	339 493	365 923	429 748	476 671	576 953	552 322
VAT Refunds	..	..	-6 416	-14 629	-33 949	-36 592	-43 264	-53 768	-69 234	-66 279
5112 Sales tax	..	0	0	0	0	0	0	0	0	0
5113 Other	..	0	0	0	0	0	0	0	0	0
5120 Taxes on specific goods and services	..	32 999	54 101	118 548	243 733	272 320	290 399	321 393	359 383	354 692
5121 Excises	..	18 849	22 614	75 236	138 261	143 701	148 561	169 237	183 714	187 024
Excise tax on beers	..	7 146	9 371	22 548	45 950	42 510	47 862	54 801	61 170	64 892
Excise tax on petroleum	..	7 857	6 515	30 941	47 043	49 761	50 013	55 791	59 311	54 865
Strategic reserves levy	..	0	0	0	4 185	9 485	10 355	10 502	11 386	10 531
Other excises taxes	..	3 846	6 728	21 746	41 084	41 946	40 331	48 143	51 848	56 736
5122 Profits of fiscal monopolies	..	0	0	0	0	0	0	0	0	0

Table 5.24. **Rwanda** *(cont.)*

Details of tax revenue / Recettes fiscales détaillées

Million RWF

	1995	2000	2005	2010	2015	2016	2017	2018	2019	2020
5123 Customs and import duties	..	14 151	31 488	43 313	105 472	128 620	141 838	152 155	175 669	167 667
Import duties	..	9 260	22 071	26 215	69 731	72 062	80 738	83 601	100 742	99 674
Rwanda road maintenance fund	..	2 531	3 644	14 843	29 620	43 062	45 768	48 805	53 109	48 166
Infrastructure development levy	..	0	0	0	3 837	10 069	11 164	12 228	14 039	13 254
African Union Levy	..	0	0	0	0	0	721	1 579	1 835	1 676
Other customs and import duties	..	2 360	5 773	2 254	2 284	3 426	3 448	5 942	5 943	4 896
5124 Taxes on exports	..	0	0	0	0	0	0	0	0	0
5125 Taxes on investment goods	..	0	0	0	0	0	0	0	0	0
5126 Taxes on specific services	..	0	0	0	0	0	0	0	0	0
5127 Other taxes on internat. trade and transactions	..	0	0	0	0	0	0	0	0	0
5128 Other taxes	..	0	0	0	0	0	0	0	0	0
5130 Unallocable between 5110 and 5120	..	0	0	0	0	0	0	0	0	0
5200 Taxes on use of goods and perform activities	..	636	816	2 612	7 961	8 058	6 897	7 335	7 261	6 592
5210 Recurrent taxes	..	636	816	2 612	7 961	8 058	6 897	7 335	7 261	6 592
5211 Paid by households: motor vehicles	..	636	816	2 612	3 252	2 947	2 691	2 269	3 473	3 563
5212 Paid by others: motor vehicles	..	0	0	0	0	0	0	0	0	0
5213 Paid in respect of other goods	..	0	0	0	4 709	5 111	4 206	5 066	3 788	3 029
5220 Non-recurrent taxes	..	0	0	0	0	0	0	0	0	0
5300 Unallocable between 5100 and 5200	..	0	0	0	0	0	0	0	0	0
6000 Other taxes	**..**	**0**	**0**	**0**	**0**	**0**	**0**	**0**	**0**	**0**
6100 Paid solely by business	..	..	..	..	..	..	..	..	..	..
6200 Other	..	..	..	..	..	..	..	..	..	..

.. Not available

Note: Year ending 31st December. From 2008, the figures for social security contributions are on a fiscal year basis beginning 1st July. For example, data for 2020 represent July 2019 to June 2020.

The data are on a cash basis.

Figures exclude tax revenues collected by sub-national governments as the data are not available.

Figures include fines related to tax revenues as it is not possible to split these out from tax revenues. These revenues are now classified as non-tax revenues following a change in the OECD classification. Rwanda considers these revenues as tax revenues.

Heading 2000: Rwanda does not include social security contributions in their tax revenue data as the Rwandan authorities do not consider them as taxes.

Source: Rwanda Revenue Authority.

StatLink https://stat.link/bltjxd

Table 5.25. **Senegal / Sénégal**

Details of tax revenue / Recettes fiscales détaillées

Million XOF

	1995	2000	2005	2010	2015	2016	2017	2018	2019	2020
Recettes fiscales totales	**..**	**559 295**	**887 248**	**1 267 799**	**1 723 131**	**1 920 344**	**1 999 742**	**2 178 126**	**2 516 373**	**2 556 434**
1000 Impôts sur revenu, bénéfices et gains en capital	**..**	**123 771**	**204 800**	**328 200**	**435 600**	**516 600**	**543 571**	**603 331**	**710 593**	**717 193**
1100 Des personnes physiques	..	64 021	102 600	192 900	261 000	314 500	260 531	313 626	352 187	354 323
1110 Sur le revenu et les bénéfices	..	63 370	101 100	191 000	257 900	310 800	260 531	313 626	352 187	354 323
1120 Sur les gains en capital	..	651	1 500	1 900	3 100	3 700	..	..	..	..
1200 Des sociétés	..	49 418	83 900	106 100	147 300	165 500	275 500	280 643	349 962	353 879
1210 Sur les bénéfices	..	49 418	83 900	106 100	147 300	165 500	275 500	280 643	349 962	353 879
1220 Sur les gains en capital	..	..	..	..	..	..	..	..	..	..
1300 Non ventilables entre 1100 et 1200	..	10 332	18 300	29 200	27 300	36 600	7 540	9 062	8 444	8 991
2000 Cotisations de sécurité sociale	**..**	**22 215**	**36 568**	**72 999**	**116 260**	**128 210**	**142 070**	**150 000**	**159 423**	**159 423**
2100 A la charge des salariés	..	..	..	..	..	..	..	..	..	..
2110 Sur la base du salaire	..	..	..	..	..	..	..	..	..	..
2120 Sur la base de l'impôt sur le revenu	..	..	..	..	..	..	..	..	..	..
2200 A la charge des employeurs	..	..	..	..	..	..	..	..	..	..
2210 Sur la base du salaire	..	..	..	..	..	..	..	..	..	..
2220 Sur la base de l'impôt sur le revenu	..	..	..	..	..	..	..	..	..	..
2300 A charge des travailleurs indép. ou sans emploi	..	..	..	..	..	..	..	..	..	..
2310 Sur la base du salaire	..	..	..	..	..	..	..	..	..	..
2320 Sur la base de l'impôt sur le revenu	..	..	..	..	..	..	..	..	..	..
2400 Non ventilables entre 2100, 2200 et 2300	..	22 215	36 568	72 999	116 260	128 210	142 070	150 000	159 423	159 423
Institution de Prévoyance Retraite du Sénégal (IPRES)	..	22 215	36 568	72 999	93 400	103 510	115 670	..	..	..
Caisse de Sécurité Sociale (CSS)	..	0	0	0	22 860	24 700	26 400	..	..	..
2410 Sur la base du salaire	..	..	..	..	..	..	..	..	..	..
2420 Sur la base de l'impôt sur le revenu	..	..	..	..	..	..	..	..	..	..
3000 Sur salaires ou main-d'œuvre	**..**	**6 668**	**9 440**	**10 800**	**20 200**	**17 310**	**13 960**	**5 283**	**8 952**	**7 996**
4000 Impôts sur le patrimoine	**..**	**11 200**	**23 200**	**39 100**	**41 500**	**51 984**	**13 050**	**14 484**	**14 758**	**17 502**
4100 Impôts périodiques sur la propriété immobilière	..	0	0	0	0	0	0	0	0	0
4110 Ménages	..	..	..	..	..	..	..	..	..	..
4120 Autres agents	..	..	..	..	..	..	..	..	..	..
4200 Impôts périodiques sur l'actif net	..	0	0	0	0	0	0	0	0	0
4210 Personnes physiques	..	..	..	..	..	..	..	..	..	..
4220 Sociétés	..	..	..	..	..	..	..	..	..	..
4300 Impôts sur mut. par décès, succ. et donations	..	2 464	5 104	12 445	8 465	11 564	3 937	4 174	3 876	6 620
4310 Impôts sur mut. par décès et successions	..	..	..	..	..	..	..	..	..	..
4320 Impôts sur les donations	..	..	..	..	..	..	..	..	..	..
4400 Impôts sur transact. mobilières et immob.	..	8 736	18 096	26 655	33 035	40 419	9 113	10 310	10 882	10 882
Droits de mutation sur vente ou echanges d'immeubles	..	..	..	15 418	15 863	14 995	..	..	..	..
Droits d'enregistrement autre que patrimoine	..	..	..	11 237	17 172	25 424	9 113	10 310	10 882	11 099
4500 Impôts non-périodiques	..	0	0	0	0	0	0	0	0	0
4510 Sur l'actif net	..	..	..	..	..	..	..	..	..	..
4520 Autres non-périodiques	..	..	..	..	..	..	..	..	..	..
4600 Autres impôts périodiques sur patrimoine	..	0	0	0	0	0	0	0	0	0
5000 Impôts sur les biens et services	**..**	**386 940**	**601 700**	**804 400**	**1 086 871**	**1 187 941**	**1 225 811**	**1 308 349**	**1 548 797**	**1 496 509**
5100 Impôts sur production, vente, transfert, etc.	..	384 590	597 700	799 400	1 078 171	1 175 841	1 214 962	1 297 281	1 535 951	1 483 770
5110 Impôts généraux	..	221 410	354 800	478 000	617 000	651 300	699 177	734 853	883 270	805 539
5111 Taxes sur la valeur ajoutée	..	221 410	354 800	478 000	617 000	651 300	699 177	734 853	883 270	805 539
5112 Impôts sur les ventes	..	0	0	0	0	0	0	0	0	0
5113 Autres impôts	..	0	0	0	0	0	0	0	0	0
5120 Impôts sur biens et services déterminés	..	163 180	242 900	321 400	461 171	524 541	515 784	562 428	652 681	678 231
5121 Accises	..	61 100	82 700	82 600	88 821	107 441	125 998	148 561	107 789	157 613
Taxe spécifique sur les produits pétroliers	..	..	62 600	63 900	61 520	74 600	83 600	91 039	69 286	97 300
Taxes sur les tabacs	..	..	8 483	9 647	14 565	15 252	13 660	16 403	19 672	20 250
Taxes sur les corps gras	..	..	4 148	978	1 964	4 712	4 330	6 413	4 034	13 953
Taxes sur les alcools	..	..	3 535	5 297	5 516	6 824	6 609	7 854	6 056	7 630
Taxe sur la cola	..	..	278	273	19	8	4	19	-6	23
Taxe sur les thés	..	..	121	154	153	228	118	70	269	123
Taxe sur le café	..	..	140	175	428	441	335	442	673	348
Taxe sur les produits comestiques	..	..	0	0	1 465	1 604	1 795	2 544	1 725	2 618
Taxe spéciale sur le ciment	..	..	0	0	0	0	10 700	14 087	0	15 369
Accises non classées ailleurs	..	..	3 395	2 176	3 189	3 771	4 848	9 690	6 082	..
5122 Bénéfices des monopoles fiscaux	..	0	0	0	0	0	0	0	0	0
5123 Droits de douane et droits à l'importation	..	90 340	138 900	181 600	227 600	234 600	263 495	290 339	365 538	337 908
5124 Taxes à l'exportation	..	0	0	0	0	0	2 891	0	0	0

Table 5.25. **Senegal / Sénégal** *(cont.)*

Details of tax revenue / Recettes fiscales détaillées

Million XOF

	1995	2000	2005	2010	2015	2016	2017	2018	2019	2020
5125 Impôts sur biens d'équipement	..	0	0	0	0	0	0	0	0	0
5126 Impôts sur services déterminés	..	11 740	21 300	45 000	71 200	76 100	95 500	105 378	78 000	100 538
Taxe sur les activités financières (TAF)	..	9 340	17 600	30 600	47 700	51 600	55 400	62 534	55 300	71 462
Redevance d'utilisation des télécommunications	..	0	0	10 000	19 500	18 600	19 600	22 289	22 700	21 214
Taxe sur les contrats d'assurances	..	2 400	3 700	4 400	4 000	5 900	6 300	6 905	0	7 862
Contribution au développement économique (CODEC)	..	0	0	0	0	0	14 200	13 649	0	0
5127 Autres impôts sur commerce et transact. internat.	..	0	0	0	0	0	0	0	0	0
5128 Autres impôts	..	0	0	12 200	73 551	106 400	27 900	18 150	101 354	82 171
Fonds de sécurisation des importations de produits pétroliers	..	..	..	12 200	69 451	104 600	26 400	17 266	96 854	81 826
Contribution spéciale des produits des mines et carrières	..	..	..	0	4 100	1 800	1 500	884	4 500	345
5130 Non ventilables entre 5110 et 5120	..	0	0	0	0	0	0	0	0	0
5200 Impôts sur utilisation des biens et exerc. activites	..	2 350	4 000	5 000	8 700	12 100	10 849	11 068	12 846	12 738
5210 Impôts périodiques	..	2 350	4 000	5 000	8 700	12 100	10 849	11 068	12 846	12 738
5211 A la charge des ménages: véhicules à moteur	..	..	..	..	..	..	..	..	..	..
5212 A la charge autres agents: véhicules à moteur	..	..	..	..	..	..	..	..	..	..
5213 Autres impôts périodiques	..	..	..	..	..	..	..	..	..	..
5220 Impôts non-périodiques	..	0	0	0	0	0	0	0	0	0
5300 Non ventilables entre 5100 et 5200	..	0	0	0	0	0	0	0	0	0
6000 Autres impôts	**..**	**8 500**	**11 540**	**12 300**	**22 700**	**18 300**	**61 280**	**96 678**	**73 851**	**157 811**
6100 A la charge exclusive des entreprises	..	..	..	..	..	..	..	..	..	..
6200 A la charge d'autres agents	..	..	..	..	..	..	..	..	..	..

.. Non disponible

Note : Année civile se terminant le 31 décembre.

Les données sont sur la base des encaissements.

Les chiffres n'incluent pas les données des recettes fiscales collectées par les collectivités locales car elles ne sont pas disponibles.

Les chiffres ne comprennent pas les taxes parafiscales car elles ne sont pas disponibles.

La rubrique 2000 comprend les cotisations de sécurité sociale de l'Institution de prévoyance retraite du Sénégal (IPRES) à partir de 2006 et les cotisations de sécurité sociale de la Caisse de Sécurité Sociale (CSS) à partir de 2012. Les cotisations de sécurité sociale au Sénégal antérieures à 2006 sont estimées.

La rubrique 5126 comprend la redevance sur l'accès ou l'utilisation du réseau des télécommunications publiques (RUTEL) classifiée comme accise au Sénégal.

Les recettes fiscales incluent les amendes et pénalités sur impôts et taxes considérées comme des recettes non fiscales. Il n'a pas été possible pour cette édition de séparer le versement des amendes et pénalités des recettes correspondant aux impôts auxquels ces amendes et pénalités se rattachent. La classification nationale du Sénégal les compte comme des recettes fiscales.

Source : Ministère de l'Économie, des Finances et du Plan.

StatLink https://stat.link/aj503n

Table 5.26. **Sierra Leone**

Details of tax revenue / Recettes fiscales détaillées

Million SLL

	1995	2000	2005	2010	2015	2016	2017	2018	2019	2020
Total tax revenue	..	..	**374 356**	**929 507**	**2 135 262**	**2 587 130**	**2 953 446**	**3 545 044**	**4 326 905**	**4 376 983**
1000 Taxes on income, profits and capital gains	..	..	**110 153**	**291 747**	**895 337**	**1 260 921**	**1 183 087**	**1 595 948**	**1 866 079**	**1 992 218**
1100 Of individuals	..	..	48 458	155 237	650 329	936 442	960 890	1 157 616	1 327 986	1 407 927
1110 On income and profits	..	..	48 458	155 237	650 329	936 442	960 890	1 157 616	1 327 986	1 407 927
Personal Income Tax	..	..	48 458	155 237	650 329	936 442	960 890	1 157 616	1 327 986	1 407 927
1120 On capital gains	..	..	0	0	0	0	0	0	0	0
1200 Corporate	..	..	61 696	136 510	245 008	324 479	222 197	438 331	538 093	584 291
1210 On profits	..	..	61 696	136 510	245 008	324 479	222 197	438 331	538 093	584 291
Corporate Tax	..	..	61 696	136 510	245 008	324 479	222 197	438 331	538 093	584 291
1220 On capital gains of corporates	..	..	0	0	0	0	0	0	0	0
1300 Unallocable between 1100 and 1200	..	..	0	0	0	0	0	0	0	0
2000 Social security contributions	..	..	..	..	..	..	..	..	..	..
2100 Employees	..	..	..	..	..	..	..	..	..	..
2110 On a payroll basis	..	..	..	..	..	..	..	..	..	..
2120 On an income tax basis	..	..	..	..	..	..	..	..	..	..
2200 Employers	..	..	..	..	..	..	..	..	..	..
2210 On a payroll basis	..	..	..	..	..	..	..	..	..	..
2220 On an income tax basis	..	..	..	..	..	..	..	..	..	..
2300 Self-employed or non-employed	..	..	..	..	..	..	..	..	..	..
2310 On a payroll basis	..	..	..	..	..	..	..	..	..	..
2320 On an income tax basis	..	..	..	..	..	..	..	..	..	..
2400 Unallocable between 2100, 2200 and 2300	..	..	..	..	..	..	..	..	..	..
2410 On a payroll basis	..	..	..	..	..	..	..	..	..	..
2420 On an income tax basis	..	..	..	..	..	..	..	..	..	..
3000 Taxes on payroll and workforce	..	..	**0**	**0**	**0**	**0**	**0**	**0**	**0**	**0**
4000 Taxes on property	..	..	..	..	..	..	..	..	..	..
4100 Recurrent taxes on immovable property	..	..	..	..	..	..	..	..	..	..
4110 Households	..	..	..	..	..	..	..	..	..	..
4120 Others	..	..	..	..	..	..	..	..	..	..
4200 Recurrent taxes on net wealth	..	..	..	..	..	..	..	..	..	..
4210 Individual	..	..	..	..	..	..	..	..	..	..
4220 Corporate	..	..	..	..	..	..	..	..	..	..
4300 Estate, inheritance and gift taxes	..	..	..	..	..	..	..	..	..	..
4310 Estate and inheritance taxes	..	..	..	..	..	..	..	..	..	..
4320 Gift taxes	..	..	..	..	..	..	..	..	..	..
4400 Taxes on financial and capital transactions	..	..	..	..	..	..	..	..	..	..
4500 Other non-reccurrent taxes on property	..	..	..	..	..	..	..	..	..	..
4510 On net wealth	..	..	..	..	..	..	..	..	..	..
4520 Other non-recurrent taxes	..	..	..	..	..	..	..	..	..	..
4600 Other recurrent taxes on property	..	..	..	..	..	..	..	..	..	..
5000 Taxes on goods and services	..	..	**264 203**	**637 760**	**1 239 925**	**1 326 210**	**1 770 360**	**1 949 097**	**2 460 826**	**2 384 764**
5100 Taxes on production, sale, transfer, etc.	..	..	264 203	637 760	1 239 925	1 326 210	1 770 360	1 949 097	2 460 826	2 384 764
5110 General taxes on goods and services	..	..	0	246 362	593 048	666 090	714 186	886 383	1 030 686	1 046 227
5111 Value added taxes	..	..	0	246 362	593 048	666 090	714 186	886 383	1 030 686	1 046 227
Domestic GST	..	..	..	109 657	238 837	298 251	302 265	335 803	444 961	467 459
GST on imports	..	..	..	136 705	354 211	367 839	411 921	550 580	585 725	578 768
5112 Sales tax	..	..	..	0	0	0	0	0	0	0
5113 Other	..	..	..	0	0	0	0	0	0	0
5120 Taxes on specific goods and services	..	..	264 203	391 397	646 877	660 119	1 056 174	1 062 713	1 430 140	1 338 537
5121 Excises	..	..	73 925	190 307	311 155	270 198	564 938	412 226	709 116	694 405
Excise on petroleum	..	..	42 347	123 439	193 084	163 624	407 005	347 155	567 476	520 115
Other excises	..	..	7 643	9 568	23 361	20 031	17 035	10 877	35 354	56 409
Road user charges	..	..	23 935	57 300	94 710	86 543	140 897	54 194	106 286	117 881
5122 Profits of fiscal monopolies	..	..	0	0	0	0	0	0	0	0
5123 Customs and import duties	..	..	185 990	189 811	329 368	381 633	485 727	650 487	711 075	644 133
Import duties	..	..	172 283	189 811	329 368	381 633	485 727	650 487	711 075	644 133
Other customs duties	..	..	13 707	0	0	0	0	0	0	0
5124 Taxes on exports	..	..	0	0	0	0	0	0	0	0
5125 Taxes on investment goods	..	..	0	0	0	0	0	0	0	0
5126 Taxes on specific services	..	..	4 288	11 279	6 354	8 288	5 510	0	9 949	0
5127 Other taxes on internat. trade and transactions	..	..	0	0	0	0	0	0	0	0
5128 Other taxes	..	..	0	0	0	0	0	0	0	0
5130 Unallocable between 5110 and 5120	..	..	0	0	0	0	0	0	0	0
5200 Taxes on use of goods and perform activities	..	..	0	0	0	0	0	0	0	0

Table 5.26. **Sierra Leone** *(cont.)*

Details of tax revenue / Recettes fiscales détaillées

Million SLL

	1995	2000	2005	2010	2015	2016	2017	2018	2019	2020
5210 Recurrent taxes	..	..	..	..	..	..	..	..	..	..
5211 Paid by households: motor vehicles	..	..	..	..	..	..	..	..	..	..
5212 Paid by others: motor vehicles	..	..	..	..	..	..	..	..	..	..
5213 Paid in respect of other goods	..	..	..	..	..	..	..	..	..	..
5220 Non-recurrent taxes	..	..	..	..	..	..	..	..	..	..
5300 Unallocable between 5100 and 5200	..	..	0	0	0	0	0	0	0	0
6000 Other taxes	**..**	**..**	**0**	**0**	**0**	**0**	**0**	**0**	**0**	**0**
6100 Paid solely by business	..	..	..	..	..	..	..	..	..	..
6200 Other	..	..	..	..	..	..	..	..	..	..

.. Not available

Note: Year ending 31st December.

The data are on a cash basis.

Figures exclude tax revenues collected by sub-national governments as the data are not available.

Heading 5121: The road user charge fund (RUC) is funded through fuel levies, vehicle licenses and vehicle registrations fees, however it is not possible to distinguish between these revenues. As fuel levies represent around 65% of these revenues, the totality of the RUC revenues is classified under heading 5121.

Heading 5126: This heading includes the foreign travel tax on air tickets until mid 2018. Its collection now forms part of the Treasury Single Account collection classified in non-tax revenues under heading "Sales of goods and services".

Source: Sierra Leone National Revenue Authority.

StatLink https://stat.link/fk1s4h

Table 5.27. **Seychelles**

Details of tax revenue / Recettes fiscales détaillées

Million SCR

	1995	2000	2005	2010	2015	2016	2017	2018	2019	2020
Total tax revenue	..	..	..	**3 595**	**5 464**	**6 108**	**6 713**	**7 464**	**7 605**	**6 761**
1000 Taxes on income, profits and capital gains	..	..	..	**1 062**	**1 696**	**1 967**	**2 255**	**2 329**	**2 360**	**2 216**
1100 Of individuals	..	..	..	254	948	939	901	965	975	1 023
1110 On income and profits	..	..	..	254	948	939	901	965	975	1 023
1120 On capital gains	..	..	..	0	0	0	0	0	0	0
1200 Corporate	..	..	..	808	748	1 029	1 354	1 364	1 385	1 193
1210 On profits	..	..	..	808	748	1 029	1 354	1 364	1 385	1 193
Companies	..	..	..	703	563	853	1 112	1 155	1 160	1 016
Sole traders	..	..	..	14	43	32	47	37	38	36
Partnerships	..	..	..	9	11	13	14	16	18	17
Witholding tax	..	..	..	58	88	83	127	96	104	103
Residential dwellings	..	..	..	0	43	47	54	59	65	22
Others	..	..	..	0	0	0	0	0	0	0
G&S Tax on rental income	..	..	..	24	0	0	0	0	0	0
1220 On capital gains	..	..	..	0	0	0	0	0	0	0
1300 Unallocable between 1100 and 1200	..	..	..	0	0	0	0	0	0	0
2000 Social security contributions	..	..	..	**329**	**215**	**212**	**255**	**540**	**398**	**436**
2100 Employees	..	..	..	21	93	106	140	185	199	213
2110 On a payroll basis	..	..	..	21	93	106	140	185	199	213
SPF - Mandatory employee contributions	..	..	..	21	93	106	140	185	199	213
2120 On an income tax basis	..	..	..	0	0	0	0	0	0	0
2200 Employers	..	..	..	21	102	106	115	148	196	212
2210 On a payroll basis	..	..	..	21	102	106	115	148	196	212
SPF - Mandatory employer contributions	..	..	..	21	102	106	115	148	196	212
2220 On an income tax basis	..	..	..	0	0	0	0	0	0	0
2300 Self-employed or non-employed	..	..	..	0	0	0	0	0	0	0
2310 On a payroll basis	..	..	..	..	..	..	..	..	..	..
2320 On an income tax basis	..	..	..	..	..	..	..	..	..	..
2400 Unallocable between 2100, 2200 and 2300	..	..	..	287	20	0	0	208	3	10
2410 On a payroll basis	..	..	..	0	0	0	0	0	0	0
2420 On an income tax basis	..	..	..	287	20	0	0	208	3	10
3000 Taxes on payroll and workforce	..	..	..	**0**	**0**	**0**	**0**	**0**	**0**	**0**
4000 Taxes on property	..	..	..	**126**	**140**	**99**	**99**	**126**	**168**	**124**
4100 Recurrent taxes on immovable property	..	..	..	0	0	0	0	0	0	0
4110 Households	..	..	..	..	..	..	..	..	..	..
4120 Others	..	..	..	..	..	..	..	..	..	..
4200 Recurrent taxes on net wealth	..	..	..	0	0	0	0	0	0	0
4210 Individual	..	..	..	..	..	..	..	..	..	..
4220 Corporate	..	..	..	..	..	..	..	..	..	..
4300 Estate, inheritance and gift taxes	..	..	..	0	0	0	0	0	0	0
4310 Estate and inheritance taxes	..	..	..	..	..	..	..	..	..	..
4320 Gift taxes	..	..	..	..	..	..	..	..	..	..
4400 Taxes on financial and capital transactions	..	..	..	126	140	99	99	126	168	124
4500 Non-recurrent taxes	..	..	..	0	0	0	0	0	0	0
4510 On net wealth	..	..	..	..	..	..	..	..	..	..
4520 Other non-recurrent taxes	..	..	..	..	..	..	..	..	..	..
4600 Other recurrent taxes on property	..	..	..	0	0	0	0	0	0	0
5000 Taxes on goods and services	..	..	..	**2 079**	**3 412**	**3 830**	**4 104**	**4 470**	**4 679**	**3 986**
5100 Taxes on production, sale, transfer, etc.	..	..	..	1 958	3 215	3 631	3 896	4 267	4 468	3 782
5110 General taxes	..	..	..	468	1 883	2 084	2 245	2 602	2 697	2 214
5111 Value added taxes	..	..	..	0	1 799	1 996	2 133	2 493	2 586	2 111
VAT - Domestic	..	..	..	..	990	1 070	1 294	1 550	1 587	1 203
VAT - Imported goods	..	..	..	..	833	950	910	968	1 003	910
VAT - Exemptions	..	..	..	..	-24	-24	-71	-25	-4	-2
5112 Sales tax	..	..	..	468	4	1	17	3	3	2
G&S Tax on locally manufactured goods (Alcohol)	..	..	..	27	0	0	0	0	0	0
G&S Tax on locally manufactured goods (tobacco)	..	..	..	12	0	0	0	0	0	0
G&S Tax on locally manufactured goods (other)	..	..	..	42	0	0	0	0	0	0
G&S Tax - Fuel/petroleum products	..	..	..	10	0	0	0	0	0	0
G&S Tax - Imported goods	..	..	..	377	0	0	0	0	0	0
G&S Tax - Arrears	..	..	..	0	4	1	17	3	3	2
5113 Other	..	..	..	0	79	87	95	106	109	102
Corporate Social Responsibility Tax (CSR)	..	..	..	..	79	87	95	106	109	102
5120 Taxes on specific goods and services	..	..	..	1 490	1 333	1 547	1 651	1 666	1 770	1 568

Table 5.27. **Seychelles** *(cont.)*

Details of tax revenue / Recettes fiscales détaillées

Million SCR

	1995	2000	2005	2010	2015	2016	2017	2018	2019	2020
5121 Excises	..	..	..	570	961	1 144	1 308	1 281	1 385	1 268
Alcohol (beverages spirits and vinegar)	..	..	..	180	278	356	363	382	419	372
Petroleum (mineral products)	..	..	..	242	493	531	655	609	628	552
Motor Vehicles (vehicles, aircraft, vessels)	..	..	..	47	44	99	135	123	148	98
Tobacco	..	..	..	102	146	157	155	166	164	202
Sugar tax on beverages	..	..	..	0	0	0	0	0	25	44
5122 Profits of fiscal monopolies	..	..	..	0	0	0	0	0	0	0
5123 Customs and import duties	..	..	..	355	326	359	283	315	313	238
Alcohol (beverages spirits and vinegar)	..	..	..	29	97	146	128	128	110	79
Petroleum (mineral products)	..	..	..	151	0	0	0	0	0	0
Textiles and textile articles	..	..	..	11	26	22	20	15	7	7
Motor Vehicles (vehicles, aircraft, vessels)	..	..	..	63	57	40	0	1	0	0
Tobacco (tobacco and manufactured tobacco)	..	..	..	2	2	2	2	2	2	3
Prepared Food (prepared foodstuffs)	..	..	..	19	19	18	11	11	13	14
Documentary Charges	..	..	..	2	2	3	2	2	3	3
Livestock Trust Fund	..	..	..	0	0	0	0	0	22	5
Other customs duties	..	..	..	79	128	133	130	160	160	129
Custom duties exemptions	..	..	..	-3	-5	-6	-10	-4	-4	-1
5124 Taxes on exports	..	..	..	0	0	0	0	0	0	0
5125 Taxes on investment goods	..	..	..	0	0	0	0	0	0	0
5126 Taxes on specific services	..	..	..	565	45	45	60	70	71	62
Gaming Tax (casino)	..	..	..	6	0	0	0	0	0	0
Tourism Marketing Tax (TMT)	..	..	..	0	45	45	60	70	71	62
G&S Tax - Professional services	..	..	..	27	0	0	0	0	0	0
G&S Tax - Tourism	..	..	..	411	0	0	0	0	0	0
G&S Tax - Telecom and utilities	..	..	..	97	0	0	0	0	0	0
G&S Tax - Insurance	..	..	..	22	0	0	0	0	0	0
5127 Other taxes on internat. trade and transactions	..	..	..	0	0	0	0	0	0	0
5128 Other taxes	..	..	..	0	0	0	0	0	0	0
5130 Unallocable between 5110 and 5120	..	..	..	0	0	0	0	0	0	0
5200 Taxes on use of goods and perform activities	..	..	..	121	197	198	208	202	211	204
5210 Recurrent taxes	..	..	..	121	197	198	208	202	211	204
5211 Paid by households: motor vehicles	..	..	..	42	95	102	118	117	129	125
Road tax and other licences	..	..	..	42	88	95	110	108	120	117
Vehicle testing	..	..	..	0	7	7	8	8	9	9
5212 Paid by others: motor vehicles	..	..	..	0	0	0	0	0	0	0
5213 Paid in respect of other goods	..	..	..	79	102	96	90	85	82	78
Trade/industry licences	..	..	..	8	8	9	11	10	10	10
Licences and other licence registration	..	..	..	5	3	3	6	4	6	3
Telecommunications and radio broadcasting licences	..	..	..	62	88	83	72	71	66	65
Casino and hotel licences	..	..	..	3	3	1	1	1	0	0
Liquor and toddy licences	..	..	..	0	0	0	0	0	0	0
5220 Non-recurrent taxes	..	..	..	0	0	0	0	0	0	0
5300 Unallocable between 5100 and 5200	..	..	..	0	0	0	0	0	0	0
6000 Other taxes	**..**	**..**	**..**	**0**	**0**	**0**	**0**	**0**	**0**	**0**
6100 Paid solely by business	..	..	..	..	..	..	..	..	..	..
6200 Other	..	..	..	..	..	..	..	..	..	..

Table 5.27. **Seychelles** *(cont.)*

Details of tax revenue / Recettes fiscales détaillées

.. Not available

Note: Year ending 31st December.

The data are on a cash basis.

Heading 1210: The Goods and Services Tax in Seychelles was also applied to rental payments, which according to *Revenue Statistics in Africa* definitions are properly classified as business taxes. These revenues are reported under the Goods and Services Tax heading in budget documents for the Seychelles.

Heading 2000:This edition includes revenues collected by the Seychelles Pensions Fund (SPF), which includes mandatory contributions classified by the OECD as social security contributions (reported under Headings 2110 and 2210). Seychelles also collected a social security tax based on income (reported under Heading 2420) which was phased out in 2010, but with a significant collection of arrears in 2018. SPF revenues are not reported as government revenues in Seychelles government documents.

Heading 5112: The Goods and Services Tax in Seychelles existed until it was replaced by a VAT in 2013. This tax imposed a 15% tax rate on sales of products and services in a long list of items enumerated in the Goods and Services Tax Act. Arrears on the Goods and Services Tax includes arrears on goods and services taxes professional services, tourism, telecom and utilities and insurance, which are reported under Heading 5126.

Heading 5123: "Other customs duties" includes the Levy on Pet Bottles, the Levy on Poultry, the Levy on Cans, and the Levy on Glass Bottles. Collections of revenues for the Livestock Trust Fund began in 2019.

Figures exclude tax revenues collected by sub-national governments as the data are not available.

Source: Seychelles Revenue Commission; Seychelles Ministry of Finance, Economic Planning and Trade; Financial Services Authority Seychelles Annual Reports; and Seychelles Pension Fund Annual Reports.

StatLink https://stat.link/6q1coa

Table 5.28. **South Africa / Afrique du Sud**

Details of tax revenue / Recettes fiscales détaillées

Million ZAR

	1995	2000	2005	2010	2015	2016	2017	2018	2019	2020
Total tax revenue	**121 920**	**211 561**	**418 823**	**706 530**	**1 170 870**	**1 242 774**	**1 326 511**	**1 423 346**	**1 467 193**	**1 393 118**
1000 Taxes on income, profits and capital gains	**65 565**	**119 979**	**220 197**	**368 118**	**608 229**	**644 259**	**700 574**	**736 734**	**751 182**	**695 192**
1100 Of individuals	49 520	87 105	122 279	219 886	393 232	418 548	453 768	489 733	523 624	500 218
1110 On income and profits	49 520	87 105	122 279	219 886	393 232	418 548	453 768	489 733	523 624	500 218
Employees tax	..	..	..	213 113	382 883	407 105	440 141	475 337	513 613	497 082
Employment Incentive Tax (ETI) refunds	..	..	..	0	-3 349	-4 905	-4 672	-4 275	-4 590	-7 081
PIT Provisional tax	..	..	..	15 719	24 200	27 313	29 427	33 426	32 138	29 149
PIT Assessment payments	..	..	..	7 425	9 970	11 594	15 011	16 230	13 158	12 831
PIT Refunds	..	..	..	-16 372	-20 474	-22 559	-26 139	-30 986	-30 695	-31 762
1120 On capital gains	..	..	..	..	..	..	..	..	..	..
1200 Corporate	14 427	23 987	82 628	132 275	191 348	200 765	214 316	215 939	215 346	194 433
1210 On profits	14 427	23 987	82 628	132 275	191 348	200 765	214 316	215 939	215 346	194 433
CIT Provisional tax	..	..	..	136 615	190 437	202 636	214 097	222 178	221 026	201 664
CIT Assessment payments	..	..	..	9 051	11 119	10 291	12 888	13 714	11 953	13 751
Royalties	..	..	..	161	369	544	434	676	633	549
CIT Refunds	..	..	..	-13 552	-10 577	-12 706	-13 103	-20 630	-18 266	-21 531
1220 On capital gains	..	..	..	..	..	..	..	..	..	..
1300 Unallocable between 1100 and 1200	1 618	8 887	15 290	15 957	23 649	24 946	32 489	31 062	12 211	541
2000 Social security contributions	**0**	**0**	**6 477**	**11 117**	**17 139**	**17 787**	**18 652**	**19 026**	**19 796**	**18 918**
2100 Employees	..	..	3 254	5 740	8 725	9 051	9 483	9 566	9 954	9 508
2110 On a payroll basis	..	..	31	363	311	314	314	106	112	99
2120 On an income tax basis	..	..	3 223	5 377	8 414	8 737	9 169	9 460	9 842	9 410
2200 Employers	..	..	3 223	5 377	8 414	8 737	9 169	9 460	9 842	9 410
2210 On a payroll basis	..	..	0	0	0	0	0	0	0	0
2220 On an income tax basis	..	..	3 223	5 377	8 414	8 737	9 169	9 460	9 842	9 410
2300 Self-employed or non-employed	..	..	0	0	0	0	0	0	0	0
2310 On a payroll basis	..	..	..	..	..	..	..	..	..	..
2320 On an income tax basis	..	..	..	..	..	..	..	..	..	..
2400 Unallocable between 2100, 2200 and 2300	..	..	0	0	0	0	0	0	0	0
2410 On a payroll basis	..	..	..	..	..	..	..	..	..	..
2420 On an income tax basis	..	..	..	..	..	..	..	..	..	..
3000 Taxes on payroll and workforce	**0**	**870**	**4 839**	**8 240**	**15 111**	**15 092**	**15 891**	**17 265**	**18 062**	**18 062**
4000 Taxes on property	**2 131**	**3 829**	**23 530**	**40 108**	**59 110**	**67 554**	**80 044**	**83 554**	**93 022**	**98 241**
4100 Recurrent taxes on immovable property	0	0	12 906	31 041	44 618	51 668	64 262	67 373	76 806	82 025
4110 Households	..	..	12 258	30 533	44 169	51 133	63 806	66 824	76 279	81 442
4120 Others	..	..	648	508	449	535	456	549	528	582
4200 Recurrent taxes on net wealth	0	0	0	0	0	0	0	0	0	0
4210 Individual	..	..	..	..	..	..	..	..	..	..
4220 Corporate	..	..	..	..	..	..	..	..	..	..
4300 Estate, inheritance and gift taxes	222	436	626	855	2 065	1 832	2 667	2 740	2 780	2 780
4310 Estate and inheritance taxes	164	417	598	794	1 918	1 612	2 303	1 894	2 174	2 174
4320 Gift taxes	57	19	28	61	147	220	364	846	605	605
4400 Taxes on financial and capital transactions	397	1 094	1 718	2 912	5 069	6 081	5 248	5 967	6 235	6 235
4500 Non-recurrent taxes	1 512	2 299	8 280	5 300	7 358	7 974	7 868	7 474	7 201	7 201
4510 On net wealth	0	0	0	0	0	0	0	0	0	0
4520 Other non-recurrent taxes	1 512	2 299	8 280	5 300	7 358	7 974	7 868	7 474	7 201	7 201
4600 Other recurrent taxes on property	0	0	0	0	0	0	0	0	0	0
5000 Taxes on goods and services	**52 938**	**84 462**	**162 918**	**278 924**	**471 281**	**498 073**	**511 366**	**566 777**	**585 132**	**562 703**
5100 Taxes on production, sale, transfer, etc.	52 938	84 462	159 589	273 602	463 423	489 342	500 917	555 577	573 556	550 389
5110 General taxes	31 729	52 054	109 274	170 548	277 551	294 694	293 900	324 702	329 415	333 372
5111 Value added taxes	31 729	52 054	109 274	170 552	277 530	294 674	293 864	324 682	329 397	333 375
Domestic VAT	18 954	52 547	126 492	202 483	303 210	314 674	333 647	368 766	392 919	390 367
VAT on Imports	12 775	25 148	42 615	78 697	148 467	151 046	150 841	169 018	181 777	161 679
VAT Refunds	0	-25 641	-59 833	-110 627	-174 147	-171 046	-190 624	-213 103	-245 298	-218 672
5112 Sales tax	0	0	0	-5	21	20	36	20	18	-3
5113 Other	0	0	0	0	0	0	0	0	0	0
5120 Taxes on specific goods and services	21 209	32 408	50 315	103 054	185 872	194 647	207 017	230 875	244 142	217 017

Table 5.28. **South Africa / Afrique du Sud** *(cont.)*

Details of tax revenue / Recettes fiscales détaillées

Million ZAR

	1995	2000	2005	2010	2015	2016	2017	2018	2019	2020
5121 Excises	15 225	24 341	35 490	76 239	137 859	143 337	155 062	172 198	183 860	166 345
Specific excise tax - Domestic	..	..	..	22 448	34 918	35 714	36 731	41 568	47 811	36 500
Ad valorem excise - Domestic	..	..	..	1 569	3 295	3 238	3 652	4 163	4 274	3 035
Fuel levy	..	..	..	32 758	56 694	61 064	68 608	74 376	78 361	76 204
Plastic bags	..	..	..	177	213	221	238	287	328	493
Electricity levy	..	..	..	5 065	8 481	8 507	8 495	8 448	8 315	7 833
Incandescent light bulb levy	..	..	..	180	52	66	62	46	34	26
CO_2 tax - motor vehicle emissions	..	..	..	205	1 429	1 177	1 347	1 376	1 355	1 248
RAF	..	..	..	13 837	32 778	33 350	35 336	41 189	42 658	39 756
Tyre Levy	..	..	..	0	0	0	593	744	724	1 248
5122 Profits of fiscal monopolies	0	0	0	0	0	0	0	0	0	0
5123 Customs and import duties	5 129	7 714	13 294	25 196	43 965	47 438	47 367	53 936	55 752	47 638
Import duties	..	..	..	..	32 130	33 855	32 742	37 649	37 595	32 890
Ad valorem import duty	..	..	..	..	8 495	8 701	5 668	10 091	10 580	8 252
Excise on imports	..	..	..	..	3 340	4 882	8 954	6 191	7 575	5 927
International Oil Pollution Levy	..	..	..	..	0	0	3	5	3	568
5124 Taxes on exports	0	0	0	61	121	116	103	62	94	70
5125 Taxes on investment goods	0	0	0	0	0	0	0	0	0	0
5126 Taxes on specific services	0	0	1 320	2 252	3 224	3 401	3 775	3 943	3 632	2 790
5127 Other taxes on internat. trade and transactions	855	353	211	-695	703	355	709	736	804	173
5128 Other taxes	0	0	0	0	0	0	0	0	0	0
5130 Unallocable between 5110 and 5120	0	0	0	0	0	0	0	0	0	0
5200 Taxes on use of goods and perform activities	0	0	3 328	5 322	7 858	8 732	10 450	11 199	11 576	12 314
5210 Recurrent taxes	..	..	3 328	5 322	7 858	8 732	10 450	11 199	11 576	12 314
5211 Paid by households: motor vehicles	..	..	2 644	4 046	6 234	6 565	8 120	8 706	9 056	9 583
5212 Paid by others: motor vehicles	..	..	661	1 012	1 558	1 641	2 030	2 176	2 264	2 396
5213 Paid in respect of other goods	..	..	23	264	66	525	299	317	256	335
5220 Non-recurrent taxes	..	..	0	0	0	0	0	0	0	0
5300 Unallocable between 5100 and 5200	0	0	0	0	0	0	0	0	0	0
6000 Other taxes	**1 286**	**2 420**	**863**	**23**	**-1**	**9**	**-17**	**-11**	**-1**	**1**
6100 Paid solely by business	0	0	0	0	0	0	0	0	0	0
6200 Other	1 286	2 420	863	23	-1	9	-17	-11	-1	1
Stamp duties and fees	..	..	..	9	0	0	0	0	0	1
Unallocated tax revenues	..	..	..	14	-1	9	-17	-11	-1	0
Memo items: *SACU expenditure*	..	..	14 145	17 906	51 022	39 448	46 542	56 921	60 265	25 295

Table 5.28. **South Africa / Afrique du Sud** *(cont.)*

Details of tax revenue / Recettes fiscales détaillées

.. Not available

Note: Year ending 31st December. Some fiscal year data have been adjusted to align to calendar years. Social security contributions and taxes at provincial and local levels are reported on a fiscal year basis beginning 1st April. For example, the data for 2020 represent April 2020 to March 2021. Data prior to 1995/96 were restated retrospectively to aggregate the revenues from TBVC States and Self-Governing Territories.

With the adoption of the interim Constitution in 1994, these were abolished.

-TBVC States: Transkei, Bophuthatswana, Venda and Ciskei.

-Self-Governing Territories: Gazankulu, Kangwane, Kwandebele, Kwazulu, Lebowa and Qwaqwa.

Tax revenues on national and provincial government level in South Africa are on a cash basis, while local authorities and public entities are on an accrual basis. Data on local government revenues were not available for the years 2019/20 and 2020/21, so for those years, projections based on the previous three years of data were used.

Tax revenues at the local and provincial levels are only available from 2003 (representing fiscal year 2003/04).

Headings 1110 and 1120: The figures include Capital Gains Tax (CGT). CGT cannot been listed separately under 1120 and 1220 because the data that South African Revenue Service (SARS) collated for CGT are for liability raised and not actual CGT collections received. The figures exclude interest and fines from 1994 onwards. Figures on ETI refunds, which started being collected in 2014, are now reported under 1110. These were included as part of Employees tax in previous editions.

Heading 2000: the social security contributions in South Africa consist of contributions to the Unemployment Insurance Fund (UIF). Standard practice in South Africa is to classify UIF under non-tax revenue. The methodology applied in the compilation of the data was to allocate 50% of the total social security contributions (UIF) to each of employees and employers.

Heading 4120: the figures refer to penalties and collection charges on property rates.

Headings 4110 and 4120: These are local government revenues for which 2019 and 2020 figures are missing and have been replaced with projections based on the previous three years of data. Recurrent taxes on immovable property were divided into collections on households (4110) and penalties and collection charges (4120).

Heading 5111: includes interests and fines.

Heading 5121: following the OECD classification, the Road Accident Fund (RAF) is classified as an excise. The national classification of South Africa classifies this revenue as a social security contribution.

Headings 5121 and 5123: The data for customs duties and excise include revenue on import duties plus specific and ad valorem excise duties that will be paid to Botswana, Eswatini, Lesotho and Namibia (BELN) through the revenue sharing agreement.

Heading 5123: SARS only started separately reporting ordinary custom duties on imported goods, specific excise duties on imported goods and ad valorem duties on imported goods from April 2012. From April 2014 onwards, the Customs Duty amounts for the specific tariff headings under Chapter 27 (Mineral Fuels) were treated as fuel levies (5121 Excises). Some estimation was used for the year 2012 due to missing information.

Heading 5124: Revenues from the International Pollution Levy were reported for the first time in this edition of *Revenue Statistics in Africa*.

Headings 5127 and 6200: include negative figures due to refund accounting adjustments.

Heading 5211: an 80:20 ratio was used to split provincial recurrent motor vehicle taxes based on research about South Africa's commercial and private household motor vehicle fleet.

Heading 6200: includes stamp duties and fees plus unallocated tax revenue.

Taxes that were discontinued and introduced (causing breaks in the data) include the following:

a. Ordinary levy discontinued in March 2003 (heading 5127).

b. Demutualisation charge has been included in heading 4400. There were two collections in March 1999 and August 1999.

c. Secondary Tax on Companies (STC) in heading 1300 effective from July 1993 and changed to Dividends Tax (DT) in April 2012.

d. Small business tax amnesty (heading 1300) effective from March 2007.

e. VAT (heading 5111) effective from September 1991 at a rate of 10% and increased to 14% in 1993. Prior to that, sales tax data was restated to VAT.

f. Levy on financial services (heading 4400) effective from January 1992.

g. Skills development levy (heading 3000) effective from May 2000.

h. Excises (5121):

- Plastic bags effective from June 2005.
- Electricity levy effective from August 2009.
- Incandescent light bulbs effective from March 2010.
- CO_2 tax effective from September 2010.

i. Air departure tax (heading 5126) effective from December 2000.

j. Universal services fund (heading 5213 paid in respect of other goods) effective from March 2006.

Source: Data on national government taxation from the South African Revenue Service (SARS); data on social security contributions, and taxes levied at the provincial and local level from the National Treasury of South Africa.

StatLink https://stat.link/0mxcu4

Table 5.29. **Togo**

Details of tax revenue / Recettes fiscales détaillées

Million XOF

	1995	2000	2005	2010	2015	2016	2017	2018	2019	2020
Recettes fiscales totales	**..**	**99 994**	**159 843**	**250 441**	**533 556**	**586 813**	**585 660**	**576 528**	**634 515**	**669 838**
1000 Impôts sur revenu, bénéfices et gains en capital	**..**	**20 928**	**37 657**	**41 200**	**88 658**	**112 797**	**100 214**	**117 078**	**136 035**	**132 485**
1100 Des personnes physiques	..	9 440	17 272	18 000	30 791	39 703	40 826	44 595	48 979	50 924
1110 Sur le revenu et les bénéfices	..	9 440	17 272	18 000	30 791	39 703	40 826	44 595	48 979	50 920
Impôt sur le revenu (IR) des transporteurs routiers	..	452	514	393	379	500	366	368	261	0
Retenue sur les revenus des capitaux mobiliers	..	1 185	2 217	6 106	8 365	12 222	9 882	11 183	11 687	9 023
IR des personnes physiques	..	7 804	14 540	11 500	22 046	26 976	30 571	33 043	36 890	41 776
IR des personnes physiques (transferts aux collectivités locales)	..	..	..	1	0	5	8	0	0	0
Taxe foncière sur les propriétés non bâties (TFPNB) - Gouv. central	..	0	0	0	0	0	0	0	56	81
Taxe foncière sur les propriétés non bâties (TFPNB) - collectivités	..	..	..	0	0	0	0	0	84	39
1120 Sur les gains en capital	..	0	0	0	0	0	0	0	0	4
Taxe sur les plus-values de cession (TPV)	..	..	..	..	..	..	..	..	0	4
1200 Des sociétés	..	11 488	20 385	23 200	57 867	73 094	59 388	72 483	87 056	81 560
1210 Sur les bénéfices	..	11 488	20 385	23 200	57 867	73 094	59 388	72 483	87 056	81 560
Impôt sur les sociétés	..	8 997	16 525	18 280	51 177	64 564	52 080	64 851	76 670	74 026
Prélèvement bénéf. industriels et commerciaux (BIC)	..	2 490	3 860	4 920	6 691	8 530	7 309	7 632	10 387	7 534
1220 Sur les gains en capital	..	0	0	0	0	0	0	0	0	0
1300 Non ventilables entre 1100 et 1200	..	0	0	0	0	0	0	0	0	0
2000 Cotisations de sécurité sociale	**..**	**..**	**..**	**..**	**..**	**..**	**..**	**..**	**..**	**..**
2100 A la charge des salariés	..	..	..	..	..	..	..	..	..	..
2110 Sur la base du salaire	..	..	..	..	..	..	..	..	..	..
2120 Sur la base de l'impôt sur le revenu	..	..	..	..	..	..	..	..	..	..
2200 A la charge des employeurs	..	..	..	..	..	..	..	..	..	..
2210 Sur la base du salaire	..	..	..	..	..	..	..	..	..	..
2220 Sur la base de l'impôt sur le revenu	..	..	..	..	..	..	..	..	..	..
2300 A charge des travailleurs indép. ou sans emploi	..	..	..	..	..	..	..	..	..	..
2310 Sur la base du salaire	..	..	..	..	..	..	..	..	..	..
2320 Sur la base de l'impôt sur le revenu	..	..	..	..	..	..	..	..	..	..
2400 Non ventilables entre 2100, 2200 et 2300	..	..	..	..	..	..	..	..	..	..
2410 Sur la base du salaire	..	..	..	..	..	..	..	..	..	..
2420 Sur la base de l'impôt sur le revenu	..	..	..	..	..	..	..	..	..	..
3000 Sur salaires ou main-d'œuvre	**..**	**1 973**	**2 463**	**5 491**	**4 551**	**5 599**	**5 018**	**4 757**	**2 262**	**770**
Taxe complémentaire à l'impôt sur le revenu	..	79	169	1 220	956	1 246	1 256	1 042	953	500
Taxes/salaires	..	1 894	2 294	4 137	3 284	3 963	3 274	3 253	1 119	142
Taxe complémentaire à l'Impôt sur le revenu (transferts aux collectivités locales)	..	..	..	134	311	389	488	463	190	128
4000 Impôts sur le patrimoine	**..**	**374**	**599**	**1 898**	**4 360**	**4 766**	**4 256**	**4 819**	**5 048**	**5 462**
4100 Impôts périodiques sur la propriété immobilière	..	374	599	1 898	4 360	4 766	4 256	4 819	5 048	5 190
Taxe foncière sur les propriétés bâties	..	278	435	655	1 465	1 507	1 315	1 410	1 531	1 698
Droits d'immatriculation des propriétés foncières	..	96	164	335	613	783	228	334	345	1 238
Taxe d'enlèvement des ordures (transferts aux collectivités locales)	..	..	..	129	315	360	331	407	360	84
Taxe foncière sur les propriétés bâties (transferts aux collectivités locales)	..	..	..	553	1 404	1 494	1 783	2 032	2 078	1 534
4110 Ménages	..	..	..	226	563	623	599	636	735	638
Taxe d'habitation (transferts aux collectivités locales)	..	..	..	226	563	623	599	636	735	638
4120 Autres agents	..	0	0	0	0	0	0	0	0	0
4200 Impôts périodiques sur l'actif net	..	0	0	0	0	0	0	0	0	0
4210 Personnes physiques	..	..	..	..	..	..	..	..	..	..
4220 Sociétés	..	..	..	..	..	..	..	..	..	..
4300 Impôts sur mut. par décès, succ. et donations	..	0	0	0	0	0	0	0	0	0
4310 Impôts sur mut. par décès et successions	..	..	..	..	..	..	..	..	..	..
4320 Impôts sur les donations	..	..	..	..	..	..	..	..	..	..
4400 Impôts sur transact. mobilières et immob.	..	0	0	0	0	0	0	0	0	272
Droits de conservation de la propriété foncière (DCPF)	..	..	..	..	..	..	..	..	..	272
4500 Impôts non-périodiques	..	0	0	0	0	0	0	0	0	0
4510 Sur l'actif net	..	..	..	..	..	..	..	..	..	..
4520 Autres non-périodiques	..	..	..	..	..	..	..	..	..	..
4600 Autres impôts périodiques sur patrimoine	..	0	0	0	0	0	0	0	0	0
5000 Impôts sur les biens et services	**..**	**74 771**	**116 641**	**196 239**	**427 424**	**454 604**	**459 815**	**439 693**	**481 493**	**515 893**
5100 Impôts sur production, vente, transfert, etc.	..	74 662	116 483	195 813	425 367	452 380	457 429	437 006	474 721	505 853

Table 5.29. **Togo** *(cont.)*

Details of tax revenue / Recettes fiscales détaillées

Million XOF

	1995	2000	2005	2010	2015	2016	2017	2018	2019	2020
5110 Impôts généraux	..	36 941	64 120	115 056	250 410	271 347	269 266	256 847	282 656	291 843
5111 Taxes sur la valeur ajoutée	..	36 073	62 989	110 316	236 011	255 323	253 663	237 537	268 602	280 325
Recettes TVA (douanes)	..	25 101	44 182	69 840	167 228	172 435	138 802	142 211	160 514	176 623
Recettes TVA (intérieure)	..	10 972	18 807	40 476	68 783	82 888	114 861	95 325	108 088	103 702
5112 Impôts sur les ventes	..	0	0	0	0	0	0	0	0	0
5113 Autres impôts	..	868	1 131	4 740	14 399	16 024	15 602	19 311	14 054	11 518
Taxe professionnelle unique	..	146	155	334	507	515	485	537	593	340
Taxe professionnelle	..	722	976	1 587	6 693	7 943	5 831	7 270	5 060	4 184
Taxe professionnelle unique (transferts aux collectivités locales)	..	..	..	206	507	572	539	597	810	719
Taxe professionnelle (transferts aux collectivités locales)	..	..	..	2 613	6 693	6 995	8 747	10 906	7 591	6 276
5120 Impôts sur biens et services déterminés	..	37 696	52 336	80 724	174 957	181 033	188 164	180 159	192 064	214 010
5121 Accises	..	12 785	14 803	16 360	35 150	43 686	43 471	44 429	38 206	52 400
Droits d'accises/produits pétroliers	..	11 773	11 852	11 738	17 972	20 945	20 337	22 978	20 614	28 910
Autres droits d'accises	..	1 012	2 950	4 622	8 246	10 906	10 955	11 835	16 237	18 323
Prélèvement pour apurement de la dette du secteur pétrolier (PADSP)	..	0	0	0	8 932	11 836	12 179	9 616	1 356	5 167
5122 Bénéfices des monopoles fiscaux	..	0	0	0	0	0	0	0	0	0
5123 Droits de douane et droits à l'importation	..	22 559	35 143	61 676	122 750	119 825	127 065	117 608	135 991	142 419
Droits de douane	..	18 519	30 023	52 941	101 730	98 020	86 383	90 186	103 536	108 532
Redevance statistique	..	2 717	3 720	6 763	13 578	14 021	32 653	18 447	23 012	24 459
Timbre douanier	..	94	138	297	424	298	283	285	290	313
Cartes et vignettes	..	186	209	237	369	600	609	872	919	448
Taxe de protection et d'entretien des infrastructures	..	1 039	1 050	1 434	2 958	3 252	3 575	3 917	3 942	4 230
Produits des crédits en douane	..	2	2	2	5	9	8	8	9	9
Prélèvement national de solidarité	..	0	0	0	3 686	3 625	3 555	3 893	4 284	4 427
Remises	..	1	0	0	0	0	0	0	0	0
Entrepôts fictifs	..	1	2	2	0	0	0	0	0	0
5124 Taxes à l'exportation	..	302	314	1 430	2 728	2 476	2 737	2 977	3 104	2 727
Taxe spéciale de réexportation	..	302	314	1 430	2 260	2 015	2 156	2 685	3 104	2 727
Redevance minière (66,67%)	..	0	0	0	468	461	580	292	0	0
5125 Impôts sur biens d'équipement	..	0	0	0	0	0	0	0	0	0
5126 Impôts sur services déterminés	..	2 049	2 076	1 258	14 329	15 046	14 891	15 146	14 763	16 464
Taxe sur les produits des jeux de hasard	..	151	206	347	913	1 047	1 185	1 184	1 343	1 265
Taxe/convention d'assurance	..	227	378	815	2 035	2 365	2 205	2 158	2 248	2 571
Taxe sur les activités financières	..	1 671	1 491	0	11 140	11 372	11 204	11 508	10 466	12 180
Taxe sur les produits des jeux de hasard (transferts aux collectivités locales)	..	..	..	94	228	262	296	296	336	316
Taxe sur les spectacles (transferts aux collectivités locales)	..	..	..	2	13	0	0	0	28	17
Taxe à l'émission des billets d'avion (TEBA)	..	0	0	0	0	0	0	0	342	115
5127 Autres impôts sur commerce et transact. internat.	..	0	0	0	0	0	0	0	0	0
5128 Autres impôts	..	0	0	0	0	0	0	0	0	0
5130 Non ventilables entre 5110 et 5120	..	25	28	33	0	0	0	0	0	0
Recettes douanières sur produits cautionnés	..	25	28	33	0	0	0	0	0	0
5200 Impôts sur utilisation des biens et exerc. activites	..	108	158	426	2 057	2 224	2 386	2 687	6 772	10 040
5210 Impôts périodiques	..	108	158	426	2 057	2 224	2 386	2 687	6 772	10 040
5211 A la charge des ménages: véhicules à moteur	..	0	0	0	0	0	0	0	223	703
Taxe sur les véhicules à moteur (TVM)	..	..	..	..	..	..	..	..	223	703
5212 A la charge autres agents: véhicules à moteur	..	2	5	0	287	308	311	312	260	74
Taxe sur les véhicules des sociétés	..	2	5	0	287	308	311	312	260	74
5213 Autres impôts périodiques	..	106	154	426	1 770	1 915	2 076	2 375	6 290	9 263
Taxe spéc. sur la fabric. et le commerce des boissons	..	106	154	162	1 145	1 158	1 300	1 521	482	8
Taxe spéc. sur la fabric. et le commerce des boissons (transferts aux collectivités locales)	..	..	..	264	625	757	776	855	697	13
Patente sur activités économiques non-salariaux des pers. phys. - Gouv. Central	..	0	0	0	0	0	0	0	1 916	7 204
Patente sur activités économiques non-salariaux des pers. phys. - Collectivités	..	0	0	0	0	0	0	0	3 194	2 038
5220 Impôts non-périodiques	..	0	0	0	0	0	0	0	0	0
5300 Non ventilables entre 5100 et 5200	..	0	0	0	0	0	0	0	0	0

Table 5.29. **Togo** (*cont.*)

Details of tax revenue / Recettes fiscales détaillées

Million XOF

	1995	2000	2005	2010	2015	2016	2017	2018	2019	2020
6000 Autres impôts	**..**	**1 949**	**2 483**	**5 612**	**8 563**	**9 048**	**16 356**	**10 180**	**9 676**	**15 228**
Droits de timbres	..	1 471	1 668	3 135	3 612	3 676	3 338	3 258	3 072	2 913
Droits d'enregistrement	..	478	816	2 436	4 949	5 158	12 498	6 553	6 392	11 950
Taxe d'enregistrement (transferts aux collectivités locales)	..	..	..	41	2	214	521	369	213	364
6100 A la charge exclusive des entreprises	..	..	..	..	..	..	..	..	..	..
6200 A la charge d'autres agents	..	..	..	..	..	..	..	..	..	..
Pour mémoire :										
Soutien à la politique pétrolière	..	0	0	3 700	5 748	4 077	6 075	13 332	7 048	622
Droits d'accise et taxes sur prod. pétr. allant à la Société autonome de financement de l'entretien routier (SAFER)	..	5 519	7 624	7 339	9 495	9 890	11 732	13 820	10 999	15 234

.. Non disponible

Note : Année civile se terminant le 31 décembre.

Les données sont sur la base des encaissements.

Les chiffres sous les rubriques 1110, 3000, 4100, 5113, 5126, 5213 et 6000 incluent les recettes recouvrées par l'administration fiscale togolaise pour le compte des collectivités locales. Ce traitement s'applique sur la période 2008-20 et les lignes concernées sont mises en exergue avec la mention « transferts aux collectivités locales ». Ces recettes sont classifiées comme des recettes du gouvernement central conformément au guide d'interprétation de l'OCDE. Le Togo ne les comptabilise pas dans les recettes du budget de l'État.

Rubrique 1110 : La collecte des recettes des taxes foncières sur les propriétés non bâties (TFPNB) a démarré en 2019.

Rubrique 1110 : L'impôt sur le revenu (IR) des transporteurs routiers a été supprimé en 2019.

Rubrique 1120 : La collecte des recettes de la taxe sur les plus-values de cession (TPV) a démarré en 2019. La collecte des recettes des patentes sur les activités économiques non-salariaux des personnes physiques a démarré en 2019.

Rubrique 2000 : Les données de cotisations de sécurité sociale ne sont pas disponibles.

Rubrique 4400 : La collecte des droits de conservation de la propriété foncière (DCPF) a demarré en 2020.

Rubrique 5121 : Le prélèvement pour l'apurement de la dette du secteur pétrolier (PADSP) est considéré comme une recette fiscale dans cette publication comme le préconise la classification OCDE (voir le *Guide d'interprétation* en Annexe A). La classification nationale du Togo considère ces recettes comme des recettes non fiscales.

Rubrique 5126 : La collecte des recettes de la taxe à l'émission des billets d'avion (TEBA) a demarré en 2019.

Rubrique 5211 : La collecte des recettes de la taxe sur les véhicules à moteur (TVM) a démarré en 2019.

Les données sur les remboursements de TVA ne sont pas disponibles car au Togo, les crédits de TVA ne font pas l'objet de remboursement avec les moyens classiques de paiement (virement, chèque, espèces, etc.). Lorsqu'un contribuable dispose d'un crédit de TVA, il adresse une demande de remboursement à l'administration fiscale qui lui délivre un certificat de détaxe. Ce certificat lui permet de payer non seulement ses déclarations ultérieures de TVA mais aussi les autres impôts.

La classification nationale du Togo considère les amendes et pénalités relatives aux impôts, les confiscations et ventes en douane et les remboursements du prélèvement communautaire de solidarité comme des recettes fiscales. Ces recettes sont classifiées comme des recettes non fiscales dans cette publication comme le préconise la classification OCDE (voir le *Guide d'interprétation* en Annexe A).

Le Soutien à la politique pétrolière (SPP) est un fond financé par un prélèvement effectué sur la TVA recouvrée par la douane, sauf pour les années 2010-12 quand le SPP était financé par une subvention de l'état.

Source : Office Togolais des Recettes.

StatLink https://stat.link/rsc43v

Table 5.30. **Tunisia / Tunisie**

Details of tax revenue / Recettes fiscales détaillées

Million TND

	1995	2000	2005	2010	2015	2016	2017	2018	2019	2020
Recettes fiscales totales	..	**7 196**	**10 146**	**17 143**	**25 613**	**26 596**	**29 810**	**33 824**	**39 450**	**38 829**
1000 Impôts sur revenu, bénéfices et gains en capital	..	**1 624**	**2 927**	**5 091**	**7 678**	**7 384**	**8 506**	**8 979**	**12 486**	**12 005**
1100 Des personnes physiques	..	1 049	1 565	2 658	5 003	5 931	6 191	6 359	8 713	8 945
1110 Sur le revenu et les bénéfices	..	1 037	1 560	2 644	4 965	5 887	6 139	6 311	8 658	8 898
Traitements et salaires	..	742	1 160	2 006	3 549	4 107	4 029	4 054	5 800	6 125
Honoraires, commissions, courtage et loyers (personnes physiques)	..	20	93	184	364	483	541	508	665	623
Intérêts dépôts des comptes spéciaux d'épargne	..	65	43	68	159	176	199	270	315	339
Revenus des capitaux mobiliers (personnes physiques)	..	32	63	75	212	269	272	310	498	573
Avances sur les marchés (personnes physiques)	..	27	24	50	313	508	624	720	821	716
Bénéfices industriels et commerciaux	..	43	56	94	119	142	146	154	201	171
Bénéfices non commerciaux	..	17	24	49	76	79	81	98	123	117
Impôt forfaitaire	..	14	16	25	36	37	39	48	64	47
Revenus agricoles	..	5	4	8	19	22	26	26	33	39
Revenus fonciers et autres	..	5	4	8	14	22	27	30	40	43
Autres impôts sur le revenu et bénéfices	..	66	73	78	105	42	156	93	99	105
1120 Sur les gains en capital	..	12	5	13	39	45	52	48	54	48
1200 Des sociétés	..	575	1 360	2 432	2 673	1 450	2 315	2 620	3 774	3 060
1210 Sur les bénéfices	..	575	1 359	2 424	2 658	1 442	2 295	2 613	3 763	3 037
Sociétés pétrolières	..	96	459	813	950	346	527	709	959	447
Sociétés non-pétrolières	..	359	644	864	1 088	806	1 299	1 149	1 984	1 877
Avances sur les marchés (sociétés)	..	33	97	356	222	46	47	57	48	55
Avance au titre des importations	..	7	28	111	198	198	268	430	468	285
Revenus des capitaux mobiliers (sociétés)	..	58	68	113	72	27	106	226	269	298
Honoraires, commissions, courtage et loyers (sociétés)	..	16	52	125	86	2	1	5	4	3
Redevances servies aux non résidents	..	3	8	39	18	9	7	4	18	27
Autres impôts sur les bénéfices	..	3	3	3	25	9	40	33	12	46
1220 Sur les gains en capital	..	0	1	7	14	7	19	7	11	23
1300 Non ventilables entre 1100 et 1200	..	0	2	2	2	4	0	0	0	0
2000 Cotisations de sécurité sociale	..	**1 551**	**2 307**	**4 629**	**7 549**	**8 415**	**9 259**	**9 826**	**11 172**	**11 982**
2100 A la charge des salariés	..	..	..	..	..	..	..	..	..	..
2110 Sur la base du salaire	..	..	..	..	..	..	..	..	..	..
2120 Sur la base de l'impôt sur le revenu	..	..	..	..	..	..	..	..	..	..
2200 A la charge des employeurs	..	..	..	..	..	..	..	..	..	..
2210 Sur la base du salaire	..	..	..	..	..	..	..	..	..	..
2220 Sur la base de l'impôt sur le revenu	..	..	..	..	..	..	..	..	..	..
2300 A charge des travailleurs indép. ou sans emploi	..	..	..	..	..	..	..	..	..	..
2310 Sur la base du salaire	..	..	..	..	..	..	..	..	..	..
2320 Sur la base de l'impôt sur le revenu	..	..	..	..	..	..	..	..	..	..
2400 Non ventilables entre 2100, 2200 et 2300	..	1 551	2 307	4 629	7 549	8 415	9 259	9 826	11 172	11 982
2410 Sur la base du salaire	..	..	..	..	..	..	..	..	..	..
2420 Sur la base de l'impôt sur le revenu	..	..	..	..	..	..	..	..	..	..
3000 Sur salaires ou main-d'œuvre	..	**107**	**114**	**199**	**315**	**345**	**375**	**405**	**457**	**445**
Fond de promotion des logements	..	71	74	124	191	215	231	246	278	287
Taxe de formation professionnelle	..	35	40	75	124	130	143	159	179	159
4000 Impôts sur le patrimoine	..	**81**	**104**	**177**	**282**	**299**	**303**	**308**	**371**	**308**
4100 Impôts périodiques sur la propriété immobilière	..	7	7	10	11	11	12	13	18	14
4110 Ménages	..	7	7	10	11	11	12	13	18	14
4120 Autres agents	..	0	0	0	0	0	0	0	0	0
4200 Impôts périodiques sur l'actif net	..	0	0	0	0	0	0	0	0	0
4210 Personnes physiques	..	..	..	..	..	..	..	..	..	..
4220 Sociétés	..	..	..	..	..	..	..	..	..	..
4300 Impôts sur mut. par décès, succ. et donations	..	0	0	0	0	0	0	0	0	0
4310 Impôts sur mut. par décès et successions	..	..	..	..	..	..	..	..	..	..
4320 Impôts sur les donations	..	..	..	..	..	..	..	..	..	..
4400 Impôts sur transact. mobilières et immob.	..	74	97	168	271	288	291	295	353	294
4500 Impôts non-périodiques	..	0	0	0	0	0	0	0	0	0
4510 Sur l'actif net	..	..	..	..	..	..	..	..	..	..
4520 Autres non-périodiques	..	..	..	..	..	..	..	..	..	..
4600 Autres impôts périodiques sur patrimoine	..	0	0	0	0	0	0	0	0	0
5000 Impôts sur les biens et services	..	**3 729**	**4 567**	**6 768**	**9 168**	**9 523**	**10 666**	**13 444**	**14 026**	**13 377**
5100 Impôts sur production, vente, transfert, etc.	..	3 665	4 458	6 612	8 977	9 300	10 442	13 222	13 803	13 179
5110 Impôts généraux	..	1 814	2 347	3 819	5 211	5 288	5 918	7 696	8 044	7 424

Table 5.30. **Tunisia / Tunisie** *(cont.)*

Details of tax revenue / Recettes fiscales détaillées

Million TND

	1995	2000	2005	2010	2015	2016	2017	2018	2019	2020
5111 Taxes sur la valeur ajoutée	..	1 792	2 301	3 750	5 068	5 118	5 722	7 425	7 797	7 201
Recettes TVA (brute)	..	..	2 419	4 163	5 684	5 771	6 106	7 787	8 093	7 706
Remboursements de la TVA	..	..	-118	-413	-617	-653	-384	-362	-296	-506
5112 Impôts sur les ventes	..	0	0	0	0	0	0	0	0	0
5113 Autres impôts	..	21	46	69	144	170	196	271	246	223
5120 Impôts sur biens et services déterminés	..	1 851	2 111	2 793	3 765	4 012	4 523	5 527	5 760	5 755
5121 Accises	..	1 023	1 340	1 814	2 397	2 876	3 226	3 621	3 692	3 717
Tabac	..	371	601	799	1 087	1 248	1 397	1 490	1 633	1 757
Boissons alcoolisées	..	147	146	174	290	336	363	431	408	376
Essences et huiles	..	260	269	268	305	649	705	757	760	727
Voitures	..	86	91	242	289	285	333	338	299	279
Produits alimentaires	..	19	28	31	41	44	50	60	66	65
Ciment	..	11	13	17	17	15	15	17	17	15
Autres accises	..	131	192	282	369	299	362	528	509	498
5122 Bénéfices des monopoles fiscaux	..	0	0	0	0	0	0	0	0	0
5123 Droits de douane et droits à l'importation	..	654	524	620	918	742	799	1 235	1 335	1 303
Hors tabac	..	565	424	428	639	429	486	894	948	920
Redevances sur prestations douanières à l'importation	..	68	81	142	155	188	204	221	234	219
Taxe conjoncturelle sur ventes du ciment importé	..	0	0	0	61	28	0	0	0	0
Droits de douane - Tabacs	..	9	12	23	27	37	51	57	71	67
Autres droits de douane	..	0	4	4	1	0	0	0	0	0
Prèlevements à l'importation	..	12	3	20	29	45	42	46	51	61
Autres taxes et prélèvements à l'importation	..	1	1	3	7	15	16	17	32	36
5124 Taxes à l'exportation	..	11	9	27	41	30	43	72	101	83
5125 Impôts sur biens d'équipement	..	0	0	0	0	0	0	0	0	0
5126 Impôts sur services déterminés	..	162	236	330	409	363	455	599	633	652
Taxe sur les télécommunications	..	72	91	136	147	153	150	178	179	193
Taxe de compensation sur les transports	..	55	84	105	126	67	138	141	142	133
Taxe sur les assurances	..	33	59	86	129	138	156	197	210	220
Autres impôts sur services déterminés	..	2	2	3	7	5	11	82	102	105
5127 Autres impôts sur commerce et transact. internat.	..	0	0	0	0	0	0	0	0	0
5128 Autres impôts	..	0	1	1	1	0	0	0	0	0
5130 Non ventilables entre 5110 et 5120	..	0	0	0	0	0	0	0	0	0
5200 Impôts sur utilisation des biens et exerc. activites	..	64	109	156	191	223	224	222	222	199
5210 Impôts périodiques	..	55	77	103	134	160	160	167	167	175
5211 A la charge des ménages: véhicules à moteur	..	35	44	60	81	91	96	101	105	105
5212 A la charge autres agents: véhicules à moteur	..	18	28	43	53	69	64	67	62	70
5213 Autres impôts périodiques	..	1	6	0	0	0	0	0	0	0
5220 Impôts non-périodiques	..	9	32	53	57	63	64	54	55	24
5300 Non ventilables entre 5100 et 5200	..	0	0	0	0	0	0	0	0	0
6000 Autres impôts	**..**	**104**	**126**	**279**	**622**	**630**	**702**	**862**	**938**	**711**
Droits de timbres	..	25	32	133	334	350	370	447	484	425
Droits d'enregistrements	..	40	67	107	181	201	214	248	256	215
Droit sur les voyages à l'étranger	..	12	12	21	33	35	38	42	43	12
Autres impôts - divers	..	28	15	17	75	43	81	125	156	58
6100 A la charge exclusive des entreprises	..	..	..	..	..	..	..	..	..	..
6200 A la charge d'autres agents	..	..	..	..	..	..	..	..	..	..

.. Non disponible

Note : Année civile se terminant le 31 décembre.

Les données sont sur la base des encaissements.

Les chiffres n'incluent pas les données des recettes fiscales collectées par les collectivités locales car elles ne sont pas disponibles.

Les impôts affectés aux Fonds spéciaux du Trésor et aux Fonds de concours sont compris dans les données pour la période 2000-20.

La rubrique 1210 exclut les redevances des compagnies pétrolières. En Tunisie, elles sont considérées comme un complément de l'impôt sur les sociétés depuis avril 2012.

Les cotisations de sécurité sociale sous la rubrique 2000 ne sont pas considérées comme des recettes fiscales en Tunisie.

Source : Ministère des Finances pour toutes les données des recettes fiscales, Ministère des Affaires Sociales pour les données de cotisations de sécurité sociale.

StatLink https://stat.link/caxnhm

Table 5.31. **Uganda / Ouganda**

Details of tax revenue / Recettes fiscales détaillées

Million UGX

	1995	2000	2005	2010	2015	2016	2017	2018	2019	2020
Total tax revenue	**521 679**	**999 659**	**1 935 472**	**4 252 022**	**9 761 430**	**11 042 365**	**12 431 317**	**14 067 588**	**16 130 627**	**15 639 910**
1000 Taxes on income, profits and capital gains	**77 170**	**181 905**	**560 351**	**1 340 327**	**3 387 902**	**3 854 687**	**4 308 416**	**4 821 107**	**5 677 950**	**5 655 860**
1100 Of individuals	52 681	136 806	392 037	958 294	2 382 729	2 767 373	3 070 385	3 479 276	4 033 859	4 182 920
1110 On income and profits	52 681	136 806	392 037	958 294	2 382 729	2 767 373	3 070 385	3 479 276	4 033 859	4 182 920
PAYE	20 329	83 471	245 325	657 920	1 613 243	1 803 532	2 114 995	2 396 113	2 811 297	3 039 830
Rental income tax	0	0	0	0	27 649	55 034	71 738	88 747	115 229	103 690
Other income tax (not counting WHT)	9 153	11 220	13 899	19 001	42 189	44 322	50 766	60 485	66 505	0
WHT on imports	14 256	23 349	47 399	68 581	152 787	165 145	154 953	179 643	194 169	166 410
WHT on general supplies	0	0	85 414	120 061	282 825	330 729	299 594	337 521	434 281	505 100
WHT on government payments	0	0	0	44 446	89 367	150 824	109 882	73 824	75 775	58 670
WHT management and professional fees	0	0	0	24 886	45 447	61 860	65 631	89 563	116 368	121 390
WHT on dividends	0	0	0	11 237	61 823	69 110	126 912	87 745	74 635	54 920
WHT non residents	0	0	0	1 356	57 106	79 583	69 924	152 988	102 942	114 490
Other WHT or unclassified	8 943	18 766	0	10 806	10 293	7 234	5 989	12 646	42 657	18 420
1120 On capital gains	..	..	..	..	..	..	..	..	..	..
1200 Corporate	24 489	40 891	160 030	315 379	714 772	732 159	764 273	884 802	1 167 745	1 392 300
1210 On profits	24 489	40 891	160 030	315 379	714 772	732 159	764 273	884 802	1 167 745	1 392 300
1220 On capital gains	..	..	..	..	..	..	..	..	..	..
1300 Unallocable between 1100 and 1200	0	4 207	8 284	66 654	290 401	355 154	473 758	457 028	476 346	80 640
2000 Social security contributions	**..**	**..**	**..**	**..**	**..**	**..**	**..**	**..**	**..**	**..**
2100 Employees	..	..	..	..	..	..	..	..	..	..
2110 On a payroll basis	..	..	..	..	..	..	..	..	..	..
2120 On an income tax basis	..	..	..	..	..	..	..	..	..	..
2200 Employers	..	..	..	..	..	..	..	..	..	..
2210 On a payroll basis	..	..	..	..	..	..	..	..	..	..
2220 On an income tax basis	..	..	..	..	..	..	..	..	..	..
2300 Self-employed or non-employed	..	..	..	..	..	..	..	..	..	..
2310 On a payroll basis	..	..	..	..	..	..	..	..	..	..
2320 On an income tax basis	..	..	..	..	..	..	..	..	..	..
2400 Unallocable between 2100, 2200 and 2300	..	..	..	..	..	..	..	..	..	..
2410 On a payroll basis	..	..	..	..	..	..	..	..	..	..
2420 On an income tax basis	..	..	..	..	..	..	..	..	..	..
3000 Taxes on payroll and workforce	**0**	**0**	**0**	**0**	**0**	**0**	**0**	**0**	**0**	**0**
4000 Taxes on property	**..**	**..**	**..**	**..**	**..**	**..**	**..**	**..**	**..**	**..**
4100 Recurrent taxes on immovable property	..	..	..	..	..	..	..	..	..	..
4110 Households	..	..	..	..	..	..	..	..	..	..
4120 Others	..	..	..	..	..	..	..	..	..	..
4200 Recurrent taxes on net wealth	..	..	..	..	..	..	..	..	..	..
4210 Individual	..	..	..	..	..	..	..	..	..	..
4220 Corporate	..	..	..	..	..	..	..	..	..	..
4300 Estate, inheritance and gift taxes	..	..	..	..	..	..	..	..	..	..
4310 Estate and inheritance taxes	..	..	..	..	..	..	..	..	..	..
4320 Gift taxes	..	..	..	..	..	..	..	..	..	..
4400 Taxes on financial and capital transactions	..	..	..	..	..	..	..	..	..	..
4500 Non-recurrent taxes	..	..	..	..	..	..	..	..	..	..
4510 On net wealth	..	..	..	..	..	..	..	..	..	..
4520 Other non-recurrent taxes	..	..	..	..	..	..	..	..	..	..
4600 Other recurrent taxes on property	..	..	..	..	..	..	..	..	..	..
5000 Taxes on goods and services	**428 807**	**815 835**	**1 372 355**	**2 861 862**	**6 350 601**	**7 184 690**	**8 062 851**	**9 213 964**	**10 457 651**	**9 867 410**
5100 Taxes on production, sale, transfer, etc.	415 342	793 285	1 308 282	2 772 331	6 201 129	7 053 046	7 920 343	9 043 464	10 285 727	9 700 030
5110 General taxes	158 745	329 755	638 773	1 371 561	3 150 723	3 580 638	3 933 635	4 503 031	4 976 098	4 767 650
5111 Value added taxes	158 745	329 755	638 773	1 371 561	3 150 723	3 580 638	3 933 635	4 503 031	4 976 098	4 767 650
VAT on imports (government taxes)	7 771	16 628	10 444	35 775	0	0	0	0	0	0
VAT on imports (non-government taxes)	67 110	178 868	365 418	763 398	1 783 518	1 952 821	2 057 107	2 416 568	2 664 812	2 498 390
VAT on phone talk time	0	0	0	93 277	151 747	181 944	205 342	213 549	200 283	154 820
VAT on beer	15 771	11 586	16 771	37 034	108 831	120 513	126 862	145 809	122 117	138 820
VAT on electricity	0	0	0	74 584	112 811	114 679	128 080	170 471	170 536	170 830
VAT on sugar	0	0	0	64 276	110 801	120 363	139 657	149 558	120 790	100 870
VAT on soft drinks	9 515	5 139	12 028	15 846	32 385	35 449	43 023	42 791	76 960	81 480
VAT on cement	0	0	0	25 161	53 086	72 014	66 491	81 095	87 557	120 190
VAT on cigarettes	13 437	6 904	6 641	1 411	16 759	9 366	9 042	9 522	4 295	430
Other VAT	45 141	140 630	263 679	359 821	923 754	1 117 807	1 303 951	1 407 037	1 756 848	1 826 180
VAT refunds	..	-30 000	-36 208	-99 023	-142 970	-144 320	-145 920	-133 370	-228 100	-324 360
5112 Sales tax	0	0	0	0	0	0	0	0	0	0

Table 5.31. **Uganda / Ouganda** (*cont.*)

Details of tax revenue / Recettes fiscales détaillées

Million UGX

	1995	2000	2005	2010	2015	2016	2017	2018	2019	2020
5113 Other	0	0	0	0	0	0	0	0	0	0
5120 Taxes on specific goods and services	256 597	463 530	669 509	1 400 770	3 050 407	3 472 408	3 986 708	4 540 433	5 309 629	4 932 380
5121 Excises	51 966	132 953	187 615	275 929	834 589	878 166	1 018 677	1 122 066	1 257 253	1 155 450
Excise tax on beer	18 483	59 938	60 704	98 864	146 853	177 678	216 717	263 072	269 276	267 890
Excise tax on phone talk time	0	0	24 901	99 490	184 175	166 780	194 297	178 966	211 878	231 260
Excise tax on soft drinks	7 134	13 348	15 304	27 907	71 799	83 125	90 009	118 869	125 992	120 530
Excise tax on cigarettes	22 267	33 572	28 632	7 698	14 979	12 617	12 072	15 591	14 912	21 020
Excise tax on spirits / waragi	742	915	6 463	10 376	53 331	58 203	98 886	157 512	155 648	104 550
Excise on international calls	0	0	0	0	65 142	34 230	33 971	33 341	34 937	27 050
Excise tax on sugar	0	0	0	17 187	17 854	18 220	37 973	30 277	35 526	40 100
Excise tax on cement	1	1	1	8 228	17 773	20 784	23 729	26 741	32 089	34 510
Other excise taxes	3 339	25 180	51 610	84 179	262 684	306 530	311 024	282 714	361 930	344 010
Tax refunds due to diesel tax exemption	0	0	0	-77 999	0	0	0	14 982	15 065	-35 470
5122 Profits of fiscal monopolies	0	0	0	0	0	0	0	0	0	0
5123 Customs and import duties	203 052	330 339	480 361	1 122 850	2 188 774	2 522 234	2 886 974	3 333 021	3 712 469	3 484 000
Petroleum duty	119 662	197 202	309 024	716 234	1 197 749	1 382 952	1 609 602	1 811 817	2 038 658	2 012 540
Surcharge on used imports	0	0	0	38 621	95 895	136 280	164 612	209 782	230 784	181 160
Non-oil imports	6 100	5 301	3 653	21 651	0	0	0	0	0	0
Commission on imports	12 150	22 746	19 567	2	0	0	0	0	0	0
Infrastructure Levy	0	0	0	0	57 268	62 936	69 107	87 669	92 569	81 530
Other import duties	65 139	105 090	153 667	346 621	841 381	940 066	1 043 652	1 223 753	1 350 458	1 208 770
Fixed duty drawbacks	0	0	-5 550	-280	-3 520	0	0	0	0	0
5124 Taxes on exports	0	0	1 165	122	13 186	15 878	13 968	12 442	20 604	14 940
5125 Taxes on investment goods	0	0	0	0	0	0	0	0	0	0
5126 Taxes on specific services	1 580	238	368	1 869	13 858	56 130	67 089	72 904	319 302	277 990
Casino and lottery tax	1 580	238	368	1 869	13 858	17 416	26 590	29 216	27 896	19 040
Bank charges	0	0	0	0	0	38 714	40 499	43 688	84 650	98 670
Levy on mobile money	0	0	0	0	0	0	0	0	49 525	59 720
Tax on over-the-top internet services	0	0	0	0	0	0	0	0	157 231	100 560
5127 Other taxes on internat. trade and transactions	0	0	0	0	0	0	0	0	0	0
5128 Other taxes	0	0	0	0	0	0	0	0	0	0
5130 Unallocable between 5110 and 5120	0	0	0	0	0	0	0	0	0	0
5200 Taxes on use of goods and perform activities	13 465	22 551	64 073	89 531	149 472	131 645	142 507	170 499	171 924	167 380
5210 Recurrent taxes	10 412	17 890	52 440	64 096	91 886	73 351	80 344	98 194	96 556	93 820
5211 Paid by households: motor vehicles	10 412	17 890	52 440	64 096	91 886	73 351	80 344	98 194	96 556	93 820
Fees and licences	10 085	17 890	52 440	64 096	91 886	73 351	80 344	98 194	96 556	93 820
Road user charges	327	0	0	0	0	0	0	0	0	0
5212 Paid by others: motor vehicles	0	0	0	0	0	0	0	0	0	0
5213 Paid in respect of other goods	0	0	0	0	0	0	0	0	0	0
5220 Non-recurrent taxes	3 053	4 660	11 633	25 434	57 586	58 294	62 164	72 305	75 368	73 560
5300 Unallocable between 5100 and 5200	0	0	0	0	0	0	0	0	0	0
6000 Other taxes	**15 702**	**1 919**	**2 766**	**49 833**	**22 927**	**2 988**	**60 050**	**32 518**	**-4 974**	**116 640**
6100 Paid solely by business	0	0	0	0	0	0	0	0	0	0
6200 Other	15 702	1 919	2 766	49 833	22 927	2 988	60 050	32 518	-4 974	116 640
Stamp duties and embossing fees	1 451	1 919	6 946	26 256	48 557	60 129	88 019	73 945	100 337	87 090
Coffee stabilisation tax	14 250	0	0	0	0	0	0	0	0	0
Government payments on behalf of private companies	0	0	0	0	0	0	0	0	0	0
Agricultural products	1	0	0	0	0	0	0	0	0	15 000
Un-allocated revenue	0	0	0	29 457	0	0	0	0	0	51 120
Tax refunds	0	0	-4 180	-5 880	-25 630	-57 141	-27 968	-41 428	-105 311	-36 570
Memo items:										
Gross domestic VAT	0	164 259	299 119	671 411	1 510 175	1 772 137	2 022 448	2 234 810	2 554 450	2 608 580
VAT on imports (non-government taxes)	0	178 868	365 418	763 398	1 783 518	1 952 821	2 057 107	2 416 570	2 664 810	2 498 390
VAT on imports (government taxes)	7 771	16 628	10 444	35 775	0	0	0	0	0	0

.. Not available

Note: Data are reported on a fiscal year basis beginning 1st July. For example, the data for 2020 represent July 2019 to June 2020.

The data are on a cash basis.

Figures exclude tax revenues collected by sub-national governments as the data are not available.

Heading 1110: Subtotals for WHT were removed from this heading in this edition in order to make the presentation clearer.

Heading 4000: Property tax is levied annually by local authorities. Revenue from property tax is not available.

Heading 5121: The "other excises taxes" category combines excise revenues from bottled water, cosmetics and mobile money transfers (all three in the "Indirect Domestic Taxes: excises" section of the Uganda Revenue Authority's budget document) with revenue from the excise duty (in the "taxes on international trade" section) and the excise duty (in the "government taxes" section).

Revenue from driver permits are considered non-tax revenue under the OECD classification, as set out in the OECD *Interpretative Guide* in Annex A. The national classification of Uganda classifies this revenue as tax revenue.

Source: Uganda Revenue Authority.

StatLink https://stat.link/prbi4x

Chapter 6

Non-tax revenue tables, 1995-2020

Chapitre 6

Tableaux des recettes non fiscales, 1995-2020

Chapter 6 / Chapitre 6

Non-tax revenue tables, 1995-2020

In all of the following tables a ("..") indicates not available or not applicable. The main series in this volume cover the years 1995 to 2020.

Figures referring to 1990-94, 1996-99, 2001-04, 2006-09 and 2011-14, in Table 6.1 and Tables 6.4 to 6.35 have been omitted because of lack of space. Complete series are, however, available on line at *http://dx.doi.org/10.1787/93add7a4-en*.

Tableaux des recettes non fiscales, 1995-2020

Dans tous les tableaux suivants le symbole («..») signifie que l'information n'est pas disponible ou qu'elle n'est pas applicable. La principale série dans ce volume couvre les années 1995 à 2020.

Les données pour les années 1990-94, 1996-99, 2001-04, 2006-09 et 2011-14 dans le tableau 6.1 et les tableaux 6.4 à 6.35 ont été omises en raison du manque d'espace. Les séries complètes sont cependant disponibles en ligne sur *http://dx.doi.org/10.1787/ef1bbbc4-fr*.

Table 6.1. **Total non-tax revenue as percentage of GDP, 1995-2020**
Tableau 6.1. **Total des recettes non fiscales en pourcentage du PIB, 1995-2020**

	1995	2000	2005	2010	2015	2016	2017	2018	2019	2020
Botswana	..	..	26.9	19.3	19.4	19.0	20.4	17.1	16.8	15.4
Burkina Faso	..	7.6	4.9	5.1	5.0	4.4	4.2	4.5	3.7	5.6
Cabo Verde	21.2	7.6	9.2	9.7	7.6	7.1	7.7	5.6	8.2	6.7
Cameroon / Cameroun	2.9	7.0	5.8	4.1	3.8	2.5	3.0	3.2	3.5	2.3
Chad / Tchad	..	..	..	5.2	5.2	4.0	5.8	6.2	5.2	5.7
Congo	..	18.4	29.3	31.4	10.8	12.6	11.6	17.5	19.2	23.1
Congo, Dem. Rep. / Congo, Rép. dém.	..	..	..	6.2	4.7	4.1	3.5	2.7	2.3	2.3
Côte d'Ivoire	0.7	0.8	1.6	1.2	2.4	1.4	1.6	1.5	1.6	1.3
Egypt / Égypte	..	..	6.6	8.1	6.8	5.4	6.0	4.6	4.2	4.3
Equatorial Guinea / Guinée équatoriale	..	..	24.4	18.8	15.0	10.3	11.2	13.6	9.3	6.2
Eswatini	10.9	12.5	15.8	8.1	14.5	12.2	14.5	11.9	13.0	15.1
Ghana	..	1.6	3.0	3.7	4.9	3.3	3.4	3.3	3.2	2.8
Kenya	..	..	1.3	1.2	1.5	1.5	1.8	1.5	1.4	2.4
Lesotho	..	..	31.3	33.4	29.5	23.9	28.7	27.0	26.3	35.1
Madagascar	0.0	2.8	5.4	3.0	1.5	1.9	2.3	2.9	2.7	3.4
Malawi	..	..	5.2	7.8	3.1	3.2	3.4	1.8	1.9	2.2
Mali	5.9	5.8	5.3	4.9	2.5	2.1	3.5	2.4	3.1	2.3
Mauritania / Mauritanie	..	..	..	6.3	6.4	4.8	4.7	6.9	5.5	6.8
Mauritius / Maurice[1]	3.4	2.7	2.4	3.7	2.8	3.2	3.7	4.3	2.9	3.3
Morocco / Maroc	..	2.2	3.0	3.6	3.9	3.5	3.5	3.7	4.3	3.4
Namibia / Namibie	..	..	..	9.4	14.0	10.8	13.7	11.8	12.7	14.6
Niger	..	4.1	6.3	4.6	5.7	5.1	6.0	7.2	7.6	8.1
Nigeria / Nigéria	..	..	..	7.7	2.9	2.1	2.5	3.0	3.6	3.1
Rwanda	..	9.9	11.1	11.6	8.6	7.6	7.2	7.8	7.2	7.7
Senegal / Sénégal	..	1.6	1.8	2.6	3.5	4.6	4.4	3.4	2.8	3.4
Seychelles	..	..	..	6.2	6.6	7.5	5.8	6.6	6.0	8.0
Sierra Leone	..	..	8.2	5.7	6.3	4.2	3.9	4.7	6.4	8.6
South Africa / Afrique du Sud	0.5	0.4	0.5	0.5	0.4	0.4	0.4	0.5	0.5	0.5
Togo	..	1.3	2.0	8.3	3.1	3.2	3.7	5.5	4.7	3.8
Tunisia / Tunisie	..	2.3	2.5	2.7	1.9	1.6	2.7	2.9	3.1	3.0
Uganda / Ouganda	3.5	4.7	5.7	1.8	1.2	1.4	1.1	1.0	1.3	1.1
Africa (31) average / Moyenne Afrique (31)[2]	**..**	**..**	**..**	**7.9**	**6.6**	**5.8**	**6.3**	**6.3**	**6.3**	**6.8**

.. Not available

Note: The figures include sub-national government non-tax revenues for Eswatini, Kenya (2014 onwards), Mauritius, and Morocco, as well as negligible amounts of non-tax revenues for South Africa in 2019 and 2020. Sub-national government non-tax revenues are not available in other countries. See the country tables in Chapter 6 for further information.

1. Data for Mauritius are on a July-June fiscal year basis except for the years 2010-15 when they were reported on a calendar year basis. Please see Chapter 5 for more details.
2. Represents an unweighted average of the 31 African countries in this publication.

.. Non disponible

Note : Les chiffres incluent les recettes non fiscales collectées par les administrations infranationales pour l'Eswatini, le Kenya (à partir de 2014), le Maroc et Maurice ansi que des montants négligeables de recettes non fiscales pour l'Afrique du Sud en 2019 et 2020. Les données des recettes non fiscales collectées par les administrations infranationales ne sont pas disponibles pour les autres pays. Voir les tableaux par pays au chapitre 6 pour plus d'informations.

1. Les données pour Maurice sont sur la base de l'année fiscale juillet-juin sauf pour les années 2010-15 où elles ont été déclarées sur la base de l'année civile. Veuillez consulter le chapitre 5 pour plus de détails.
2. Représente une moyenne non pondérée des 31 pays africains inclus dans cette publication.

StatLink https://stat.link/vng6we

Table 6.2. **Tax revenue of main headings as percentage of GDP, 2020**
Tableau 6.2. **Recettes fiscales des principales rubriques en pourcentage du PIB, 2020**

	Grants / Dons	Property income / Revenus de la propriété				Sales of goods and services / Ventes de biens et de services	Fines, penalties and forfeits / Amendes, pénalités et confiscations	Miscellaneous and unidentified revenue / Recettes diverses et non identifiées
		Total	Rents and royalties / Loyers et redevances	Interest and dividends / Intérêts et dividendes	Other property income / Autres revenus de la propriété			
Botswana	0.0	5.8	1.2	4.6	0.0	0.3	0.0	9.3
Burkina Faso	3.2	1.6	1.0	0.6	0.0	0.4	0.1	0.3
Cabo Verde	3.2	0.7	..	..	..	2.3	0.1	0.4
Cameroon / Cameroun	0.2	1.7	1.6	0.1	0.0	0.1	0.3	0.0
Chad / Tchad	4.0	1.2	1.1	0.0	0.0	0.1	0.1	0.3
Congo	1.7	21.4	21.2	0.0	0.2	0.0	0.0	0.0
Congo, Dem. Rep. / Congo, Rép. dém.	1.0	0.9	0.9	0.1	0.0	0.3	0.1	0.0
Côte d'Ivoire	0.5	0.3	0.2	0.1	0.0	0.2	0.0	0.3
Egypt / Égypte	0.0	1.2	0.3	0.9	0.0	1.3	0.0	1.7
Equatorial Guinea / Guinée équatoriale	0.0	5.9	3.9	1.7	0.2	0.3	0.0	0.1
Eswatini	0.4	1.8	0.1	1.5	0.2	0.2	0.1	12.6
Ghana	0.3	1.3	0.6	0.6	0.0	1.2	0.0	0.1
Kenya	0.2	1.6	0.0	0.9	0.7	0.5	0.0	0.2
Lesotho	3.1	5.0	4.6	0.3	0.0	0.4	0.0	26.6
Madagascar	3.1	0.3	0.1	0.2	0.0	0.0	0.0	0.1
Malawi	1.3	0.3	0.0	0.3	0.0	0.5	0.0	0.0
Mali	1.3	0.6	0.0	0.6	0.0	0.2	0.1	0.0
Mauritania / Mauritanie	2.1	4.1	3.5	0.6	0.0	0.1	0.2	0.3
Mauritius / Maurice	0.9	1.2	0.2	0.2	0.8	0.8	0.1	0.2
Morocco / Maroc	0.0	0.8	0.3	0.5	0.0	1.2	0.1	1.2
Namibia / Namibie	0.2	1.3	1.0	0.3	0.0	0.4	0.1	12.6
Niger	6.8	0.4	0.2	0.2	0.0	0.1	0.0	0.8
Nigeria / Nigéria	1.1	2.0	2.0	0.0	0.0	0.0	0.0	0.0
Rwanda[1]	4.9	..	..	..	..	..	..	2.8
Senegal / Sénégal	2.3	0.8	0.4	0.3	0.0	0.1	0.0	0.2
Seychelles	2.1	3.6	1.5	2.1	0.1	2.0	0.0	0.2
Sierra Leone	5.8	0.9	0.9	0.0	0.0	0.9	0.0	1.0
South Africa / Afrique du Sud	0.0	0.4	0.3	0.1	0.0	0.0	0.1	0.0
Togo	2.3	0.8	0.2	0.6	0.0	0.6	0.0	0.2
Tunisia / Tunisie	0.7	1.5	0.6	0.9	0.0	0.0	0.4	0.4
Uganda / Ouganda	0.8	0.0	0.0	0.0	0.0	0.3	0.0	0.0
Africa (31) average / Moyenne Afrique (31)[2]	**1.7**	**2.3**	**1.7**	**0.6**	..	**0.5**	**0.1**	**2.3**

.. Not available

Note: The figures include sub-national government non-tax revenues for Eswatini, Kenya (2014 onwards), Mauritius, and Morocco, as well as negligible amounts of non-tax revenues for South Africa in 2019 and 2020. Sub-national government non-tax revenues are not available in other countries. See the country tables in Chapter 6 for further information.

1. Data for property income, sales of goods and services and fines, penalties and forfeits are included in miscellaneous and unidentified revenue.
2. Represents an unweighted average of the 31 African countries in this publication.

.. Non disponible

Note : Les chiffres incluent les recettes non fiscales collectées par les administrations infranationales pour l'Eswatini, le Kenya (à partir de 2014), le Maroc et Maurice ansi que des montants négligeables de recettes non fiscales pour l'Afrique du Sud en 2019 et 2020. Les données des recettes non fiscales collectées par les administrations infranationales ne sont pas disponibles pour les autres pays.Voir les tableaux par pays au chapitre 6 pour plus d'informations.

1. Les données relatives aux revenus de propriété, les ventes de biens et de services, les amendes, les pénalités et les confiscations sont incluses dans la rubrique « recettes diverses et non identifiées ».
2. Représente une moyenne non pondérée des 31 pays africains inclus dans cette publication.

StatLink https://stat.link/17dzcn

Table 6.3. **Tax revenue of main headings as percentage of total non-tax revenue, 2020**
Tableau 6.3. **Recettes fiscales des principales rubriques en pourcentage du total des recettes non fiscales, 2020**

	Grants / Dons	Property income / Revenus de la propriété				Sales of goods and services / Ventes de biens et de services	Fines, penalties and forfeits / Amendes, pénalités et confiscations	Miscellaneous and unidentified revenue / Recettes diverses et non identifiées
		Total	Rents and royalties / Loyers et redevances	Interest and dividends / Intérêts et dividendes	Other property income / Autres revenus de la propriété			
Botswana	0.1	37.7	7.6	30.1	0.0	1.7	0.2	60.2
Burkina Faso	56.6	29.3	18.8	10.5	0.0	6.6	2.2	5.2
Cabo Verde	47.7	10.2	..	..	..	33.5	2.0	6.6
Cameroon / Cameroun	7.6	72.8	69.4	3.5	0.0	5.8	13.2	0.6
Chad / Tchad	70.9	20.4	19.8	0.0	0.6	1.6	1.4	5.7
Congo	7.3	92.7	91.7	0.0	1.1	0.0	0.0	0.0
Congo, Dem. Rep. / Congo, Rép. dém.	43.9	39.1	36.6	2.5	0.0	12.6	3.8	0.6
Côte d'Ivoire	41.3	21.2	12.6	8.6	0.0	16.4	0.0	21.2
Egypt / Égypte	0.7	27.5	7.0	20.4	0.2	31.1	1.1	39.4
Equatorial Guinea / Guinée équatoriale	0.2	93.8	63.2	27.0	3.6	5.0	0.0	1.0
Eswatini	2.5	12.0	0.8	10.1	1.1	1.4	0.5	83.7
Ghana	11.2	45.0	22.7	22.3	0.0	41.8	0.0	1.9
Kenya	7.7	64.4	0.5	36.6	27.3	21.2	0.5	6.2
Lesotho	8.9	14.1	13.2	1.0	0.0	1.2	0.0	75.8
Madagascar	89.4	7.9	1.8	6.1	0.0	0.9	0.0	1.8
Malawi	62.6	13.9	0.0	13.9	0.0	21.8	1.7	0.0
Mali	57.2	27.4	0.7	26.2	0.5	8.0	5.4	2.0
Mauritania / Mauritanie	30.6	59.3	50.8	8.5	0.0	2.0	3.5	4.7
Mauritius / Maurice	28.6	36.8	6.4	5.1	25.3	25.5	2.1	7.0
Morocco / Maroc	0.7	23.4	7.8	15.6	0.0	35.6	4.0	36.2
Namibia / Namibie	1.0	9.1	6.7	2.4	0.0	3.0	0.4	86.5
Niger	83.3	5.2	3.0	2.1	0.1	1.3	0.5	9.7
Nigeria / Nigéria	35.3	64.6	64.6	0.0	0.0	0.0	0.0	0.1
Rwanda[1]	63.7	..	..	..	..	..	..	36.3
Senegal / Sénégal	68.4	22.9	12.9	10.0	0.0	2.3	0.0	6.4
Seychelles	26.0	45.5	18.6	25.9	1.1	25.7	0.0	2.9
Sierra Leone	67.4	10.3	10.3	0.0	0.0	10.3	0.0	12.1
South Africa / Afrique du Sud	5.4	72.5	49.0	23.6	0.0	5.6	15.0	1.5
Togo	60.1	20.0	4.3	15.7	0.0	15.1	0.4	4.5
Tunisia / Tunisie	21.7	49.2	19.5	29.7	0.0	0.9	13.2	15.0
Uganda / Ouganda	74.7	0.9	0.9	0.0	0.0	24.4	0.0	0.0
Africa (31) average / Moyenne Afrique (31)[2]	**34.9**	**35.0**	**21.4**	**12.3**	..	**12.1**	**2.4**	**17.2**

.. Not available

Note: The figures include sub-national government non-tax revenues for Eswatini, Kenya (2014 onwards), Mauritius, and Morocco, as well as negligible amounts of non-tax revenues for South Africa in 2019 and 2020. Sub-national government non-tax revenues are not available in other countries. See the country tables in Chapter 6 for further information.

1. Data for property income, sales of goods and services and fines, penalties and forfeits are included in miscellaneous and unidentified revenue.
2. Represents an unweighted average of the 31 African countries in this publication.

.. Non disponible

Note : Les chiffres incluent les recettes non fiscales collectées par les administrations infranationales pour l'Eswatini, le Kenya (à partir de 2014), le Maroc et Maurice ansi que des montants négligeables de recettes non fiscales pour l'Afrique du Sud en 2019 et 2020. Les données des recettes non fiscales collectées par les administrations infranationales ne sont pas disponibles pour les autres pays.Voir les tableaux par pays au chapitre 6 pour plus d'informations.

1. Les données relatives aux revenus de propriété, les ventes de biens et de services, les amendes, les pénalités et les confiscations sont incluses dans la rubrique « recettes diverses et non identifiées ».
2. Représente une moyenne non pondérée des 31 pays africains inclus dans cette publication.

StatLink https://stat.link/i126l3

Table 6.4. **Total non-tax revenue in millions of US dollars at market exchange rates, 1995-2020**

Tableau 6.4. **Totale des recettes non fiscales en millions de dollars américains au taux de change du marché, 1995-2020**

	1995	2000	2005	2010	2015	2016	2017	2018	2019	2020
Botswana	..	..	2 650	2 558	2 704	2 920	3 333	2 897	2 734	2 408
Burkina Faso	..	225	304	514	594	569	594	725	593	971
Cabo Verde	114	46	100	161	122	118	137	111	163	115
Cameroon / Cameroun	295	720	1 140	1 134	1 220	860	1 078	1 293	1 407	951
Chad / Tchad	..	..	..	561	572	411	582	685	568	608
Congo	..	667	1 946	4 126	1 279	1 284	1 284	2 386	2 450	2 387
Congo, Dem. Rep. / Congo, Rép. dém.	..	..	..	1 337	1 784	1 501	1 336	1 279	1 164	1 144
Côte d'Ivoire	108	121	386	414	1 108	677	808	879	910	814
Egypt / Égypte	..	..	6 196	18 520	22 574	17 981	14 230	11 609	12 794	15 564
Equatorial Guinea / Guinée équatoriale	..	..	1 995	3 062	1 978	1 157	1 369	1 785	1 057	626
Eswatini	208	212	508	367	580	482	649	549	568	625
Ghana	..	178	730	1 612	2 419	1 849	2 074	2 195	2 161	1 951
Kenya	..	..	424	514	1 037	1 120	1 383	1 329	1 383	2 466
Lesotho	..	..	465	788	651	531	676	632	604	724
Madagascar	0	128	315	297	172	229	298	402	383	448
Malawi	..	..	262	723	268	265	279	173	197	246
Mali	197	173	329	519	334	297	537	404	538	406
Mauritania / Mauritanie	..	..	..	357	397	310	322	505	432	555
Mauritius / Maurice	140	128	161	372	323	386	475	593	405	413
Morocco / Maroc	..	873	1 889	3 323	3 961	3 592	3 809	4 311	5 104	3 901
Namibia / Namibie	..	..	..	1 088	1 572	1 219	1 791	1 578	1 531	1 609
Niger	..	93	275	363	548	528	668	920	983	1 119
Nigeria / Nigéria	..	..	..	28 431	14 055	8 508	9 392	12 573	16 098	13 200
Rwanda	..	203	328	712	736	661	670	756	744	792
Senegal / Sénégal	..	96	200	412	621	882	915	784	647	826
Seychelles	..	..	..	60	93	112	91	108	100	96
Sierra Leone	..	..	133	146	268	163	145	191	259	350
South Africa / Afrique du Sud	790	596	1 399	2 211	1 406	1 375	1 643	2 093	2 034	1 752
Togo	..	27	61	384	174	193	234	391	342	287
Tunisia / Tunisie	..	529	831	1 257	891	716	1 145	1 229	1 305	1 275
Uganda / Ouganda	241	367	665	438	361	400	346	316	457	416

.. Not available

Note: This table is derived by dividing the total non-tax revenue figures for each country (in millions of national currency) in Table 6.1 by the exchange rate figures shown in Table 4.19.

.. Non disponible

Note : Ce tableau est obtenu en divisant les chiffres des recettes non fiscales en millions de monnaie nationale du tableau 6.1 pour chaque pays par les tauxde change du tableau 4.19.

StatLink https://stat.link/9jq3sy

Table 6.5. **Botswana**

Details of non-tax revenue / Recettes non fiscales détaillées

Million BWP

	1995	2000	2005	2010	2015	2016	2017	2018	2019	2020
Total non-tax revenue	..	..	**14 034**	**17 412**	**27 953**	**31 412**	**34 363**	**29 941**	**29 844**	**27 330**
Grants	..	..	0	210	74	1	170	1	24	28
Grants	..	..	0	210	74	1	170	1	24	28
IMF Gold Sales	..	..	0	0	0	0	0	0	0	0
Property income	..	..	9 159	9 914	11 152	18 424	15 092	14 171	15 114	10 296
Rents and royalties	..	..	1 589	2 071	3 223	3 320	5 648	3 403	3 476	2 069
Mineral Royalties	..	..	1 577	2 057	3 215	3 307	5 638	3 383	3 463	2 062
Royalties and Dividends	..	..	0	0	0	0	0	0	0	0
Rent of Land	..	..	12	14	8	13	10	20	13	7
Interest and dividends	..	..	7 569	7 842	7 929	15 104	9 444	10 768	11 638	8 227
Mineral Dividends	..	..	6 573	7 054	6 766	11 976	7 740	9 905	6 547	4 196
Bank of Botswana Revenue	..	..	741	700	1 133	2 842	1 573	740	5 049	4 009
Profits From Public Enterprises	..	..	171	61	18	67	107	117	10	21
Interest: Parastatals (DDF)	..	..	38	20	8	215	19	1	29	0
Interest: Local Authorities	..	..	1	0	0	0	0	0	0	0
Interest: Deposits	..	..	46	8	4	4	4	5	3	0
Other property income	..	..	0	0	0	0	0	0	0	0
Sales of goods and services	..	..	908	1 047	811	1 137	1 183	930	656	478
Motor vehicle revenues	..	..	342	363	50	40	44	36	40	34
Petrol, Oil and Lubricants - Revenue	..	..	54	182	231	259	184	217	111	67
Water revenues	..	..	167	42	2	2	2	2	2	3
Fees and charges	..	..	84	107	129	123	599	123	137	68
Rent of Buildings & Equipment	..	..	73	86	97	95	97	97	99	100
Sale of Livestock	..	..	2	5	2	1	4	2	1	1
Registrations, licences and certificates	..	..	19	22	33	34	29	33	39	29
Other sales of goods and services	..	..	167	242	269	583	225	419	227	176
Fines, penalties and forfeits	..	..	36	31	93	65	46	42	60	62
Traffic fines	..	..	0	0	44	25	1	0	0	0
Court fines	..	..	19	20	38	23	22	22	23	34
Bond revenues	..	..	1	1	1	3	3	1	2	1
Income tax penalty	..	..	11	0	0	0	0	0	0	0
Other fines, penalties and forfeits	..	..	5	10	11	14	20	19	36	27
Miscellaneous and unidentified revenue	..	..	3 931	6 210	15 823	11 784	17 871	14 797	13 991	16 466
SACU Revenue	..	..	3 930	6 207	15 818	11 773	17 864	14 789	13 976	16 459
Recovery of Arrears of Revenue	..	..	0	3	5	10	6	8	14	6
Revenue from Local Authorities	..	..	0	0	0	0	0	0	0	0
Reimbursement of Medical Claims (Revenue)	..	..	1	1	1	1	1	1	1	0
Total tax and non-tax revenue	..	..	22 073	31 712	47 285	55 551	56 833	53 229	54 201	49 303

.. Not available

Note: Data are on a fiscal year basis beginning 1st April. For example, the data for 2020 represent April 2020 to March 2021.

Data are reported on a cash basis.

Figures exclude non-tax revenues collected by sub-national governments as the data are not available.

Source: Botswana Ministry of Finance and Economic Development, and Statistics Botswana.

StatLink https://stat.link/h0m29t

Table 6.6. **Burkina Faso**

Details of non-tax revenue / Recettes non fiscales détaillées

Million XOF

	1995	2000	2005	2010	2015	2016	2017	2018	2019	2020
Total des recettes non fiscales	**..**	**160 511**	**160 032**	**254 019**	**351 209**	**337 426**	**345 257**	**402 658**	**347 502**	**557 963**
Dons	..	143 716	131 541	198 940	230 041	180 190	194 303	215 091	134 275	315 959
Revenus de la propriété	..	6 326	9 148	15 447	57 875	74 704	87 166	104 718	116 802	163 537
Loyers et redevances	..	411	508	12 453	37 938	45 182	53 727	65 780	68 748	104 726
Droits sur les titres miniers et redevances minières	..	324	508	12 453	37 938	45 182	53 727	65 780	68 748	104 726
Redevance surété	..	87	0	0	0	0	0	0	0	0
Intérêts et dividendes	..	5 915	8 640	2 993	19 937	29 522	33 438	38 937	48 054	58 811
Intérêts en douane	..	42	36	40	493	295	212	124	2 023	201
Portefeuille de l'État et plus value	..	5 873	8 604	2 954	19 443	29 227	33 227	38 813	46 032	58 611
Autres revenus de la propriété	..	0	0	0	0	0	0	0	0	0
Ventes de biens et de services	..	6 408	11 996	24 510	39 979	44 358	40 816	38 088	38 838	37 081
Diverses prestations de services	..	2 364	4 876	10 831	19 016	20 865	15 311	11 448	9 946	11 741
Location de biens	..	8	35	398	76	57	222	254	161	169
Frais douanes	..	2 493	5 031	6 667	9 795	12 533	14 121	14 173	13 952	13 855
Frais visas, papiers d'identite et permis de conduire	..	431	1 007	2 986	4 582	5 201	5 072	4 793	5 094	3 395
Autres frais administratifs	..	1 113	1 048	3 629	6 511	5 702	6 089	7 421	9 685	7 922
Amendes, pénalités et confiscations	..	1 272	2 689	4 505	8 863	19 025	3 033	4 225	18 162	12 431
Amendes et pénalités dues au retard de paiement des taxes, impôts et redevances proportionnelles	..	0	0	0	1 699	1 274	778	1 127	747	1 795
Amendes et confiscations douanières	..	403	1 058	1 147	0	0	0	38	156	320
Recettes contentieuses (amendes) en matières forestière, de faune et de pêche	..	2	62	143	263	299	257	260	152	146
Amendes forfaitaires de la Gendarmerie et de la Police	..	110	265	167	203	385	384	481	267	300
Amendes et confiscation de l'IGAE	..	346	85	86	117	14 909	268	327	377	717
Amendes et confiscations (CNLF)	..	131	171	574	101	54	133	165	182	348
Frais et amendes de justice	..	1	1	243	32	65	46	64	37	21
Autres amendes et confiscations	..	0	0	1	8	16	19	5	14 844	7 432
Pénalités sur les marchés administratifs	..	85	435	657	311	618	381	1 293	661	674
Créances diverses	..	193	610	1 487	6 128	1 404	766	465	740	678
Recettes diverses et non identifiées	..	2 790	4 658	10 618	14 451	19 148	19 939	40 536	39 424	28 956
Reversement des intérêts	..	2 382	2 071	3 618	2 534	785	5 309	4 133	2 088	2 263
Autres produits	..	408	2 588	7 000	11 917	18 363	14 629	36 404	37 336	26 693
Total des recettes fiscales et non fiscales	..	375 113	540 193	952 872	1 369 969	1 498 795	1 671 321	1 887 343	1 970 048	2 218 141

.. Non disponible

Note : Année civile se terminant le 31 décembre.

Les données sont sur la base des encaissements.

Les chiffres n'incluent pas les recettes non fiscales collectées par les collectivités locales car elles ne sont pas disponibles. Cependant, ils incluent des recettes collectées par l'administration centrale au profit des collectivités locales.

Les recettes provenant de la taxe de location de biens, des droits sur les titres miniers, redevances minières et des frais administratifs sont incluses dans les recettes non fiscales comme le préconise la classification OCDE (voir le *Guide d'interprétation* en Annexe A). La classification nationale du Burkina Faso les comptabilise comme des recettes fiscales.

Source : Ministère de l'Économie, des Finances et du Développement du Burkina Faso.

StatLink https://stat.link/79o5n2

Table 6.7. **Cabo Verde**

Details of non-tax revenue / Recettes non fiscales détaillées

Million CVE

	1995	2000	2005	2010	2015	2016	2017	2018	2019	2020
Total des recettes non fiscales	**8 744**	**5 372**	**8 902**	**13 396**	**12 116**	**11 777**	**13 405**	**10 368**	**16 034**	**11 105**
Dons	6 848	3 931	6 610	9 440	3 958	4 507	6 193	2 265	6 145	5 302
Transferts courants de gouvernements étrangers	6 848	0	0	0	370	461	278	851	551	571
Aide budgétaire	0	..	..	..	0	0	0	0	0	0
Aide alimentaire	1 064	..	..	..	0	0	0	0	0	0
Dons directs	5 161	..	..	..	353	449	266	846	548	571
Autre transfert courants	623	..	..	..	17	13	12	5	4	0
Transferts en capital de gouvernements étrangers	0	3 931	6 610	9 440	3 588	4 046	5 914	1 414	5 594	4 730
Aide budgétaire	..	0	551	3 085	1 282	1 312	2 701	1 103	2 006	2 287
Aide alimentaire	..	672	750	338	0	60	283	154	231	106
Dons directs	..	3 259	5 138	6 018	2 048	2 542	2 930	158	3 357	2 336
Autre dons en capital	..	0	171	0	259	132	0	0	0	2
Revenus de la propriété	487	364	95	316	1 022	1 083	976	1 793	2 632	1 135
Loyers et redevances	..	..	..	..	..	..	..	..	..	..
Intérêts et dividendes	..	..	..	..	..	..	..	..	..	..
Autres revenus de la propriété	..	..	..	..	..	..	..	..	..	..
Ventes de biens et de services	382	592	1 496	3 077	4 652	5 042	5 189	5 509	5 987	3 719
Frais	192	448	1 445	3 003	4 492	4 738	4 995	5 293	5 841	3 628
Ventes	190	144	51	74	160	303	194	216	146	91
Amendes, pénalités et confiscations	64	54	169	376	404	679	498	369	433	220
Recettes diverses et non identifiées	963	431	532	187	2 079	467	550	431	838	730
Autres transferts	425	413	150	41	36	35	28	24	242	192
Autres recettes diverses et non spécifiées	538	18	382	146	2 043	432	521	407	595	538
Total des recettes fiscales et non fiscales	15 034	16 346	27 731	39 686	42 807	43 982	48 959	50 706	57 481	44 236

.. Non disponible

Note : Année civile se terminant le 31 décembre.

Les données sont sur la base des encaissements.

Les chiffres n'incluent pas les données des recettes non fiscales collectées par les collectivités locales car elles ne sont pas disponibles.

La présente publication n'inclut pas le produit de la vente d'actifs non financiers rapporté dans les documents budgétaires du Cabo Verde. La classification nationale du Cabo Verde compte le produit de la vente d'actifs non financiers comme une recette non fiscale. Selon la classification de l'OCDE (voir le *Guide d'interprétation* en Annexe B), le produit de la vente d'actifs n'est pas considéré comme une recette (fiscale ou non fiscale) car il ne représente pas une augmentation de la valeur nette résultant d'une transaction.

Source : Ministère des Finances et du Plan du Cabo Verde.

StatLink https://stat.link/u3jw5s

Table 6.8. **Cameroon / Cameroun**

Details of non-tax revenue / Recettes non fiscales détaillées

Million XAF

	1995	2000	2005	2010	2015	2016	2017	2018	2019	2020
Total des recettes non fiscales	**153 206**	**527 053**	**600 552**	**560 690**	**721 082**	**509 962**	**626 311**	**717 707**	**824 233**	**546 454**
Dons	..	6 900	91 404	78 805	18 089	54 100	64 800	86 700	133 300	41 700
Revenus de la propriété	90 400	404 500	446 825	442 296	465 541	396 033	398 521	510 077	551 526	398 084
Loyers et redevances	90 400	404 500	410 657	437 650	445 587	376 734	388 483	499 042	527 789	379 185
Redevance pétrolière	87 610	399 300	367 955	418 971	384 630	316 005	319 434	413 325	471 518	321 370
Droits de passage du pipeline	0	0	14 065	9 080	36 201	31 953	27 891	29 543	35 013	36 818
Autres loyers et redevances	2 790	5 200	28 637	9 599	24 756	28 776	41 158	56 175	21 257	20 997
Intérêts et dividendes	..	..	36 169	4 646	19 954	19 299	10 038	11 035	23 737	18 899
Autres revenus de la propriété	..	..	0	0	0	0	0	0	0	0
Ventes de biens et de services	26 700	33 500	40 262	37 732	188 402	29 094	21 737	48 055	56 291	31 607
Amendes, pénalités et confiscations	..	..	444	1 857	26 849	15 487	43 386	57 334	61 259	71 960
Recettes diverses et non identifiées	36 106	82 153	21 616	0	22 201	15 248	97 867	15 541	21 857	3 102
Total des recettes fiscales et non fiscales	634 589	1 337 553	1 735 808	2 132 385	3 409 008	3 253 870	3 561 490	3 864 201	4 046 395	3 560 542

.. Non disponible

Note : Année civile se terminant le 31 décembre.

Les données sont sur la base des encaissements.

Les chiffres n'incluent pas les recettes non fiscales collectées par les collectivités locales car elles ne sont pas disponibles.

Les revenus de la propriété comprennent les taxes domaniales, la taxe à l'extraction des carrières et la redevance à la production des eaux comme le préconise la classification OCDE (voir le *Guide d'interprétation* en Annexe B). La classification nationale du Cameroun les comptabilise comme des recettes fiscales.

Les recettes diverses et non identifiées comprennent les transferts de capitaux non compris ailleurs et transferts volontaires autres que les dons.

Source : Ministère des Finances du Cameroun.

StatLink https://stat.link/5tego7

Table 6.9. **Chad / Tchad**

Details of non-tax revenue / Recettes non fiscales détaillées

Million XAF

	1995	2000	2005	2010	2015	2016	2017	2018	2019	2020
Total des recettes non fiscales	..	..	..	**277 272**	**337 904**	**243 337**	**337 881**	**380 062**	**332 670**	**349 718**
Dons	..	..	..	68 799	221 884	175 497	235 922	199 244	106 891	248 109
Revenus de la propriété	..	..	..	193 129	87 733	44 164	69 280	149 077	200 942	71 264
Loyers et redevances	..	..	..	190 753	86 094	43 333	66 082	146 899	198 643	69 282
Redevances et dividendes pétroliers	..	..	..	185 445	86 094	20 363	56 138	58 653	88 201	65 252
Autres recettes pétrolières	..	..	..	5 308	0	22 970	9 944	88 246	110 442	4 030
Intérêts et dividendes	..	..	..	0	0	0	0	0	0	0
Autres revenus de la propriété	..	..	..	2 377	1 639	831	3 198	2 178	2 299	1 982
Ventes de biens et de services	..	..	..	4 162	10 591	6 837	3 694	2 416	15 873	5 583
Amendes, pénalités et confiscations	..	..	..	6 474	1 528	4 038	2 759	5 678	4 419	4 757
Recettes diverses et non identifiées	..	..	..	4 708	16 168	12 801	26 226	23 648	4 545	20 004
Total des recettes fiscales et non fiscales	..	..	..	1 050 538	712 081	527 746	699 833	862 843	852 043	1 251 608

.. Non disponible

Note : Année civile se terminant le 31 décembre.

Les données sont sur la base des encaissements.

Les chiffres n'incluent pas les recettes fiscales collectées par les collectivités locales car elles ne sont pas disponibles.

Les recettes provenant des amendes fiscales, des valeurs mobilières de l'État et de la redevance audiovisuelle sont incluses dans les recettes non fiscales comme le préconise la classification OCDE (voir le *guide d'interprétation* en Annexe A). La classification nationale du Tchad les comptabilise comme des recettes fiscales.

Les recettes provenant des amendes fiscales sont comptabilisées dans la rubrique amendes, pénalités et confiscations. Les recettes provenant des valeurs mobilières de l'État et de la redevance audiovisuelle sont comptabilisées dans la rubrique "ventes de biens et de services".

Source : Ministère des Finances et du Budget du Tchad.

StatLink https://stat.link/s28tqm

Table 6.10. **Congo**

Details of non-tax revenue / Recettes non fiscales détaillées

Million XAF

	1995	2000	2005	2010	2015	2016	2017	2018	2019	2020
Total des recettes non fiscales	..	**474 909**	**1 025 700**	**2 039 707**	**756 251**	**761 309**	**745 674**	**1 324 923**	**1 435 169**	**1 372 050**
Dons	..	6 800	5 900	4 100	41 400	40 400	29 600	5 900	56 600	99 521
Revenus de la propriété	..	468 109	1 019 800	2 034 514	713 099	720 025	715 490	1 318 180	1 378 325	1 272 119
Loyers et redevances	..	468 109	1 019 800	2 034 462	707 304	704 803	708 108	1 305 772	1 362 637	1 257 693
Recettes pétrolières	..	468 109	1 019 800	2 032 755	699 478	699 937	679 323	1 288 100	1 346 809	1 245 817
Redevance pétrolière	..	..	..	0	70	118	71	77	13	8
Redevance minière	..	..	..	2	60	12	42	1	1	9
Redevance forestière	..	..	..	1 705	7 696	4 735	28 673	17 594	15 814	11 859
Intérêts et dividendes	..	..	..	0	0	0	0	0	0	0
Autres revenus de la propriété	..	..	..	53	5 796	15 223	7 382	12 407	15 688	14 426
Ventes de biens et de services	..	..	..	16	30	12	419	48	207	5
Amendes, pénalités et confiscations	..	..	..	1 077	1 721	872	165	795	37	405
Recettes diverses et non identifiées	..	..	..	0	0	0	0	0	0	0
Total des recettes fiscales et non fiscales	..	573 593	1 232 116	2 494 005	1 660 585	1 562 055	1 442 684	1 891 343	2 044 271	1 957 867

.. Non disponible

Note : Année civile se terminant le 31 décembre.

Les données sont sur la base des encaissements.

Les chiffres n'incluent pas les recettes non fiscales collectées par les collectivités locales car elles ne sont pas disponibles.

Les données des dons et des recettes pétrolières sont issues de la base de données de la publication PEM 2022 (Perspectives de l'économie mondiale, avril 2022) pour les dons publiée par le FMI.

A partir de 2017, les loyers et redevances incluent la redevance bois et la redevance diamant collectées par la Direction Générale des douanes et des droits indirects.

Source : Ministère des Finances et du Budget de la République du Congo.

StatLink https://stat.link/bw6zm5

Table 6.11. **Congo, Dem. Rep. / Congo, Rép. dém.**

Details of non-tax revenue / Recettes non fiscales détaillées

Million CDF

	1995	2000	2005	2010	2015	2016	2017	2018	2019	2020
Total des recettes non fiscales	**..**	**..**	**..**	**1 212 847**	**1 652 391**	**1 537 085**	**1 958 695**	**2 075 240**	**1 917 966**	**2 118 779**
Dons	..	0	110 362	656 421	1 108 062	1 050 733	1 095 000	851 000	638 806	930 571
Revenus de la propriété	..	..	..	397 162	328 729	262 614	603 531	796 073	841 845	828 625
Loyers et redevances	..	..	..	357 515	290 419	240 294	558 220	734 297	765 511	775 571
Royalties des sociétés pétrolières	..	..	..	39 705	19 050	15 218	29 084	41 483	34 353	27 259
Redevance et royalty minières	..	..	..	139 802	143 702	114 681	279 414	408 754	385 847	545 897
Droits superficie annuels (mines)	..	..	..	25 464	20 689	18 958	46 510	13 970	10 199	11 730
Bonus de signature - renouvellement (hydrocarbures)	..	..	..	4 566	624	1 015	31 462	736	1 041	1 652
Redevance annuelle sur l'exploitation et autres (télécommunications)	..	..	..	50 603	38 635	50 464	55 098	53 312	94 410	108 156
Autorisation de concessions,extraction et autres autorisations (télécommunications)	..	..	..	9 126	5 789	113	31	131 631	101 098	2 396
Permis ressources forestières et faune	..	..	..	3 541	387	638	6 566	771	2 171	3 484
Marge distribuable (recettes pétrolières)	..	..	..	84 491	52 694	34 918	102 933	83 408	127 330	65 303
Redevances superficiaires sur permis d'exploration et sur concession (hydrocarbures)	..	..	..	10	8 791	4 280	5 878	30	8 502	8 355
Autres loyers	..	..	..	207	58	9	1 243	202	558	1 338
Intérêts et dividendes	..	..	..	39 301	37 159	22 228	45 162	40 811	75 305	52 225
Dividendes on shore (recettes pétrolières)	..	..	..	8 068	14 665	3 916	5 867	10 994	20 246	15 852
Participations off shore (recettes pétrolières)	..	..	..	25 347	15 806	10 463	30 839	24 271	41 892	19 716
Autres dividendes et participations	..	..	..	5 886	6 688	7 848	8 457	5 546	13 167	16 657
Autres revenus de la propriété	..	..	..	345	1 152	92	149	20 965	1 029	829
Ventes de biens et de services	..	..	..	123 462	163 712	156 955	185 267	325 778	285 401	267 178
Vente des imprimés	..	158	7	1 106	690	218	52	219	75	158
Taxe de numérotation	..	..	..	16 464	26 110	26 898	40 126	51 014	45 573	44 887
Taxe de régulation et taxe de modification des titres obtenus / télécommunications	..	..	..	13 180	36 198	38 820	21 884	20 191	18 050	19 019
Passeport, visa et carte de travail	..	..	..	20 859	31 053	25 967	32 300	45 946	42 369	27 344
Taxes sur le gardiennage par la Police Nationale Congolaise	..	..	..	4 247	11 337	10 597	16 059	23 016	34 594	32 749
Contrôle des produits d'origine toxique, soporifique et stupéfiante	..	..	..	647	7 328	6 862	6 248	7 736	7 075	59 715
Redevance sur la désinfection et le contrôle sanitaire des friperies	..	..	..	3 828	3 111	2 586	3 081	14 156	53 800	17 897
Agréments	..	..	..	1 181	559	317	525	995	1 364	1 309
Autres	..	..	..	61 949	44 803	43 588	62 660	158 037	77 742	60 059
Loyers, Institut National de Sécurité Sociale (INSS)	..	..	..	0	2 524	1 101	2 331	4 468	4 759	4 040
Amendes, pénalités et confiscations	..	..	..	35 178	50 759	66 125	73 995	101 166	150 624	80 584
Amendes et pénalités (DGI)	..	418	2	15 455	15 160	40 058	18 504	65 525	90 865	43 701
Amendes et pénalités (DGDA)	..	2	40	1 561	4 093	2 525	3 492	1 910	1 633	1 246
Amendes et pénalités (DGRAD)	..	..	..	18 162	31 505	23 541	52 000	33 732	58 126	35 638
Recettes diverses et non identifiées	..	..	..	625	1 129	658	902	1 222	1 289	11 821
Total des recettes fiscales et non fiscales	..	13 951	303 088	2 890 017	5 138 737	4 774 839	5 852 424	7 976 245	8 271 235	8 696 136

.. Non disponible

Note : Année civile se terminant le 31 décembre.

Les données sont sur la base des encaissements.

Les chiffres n'incluent pas les données des recettes non fiscales collectées par les collectivités locales car elles ne sont pas disponibles.

Les données des dons sont issues de la base de données de la publication PEM 2022 (*Perspectives de l'économie mondiale* 2022, avril 2022) publiée par le FMI.

La classification des données de la DGRAD a été révisée et affinée suite à la provision d'un nouvel ensemble de données couvrant 2008 à 2020. La révision de la classification a résulté à un plus grand nombre de recettes de la DGRAD classifié comme des recettes fiscales par rapport aux années précédentes.

Les données autres que les dons sont disponibles à partir de 2008.

Les recettes provenant de la vente des imprimés sont incluses dans les recettes non fiscales comme le préconise la classification OCDE (voir le *Guide d'interprétation* en Annexe B). La classification nationale en République Démocratique du Congo classifie les recettes de la vente des imprimés comme des recettes fiscales.

Certaines recettes – considérées comme des taxes en République Démocratique du Congo – sont considérées comme des frais administratifs et sont classifiés comme des recettes non fiscales comme le préconise la classification OCDE (voir le *guide d'interprétation* en Annexe B).

Source : Ministère des Finances de la République Démocratique du Congo; FMI, *Perspectives de l'économie mondiale*, avril 2022.

StatLink https://stat.link/ixyk0t

Table 6.12. **Côte d'Ivoire**

Details of non-tax revenue / Recettes non fiscales détaillées

Million XOF

	1995	2000	2005	2010	2015	2016	2017	2018	2019	2020
Total des recettes non fiscales	**54 156**	**86 004**	**203 671**	**205 073**	**654 836**	**401 313**	**469 133**	**488 004**	**533 356**	**467 932**
Dons	35 000	33 500	94 628	106 540	282 200	253 518	266 126	246 158	274 912	193 269
Revenus de la propriété	1 356	4 204	5 555	76 308	285 955	68 211	135 029	145 071	135 074	98 988
Loyers et redevances	1 356	4 204	5 555	44 902	255 515	57 736	119 272	121 350	107 057	58 889
Revenus du domaine	0	0	0	283	2 111	2 972	2 152	2 160	3 578	4 104
Taxe d'exploitation pétrolière	0	0	0	27 275	30 851	23 555	27 595	36 888	44 522	28 012
Bonus de signature pétrolière	0	0	0	0	0	0	0	6 039	8 088	0
Taxes domaniales (hors taxe ad-valorem 2012-2020)	1 356	4 204	5 555	7 696	37 224	25 697	24 251	31 812	23 425	26 632
Autres loyers et redevances	0	0	0	9 647	185 329	5 512	65 273	44 451	27 444	142
Intérêts et dividendes	0	0	0	27 981	30 440	10 475	15 757	23 721	28 017	40 099
Autres revenus de la propriété	0	0	0	3 426	0	0	0	0	0	0
Ventes de biens et de services	0	0	13 200	21 700	35 414	43 920	27 870	47 111	57 937	76 599
Redevance Radiodiffusion Télévision Ivoirienne (RTI)	..	..	0	4 107	6 244	7 275	8 270	8 587	10 342	9 493
Taxe audiovisuelle	..	..	0	0	0	0	0	0	0	0
Péages routiers	..	..	0	0	0	0	0	0	0	16 461
Autres ventes de biens et de services	..	..	13 200	17 592	29 170	36 645	19 600	38 524	47 595	50 645
Amendes, pénalités et confiscations	0	0	0	173	0	0	0	0	0	0
Recettes diverses et non identifiées	17 800	48 300	90 288	353	51 267	35 664	40 108	49 664	65 433	99 076
Total des recettes fiscales et non fiscales	978 628	1 255 611	1 610 948	2 240 542	4 069 254	4 137 768	4 452 816	4 682 693	5 061 198	5 202 418

.. Non disponible

Note : Année civile se terminant le 31 décembre.

Les données sont sur la base des encaissements.

Les chiffres n'incluent pas les données des recettes non fiscales collectées par les collectivités locales car elles ne sont pas disponibles.

Les recettes des taxes domaniales, la taxe ad valorem et la taxe d'exploitation sont considérées comme des recettes non fiscales selon la classification OCDE (voir le *Guide d'interprétation* en Annexe B). La classification nationale de la Côte d'Ivoire les compte comme des recettes fiscales.

Les recettes des taxes domaniales sont hors taxe ad-valorem pour la période 2012 à 2016, période pour laquelle il a été possible de distinguer ces recettes.

La taxe audiovisuelle et la redevance radiodiffusion télévision ivoirienne (RTI) sont considérées comme des recettes non fiscales selon la classification OCDE (voir le *Guide d'interprétation* en Annexe B). La classification nationale de la Côte d'Ivoire les compte comme des recettes fiscales.

Les recettes diverses et non identifiées comprennent les transferts de capitaux non compris ailleurs et transferts volontaires autres que les dons.

Source : Ministère de l'Économie et des Finances.

StatLink https://stat.link/to0vgj

Table 6.13. **Egypt / Égypte**

Details of non-tax revenue / Recettes non fiscales détaillées

Million EGP

	1995	2000	2005	2010	2015	2016	2017	2018	2019	2020
Total non-tax revenue	**..**	**..**	**37 270**	**102 149**	**166 134**	**146 526**	**208 760**	**205 853**	**225 222**	**250 335**
Grants	..	..	2 114	3 830	25 243	3 405	17 394	1 914	1 848	1 806
Grants from foreign governments	..	..	2 114	3 497	24 942	3 236	17 040	1 006	1 100	1 007
Grants from international organisations	..	..	0	332	302	169	354	908	747	798
Property income	..	..	18 672	55 533	83 283	71 429	87 311	74 150	75 222	68 950
Rents and royalties	..	..	1 114	7 216	8 252	6 890	11 917	18 262	20 964	17 488
Royalties on petroleum	..	..	0	2 750	5 964	4 139	7 372	11 610	14 148	11 178
Royalties on Suez Canal	..	..	1 068	1 354	1 945	2 059	3 360	5 163	5 157	4 600
Mining royalties	..	..	17	46	230	506	939	1 205	1 208	1 420
Other royalties	..	..	30	3 066	113	187	246	284	451	291
Interest and dividends	..	..	17 233	48 315	74 894	64 264	75 244	55 616	53 812	50 952
Suez Canal Authority (SCA)	..	..	9 651	12 729	19 214	14 755	29 381	23 718	30 308	18 354
Central Bank of Egypt (CBE)	..	..	4 999	205	13 417	29 462	19 427	5 233	0	0
Economic authorities	..	..	402	1 431	10 093	7 820	10 989	8 297	10 817	12 045
Public and private companies and enterprises	..	..	245	3 272	3 295	3 433	5 230	6 867	5 408	8 631
Egyptian General Petroleum Corporation (EGPC)	..	..	154	25 546	25 414	7 820	5 944	8 144	1 278	2 093
Other dividends and interests	..	..	1 782	5 130	3 460	974	4 273	3 358	6 001	9 830
Other property income	..	..	324	2	137	276	150	272	447	509
Sales of goods and services	..	..	8 979	25 661	27 583	30 547	53 859	62 243	73 342	77 956
Administrative fees	..	..	1 505	2 681	4 482	4 453	7 559	10 437	12 520	10 463
Development fees	..	..	294	841	931	920	534	403	1 991	2 352
Service fees	..	..	3 170	3 572	8 352	9 160	11 533	15 343	17 147	15 757
Capital revenues	..	..	3 986	16 962	13 610	15 824	26 934	35 803	41 252	48 099
Licences	..	..	0	1 557	128	74	7 187	125	276	1 136
Other sales of goods and services	..	..	24	49	80	116	113	134	156	149
Fines, penalties and forfeits	..	..	343	653	1 193	1 823	2 748	1 732	2 379	2 871
Miscellaneous and unidentified revenue	..	..	7 163	16 472	28 831	39 322	47 448	65 814	72 431	98 753
Current revenues from special accounts and funds	..	..	4 842	12 268	17 797	19 627	26 223	35 732	36 128	42 787
Voluntary transfers other than grants	..	..	1 084	684	901	1 455	2 956	2 143	2 316	2 262
Current revenues	..	..	1 114	3 312	9 827	17 968	17 964	27 576	33 685	53 405
Other revenues	..	..	123	208	306	273	305	363	303	300
Total tax and non-tax revenue	..	..	126 128	295 578	525 080	540 311	737 992	870 942	989 339	1 026 808

.. Not available

Note: Fiscal year ends on 30 June. For example, the data for 2020 represent July 2019 to June 2020.

Data are reported on a cash basis.

Figures exclude non-tax revenues collected by sub-national governments as the data are not available.

Royalties on the Suez Canal as well as other royalties and administrative fees are reported as tax revenues in Egypt. In accordance with the OECD classification, as set out in the *Interpretative Guide* in Annex A, these revenues are considered non-tax revenues.

Source: Ministry of Finance.

StatLink https://stat.link/uzkdh5

Table 6.14. **Equatorial Guinea / Guinée équatoriale**

Details of non-tax revenue / Recettes non fiscales détaillées

Million XAF

	1995	2000	2005	2010	2015	2016	2017	2018	2019	2020
Total non-tax revenue	..	..	**1 051 820**	**1 515 259**	**1 169 328**	**685 668**	**794 644**	**991 642**	**619 121**	**360 207**
Grants	..	..	17 533	0	0	0	0	0	1 648	576
Property income	..	..	1 012 089	1 489 017	1 087 688	649 765	742 191	962 877	595 780	337 860
Rents and royalties	..	..	518 258	957 200	688 968	421 568	484 757	604 305	373 890	227 588
Petroleum royalties	..	..	462 289	951 507	680 217	415 597	478 744	590 596	355 668	211 397
Surface royalties	..	..	51 284	844	1 842	619	530	1 794	400	84
Fishing and concessional royalties	..	..	2 021	4 850	6 909	5 352	5 483	11 915	17 822	16 107
GEOGAM gas sales	..	..	2 664	0	0	0	0	0	0	0
Interest and dividends	..	..	491 560	437 662	380 575	206 307	244 266	328 453	206 847	97 177
Shareholder participation in oil revenues	..	..	476 917	257 392	237 800	103 899	99 609	134 422	108 655	63 718
Oil dividends	..	..	0	146 345	134 965	84 190	132 925	185 706	93 018	26 545
Non-oil dividends	..	..	1 622	17 314	7 538	17 339	11 522	7 794	1 454	3 762
Interest on reserve funds	..	..	12 554	6 977	43	45	12	498	3 561	2 997
Other interest (banking, deferrals)	..	..	467	9 635	52	43	8	1	0	0
INSESO: Interest and dividends	..	..	..	..	178	792	191	32	160	155
Other property income	..	..	2 271	94 155	18 145	21 889	13 168	30 119	15 043	13 094
Contributions of public companies and independent entitites	..	..	0	1 624	4 149	21 889	9 744	26 104	15 037	13 090
Other oil-related property income	..	..	2 271	92 531	13 997	0	3 424	4 015	6	5
Sales of goods and services	..	..	4 912	15 935	24 901	27 212	20 154	17 470	17 345	18 095
Administrative fees and government services	..	..	4 344	13 975	19 669	19 335	15 052	14 234	13 929	13 890
Consular fees	..	..	294	1 357	973	875	561	1 694	123	106
Tolls	..	..	184	458	2 714	509	0	383	2 249	2 356
Rentals of government buildings	..	..	90	145	132	191	69	139	42	10
INSESO: Medical goods and services	..	..	..	..	1 355	6 042	1 147	875	850	1 619
INSESO: Other goods and services	..	..	..	..	59	262	139	144	151	113
INSESO: Provincial medical fees	..	..	..	..	0	0	3 186	0	0	0
Fines, penalties and forfeits	..	..	0	0	258	199	462	451	319	85
INSESO: Sanctions, arrears and penalties	..	..	..	..	258	199	462	451	319	85
Miscellaneous and unidentified revenue	..	..	17 286	10 307	56 481	8 492	31 837	10 843	4 029	3 591
INSESO: Other revenues	..	..	0	0	0	0	256	256	4	0
Other revenues, excluding INSESO	..	..	17 286	10 307	56 481	8 492	31 581	10 587	4 025	3 591
Total tax and non-tax revenue	..	..	1 407 860	2 127 636	2 105 235	1 157 882	1 265 740	1 471 741	1 270 542	850 596

.. Not available

Note: Year ending 31st December.
Data are reported on a cash basis.

Source: Ministry of Finance, Economy and Planning; Instituto Nacional de Seguridad Social de Guinea Ecuatorial (INSESO).

StatLink https://stat.link/vbw5en

Table 6.15. **Eswatini**

Details of non-tax revenue / Recettes non fiscales détaillées

Million SZL

	1995	2000	2005	2010	2015	2016	2017	2018	2019	2020
Total non-tax revenue	**789**	**1 549**	**3 285**	**2 680**	**7 662**	**6 900**	**8 627**	**7 434**	**8 471**	**9 999**
Grants	1	3	7	12	121	166	248	137	170	249
Property income	26	95	67	553	494	1 196	1 038	1 069	1 784	1 200
Rents and royalties	0	0	0	3	72	75	81	81	143	83
Land concession rents, postal revenue	0	0	0	0	0	0	0	0	0	0
Rents attributed to social security funds	0	0	0	3	72	75	81	81	143	83
Interest and dividends	19	91	65	548	391	878	896	919	1 546	1 006
Local interest collected by central government	7	21	25	538	60	7	-30	28	16	20
Central bank profit	6	0	0	0	245	287	244	0	430	43
External interest and interest on capital	5	69	13	0	0	2	4	3	2	4
Dividends	1	1	27	8	11	115	115	106	207	108
Interest and dividends collected by social security funds	0	0	0	1	75	467	564	783	891	831
Other property income	7	4	1	1	31	244	62	69	95	110
Quitrents	0	0	0	0	0	0	0	0	0	0
Local government property income	7	4	1	1	31	244	62	69	95	110
Sales of goods and services	16	40	63	115	73	216	154	325	137	139
Sundry fees	7	13	40	38	6	144	64	246	39	67
Passports, citizenship and resident permits	3	5	5	25	25	29	35	33	40	22
Rental of government real estate	2	3	6	7	11	12	13	13	13	12
Driver's licences, motor vehicle certification	0	1	3	8	11	15	14	15	16	16
Hospital and medical services	0	5	4	6	6	7	7	8	8	6
Hire of government plants and vehicles	0	0	0	21	0	0	0	0	0	0
Aviation fees	1	12	1	0	0	0	0	0	0	0
Sale of government furniture and vehicles	0	0	0	6	7	1	10	2	2	5
Sale of agricultural products and services	1	2	1	1	2	3	3	3	3	3
Public service transport fees	1	0	1	1	1	1	1	1	1	1
Sale of government publications	0	0	0	1	1	2	1	1	1	2
Prison industry sales	0	0	0	0	0	0	0	0	0	0
Local government sales of goods and services	0	0	1	1	2	3	5	5	14	8
Fines, penalties and forfeits	2	4	11	28	33	42	43	46	49	46
Traffic fines	1	2	5	15	13	14	15	15	16	21
Judicial fines and other penalties	0	1	4	10	18	22	24	24	25	19
Interest and penalties on late tax payments	0	0	1	1	2	5	5	4	5	6
PAYE penalties[1]	0	1	1	1	0	0	0	0	0	0
Fines, penalties and forfeits (local non-tax revenue)	0	0	0	0	0	0	0	3	2	0
Miscellaneous and unidentified revenue	744	1 407	3 138	1 972	6 942	5 280	7 143	5 856	6 332	8 365
SACU revenue	744	1 406	3 136	1 969	6 931	5 252	7 109	5 844	6 318	8 349
SACU penalties	0	0	1	2	9	12	18	9	7	10
Miscellaneous and unidentified revenue (local non-tax revenue)	0	0	0	2	3	16	16	3	7	6
Total tax and non-tax revenue	1 534	2 876	5 691	7 267	15 569	16 040	18 727	18 325	20 364	21 916

Note: Data are reported on a fiscal year basis beginning 1st April. For example, the data for 2020 represent April 2020 to March 2021.

Data are reported on a cash basis.

Revenues from motor vehicle licences, the change of ownership fees and the registration of new motor vehicles are considered as tax revenue under the OECD classification as set out in the *OECD Interpretative Guide* in Annex A and are classified under heading 5211 (Recurrent taxes paid by households: motor vehicles). The national classification of Eswatini classifies these revenues as non-tax revenues.

Revenues from business and sundry licences are considered as tax revenue under the OECD classification, as set out in the *OECD Interpretative Guide* in Annex A and are classified under heading 5211 (Recurrent taxes paid on use of goods and perform activities other than on motor vehicles). The national classification of Eswatini classifies these revenues as non-tax revenues.

Revenues from the registrations of specific goods (e.g. firearms) are considered as tax revenue under the OECD classification, as set out in the *OECD Interpretative Guide* in Annex A and are classified under heading 5220 (Non-recurrent taxes on use of goods and perform activities). The national classification of Eswatini classifies these revenues as non-tax revenues.

Revenues from the education loans' repayments do not represent an increase of net worth resulting from a transaction and therefore are not considered as revenues under the OECD classification, as set out in the *OECD Interpretative Guide* in Annex B.

Grants data are not available up to 2011.

Revenue from PAYE Penalties, tax interests and penalties on taxes are considered as non-tax revenue under the OECD classification, as set out in the *OECD Interpretative Guide* in Annex A. The national classification of Eswatini classifies it as tax revenues.

1. Revenue from PAYE Penalties, tax interests and penalties on taxes are considered as non-tax revenue under the OECD classification, as set out in the *OECD Interpretative Guide* in Annex A. The national classification of Eswatini classifies it as tax revenues.

Source: Eswatini Revenue Authority; Local Government; Eswatini National Provident Fund and Public Service Pension Fund; Ministry of Economic Planning and Development; Central Government.

StatLink https://stat.link/n651b9

Table 6.16. **Ghana**

Details of non-tax revenue / Recettes non fiscales détaillées

Million GHS

	1995	2000	2005	2010	2015	2016	2017	2018	2019	2020
Total non-tax revenue	**..**	**97**	**661**	**2 306**	**8 978**	**7 233**	**9 027**	**10 071**	**11 272**	**10 922**
Grants	..	57	535	1 080	2 689	1 141	1 535	1 135	986	1 229
Project grants	..	24	284	591	1 744	1 034	1 535	1 121	986	1 229
Programme grants	..	34	135	288	945	106	0	14	0	0
International debt relief	..	0	116	201	0	0	0	0	0	0
Property income	..	7	18	347	3 003	2 228	3 669	5 075	5 517	4 916
Rents and royalties	..	0	0	0	908	757	1 346	1 969	2 328	2 476
Mineral royalties (aside from oil)	..	..	..	..	518	578	749	744	1 057	1 376
Oil revenues	..	..	..	..	384	176	589	1 213	1 252	1 092
Lodgements to MDAs and MMDAs: surface rentals from oil/PHF interest	..	..	..	..	6	3	8	12	19	7
Lodgements to MDAs and MMDAs: fees from granting of new stability agreements	..	..	..	..	0	0	0	0	0	0
Revenue from oil companies (includes corporate tax)	..	..	..	..	0	0	0	0	0	0
Interest and dividends	..	7	18	347	2 095	1 471	2 322	3 106	3 189	2 441
Lodgements to MDAs and MMDAs: dividend, interest and profits from oil companies	..	0	0	0	995	491	1 586	2 531	2 691	1 696
Lodgements to MDAs and MMDAs: dividend, interest and profits aside from oil companies	..	7	18	347	726	556	331	139	106	275
SSNIT revenue - Investment income	..	0	0	0	375	425	406	436	392	469
Other property income	..	0	0	0	0	0	0	0	0	0
Sales of goods and services	..	32	108	879	3 195	3 833	3 401	3 719	4 576	4 568
Retentions by MDAs and MMDAs	..	23	78	685	2 531	3 368	2 849	3 165	3 953	4 003
Lodgements to MDAs and MMDAs: fees and charges	..	10	30	194	663	466	553	555	623	565
Lodgements to MDAs and MMDAs: gas receipts	..	0	0	0	2	0	0	0	0	0
Fines, penalties and forfeits	..	0	0	0	0	0	0	0	0	0
Miscellaneous and unidentified revenue	..	0	0	0	91	31	422	142	194	209
Yield from budget capping policy	..	..	..	..	0	0	0	101	115	120
SSNIT revenue - Miscellaneous income	..	..	..	..	91	31	422	41	79	89
Total tax and non-tax revenue	..	584	3 004	9 001	32 570	35 984	44 369	52 256	58 311	62 390

.. Not available

Note: Year ending 31st December.

Data are reported on a cash basis.

Figures exclude non-tax revenues collected by sub-national governments as the data are not available.

Revenues for MDAs (Municipalities, Departments and Agencies) and MMDAs (Metropolitan, Municipal and District Assemblies) contain a mixture of revenues collected at the local level, and revenues collected at a federal level. These are reported as revenues to the central government.

Yield from budget capping policy has been added to the classification in this edition. The Earmarked Funds and Capping Realignment Bill was passed into law in 2017.

Source: Ghana Statistical Service.

StatLink https://stat.link/p59don

Table 6.17. **Kenya**

Details of non-tax revenue / Recettes non fiscales détaillées

Million KES

	1995	2000	2005	2010	2015	2016	2017	2018	2019	2020
Total non-tax revenue	..	..	**32 767**	**40 293**	**96 279**	**111 693**	**141 806**	**135 970**	**140 596**	**256 791**
Grants	..	..	14 905	20 710	12 020	29 597	26 962	26 484	19 692	19 820
Grants from foreign governments	..	..	14 905	9 215	2 644	3 228	2 345	2 696	2 289	4 151
Grants from International orgs	..	..	0	11 495	9 376	26 369	24 617	23 788	17 402	15 669
Property income	..	..	5 255	9 921	16 216	22 309	34 049	43 670	49 280	165 386
Rents and royalties	..	..	727	1 184	695	743	665	1 606	1 576	1 398
Rent of land	..	..	674	1 108	8	25	38	753	610	472
Kenya Airports Authority (KAA) concession fees	..	..	53	77	113	114	127	131	134	120
Base titanium royalty	..	..	0	0	338	356	295	491	520	509
Mining royalties	..	..	0	0	136	143	118	95	117	193
Royalties from soda ash	..	..	0	0	100	105	87	135	195	105
Interest and dividends	..	..	2 027	8 736	10 781	18 225	28 053	34 137	39 704	93 887
Profits and dividends	..	..	1 185	8 354	9 002	15 919	26 022	32 023	37 526	92 090
Interests	..	..	843	382	1 779	2 306	2 032	2 114	2 178	1 797
Other property income	..	..	2 500	0	4 740	3 341	5 330	7 927	8 000	70 101
Surplus funds from regulatory authority	..	..	2 500	0	4 740	3 341	5 330	7 927	8 000	70 101
Sales of goods and services	..	..	1 548	2 302	45 303	47 042	46 601	48 585	55 518	54 472
Work permits	..	..	0	0	4 098	5 226	5 363	2	8 333	3 694
Road transit toll	..	..	293	457	562	674	737	766	840	912
Immigration visas and other consular fees	..	..	0	0	2 822	3 063	3 144	8 980	5 083	6 058
Fees under traffic act	..	..	304	1 188	0	0	0	1 326	1 647	1 574
Land administration fees	..	..	55	0	1 826	586	915	722	959	1 095
Motor driver's licences	..	..	376	656	0	0	1 270	0	0	0
Passport fees	..	..	0	0	570	845	867	1 116	2 461	1 333
Rent of government buildings and housing	..	..	520	0	135	213	332	157	260	0
Other fees for administrative services	..	..	0	0	556	542	556	1 756	2 436	2 139
Hire of security service fees	..	..	0	0	372	321	330	854	566	893
Registration of organisations, professionals and agreements	..	..	0	0	296	360	369	36	121	864
Registration of births, deaths and marriages	..	..	0	0	214	193	198	370	313	211
Other non-tax revenue collected by local government	..	..	..	..	33 850	35 020	32 520	32 500	32 500	35 700
Fines, penalties and forfeits	..	..	200	229	1 459	1 470	1 098	1 124	1 567	1 283
Miscellaneous and unidentified revenue	..	..	10 859	7 131	21 281	11 275	33 097	16 108	14 539	15 830
Contribution from government employees to social and welfare schemes within government	..	..	558	341	871	462	390	203	213	193
National Social Security Fund	..	..	4 097	6 790	9 210	9 486	9 491	9 988	14 036	14 771
Other Miscellaneous	..	..	6 204	0	11 200	1 327	23 216	5 917	290	866
Total tax and non-tax revenue	..	..	309 968	580 456	1 181 498	1 343 464	1 541 463	1 618 568	1 748 041	1 868 392

.. Not available

Note: Data are reported on a fiscal year basis beginning 1st July. For example, the data for 2020 represent July 2019 to June 2020.

Data are reported on a cash basis.

Detailed non-tax revenue data are not readily available for 2001, 2002, 2003, 2004, 2006, 2011 and 2012. Figures exclude non-tax revenues collected by sub-national governments as the data are not available.

The national classification of Kenya classifies revenues from the airport revenue, aviation revenue, petroleum development levy, FMV, road maintenance levy, sugar levy, petroleum regulatory levy, merchant superintendent shipping levy, railway development levy, revenue Stamps, KEBS and land rates as non-tax revenues. They are considered in this publication as tax revenues under the OECD classification, as set out in the *OECD Interpretative Guide* in Annex A.

Source: Kenya Revenue Authority Statistical Service.

StatLink https://stat.link/t71jsq

Table 6.18. **Lesotho**

Details of non-tax revenue / Recettes non fiscales détaillées

Million LSL

	1995	2000	2005	2010	2015	2016	2017	2018	2019	2020
Total non-tax revenue	..	..	**2 975**	**5 668**	**8 978**	**7 458**	**8 787**	**8 691**	**8 929**	**11 850**
Grants	..	..	222	1 306	966	1 229	1 005	1 373	1 256	1 049
Property income	..	..	270	1 583	1 394	1 449	1 457	1 613	1 330	1 677
Rents and royalties	..	..	270	897	993	1 088	1 244	1 294	1 154	1 559
Water royalties	..	..	236	432	740	837	941	937	793	1 074
Mining and other royalties	..	..	34	465	252	251	304	357	361	485
Interest and dividends	..	..	0	686	401	362	213	319	176	118
Mining dividends	..	..	..	126	254	140	64	319	16	118
Non-mining dividends	..	..	..	560	147	222	149	0	160	0
Other property income	..	..	0	0	0	0	0	0	0	0
Sales of goods and services	..	..	170	149	216	256	169	166	115	143
Fines, penalties and forfeits	..	..	7	2	4	4	3	0	1	1
Fines for traffic offences	..	..	7	2	4	4	3	0	1	1
Miscellaneous and unidentified revenue	..	..	2 306	2 628	6 398	4 519	6 154	5 538	6 226	8 981
SACU revenue	..	..	2 306	2 628	6 398	4 519	6 154	5 538	6 226	8 981
Total tax and non-tax revenue	..	..	4 437	8 601	14 850	13 453	14 882	15 980	16 177	18 621
Total non-tax revenue excluding grants	..	..	2 753	4 362	8 012	6 229	7 783	7 317	7 673	10 801

.. Not available

Note: Data are on a fiscal year basis beginning 1st April. For example, the data for 2020 represent April 2020 to March 2021.

Data are reported on a cash basis.

Source: Revenue Services Lesotho for all revenues except for transfers from the SACU Common Revenue Pool. Lesotho Ministry of Finance budget reports for SACU revenues.

StatLink https://stat.link/14jzh0

Table 6.19. **Madagascar**

Details of non-tax revenue / Recettes non fiscales détaillées

Million MGA

	1995	2000	2005	2010	2015	2016	2017	2018	2019	2020
Total des recettes non fiscales	**0**	**172 677**	**630 632**	**619 717**	**504 711**	**726 921**	**929 098**	**1 340 511**	**1 385 109**	**1 697 961**
Dons	0	153 554	547 855	351 388	423 925	611 340	806 948	1 207 985	1 240 807	1 518 154
Dons - programmes des gouvernements étrangers	..	0	49 571	0	39 869	226 095	292 600	410 118	356 627	433 406
Dons - projets des institutions internationales	..	153 554	438 520	336 704	384 056	385 245	514 348	797 867	884 180	1 084 747
Ressources PPTE	..	0	59 764	14 684	0	0	0	0	0	0
Revenus de la propriété	0	17 649	26 100	266 340	59 980	94 467	107 633	109 916	119 659	134 090
Loyers et redevances	..	5 649	17 092	241 311	14 064	12 024	8 634	14 663	12 931	30 651
Intérêts et dividendes	..	12 000	9 008	25 029	45 916	82 443	98 999	95 253	106 728	103 439
Autres revenus de la propriété	..	0	0	0	0	0	0	0	0	0
Ventes de biens et de services	0	1 474	5 204	1 989	5 225	20 389	4 886	3 778	4 757	15 032
Amendes, pénalités and confiscations	0	0	0	0	0	0	0	0	0	0
Recettes diverses et non identifiées	0	0	51 473	0	15 581	725	9 631	18 832	19 886	30 685
Total des recettes fiscales et non fiscales	219 280	775 877	1 674 190	2 600 566	3 646 406	4 498 866	5 402 966	6 617 859	7 247 670	6 900 804

.. Non disponible

Note : Année civile se terminant le 31 décembre.

Les données sont sur la base des encaissements.

Les chiffres n'incluent pas les recettes non fiscales collectées par les collectivités locales car elles ne sont pas disponibles.

Source : Ministère de l'Économie et des Finances de Madagascar.

StatLink https://stat.link/sylvwg

Table 6.20. **Malawi**

Details of non-tax revenue / Recettes non fiscales détaillées

Million MWK

	1995	2000	2005	2010	2015	2016	2017	2018	2019	2020
Total non-tax revenue	**..**	**..**	**29 851**	**105 601**	**124 112**	**159 138**	**202 474**	**126 362**	**145 819**	**183 231**
Grants	..	..	24 227	78 448	79 392	131 007	147 706	70 155	109 255	114 705
Grants from foreign governments - Current	..	..	6 885	18 782	20 769	12 323	8 962	0	0	..
Grants from foreign governments - Capital	..	..	4 039	25 844	47 519	49 542	73 505	44 300	0	..
Grants from international orgs - Current	..	..	8 097	33 822	10 711	67 302	65 239	25 855	30 705	..
Grants from international orgs - Capital	..	..	5 206	0	393	1 840	0	0	78 551	..
Property income	..	..	760	3 466	32 815	13 653	22 837	20 083	7 555	25 470
Rents and royalties	..	..	0	0	0	0	0	0	0	0
Interest and dividends	..	..	760	3 466	32 815	13 653	22 837	20 083	7 555	25 470
Parastatal dividends	..	..	760	3 466	32 815	13 653	22 837	20 083	7 555	25 470
Other property income	..	..	0	0	0	0	0	0	0	0
Sales of goods and services	..	..	3 108	13 724	11 397	14 478	20 607	34 639	27 064	39 965
Fertiliser sales revenue	..	..	0	736	0	0	0	0	0	0
Receipts from fertiliser option	..	..	0	0	0	0	0	0	0	0
Maize sales	..	..	468	0	0	0	0	0	0	0
Departmental receipts	..	..	2 640	12 988	11 397	14 478	20 607	34 639	27 064	39 965
Fines, penalties and forfeits	..	..	15	205	509	0	0	1 485	1 945	3 091
Penalties	..	..	15	205	509	..	..	1 485	1 945	3 091
Miscellaneous and unidentified revenue	..	..	1 742	9 758	0	0	11 325	0	0	0
Other current transfers not elsewhere classified	..	..	1 742	9 758	..	..	11 325	..	..	..
Total tax and non-tax revenue	..	..	81 034	258 346	609 438	763 359	998 258	1 007 257	1 132 530	1 227 747

.. Not available

Note: Data are on a fiscal year basis beginning 1st July. For example, the data for 2020 represent July 2019 to June 2020.

Data are reported on a cash basis.

Figures exclude revenues from business licenses and permits collected by city and district councils from business entities within their jurisdictions.

Source: Ministry of Finance, Economic Planning and Development of Malawi.

StatLink https://stat.link/tn59um

Table 6.21. **Mali**

Details of non-tax revenue / Recettes non fiscales détaillées

Million XOF

	1995	2000	2005	2010	2015	2016	2017	2018	2019	2020
Total des recettes non fiscales	**97 332**	**122 795**	**173 446**	**256 632**	**197 471**	**175 908**	**311 733**	**224 545**	**315 381**	**233 488**
Dons	86 170	102 481	138 317	190 540	112 124	98 310	159 914	136 049	208 841	133 452
Dons - gouvernements étrangers	0	0	0	22 263	20 665	8 639	14 208	6 129	8 056	6 563
Dons - institutions internationales	86 170	102 481	115 684	160 368	79 066	71 942	127 477	110 927	183 184	100 243
Ressources PPTE	0	0	22 633	7 909	12 393	17 729	18 229	18 993	17 601	26 646
Ressources exceptionnelles: reconversion dette monétaire fonds de concours	0	0	0	0	0	0	0	0	0	0
Revenus de la propriété	1 753	9 669	12 421	34 564	46 966	33 747	115 029	48 426	60 765	63 927
Loyers et redevances	1 168	358	507	650	1 735	750	81 041	21 023	15 877	1 665
Concessions ordinaires	143	336	257	262	1 315	276	80 510	20 425	15 049	1 092
Redevances superficiaires	7	22	241	388	262	240	421	371	465	353
Taxe d'extraction	1 018	0	9	0	158	234	110	107	364	219
Autres loyers et redevances - extrabudgétaires	0	0	0	0	0	0	0	121	..	..
Intérêts et dividendes	585	9 311	11 914	32 873	44 810	32 544	33 252	25 157	43 745	61 204
Revenus des valeurs mobilières, des titres et des dividendes	585	9 296	11 908	30 500	41 261	29 761	8 059	7 201	24 624	23 297
Autres intérêts et dividendes (budget d'état)	0	15	6	0	0	0	21 563	15 726	17 093	35 052
Interêts des comptes bancaires (INPS)	0	0	0	2 373	3 549	2 783	3 630	2 230	2 029	2 855
Autres revenus de la propriété	0	0	0	1 041	420	453	736	2 246	1 142	1 059
Autres revenus de la propriété (CMSS)	..	..	..	0	140	142	87	47	101	73
Autres revenus de la propriété (INPS)	..	..	..	1 041	281	311	649	2 199	1 041	986
Ventes de biens et de services	4 027	3 924	7 488	13 208	22 849	23 991	19 947	21 868	22 642	18 621
Prestations, évacuations, importations, exportations - extrabudgétaires	0	0	0	0	0	0	0	3 351	0	0
Droits de chancellerie	834	886	1 949	2 152	4 310	3 033	3 914	4 255	9 033	4 793
Passeports et cartes d'identités	288	473	1 466	2 609	2 680	1 494	1 352	3 251	5 345	2 836
Recettes sur rôles (Trésor - BN)	1 503	981	154	91	0	0	0	0	0	0
Frais d'administration, voitures	440	497	591	813	1 200	1 342	1 355	1 137	1 163	621
Ventes en douanes	5	15	24	117	26	66	18	19	87	20
Location des immeubles de l'état	27	393	36	0	0	29	0	0	0	0
Autres ventes de biens et de services (budget d'état)	930	679	197	6 460	12 598	14 571	8 206	6 584	2 917	2 004
Recettes de la Caisse Malienne de Sécurité Sociale (CMSS) - hors cotisations	0	0	403	699	995	1 672	1 146	779	1 225	1 629
Recettes de l'Institut National de Prévoyance Sociale (INPS) - hors cotisations	0	0	2 668	267	1 040	1 784	3 956	1 436	2 872	6 717
Location des immeubles de l'état - extrabudgétaires	..	..	0	0	0	0	0	517	0	0
Autres ventes de biens et de services - extrabudgétaires	..	..	0	0	0	0	0	540	0	0
Amendes, pénalités et confiscations	2 159	2 786	4 656	8 010	12 764	15 196	7 289	8 753	16 288	12 709
Pénalités sur impots directs	160	352	1 154	3 939	4 753	7 580	3 529	2 983	4 481	3 473
Pénalités sur impôts indirects	1 130	1 528	2 602	1 418	3 101	3 794	1 247	1 800	5 197	4 024
Amendes et confiscations	717	710	592	1 268	2 738	2 357	1 301	1 487	2 007	2 156
Transactions forestières, pêche et chasse	18	98	45	153	0	0	0	0	0	0
Frais et amendes judiciaires	134	98	243	249	397	386	302	296	0	210
Autres pénalités (budget d'état)	0	0	20	77	624	69	51	50	96	97
Pénalités et frais contentieux (INPS)	0	0	0	906	1 151	1 010	859	2 137	4 507	2 747
Recettes diverses et non identifiées	3 223	3 935	10 564	10 309	2 769	4 665	9 554	9 448	6 846	4 779
Compensations des moins values de recettes	0	0	5 260	0	0	0	0	0	0	0
Amendes arbitrées	117	268	41	66	41	80	94	60	89	62
Autres recettes diverses	3 106	3 667	5 263	10 243	2 728	4 585	9 460	8 099	6 756	4 717
Autres recettes diverses - extrabudgétaires	..	..	..	..	..	..	..	1 289	..	..
Total des recettes fiscales et non fiscales	221 535	362 157	650 221	1 004 877	1 372 331	1 547 057	1 803 523	1 488 463	2 086 370	2 053 836

.. Non disponible

Note : Année civile se terminant le 31 décembre.

Les données sont sur la base des encaissements.

Les chiffres n'incluent pas les recettes non fiscales collectées par les collectivités locales car elles ne sont pas disponibles.

Certains chiffres sur les recettes non fiscales du Mali ne sont pas disponibles pour 2019 et 2020. Cela affecte les statistiques sur les concessions ordinaires, certaines recettes des ventes de biens et services, et certaines autres recettes non budgétaires.

Source : Ministère de l'Économie et des Finances et la Direction Nationale du Trésor et de la Comptabilité Publique du Mali.

StatLink https://stat.link/pzgjko

Table 6.22. **Mauritania / Mauritanie**

Details of non-tax revenue / Recettes non fiscales détaillées

Million MRU

	1995	2000	2005	2010	2015	2016	2017	2018	2019	2020
Total des recettes non fiscales	**..**	**..**	**..**	**9 833**	**12 868**	**10 914**	**11 469**	**18 008**	**15 862**	**20 145**
Dons	..	..	..	830	1 988	1 600	1 096	201	2 211	6 159
Dons courants états étrangers	..	..	..	0	1 988	1 600	1 096	0	0	..
Dons courants organismes	..	..	..	830	0	0	0	201	2 211	..
Revenus de la propriété	..	..	..	8 172	9 551	7 936	9 343	15 148	11 783	11 952
Loyers et redevances	..	..	..	6 843	8 112	6 900	8 180	13 840	10 612	10 242
Accords de pêche	..	..	..	3 945	4 068	4 966	5 048	5 859	6 665	6 971
Droits d'accès pêche	..	..	..	208	318	850	1 524	1 643	869	364
Licences télécom et sanctions	..	..	..	3	1 906	451	464	452	347	993
Mine : permis d'exploitation et de recherche	..	..	..	1 562	635	613	620	615	902	1 389
Pétrole : bonus de signature	..	..	..	73	0	0	460	5 141	1 637	0
Pétrole : redevances et autres	..	..	..	1 035	1 150	11	24	85	123	514
Redevances et concessions domaniales	..	..	..	16	35	10	39	45	69	11
Intérêts et dividendes	..	..	..	1 329	1 439	1 035	1 161	1 308	1 171	1 710
Autres revenus de la propriété	..	..	..	0	0	0	3	0	0	0
Ventes de biens et de services	..	..	..	127	486	468	447	508	458	393
Visas	..	..	..	0	150	231	162	179	178	92
Passeports	..	..	..	0	102	86	149	167	93	67
Cartes grises et permis de conduire	..	..	..	0	54	34	24	40	59	51
Frais administratifs	..	..	..	106	181	118	92	98	106	100
Frais universités, instituts et centres nationaux	..	..	..	21	0	0	20	24	21	84
Amendes, pénalités et confiscations	..	..	..	206	393	458	366	519	476	705
Amendes de pêche	..	..	..	75	57	57	130	80	139	160
Autres amendes	..	..	..	131	336	401	236	439	336	544
Recettes diverses et non identifiées	..	..	..	498	450	453	218	1 632	934	937
Total des recettes fiscales et non fiscales	..	..	..	25 015	41 961	42 871	46 622	58 374	55 795	58 746

.. Non disponible

Note : Année civile se terminant le 31 décembre.

Les données sont sur la base des encaissements.

Les chiffres n'incluent pas les recettes des droits de conservation foncière. Elles sont incluses dans les recettes fiscales comme le préconise la classification OCDE (voir le *guide d'interprétation* en Annexe A) mais considérées comme des recettes non fiscales en Mauritanie.

Les données des dons pour 2020 sont issues de la base de données de la publication PEM 2022 (*Perspectives de l'économie mondiale*, avril 2022) par le FMI.

Source : Ministère des Finances de la Mauritanie.

StatLink https://stat.link/di4xyk

Table 6.23. **Mauritius / Maurice**

Details of non-tax revenue / Recettes non fiscales détaillées

Million MUR

	1995	2000	2005	2010	2015	2016	2017	2018	2019	2020
Total non-tax revenue	**2 467**	**3 293**	**4 590**	**11 458**	**11 320**	**13 644**	**16 627**	**20 279**	**14 070**	**15 348**
Grants	262	161	444	1 991	1 202	345	2 920	2 635	1 998	4 386
Grants from foreign governments	..	..	..	2	183	122	1 915	2 248	1 580	4 140
Grants from international organizations	..	..	..	1 989	1 019	223	1 005	387	418	246
Property income	1 671	2 370	2 395	5 020	3 604	5 048	4 583	5 060	4 151	5 655
Rents and royalties	..	..	..	1 284	752	961	960	1 171	1 192	982
Interest and dividends	..	..	..	979	873	679	534	1 051	430	784
Interest	..	..	..	392	382	360	236	271	244	232
Dividends	..	..	..	587	492	319	298	780	186	552
Other property income	1 671	2 370	2 395	2 756	1 979	3 408	3 089	2 838	2 529	3 889
Other property income - Budgetary	1 196	1 692	1 235	1 549	1 392	2 289	1 810	1 039	1 138	2 152
Other property income - Extra-budgetary	26	58	136	349	33	22	63	235	235	414
Other property income - Social security funds	424	544	973	777	529	1 058	1 169	1 531	1 103	1 278
Other property income - Regional government	0	0	6	11	5	5	13	12	19	13
Other property income - Local government	25	76	45	71	20	34	34	20	34	32
Sales of goods and services	442	626	1 385	2 028	3 633	3 800	3 889	4 056	4 358	3 913
Work/occupational permits	0	0	47	95	194	203	205	266	277	221
Extra-budgetary fees, charges, and non-industrial sales	140	177	397	543	1 219	1 054	1 180	1 671	1 362	1 405
Fees, charges, and non-industrial sales by social security funds	17	20	40	51	78	156	159	0	271	106
Regional government sales of goods and services	0	0	6	5	4	4	9	11	7	13
Local government sales of goods and services	22	60	96	113	353	713	678	445	619	553
Other sales of goods and services	264	370	799	1 222	1 786	1 669	1 658	1 663	1 821	1 615
Fines, penalties and forfeits	27	65	152	272	292	247	305	284	359	320
Budgetary fines, penalties and forfeits	27	65	151	269	290	244	251	238	339	302
Extra-budgetary fines, penalties and forfeits	0	0	0	0	0	0	49	34	0	0
Regional government fines, penalties and forfeits	0	0	1	3	2	2	5	5	5	5
Local government fines, penalties and forfeits	0	0	0	0	0	0	0	8	15	13
Miscellaneous and unidentified revenue	65	70	214	2 147	2 588	4 205	4 931	8 244	3 204	1 074
Budgetary miscellaneous and unidentified revenue	26	10	13	1 803	157	167	250	242	229	156
Extra-budgetary miscellaneous and unidentified revenue	36	44	185	293	1 092	1 771	4 460	3 085	1 209	524
Miscellaneous and unidentified revenue for social security funds	0	4	0	3	0	0	0	0	0	0
Regional government miscellaneous and unidentified revenue	0	0	0	1	0	1	52	1	0	4
Local government miscellaneous and unidentified revenue	4	13	16	47	0	0	0	3	11	18
Transfers from special funds	0	0	0	0	1 339	2 266	171	4 914	1 755	372
Total tax and non-tax revenue	14 729	25 439	39 417	69 862	90 544	95 983	105 211	116 031	117 456	112 623

.. Not available

Note: Data are on a fiscal year basis beginning 1st July for years prior to 2010 (for example the data for 2009 represent July 2008 to June 2009) and are on a calendar year basis from 2010-15. Mauritius went back to a July-June fiscal year in 2015. Figures for 2016 correspond to the July-June 2015/16 fiscal year, while figures for 2015 correspond to the January-December calendar year. The calendar year 2015 is not used in national budget reporting by Mauritius, which means that official figures are not available for all revenue categories for this period.

Where data was missing for 2015, quarterly revenue figures at the aggregate level were used along with fiscal year revenue data to produce estimates.

Data are reported on a cash basis.

Figures taken from the Digest of Public Finance Statistics were adjusted in order to ensure that the sum of the revenues for different levels of governments would be equal to consolidated total revenues reported for the general government of Mauritius.

For the years 1989/90-2005/06, budgetary rents and royalties, interest and dividends are all reported under the heading "Other property income - Budgetary". For the years 2006/07 onwards, budgetary rents and royalties, interest and dividends are reported under separate headings.

Grants revenue is slightly different in this edition than in the previous edition for the years from 2017/18 onwards since the data now reflect consolidated general government revenues rather than consolidated central government revenues.

Sales of goods and services corresponds to the category "122 Fees, charges and non-industrial sales" in the Digest of Public Sector Statistics for the years up to 2006/07. For subsequent years, this excludes a number of sub-categories, such as licence fees, and work permits which are classified under other revenue categories.

Revenues reported as "Transfers from special funds" in fact represent funds raised from various sources, including tax revenues, non-tax revenues, and inter-governmental transfers which are not properly classified as revenues. Special Funds are special purpose vehicles set up by way of legislation for a specific purpose, i.e., to finance a dedicated programme or projects. Funds are transferred to the Fund from the Consolidated Fund through an appropriate expenditure item in the budget. Such Funds also generate their own revenue in terms of, for example, a levy imposed on petroleum products or contributions from international institutions and friendly countries. As such, once the dedicated programme or projects are completed, the available balance in the Special Funds are transferred to the Consolidated Fund and reported as revenues in budget documents for Mauritius.

Source: Mauritius Revenue Authority for the central government budgetary tax data from 2007 to 2014. Statistics Mauritius for extra-budgetary, local government, regional government and social security revenues from 1990 to 2020, as well as for budgetary central government tax revenues up to 2006; Ministry of Finance budget estimates for detailed revenue figures for the periods July 2005-June 2008, for 2016-20, and for the figures used to estimate calendar year 2015 revenues.

StatLink https://stat.link/elqvwm

Table 6.24. **Morocco / Maroc**

Details of non-tax revenue / Recettes non fiscales détaillées

Million MAD

	1995	2000	2005	2010	2015	2016	2017	2018	2019	2020
Total des recettes non fiscales	..	**9 278**	**16 745**	**27 970**	**38 673**	**35 225**	**36 921**	**40 466**	**49 088**	**37 043**
Dons	..	2	1 163	199	0	0	0	0	0	276
Revenus de la propriété	..	3 125	4 878	9 786	8 934	9 425	8 604	9 836	10 401	8 687
Loyers et redevances	..	1 507	2 892	3 868	5 192	4 237	4 583	4 738	4 865	2 901
Redevance gazoduc	..	298	1 369	1 442	1 765	999	1 016	1 538	1 011	455
Redevances et contributions pour licence de pêche en haute mer	..	94	38	329	520	593	739	235	773	93
Redevances pour l'occupation du domaine public	..	132	214	331	281	195	257	273	260	98
Autres redevances	..	7	8	63	6	10	8	6	10	4
Loyers et redevances reçues par les collectivités locales	..	977	1 262	1 703	2 620	2 440	2 563	2 686	2 809	2 251
Intérêts et dividendes	..	1 618	1 986	5 918	3 742	5 188	4 021	5 098	5 537	5 786
Dividendes des monopoles	..	1 008	1 540	5 584	3 236	4 675	3 526	4 650	5 197	5 354
Intérêts sur placements et avances	..	419	198	96	195	199	174	119	4	7
Interêts et dividendes reçus par collectivités locales	..	191	248	239	311	315	322	329	336	425
Autres revenus de la propriété	..	0	0	0	0	0	0	0	0	0
Ventes de biens et de services	..	4 573	7 315	10 286	16 009	14 746	16 890	17 990	20 791	13 182
Cartes d'identités, passeports et documents divers	..	453	511	567	498	718	759	950	1 111	746
Produits de certains établissements publics	..	1 544	3 038	2 990	5 462	3 149	4 432	4 425	7 487	4 194
Revenus des immeubles domaniaux (loyers, charges locatives, etc.)	..	137	172	250	265	312	302	335	327	275
Autres produits et divers	..	175	824	646	965	791	1 199	1 661	825	777
Ventes de biens et de services par collectivités locales	..	2 265	2 770	5 832	8 819	9 777	10 198	10 619	11 040	7 190
Amendes, pénalités et confiscations	..	398	851	2 802	2 994	3 179	2 973	3 963	5 872	1 496
Amendes et condamnations pécuniaires	..	17	42	21	61	68	63	66	63	45
Amendes transactionnelles	..	36	90	130	706	593	471	481	425	124
Autres (produits des confiscations, pénalités et amendes autres que fiscales)	..	6	9	1	0	0	0	0	0	0
Majorations et pénalités	..	339	709	2 650	2 226	2 518	2 439	3 416	5 385	1 328
Recettes diverses et non identifiées	..	1 180	2 539	4 897	10 736	7 875	8 454	8 678	12 024	13 402
Fonds de concours	..	147	968	3 597	3 453	2 187	2 250	1 944	1 973	6 922
Recettes en atténuation des dépenses de la dette	..	801	879	480	4 386	1 894	691	963	3 164	1 526
Reversements sur traitements et salaires	..	55	157	99	62	60	1 300	957	919	829
Créances sur le trésor prescrites	..	30	224	39	97	163	260	305	866	67
Autres (divers remboursement à l'État)	..	7	29	6	254	254	46	11	12	11
Recettes diverses et non identifiées des collectivités locales	..	139	281	677	2 484	3 316	3 907	4 498	5 089	4 048
Total des recettes fiscales et non fiscales	..	100 178	154 185	244 738	303 742	313 649	334 103	353 162	375 614	345 053

.. Non disponible

Note : Année civile se terminant le 31 décembre.

Les données sont sur la base des encaissements.

Les recettes des majorations et pénalités relatives aux impôts sont considérées comme des recettes non fiscales comme le préconise la classification OCDE (voir le *Guide d'interprétation* : annexes A et B). La classification nationale du Maroc les compte comme des recettes fiscales.

Source : Ministère de l'Économie et des Finances.

StatLink https://stat.link/3cgsnp

Table 6.25. **Namibia / Namibie**

Details of non-tax revenue / Recettes non fiscales détaillées

Million NAD

	1995	2000	2005	2010	2015	2016	2017	2018	2019	2020
Total non-tax revenue	**..**	**..**	**..**	**7 948**	**20 781**	**17 447**	**23 812**	**21 336**	**22 799**	**25 728**
Grants	..	..	..	24	152	0	1	72	98	266
Property income	..	..	..	1 373	2 568	2 474	3 026	2 571	2 653	2 331
Rents and royalties	..	..	..	1 015	1 482	1 477	1 691	1 869	1 520	1 713
Diamond royalties	..	..	..	602	1 060	978	1 203	1 255	707	881
Other mineral royalties	..	..	..	280	309	391	343	347	546	619
Fishing quota levies	..	..	..	133	113	108	145	267	267	213
Interest and dividends	..	..	..	358	1 086	997	1 335	702	1 133	618
Other property income	..	..	..	0	0	0	0	0	0	0
Sales of goods and services	..	..	..	534	628	835	1 092	1 228	1 027	780
Fines, penalties and forfeits	..	..	..	43	78	67	95	90	99	99
Miscellaneous and unidentified revenue	..	..	..	5 975	17 355	14 071	19 598	17 375	18 922	22 252
SACU Revenue Pool Share	..	..	..	5 975	17 355	14 071	19 598	17 375	18 922	22 252
Total tax and non-tax revenue	..	..	..	23 682	52 754	51 490	59 306	56 504	59 046	58 490

.. Not available

Note: Data are on a fiscal year basis beginning 1st April. For example, the data for 2020 represent April 2020 to March 2021.

Data are reported on a cash basis.

Figures exclude tax revenues collected by sub-national governments as the data are not available.

Source: Namibia Revenue Agency.

StatLink https://stat.link/i2rypx

Table 6.26. **Niger**

Details of non-tax revenue / Recettes non fiscales détaillées

Million XOF

	1995	2000	2005	2010	2015	2016	2017	2018	2019	2020
Total des recettes non fiscales	..	**65 671**	**145 019**	**179 681**	**323 732**	**313 103**	**388 162**	**510 606**	**576 125**	**643 414**
Dons	..	59 240	134 000	130 144	232 611	270 255	342 117	428 900	514 000	535 990
Revenus de la propriété	..	4 751	5 998	28 436	40 249	31 921	28 929	47 496	30 975	33 590
Loyers et redevances	..	4 673	5 156	14 977	32 963	19 974	16 095	38 235	16 258	19 506
Bonus de signature	..	0	0	0	17 044	0	0	22 974	0	0
Redevance minière (RM)	..	4 519	4 732	14 381	11 323	13 105	8 850	7 214	6 877	9 801
Redevance superficaire pétrole	..	0	0	0	2 776	3 093	3 138	3 046	4 443	4 516
Publicité foncière	..	50	281	429	950	1 476	2 149	2 650	1 801	3 704
Redevance superficaire mine	..	0	0	0	449	1 001	1 117	1 463	2 191	1 060
Retenue pour logements	..	6	3	25	173	165	228	139	182	43
Concessions provisoires	..	0	73	86	164	740	190	288	286	69
Permis de coupe de bois	..	65	18	42	52	358	295	191	277	203
Bornage de terrains	..	4	13	9	20	23	23	190	124	109
Concessions définitives	..	29	35	5	12	12	103	82	76	1
Intérêts et dividendes	..	0	653	13 166	6 996	11 613	12 459	8 864	14 333	13 648
Dividendes	..	..	653	12 081	2 990	3 990	7 542	5 263	10 558	9 369
Bénéfices pétroliers	..	..	0	0	3 577	3 674	4 042	3 430	3 651	3 553
Intérêts créditeurs	..	..	0	1 084	430	3 949	876	170	124	726
Autres revenus de la propriété	..	78	189	293	290	334	375	398	384	436
Droits d'occupation du domaine public	..	78	189	293	290	334	375	398	384	436
Ventes de biens et de services	..	85	281	289	36 492	2 730	4 733	15 429	7 503	8 270
Vente de licence de téléphonie cellulaire	..	0	0	0	34 000	0	0	10 000	2 000	0
Commission sur transferts banque centrale (BCEAO)	..	0	0	42	1 090	799	3 093	3 905	3 826	5 255
Vente passeports/visa interpol	..	0	0	0	469	961	760	731	1 076	913
Vaccination internationale	..	0	0	0	239	275	217	179	154	172
Emission cartes grises/transport	..	0	0	0	143	121	180	3	51	143
Recettes des régies forestières	..	30	110	159	127	46	26	20	13	13
Ventes imprimés DGI/DGD	..	0	0	0	104	51	74	43	13	215
Droit de chancellerie	..	0	4	3	76	8	10	17	10	11
Location d'immeubles	..	9	135	63	9	27	21	29	22	447
Autres ventes de biens et services	..	46	32	21	235	442	352	503	337	320
Diverses prestations exceptionnelles	..	0	0	0	0	0	0	0	0	781
Amendes, pénalités et confiscations	..	1 348	1 700	3 816	6 744	4 215	7 433	9 612	10 908	3 420
Amendes et pénalités de la DGI	..	1 188	1 062	2 296	4 035	2 281	5 167	7 727	8 162	368
Amendes et frais de police	..	0	76	482	1 230	820	895	909	1 553	1 739
Amendes et confiscations	..	159	122	214	842	628	602	561	471	628
Amendes, frais et pénalités (gendarmerie et police)	..	0	402	769	595	428	707	266	431	491
Amendes et saisies forêts et chasse	..	1	27	45	26	9	8	32	212	68
Amendes et frais de justice	..	0	4	8	9	42	42	85	52	112
Amendes et saisies sur contrôle des prix-poids-mesure	..	0	6	1	8	7	13	32	26	14
Recettes diverses et non identifiées	..	248	3 040	16 995	7 635	3 983	4 950	9 168	12 739	62 144
Autres recettes diverses - Trésor National	..	0	0	16 461	4 921	3 021	3 681	8 539	12 386	61 751
Autres recettes diverses	..	248	250	420	779	962	1 269	251	188	307
Reversements UEMOA et produits divers ARC	..	0	2 790	114	1 935	0	0	0	0	0
Commissariat à l'Organisation du Hadjj et de la Oumra (COHO)	..	0	0	0	0	0	0	378	166	86
Total des recettes fiscales et non fiscales	..	181 490	335 237	553 142	1 044 271	958 003	1 003 606	1 307 277	1 362 476	1 417 390

.. Non disponible

Note : Année civile se terminant le 31 décembre.

Les données sont sur la base des encaissements.

Les chiffres n'incluent pas les données des recettes non fiscales collectées par les collectivités locales car elles ne sont pas disponibles.

Les données pour la période 2000-04 doivent être interprétées avec prudence car les données non fiscales collectées par la Direction Générale du Trésor et de la Comptabilité Publique (DGTCP) ne sont pas disponibles pour cette période. Selon la classification OCDE (voir le *guide d'interprétation* en Annexe B) produit de la vente d'immeuble bâtis n'est pas considéré comme une recette (fiscale ou non fiscale) car il ne représente pas une augmentation de la valeur nette résultant d'une transaction. La classification du Niger compte ces recettes comme des recettes non fiscales.

Selon la classification OCDE (voir le *guide d'interprétation* en Annexe B), le produit de la vente d'immeuble bâtis n'est pas considéré comme une recette (fiscale ou non fiscale) car il ne représente pas une augmentation de la valeur nette résultant d'une transaction. La classification du Niger compte ces recettes comme des recettes non fiscales.

Source : Direction Générale des Impôts.

StatLink https://stat.link/7dknjy

Table 6.27. **Nigeria / Nigéria**

Details of non-tax revenue / Recettes non fiscales détaillées

Million NGN

	1995	2000	2005	2010	2015	2016	2017	2018	2019	2020
Total non-tax revenue	..	..	..	**4 273 105**	**2 716 478**	**2 156 625**	**2 872 115**	**3 848 472**	**5 231 907**	**4 741 408**
Grants	..	..	..	335	49 288	125 059	141 055	88 292	591 157	1 672 193
Property income	..	..	..	4 266 330	2 622 660	2 007 436	2 731 060	2 636 270	3 127 320	3 065 216
Rents and royalties	..	..	..	4 266 330	2 622 660	2 007 436	2 731 060	2 636 270	3 127 320	3 065 216
Revenue from oil	..	..	..	3 574 420	2 059 110	1 607 090	2 100 870	1 395 650	1 734 790	873 135
Revenue from royalties	..	..	..	691 910	563 550	400 346	628 690	1 235 200	1 387 220	1 273 232
Revenue from fees and licences	..	..	..	0	0	0	1 500	5 420	5 310	918 849
Interest and dividends	..	..	..	0	0	0	0	0	0	0
Other property income	..	..	..	0	0	0	0	0	0	0
Sales of goods and services	..	..	..	0	0	0	0	0	0	0
Fines, penalties and forfeits	..	..	..	0	0	0	0	0	0	0
Miscellaneous and unidentified revenue	..	..	..	6 440	44 530	24 130	0	1 123 910	1 513 430	3 999
Total tax and non-tax revenue	..	..	..	8 296 702	8 477 903	7 570 536	9 419 129	12 015 509	13 911 584	13 267 524

.. Not available

Note: Year ending 31st December.

Data are reported on a cash basis.

"Revenue from oil" refers to government share of revenues from revenue sharing agreements with oil and exploration companies.

"Revenue from fees and licenses" refers to government fees collected in exchange for granting Oil Prospecting Licenses (OPL) and Oil Mining Leases (OML).

"Revenue from royalties" includes royalties charged to oil and mineral exploration companies.

Miscellaneous and unidentified revenue includes some revenues from dividends and issued profits from state-owned enterprises.

Source: Federal Inland Revenue Service.

StatLink https://stat.link/jnvysl

Table 6.28. **Rwanda**

Details of non-tax revenue / Recettes non fiscales détaillées

Million RWF

	1995	2000	2005	2010	2015	2016	2017	2018	2019	2020
Total non-tax revenue	**..**	**79 888**	**182 339**	**415 465**	**529 400**	**520 541**	**556 992**	**650 724**	**669 370**	**747 401**
Grants	..	76 710	164 477	397 352	374 600	339 336	359 731	398 686	427 498	475 830
Property income	..	..	..	..	..	..	..	..	..	..
Rents and royalties	..	..	..	..	..	..	..	..	..	..
Interest and dividends	..	..	..	..	..	..	..	..	..	..
Other property income	..	..	..	..	..	..	..	..	..	..
Sales of goods and services	..	..	..	..	..	..	..	..	..	..
Fines, penalties and forfeits	..	..	..	..	..	..	..	..	..	..
Miscellaneous and unidentified revenue	..	3 178	17 862	18 113	154 800	181 205	197 261	252 038	241 872	271 571
Total tax and non-tax revenue	..	148 797	356 945	856 189	1 526 632	1 636 177	1 805 009	2 052 226	2 281 100	2 390 379

.. Not available

Note: Year ending 31st December.

Data are reported on a cash basis.

Figures exclude non-tax revenues collected by sub-national governments as the data are not available.

Figures exclude fines related to tax revenues as it is not possible to split these out from tax revenues. Revenues from fines related to taxes are classified as non-tax revenues under the OECD classification, as set out in the *OECD Interpretative Guide* in Annex A. Rwanda classifies these revenues as tax revenues.

Miscellaneous and unidentified revenue includes non-tax fines, administrative fees and revenue from public property and public assets for Rwanda. These data could not be disaggregated to allocate revenue to the relevant non-tax revenue categories.

Source: Rwanda Revenue Authority.

StatLink https://stat.link/kctd1y

Table 6.29. **Senegal / Sénégal**

Details of non-tax revenue / Recettes non fiscales détaillées

Million XOF

	1995	2000	2005	2010	2015	2016	2017	2018	2019	2020
Total des recettes non fiscales	**..**	**68 000**	**105 200**	**203 550**	**366 943**	**522 831**	**531 764**	**435 068**	**378 817**	**474 534**
Dons	..	64 000	75 600	161 850	232 034	244 348	264 530	256 444	224 326	324 523
Revenus de la propriété	..	0	26 500	39 600	84 990	83 413	68 791	76 831	100 798	108 435
Loyers et redevances	..	..	14 600	20 300	35 790	31 943	25 178	43 880	64 854	61 187
Intérêts et dividendes	..	..	11 900	19 300	49 200	51 470	43 613	32 952	35 944	47 248
Autres revenus de la propriété	..	..	0	0	0	0	0	0	0	0
Ventes de biens et de services	..	0	0	0	0	0	9 123	10 310	10 997	11 135
Amendes, pénalités et confiscations	..	0	0	0	28 220	0	11	45	0	0
Recettes diverses et non identifiées	..	4 000	3 100	2 100	21 700	195 070	189 310	91 438	42 697	30 442
Recettes exceptionnelles (Swapp et Sonatel)	..	0	0	0	0	139 770	..	..	..	..
Divers reversements	..	4 000	3 100	2 100	21 700	55 300	..	..	..	..
Total des recettes fiscales et non fiscales	..	627 295	992 448	1 471 349	2 090 075	2 443 175	2 531 506	2 613 194	2 895 190	3 030 968

.. Non disponible

Note : Année civile se terminant le 31 décembre.

Les données sont sur la base des encaissements.

Les chiffres n'incluent pas les données des recettes fiscales collectées par les collectivités locales car elles ne sont pas disponibles.

Les recettes des amendes et les pénalités sur impôts et taxes sont considérées comme des recettes non fiscales. Cependant, il n'a pas été possible de séparer le versement des amendes et pénalités des recettes correspondant aux impôts auxquels ces amendes et pénalités se rattachent et sont donc exlues de cette rubrique. La classification nationale du Sénégal les compte comme des recettes fiscales. Les montants des années 2017 à 2020 concernent uniquement les recouvrements de la DGID.

Les recettes diverses et non identifiées comprennent les transferts de capitaux non compris ailleurs.

Source : Ministère de l'Économie, des Finances et du Plan.

StatLink https://stat.link/xy3m1l

Table 6.30. **Seychelles**

Details of non-tax revenue / Recettes non fiscales détaillées

Million SCR

	1995	2000	2005	2010	2015	2016	2017	2018	2019	2020
Total non-tax revenue	..	..	..	**725**	**1 237**	**1 488**	**1 247**	**1 511**	**1 408**	**1 684**
Grants	..	..	..	101	144	271	173	281	94	438
Property income	..	..	..	357	519	602	539	731	798	766
Rents and royalties	..	..	..	115	215	226	247	267	252	313
Fishing licence fees	..	..	..	93	0	0	0	0	0	98
Annual EU fishing licence fees to access Seychelles EEZ	..	..	..	0	43	36	37	42	1	23
EU fishing licence: vessel fee	..	..	..	0	37	33	29	35	79	3
Non EU fishing licence fees	..	..	..	0	60	64	72	72	1	74
Local fishing licence fees	..	..	..	0	1	1	0	2	54	1
SPF - Rental income	..	..	..	22	74	93	108	115	118	114
Interest and dividends	..	..	..	241	304	375	292	465	546	436
Income from interest and dividends (main budget)	..	..	..	206	228	304	207	377	442	338
FSA rental income (dividends)	..	..	..	0	11	14	23	29	33	30
SPF - Interest income	..	..	..	22	51	46	48	44	51	45
SPF - Investment/dividend income	..	..	..	12	14	12	14	14	21	22
Other property income	..	..	..	0	0	1	0	0	0	18
Sales of goods and services	..	..	..	191	462	565	489	466	465	432
Fines, penalties and forfeits	..	..	..	0	0	0	0	0	0	0
Miscellaneous and unidentified revenue	..	..	..	77	111	50	46	33	50	48
Total tax and non-tax revenue	..	..	..	4 321	6 701	7 596	7 960	8 975	9 013	8 446

.. Not available

Note: Year ending 31st December.

Data are reported on a cash basis.

Figures exclude non-tax revenues collected by sub-national governments as the data are not available.

In addition to the revenues labelled "SPF" under "Rents and royalties" and "Interest and dividends", some, generally negligible, SPF revenues are counted under "Other property income", "Sales of goods and services", and "Miscellaneous and unidentified revenue". SPF revenues are not reported as government revenues in Seychelles government documents.

"Rents and royalties" includes fishing licences fees considered as non-tax revenues in accordance with the OECD classification, as set out in the *OECD Interpretative Guide* in Annex A. The Seychelles classifies these revenues as tax revenues.

"Interest and dividends" includes revenues from the Financial Services Authority (FSA). FSA revenues are not reported as government revenues in Seychelles government documents.

Source: Seychelles Revenue Commission; Seychelles Ministry of Finance, Economic Planning and Trade; Financial Services Authority Seychelles Annual Reports; and Seychelles Pension Fund Annual Reports.

StatLink https://stat.link/tck6v7

Table 6.31. **Sierra Leone**

Details of non-tax revenue / Recettes non fiscales détaillées

Million SLE

	1995	2000	2005	2010	2015	2016	2017	2018	2019	2020
Total non-tax revenue	..	..	**393 496**	**581 304**	**1 359 374**	**1 026 117**	**1 075 211**	**1 516 270**	**2 338 842**	**3 444 342**
Grants	..	..	351 870	497 848	1 164 553	727 000	683 151	632 856	1 248 642	2 320 695
Programme	..	..	250 568	265 435	656 091	193 000	163 886	238 856	751 432	1 723 912
Elections Basket Fund	..	..	0	0	0	0	0	8 000	0	0
Project	..	..	101 302	232 413	508 462	534 000	519 264	386 000	497 210	596 783
Property income	..	..	15 869	34 475	126 649	210 168	229 646	317 691	341 425	354 134
Rents and royalties	..	..	15 869	34 475	126 649	210 168	229 646	317 691	341 425	354 134
Royalty on rutile	..	..	318	883	7 836	0	48 733	54 374	70 076	80 193
Royalty on bauxite and zircon	..	..	1 683	4 098	6 476	0	9 148	15 664	10 805	13 242
Royalty on diamonds and gold	..	..	0	6 360	28 485	104 872	20 603	71 619	77 638	89 875
Royalty on iron ore	..	..	0	0	6 119	0	25 568	3 468	3 453	0
Other mining licences and royalties	..	..	8 243	12 848	37 613	50 644	50 864	77 648	71 437	74 612
Royalty of fisheries	..	..	5 625	10 285	40 121	54 652	74 730	94 919	108 016	96 212
Interest and dividends	..	..	0	0	0	0	0	0	0	0
Other property income	..	..	0	0	0	0	0	0	0	0
Sales of goods and services	..	..	0	0	0	0	0	227 005	354 581	353 517
Treasury Single Account	..	..	..	..	..	..	..	227 005	354 581	353 517
Fines, penalties and forfeits	..	..	0	0	0	0	0	0	0	0
Miscellaneous and unidentified revenue	..	..	25 756	48 981	68 172	88 949	162 415	338 718	394 194	415 997
Total tax and non-tax revenue	..	..	767 852	1 510 810	3 494 635	3 613 247	4 028 658	5 061 314	6 665 747	7 821 325

.. Not available

Note: Year ending 31st December.

Data are reported on a cash basis.

"Miscellaneous and unidentified revenue" includes revenues from parastatals & other MDAs as well as other revenues including freight levy. The freight levy forms part of the Treasury Single Account collection since 2018.

"Sales of goods and services" includes revenues by key government agencies from various sources largely relating to regulatory fees, that are centralised into the Treasury Single Account.

Source: Sierra Leone National Revenue Authority.

StatLink https://stat.link/vgs8l3

Table 6.32. **South Africa / Afrique du Sud**

Details of non-tax revenue / Recettes non fiscales détaillées

Million ZAR

	1995	2000	2005	2010	2015	2016	2017	2018	2019	2020
Total non-tax revenue	**2 864**	**4 135**	**8 899**	**16 192**	**17 934**	**20 234**	**21 886**	**27 705**	**29 398**	**28 845**
Grants	135	637	1 118	1 012	1 467	1 800	1 458	1 276	1 155	1 545
Property income	1 881	1 378	5 208	8 170	10 113	11 189	12 726	16 845	20 986	20 927
Rents and royalties	217	0	271	4 448	3 772	5 948	7 834	9 049	11 831	14 133
Interest and dividends	1 664	1 378	4 937	3 721	6 341	5 240	4 891	7 796	9 154	6 794
Interest	954	714	2 570	2 524	4 487	3 981	3 485	6 834	8 276	6 502
Dividends	710	664	2 366	1 197	1 853	1 259	1 406	963	878	292
Other property income	0	0	0	0	0	0	0	0	0	0
Sales of goods and services	600	2 006	2 243	2 335	2 159	2 592	2 629	2 321	2 715	1 611
Fines, penalties and forfeits	124	114	280	4 425	3 665	4 206	4 786	6 877	4 144	4 340
Interest on overdue tax: Individuals	..	..	..	1 225	993	1 301	1 698	1 991	1 563	1 563
Interest on overdue tax: Companies	..	..	..	1 744	1 707	2 239	2 622	3 135	2 214	2 214
Other Fines, Penalties and Forfeitures	124	114	280	1 457	965	667	466	1 752	367	563
Miscellaneous and unidentified revenue	123	0	50	251	531	448	287	386	399	422
Total tax and non-tax revenue	124 784	215 696	427 722	722 722	1 188 804	1 263 007	1 348 397	1 451 051	1 496 592	1 421 963
Memo items: *SACU expenditure*	..	..	14 145	17 906	51 022	39 448	46 542	56 921	60 265	25 295

.. Not available

Note: Data are reported on a fiscal year basis beginning 1st April. For example, the data for 2020 represent April 2020 to March 2021.

Data are reported on a cash basis.

Figures exclude non-tax revenues collected by sub-national governments as the data are not available.

Grants include total grants and donations received mainly from foreign governments and multilateral institutions. This flow does not go through the Government Revenue fund but it is earmarked for specific projects implemented across government (by line departments). Unaudited estimates for grants are used for the fiscal year 2020/21.

Memo items: the Southern African Customs Union (SACU) expenditure records the difference between South Africa contributions to the SACU pool and the South Africa revenue share from the SACU pool that includes the balance of the "surplus/deficit" for that fiscal year and allocations to the SACU secretariat. The figures for 2013/14 figures differ from numbers published in South African tax statistics since some Fuel Levy imports were included in that year.

Source: National Treasury of South Africa. Data for grants are from the financial statements of the Reconstruction and Development Fund Programme (RDP) Fund administered by the office of Accountant General.

StatLink https://stat.link/n8aloz

Table 6.33. **Togo**

Details of non-tax revenue / Recettes non fiscales détaillées

Million XOF

	1995	2000	2005	2010	2015	2016	2017	2018	2019	2020
Total des recettes non fiscales	..	**18 987**	**31 939**	**189 745**	**102 957**	**114 513**	**135 695**	**216 888**	**200 351**	**165 057**
Dons	..	4 292	13 110	80 357	57 238	75 601	88 527	105 895	122 423	99 203
Dons projets	..	4 292	13 110	62 257	47 539	64 333	40 208	72 712	60 355	62 008
Dons programmes	..	0	0	18 100	9 699	11 267	48 319	33 183	62 068	37 195
Revenus de la propriété	..	10 040	11 942	92 473	25 555	21 201	31 185	41 010	37 962	32 940
Loyers et redevances	..	5 548	3 221	42 400	3 837	3 640	4 125	3 426	6 843	7 016
Redevances minières	..	0	0	0	1 270	1 372	1 850	2 322	1 777	1 872
Redevances de réhabilitation de l'Aéroport International Gnassingbé Eyadéma (AIGE)	..	5 548	3 221	0	2 240	1 819	1 828	665	3 543	4 714
Redevance contour global	..	0	0	0	0	408	447	332	330	431
Autres recettes domaniales	..	0	0	42 400	327	42	0	106	1 194	0
Intérêts et dividendes	..	4 492	8 721	50 073	21 718	17 560	27 061	37 584	31 119	25 924
Dividendes	..	2 416	2 696	6 745	16 179	11 335	21 784	31 592	25 366	18 975
Intérêts de placement	..	771	1 838	985	4 307	307	1	1	5	89
Produits divers (commissions, transferts BCEAO et intérêts)	..	0	0	0	201	4 642	4 649	5 234	5 181	6 152
Autres produits financiers	..	1 304	4 187	42 344	1 032	1 276	627	758	567	708
Autres revenus de la propriété	..	0	0	0	0	0	0	0	0	0
Ventes de biens et de services	..	1 365	850	140	7 692	9 017	8 623	57 099	25 308	24 926
Loyers d'immeuble	..	0	0	0	201	1 626	267	386	228	253
Redevances téléphoniques	..	0	0	0	2 000	1 500	1 573	50 440	15 500	15 500
Recettes de services	..	1 365	850	140	4 752	5 286	6 047	6 064	9 349	9 174
Recettes consulaires	..	0	0	0	739	605	736	210	230	0
Amendes, pénalités et confiscations	..	1 222	633	495	1 359	953	1 318	1 148	1 679	636
Amendes et pénalités (recettes fiscales)	..	955	495	262	989	754	1 129	821	1 132	320
Amendes et pénalités (recettes douanières)	..	267	138	232	369	199	189	326	547	316
Recettes diverses et non identifiées	..	2 069	5 403	16 280	11 114	7 741	6 042	11 737	12 978	7 351
Confiscations et ventes en douane	..	0	0	0	954	4 226	2 459	9 616	6 488	2 013
Ordre de recettes (gestion antérieure)	..	0	0	0	6	262	53	43	0	0
Ordre de recettes (gestion courante)	..	0	0	0	95	53	65	175	27	321
Divers reversements	..	785	1 216	0	9 754	2 985	3 207	1 114	6 368	2 941
Autres recettes non fiscales	..	1 284	4 187	16 280	305	216	259	789	96	2 076
Total des recettes fiscales et non fiscales	..	118 981	191 782	440 185	636 513	701 326	721 355	793 416	834 865	834 894

.. Non disponible

Note : Année civile se terminant le 31 décembre.

Les données sont sur la base des encaissements.

Les recettes non fiscales incluent les recettes des autres ministères ou directions, autres que le Ministère de l'économie et des finances.

Les chiffres n'incluent pas des autres recettes collectées par les collectivités locales pour leur propre compte, car elles ne sont pas disponibles. La classification nationale du Togo considère le Prélèvement pour apurement de la dette du secteur pétrolier (PADSP) comme une recette non fiscale. Cette recette est considérée comme une recette fiscale dans cette publication comme le préconise la classification OCDE (voir le *Guide d'interprétation* en Annexe A).

Les amendes et pénalités sur les impôts et les droits de douanes sont classifiées comme des recettes non fiscales dans cette publication comme le préconise la classification OCDE (voir le *Guide d'interprétation* en Annexe B). La classification nationale du Togo comptabilise ces recettes comme des recettes fiscales et des recettes douanières, respectivements.

Les confiscations et ventes en douane comprennent les reversements du prélèvement communautaire de solidarité qui sont classifiés comme des recettes non fiscales dans cette publication comme le préconise la classification OCDE (voir le *guide d'interprétation* en Annexe B. La classification nationale du Togo considère ces recettes comme des recettes fiscales douanières. Avant 2014, ces recettes étaient comptabilisés dans la rubrique « Amendes et pénalités (recettes douanières) ».

Source : Office Togolais des Recettes.

StatLink https://stat.link/805kdv

Table 6.34. **Tunisia / Tunisie**

Details of non-tax revenue / Recettes non fiscales détaillées

Million TND

	1995	2000	2005	2010	2015	2016	2017	2018	2019	2020
Total des recettes non fiscales	..	**725**	**1 078**	**1 799**	**1 749**	**1 539**	**2 770**	**3 254**	**3 828**	**3 584**
Dons	..	7	70	54	292	130	201	236	249	779
Revenus de la propriété	..	525	703	1 299	863	915	1 623	2 105	2 237	1 762
Loyers et redevances	..	185	295	435	350	388	1 251	1 353	1 043	698
Redevances pétrolières et du gaz	..	177	284	415	328	366	1 224	1 324	1 017	675
Loyers	..	8	11	19	22	23	27	29	26	23
Intérêts et dividendes	..	341	408	864	513	527	372	752	1 194	1 065
Intérêts	..	56	87	56	41	8	53	72	72	64
Transferts des entreprises publiques et bénéfices de la Banque Centrale	..	274	311	796	430	447	262	631	1 068	933
Remises sur crédit	..	3	3	2	3	4	4	4	3	3
Autres intérêts et dividendes non compris ailleurs	..	9	8	10	39	68	53	44	50	65
Autres revenus de la propriété	..	0	0	0	0	0	0	0	0	0
Ventes de biens et de services	..	22	38	40	28	32	42	72	53	34
Ventes de produits divers	..	21	37	38	26	30	40	70	50	31
Frais administratifs	..	1	1	2	2	2	2	2	2	3
Amendes, pénalités et confiscations	..	87	127	186	378	273	708	532	998	473
Recettes diverses et non identifiées	..	85	139	220	189	190	197	309	292	537
Total des recettes fiscales et non fiscales	..	7 922	11 223	18 942	27 362	28 135	32 580	37 078	43 278	42 413

.. Non disponible

Note : Année civile se terminant le 31 décembre.

Les données sont sur la base des encaissements.

Les chiffres n'incluent pas les données des recettes non fiscales collectées par les collectivités locales car elles ne sont pas disponibles.

Les dons affectés pour les Fonds spéciaux du Trésor et les Fonds de concours sont compris dans les données des dons des gouvernements et institutions étrangers.

Les recettes diverses et non identifiées incluent entre autres des recettes accidentelles à divers titres et des recettes non fiscales des Fonds spéciaux du Trésor et des Fonds de concours.

Source : Ministère des Finances.

StatLink https://stat.link/uakpt2

Table 6.35. **Uganda / Ouganda**

Details of non-tax revenue / Recettes non fiscales détaillées

Million UGX

	1995	2000	2005	2010	2015	2016	2017	2018	2019	2020
Total non-tax revenue	**234 550**	**568 523**	**1 194 038**	**921 459**	**1 109 069**	**1 400 151**	**1 239 490**	**1 161 102**	**1 688 568**	**1 548 076**
Grants	234 000	566 605	1 177 119	863 608	930 809	1 147 209	949 743	774 198	1 201 553	1 156 386
Budget support	89 300	255 205	817 409	467 338	258 151	339 676	259 263	154 513	594 860	455 205
Project grants	144 700	311 400	359 710	396 270	672 658	807 533	690 480	619 684	606 693	701 181
Property income	0	0	2 355	4 061	8 684	10 914	16 930	17 766	16 893	13 340
Rents and royalties	..	..	2 355	4 061	8 684	10 914	16 930	17 766	16 893	13 340
Mining royalties	..	..	2 355	4 061	8 684	10 914	16 930	17 766	16 893	13 340
Interest and dividends	..	..	0	0	0	0	0	0	0	0
Other property income	..	..	0	0	0	0	0	0	0	0
Sales of goods and services	550	1 919	14 564	53 790	169 575	242 029	272 818	369 138	470 122	378 350
Driver's permits[1]	550	1 919	3 877	12 373	15 921	18 245	33 561	37 335	39 425	39 110
Migration fees	..	..	3 822	23 317	90 913	123 251	121 892	140 196	139 778	122 840
Passport fees	..	..	2 523	4 614	12 800	21 660	21 065	25 950	37 338	40 140
Uganda Registration Services Bureau	..	..	0	0	23 470	24 417	32 549	21 461	56 259	37 490
Other administrative fees	..	..	4 342	13 486	26 472	54 456	63 750	144 196	197 322	138 770
Fines, penalties and forfeits	0	0	0	0	0	0	0	0	0	0
Miscellaneous and unidentified revenue[2]	0	0	0	0	0	0	0	0	0	0
Total tax and non-tax revenue	756 229	1 568 183	3 129 509	5 173 480	10 870 499	12 442 517	13 670 807	15 228 690	17 819 195	17 187 986

.. Not available

Note: Data are reported on a fiscal year basis beginning 1st July. For example, the data for 2020 represent July 2019 to June 2020.

Data are reported on a cash basis.

Figures exclude non-tax revenues collected by sub-national governments as the data are not available.

1. Revenue from drivers permits are considered as non-tax revenue according the OECD classification described in the *OECD Interpretative Guide*. The national classification of Uganda classifies it as tax revenues.
2. This category includes non-tax fines, administrative fees and revenue from public property and public assets. These data could not be disaggregated to allocate revenue to the relevant non-tax revenue categories.

Source: Uganda Revenue Authority.

StatLink https://stat.link/4xki2v

Revenue Statistics in Africa 1990-2020/Statistiques des recettes publiques en Afrique 1990-2020

Annex A

The OECD classification of taxes and interpretative guide[1]

Table of contents

A.1. The OECD Classification of Taxes

1. **1000. Taxes on income, profits and capital gains**
    - 1100. Taxes on income, profits and capital gains of individuals
        - 1110. On income and profits
        - 1120. On capital gains
    - 1200. Corporate taxes on income, profits and capital gains
        - 1210. On income and profits
        - 1220. On capital gains
    - 1300. Unallocable as between 1100 and 1200
2. **2000. Social security contributions**
    - 2100. Employees
        - 2110. On a payroll basis
        - 2120. On an income tax basis
    - 2200. Employers
        - 2210. On a payroll basis
        - 2220. On an income tax basis
    - 2300. Self-employed or non-employed
        - 2310. On a payroll basis
        - 2320. On an income tax basis
    - 2400 Unallocable as between 2100, 2200 and 2300
        - 2410. On a payroll basis
        - 2420. On an income tax basis
3. **3000. Taxes on payroll and workforce**
4. **4000. Taxes on property**
    - 4100. Recurrent taxes on immovable property
        - 4110. Households
        - 4120. Other
    - 4200 Recurrent taxes on net wealth
        - 4210. Individual
        - 4220. Corporate
    - 4300. Estate, inheritance and gift taxes
        - 4310. Estate and inheritance taxes
        - 4320. Gift taxes
    - 4400. Taxes on financial and capital transactions
    - 4500. Other non-recurrent taxes on property
        - 4510. On net wealth
        - 4520. Other non-recurrent taxes
    - 4600. Other recurrent taxes on property

5. **5000. Taxes on goods and services**

5100. Taxes on production, sale, transfer, leasing and delivery of goods and rendering of services

5110. General taxes

5111. Value added taxes

5112. Sales taxes

5113. Turnover and other general taxes on goods and services

5120. Taxes on specific goods and services

5121. Excises

5122. Profits of fiscal monopolies

5123. Customs and import duties

5124. Taxes on exports

5125. Taxes on investment goods

5126. Taxes on specific services

5127. Other taxes on international trade and transactions

5128. Other taxes on specific goods and services

5130. Unallocable as between 5110 and 5120

5200. Taxes on use of goods, or on permission to use goods or perform activities

5210. Recurrent taxes

5211. Paid by households in respect of motor vehicles

5212. Paid by others in respect of motor vehicles

5213. Other recurrent taxes

5220. Non-recurrent taxes

5300. Unallocable as between 5100 and 5200

6. **6000. Other taxes**

6100. Paid solely by business

6200. Paid by other than business or unidentifiable

A.2. Coverage

General criteria

1. In the OECD classification, the term "taxes" is confined to compulsory unrequited payments to the general government or to a supranational authority. Taxes are unrequited in the sense that benefits provided by government to taxpayers are not normally in proportion to their payments.

2. The term "tax" does not include fines, penalties and compulsory loans paid to government. Borderline cases between tax and non-tax revenues in relation to certain fees and charges are discussed in §12–15.

3. General government consists of the central administration, agencies whose operations are under its effective control, state and local governments and their administrations, certain social security schemes and autonomous governmental entities, excluding public enterprises. This definition of government follows that of the 2008 *System of National Accounts* (SNA).[2] In that publication, the general government sector and its sub-sectors are defined in Chapter 4, paragraphs 4.117 to 4.165.

4. Extra-budgetary units are part of the general government system. These are general government entities with individual budgets that are not fully covered by the main or general budget. These entities operate under the authority or control of a central, state, or local government. Extra-budgetary entities may have their own revenue sources, which may be supplemented by grants (transfers) from the general budget or from other sources. Even though their budgets may be subject to approval by the legislature, similar to that of budgetary accounts, they have discretion over the volume and composition of their spending. Such entities may be established to carry out specific government functions, such as road construction, or the nonmarket production of health or education services. Budgetary arrangements vary widely across countries, and various terms are used to describe these entities, but they are often referred to as "extra-budgetary funds" or "decentralised agencies."

5. Compulsory, unrequited payments collected by national governments and paid to supranational authorities are also included as taxes under the definition in paragraph 1. Taxes that are collected by national governments and paid to a supranational authority are included as tax revenues at the level of the supranational authority in the SNA2008 (paragraphs 22.60-61, 22.88 and 22.99 refer) and the ESA2010 (paragraph 20.165 refers). In Revenue Statistics, these taxes include customs duties, contributions to the EU Single Resolution Fund, and any other taxes collected by EU member states on behalf of the European Union. They are included in the tax revenue amounts in the country tables (Chapter 5) of the country in which they are collected and are attributed to the supranational level of government (see §102).

6. In countries where the church forms part of general government, church taxes are included, provided they meet the criteria set out in §1 above. As the data refer to receipts of general government and to supranational authorities, levies paid to non-government bodies, welfare agencies or social insurance schemes outside general government, trade unions or trade associations, even where such levies are compulsory, are excluded. Compulsory payments to general government earmarked for such bodies are, however, included, provided that the government is not simply acting in an agency capacity.[3] Profits from fiscal monopolies are distinguished from those of other public enterprises and are treated as taxes because they reflect the exercise of the taxing power of the state by the use of monopoly

powers (see §66–68), as are profits received by the government from the purchase and sale of foreign exchange at different rates (see §76).

7. Taxes paid by governments (e.g., social security contributions and payroll taxes paid by governments in their capacity as an employer, consumption taxes on their purchases or taxes on their property) are not excluded from the data provided. However, where it is possible to identify the amounts of revenue involved,[4] they are shown in Table 5.40 of this Report.

8. The relationship between this classification and that of the System of National Accounts (SNA) is set out in Sections A.9 and A.11 below. Because of the differences between the two classifications, the data shown in national accounts are sometimes calculated or classified differently from the practice set out in this guide. These and other differences are mentioned where appropriate (e.g., in §31 below) but it is not possible to refer to all of them. There may also be some differences between this classification and that employed domestically by certain national administrations (e.g., see §13 below), so that OECD and national statistics data may not always be consistent: any such differences, however, are likely to be very slight in terms of amounts of revenues involved.

Social security contributions

9. Compulsory social security contributions, as defined in §40, and paid to general government, are treated here as tax revenues. They may, however, differ from other taxes in that the receipt of social security benefits depends, in most countries, upon appropriate contributions having been made, although the size of the benefits is not necessarily related to the amount of the contributions. Better comparability between countries is obtained by treating social security contributions as taxes, but they are listed under a separate heading so that they can be distinguished in any analysis.

10. The strict dividing line between tax revenues (compulsory unrequited payments to general government or a supranational authority) and non-tax compulsory payments (NTCPs) (payments that are either requited or made to other institutions) is clearly defined. However, within the range of different compulsory payments to governments existing across countries, it is not always straightforward in practice to decide whether specific payments are either taxes or NTCPs. For example, compulsory pension savings that are controlled by general government and that accumulate on an individual account earning a market return or a rate that compensates for inflation would at first sight be categorised as NTCPs as opposed to taxes. However, even these payments might still be 'unrequited' and therefore classify as taxes instead of NTCPs (for example if these pension savings are not paid out when the taxpayer dies before reaching the pension age and the funds are then used to provide a minimum pension to all taxpayers that are insured). These issues result in the social security revenue figures reported for most countries being based on the premise that all types of compulsory payments to general government are judged to some extent to have a re-distributional element. It should be noted that this conclusion is based on a typically broad interpretation of the term 'unrequited' in the tax definition.

11. Social security contributions which are either voluntary or not payable to general government (see §1) are not treated as taxes, though in some countries, as indicated in the country footnotes, there are difficulties in completely eliminating voluntary contributions and certain compulsory payments to the private sector from the revenue figures. Imputed social security contributions are also not treated as taxes.

Fees, user charges and licence fees

12. Apart from vehicle licence fees, which are universally regarded as taxes, it is not easy to distinguish between those fees and user charges which are to be treated as taxes and those which are not, since, whilst a fee or charge is levied in connection with a specific service or activity, the strength of the link between the fee and the service provided may vary considerably, as may the relation between the amount of the fee and the cost of providing the service. Where the recipient of a service pays a fee clearly related to the cost of providing the service, the levy may be regarded as requited and under the definition of §1 would not be considered as a tax. In the following cases, however, a levy could be considered as 'unrequited':

a) where the charge greatly exceeds the cost of providing the service;

b) where the payer of the levy is not the receiver of the benefit (e.g., a fee collected from slaughterhouses to finance a service which is provided to farmers);

c) where government is not providing a specific service in return for the levy which it receives even though a licence may be issued to the payer (e.g., where the government grants a hunting, fishing or shooting licence which is not accompanied by the right to use a specific area of government land);

d) where benefits are received only by those paying the levy but the benefits received by each individual are not necessarily in proportion to his payments (e.g., a milk marketing levy paid by dairy farmers and used to promote the consumption of milk).

13. In marginal cases, however, the application of the criteria set out in §1 can be particularly difficult. The solution adopted — given the desirability of international uniformity and the relatively small amounts of revenue usually involved — is to follow the predominant practice among tax administrations rather than to allow each country to adopt its own view as to whether such levies are regarded as taxes or as non-tax revenue.[5]

14. A list of the main fees and charges in question and their normal[6] treatment in this publication is as follows:

Non-tax revenues:	court fees; driving licence fees; harbour fees; passport fees; radio and television licence fees where public authorities provide the service
Taxes within heading 5200	permission to perform such activities as distributing films; hunting, fishing and shooting; providing entertainment or gambling facilities; selling alcohol or tobacco; permission to own dogs or to use or own motor vehicles or guns; severance taxes

15. In practice, it may not always be possible to isolate tax receipts from non-tax revenue receipts when they are recorded together. If it is estimated that the bulk of the receipts derive from non-tax revenues, the whole amount involved is treated as a non-tax revenue; otherwise, such government receipts are included and classified according to the rules provided in §33 below.

Royalties

16. The ownership of subsoil assets in the form of deposits of minerals or fossil fuels (coal, oil, or natural gas) depends upon the way in which property rights are defined by law and also on international agreements in the case of deposits below international waters. In some cases, either the ground below which the mineral deposits are located, the deposits themselves or both may belong to a local or central government unit.

17. In such cases, these general government units may grant leases to other institutional units that permit them to extract these deposits over a specified period of time in return for a payment or series of payments. These payments are often described as 'royalties' but they are essentially rent that accrues to owners of natural resources in return for putting these assets at the disposal of other units for specified periods of time. The rent may take the form of periodic payments of fixed amounts, irrespective of the rate of extraction, or, more commonly, they may be a function of the quantity, volume, or value of the asset extracted. Enterprises engaged in exploration on government land may make payments to general government units in exchange for the right to undertake test drilling or otherwise investigate the existence and location of subsoil assets. Such payments are also recorded as rents even though no extraction may take place. These payments are therefore classified as non-tax revenues.

18. The same principles apply when other institutional units are granted leases that permit them to fell timber in natural forests on land owned by general government units. These payments are also classified as non-tax revenues.

19. These rents or royalties paid to general government should not be confused with taxes on income and profits, severance taxes, business licenses, or other taxes. If the payments are levied on the profits from the extraction activity, then they should be classified as taxes on incomes, profits and gains (1000). In addition, any severance payments that are imposed on the extraction of minerals and fossil fuels from reserves owned privately or by another government should be classified as taxes. Payments related to the gross value of production should be classified as other taxes on goods and services (5128). Payments for a license or permit to conduct extraction operations should be classified as taxes on use of goods and on permission to use goods or perform activities (5213).

Fines and penalties

20. In principle, fines and penalties charged on overdue taxes or penalties imposed for the attempted evasion of taxes should not be recorded as tax revenues. However, it may not be possible to separate payments of fines or other penalties from the revenues from the taxes to which they relate. In this case, the fines and penalties relating to a particular tax are recorded together with the revenues from that tax and fines and penalties paid with revenue from unidentifiable taxes are classified as other taxes in Category 6000. Fines not relating to tax offences (e.g., for parking offences), or not identifiable as relating to tax offences, are also not treated as tax revenues.

A.3. Basis of reporting

Accrual or cash reporting

21. The data reported in the *Revenue Statistics* publications for recent years are predominantly recorded on an accrual basis for OECD countries, i.e. recorded at the time that the tax liability was created. Further information is provided in the footnotes to the country table in Chapter 5 of the Report.

22. However, data for earlier years and for non-OECD countries are still predominantly recorded on a cash basis, i.e. at the time at which the payment was received by government. Thus, for example, taxes withheld by employers in one year but paid to the government in the following year and taxes due in one year but actually paid in the following year are both included in the receipts of the second year. Corrective transactions, such as refunds,

repayments and drawbacks, are deducted from gross revenues of the period in which they are made.

23. Data on tax revenues are recorded without offsets for the administrative expenses connected with tax collection. Similarly, where the proceeds of tax are used to subsidise particular members of the community, the subsidy is not deducted from the yield of the tax, though the tax may be shown net of subsidies in the national records of some countries.

24. As regards fiscal monopolies (heading 5122), only the amount actually transferred to the government is included in government revenues. However, if any expenditures of fiscal monopolies are considered to be government expenditures (e.g., social expenditures undertaken by fiscal monopolies at the direction of the government) they are added back for the purpose of arriving at tax revenue figures (see §66 below).

The distinction between tax and expenditure provisions[7]

25. Because this publication is concerned only with the revenue side of government operations, no account being taken of the expenditure side, a distinction has to be made between tax and expenditure provisions. Normally there is no difficulty in making this distinction as expenditures are made outside the tax system and the tax accounts and under legislation separate from the tax legislation. In borderline cases, cash flow is used to distinguish between tax provisions and expenditure provisions. Insofar as a provision affects the flow of tax payments from the taxpayer to the government, it is regarded as a tax provision and is taken into account in the data shown in this publication. A provision which does not affect this flow is seen as an expenditure provision and is disregarded in the data recorded in this publication.

26. Tax allowances, exemptions and deductions against the tax base clearly affect the amount of tax paid to the government and are therefore considered as tax provisions. At the other extreme, those subsidies which cannot be offset against tax liability and which are clearly not connected with the assessment process, do not reduce tax revenues as recorded in this publication. Tax credits are amounts deductible from tax payable (as distinct from deductions from the tax base). Two types of tax credits are distinguished, those (referred to here as wastable tax credits) which are limited to the amount of the tax liability and therefore cannot give rise to a payment by the authorities to the taxpayer, and those (referred to as non-wastable tax credits) which are not so limited, so that the excess of the credit over the tax liability can be paid to the taxpayer.[8] A wastable tax credit, like a tax allowance, clearly affects the amount of tax paid to the government, and is therefore considered as a tax provision. The practice followed for non-wastable tax credits[9] is to distinguish between the 'tax expenditure component',[10] which is that portion of the credit that is used to reduce or eliminate a taxpayer's liability, and the 'transfer component', which is the portion that exceeds the taxpayer's liability and is paid to that taxpayer. Reported tax revenues should be reduced by the amount of the tax expenditure component but not by the amount of the transfer component. In addition, the amounts of the tax expenditure and transfer components should be reported as memorandum items in the country tables. Countries that are unable to distinguish between the tax expenditure and transfer components should indicate whether or not the tax revenues have been reduced by the total of these components, and provide any available estimates of the amounts of the two components. Further information is given in Chapter 1 of the Report, which illustrates the effect of alternative treatments of non-wastable tax credits on tax to GDP.

Calendar and fiscal years

27. National authorities whose fiscal years do not correspond to the calendar year show data, where possible, on a calendar year basis to permit maximum comparability with the data of other countries. There remain a few countries where data refer to fiscal years. For these the GDP data used in the comparative tables also correspond to the fiscal years.

A.4. General classification criteria

The main classification criteria

28. The classification of receipts among the main headings (1000, 2000, 3000, 4000, 5000 and 6000) is generally governed by the base on which the tax is levied: 1000 income, profits and capital gains; 2000 and 3000 earnings, payroll or number of employees; 4000 property; 5000 goods and services; 6000 multiple bases, other bases or unidentifiable bases. Where a tax is calculated on more than one base, the receipts are, where possible, split among the various headings (see §33 and §84). The headings 4000 and 5000 cover not only taxes where the tax base is the property, goods or services themselves but also certain related taxes. Thus, taxes on the transfer of property are included in 4400[11] and taxes on the use of goods or on permission to perform activities in 5200. In headings 4000 and 5000 a distinction is made in certain sub-headings between recurrent and non-recurrent taxes: recurrent taxes are defined as those levied at regular intervals (usually annually) and non-recurrent taxes are levied once and for all (see also §48 to §51, §54, §55 and §81 for particular applications of this distinction).

29. Earmarking of a tax for specific purposes does not affect the classification of tax receipts. However, as explained in §40 on the classification of social security contributions, the conferment of an entitlement to social benefits is crucial to the definition of the 2000 main heading.

30. The way that a tax is levied or collected (e.g., by use of stamps) does not affect classification.

Classification of taxpayers

31. In certain sub-headings, distinctions are made between different categories of taxpayers. These distinctions vary from tax to tax:

a) *Between individuals and corporations in relation to income and net wealth taxes*

The basic distinction is that corporation income taxes, as distinct from individual income taxes, are levied on the corporation as an entity, not on the individuals who own it, and without regard to the personal circumstances of these individuals. The same distinction applies to net wealth taxes on corporations and those on individuals. Taxes paid on the profits of partnerships and the income of institutions, such as life insurance or pension funds, are classified according to the same rule. They are classified as corporate taxes (1200) if they are charged on the partnership or institution as an entity without regard to the personal circumstances of the owners. Otherwise, they are treated as individual taxes (1100). Usually, there is different legislation for the corporation taxes and for the individual taxes.[12] The distinction made here between individuals and corporations does not follow the sector classification between households, enterprises, and so on of the System of National Accounts for income and outlay accounts. The SNA classification requires certain unincorporated businesses[13] to be excluded from the household sector and included with non-financial enterprises and financial institutions. The tax on the profits of these businesses, however, cannot always be separated from the tax on the other income of their owners, or can be separated only on an arbitrary basis. No attempt at this separation is made here and the whole of the individual income tax is shown together without regard to the nature of the income chargeable.

b) *Between households and others in relation to taxes on immovable property*

Here the distinction is that adopted by the SNA for the production and consumption expenditure accounts. The distinction is between households as consumers (i.e. excluding non-incorporated business) on the one hand and producers on the other hand. However, taxes on dwellings occupied by households, whether paid by owner-occupiers, tenants or landlords, are classified under households. This follows the common distinction made between taxes on domestic property versus taxes on business property. Some countries are not, however, in a position to make this distinction.

c) *Between households and others in relation to motor vehicle licences*

Here the distinction is between households as consumers on the one hand and producers on the other, as in the production and consumption expenditure accounts of the SNA.

d) *Between business and others in relation to the residual taxes (6000)*

The distinction is the same as in c) above between producers on the one hand and households as consumers on the other hand. Taxes which are included under the heading 6000 because they involve more than one tax base or because the tax base does not fall within any of the previous categories but which are identifiable as levyable only on producers and not on households are included under 'business'. The rest of the taxes which are included under the heading 6000 are shown as 'other' or non-identified.

Surcharges

32. Receipts from surcharges in respect of particular taxes are usually classified with the receipts from the relevant tax whether or not the surcharge is temporary. If, however, the surcharge has a characteristic which would render it classifiable in a different heading of the OECD list, receipts from the surcharge are classified under that heading separately from the relevant tax.

Unidentifiable tax receipts and residual sub-headings

33. A number of cases arise where taxes cannot be identified as belonging entirely to a heading or sub-heading of the OECD classification and the following practices are applied in such cases:

a) The heading is known, but it is not known how receipts should be allocated between sub-headings: receipts are classified in the appropriate residual sub-heading (1300, 2400, 4520, 4600, 5128, 5130, 5300 or 6200).

b) It is known that the bulk of receipts from a group of taxes (usually local taxes) is derived from taxes within a particular heading or sub-heading, but some of the taxes in the group whose amount cannot be precisely ascertained may be classifiable in other headings or sub-headings: receipts are shown in the heading or sub-heading under which most of the receipts fall.

c) Neither the heading nor sub-heading of a tax (usually local) can be identified: the tax is classified in 6200 unless it is known that it is a tax on business in which case it is classified in 6100.

A.5. Commentaries on items of the list

1000 — *Taxes on income, profits and capital gains*

34. This heading covers taxes levied on the net income or profits (i.e. gross income minus allowable tax reliefs) of individuals and enterprises. Also covered are taxes levied on the capital gains of individuals and enterprises, and gains from gambling.

35. Included in the heading are:

a) taxes levied predominantly on income or profits, though partially on other bases. Taxes on various bases which are not predominantly income or profits are classified according to the principles laid down in §33 and §84;

b) taxes on property, which are levied on a presumed or estimated income as part of an income tax (see also §48(a), (c) and (d));

c) compulsory payments to social security fund contributions that are levied on income but do not confer an entitlement to social benefits. When such contributions do confer an entitlement to social benefits, they are included in heading 2000 (see §40);

d) receipts from integrated scheduler income tax systems are classified as a whole in this heading, even though certain of the scheduler taxes may be based upon gross income and may not take into account the personal circumstances of the taxpayer.

36. The main subdivision of this heading is between levies on individuals (1100) and those on corporate enterprises (1200). Under each subdivision a distinction is made between taxes on income and profits (1110 and 1210), and taxes on capital gains (1120 and 1220). If certain receipts cannot be identified as appropriate to either 1100 or 1200, or if in practice this distinction cannot be made (e.g., because there are no reliable data on the recipients of payments from which withholding taxes are deducted) they are classified in 1300 as not-allocable.

Treatment of credits under imputation systems

37. Under imputation systems of corporate income tax, a company's shareholders are wholly or partly relieved of their liability to income tax on dividends paid by the company out of income or profits liable to corporate income tax. In countries with such systems,[14] part of the tax on the company's profits is available to provide relief against the shareholders' own tax liability. The relief to the shareholder takes the form of a tax credit, the amount of which may be less than, equal to, or more than the shareholder's overall tax liability. If the tax credit exceeds this tax liability the excess may be payable to the shareholder. As this type of tax credit is an integral part of the imputation system of corporate income tax, any payment to the shareholders is treated as a repayment of tax and not as expenditure (compare the treatment of other tax credits described in §26).

38. As the tax credit under imputation systems (even when exceeding tax liability) is to be regarded as a tax provision, the question arises whether it should be deducted from individual income tax receipts (1110) or corporate income tax receipts (1210). In this Report, the full amount of corporate income tax paid is shown under 1210 and no imputed tax is included under 1110. Thus, the full amount of the credit reduces the amount of 1110 whether the credit results in a reduction of personal income tax liability or whether an actual refund is made because the credit exceeds the income tax liability. (Where, however, such tax credits are deducted from corporation tax in respect of dividends paid to corporations the amounts are deducted from the receipts of 1210).

1120 and 1220 — Taxes on capital gains

39. These sub-headings comprise taxes imposed on capital gains, 1120 covering those levied on the gains of individuals and 1220 those levied on the gains of corporate enterprises, where receipts from such taxes can be separately identified. In many countries, this is not the case and the receipts from such taxes are then classified with those from the income tax. Heading 1120 also includes taxes on gains from gambling.

2000 — Social security contributions

40. Classified here are all compulsory payments to general government that confer an entitlement to receive a (contingent) future social benefit. Such payments are usually earmarked to finance social benefits and are often paid to institutions of general government that provide such benefits. However, such earmarking is not part of the definition of social security contributions and is not required for a tax to be classified here. However, conferment of an entitlement is required for a tax to be classified under this heading. So, levies on income or payroll that are earmarked for social security funds but do not confer an entitlement to benefit are excluded from this heading and shown under personal income taxes (1100) or taxes on payroll and workforce (3000). Taxes on other bases, such as goods and services, which are earmarked for social security benefits are not shown here but are classified according to their respective bases because they generally confer no entitlement to social security benefits.

41. Contributions for the following types of social security benefits would, *inter alia*, be included: unemployment insurance benefits and supplements, accident, injury and sickness benefits, old-age, disability and survivors' pensions, family allowances, reimbursements for medical and hospital expenses or provision of hospital or medical services. Contributions may be levied on both employees and employers.

42. Contributions may be based on earnings or payroll ('on a payroll basis') or on net income after deductions and exemptions for personal circumstances ('on an income tax basis'), and the revenues from the two bases should be separately identified if possible. However, where contributions to a general social security scheme are on a payroll basis, but the contributions of particular groups (such as the self-employed) cannot be assessed on this basis and net income is used as a proxy for gross earnings, the receipts may still be classified as being on a payroll basis. In principle, this heading excludes voluntary contributions paid to social security schemes. When separately identifiable these are shown in the memorandum item on the financing of social security benefits. In practice, however, they cannot always be separately identified from compulsory contributions, in which case they are included in this heading.

43. Contributions to social insurance schemes which are not institutions of general government and to other types of insurance schemes, provident funds, pension funds, friendly societies or other saving schemes are not considered as social security contributions. Provident funds are arrangements under which the contributions of each employee and of the corresponding employer on his/her behalf are kept in a separate account earning interest and withdrawable under specific circumstances. Pension funds are separately organised schemes negotiated between employees and employers and carry provisions for different contributions and benefits, sometimes more directly tied to salary levels and length of service than under social security schemes. When contributions to these schemes are compulsory or quasi-compulsory (e.g., by virtue of agreement with professional and union organisations) they are shown in the memorandum item (refer to Table 5.39 of the Report).

44. Contributions by government employees and by governments in respect of their employees, to social security schemes classified within general government are included in this heading. Contributions to separate schemes for government employees, which can be regarded as replacing general social security schemes, are also regarded as taxes.[15] Where, however, a separate scheme is not seen as replacing a general scheme and has been negotiated between the government, in its role as an employer, and its employees, it is not regarded as social security and contributions to it are not regarded as taxes, even though the scheme may have been established by legislation.

45. This heading excludes 'imputed' contributions, which correspond to social benefits paid directly by employers to their employees or former employees or to their representatives (e.g., when employers are legally obliged to pay sickness benefits for a certain period).

46. Contributions are divided into those of employees (2100), employers (2200), and self-employed or non-employed (2300), and then further sub-divided according to the basis on which they are levied. Employees are defined for this purpose as all persons engaged in activities of business units, government bodies, private non-profit institutions, or other paid employment, except the proprietors and their unpaid family members in the case of unincorporated businesses. Members of the armed forces are included, irrespective of the duration and type of their service, if they contribute to social security schemes. The contributions of employers are defined as their payments on account of their employees to social security schemes. Where employees or employers are required to continue the payment of social security contributions when the employee becomes unemployed these contributions, data permitting, are shown in 2100 and 2200 respectively. Accordingly, the sub-heading 2300 is confined to contributions paid by the self-employed and by those outside of the labour force (e.g., disabled or retired individuals).

3000 — Taxes on payroll and workforce

47. These consist of taxes payable by enterprises assessed either as a proportion of the wages or salaries paid or as a fixed amount per person employed. They do not include compulsory social security contributions paid by employers or any taxes paid by employees themselves out of their wages or salaries

4000 — Taxes on property

48. This heading covers recurrent and non-recurrent taxes on the use, ownership or transfer of property. These include taxes on immovable property or net wealth, taxes on the change of ownership of property through inheritance or gift and taxes on financial and capital transactions. The following kinds of tax are excluded from this heading:

a) taxes on capital gains resulting from the sale of a property (1120 or 1220);

b) taxes on the use of goods or on permission to use goods or perform activities (5200); see §78;

c) taxes on immovable property levied on the basis of a presumed net income which take into account the personal circumstances of the taxpayer. They are classified as income taxes along with taxes on income and capital gains derived from property (1100);

d) taxes on the use of property for residence, where the tax is payable by either proprietor or tenant and the amount payable is a function of the user's personal circumstances (pay, dependants, and so on). They are classified as taxes on income (1100);

e) taxes on building in excess of permitted maximum density, taxes on the enlargement, construction or alteration of certain buildings beyond a permitted value and taxes on building construction. They are classified as taxes on permission to perform activities (5200);

f) taxes on the use of one's own property for special trading purposes like selling alcohol, tobacco, meat or for exploitation of land resources (e.g., United States severance taxes). They are classified as taxes on permission to perform activities (5200).

4100 — Recurrent taxes on immovable property

49. This sub-heading covers taxes levied regularly in respect of the use or ownership of immovable property.

- these taxes are levied on land and buildings;
- they can be in the form of a percentage of an assessed property value based on a national rental income, sales price, or capitalised yield; or in terms of other characteristics of real property, (for example size or location) from which a presumed rent or capital value can be derived.
- such taxes can be levied on proprietors, tenants, or both. They can also be paid by one level of government to another level of government in respect of property under the jurisdiction of the latter.
- debts are not taken into account in the assessment of these taxes, and they differ from taxes on net wealth in this respect.

50. Taxes on immovable property are further sub-divided into those paid by households (4110) and those paid by other entities (4120), according to the criteria set out in §31(*b*) above.

4200 — Recurrent taxes on net wealth

51. This sub-heading covers taxes levied regularly (in most cases annually) on net wealth, i.e. taxes on a wide range of movable and immovable property, net of debt. It is sub-divided into taxes paid by individuals (4210) and taxes paid by corporate enterprises (4220) according to the criteria set out in §31(*a*) above. If separate figures exist for receipts paid by institutions, the tax payments involved are added to those paid by corporations.

4300 — Estate, inheritance and gift taxes

52. This sub-heading is divided into taxes on estates and inheritances (4310) and taxes on gifts (4320).[16] Estate taxes are charged on the amount of the total estate whereas inheritance taxes are charged on the shares of the individual recipients; in addition the latter may take into account the relationship of the individual recipients to the deceased.

4400 — Taxes on financial and capital transactions

53. This sub-heading comprises, *inter alia*, taxes on the issue, transfer, purchase and sale of non-financial and financial assets (including foreign exchange or securities), taxes on cheques and other forms of payment, and taxes levied on specific legal transactions such as validation of contracts and the sale of immovable property. The heading does not include:

a) taxes on the use of goods or property or permission to perform certain activities (5200);

b) fees paid to cover court charges, charges for birth, marriage or death certificates, which are normally regarded as non-tax revenues (see §12);
c) taxes on capital gains (1000);
d) recurrent taxes on immovable property (4100);
e) recurrent taxes on net wealth (4200);
f) once-and-for-all levies on property or wealth (4500);
g) stamp taxes not related to financial and capital transactions
   i. Stamp taxes on the sale of specific products, such as alcoholic beverages or tobacco (5121);
   ii. Stamp taxes restricted by law to imported products (5123) or to exported products (5124); or
   iii. Stamp taxes not falling exclusively on a single category of transaction (6000).

4500 — Other non-recurrent taxes on property

54. This sub-heading covers once-and-for-all, as distinct from recurrent, levies on property. It is divided into taxes on net wealth (4510) and other non-recurrent taxes on property (4520). Heading 4510 would include taxes levied to meet emergency expenditures, or for redistribution purposes. Heading 4520 would cover taxes levied to take account of increases in land value due to permission given to develop or provision of additional local facilities by general government, any taxes on the revaluation of capital and once-and-for-all taxes on particular items of property.

4600 — Other recurrent taxes on property

55. These rarely exist in OECD member countries, but the heading would include taxes on goods such as cattle, jewellery, windows, and other external signs of wealth.

5000 — Taxes on goods and services

56. All taxes and duties levied on the production, extraction, sale, transfer, leasing or delivery of goods, and the rendering of services (5100), or in respect of the use of goods or permission to use goods or to perform activities (5200) are included here. The heading thus covers:

a) multi-stage cumulative taxes;
b) general sales taxes — whether levied at manufacture/production, wholesale or retail level;
c) value-added taxes;
d) excises;
e) taxes levied on the import and export of goods;
f) taxes levied in respect of the use of goods and taxes on permission to use goods, or perform certain activities;
g) taxes on the extraction, processing or production of minerals and other products.

57. Borderline cases between this heading and heading 4000 (taxes on property) and 6100 (other taxes on business) are referred to in §48, §53 and §80. Residual sub-headings (5300) and (5130) cover tax receipts which cannot be allocated between 5100 and 5200 and between 5110 and 5120, respectively; see §33.

5100 — *Taxes on the production, sale, transfer, leasing and delivery of goods and rendering of services*

58. This sub-heading consists of all taxes, levied on transactions in goods and services on the basis of their intrinsic characteristics (e.g., value, weight of tobacco, strength of alcohol, and so on) as distinct from taxes imposed on the use of goods, or permission to use goods or perform activities, which fall under 5200.

5110 — *General taxes on goods and services*

59. This sub-heading includes all taxes, other than import and export duties (5123 and 5124), levied on the production, leasing, transfer, delivery or sales of a wide range of goods and/or the rendering of a wide range of services, irrespective of whether they are domestically produced or imported and irrespective of the stage of production or distribution at which they are levied. It thus covers value-added taxes, sales taxes and multi-stage cumulative taxes. Receipts from border adjustments in respect of such taxes when goods are imported are added to gross receipts for this category, and repayments of such taxes when goods are exported are deducted. These taxes are subdivided into 5111 value-added taxes, 5112 sales taxes, 5113 turnover and other general taxes on goods and services.

60. Borderline cases arise between this heading and taxes on specific goods (5120) when taxes are levied on a large number of goods, for example, the United Kingdom purchase tax (repealed in 1973) and the Japanese commodity tax (repealed in 1988). In conformity with national views, the former United Kingdom purchase tax is classified as a general tax (5112) and the former Japanese commodity tax as excises (5121).

5111 — *Value-added taxes*

61. All general consumption taxes charged on value-added are classified in this sub-heading, irrespective of the method of deduction and the stages at which the taxes are levied. In practice, all OECD countries with value-added taxes normally allow immediate deduction of taxes on purchases by all but the final consumer and impose tax at all stages. In some countries the heading may include certain taxes, such as those on financial and insurance activities, either because receipts from them cannot be identified separately from those from the value-added tax, or because they are regarded as an integral part of the value-added tax, even though similar taxes in other countries might be classified elsewhere (e.g., 5126 as taxes on services or 4400 as taxes on financial and capital transactions).

5112 — *Sales taxes*

62. All general taxes levied at one stage only, whether at manufacturing or production, wholesale or retail stage are classified here.

5113 — *Turnover and other general taxes on goods and services*

63. These are multi-stage cumulative taxes and taxes where elements of consumption taxes are combined with multistage taxes. These taxes are levied each time a transaction takes place without deduction for taxes paid on inputs. Multi-stage taxes can be combined with elements of value-added or sales taxes.

5120 — *Taxes on specific goods and services*

64. Excises, profits generated and transferred from fiscal monopolies, and customs and imports duties as well as taxes on exports, foreign exchange transactions, investment goods

and betting stakes and special taxes on services, which do not form part of a general tax of 5110, are included in this category.

5121 — *Excises*

65. Excises are taxes levied as a product specific unit tax on a predefined limited range of goods. Excises are usually levied at differentiated rates on nonessential or luxury goods, alcoholic beverages, tobacco, and energy. Excises may be imposed at any stage of production or distribution and are usually assessed as a specific charge per unit based on characteristics by reference to the value, weight, strength, or quantity of the product. Included are special taxes on individual products such as sugar, sugar beets, matches, and chocolates; taxes levied at varying rates on a certain range of goods; and taxes levied on tobacco goods, alcoholic drinks, motor fuels, and hydrocarbon oils. If a tax collected principally on imported goods also applies, or would apply, under the same law to comparable domestically produced goods, then the revenue from this tax is classified as arising from excises rather than from import duties. This principle applies even if there is no comparable domestic production or no possibility of such production. Taxes on the use of utilities such as water, electricity, gas, and energy are regarded as excises rather than taxes on specific services (5126). Excises exclude those taxes that are levied as general taxes on goods and services (5110); profits of fiscal monopolies (5122); customs and other import duties (5123); or taxes on exports (5124).

5122 — *Profits of fiscal monopolies*

66. This sub-heading covers that part of the profits of fiscal monopolies which is transferred to general government or which is used to finance any expenditures considered to be government expenditures (see §24). Amounts are shown when they are transferred to general government or used to make expenditures considered to be government expenditures.

67. Fiscal monopolies reflect the exercise of the taxing power of government by the use of monopoly powers. Fiscal monopolies are non-financial public enterprises exercising a monopoly in most cases over the production or distribution of tobacco, alcoholic beverages, salt, matches, playing cards and petroleum or agricultural products (i.e. on the kind of products which are likely to be, alternatively or additionally, subject to the excises of 5121), to raise the government revenues which in other countries are gathered through taxes on dealings in such commodities by private business units. The government monopoly may be at the production stage or, as in the case of government-owned and controlled liquor stores, at the distribution stage.

68. Fiscal monopolies are distinguished from public utilities such as rail transport, electricity, post offices, and other communications, which may enjoy a monopoly or quasi-monopoly position but where the primary purpose is normally to provide basic services rather than to raise revenue for government. Transfers from such other public enterprises to the government are considered as non-tax revenues. The traditional concept of fiscal monopoly is not generally extended to include state lotteries, the profits of which are usually accordingly regarded as non-tax revenues. However, they can be included as tax revenues if the prime reason for their operation is to raise revenues to finance government expenditure. Fiscal monopoly profits are distinguished from export and import monopoly profits (5127) transferred from marketing boards or other enterprises dealing with international trade.

5123 — *Customs and other import duties*

69. Taxes, stamp duties and surcharges restricted by law to imported products are included here. Also included are levies on imported agricultural products which are imposed in member countries of the European Union and amounts paid by certain of these countries under the Monetary Compensation Accounts (MCA) system.[17] Customs duties collected by European Union member states on behalf of the European Union are reported under this heading at the supranational level of government in the country tables (in Chapter 5 of the Report). Excluded here are taxes collected on imports as part of a general tax on goods and services, or an excise applicable to both imported and domestically produced goods.

5124 — *Taxes on exports*

70. In the 1970s, export duties were levied in Australia, Canada and Portugal as a regular measure and they have been used in Finland for counter-cyclical purposes. Some member countries of the European Union pay, as part of the MCA system, a levy on exports (see note 16 to §69). Where these amounts are identifiable, they are shown in this heading. This heading does not include repayments of general consumption taxes or excises or customs duties on exported goods, which should be deducted from the gross receipts under 5110, 5121 or 5123, as appropriate.

5125 — *Taxes on investment goods*

71. This sub-heading covers taxes on investment goods, such as machinery. These taxes may be imposed for a number of years or temporarily for counter-cyclical purposes. Taxes on industrial inputs which are also levied on consumers [e.g., the Swedish energy tax which is classified under (5121)] are not included here.

5126 — *Taxes on specific services*

72. All taxes assessed on the payment for specific services, such as taxes on insurance premiums, banking services, gambling and betting stakes (e.g., from horse races, football pools, lottery tickets), transport, entertainment, restaurant and advertising charges, fall into this category. Taxes on entry to casinos, races, other similar events or venues as well as stamp taxes on specific services are also classified under this heading. Taxes levied on the gross income of companies providing a specific service (e.g. transportation [including airport and other passenger taxes] insurance, banking, entertainment, restaurants, and advertising) are also classified under this heading.

73. Tax revenues from bank levies and payments to deposit insurance and financial stability schemes are also included here:

- Compulsory payments of stability fees, bank levies and deposit insurance should generally be treated as tax revenues where the payments are made to general government or supranational authorities and are allocated to the governments' consolidated or general funds so that the government is free to make immediate use of the money for the purposes that it chooses. This principle would apply regardless of whether the government is promising to make payments to guarantee the banks' customer deposits in some future contingency.
- If the compulsory payments are made to general government and placed in funds that are earmarked to be entirely channelled back to the sector of the economy that comprises the companies that are subject to the payment, they would still generally be treated as tax revenues on the grounds that the funds would be available for

the government and would reduce its budget deficit, the fee is unrequited for an individual entity and the amounts raised could be unrelated to any eventual pay out to depositors or expenditure on wider support for the financial sector.

- Payments to made to the smaller long-standing schemes for insuring 'retail' deposits, where the payment levels are consistent with the costs of insurance should be classified as fee for service.
- Any payments which involve governments realising the assets of a failed institution or receiving a priority claim on its assets in liquidation in order to fund payments of compensation to customers for their lost deposits would be treated as a fee for a service as opposed to tax revenues.
- Compulsory payments that are made to funds operated outside the government sector and non-state institutions backed by the deposit takers and all payments to voluntary schemes should not be treated as tax revenues.
- Contributions made to the EU Single Resolution Fund are also included here and recorded under the supranational level of government in the country tables.

74. Excluded from this sub-heading are:

a) taxes on services forming part of a general tax on goods and services (5110);

b) taxes on electricity, gas and energy (5121 as excises);

c) taxes on individual gains from gambling (1120 as taxes on capital gains of individuals and non-corporate enterprises) and lump-sum taxes on the transfer of private lotteries or on the permission to set up lotteries (5200);[18]

d) taxes on cheques and on the issue, transfer or redemption of securities (4400 as taxes on financial and capital transactions);

e) general taxes on turnover (5113).

5127 — *Other taxes on international trade and transactions*

75. This sub-heading covers revenue received by the government from the purchase and sale of foreign exchange at different rates. When the government exercises monopoly powers to extract a margin between the purchase and sales price of foreign exchange, other than to cover administrative costs, the revenue derived constitutes a compulsory levy exacted in indeterminate proportions from both purchaser and seller of foreign exchange. It is the common equivalent of an import duty and export duty levied in a single exchange rate system or of a tax on the sale or purchase of foreign exchange. Like the profits of fiscal monopolies and import or export monopolies transferred to government, it represents the exercise of monopoly powers for tax purposes and is included in tax revenues.

76. The sub-heading covers also the profits of export or import monopolies, which do not however exist in OECD countries, taxes on purchase or sale of foreign exchange, and any other taxes levied specifically on international trade or transactions.

5128 — *Other taxes on specific goods and services*

77. This item includes taxes on the extraction of minerals, fossil fuels and other exhaustible resources from deposits owned privately or by another government together with any other unallocable receipts from taxes on specific goods and services. Taxes on the extraction of exhaustible resources are usually a fixed amount per unit of quality or weight, but can be a percentage of value. The taxes are recorded when the resources are extracted. Payments

from the extraction of exhaustible resources from deposits owned by the government unit receiving the payment are classified as rent.

5200 — *Taxes on use of goods or on permission to use goods or perform activities*

78. This sub-heading covers taxes which are levied in respect of the use of goods as distinct from taxes on the goods themselves. Unlike the latter taxes – reported under 5100 –, they are not assessed on the value of the goods but usually as fixed amounts. Taxes on permission to use goods or to perform activities are also included here, as are pollution taxes not based upon the value of particular goods. It is sometimes difficult to distinguish between compulsory user charges and licence fees which are regarded as taxes and those which are excluded as non-tax revenues. The criteria which are employed are noted in §12–13.

79. Although the sub-heading refers to the 'use' of goods, registration of ownership rather than use may be what generates liability to tax, so that the taxes of this heading may apply to the ownership of animals or goods rather than their use (e.g., race horses, dogs and motor vehicles) and may apply even to unusable goods (e.g., unusable motor vehicles or guns).

80. Borderline cases arise with:

a) taxes on the permission to perform business activities which are levied on a combined income, payroll or turnover base and, accordingly, are classified following the rules in §84;

b) taxes on the ownership or use of property of headings 4100, 4200 and 4600. The heading 4100 is confined to taxes on the ownership or tenancy of immovable property and – unlike the taxes of 5200 – they are related to the value of the property. The net wealth taxes and taxes on chattels of 4200 and 4600 respectively are confined to the ownership rather than the use of assets, apply to groups of assets rather than particular goods and again are related to the value of the assets,

5210 — *Recurrent taxes on use of goods and on permission to use goods or perform activities*

81. The principal characteristic of taxes classified here is that they are levied at regular intervals and that they are usually fixed amounts. The most important item in terms of revenue receipts is vehicle licence taxes. This sub-heading also covers taxes on permission to hunt, shoot, fish or to sell certain products and taxes on the ownership of dogs and on the performance of certain services, provided that they meet the criteria set out in §12–13. The sub-divisions of 5210 are:

- user taxes on motor vehicles paid by households (5211);
- taxes on motor vehicles paid by others (5212); and
- other recurrent taxes (5213). This sub-heading covers business and professional licences paid by enterprises in order to obtain a licence to carry on a particular kind of business or profession when the levies are on a recurring basis. Licences such as taxi and casino licences are included. Dog licences and recurrent general licences for hunting, shooting and fishing where the right to carry out these activities is not granted as part of a normal commercial transaction are also included under this heading.

82. Excluded from sub-heading 5213 are:

a) licences where the right to carry out such activities is granted as part of a normal commercial transaction (e.g., the granting of the licence is accompanied by the right to use a specific area which is owned by government);

b) payments relating to the checks carried out by the government on the suitability and or safety of the business premises or equipment, or on the quality or standard of goods or services produced as a condition for granting such a licence. These payments are not unrequited and should be treated as payments for services rendered, unless the amounts charged for the licences are out of all proportion to the costs of the checks carried out by governments.

5220 — Non-recurrent taxes on use of goods and on permission to use goods or perform activities

83. This section covers non-recurrent taxes levied on the use of goods or on permission to use goods or perform activities and taxes levied each time goods are used. It includes taxes levied on the emission or discharge into the environment of noxious gases, liquids or other harmful substances.

- Payments for tradable emission permits issued by governments under cap and trade schemes should be recorded here at the time the emissions occur. No revenue should be recorded for permits that governments issue free of charge. The accrual basis of recording means that there can be a timing difference between the cash being received by government for the permits and the time the emission occurs. In the national accounts, this timing gives rise to a financial liability for government during the period.
- Payments made for the collection and disposal of waste or noxious substances by public authorities should be excluded as they constitute a sale of services to enterprises.

84. Other taxes falling under heading 5200 that are not levied recurrently are also included here. Thus, once-and-for-all payments for permission to sell liquor or tobacco or to set up betting shops are included provided they meet the criteria set out in §12–13.

6000 — Other taxes

85. Taxes levied on a base, or bases, other than those described under headings 1000, 3000, 4000 and 5000, or on bases of which cannot be considered to be related to any one of these headings, are included here. Where taxes are levied on a multiple base and it is possible to estimate the receipts related to each base the separate amounts are included under the appropriate headings. If separate amounts cannot be estimated and it is known that most of the receipts are derived from one base, the whole of the receipts are classified according to that base. Otherwise, they are classified here. Other revenues included here are presumptive taxes not included elsewhere in the classification system, taxes on individuals in the form of a poll tax or capitation tax, stamp taxes not related to financial and capital transactions nor falling exclusively on a single category of transaction, expenditure taxes where personal deductions or exemptions are applied and unidentifiable tax receipts. A subdivision is made between taxes levied wholly or predominantly on business (6100) and those levied on others (6200).

A.6. Conciliation with National Accounts

86. This section of the tables provides a re-conciliation between the OECD calculation of total tax revenues and the total of all taxes and social contributions paid to general government as recorded in the country's National Accounts. Where the country is a member of the European Union (EU), the comparison is between the OECD calculation of total tax revenues and the sum of tax revenues and social contributions recorded in the combination of the general government and the institutions of the EU sectors of the National Accounts.

A.7. Memorandum item on the financing of social security benefits

87. In view of the varying relationship between taxation and social security contributions and the cases referred to in §40 to §46, a memorandum item collects together all payments earmarked for social security-type benefits, other than voluntary payments to the private sector. Data are presented as follows (refer Table 5.39 of the Report):

a) Taxes of 2000 series.

b) Taxes earmarked for social security benefits.

c) Voluntary contributions to the government.

d) Compulsory contributions to the private sector.

Guidance on the breakdown of (a) to (d) above is provided in §40 to §46.

A.8. Memorandum item on identifiable taxes paid by government

88. Identifiable taxes actually paid by government are presented in a memorandum item classified by the main headings of the OECD classification of taxes. In the vast majority of countries, only social security contributions and payroll taxes paid by government can be identified. These are, however, usually the most important taxes paid by governments (refer to Table 5.40 of the Report).

A.9. Relation of OECD classification of taxes to national accounting systems

89. A system of national accounts (SNA) seeks to provide a coherent framework for recording and presenting the main flows relating respectively to production, consumption, accumulation and external transactions of a given economic area, usually a country or a major region within a country. Government revenues are an important part of the transactions recorded in SNA. The final version of the 2008 SNA was jointly published by five international organisations: the United Nations, the International Monetary Fund, the European Union, the Organisation for Economic Co-operation and Development, and the World Bank in August 2009. The *System* is a comprehensive, consistent and flexible set of macroeconomic accounts. It is designed for use in countries with market economies, whatever their stage of economic development, and also in countries in transition to market economies. The important parts of the SNA's conceptual framework and its definitions of the various sectors of the economy have been reflected in the OECD's classification of taxes.

90. There are, however, some differences between the OECD classification of taxes and SNA concepts that are listed below. They arise because the aim of the former is to provide the maximum disaggregation of statistical data on what are generally regarded as taxes by tax administrations.

a) OECD includes compulsory social security contributions paid to general government in total tax revenues. Imputed and voluntary contributions plus those paid to private funds are not treated as taxes (§9 and §11 above);

b) there are different points of view on whether or not some levies and fees are classified as taxes (§12 and §13 above);

c) OECD excludes imputed taxes or subsidies resulting from the operation of official multiple exchange rates or from the central bank paying a rate of interest on required reserves that is different from other market rates;

d) there are differences in the treatment of non-wastable tax credits

91. As noted in §1 and §2, headings 1000 to 6000 of the OECD list of taxes cover all unrequited payments to general government or to a supranational authority, other than compulsory loans and fines. Such unrequited payments including fines, but excluding compulsory loans can be obtained from adding together the following figures in the 2008 SNA

- value-added type taxes (D.211);
- taxes and duties on imports, excluding VAT (D.212);
- export taxes (D.213);
- taxes on products, excluding VAT, import and export taxes (D.214);
- other taxes on production (D.29);
- taxes on income (D.51);
- other current taxes (D.59);
- actual social contributions (D.611 and D613), excluding voluntary contributions and payments to employment-related schemes that are not social security schemes
- capital taxes (D.91).

A.10. The OECD classification of taxes and the International Monetary Fund (GFS) system

92. The coverage and valuation of tax revenues in the GFS system and the 2008 SNA are very similar. Therefore, the differences between the OECD classification and that of the 2008 SNA (see §90 above) also apply to the GFS. In addition the International Monetary Fund subdivides the OECD 5000 heading into section IV (Domestic Taxes on Goods and Services) and section V (Taxes on International Trade and Transactions). This reflects the fact that while the latter usually yield insignificant amounts of revenue in OECD countries, this is not the case in many non-OECD countries.

A.11. Comparison of the OECD classification of taxes with other international classifications

93. The table below describes an item by item comparison of the OECD classification of taxes and the classifications used in the following:

a) System of National Accounts (2008 SNA);

b) European System of Accounts (2010 ESA);

c) IMF Government Finance Statistics Manual (GFSM2014).

94. These comparisons represent those that would be expected to apply in the majority of cases. However in practice some flexibility should be used in their application. This is because in particular cases, countries can adopt varying approaches to the classification of revenues in National Accounts.

OECD Classification	2008 SNA	2010 ESA	GFSM2014
1000 Taxes on income, profits and capital gains			
1100 Individuals			
1110 Income and profits	D51-8.61a	D51A	1111
1120 Capital gains	D51-8.61c, d	D51C, D	1111
1200 Corporations			
1210 Income and profits	D51-8.61b	D51B	1112
1220 Capital gains	D51-8.61c	D51C	1112
1300 Unallocable as between 1100 and 1200			1113
2000 Social security contributions			
2100 Employees	D613-8.85	D613	1211
2200 Employers	D611-8.83	D611	1212
2300 Self-employed, non-employed	D613-8.85	D613	1213
2400 Unallocable as between 2100, 2200 and 2300			1214
3000 Taxes on payroll and workforce	D29-7.97a	D29C	112
4000 Taxes on property			
4100 Recurrent taxes on immovable property			
4110 Households	D59-8.63a	D59A	1131
4120 Other	D29-7.97b	D29A	1131
4200 Recurrent net wealth taxes			
4210 Individual	D59-8.63b	D59A	1132
4220 Corporations	D59-8.63b	D59A	1132
4300 Estate, inheritance and gift taxes			
4310 Estate and inheritance taxes	D91-10.207b	D91A	1133
4320 Gift taxes	D91-10.207b	D91A	1133
4400 Taxes on financial and capital transactions	D59-7.96d; D29-7.97e	D214B, C	114114; 1161
4500 Other non-recurrent taxes on property	D91-10.207a	D91B	1135
4600 Other recurrent taxes on property	D59-8.63c	D59A	1136
5000 Taxes on goods and services			
5100 Taxes on production, sale and transfer of goods and services			
5110 General taxes on goods and services			
5111 Value-added taxes	D211-7.89	D211; D29G	11411
5112 Sales taxes	D2122-7.94a; D214-7.96a	D21224; D214I	11412
5113 Other general taxes on goods and services	D214-7.96a	D214I	11413
5120 Taxes on specific goods and services			
5121 Excises	D2122-7.94b; D214-7.96b	D21223; D214A, B, D	1142
5122 Profits of fiscal monopolies	D214-7.96e	D214J	1143
5123 Customs and other import duties	D2121-7.93	D2121; D21221, 2	1151
5124 On exports	D213-7.95a	D214K	1152-4
5125 On investment goods			
5126 On specific services	D2122-7.94c; D214-7.96c	D21225; D214E, F, G, H; D29F	1144; 1156
5127 Other taxes on international trade and transactions	D2122-7.94d D29-7.95b D29-7.97g D59-8.64d	D21226; D29D; D59E	1153; 1155-6
5128 Other taxes on specific goods and services			1146
5130 Unallocable between 5110 and 5120			
5200 Taxes on use of goods and on permission to use goods or perform activities			
5210 Recurrent taxes on use of goods and on permission to use goods or perform activities			
5211 Motor vehicle taxes households	D59-8.64c	D59D	11451
5212 Motor vehicles taxes others	D29-7.97d	D214D; D29B	11451
5213 Other recurrent taxes on use of goods and on permission to use goods or perform activities	D29-7.97c, d, f D59-8.64c	D29B, E, F; D59D	11452
5220 Non-recurrent taxes on permission to use goods or perform activities			11452
5300 Unallocable as between 5100 and 5200			
6000 Other taxes			
6100 Payable solely by business			1161
6200 Payable by other than business, or unidentifiable	D59-8.64a, b	D59B, C	1162

A.12. Attribution of tax revenues by sub-sectors of general government

95. The OECD classification requires a breakdown of tax revenues by sub-sectors of government. The definition of each sub-sector and the criteria to be used to attribute tax revenues between these sub-sectors are set out below. They follow the guidance of the 2008 SNA and GFSM 2014.

Sub-sectors of general government to be identified

a) Central government

96. The central government sub-sector includes all governmental departments, offices, establishments and other bodies which are agencies or instruments of the central authority whose competence extends over the whole territory, with the exception of the administration of social security funds. Central government therefore has the authority to impose taxes on all resident and non-resident units engaged in economic activities within the country.

b) State, provincial or regional government

97. This sub-sector consists of intermediate units of government exercising a competence at a level below that of central government. It includes all such units operating independently of central government in a part of a country's territory encompassing a number of smaller localities, with the exception of the administration of social security funds. In unitary countries, regional governments may be considered to have a separate existence where they have substantial autonomy to raise a significant proportion of their revenues from sources within their control and their officers are independent of external administrative control in the actual operation of the unit's activities.

98. At present, federal countries comprise the majority of cases where revenues attributed to intermediate units of government are identified separately. Colombia and Spain are the only two unitary countries in this position. In the remaining unitary countries, regional revenues are included with those of local governments.

c) *Local government*

99. This sub-sector includes all other units of government exercising an independent competence in part of the territory of a country, with the exception of the administration of social security funds. It encompasses various urban and/or rural jurisdictions (e.g., local authorities, municipalities, cities, boroughs, districts).

d) Social security funds

100. Social security funds form a separate sub-sector of general government. The social security sub-sector is defined in the 2008 SNA by the following extracts from paragraphs 4.124 to 4.126 and 4.147:

> *"Social security schemes are social insurance schemes covering the community as a whole or large section of the community that are imposed and controlled by government units. The schemes cover a wide variety of programmes, providing benefits in cash or in kind for old age, invalidity or death, survivors, sickness and maternity, work injury, unemployment, family allowance, health care, etc. There is not necessarily a direct link between the amount of the contribution paid by an individual and the benefits he or she may receive." (Paragraph 4.124).*

"When social security schemes are separately organised from the other activities of government units and hold their assets and liabilities separately from the latter and engage in financial transactions on their own account they qualify as institutional units that are described as social security funds." (Paragraph 4.125).

"The amounts raised, and paid out, in social security contributions and benefits may be deliberately varied in order to achieve objectives of government policy that have no direct connection with the concept of social security as a scheme to provide social benefits to members of the community. They may be raised or lowered in order to influence the level of aggregate demand in the economy, for example. Nevertheless, so long as they remain separately constituted funds, they must be treated as separate institutional units in the SNA. (Paragraph 4.126).

"The social security funds sub-sector (of general government) consists of the social security funds operating at all levels of government. Such funds are social insurance schemes covering the community as a whole or large section of the community that are imposed by government units." (Paragraph 4.147).

101. This definition of social security funds is followed in the OECD classification with the two following exceptions which are excluded

- Schemes imposed by government and operated by bodies outside the general government sector, as defined in §3 of this manual; and
- Schemes to which all contributions are voluntary.

Supranational Authorities

102. This sub-sector covers the revenue-raising operations of supra-national authorities within a country. In practice, the only relevant supranational authority in the OECD area is that of the institutions of the European Union (EU). Tax revenues collected by member countries and paid to the EU are included in the *Revenue Statistics* at the supranational level of government. Income taxes and social security contributions collected by European Institutions and paid by European civil servants who are resident of EU member countries should not be included.

Criteria to be used for the attribution of tax revenues

103. When a government collects taxes and pays them over in whole or in part to other governments, it is necessary to determine whether the revenues should be considered to be those of the collecting government which it distributes to others as grants, or those of the beneficiary governments which the collecting government receives and passes on only as their agent. The criteria to be used in the attribution of revenues are set out in §104 to §107 which replicate paragraphs 3.70 to 3.73 from the 2008 SNA.

104. In general, a tax is attributed to the government unit that

a) exercises the authority to impose the tax (either as a principal or through the delegated authority of the principal),

b) has final discretion to set and vary the rate of the tax

105. Where an amount is collected by one government for and on behalf of another government, and the latter government has the authority to impose the tax, and set and vary its rate, then the former is acting as an agent for the latter and the tax is reassigned. Any amount retained by the collecting government as a collection charge should be treated as a payment for a service. Any other amount retained by the collecting government, such as under a tax-sharing arrangement, should be treated as a current grant. If the collecting

government was delegated the authority to set and vary the rate, then the amount collected should be treated as tax revenue of this government.

106. Where different governments jointly and equally set the rate of a tax and jointly and equally decide on the distribution of the proceeds, with no individual government having ultimate overriding authority, then the tax revenues are attributed to each government according to its respective share of the proceeds. If an arrangement allows one government unit to exercise ultimate overriding authority, then all of the tax revenue is attributed to that unit.

107. There may also be the circumstance where a tax is imposed under the constitutional or other authority of one government, but other governments individually set the tax rate in their jurisdictions. The proceeds of the tax generated in each respective government's jurisdiction are attributed as tax revenues of that government.

108. The levies paid by the member states of the EU take the form specific levies which include

a) custom duties and levies on agricultural goods (5123),

b) gross monetary compensation accounts (5123 if relating to imports and 5124 if relating to exports);

c) contributions to the Single Resolution Fund (5126); and

d) Steel, coal, sugar and milk levies (5128).

109. The custom duties collected by member states on behalf of the EU are recorded

- on a gross of collection fee basis;
- using figures adjusted so that duties are shown on a 'final destination' as opposed to a 'country of first entry' basis where such adjustments can be made. These adjustments concern in particular duties collected at important (sea) ports. Although the EU duties are collected by the authorities of the country of first entry, when possible these duties should be excluded from the revenue of the collecting country and be included in the revenue of the country of final destination

110. These are the specific EU levies that most clearly conform to the attribution criterion described in §102 above. Consequently, these amounts are footnoted as a memorandum item to the EU member state country tables (in Chapter 5) and are shown as supranational revenues against each of the tax headings identified in §108.

Notes

1. References in this OECD Interpretative Guide to Sections or Parts of "this Report" refer to OECD (2022), Revenue Statistics 2022, OECD Publishing, Paris.
2. All references to SNA are to the 2008 edition.
3. See section A.12 of this guide for a discussion of the concept of agency capacity.
4. It is usually possible to identify amounts of social security contributions and payroll taxes, but not other taxes paid by government.
5. If, however, a levy which is considered as non-tax revenue by most countries is regarded as a tax — or raises substantial revenue — in one or more countries, the amounts collected are footnoted at the end of the relevant country tables, even though the amounts are not included in total tax revenues.

6. Names, however, can frequently be misleading. For example, though a passport fee would normally be considered a non-tax revenue, if a supplementary levy on passports (as is the case in Portugal) were imposed in order to raise substantial amounts of revenue relative to the cost of providing the passport, the levy would be regarded as a tax under 5200.
7. A more detailed explanation of this distinction can be found in the special feature, 'Current issues in reporting tax revenues', in the 2001 edition of the *Revenue Statistics*.
8. Sometimes the terms 'non-refundable' and 'refundable' are used, but it may be considered illogical to talk of 'refundable' when nothing has been paid.
9. A different treatment, however, is accorded to non-wastable tax credits under imputation systems of corporate income tax (§37–39).
10. This is not strictly a true tax expenditure in the formal sense. Such tax expenditures require identification of a benchmark tax system for each country or, preferably, a common international benchmark. In practice it has not been possible to reach agreement on a common international benchmark.
11. Unless based on the profit made on a sale, in which case they would be classified as capital gains taxes under 1120 or 1220.
12. In some countries the same legislation applies to both individual and corporate enterprises for particular taxes on income. However, the receipts from such taxes are usually allocable between individuals and enterprises and can therefore be shown in the appropriate sub-heading.
13. For example, "... sufficiently self-contained and independent that they behave in the same way as corporations... (including) keeping a complete set of accounts" (2008 SNA, section 4.44).
14. In Canada — a country also referred to as having an imputation system — the (wastable) tax credit for the shareholder is in respect of domestic corporation tax deemed to have been paid whether or not a corporation tax liability has arisen. As there is no integral connection between the corporation tax liability and the credit given against income tax under such systems, these credits for dividends are treated, along with other tax credits, on the lines described in §26.
15. This may also apply where a scheme for government employees existed prior to the introduction of a general social security scheme.
16. In the 2008 SNA these are regarded as capital transfers and not as taxes (see section A.8).
17. This is the system by which the European Union adjusts for differences between the exchange rates used to determine prices under the Common Market Agricultural Policy and actual exchange rates. Payments under the system may relate to imports or exports and where these amounts are separately identifiable they are shown under the appropriate heading (5123 or 5124). In this Report, these amounts are shown gross (i.e. without deducting any subsidies paid out under the MCA system).
18. Transfers of profits of State lotteries are regarded as non-tax revenues (see also §68).

Revenue Statistics in Africa 1990-2020/Statistiques des recettes publiques en Afrique 1990-2020

Annexe A

Classification des impôts de l'OCDE et Guide d'interprétation[1]

Table des matières

A.1. Classification des impôts de l'OCDE

1. 1000 Impôts sur le revenu, les bénéfices et les gains en capital
   - 1100 Impôts sur le revenu, les bénéfices et les gains en capital des personnes physiques
     - 1110 Sur le revenu et les bénéfices
     - 1120 Sur les gains en capital
   - 1200 Impôts sur le revenu, les bénéfices et les gains en capital des sociétés
     - 1210 Sur le revenu et les bénéfices
     - 1220 Sur les gains en capital
   - 1300 Non ventilables entres les rubriques 1100 et 1200
2. 2000 Cotisations de sécurité sociale
   - 2100 A la charge des salariés
     - 2110 Sur la base du salaire
     - 2120 Sur la base de l'impôt sur le revenu
   - 2200 A la charge des employeurs
     - 2210 Sur la base du salaire
     - 2220 Sur la base de l'impôt sur le revenu
   - 2300 A la charge des travailleurs indépendants ou des personnes n'occupant pas d'emploi
     - 2310 Sur la base du salaire
     - 2320 Sur la base de l'impôt sur le revenu
   - 2400 Non ventilables entre les rubriques 2100, 2200 et 2300
     - 2410 Sur la base du salaire
     - 2420 Sur la base de l'impôt sur le revenu
3. 3000 Impôts sur les salaires et la main-d'œuvre
4. 4000 Impôts sur le patrimoine
   - 4100 Impôts périodiques sur la propriété immobilière
     - 4110 Ménages
     - 4120 Autres agents
   - 4200 Impôts périodiques sur l'actif net
     - 4210 Personnes physiques
     - 4220 Sociétés
   - 4300 Impôts sur les mutations par décès, les successions et les donations
     - 4310 Impôts sur les mutations par décès et les successions
     - 4320 Impôts sur les donations
   - 4400 Impôts sur les transactions mobilières et immobilières
   - 4500 Autres impôts non périodiques sur le patrimoine
     - 4510 Impôts sur l'actif net
     - 4520 Autres impôts non périodiques

4600 Autres impôts périodiques sur le patrimoine

5. 5000 Impôts sur les biens et services

5100 Impôts sur la production, la vente, le transfert, la location et la livraison des biens et la prestation de services

5110 Impôts généraux

5111 Taxes sur la valeur ajoutée

5112 Impôts sur les ventes

5113 Impôts sur le chiffre d'affaires et autres impôts généraux sur les biens et services

5120 Impôts sur des biens et des services déterminés

5121 Accises

5122 Bénéfices des monopoles fiscaux

5123 Droits de douane et autres droits à l'importation

5124 Taxes à l'exportation

5125 Impôts sur les biens d'équipement

5126 Impôts sur des services déterminés

5127 Autres impôts sur les transactions et les échanges internationaux

5128 Autres impôts sur des biens et services déterminés

5130 Non ventilables entre les rubriques 5110 et 5120

5200 Impôts sur l'utilisation des biens ou l'autorisation d'utiliser des biens ou d'exercer des activités

5210 Impôts périodiques

5211 A la charge des ménages au titre de véhicules à moteur

5212 A la charge d'autres agents au titre de véhicules à moteur

5213 Autres impôts périodiques

5220 Impôts non périodiques

5300 Non ventilables entre les rubriques 5100 et 5200

6. 6000 Autres impôts

6100 A la charge exclusive des entreprises

6200 A la charge d'autre agents que les entreprises ou non identifiables

A.2. Champ couvert

Principes généraux

1. Dans la classification de l'OCDE, le terme « impôts » désigne uniquement les versements obligatoires effectués sans contrepartie au profit des administrations publiques ou à une autorité supranationale. Les impôts n'ont pas de contrepartie en ce sens que, normalement, les prestations fournies par les administrations au contribuable ne sont pas proportionnelles à ses versements.

2. Le terme « impôts » ne couvre pas les amendes, les pénalités, ni les prêts obligatoires aux administrations. Les cas dans lesquels la délimitation entre recettes fiscales et non fiscales est délicate à tracer, pour certains droits et taxes d'utilisation, sont examinés dans les § 12 à 15.

3. Les administrations publiques comprennent l'administration centrale et les organismes dont les opérations sont sous son contrôle effectif, les administrations régionales et locales et leurs services, les organismes de sécurité sociale et les entités publiques autonomes, à l'exception des entreprises publiques. Cette définition des administrations est calquée sur celle du Système de comptabilité nationale 2008 (SCN)[2]. Dans cette publication, les administrations publiques et leurs sous-secteurs sont décrits dans le chapitre 4, paragraphes 4.117 à 4.165.

4. Les unités extrabudgétaires sont des composantes du système des administrations publiques. Il s'agit d'entités d'administration publique dotées de budgets distincts, qui ne sont pas intégralement financés par le budget central ou général. Ces organismes fonctionnent sous l'autorité ou le contrôle d'une administration centrale, d'un État fédéré ou d'une collectivité locale. Les entités extrabudgétaires peuvent disposer de leurs propres sources de recettes, qui peuvent être complétées par des dotations (transferts) provenant du budget général ou d'autres sources. Même si leurs budgets peuvent être soumis à l'approbation du corps législatif, comme les comptes budgétaires, elles disposent d'une certaine latitude quant au volume et à la composition de leurs dépenses. Ces entités peuvent être mises en place pour exercer des fonctions spécifiques des administrations publiques, telles que la construction de routes ou la production non marchande de services de santé ou d'éducation. Les dispositions budgétaires peuvent varier grandement suivant les pays, et différents termes sont utilisés pour décrire ces entités, mais elles sont souvent qualifiées de « fonds extrabudgétaires » ou d'« organismes autonomes ».

5. Les paiements obligatoires, sans contrepartie, perçus par les gouvernements nationaux et versés aux autorités supranationales sont également traitées comme des impôts au titre de la définition du paragraphe 1. Les recettes fiscales qui sont perçues par les gouvernements nationaux et payées à une autorité supranationale sont attribuées en tant que recettes fiscales à l'autorité supranationale dans le SCN 2008 (voir paragraphes 22.60-61, 22.88 et 22.99) et le SEC 2010 (voir paragraphe 20.165). Dans les Statistiques des recettes publiques, ces recettes fiscales comprennent les droits de douane, les contributions au Fonds de résolution unique de l'UE et toute autre taxe perçue par les États membres de l'UE au nom de l'Union européenne. Elles sont incluses dans les montants des recettes fiscales dans les tableaux par pays (chapitre 5) du pays dans lequel elles sont perçues et sont attribuées à l'autorité supranationale (voir § 102).

6. Dans les pays où les églises font partie des administrations publiques, les impôts sur les cultes sont inclus dans ces paiements, à condition qu'ils répondent aux critères énoncés au

§ 1 ci-dessus. Comme les données se réfèrent aux montants encaissés par les administrations publiques et les autorités supranationales, les contributions versées à des organismes privés, aux organismes sociaux ou régimes de sécurité sociale extérieurs aux administrations publiques, aux syndicats ou aux associations professionnelles sont exclues, même si elles sont obligatoires. Sont toutefois inclus les versements obligatoires aux administrations publiques dont le montant est affecté à ces organismes, à condition que l'administration ne fasse pas simplement office d'agent collecteur[3]. On a distingué les bénéfices des monopoles fiscaux de ceux d'autres entreprises publiques et on les a considérés comme des impôts parce qu'ils reflètent l'exercice du pouvoir d'imposition de l'État par l'intermédiaire du monopole (voir § 66 à 68), comme le sont les bénéfices de l'État provenant de l'achat et de la vente de monnaies étrangères à des taux différents (voir § 76).

7. Les impôts payés par les administrations elles-mêmes (tels que les cotisations de sécurité sociale et les impôts sur les salaires payés par les administrations en tant qu'employeurs (2200 et 3000), les impôts sur la consommation qu'elles acquittent à l'occasion de leurs achats ou les impôts sur leur patrimoine) sont inclus dans les données présentées. Toutefois, lorsqu'il est possible de les isoler, les montants provenant de ces impôts[4] sont indiqués dans le Tableau 5.40 de ce Rapport.

8. Les rapports entre cette classification et celle du Système de comptabilité nationale (SCN) sont indiqués dans les sections A.9 et A.11. À cause des différences qui existent entre les deux classifications, les statistiques de la comptabilité nationale ne sont pas toujours établies ou classées suivant la pratique adoptée dans le présent guide. Ces différences et d'autres encore sont mentionnées dans les cas appropriés (voir par exemple § 31), mais il est impossible de toutes les signaler. Il peut y avoir aussi certaines différences entre cette classification et celle utilisée par certaines administrations nationales (voir par exemple § 13), aussi les statistiques nationales et celles de l'OCDE ne peuvent pas toujours être compatibles ; ces différences, cependant, sont vraisemblablement très insignifiantes dans les montants des recettes en cause.

Cotisations de sécurité sociale

9. Les cotisations obligatoires de sécurité sociale, définies au § 40, qui sont versées aux administrations publiques, font partie des recettes fiscales. Mais elles peuvent différer toutefois des autres impôts du fait que le paiement des prestations de sécurité sociale dépend dans la plupart des pays du versement des cotisations appropriées, encore qu'il n'y ait pas forcément un lien entre l'importance des prestations et le montant des cotisations. La comparabilité entre les pays sera meilleure si on considère les cotisations de sécurité sociale comme des impôts ; elles figurent cependant sous une rubrique distincte de façon à permettre un traitement séparé pour n'importe quelle analyse.

10. La distinction stricte entre les recettes fiscales (qui sont des paiements obligatoires sans contrepartie aux administrations publiques ou à une autorité supranationale) et les prélèvements obligatoires non fiscaux (PONF) (qui sont soit des paiements avec contrepartie aux administrations publiques, soit des paiements destinés à d'autres organismes) est clairement définie. Néanmoins, dans la palette des divers prélèvements obligatoires destinés aux administrations publiques qui existent dans les différents pays, il n'est pas toujours évident de déterminer en pratique si tel ou tel prélèvement est un impôt ou un PONF. Ainsi, l'épargne-retraite obligatoire qui est placée sous le contrôle des administrations publiques et qui s'accumule sur un compte individuel rémunéré à un taux correspondant au rendement du marché ou destiné à compenser l'inflation semble, à première vue, constituer une forme

de PONF, et non d'impôt. Toutefois, ces paiements peuvent encore être considérés comme « sans contrepartie » et, par conséquent, être classés dans les impôts et non dans les PONF (par exemple si cette épargne-retraite n'est pas remboursée au cas où le contribuable décède avant d'atteindre l'âge de la retraite, et si les fonds en question sont utilisés ensuite pour verser une pension minimale à tous les contribuables qui sont assurés). En conséquence, les chiffres relatifs aux recettes de sécurité sociale indiqués pour la plupart des pays reposent sur l'hypothèse que l'on considère que tous les types de prélèvements obligatoires destinés aux administrations publiques comportent, dans une certaine mesure, un élément redistributif. Il convient de noter que cette conclusion découle d'une interprétation généralement large du terme « sans contrepartie » dans la définition de l'impôt.

11. Les cotisations de sécurité sociale qui sont facultatives ou qui ne sont pas versées à des administrations publiques (voir § 1) ne sont pas considérées comme des impôts, bien que dans certains pays (comme il est indiqué dans les notes correspondantes), il soit difficile d'éliminer complètement les cotisations facultatives et certains versements obligatoires au secteur privé des statistiques relatives aux recettes publiques. Les cotisations de sécurité sociale imputées ne sont pas considérées comme des impôts.

Droits, taxes d'utilisation et droits de licence

12. Si l'on excepte les droits perçus sur les permis de circulation des véhicules à moteur, qui sont universellement considérés comme des impôts, il n'est pas facile de distinguer les droits et taxes d'utilisation qui doivent être traitées comme des impôts de celles qui ne doivent pas l'être. Si, en effet, un droit ou une taxe est perçu au titre d'un service ou d'une activité déterminée, le lien entre ce prélèvement et la prestation fournie peut être plus ou moins important, de même que la relation entre le montant du prélèvement et le coût de la prestation. Lorsque le bénéficiaire d'une prestation acquitte un droit dont le montant est clairement lié au coût de la prestation fournie, on peut considérer que le prélèvement comporte une contrepartie, et d'après la définition donnée au § 1, il ne sera pas traité comme un impôt. Toutefois, dans les cas suivants, les prélèvements seraient 'sans contrepartie':

a) lorsque le prélèvement est très supérieur au coût de la prestation fournie ;

b) lorsque le redevable de la contribution n'est pas le bénéficiaire de la prestation correspondante (par exemple, un droit perçu sur l'abattage du bétail pour financer un service qui est fourni aux agriculteurs) ;

c) lorsque l'État ne fournit pas un service déterminé en contrepartie du droit qu'il perçoit, même si un permis est délivré à celui qui acquitte le droit (par exemple, lorsque l'État délivre des permis de chasse, de pêche ou de port d'armes qui ne sont pas assortis du droit d'utiliser une parcelle déterminée de terres appartenant à l'État) ;

d) lorsque les bénéficiaires de la prestation sont les personnes qui ont acquitté le droit, mais que la prestation dont chacun bénéficie n'est pas nécessairement en rapport avec le montant de ses propres versements (par exemple, le droit de commercialisation du lait acquitté par les fermiers qui sert à promouvoir la consommation de lait.

13. Dans des cas limites, cependant, l'application des critères énoncés au § 1 peut être particulièrement difficile. La solution adoptée, dans un souci d'uniformité entre les pays et eu égard aux montants relativement faibles des recettes en cause, consiste à s'en tenir

à la pratique prépondérante des administrations fiscales plutôt que de laisser chaque pays décider si ces prélèvements sont des impôts ou des recettes non fiscales[5].

14. On trouvera ci-après la liste des principaux droits et taxes en question et leur traitement normal[6] dans la présente publication :

Recettes non fiscales :	frais de justice ; droits de délivrance de permis de conduire ; droits portuaires ; redevances de passeport ; redevances de radio et de télévision lorsque le service est assuré par les pouvoirs publics.
Impôts du sous-groupe 5200:	autorisation d'exercer certaines activités telles que : distribution de films ; chasse, pêche et utilisation d'armes à feu ; organisation de spectacles ou de jeux et paris ; vente de boissons alcoolisées ou de tabacs ; autorisation de posséder des chiens et d'utiliser ou posséder des véhicules à moteur ou des armes à feu ; taxes d'extraction.

15. Dans la pratique, il se peut qu'il ne soit pas toujours possible d'isoler les recettes fiscales des recettes non fiscales quand elles sont enregistrées ensemble. Si l'on estime qu'il s'agit surtout de recettes non fiscales, l'ensemble sera traité comme tel ; dans le cas contraire, les recettes seront comptabilisées et classées conformément aux règles énoncées au § 33.

Redevances

16. La propriété des gisements prenant la forme de minéraux ou de combustibles fossiles (charbon, pétrole ou gaz naturel) dépend de la façon dont les droits de propriété sont définis par la loi, et aussi par les conventions internationales quand les gisements sont situés sous les eaux internationales. Dans certains cas, soit le terrain sous lequel les gisements sont situés, soit les gisements eux-mêmes, soit les deux peuvent appartenir à une administration publique centrale ou locale.

17. Ces unités des administrations publiques peuvent alors consentir un bail à d'autres unités institutionnelles en les autorisant à exploiter ces gisements pendant une période déterminée, en contrepartie d'un paiement ou d'une série de paiements. Ces paiements sont souvent qualifiés de redevances (« royalties »), mais ils n'en constituent pas moins essentiellement des loyers, qui reviennent aux propriétaires des ressources naturelles considérées parce qu'ils mettent ces actifs à la disposition d'autres unités institutionnelles pour des durées déterminées. Ces loyers peuvent prendre la forme de versements périodiques d'un montant fixe, indépendant du rythme d'extraction ; plus vraisemblablement, ils peuvent être fonction de la quantité, du volume ou de la valeur des actifs extraits. Les entreprises engagées dans des activités de prospection sur des terrains publics peuvent effectuer des paiements aux unités de l'administration publique concernées, en contrepartie de l'autorisation de procéder à des forages d'essai ou de réaliser par d'autres moyens des recherches concernant l'existence et la localisation de gisements. Ces paiements sont également considérés comme des loyers, même en l'absence d'extraction. Ils sont donc classés dans les recettes non fiscales.

18. Les mêmes principes s'appliquent lorsque d'autres unités institutionnelles se voient consentir un bail leur permettant de couper du bois dans des forêts naturelles sur des terrains appartenant à des unités des administrations publiques. Ces paiements sont également classés dans les recettes non fiscales.

19. Ces loyers ou redevances versés aux administrations publiques ne doivent pas être confondus avec les impôts sur le revenu et les bénéfices, les taxes d'extraction, les taxes professionnelles ou d'autres impôts. Si ces paiements sont prélevés sur les bénéfices tirés des activités d'extraction, ils doivent être classés dans les impôts sur le revenu, les bénéfices et les gains en capital (1000). En outre, toute taxe d'extraction relative à des

minéraux ou des combustibles fossiles extraits de réserves privées ou appartenant à d'autres administrations publiques doit être classée dans les impôts. Les paiements liés à la valeur brute de la production doivent être classés dans les autres impôts sur des biens et services déterminés (5128). Les paiements effectués en contrepartie d'une autorisation ou d'un permis d'extraction doivent être classés dans les impôts sur l'utilisation des biens ou l'autorisation d'utiliser des biens ou d'exercer des activités (5200).

Amendes et pénalités

20. En principe, les amendes et pénalités portant sur les impôts impayés ou les pénalités appliquées en cas de tentative d'évasion fiscale ne doivent pas être enregistrées comme des recettes fiscales. Cependant, il se peut qu'il ne soit pas possible de séparer le versement des amendes et pénalités des recettes correspondant aux impôts auxquels ces amendes et pénalités se rattachent. Dans ce cas, les amendes et pénalités associés à un impôt particulier sont enregistrées avec les recettes correspondant à cet impôt alors que les amendes et pénalités liées à des recettes correspondant à des impôts non-identifiés sont classées comme autres impôts dans la catégorie 6000. Les amendes qui ne concernent pas des infractions fiscales (comme les infractions au stationnement), ou qui ne sont pas identifiables en tant que telles, ne sont pas non plus considérées comme des recettes fiscales.

A.3. Bases de comptabilisation

Droits constatés ou décaissements

21. Les données enregistrées dans les publications des *Statistiques des recettes publiques* pour les années récentes sont essentiellement indiquées en droits constatés pour les pays de l'OCDE, c'est-à-dire qu'elles sont enregistrées au moment du fait générateur de l'impôt. D'autres informations sont fournies dans les notes des tableaux par pays au chapitre 5 de ce Rapport.

22. Toutefois, les données des années antérieures et qui concernent les pays non OCDE sont encore principalement comptabilisées sur la base des décaissements, c'est-à-dire au moment où l'administration reçoit le versement. Ainsi, les impôts retenus à la source par les employeurs au cours d'un exercice, mais versés à l'administration au cours de l'exercice suivant, et les impôts dus au titre d'une année mais effectivement versés l'année suivante, figurent les uns et les autres dans les recettes du second exercice. Les restitutions, remboursements et retraits résultant d'opérations rectificatives sont déduits des recettes brutes de la période au cours de laquelle ces opérations sont effectuées.

23. Les données relatives aux recettes fiscales sont comptabilisées, sans déduction compensatoire des dépenses administratives liées au recouvrement de l'impôt. De même, lorsque le produit d'un impôt sert à subventionner certains membres de la collectivité, la subvention n'est pas déduite du rendement de l'impôt, encore que certains pays fassent figurer dans leurs données l'impôt après déduction des subventions.

24. Pour les monopoles fiscaux (sous-groupe 5122), seul le montant effectivement transféré à l'État est inclus dans les recettes publiques. Toutefois, les dépenses des monopoles fiscaux qui sont considérées comme des dépenses publiques (par exemple, des dépenses de caractère social engagées par les monopoles fiscaux à l'instigation de l'État) sont ajoutées après coup pour calculer le montant des recettes fiscales (voir § 66).

La distinction entre dispositions fiscales et dépenses directes[7]

25. Étant donné que la présente publication ne vise que les recettes publiques en faisant abstraction des dépenses, il convient de distinguer entre les dispositions fiscales et les dépenses directes. Normalement, cette distinction ne soulève aucune difficulté, car les dépenses directes sont effectuées en dehors du système fiscal et des comptes fiscaux et en vertu de dispositions législatives distinctes. Dans les cas limites, on recourt, pour établir la distinction, au principe de la comptabilisation sur la base des paiements. Dans la mesure où une disposition affecte le montant des paiements du contribuable à l›État, elle est considérée comme une disposition fiscale dont il est tenu compte dans les données figurant dans cette publication. Une disposition qui n›affecte pas ce montant est considérée comme une dépense directe dont il n›est pas tenu compte dans les données reproduites dans cette publication.

26. Il est clair que les abattements fiscaux, exonérations et déductions de l'assiette de l'impôt modifient le montant de l'impôt acquitté à l'État ; il s'agit donc de dispositions fiscales. Inversement, les formes d'aides qui ne sont pas imputables sur l'impôt et n'ont donc aucun lien avec le processus d'imposition, ne réduisent pas les recettes publiques qui sont consignées dans ce volume. Les crédits d'impôt sont des montants déductibles de l'impôt à acquitter (par opposition aux déductions, qui sont opérées sur l'assiette de l'impôt). On distingue deux catégories de crédits d'impôt : ceux (que l'on qualifiera ici de 'non récupérables') qui sont limités au montant de l'impôt à acquitter et ne peuvent donc donner lieu à un versement de l'administration au contribuable, et ceux (qualifiés ici de 'récupérables') qui n'ont pas cette limite, de sorte que l'excédent du crédit sur l'impôt peut être versé au contribuable[8]. Le crédit d'impôt non récupérable, comme un abattement fiscal, affecte évidemment le montant de l'impôt acquitté à l'État ; aussi est-il considéré comme une disposition fiscale. La solution adoptée pour les crédits d'impôts récupérables[9] consiste à distinguer l'élément de « dépense fiscale »[10], qui est la part du crédit utilisée pour réduire ou supprimer l'impôt dû par le contribuable, et l'« élément de transfert », qui correspond à la part excédant l'impôt dû par le contribuable et qui lui est reversée. Les recettes fiscales rapportées doivent être diminuées du montant de l'élément de dépense, mais non de l'élément de transfert. En outre, les montants de l'élément de dépense fiscale et de l'élément de transfert doivent être indiqués pour mémoire dans les tableaux par pays. Les pays qui ne sont pas en mesure de faire la distinction entre l'élément de dépense fiscale et l'élément de transfert doivent indiquer si leurs recettes fiscales ont été ou non diminuées du montant total de ces éléments, et fournir toutes les estimations dont ils disposent concernant les montants de ces deux éléments. Des informations complémentaires figurent dans le chapitre 1 de ce Rapport, qui fait apparaître les effets des différents traitements possibles des crédits d'impôts récupérables sur les ratios impôt rapportant les impôts au PIB.

Année civile et année fiscale (exercice budgétaire)

27. Les autorités nationales dont l'exercice budgétaire ne correspond pas à l'année civile fournissent, autant que possible, leurs données sur la base de l'année civile afin de faciliter au maximum la comparaison avec les données des autres pays. Les données d'un petit nombre de pays se réfèrent à l'exercice budgétaire. Pour ceux-ci, les statistiques de PIB utilisées dans les tableaux comparatifs portent aussi sur les exercices budgétaires.

A.4. Principes généraux de classification

Les fondements essentiels de la classification

28. Les recettes sont classées par groupes principaux (1000, 2000, 3000, 4000, 5000, 6000) suivant l'assiette de l'impôt : 1000 revenus, bénéfices et gains en capital ; 2000 et 3000 salaires et nombre d'employés ; 4000 patrimoine ; 5000 biens et services ; 6000 assiettes diverses, autres ou non identifiables. Lorsqu'un impôt est calculé en fonction de plusieurs assiettes, les recettes sont, chaque fois que c'est possible, réparties entre les divers groupes (voir § 33 et § 84). Les groupes 4000 et 5000 ne comprennent pas seulement les impôts ayant pour assiette le patrimoine, les biens ou les services eux-mêmes, mais aussi certains impôts connexes. Ainsi, les impôts sur les mutations du patrimoine sont classés dans le groupe 4400[11] et les impôts sur l'utilisation des biens, ou l'autorisation d'exercer une activité, dans le groupe 5200. Dans les groupes 4000 et 5000, une distinction est faite dans certains sous-groupes entre impôts périodiques et impôts non périodiques : on entend par impôts périodiques ceux qui sont perçus à intervalles réguliers (ordinairement tous les ans) et par impôts non périodiques ceux qui ne sont perçus qu'une seule fois (voir aussi les § 48 à 51, § 54, § 55, et § 81 pour une application particulière de cette distinction).

29. L'affectation spéciale de certaines recettes fiscales n'influe pas sur leur classification. Toutefois comme explicité au § 40 sur la classification des cotisations de sécurité sociale, l'octroi d'un droit aux prestations sociales est crucial dans la définition de la rubrique principale 2000.

30. La manière selon laquelle un impôt est perçu ou recouvré (par exemple, au moyen de timbres) n'affecte pas sa classification.

Classification des contribuables

31. Dans certains sous-groupes, des distinctions sont faites entre les différentes catégories de contribuables. Ces distinctions varient d'un impôt à l'autre :

a) *Ventilation des impôts sur le revenu et sur l'actif net entre personnes physiques et sociétés*

La distinction fondamentale entre les impôts sur le revenu des sociétés et les impôts sur le revenu des personnes physiques est que les premiers sont perçus sur la société en tant qu'entité et non sur les personnes physiques qui en sont propriétaires, donc sans tenir compte de la situation personnelle de celles-ci. La même distinction est applicable aux impôts sur l'actif net des sociétés et des personnes physiques. Les impôts perçus sur les bénéfices des sociétés de personnes et sur le revenu de certaines institutions comme les caisses d'assurance-vie ou de retraite, sont classés selon le même principe. Ils sont compris dans les impôts sur les sociétés (1200) lorsqu'ils sont perçus sur la société de personnes ou l'institution en tant qu'entité sans que la situation personnelle des propriétaires entre en ligne de compte ; dans les autres cas, ils sont considérés comme des impôts sur les personnes physiques (1100). Ordinairement, les impôts sur les sociétés et les impôts sur les personnes physiques sont régis par des dispositions législatives différentes[12]. La distinction qui est faite ici entre personnes physiques et sociétés ne reprend pas la classification par secteur (ménages, entreprises, etc.) adoptée dans les comptes de revenus et de dépenses du SCN. Cette dernière classification exclut du secteur des ménages certaines entreprises non constituées en sociétés[13] et les fait figurer parmi les entreprises non financières et les institutions financières. Toutefois, l'impôt sur les bénéfices de ces entreprises ne peut pas toujours être isolé de l'impôt sur les autres revenus des propriétaires de ces entreprises, ou ne peut l'être que d'une façon arbitraire. On n'a pas cherché ici à faire la distinction et l'impôt sur le revenu des personnes physiques figure globalement, quelle que soit la nature du revenu imposable.

b) *Ventilation des impôts sur les biens immobiliers entre ménages et autres agents*

En l'occurrence, la distinction est celle qui a été adoptée par le SCN dans les comptes de production et de consommation. On distingue, en effet, les ménages en tant que consommateurs d'une part (c'est-à-dire à l'exclusion des entreprises individuelles), et les producteurs d'autre part. Cependant, les impôts sur les logements occupés par les ménages, qu'ils soient à la charge des propriétaires qui les occupent, du locataire ou du propriétaire, sont classés comme étant à la charge des ménages. C'est la distinction faite habituellement entre les impôts sur les biens des personnes et les impôts sur les biens des entreprises. Toutefois, certains pays ne sont pas en mesure d'établir cette distinction.

c) *Ventilation des permis de circuler des véhicules à moteur entre taxes à la charge des ménages et à la charge d'autres agents*

On distingue ici les ménages en tant que consommateurs d'une part, et producteurs d'autre part, comme dans les comptes de production et de consommation du SCN.

d) *Ventilation des autres impôts (6000) entre les entreprises et les autres agents*

Il est fait la même distinction qu'au point (c) ci-dessus entre les producteurs, d'une part, et les ménages consommateurs d'autre part. Les impôts qui figurent dans le groupe 6000 parce qu'ils ne comportent pas une assiette unique ou parce que leur assiette ne relève d'aucune des catégories précédentes, mais qui ne sont manifestement perçus que sur les producteurs et non sur les ménages, sont classés comme étant 'à la charge des entreprises'. Les autres impôts du groupe 6000 figurent sous la rubrique 'à la charge d'autres agents' ou 'non identifiés'.

Surtaxes

32. Les recettes des surtaxes relatives à des impôts particuliers sont classées ordinairement avec les recettes de l'impôt correspondant, que la surtaxe ait ou non un caractère temporaire. Toutefois, si l'une des caractéristiques de la surtaxe permet de la classer sous une rubrique différente de la classification de l'OCDE, les recettes de cette surtaxe sont classées sous cette rubrique et non pas avec les recettes de l'impôt correspondant

Recettes fiscales non identifiables et sous-groupes résiduels

33. Il arrive parfois qu'on ne puisse déterminer si des impôts relèvent entièrement d'un groupe ou d'un sous-groupe de la classification de l'OCDE ; dans ces cas on applique les méthodes suivantes :

a) le groupe est connu, mais on ne sait pas comment répartir les recettes entre les sous-groupes ; les recettes sont alors classées dans le sous-groupe résiduel approprié (1300, 2400, 4520, 4600, 5128, 5130, 5300 ou 6200) ;

b) on sait que l'ensemble des recettes d'un groupe d'impôts (ordinairement des impôts locaux) provient d'impôts relevant d'un groupe ou sous-groupe particulier, mais certains impôts du groupe, dont le montant ne peut être déterminé avec précision, peuvent être classés dans d'autres groupes ou sous-groupes ; dans ce cas les recettes sont comptabilisées dans le groupe ou sous-groupe dont relève l'essentiel des recettes ;

c) il est impossible d'identifier le groupe ou le sous-groupe d'un impôt (ordinairement un impôt local) ; l'impôt est alors classé dans le groupe 6200, à moins qu'il ne s'agisse d'un impôt manifestement à la charge des entreprises, auquel cas il est classé dans le sous-groupe 6100.

A.5. Commentaires sur les postes de la liste

1000 — Impôts sur le revenu, les bénéfices et les gains en capital

34. Ce groupe couvre les impôts prélevés sur le revenu ou le bénéfice net (c'est-à-dire le revenu brut déduction faite des abattements autorisés) des personnes physiques et des entreprises. Sont aussi couverts les impôts prélevés sur les gains en capital des personnes physiques et des entreprises et sur les gains provenant de jeux.

35. Ce groupe comprend :

a) les impôts perçus principalement sur les revenus ou les bénéfices, bien qu'ils puissent l'être partiellement sur d'autres bases. Les impôts qui ont une autre assiette principale que le revenu ou les bénéfices sont classés selon les principes énoncés aux § 33 et § 84 ;

b) les impôts sur la propriété immobilière, qui sont perçus sur la base d'un revenu présumé ou estimé faisant partie de l'assiette de l'impôt sur le revenu (voir aussi § 48 (a), (c) et (d)) ;

c) les versements obligatoires aux caisses de sécurité sociale qui sont prélevés sur les revenus mais ne donnent pas droit à des prestations sociales. Lorsque ces contributions donnent droit à des prestations sociales, elles figurent à la rubrique 2000 (voir § 40) ;

d) les recettes provenant d'impôts cédulaires sur le revenu intégrés dans le régime général qui sont globalement classés dans ce groupe, bien que certains de ces impôts soient sur le revenu brut et ne tiennent pas toujours compte de la situation personnelle du contribuable.

36. Les impôts figurant dans ce groupe sont subdivisés en deux grands sous-groupes, les impôts sur le revenu des personnes physiques (1100) et les impôts sur le revenu des sociétés (1200), une ventilation étant faite dans chacun d'eux entre les impôts sur le revenu et les bénéfices (1110 et 1210) et les impôts sur les gains en capital (1120 et 1220). Si certaines recettes ne peuvent être identifiées comme relevant soit du sous-groupe 1100, soit du sous-groupe 1200, ou si cette distinction ne peut être faite dans la pratique (parce qu'il n'y a pas de données fiables sur les bénéficiaires des paiements sur lesquels la retenue à la source est faite), elles sont classées dans le sous-groupe 1300 (non ventilables).

Traitement des crédits d'impôt dans les systèmes d'imputation

37. Dans les régimes d'imputation de l'impôt sur les bénéfices des sociétés, les actionnaires bénéficient d'une compensation totale ou partielle d'imposition sur les dividendes que la société leur a versés et pour lesquels elle a acquitté l'impôt sur le revenu des sociétés. Dans les pays qui appliquent un tel régime,[14] une fraction de l'impôt sur les bénéfices des sociétés sert à alléger l'impôt dû par l'actionnaire. Cet allégement prend la forme d'un crédit d'impôt, dont le montant peut être inférieur, égal ou supérieur au montant total de l'impôt dont il est redevable. Si le crédit d'impôt dépasse ce montant, l'excédent peut être versé à l'actionnaire. Comme ce type de crédit d'impôt fait partie intégrante des systèmes d'imputation de l'impôt sur le revenu des sociétés, tout paiement à l'actionnaire est considéré

comme un remboursement d'impôt et non comme une dépense (se référer au traitement des autres crédits d'impôt exposé au § 26).

38. Puisque, dans les systèmes d'imputation, le crédit d'impôt (même lorsqu'il dépasse l'impôt dû) est censé être une disposition fiscale, on peut se demander s'il doit être déduit des recettes de l'impôt sur le revenu des personnes physiques (1110) ou de celles de l'impôt sur les bénéfices de sociétés (1210). Dans ce Rapport le montant intégral de l'impôt acquitté sur les bénéfices des sociétés figure sous le poste 1210 et aucun impôt imputé n'est inclus dans le poste 1110. Le montant total du crédit d'impôt réduit donc le montant des recettes du poste 1110, que ce crédit se traduise par une réduction de l'impôt dû sur le revenu des personnes physiques ou par un remboursement réel du fait que le crédit dépasse le montant de l'impôt. (Cependant, lorsque ces crédits sont déduits de l'impôt sur les sociétés au titre de dividendes versés à des sociétés, le montant est déduit des recettes du poste 1210).

1120 et 1220 — Impôts sur les gains en capital

39. Ces postes comprennent les impôts perçus sur les gains en capital, le sous-groupe 1120 comptabilisant les impôts prélevés sur les gains des personnes physiques et le sous-groupe 1220 ceux qui sont perçus sur les gains des entreprises constituées sous forme de sociétés, lorsque ces recettes peuvent être ventilées. Ce n'est pas le cas dans de nombreux pays et les recettes de ces impôts sont alors classées avec celles de l'impôt sur le revenu. Les impôts sur les gains provenant de jeux sont aussi classés sous le poste 1120.

2000 — Cotisations de sécurité sociale

40. Figurent dans ce groupe tous les versements obligatoires aux administrations publiques qui donnent le droit de bénéficier d'une prestation sociale future (éventuelle). Ces versements sont généralement affectés au financement de prestations sociales et souvent effectués au profit d'institutions ou d'administrations publiques qui fournissent de telles prestations. Cependant, cette affectation n'entre pas dans la définition des cotisations de sécurité sociale et n'est pas nécessaire pour qu'un impôt soit classé dans cette rubrique. Cependant, il faut qu'un impôt confère un droit pour être classé dans cette rubrique. Par conséquent, les prélèvements sur les revenus ou la masse salariale qui sont affectés aux caisses de sécurité sociale mais ne donnent aucun droit à des prestations sont exclus de cette rubrique et figurent à celle des impôts sur le revenu des personnes physiques (1100) ou des impôts sur les salaires et la main-d'œuvre (3000). Les impôts assis sur d'autres bases, telles que les biens et services, qui sont affectés à des prestations de sécurité sociale, ne sont pas indiqués ici, mais sont classés en fonction de leurs bases respectives parce qu'en général ils ne donnent pas droit à des prestations de sécurité sociale.

41. Seraient entre autres incluses les cotisations au titre des catégories suivantes de prestations de sécurité sociale : les allocations d'assurance-chômage et les compléments, les allocations pour accidents, blessures et maladie, les pensions de retraite, d'invalidité et de survivant, les allocations familiales, les remboursements de dépenses médicales et d'hospitalisation ou la fourniture de services médicaux ou hospitaliers. Les cotisations peuvent être collectées à la fois auprès des employés et des employeurs.

42. Les cotisations peuvent être assises sur les gains ou la masse salariale (« sur la base du salaire ») ou sur le revenu net après déductions et exemptions en fonction de la situation personnelle (« sur la base de l'impôt sur le revenu ») et les recettes correspondant à ces deux bases doivent être identifiées séparément si possible. Cependant, lorsque les cotisations à un régime général de sécurité sociale sont assises sur la masse salariale, mais que les

cotisations de groupes particuliers (tels que les travailleurs indépendants) ne peuvent être évaluées sur cette base et que le revenu net est utilisé comme valeur rapprochée des gains bruts, les recettes peuvent encore être considérées comme assises sur la masse salariale. En principe, cette rubrique exclut les cotisations facultatives à des régimes de sécurité sociale. Lorsqu'elles peuvent être identifiées séparément, elles figurent pour mémoire dans le tableau indiquant le financement des prestations de sécurité sociale. Toutefois, en pratique, elles ne peuvent pas toujours être distinguées des cotisations facultatives, et dans ce cas elles figurent à cette rubrique.

43. Les cotisations à des régimes d'assurance sociale qui ne relèvent pas des pouvoirs publics et à d'autres régimes d'assurance ou de prévoyance, aux caisses de retraite, sociétés de secours mutuel ou autres systèmes d'épargne, ne sont pas considérées comme des cotisations de sécurité sociale. Les caisses de prévoyance résultant d'arrangements aux termes desquels les cotisations de chaque salarié et celles que l'employeur verse en son nom sont comptabilisées séparément dans un compte productif d'intérêts d'où elles peuvent être retirées dans des conditions bien déterminées. Les caisses de retraite sont des régimes autonomes organisés par négociations entre salariés et employeurs, qui comportent diverses contributions et prestations, parfois liées plus directement au salaire et à la durée d'activité que dans les régimes de sécurité sociale. Lorsque les cotisations à ces régimes sont obligatoires ou quasi obligatoires (par exemple en vertu d'un accord entre organisations professionnelles et syndicales), elles sont comptabilisées dans le poste pour mémoire (voir le Tableau 5.39 du Rapport).

44. Les cotisations versées par les agents des administrations et par les administrations au titre de leurs agents à des régimes de sécurité sociale relevant des pouvoirs publics sont incluses dans ce groupe. Sont aussi assimilées à des impôts les cotisations à des régimes particuliers réservés aux agents des administrations qui sont censés remplacer un régime général de la sécurité sociale[15]. Par contre, lorsqu'un régime distinct n'est pas censé remplacer un régime général et résulte de négociations entre l'administration, agissant en qualité d'employeur, et ses agents, il n'est pas considéré comme un régime de sécurité sociale et les cotisations à ce titre ne sont pas assimilées à des impôts, même si le régime a été institué par des dispositions législatives.

45. Cette rubrique ne comprend pas les cotisations 'imputées', qui correspondent aux prestations sociales versées directement par les employeurs à leurs salariés, ou anciens salariés, ou à leurs représentants (par exemple, lorsque des employeurs sont légalement tenus de verser des prestations maladies pendant une certaine période).

46. Le groupe comprend les cotisations à la charge des salariés (2100), à la charge des employeurs (2200), et à la charge des travailleurs indépendants ou des personnes n'occupant pas d'emploi (2300). À cet effet, on entend par salariés toutes les personnes qui exercent une activité dans des entreprises, des administrations, des institutions privées sans but lucratif, ou qui occupent d'autres emplois rémunérés, à l'exception des propriétaires et des membres de leur famille non rémunérés dans le cas d'entreprises individuelles. Sont également compris les membres des forces armées, quelle que soit la durée et la nature de leurs services, s'ils cotisent à un régime de sécurité sociale. Par cotisations à la charge des employeurs, on entend les versements qu'ils effectuent au régime de sécurité sociale pour le compte de leurs salariés. Si, en cas de chômage, les salariés ou employeurs sont tenus de continuer à effectuer ces versements, ces derniers doivent figurer respectivement dans les sous-groupes 2100 et 2200. En conséquence, le sous-groupe 2300 est réservé aux cotisations

versées par les travailleurs indépendants et par ceux qui n'appartiennent pas à la population active (comme les handicapés ou les retraités).

3000 — Impôts sur les salaires et la main-d'œuvre

47. Il s'agit d'impôts que doivent acquitter les entreprises, déterminés en proportion des salaires et des traitements payés, ou d'après un montant fixe par personne employée. Ils ne comprennent pas les cotisations obligatoires de sécurité sociale payées par les employeurs, ni les impôts payés par les salariés sur leurs traitements et leurs salaires.

4000 — Impôts sur le patrimoine

48. Ce groupe couvre les impôts périodiques et non périodiques sur l'utilisation, la propriété ou la mutation des biens. Sont comptabilisés ici les impôts sur la propriété immobilière et sur l'actif net, les impôts sur les mutations par décès, les successions et les donations, et les impôts sur les transactions mobilières et immobilières. Sont exclus de ce groupe :

a) les impôts sur les gains en capital provenant de la vente d'un bien (1120 ou 1220) ;

b) les impôts sur l'utilisation des biens ou l'autorisation d'utiliser des biens ou d'exercer des activités (5200) [voir § 78] ;

c) les impôts immobiliers perçus sur la base d'un revenu net présumé qui tiennent compte de la situation personnelle du contribuable. Ces impôts sont classés dans le groupe 1100 en tant qu'impôts sur le revenu, avec les impôts sur le revenu et les gains en capital provenant des biens immobiliers ;

d) les impôts sur l'utilisation de biens immobiliers aux fins d'habitation qui sont à la charge du propriétaire ou du locataire et dont le montant est fonction de la situation personnelle de l'utilisateur (salaire, personnes à charge, etc.). Ils sont classés dans le groupe 1100 en tant qu'impôts sur le revenu ;

e) les impôts sur les constructions dépassant la densité autorisée, les impôts sur l'extension, la construction ou la modification de certains immeubles au-delà d'une valeur autorisée et les impôts sur la construction d'immeubles. Ces impôts sont classés dans le poste 5200 en tant qu'impôts sur l'autorisation d'exercer certaines activités ;

f) les impôts sur l'utilisation de biens immobiliers par le propriétaire à des fins commerciales particulières, comme la vente de boissons alcoolisées, de tabac, de viande, ou pour l'exploitation de sols ou terrains (par exemple aux États-Unis, les taxes d'extraction). Ils sont classés dans le poste 5200 en tant qu'impôts sur l'autorisation d'exercer certaines activités.

4100 — Impôts périodiques sur la propriété immobilière

49. Ce sous-groupe comprend les impôts prélevés régulièrement au titre de l'utilisation ou de la propriété de biens immobiliers.

- ces impôts sont prélevés sur les terrains et les bâtiments ;
- ces impôts sont calculés en pourcentage de la valeur du bien évalué d'après un revenu locatif fictif, le prix de vente ou le rendement capitalisé, ou en fonction d'autres caractéristiques du bien, comme sa dimension ou son emplacement, d'où l'on peut déduire une valeur locative présumée ou la valeur du capital.

- ces impôts sont à la charge du propriétaire, du locataire ou des deux. Ils peuvent également être payés par une administration à une autre administration au titre d'un bien relevant de la compétence de cette dernière.
- il n'est pas tenu compte des dettes pour la détermination de l'assiette de ces impôts, contrairement aux impôts sur l'actif net.

50. Les impôts sur la propriété immobilière sont en outre subdivisés en impôts acquittés par les ménages (4110) et impôts acquittés par d'autres agents (4120), suivant les critères exposés au § 31*(b)* ci-dessus.

4200 — Impôts périodiques sur l'actif net

51. Ce sous-groupe comprend les impôts prélevés régulièrement (dans la plupart des cas annuellement) sur l'actif net, c'est-à-dire les impôts perçus sur un large éventail de biens mobiliers et immobiliers, endettement déduit. Il est subdivisé en impôts acquittés par des personnes physiques (4210), et en impôts acquittés par des sociétés (4220) selon les critères exposés plus haut au § 31(a). Si les recettes provenant des institutions sont comptabilisées à part, les paiements concernés doivent être ajoutées aux impôts des entreprises.

4300 — Impôts sur les mutations par décès, les successions et les donations

52. Ce sous-groupe comprend les impôts sur les mutations par décès et les successions (4310) et les impôts sur les donations (4320).[16] Les impôts sur les mutations par décès sont calculés soit sur l'ensemble de la masse successorale, soit en fonction de la part de chacun des bénéficiaires (« part héréditaire ») ; en outre, ces derniers impôts peuvent tenir compte du degré de parenté entre chacun des bénéficiaires et le défunt.

4400 — Impôts sur les transactions mobilières et immobilières

53. Sont compris, entre autres, dans ce sous-groupe les impôts sur l'émission, le transfert, l'achat et la vente d'actifs financiers et non financiers (y compris de devises étrangères ou de valeurs mobilières), les impôts sur les chèques et d'autres formes de paiement, ainsi que les droits perçus à l'occasion d'actes juridiques déterminés, comme la validation de contrats et la vente de biens immobiliers. Sont exclus :

a) les impôts sur l'utilisation de biens, mobiliers ou immobiliers, ou l'autorisation d'exercer certaines activités (5200) ;

b) les droits acquittés au titre de frais de justice, ou pour la délivrance de certificats de naissance, de mariage ou de décès, car ces droits sont considérés comme des recettes non fiscales (voir § 12) ;

c) les impôts sur les gains en capital (1000) ;

d) les impôts périodiques sur la propriété immobilière (4100) ;

e) les impôts périodiques sur l'actif net (4200) ;

f) les prélèvements sur le patrimoine ou sur l'actif net effectués une fois pour toutes (4500) ;

g) les droits de timbre non liés à des transactions financières et immobilières

   i. Droits de timbre sur la vente de produits spécifiques, comme les boissons alcoolisées ou le tabac (5121) ;

   ii. Droits de timbre limités par la loi aux produits importés (5123) ou aux produits exportés (5124) ; ou

iii. Droits de timbre qui ne grèvent pas exclusivement une seule catégorie de transaction (6000).

4500 — *Autres impôts non périodiques sur le patrimoine*

54. Ce sous-groupe comprend les prélèvements sur le patrimoine effectués une fois pour toutes (par opposition aux prélèvements périodiques). Il est subdivisé en impôts sur l'actif net (4510) et en autres impôts non périodiques sur le patrimoine (4520). Le poste 4510 inclurait les impôts perçus pour couvrir des dépenses exceptionnelles ou à des fins de redistribution. Le poste 4520 comprendrait les impôts prélevés pour tenir compte d'une plus-value prise par les terrains du fait que les administrations publiques ont autorisé l'extension ou l'aménagement d'installations locales, ainsi que les impôts sur la réévaluation du capital ou les impôts perçus une seule fois sur certains biens déterminés.

4600 — *Autres impôts périodiques sur le patrimoine*

55. Ils sont rares dans des pays Membres de l'OCDE ; ce sous-groupe comprendrait les impôts sur des biens tels que le cheptel, les bijoux, les fenêtres et les signes extérieurs de richesse.

5000 — *Impôts sur les biens et services*

56. Ce poste couvre tous les impôts et droits perçus sur la production, l'extraction, la vente, le transfert, la location ou la livraison de biens et la prestation de services (5100), ou sur l'utilisation ou l'autorisation d'utiliser des biens ou d'exercer des activités (5200). Ce groupe comprend donc :

a) les taxes cumulatives en cascade ;
b) les taxes générales sur les ventes — perçues au stade de la production ou de la fabrication, du gros ou du détail ;
c) les taxes sur la valeur ajoutée ;
d) les accises ;
e) les taxes perçues à l'importation et à l'exportation de biens ;
f) les impôts perçus sur l'utilisation de biens et sur l'autorisation d'utiliser des biens ou d'exercer certaines activités ;
g) les impôts sur l'extraction, le traitement ou la production de minéraux et autres produits.

57. Les cas douteux de délimitation entre ce groupe et le groupe 4000 (impôts sur le patrimoine) et le sous-groupe 6100 (autres impôts à la charge des entreprises) sont examinés aux § 48, § 53 et § 80. Des postes résiduels (5300 et 5130) ont été prévus pour comptabiliser les recettes fiscales qui ne peuvent être ventilées respectivement entre les postes 5100 et 5200 et entre les postes 5110 et 5120 (voir § 33).

5100 — *Impôts sur la production, la vente, le transfert, la location et la livraison de biens et la prestation de services*

58. Ce sous-groupe comprend tous les impôts perçus sur les transactions afférentes à des biens ou services, en fonction de leurs caractéristiques propres (comme la valeur, le poids du tabac, le degré d'alcool, etc.), à la différence des impôts perçus au titre de l'utilisation ou de l'autorisation d'utiliser des biens ou d'exercer des activités, qui entrent dans le sous-groupe 5200.

5110 — *Impôts généraux sur les biens et services*

59. Ce sous-groupe comprend tous les impôts, autres que les droits à l'importation et à l'exportation (5123 et 5124), perçus sur la production, la location, le transfert, la livraison ou la vente d'une gamme de biens ou la prestation d'une gamme de services, qu'ils soient produits dans le pays ou importés, et quel que soit le stade de la production ou de la distribution aux quel ils sont perçus. Il couvre ainsi les taxes sur la valeur ajoutée, les taxes sur les ventes et les taxes de caractère cumulatif en cascade. On a ajouté aux recettes brutes de cette catégorie les recettes provenant de la compensation à la frontière de ces impôts lorsque les biens sont importés, et déduit les remboursements d'impôts effectués lorsque les marchandises sont exportées. Ces impôts sont ventilés en : taxes sur la valeur ajoutée (5111), impôts sur les ventes (5112), impôts sur le chiffre d'affaires et autres impôts généraux sur les biens et services (5113).

60. Certains cas se trouvent à la limite entre ce sous-groupe et celui des impôts sur des biens et services déterminés (5120) lorsque ces impôts sont perçus sur un grand nombre de biens, comme dans le cas de la « *purchase tax* » au Royaume-Uni (abrogée en 1973) et l'impôt japonais sur les biens marchands (abrogé en 1988). Conformément aux options nationales, la « *purchase tax* » britannique est classée impôt général (5112) et l'impôt japonais dans les accises (5121).

5111 — *Taxes sur la valeur ajoutée*

61. Sont classés dans ce sous-groupe tous les impôts généraux sur la consommation prélevée sur la valeur ajoutée, quels que soient le mode de déduction et les stades auxquels ils sont perçus. En pratique, tous les pays de l'OCDE où existe une taxe sur la valeur ajoutée autorisent normalement la déduction immédiate des taxes sur les achats par tous les redevables, à l'exception du consommateur final, et imposent la taxe à tous les stades. Dans certains pays, le poste peut inclure aussi certains impôts, comme les taxes sur les activités financières et les assurances, soit parce que les recettes correspondantes ne peuvent être dissociées de celles de la taxe sur la valeur ajoutée, soit parce qu'elles sont considérées comme faisant partie intégrante de la taxe sur la valeur ajoutée, même si les taxes similaires qui existent dans d'autres pays peuvent être classées autrement (par exemple, sous le poste 5126 comme impôts sur les services ou sous le poste 4400 comme impôts sur les transactions mobilières et immobilières).

5112 — *Impôts sur les ventes*

62. Sont classés ici tous les impôts perçus à un stade unique, que ce soit celui de la fabrication, de la production, du gros ou du détail.

5113 — *Impôts sur le chiffre d'affaires et autres impôts généraux sur les biens et services*

63. Il s'agit des taxes cumulatives en cascade et des taxes qui combinent des éléments de taxe sur la consommation et des taxes en cascade. Ces impôts sont prélevés sur chaque transaction sans déduction des taxes acquittées en amont. Les taxes en cascade peuvent être combinées avec des éléments de taxe sur la valeur ajoutée ou d'impôts sur les ventes.

5120 — *Impôts sur des biens et des services déterminés*

64. Ce sous-groupe couvre les accises, les bénéfices engendrés et transférés par les monopoles fiscaux, et les droits de douane et à l'importation, ainsi que les taxes à

l'exportation, les opérations de change, les biens d'équipement et les paris, et aussi les impôts spéciaux sur les services qui ne font pas partie d'un impôt général du sous-groupe 5110.

5121 — *Accises*

65. Les accises sont des impôts spécifiques perçus par unité produite sur une gamme limitée de biens prédéfinie. Les accises sont généralement prélevées à des taux différenciés sur des biens non essentiels ou de luxe, les boissons alcoolisées, les produits à base de tabac et l'énergie. Les accises peuvent être perçues à un stade quelconque de la production ou de la distribution et sont calculées généralement sur la base d'un prélèvement spécifique par unité correspondant aux caractéristiques du produit considéré, par référence à sa valeur, son poids, son degré ou son volume. Cette subdivision couvre ainsi les impôts spéciaux sur certains produits tels que le sucre, la betterave, les allumettes et le chocolat ; les impôts prélevés à des taux variables sur une gamme déterminée de produits ; ainsi que les impôts perçus sur les produits à base de tabac, les boissons alcoolisées, les combustibles et les hydrocarbures. Si un impôt frappant principalement des produits importés doit ou devrait également être perçu sur des produits nationaux comparables, suivant la même législation, les recettes de cet impôt doivent alors être classées dans la catégorie des accises et non dans celle des droits à l'importation. Ce principe vaut également même s'il n'existe pas, ou ne peut exister, de production nationale comparable. Les impôts prélevés sur la consommation de services d'utilité publique (eau, électricité, gaz et autres formes d'énergie) sont considérés comme des accises, et non comme des impôts sur des services déterminés (5126). Ne sont pas inclus dans les accises les prélèvements entrant dans les catégories des impôts généraux sur les biens et services (5110), des bénéfices des monopoles fiscaux (5122), des droits de douane et autres droits à l'importation (5123) ou des taxes à l'exportation (5124).

5122 — *Bénéfices des monopoles fiscaux*

66. Ce sous-groupe couvre la fraction des bénéfices des monopoles fiscaux qui est transférée aux administrations publiques ou qui sert à financer des dépenses considérées comme dépenses publiques (voir § 24). Les montants sont comptabilisés lorsqu'ils sont transférés aux administrations publiques ou utilisés pour effectuer des dépenses considérées comme des dépenses publiques.

67. Les monopoles fiscaux reflètent l'exercice du pouvoir d'imposition de l'État par l'intermédiaire du monopole. Les monopoles fiscaux sont des entreprises publiques non financières, qui exercent dans la plupart des cas un monopole sur la production ou la distribution du tabac, des boissons alcoolisées, du sel, des allumettes, des cartes à jouer et des produits pétroliers ou agricoles (c'est-à-dire, sur le genre de produits qui peuvent être soumis, principalement ou accessoirement, aux accises du poste 5121), pour procurer des recettes publiques qui, dans d'autres pays, sont obtenues par le biais d'impôts frappant les transactions sur ces produits d'entreprises privées. Le monopole d'État peut être exercé au stade de la production, ou au stade de la distribution comme dans le cas des magasins de vente de boissons alcoolisées qui appartiennent à l'État et sont contrôlés par lui.

68. Les monopoles fiscaux sont différents des services publics, comme les chemins de fer, l'électricité, les postes et autres moyens de communication, qui peuvent avoir une position de monopole ou de quasi-monopole, mais dont l'objet principal est, normalement, de fournir des services essentiels et non pas de procurer des recettes à l'État. Les transferts à l'administration de ces autres entreprises publiques sont considérés comme des recettes

non fiscales. La notion traditionnelle de monopole fiscal n'a généralement pas été élargie pour inclure les loteries nationales, dont les bénéfices sont habituellement considérés comme des recettes non fiscales. Cependant, ces bénéfices peuvent être considérés comme des recettes fiscales quand la raison principale de la mise en œuvre de ces loteries est l'augmentation des recettes pour financer les dépenses publiques. On distingue les bénéfices des monopoles fiscaux des bénéfices des monopoles d'exportation et d'importation (5127), qui sont transférés des offices de commercialisation ou d'autres entreprises s'occupant du commerce international.

5123 — *Droits de douane et autres droits à l'importation*

69. Figurent ici les taxes, droits de timbre et surtaxes qui, selon la loi sont perçus exclusivement sur des produits importés. Sont aussi inclus dans ce poste les droits perçus sur l'importation de denrées agricoles dans les pays Membres de l'Union Européenne et les montants acquittés par certains de ces pays en vertu du Système de Montants Compensatoires[17]. Les droits de douane collectés par les États membres de l'Union européenne pour le compte de l'Union européenne sont reportés sous cette rubrique au niveau de l'autorité supranationale dans les tableaux par pays (chapitre 5 de ce Rapport). Sont exclues ici les taxes perçues sur les importations au titre d'un impôt général sur les biens et les services ou d'une accise applicable aussi bien aux produits importés qu'aux produits fabriqués dans le pays.

5124 — *Taxes à l'exportation*

70. Pendant les années 70, les droits à l'exportation étaient perçus normalement en Australie, au Canada et au Portugal, et ils étaient utilisés en Finlande à des fins conjoncturelles. Certains pays Membres de l'Union Européenne acquittent, dans le cadre du système des montants compensatoires, une taxe sur les exportations (voir la note 16 du § 69). Lorsque ces montants sont identifiables, ils sont inclus dans ce poste. Ce dernier ne comprend pas les remboursements effectués au titre d'impôts généraux sur la consommation d'accises ou de droits de douane sur des biens exportés, qui doivent être déduits des recettes brutes comptabilisées, selon le cas, sous le poste 5110, 5121 ou 5123.

5125 — *Impôts sur les biens d'équipement*

71. Ce sous-groupe comprend les impôts perçus sur les biens d'équipement, comme les machines. Ils peuvent exister depuis un certain nombre d'années ou avoir un caractère temporaire et être prélevés à des fins conjoncturelles. Ne sont pas inclus les impôts sur les 'inputs' industriels qui frappent aussi les consommateurs (comme l'impôt suédois sur l'énergie qui est classé sous le poste 5121).

5126 — *Impôts sur des services déterminés*

72. Sous ce poste figurent tous les impôts calculés sur la rémunération de services spécifiques, comme les taxes sur les primes d'assurance, les taxes sur les services bancaires, sur les jeux et paris (par exemple : courses de chevaux, pronostics de football, billets de loterie nationale), les transports, les spectacles, les restaurants et la publicité. Les impôts prélevés à l'entrée dans un casino, sur un champ de courses ou lors d'événements ou dans des lieux similaires, ainsi que les droits de timbre sur des services déterminés sont également classés sous ce poste. Les impôts prélevés sur le revenu brut des sociétés prestataires d'un service déterminé (exemple : transports [y compris les taxes d'aéroport et autres taxes

d'embarquement], assurance, banque, spectacles, restaurants et publicité) sont eux aussi classés sous ce poste.

73. Les recettes fiscales provenant des prélèvements sur les banques et des contributions aux mécanismes de garantie des dépôts et de stabilité financière sont également classés ici :

- Les redevances de stabilité, les prélèvements sur les banques et les contributions à la garantie des dépôts, qu'il est obligatoire d'acquitter, doivent généralement être traitées comme des recettes fiscales lorsque les versements sont effectués au profit de l'administration publique ou d'une autorité supranationale et affectés au budget consolidé ou général des administrations de sorte que les pouvoirs publics soient libres d'utiliser les fonds sans délai aux fins qu'ils jugent opportunes. Ce principe s'appliquerait indépendamment du fait que l'administration promette ou non d'effectuer des versements pour garantir les dépôts des clients des établissements bancaires si la situation l'exigeait à l'avenir.
- Si les paiements obligatoires sont effectués au profit de l'administration publique et imputés à des budgets dont les ressources doivent être entièrement réaffectées au secteur de l'économie qui englobe les entreprises assujetties à ces paiements, ceux-ci seront toujours traités, en règle générale, comme des recettes fiscales étant donné que les fonds seraient disponibles pour l'administration et réduiraient son déficit budgétaire, que la redevance est sans contrepartie pour les entités individuelles et que les montants collectés pourraient être dissociés de tout versement en faveur des déposants ou de toute dépense visant à soutenir plus largement le secteur financier.
- Les contributions aux mécanismes traditionnels de moindre envergure destinés à garantir les dépôts de détail, contributions dont le montant est aligné sur le coût de la garantie, doivent être classées en tant que redevances pour services rendus.
- Tout versement au titre de la réalisation par une administration des actifs d'un établissement en faillite ou du recouvrement par cette administration d'une créance prioritaire sur les actifs de l'établissement en cours de liquidation, effectué en vue de financer l'indemnisation des clients ayant perdu leurs dépôts, serait traité comme une redevance par opposition aux recettes fiscales.
- Les versements obligatoires effectués à des fonds gérés en dehors du secteur public et à des institutions non étatiques soutenues par les déposants, ainsi que tous les versements à des régimes volontaires, ne doivent pas être traités comme des recettes fiscales.
- Les contributions au Fonds de résolution unique de l'UE sont également incluses ici et attribuées à l'autorité supranationale dans les tableaux par pays.

74. Ne figurent pas sous ce poste :

a) les impôts sur les services qui font partie d'un impôt général sur les biens et services et sont classés sous le poste 5110 ;

b) les taxes sur l'électricité, le gaz et l'énergie (classées sous le poste 5121 en tant qu'accises) ;

c) les taxes sur les gains personnels tirés de jeux et paris (qui sont classées sous le poste 1120, en tant qu'impôts sur les gains en capital des personnes physiques et entreprises individuelles) et les montants forfaitaires perçus sur le transfert de loteries privées ou sur l'autorisation de créer des loteries (5200)[18] ;

d) les impôts sur les chèques et sur l'émission, le transfert ou le remboursement de valeurs mobilières, (qui sont classés sous le poste 4400, en tant qu'impôts sur les transactions mobilières et immobilières) ;

e) les impôts généraux sur le chiffre d'affaires (5113).

5127 — *Autres impôts sur les transactions et les échanges internationaux*

75. Ce sous-groupe couvre les recettes perçues par l'État sur l'achat et la vente de monnaies étrangères à des taux différents. Lorsque l'État exerce le privilège exclusif dont il dispose pour s'assurer une marge entre le prix d'achat et le prix de vente de devises qui ne se réduit pas à la simple couverture des frais administratifs, ce bénéfice représente un prélèvement obligatoire imposé dans des proportions indéterminées à l'acheteur et au vendeur des monnaies étrangères. Il équivaut normalement au droit à l'importation et au droit à l'exportation perçus dans un système de taux de change unique, ou à une taxe sur la vente ou l'achat de monnaies étrangères. Comme les bénéfices des monopoles fiscaux et des monopoles d'importation ou d'exportation transférés à l'État, il représente l'exercice d'un monopole aux fins d'imposition et est inclus dans les recettes fiscales.

76. Ce sous-groupe comprend aussi les bénéfices des monopoles d'exportation ou d'importation, bien qu'il n'en existe pas dans les pays de l'OCDE, les impôts sur l'achat ou la vente de devises et tous les autres impôts perçus spécifiquement sur les opérations ou les échanges internationaux.

5128 — *Autres impôts sur des biens et services déterminés*

77. Cette rubrique comprend les impôts sur l'extraction de minéraux, combustibles fossiles et autres ressources non renouvelables provenant de gisements privés ou détenus par une autre administration, ainsi que toute autre recette non ventilable provenant des impôts sur des biens et services déterminés. Les impôts sur l'extraction de ressources non renouvelables correspondent généralement à un montant forfaitaire par unité de qualité ou de poids, mais peuvent être calculés ad valorem. Les impôts sont comptabilisés à la date d'extraction des ressources. Les versements tirés de l'extraction de ressources non renouvelables issues de gisements appartenant à l'administration publique qui perçoit ces versements sont classés en tant que loyers.

5200 — *Impôts sur l'utilisation des biens ou l'autorisation d'utiliser des biens ou d'exercer des activités*

78. Ce sous-groupe comprend les taxes prélevées en raison de l'utilisation de biens, indépendamment des impôts frappant les biens eux-mêmes. Contrairement à ceux-ci (5100), les impôts du sous-groupe 5200 ne sont pas calculés d'après la valeur des biens, mais ordinairement d'après un montant forfaitaire. Sont aussi couverts les impôts perçus au titre du droit d'utiliser des biens ou d'exercer des activités, comme les taxes sur la pollution qui ne reposent pas sur la valeur de biens déterminés. Il est parfois difficile de distinguer les taxes d'utilisation et droits de licence obligatoires, qui sont considérés comme des impôts, de ceux qui ne le sont pas parce qu'ils sont assimilés à des recettes non fiscales ; les critères appliqués sont ceux indiqués aux § 12 et 13.

79. Bien que le sous-groupe se réfère à l'utilisation des biens, le fait générateur de l'impôt peut être aussi bien l'enregistrement de la propriété, de sorte que les impôts relevant de ce sous-groupe peuvent viser la possession d'animaux ou de biens plutôt que leur utilisation

(par exemple, les chevaux de course, les chiens, les véhicules à moteur) et même s'appliquer à des biens inutilisables (comme les véhicules à moteur ou les fusils inutilisables).

80. Les cas limites concernent :

a) les impôts sur l'autorisation d'exercer des activités commerciales, qui sont classés selon les règles exposées au § 84 lorsqu'ils ont une assiette mixte associant le revenu, les salaires versés ou le chiffre d'affaires ;

b) les impôts sur la propriété ou l'utilisation de la propriété de biens visés par les postes 4100, 4200 et 4600. Le poste 4100 ne vise que les impôts sur la propriété ou la location de biens immobiliers et, contrairement aux impôts du sous-groupe 5200, ils sont fonction de la valeur du bien. Les impôts sur l'actif net et les impôts sur les biens meubles des sous-groupes 4200 et 4600 visent la propriété et non pas l'utilisation des biens, couvrent un groupe d'actifs et non pas de biens particuliers et sont aussi fonction de la valeur du bien.

5210 — Impôts périodiques sur l'utilisation de biens ou sur l'autorisation d'utiliser des biens ou d'exercer certaines activités

81. Ces impôts ont pour principale caractéristique d'être perçus à intervalles réguliers et de représenter ordinairement des montants forfaitaires. Le poste le plus important, du point de vue du volume des recettes, est constitué par les permis de circulation des véhicules. Ce sous-groupe inclut aussi les taxes perçues lors de la délivrance de permis de chasse, de tir ou de pêche, ou l'autorisation de vendre certains produits, ainsi que les taxes sur la possession de chiens et sur la prestation de certains services à condition qu'elles répondent aux critères définis aux § 12 et 13. Les subdivisions du poste 5210 comprennent :

- les taxes d'utilisation de véhicules à moteur à la charge des ménages (5211) ;
- les taxes d'utilisation de véhicules à moteur à la charge d'autres agents (5212) ; et
- les autres impôts périodiques (5213). Ce poste couvre les licences commerciales et professionnelles achetées par des entreprises pour obtenir le droit d'exercer un type déterminé d'activité ou de profession lorsque ces droits sont perçus sur une base périodique. Il englobe aussi les licences de taxi et de casino. Enfin, ce poste inclut les plaques de chiens et permis généraux de chasse, de port d'armes et de pêche, lorsque le droit d'exercer ces activités n'est pas accordé au titre d'une opération commerciale normale.

82. Le poste 5213 exclut :

a) les permis lorsque le droit d'exercer ces activités est accordé au titre d'une opération commerciale normale (par exemple, la délivrance du permis s'accompagne du droit d'utiliser une parcelle déterminée de terrain appartenant à l'État) ;

b) les paiements liés aux contrôles effectués par l'État pour vérifier l'adéquation et/ou la sécurité des locaux ou des équipements professionnels, ou la qualité ou la norme de biens ou de services produits en contrepartie de l'octroi de ce permis. Ces paiements ne sont pas sans contrepartie et doivent être considérés comme des paiements au titre de services rendus, sauf si les montants facturés pour les permis sont disproportionnés par rapport aux coûts des contrôles effectués par l'État.

5220 — Impôts non périodiques sur l'utilisation de biens ou sur l'autorisation d'utiliser des biens ou d'exercer certaines activités

83. Cette rubrique recouvre les taxes non périodiques perçues sur l'utilisation de biens ou sur l'autorisation d'utiliser des biens ou d'exercer certaines activités et celles qui sont

prélevées chaque fois que des biens sont utilisés. Les impôts prélevés sur l'émission ou le rejet dans l'environnement de gaz toxiques, liquides nocifs ou autres substances dangereuses figurent ici.

- Les paiements au titre des permis d'émission négociables délivrés par les administrations publiques dans le cadre des dispositifs de plafonnement et d'échange doivent également être comptabilisés sous cette rubrique au moment où les émissions sont produites. Les permis délivrés gratuitement par les administrations ne donnent lieu à aucun enregistrement comptable de recettes. La comptabilisation en droits constatés implique un éventuel délai entre la date à laquelle l'administration perçoit le règlement des permis et la date à laquelle les émissions sont produites. Dans les comptes nationaux, ce délai se traduit pour l'administration par un engagement financier sur la période.
- Il convient d'exclure les paiements effectués au titre de la collecte et de l'élimination de déchets ou de substances nocives par les autorités publiques, étant donné qu'il s'agit là de vente de services aux entreprises.

84. D'autres impôts non périodiques qui relèvent du poste 5200 sont aussi classés dans cette rubrique. Ainsi figurent les paiements uniques effectués au titre de l'autorisation de vendre des boissons alcoolisées ou des tabacs ou d'ouvrir des guichets de « paris mutuels », à condition qu'ils répondent aux critères définis aux § 12 et 13.

6000 — Autres impôts

85. Ce groupe couvre les impôts prélevés sur une ou plusieurs assiettes différentes de celles qui sont indiquées pour les groupes 1000, 3000, 4000 et 5000, ou sur des assiettes qui ne peuvent être considérées comme liées à l'une de celles afférentes à ces groupes. Lorsque des impôts sont perçus sur plusieurs assiettes différentes, et qu'il est possible d'évaluer les recettes liées à chaque assiette, les montants correspondants sont inclus dans le groupe approprié. S'il est impossible d'évaluer le montant correspondant à chaque assiette, et si l'on sait que l'essentiel des recettes provient des impôts perçus sur une assiette donnée, la totalité des recettes est classée en fonction de cette assiette. Sinon, les impôts sont classés dans le présent groupe. Sont également inclus dans ce groupe les impôts forfaitaires non inclus ailleurs dans le système de classification, les impôts prélevés sur les personnes physiques sous la forme de taxe civique ou d'impôt de capitation, les droits de timbre qui ne sont pas liés à des transactions mobilières ou immobilières et qui n'entrent pas exclusivement dans une catégorie de transactions, les impôts sur les dépenses dès lors qu'ils s'accompagnent d'abattements et d'exonérations individuels, ainsi que les recettes fiscales non identifiables. Ce poste est divisé en impôts exclusivement ou principalement à la charge des entreprises (6100) et en impôts à la charge d'autres contribuables (6200).

A.6. Conciliation avec les comptes nationaux

86. Cette section des tableaux permet de concilier les calculs des recettes fiscales totales de l'OCDE et l'ensemble des impôts et cotisations sociales versés aux administrations publiques qui sont enregistrés dans les comptes nationaux par pays. Lorsque le pays en question est membre de l'Union européenne (UE), la comparaison est effectuée entre les calculs des recettes fiscales totales des pays de l'OCDE et la somme des recettes fiscales et cotisations de sécurité sociale perçues par les administrations publiques et les institutions des secteurs de l'Union européenne des comptes nationaux.

A.7. Poste pour mémoire relatif au financement des prestations de sécurité sociale

87. Le rapport entre les impôts et les cotisations de sécurité sociale étant variable, et en raison des problèmes évoqués aux § 40 à 46, on a réuni dans un poste pour mémoire l'ensemble des versements affectés à des prestations du type sécurité sociale, en dehors des versements facultatifs au secteur privé. Les données sont présentées de la façon suivante (voir le Tableau 5.39 du Rapport)

a) impôts du groupe 2000 ;

b) impôts affectés aux prestations de sécurité sociale ;

c) cotisations facultatives à l'administration ;

d) cotisations obligatoires au secteur privé.

Les § 40 à 46 ci-dessus contiennent des directives pour la ventilation entre ces quatre catégories

A.8. Poste pour mémoire relatif aux impôts identifiables payés par les administrations

88. Les impôts effectivement payés par les administrations elles-mêmes et que l'on peut identifier sont indiqués dans un poste pour mémoire et classés suivant les grandes rubriques de la classification des impôts de l'OCDE. Dans la très grande majorité des pays, seuls peuvent être identifiées en l'occurrence les cotisations de sécurité sociale et les impôts sur les salaires, mais il s'agit là en général des impôts les plus importants acquittés par les administrations (voir le Tableau 5.40 du Rapport).

A.9. Rapport de la classification des impôts de l'OCDE avec les systèmes nationaux de comptabilité nationale

89. Un système de comptabilité nationale (SCN) tend à fournir un cadre cohérent pour enregistrer et présenter les principaux flux relatifs à la production, à la consommation, à l'accumulation et aux transactions extérieures d'une zone économique donnée, d'ordinaire un pays ou une grande région d'un pays. Les recettes publiques sont une partie importante des transactions enregistrées dans le SCN. La version finale du SCN 2008 a été diffusée conjointement par cinq organisations internationales : les Nations Unies, le Fonds Monétaire International, l'Union européenne, l'Organisation de Coopération et de Développement Économiques et la Banque Mondiale, en août 2009. Le *Système* est un ensemble complet, cohérent et souple de comptes macro-économiques. Il est élaboré pour être utilisé dans les pays à économie de marché quel que soit leur niveau de développement économique ainsi que dans les pays en transition vers l'économie de marché. De larges extraits du cadre théorique ainsi que les définitions des divers secteurs de l'économie du SCN figurent dans la classification des impôts de l'OCDE.

90. Il existe cependant un certain nombre de différences entre la classification des impôts de l'OCDE et les concepts du SCN qui sont indiqués ci-dessous. Ils proviennent du fait que l'objectif de cette classification est de permettre une ventilation aussi large que possible des données statistiques pour ce que les administrations fiscales conviennent de considérer de manière générale comme des impôts.

a) l'OCDE inclut les cotisations obligatoires de sécurité sociale payées aux administrations publiques dans les recettes fiscales totales. Les cotisations sociales facultatives et imputées ainsi que celles versées aux caisses privées ne sont pas considérées comme des impôts (§ 9 et 11 ci-dessus) ;

b) les avis diffèrent sur la question de savoir s'il y a lieu de classer certains prélèvements et redevances dans les impôts (§ 12 et 13 ci-dessus) ;

c) l'OCDE exclut les impôts imputés ou les subventions résultant d'opérations de taux de change officiels multiples et ceux résultant du fait que la banque centrale paye un taux d'intérêt sur les réserves obligatoires différent des autres taux du marché ;

d) il existe des différences dans le traitement des crédits d'impôt récupérables.

91. Comme on l'a noté aux § 1 et 2, les groupes 1000 à 6000 de la classification de l'OCDE comprennent tous les versements sans contrepartie aux administrations publiques ou à une autorité supranationale, à l'exclusion des prêts obligatoires et des amendes. On peut obtenir le total de ces versements sans contrepartie, amendes incluses, mais prêts obligatoires exclus, en additionnant les postes suivants du SCN 2008 :

- impôts du type valeur ajoutée (D.211) ;
- droits et taxes sur les importations à l'exclusion de la TVA (D.212) ;
- droits sur les exportations (D.213) ;
- taxes sur les produits, à l'exclusion de la TVA, des droits sur les importations et les exportations (D.214) ;
- autres impôts sur la production (D.29) ;
- impôts sur le revenu (D.51) ;
- autres impôts périodiques (D.59) ;
- cotisations de sécurité sociale effectives (D.611 et D613), à l'exclusion des cotisations volontaires et des versements à des régimes d'assurance sociale liés à l'emploi qui ne sont pas des régimes de sécurité sociale ;
- impôts sur le capital (D.91).

A.10. La classification des impôts de l'OCDE et le système du Fonds monétaire international (SFP)

92. Le périmètre et l'évaluation des recettes fiscales dans le système de statistiques de finances publiques (SFP) et dans le système de comptabilité nationale de 2008 (SCN 2008) sont très proches. Par conséquent, les différences entre la classification de l'OCDE et celle du SCN 2008 (voir § 90 ci-dessus) sont également valables pour les SFP. En outre, le Fonds monétaire international subdivise le groupe 5000 de la classification de l'OCDE en une section iv (Taxes intérieures sur les biens et services) et une section v (Taxes sur les transactions et les échanges internationaux). Cela tient à ce que le rendement de ces dernières taxes représente généralement des sommes infimes dans les pays de l'OCDE ce qui n'est pas le cas dans beaucoup de pays non membres.

A.11. Comparaison de la classification des impôts de l'OCDE et des autres classifications internationales des recettes publiques

93. Le tableau ci-dessous décrit point par point la comparaison entre la classification des impôts de l'OCDE et les classifications suivantes :

a) Système des comptes nationaux (SCN 2008) ;

b) Système européen des comptes (SEC 2010) ;

c) Manuel de statistiques des finances publiques du Fonds monétaire international (MSFP 2014).

94. Ces comparaisons correspondent à celles qui devraient s'appliquer dans la majorité des cas. Toutefois, en pratique il faut faire preuve d'une certaine souplesse dans leur application. En effet, dans certains cas, les pays peuvent adopter des méthodes diverses de classification des recettes dans les comptes nationaux.

OECD Classification	2008 SNA	2010 ESA	GFSM2014
1000 Impôts sur le revenu, les bénéfices et les gains en capital			
1100 Personnes physiques			
1110 Sur le revenu et les bénéfices	D51-8.61a	D51A	1111
1120 Sur les gains en capital	D51-8.61c, d	D51C, D	1111
1200 Sociétés			
1210 Sur le revenu et les bénéfices	D51-8.61b	D51B	1112
1220 Sur les gains en capital	D51-8.61c	D51C	1112
1300 Non ventilables entre les rubriques 1100 et 1200			1113
2000 Cotisations de sécurité sociale			
2100 Salariés	D613-8.85	D613	1211
2200 Employeurs	D611-8.83	D611	1212
2300 A la charge des travailleurs indépendants ou des personnes sans occupation	D613-8.85	D613	1213
2400 Non ventilables entre les rubriques 2100, 2200 et 2300			1214
3000 Impôts sur les salaires et la main-d'œuvre	D29-7.97a	D29C	112
4000 Impôts sur le patrimoine			
4100 Impôts périodiques sur la propriété immobilière			
4110 Ménages	D59-8.63a	D59A	1131
4120 Autres agents	D29-7.97b	D29A	1131
4200 Impôts périodiques sur l'actif net			
4210 Personnes physiques	D59-8.63b	D59A	1132
4220 Sociétés	D59-8.63b	D59A	1132
4300 Impôts sur les mutations par décès, les successions et les donations			
4310 Impôts sur les mutations par décès et les successions	D91-10.207b	D91A	1133
4320 Impôts sur les donations	D91-10.207b	D91A	1133
4400 Impôts sur les transactions mobilières et immobilières	D59-7.96d; D29-7.97e	D214B, C	114114; 1161
4500 Autres impôts non périodiques sur le patrimoine	D91-10.207a	D91B	1135
4600 Autres impôts périodiques sur le patrimoine	D59-8.63c	D59A	1136
5000 Impôts sur les biens et services			
5100 Impôts sur les biens et services			
5110 Impôts généraux sur les biens et services			
5111 Taxes sur la valeur ajoutée	D211-7.89	D211; D29G	11411
5112 Impôts sur les ventes	D2122-7.94a; D214-7.96a	D21224; D214I	11412
5113 Autres impôts généraux sur les biens et services	D214-7.96a	D214I	11413
5120 Impôts sur des biens et services déterminés			
5121 Accises	D2122-7.94b; D214-7.96b	D21223; D214A, B, D	1142
5122 Bénéfices des monopoles fiscaux	D214-7.96e	D214J	1143
5123 Droits de douane et autres droits à l'importation	D2121-7.93	D2121; D21221, 2	1151
5124 Taxes à l'exportation	D213-7.95a	D214K	1152-4
5125 Impôts sur les biens d'équipements			
5126 Impôts sur les services déterminés	D2122-7.94c; D214-7.96c	D21225; D214E, F, G, H; D29F	1144; 1156

OECD Classification	2008 SNA	2010 ESA	GFSM2014
5127 Autres impôts sur les transactions et les échanges internationaux	D2122-7.94d D29-7.95b D29-7.97g D59-8.64d	D21226; D29D; D59E	1153; 1155-6
5128 Autres impôts sur des et services déterminés			1146
5130 Non ventilable entre les rubriques 5110 et 5120			
5200 Impôts sur l'utilisation des biens ou l'autorisation d'utiliser des biens ou d'exercer des activités			
5210 Impôts périodiques sur l'utilisation des biens ou l'autorisation d'utiliser des biens ou d'exercer des activités			
5211 A la charge des ménages au titre de véhicules à moteurs	D59-8.64c	D59D	11451
5212 A la charge d'autres agents au titre de véhicules à moteurs	D29-7.97d	D214D; D29B	11451
5213 Autres impôts périodiques sur l'utilisation des biens u l'autorisation d'utiliser des biens ou d'exercer des activités	D29-7.97c, d, f D59-8.64c	D29B, E, F; D59D	11452
5220 Impôts non périodiques			11452
5300 Non ventilable entre les rubriques 5100 et 5200			
6000 Autres impôts			
6100 A la charge exclusive des entreprises			1161
6200 A la charge d'autres agents que les entreprises ou non identifiables	D59-8.64a, b	D59B, C	1162

A.12. Répartition des recettes fiscales par sous-secteurs d'administration publique

95. La classification de l'OCDE appelle une ventilation des recettes fiscales par sous-secteurs d'administration. On trouvera ci-après la définition de chaque sous-secteur et les critères à utiliser pour répartir entre eux les recettes fiscales. Ces définitions et critères suivent les orientations qui figurent dans le SCN 2008 et le MSFP 2014.

Sous-secteurs des administrations publiques à identifier

Administration centrale

96. Le sous-secteur des administrations centrales groupe tous les ministères, bureaux, établissements et autres organismes qui sont des services ou des moyens d'action du pouvoir central et dont la compétence s'étend à la totalité du territoire, à l'exception de l'administration des caisses de sécurité sociale. L'administration centrale a donc le pouvoir de prélever des impôts sur toutes les unités résidentes et non résidentes exerçant des activités économiques à l'intérieur du pays.

Administration d'un État fédéré, d'une province ou d'une région

97. Ce sous-secteur comprend les unités administratives intermédiaires et inclut toutes les unités administratives dont la compétence s'exerce indépendamment de l'Administration centrale sur une partie du territoire englobant un certain nombre de petites localités, à l'exception des caisses de sécurité sociale. Dans les pays unitaires, les administrations régionales peuvent être considérées comme dotées d'une existence distincte lorsqu'elles disposent d'une autonomie substantielle pour percevoir une part importante de leurs recettes de sources placées sous leur contrôle et lorsque leurs agents ne sont pas soumis à un contrôle administratif externe dans l'exercice des activités de l'unité.

98. Actuellement, les pays à structure fédérale représentent la majorité des cas dans lesquels les recettes attribuées aux unités administratives intermédiaires sont identifiées séparément. La Colombie et l'Espagne sont les deux seuls pays à structure unitaire qui se trouvent dans

cette situation. Dans les autres pays unitaires, les recettes des administrations régionales sont incluses dans celles des administrations locales.

Collectivités locales

99. Ce sous-secteur comprend toutes les autres unités administratives exerçant une compétence indépendante sur une partie du territoire d'un pays, à l'exception des administrations des caisses de sécurité sociale. Il englobe les diverses circonscriptions urbaines et/ou rurales (par exemple les collectivités locales, les municipalités, les villes, les bourgs ou les districts).

Caisses de sécurité sociale

100. Les caisses de sécurité sociale constituent un sous-secteur distinct des administrations publiques. Le sous-secteur de la sécurité sociale est défini dans le SCN de 2008 par les extraits suivants des paragraphes 4.124 à 4.126 et 4.147 :

« Les systèmes de sécurité sociale sont des systèmes d›assurance sociale qui couvrent l›ensemble de la collectivité ou d›importants sous-ensembles de la collectivité : ces systèmes sont imposés et contrôlés par les administrations publiques. Ces systèmes couvrent une grande variété de programmes qui consistent à fournir des prestations, en espèces ou en nature, au titre des circonstances suivantes : vieillesse, invalidité ou décès, survie, maladie et maternité, accident du travail, chômage, allocations familiales, soins de santé etc. Il n'existe pas nécessairement de lien direct entre le montant de la cotisation versée par un particulier et les prestations qu'il est susceptible de recevoir » (paragraphe 4.124).

« Lorsque les systèmes de sécurité sociale ont une organisation distincte des autres activités des administrations publiques et détiennent des actifs et des engagements indépendamment de ces dernières et effectuent des opérations financières pour leur propre compte, ils peuvent être considérés comme des unités institutionnelles désignées sous le nom de caisses de sécurité sociale » (paragraphe 4.125).

« Il est possible de faire varier de façon discrétionnaire les montants prélevés et versés sous forme de cotisations de sécurité sociale et de prestations afin d›atteindre des objectifs de politique publique qui n›ont pas de lien direct avec la notion de sécurité sociale en tant que système visant à fournir des prestations à des membres de la collectivité. Ainsi, ces cotisations ou prestations peuvent être augmentées ou diminuées afin d›influer sur le niveau de la demande globale au sein de l›économie. Néanmoins, tant que ces caisses restent indépendantes, elles doivent être traitées comme des unités institutionnelles distinctes dans le SCN » (paragraphe 4.126).

« Le sous-secteur des administrations de sécurité sociale comprend les administrations de sécurité sociale opérant à tous les niveaux des administrations publiques. Les administrations de sécurité sociale sont des systèmes couvrant l›ensemble de la collectivité ou d›importants sous-ensembles de la collectivité qui sont rendus obligatoires et contrôlés par des administrations publiques » (paragraphe 4.147).

101. Cette définition des administrations de sécurité sociale est suivie dans la classification de l'OCDE à l'exception des régimes suivants :

- Les régimes imposés par l'administration et exploités par des organismes extérieurs au secteur des administrations publiques, tel qu'il est défini au § 3 de ce manuel et
- Les régimes qui perçoivent des cotisations facultatives.

Autorités supranationales

102. Ce sous-secteur s'applique aux activités de collecte de recettes publiques des autorités supranationales sur le territoire d'un pays. En pratique, le seul cas d'autorité supranationale de la zone de l'OCDE est celui des institutions de l'Union européenne (UE). Les recettes fiscales collectées par les pays membres et versées à l'UE sont incluses dans les statistiques des recettes publiques au niveau de l'autorité supranationale. Les impôts sur le revenu et les cotisations de sécurité sociale perçus par les institutions européennes et payés par les fonctionnaires européens qui résident dans les pays membres de l'UE ne doivent pas être inclus.

Critères à utiliser pour l'attribution des recettes fiscales

103. Lorsqu'une administration collecte l'impôt et le reverse, en totalité ou en partie, à d'autres administrations, il est nécessaire de déterminer si ces recettes doivent être considérées comme étant celles de l'administration qui les perçoit et les répartit entre d'autres administrations ou celles des administrations bénéficiaires auxquelles l'administration qui les a perçues les a transférées en simple qualité d'agent. Les critères à utiliser dans l'attribution des recettes sont indiqués aux § 104 à 107, qui reprennent les paragraphes 3.70 à 3.73 du SCN 2008.

104. En général, un impôt est attribué à l'Unité administrative qui :

a) exerce le pouvoir de percevoir l'impôt (soit en tant que détenteur de ce pouvoir soit par délégation de l'autorité qui le détient),

b) dispose du pouvoir discrétionnaire final de fixer et de faire varier le taux de l'impôt.

105. Lorsqu'une somme est collectée par une administration au profit d'une autre administration et en son nom, et que cette dernière a le pouvoir de percevoir l'impôt et de fixer et de faire varier son taux, la première intervient comme agent pour le compte de la dernière et l'impôt est réaffecté. Toute somme retenue par l'administration collectrice au titre des frais de recouvrement doit être considérée comme la rémunération d'un service rendu. Toute autre somme conservée par l'administration collectrice, notamment dans le cadre d'un accord de partage d'impôt, doit être considérée comme une subvention courante. Si l'administration collectrice s'est vu déléguer le pouvoir de fixer et de faire varier le taux, le montant recouvré doit être considéré comme une recette fiscale de cette administration.

106. Lorsque des administrations différentes fixent conjointement et sur un pied d'égalité la répartition du produit de cet impôt, aucune administration ne disposant d'un pouvoir prépondérant en dernier ressort, les recettes fiscales sont attribuées à chaque administration en fonction de sa part respective du produit de l'impôt. Si un accord permet à une unité administrative d'exercer un pouvoir prépondérant en dernier ressort, la totalité des recettes fiscales est attribuée à cette unité.

107. Dans certains cas aussi, un impôt est perçu dans le cadre des compétences d'une administration qui résulte de la constitution ou d'autres dispositions mais d'autres administrations fixent individuellement le taux d'imposition sur leurs territoires. Le produit de l'impôt généré sur les territoires respectifs de chaque administration est attribué à l'administration en question comme constituant ses recettes fiscales.

108. Les versements effectués par les États membres de l'Union européenne prennent la forme de prélèvements spécifiques qui comprennent :

a) les droits de douane et les prélèvements agricoles (5123),

b) les montants compensatoires monétaires bruts (5123 si relatifs aux importations et 5124 si relatifs aux exportations),

c) les contributions au Fonds de résolution unique (5126), et

d) les prélèvements de la CECA, les cotisations sucre et les taxes de coresponsabilité sur le lait (5128).

109. Les droits de douane collectés par les États membres pour le compte de l'Union européenne sont comptabilisés :

a) sur une base qui ne tient pas compte des droits d'encaissement,

b) en utilisant des chiffres corrigés de manière à exprimer les droits sur la base de la « destination finale » et non du « pays de première entrée » lorsque de telles corrections sont possibles. Ces corrections concernent en particulier les droits prélevés dans des ports (maritimes) importants. Bien que les droits de l'UE soient prélevés par les autorités du pays de première entrée, ces droits doivent être dans la mesure du possible déduits des recettes du pays qui les recouvre et inclus dans les recettes du pays de destination finale.

110. Ce sont les prélèvements spécifiques de l'UE qui se conforment le plus clairement au critère d'attribution décrit au § 102 ci-dessus. Par conséquent, ces montants sont indiqués en note de bas de page dans les tableaux par pays des États membres de l'UE (au chapitre 5) et figurent en tant que recettes supranationales dans chacune des rubriques fiscales identifiées au § 108.

Notes

1. Les références dans cette annexe aux chapitres ou aux sections de « ce rapport » sont issues de OCDE (2022), Statistiques des recettes publiques 2022, Éditions OCDE, Paris.
2. Toutes les références au SCN concernent l'édition de 2008.
3. Se reporter à la section A.12 de ce manuel pour l'examen de cette notion.
4. Il est en général possible d'identifier les montants des cotisations de sécurité sociale et les impôts sur les salaires, mais pas les autres impôts payés par les administrations.
5. En revanche, si un ou plusieurs pays considèrent comme un impôt un droit que la plupart des pays font entrer dans les recettes non fiscales ou qui procure des recettes substantielles, les montants ainsi perçus figureront dans une note de renvoi à la fin des tableaux par pays correspondants, même s'ils ne sont pas inclus dans le total des recettes fiscales.
6. Les appellations peuvent cependant être souvent trompeuses. Ainsi, une redevance de passeport sera normalement considérée comme une recette non fiscale, alors qu'un prélèvement additionnel sur les passeports (comme c'est le cas au Portugal), qui a pour but de procurer un montant substantiel de recettes eu égard au coût de délivrance du passeport, sera considéré comme un impôt du sous-groupe 5200.
7. On trouvera des précisions sur cette distinction dans l'étude spéciale intitulée « L'information sur les recettes fiscales : problèmes actuels », de l'édition de 2001 des *Statistiques des recettes publiques*.
8. On utilise parfois les expressions « non remboursable » et « remboursable » mais il peut paraître illogique de parler de « remboursement » lorsque rien n'a été versé.
9. Toutefois, dans les systèmes d'imputation de l'impôt sur les sociétés, les crédits d'impôts récupérables sont traités différemment (§ 37 à 39).
10. Il ne s'agit pas d'une véritable dépense fiscale au sens strict. De telles dépenses fiscales supposent que l'on identifie un système fiscal de référence pour chaque pays ou, de préférence, une norme internationale commune. En pratique, il n'a pas été possible de parvenir à un accord sur une norme internationale commune.

11. Sauf s'ils sont calculés sur le bénéfice résultant de la vente, auquel cas ils seraient classés parmi les impôts sur les gains en capital dans le sous-groupe 1120 ou 1220.

12. Dans certains pays, la même législation est applicable aux personnes physiques et aux entreprises dans le cas d'impôts sur le revenu particulier. Cependant, les recettes procurées par ces impôts peuvent, en général, être ventilées et figurent donc dans les deux sous-groupes appropriés.

13. Ainsi, « celles qui sont suffisamment autonomes et indépendantes pour que leur fonctionnement soit comparable à celui d'une société… (y compris) la tenue de comptes complets » (2008 SCN section 4.44).

14. Au Canada - un pays également désigné comme ayant un système d'imputation - le crédit d'impôt (récupérable) pour l'actionnaire concerne l'impôt sur les sociétés national considéré comme payé, qu'un impôt sur les sociétés ait été créé ou non. Comme il n'existe pas de lien essentiel entre l'impôt sur les sociétés à payer et le crédit imputé sur l'impôt sur le revenu selon ces systèmes, ces crédits pour dividendes sont traités, avec d'autres crédits d'impôt, selon les lignes décrites au § 26.

15. Il peut en être ainsi lorsqu'un régime en faveur des administrations existait avant l'instauration d'un régime général de sécurité sociale.

16. Dans le SCN 2008, ces transferts sont considérés comme des transferts de capital et non comme des impôts (voir section A.8).

17. Système selon lequel l'Union Européenne ajuste les effets des différences entre les taux de change utilisés pour fixer les prix des produits agricoles dans le cadre de la politique agricole commune, et le taux de change réel. Les paiements effectués selon ce système portent sur les importations ou les exportations; lorsqu'ils sont identifiables, ces montants figurent dans la rubrique appropriée (5123 ou 5124). Dans ce guide, sont inclus les montants bruts, c'est-à-dire sans déduction d'aucune prime payée dans le cadre du système des montants compensatoires.

18. Les transferts de bénéfices de loteries d'État sont considérés comme des recettes non fiscales (voir aussi § 68).

Revenue Statistics in Africa 1990-2020/Statistiques des recettes publiques en Afrique 1990-2020

Annex B

Interpretative guide to non-tax revenue in Revenue Statistics in Africa

Table of contents

B.1. Coverage

The definition of non-tax revenues and the main subcategories identified in this publication generally correspond to the concepts laid out in the 2014 IMF Government Finance Statistics Manual (GFSM). Non-tax revenues refer to increases in government net worth resulting from transactions other than tax revenues. They exclude funds arising from the repayment of previous lending by governments or from borrowing, or proceeds derived from sales of fixed capital assets, stocks, land and intangible assets or private gifts.

Non-tax revenues are made up of grants; property income; sales of goods and services; and miscellaneous and unidentified revenue..

B.2. Grants

The GFSM 2014 states "Grants are transfers receivable by government units from non-resident government units or international organisations without the receipt of any goods, services, or assets in return. Grants are normally receivable in cash, but may also take the form of the receipt of goods or services (in kind)". These transfers are non refundable and unrequited. Grants encompass reparations and gifts given for particular projects or programmes. The term "grants" is not used to refer to transfers to or from non-governmental units and excludes inter-governmental transfers. The remission of funds collected by one government for another in an agency capacity should not be shown as receipt of a grant by the beneficiary government but as its direct receipt of revenue.

B.3. Property income

This category includes income to government arising from their ownership of property, enterprises, financial assets, or intangible assets when government units place them at the disposal of other units. Sales of non-financial assets such as the sales of lands are not recorded as revenue because disposal of such an asset does not increase net worth. Similarly, repayments on loans and loan disbursements are not revenue. Property income may take the form of dividends, interest, land rents, royalties, or withdrawals from entrepreneurial income. The main components are:

- Interest and dividends: Interest is the revenue earned by the government unit from a financial asset by putting it at the disposal of another institutional unit. Dividends are the revenue earned by placing equity funds at the disposal of a corporation (resident or non-resident corporation). This category also consists of profits of state-owned enterprises except those classified as fiscal monopolies (see §66-§68 of the *OECD Interpretative Guide* to tax revenue in Annex A), export and import monopoly profits (see §75-§76 of the same document) or those providing public utilities such as rail transport, electricity, post offices and other communications. In this category are included revenue from public financial institutions such as the central banks' profits, profits transferred or distributed from the operation of monetary authority functions outside the central bank and the profits of state lotteries transferred to the government. Transfers from public utilities enterprises are recorded as non-tax revenue under "sales of goods and services" whereas profits for fiscal, export or import monopolies are classified as tax revenue.
- Rents or royalties: Rent is the revenue generated from natural resources, such as land, mining, or oil resources, when a government unit places these at the disposal of private or foreign entities. The rents received relate to a resource lease-giving agreement for the exploitation and extraction of a natural resource by the lessee in return for a payment.

Payments for exploration rights are also treated as rent. Rents should not be confused with other payments a government may receive related to the exploitation of subsoil and similar assets, such as severance taxes, business licenses, or other taxes (e.g. value added taxes, excises, taxes on exports, or taxes on mining private land - see §77 of Annex A, etc.) They should also not be taken to mean incomes from the rental of buildings and equipment, which are treated as sales of goods and services. Revenues from rents and royalties are in some cases difficult to establish and depend on the agreement between the government unit and the lessee. For example rents, royalties and taxes such as corporate income taxes and VAT are sometimes encompassed in a single payment to the general government. In such cases the revenue should be classified under the category to which the majority of revenue belongs.

- Other property income: This includes revenue earned by a government unit placing funds at a disposal of quasi-corporations.[1] Conceptually this source of revenue is equivalent to that of dividends from a corporation but by definition, quasi-corporations cannot distribute income in the form of dividends. This category of "other property income" also includes retained or reinvested earnings, i.e. the percentage of distributable revenue not paid out as dividends, but retained by the corporation or quasi-corporation on foreign investment; property income from investment income disbursements and unidentified property income.

B.4. Sales of goods and services

Revenue under the category "sales of goods and services" is generally reported on a gross basis, without deduction of costs. Since these costs can represent a significant proportion of revenues, they cannot be regarded in total as funds available for governments to finance their general activities. This contrasts with tax revenues, where the collection costs are usually a small proportion of revenue. This difference implies that it may not be meaningful to sum tax and non-tax revenues as part of a calculation of generally available funds.

The proceeds of sales of nonfinancial assets such as the sale of buildings or lands are not classified as revenues since their disposal does not increase the net worth.

Sales of goods and services consist of:

- Sales by market establishments.[2]
- Administrative fees for services (i.e. fees for drivers' licences; passports; visas; court fees; harbour fees; fees for birth, marriage or death certificates; patent registrations; and radio and television licenses when public authorities provide general broadcasting services).
- Administrative fees that are sales of services associated with a regulatory function of government (such as fees for the inspection of premises before delivering a business licence) and considered to be proportional to the cost of producing the service are included in this category. If the fee in return for the service provided by the government unit is disproportionate, then the fee will be classified as a tax. Specific examples of fees that are considered taxes include fees for permission to perform activities such as hunting, fishing and shooting; and fees for business registration where this is a legal requirement for the business to operate.
- Sales by nonmarket establishments such as fees at government hospitals, tuition fees at government schools and admission fees to museums and parks.
- Leasing of buildings and equipment.

B.5. Fines, penalties and forfeits

The GFSM 2014 states "Fines and penalties are compulsory transfers imposed by courts of law or bodies for violations of laws or administrative rules. Out-of-court agreements are also included (...). Forfeits are amounts deposited with a general government unit pending a legal or administrative proceeding, and that will be transferred to the unit upon resolution". For example traffic fines are included here. Fines and penalties charged on overdue taxes or penalties imposed for the evasion of taxes should be recorded in this category and not as taxes. However if it is not possible to separate the amounts paid in taxes and fines, the whole amount should be classified under the tax to which the fine relates (see §14 of Annex A for further explanation).

B.6. Other social contributions

This category includes the actual and imputed contributions to social insurance schemes operated by governments as employers on behalf of their employees that do not create a future defined liability. This category also includes the sum of the total voluntary contributions.[3] Excluded from this category are any contributions to funds in which the contributions of each participant and of his employer on his behalf are kept in a separate account earning interest and withdrawable under specified circumstances or any contributions to a pension fund autonomous to the general government. This category is not included in this publication.

B.7. Miscellaneous and unidentified revenue

This category consists of unidentified non-tax revenues or those that do not fit into any of the other categories listed above. It includes revenues such as gifts and transfers from individuals, private non-profit institutions, nongovernmental foundations, corporations, or sources other than governments and international organisations. Major non-recurrent payments receivable in compensation for extensive damages or serious injuries not covered by insurance policies are also included, such as payments of compensation for damages caused by major explosions; oil spillages; or payments receivable for damage to property other than payments from an insurance settlement.

Notes

1. Quasi-corporations are unincorporated enterprises that exercise some functions of corporations, but have not been granted separate legal personality by statute.
2. A market establishment is an establishment that charges economically significant prices.
3. The IMF includes these contributions as part of their total of social security contributions.

Revenue Statistics in Africa 1990-2020/Statistiques des recettes publiques en Afrique 1990-2020

Annexe B

Guide d'interprétation des recettes non fiscales dans les Statistiques des recettes publiques en Afrique

Table des matières

B.1. Champ couvert

La définition des recettes non fiscales et des principales sous-catégories décrites dans la présente publication coïncident en grande partie avec les notions retenues dans le manuel des statistiques de finances publiques du FMI de 2014 (manuel SFP 2014). Les recettes non fiscales désignent des augmentations de la valeur nette résultant d'une transaction et qui ne sont pas des recettes fiscales. Elles excluent les fonds relatifs au remboursement de prêts consentis antérieurement par les administrations ou liés à des emprunts, ainsi que le produit de la cession d'actifs immobilisés, d'éléments de stocks, de terrains, d'actifs immatériels et les dons à titre privé.

Les recettes non fiscales se composent des dons ; des revenus de la propriété, des ventes de biens et de services ; des amendes, pénalités et confiscations ; et des recettes diverses et non identifiées.

B.2. Dons

Selon le manuel SFP 2014, les dons sont des transferts qu'une administration publique reçoit d'une autre administration publique étrangère ou d'une organisation internationale, sans recevoir de cette dernière un bien, un service ou un actif en contrepartie directe. Les dons sont habituellement reçus en espèces, mais peuvent aussi prendre la forme de biens ou de services (en nature). Ces transferts sont non remboursables et sans contrepartie. Les dons recouvrent les réparations et dons assignés à des projets ou programmes particuliers. Le terme de « dons » n'est pas employé pour désigner les transferts réalisés par des entités autres que des administrations publiques ou effectués en leur faveur et exclut les transferts entre administrations. Le versement de fonds collectés par une administration qui agit en qualité de mandataire ne devrait pas entrer dans la catégorie des dons perçus par l'administration bénéficiaire, mais bien s'ajouter aux recettes directement perçues par cette dernière.

B.3. Revenus de la propriété

Cette catégorie regroupe les recettes publiques découlant de la détention de biens fonciers, de parts de sociétés, d'actifs financiers ou d'actifs immatériels que certaines unités administratives ont mis à la disposition d'autres unités administratives. Les cessions d'actifs non financiers comme la vente de terrains ne sont pas enregistrées en tant que recettes parce que la cession de tels actifs n'a pas d'effet sur la valeur nette. De même, les remboursements de prêts et les prêts octroyés ne sont pas des recettes. Les revenus de la propriété peuvent prendre la forme de dividendes, d'intérêts, de revenus fonciers, de redevances, ou de prélèvements sur des revenus d'entreprises. Les principales composantes en sont les suivantes :

- Intérêts et dividendes : Les intérêts sont les revenus perçus par une unité administrative au titre d'un actif financier qu'elle met à la disposition d'une autre unité institutionnelle. Les dividendes sont les recettes perçues par une unité qui met des capitaux à la disposition d'une société (qu'elle soit ou non un résident du pays concerné). Cette catégorie recouvre également les bénéfices d'entreprises détenues par une administration, en excluant les monopoles fiscaux (voir paragraphes 66 à 68 du Guide d'interprétation de l'OCDE en Annexe A), les monopoles d'exportation et d'importation (voir paragraphes 75 et 76 du même document) ainsi que les entreprises qui fournissent des services publics comme les chemins de fer, l'électricité, les postes et autres moyens de communication. Sont regroupés dans cette catégorie les revenus provenant d'institutions financières publiques comme les bénéfices de la banque centrale, les bénéfices transférés ou distribués au titre de fonctions de l'autorité monétaire exercées en dehors de la banque centrale et les bénéfices liés aux loteries nationales qui sont transférés à l'administration. Les transferts émanant d'entreprises qui assurent des services publics sont comptabilisés dans la rubrique « ventes de biens et de services » alors que les bénéfices des monopoles fiscaux, d'exportation ou d'importation constituent des recettes fiscales.

- Loyers et redevances : Les loyers sont des revenus générés lorsqu'une unité administrative met à la disposition d'autres entités privées ou étrangères des ressources naturelles, comme des terrains ou des gisements de minéraux ou de pétrole. Les loyers perçus sont liés à des accords de concession relatifs à l'exploitation et à l'extraction d'une ressource naturelle par un concessionnaire en contrepartie d'un paiement. Les paiements en échange de droits de prospection doivent également être traités comme des loyers. Les loyers sont à distinguer des autres paiements qu'une administration publique peut recevoir pour l'exploitation d'actifs du sous-sol et d'autres actifs du même type, par exemple les paiements de taxes d'extraction, patentes ou autres impôts (taxes sur la valeur ajoutée, accises, taxes à l'exportation, ou impôts ou taxes sur les terres privées minières - voir §77 de l'annexe A, etc.) Il ne faut pas non plus confondre loyers et revenus de la location de bâtiments et d'équipements, par exemple, qui sont classés dans les ventes de biens et de services. Les revenus liés aux loyers et redevances sont parfois difficiles à déterminer car ils dépendent de la nature de l'accord conclu entre l'unité administration et le concessionnaire. À titre d'exemple, un versement unique effectué en faveur des administrations publiques peut regrouper le paiement de loyers, de redevances et d'autres obligations fiscales comme l'impôt sur les bénéfices des sociétés ou la TVA. Dans un tel cas, le paiement est classé dans la catégorie qui correspond à la majeure partie du versement considéré.
- Autres revenus de la propriété : Cette catégorie inclut les recettes perçues par une unité administrative qui met des capitaux à la disposition de quasi-sociétés[1]. Cette source de recettes est en substance équivalente à des dividendes versés par une société mais, par définition, les quasi-sociétés ne distribuent pas de bénéfices sous forme de dividendes. Cette catégorie englobe de plus les bénéfices non distribués ou réinvestis, à savoir la fraction du bénéfice distribuable qui n'a pas été versée sous forme de dividendes, mais conservée par la société ou quasi-société sur des investissements étrangers ; les revenus de la propriété provenant de versements de revenus d'investissements et revenus de la propriété non identifiés.

B.4. Ventes de biens et de services

Les recettes qui entrent dans cette catégorie sont enregistrées en valeur brute, sans déduction de coûts. Dans la mesure où les coûts peuvent représenter une part importante des recettes, le montant total des ventes biens et de services ne peut pas être considéré comme un montant dont l'administration dispose dans son intégralité pour financer ses activités générales. C'est une différence notable avec les recettes fiscales, auxquelles sont associés des coûts de recouvrement qui ne représentent le plus souvent qu'une faible part des recettes. De ce fait, le montant obtenu par addition des recettes fiscales et non fiscales ne fournit pas forcément une bonne évaluation des fonds généralement disponibles.

Le produit généré par la cession d'actifs non financiers tels que des bâtiments ou des terrains n'est pas enregistré en tant que recettes étant donné que la cession de tels actifs n'a pas d'effet sur la valeur nette.

Les ventes de biens et de services se composent des éléments suivants :

- les ventes des établissements marchands[2].
- les droits administratifs pour services fournis (droits sur les permis de conduire, sur les passeports, sur les visas ; droits de procédure ; droits portuaires ; droits pour l'établissement d'actes de naissance, de mariage, de décès ; frais de dépôt de brevet ; licences de radio et télévision lorsque les autorités publiques fournissent des services généraux de radiodiffusion).
- Les droits administratifs qui sont des ventes de biens et de services associés à une fonction régulatrice des administrations publiques (comme les droits perçus au titre d'une inspection d'installations menée en vue de la délivrance d'un permis d'exploitation) sont inclus lorsqu'ils sont considérés comme étant proportionnels au coût de production du service en question. Lorsque les droits perçus en contrepartie d'un service fourni par l'administration sont disproportionnés par rapport aux coûts, ils sont considérés comme des impôts. Parmi les droits ainsi classés dans la catégorie des recettes fiscales figurent notamment les droits perçus pour l'octroi de permis d'exercer des activités telles que la chasse, la pêche et l'utilisation d'armes à feu ; et les droits d'enregistrement d'une société dès lors que les entreprises sont tenues par la loi de procéder à un tel enregistrement pour pouvoir exercer leur activité.
- les ventes par les établissements non marchands, comme les droits prélevés par les hôpitaux publics, les droits de scolarité des écoles publiques et les droits d'entrée aux musées et parcs.
- la location de bâtiments et d'équipements.

B.5. Amendes, pénalités et confiscations

Le manuel des statistiques de finances publiques du FMI de 2014 définit les amendes et pénalités comme des transferts obligatoires imposés aux unités par des tribunaux ou des organismes pour infraction à la loi ou aux règlements administratifs. Les accords extra-judiciaires sont également inclus. Les confiscations sont les montants déposés auprès d'une unité d'administration publique pendant le déroulement d'une procédure judiciaire ou administrative puis transférés à cette unité au moment du règlement de celle-ci. À titre d'exemple, les amendes sanctionnant les contraventions au code de la route entrent dans cette catégorie. Les amendes et pénalités appliquées au titre d'arriérés d'impôts ou les pénalités pour fraude fiscale devraient également être comptabilisées ici et non comme des recettes fiscales. Toutefois, s'il est impossible de distinguer les montants qui correspondent respectivement à l'impôt et aux pénalités, la somme totale est rattachée aux recettes générées par l'impôt qui a motivé l'application des pénalités (voir paragraphe 14 en Annexe A pour plus de précisions).

B.6. Autres cotisations sociales

Cette catégorie englobe les cotisations sociales effectives et imputées aux régimes d'assurance sociale gérés par des administrations publiques en qualité d'employeurs pour le compte de leurs employés qui ne génèrent pas de passif défini dans des périodes futures. Cette catégorie inclut également la somme des contributions volontaires totales[3]. Toutefois, sont exclues les cotisations à des fonds dans lesquels les cotisations de chaque salarié et celles que l'employeur verse en son nom sont comptabilisées séparément dans un compte productif d'intérêts d'où elles peuvent être retirées dans des conditions biens déterminées, ainsi que les cotisations à des fonds de pension autonomes vis-à-vis des administrations publiques. Cette catégorie n'est pas incluse aux fins de la présente publication.

B.7. Recettes diverses et non identifiées

Cette catégorie regroupe toutes les recettes non fiscales qui ne peuvent être identifiées ou qui n'entrent dans aucune des catégories décrites précédemment. Elle englobe des dons et transferts provenant de personnes physiques, d'institutions privées sans but lucratif, de fondations non gouvernementales, de sociétés ou de sources autres que les administrations publiques et les organisations internationales. Les paiements non récurrents d'un montant élevé reçus par les administrations publiques en compensation de dommages importants non couverts par des polices d'assurance sont également inclus, ainsi que des paiements d'indemnités en compensation de dommages causés par des explosions de grande ampleur, le déversement d'hydrocarbures, ou des paiements exigibles en cas de dommages matériels autres que les paiements au titre d'une indemnisation par une assurance.

Notes

1. Les quasi-sociétés sont des entreprises non constituées en sociétés qui exercent certaines de leurs activités comme des sociétés, mais n'ont pas reçu de personnalité juridique distincte en vertu de la loi.
2. Un établissement marchand est une entité qui pratique des prix économiquement significatifs.
3. Le FMI comptabilise ces cotisations dans le total des cotisations de sécurité sociale.

www.ingramcontent.com/pod-product-compliance
Lightning Source LLC
Chambersburg PA
CBHW061156240926
51846CB00006B/1031
9789264448087